COSMIC TELEPATHY
The Wisdom beyond Thought
and Audible Sound
of the Past for the Future

Sventovid

Cosmic Telepathy series

Book 1
**Life without Food and the Timelessness
of Spiritual Messages**
of the North American Indians

Book 2
**The Boundless Singing Links
of Body and Spirit**
of the Mexican Mayans

Book 3
**The Alchemy of Harmony between
the Earth and the Sky**
*of Prehistoric Wisdom
and Siberian Shamans*

Book 4
**The Mysteries of Life,
Death, and Soul**
*in the Ancient Vedic Lore
of the Balinese in Indonesia*

Book 5
**The Timeless Weave
of Mind and Abundance**
*of the Hawaiian
Ka-huna Tradition*

Book 6
**Spiritual and Sound Surgery
in the Portals of Attunement**
of the Aboriginal People of Australia, Brazilians, and Filipinos

Book 7
**The Magic of the Stars
and the Keys to Life**
*of the Ancient Egyptians
and Ancient Greeks*

Book 8
**The Sound Yarn of Love
in the Fabric of Relationships**
*in Indo-European, Slavic, Celtic-Illyrian,
and Ancient Slovene Heritages*

Book 9
**The Light-Sound Threads of Songs,
Myths, and Fairy Tales**
of the Ancient Slovenes

Book 2

••••••••••••

The Boundless Singing Links of Body and Spirit
of the Mexican Mayans

Part II

The Sound Alchemy, Spirit, Soul,
and Consciousness of the Ancient Mayans

••••••••••••

MIRA OMERZEL - MIRIT, PH.D.

Series COSMIC TELEPATHY
The Wisdom beyond Thought and Audible Sound of the Past for the Future
Mira Omerzel - Mirit, Ph.D.

Book 2
The Boundless Singing Links of Body and Spirit of the Mexican Mayans

Part II
The Sound Alchemy, Spirit, Soul, and Consciousness of the Ancient Mayans

---

Knjižna serija KOZMIČNA TELEPATIJA
ali modrost onkraj misli in slišnega zvoka
preteklosti za prihodnost

2. knjiga
Brezmejne pojoče vezi telesa in duha mehiških Majev

II. del
Zvočna alkimija, duh, duša in zavest starih Majev

The original was first published in Slovenia by SVENTOVID/Ig, 2012.

Edited by: Danijel Bogataj, Andra Lujić
Translated by: Andra Lujić
Proofreader: Ivana Edmonds
Book Design: Ganeša, David Čelović s.p.
Photo: Mira Omerzel - Mirit, Danijel Bogataj

Published by: Inštitut Sventovid, Škrilje 50c, Ig, Slovenia
© Institut Sventovid 2020

Printed on demand
€26.50

CIP - Kataložni zapis o publikaciji
Narodna in univerzitetna knjižnica, Ljubljana

130.33

OMERZEL, Mira
   The boundless singing links of body and spirit of the Mexican Mayans. Pt. 2, The sound alchemy, spirit, soul, and consciousness of the ancient Mayans / Mira Omerzel-Mirit ; [translated by Andra Lujić ; photo Mira Omerzel-Mirit, Danijel Bogataj]. - Ig : Inštitut Sventovid, 2020. - (Series Cosmic telepathy : the wisdom beyond thought and audible sound of the past for the future ; book 2)

Prevod dela: Brezmejne pojoče vezi telesa in duha mehiških majev. Del 2, Zvočna alkimija, duh, duša in zavest starih Majev
ISBN 978-961-7084-05-4
COBISS.SI-ID 19537667

**About audible and inaudible sound waves
of awakened consciousness**

The voice of my internalised wisdom whispers to me:
Sound is the deepest mystery.

Mirit

Richly decorated priest's flute with a mask in the middle.

ODE TO SOUND

Offer me the soothing song of the soul

Sound, song, and word should contain the volume of the soul,
the expanse of the Universe,
the invisible Blueprint and Divine Will,
the bliss of fullness and silence,
the richness of the unknown
and the wholly new,
yet old and **eternal** at its core,
the very essence of **the clearly understandable and divine;**
the purity and power of the piercing,
not totally comprehensible to the mind;
the inter-dimensional expanse of thoughts,
the deep magic of reality,
the elfin thread of all-connectedness.
May they be suffused with **the weave of freedom**
and infinity,
yet also with the fabric of finity and new birth.

Sound is the messenger of the Divine Source,
of the Earth and body,
offering
perfection,
efficacy
and the elixir of life.
It is the gatekeeper into the immortal,
the key to abundance,
the revered **euphony**
and intangible harmony.

Those who play or sing – who resonate within sound images and listen,
they unveil **lovingness**
and reveal themselves as **beneficent remedies,**
which are the whisper of the soul
and food for the body.

Mellifluous harmony is the abundance of the beginning and the end,
of time and timelessness,
of rhythm and silence.
Sound is the harbinger of silence and enlightened thought,
the echo of a loving willingness and beneficent **compassion**,
which is **the light of the sound,**
the lullaby of the stars
and the alarm call of the Sun.
Sound is the language of the Universe,
the solace of life,
the earthly healing balm.
Truly worth and piercing is the voice of the Master,
echoing across the octaves of the Universe,
mirrored in the audible and inaudible,
tangible and intangible,
visible and invisible.

Sound waves are the language of thoughts and movement,
the taste of bliss,
the fragrance of the Sky and the Earth,
of the stars, trees, and grasses.
Sound comes from the same Source and **from the same sound yarn**
as **imagination** and inspiring **dreams,**
ideas, visions, healing and the silent work of spirit.
It resonates and sings like every **light-sound string of body and cell,**
talking with **the celestial lyre,**
with **this divine instrument of sonic waves,**
which to the Earth brings the sound of planetary desires and dreams,
creating the game of life, whether drama or comedy,
inviting us to the spiritual university of wisdom and to the symphony of feelings.
Within this show of life, we are **pupils, directors, actors and main creators,**
seeking answers to the questions
of **why, whence, and who we are.**

If sound lacks all of this,
it is without effect and meaning,
an empty shell,
emptied content;
its rhythm is without the grace of the heart
and without Divine inspiration
which breathes and sings incessantly
across the fields and seas of spirit,
across embodied forms and all bodies,
vocalising all the quests of our life,
nourishing them,
binding human love to the breath of the Universe.

The song of our ancestors resonated in a similar way,
when they sailed the boats of awakened tune,
seeking within music **the sparks of transformation's fiery flame,**
which changes the world and awakens within people
the most sacred sparks and intentions.
Truly **effective** sound images are **directed by the Divine Intelligence,**
the soul receives them and
captures them onto **the screens of cosmic telepathy,**
while **the mind** fulfils their contents and messages,
edits them, makes them audible.

The guided sound of shamans and mediums is magical
and **penetrating,** just like their power and heartful **creative force**
which never dries up,
never wearies and never disappears,
for it is eternally present, complete, and **indivisible;**
the harmonising sound of musician-priests mirrors the rhythm of the
Universe,
the voice of the Earth and the breath of a living being.
The noble sound of a healer and wise shaman
is a much welcome support and the potion of life,
the pulse of a complementary vicinity of death,
which gives rebirth and birth,
which enacts and fulfils.
May it be so in the future too!
May the divine euphony never dry up!

May it ceaselessly undulate through all living and non-living forms,
may it ennoble stones, planets, and matter,
and tirelessly bring to people **a full awareness,
which gives solace and serenity,**
guiding through the labyrinth and riddles of life,
blessing and bringing the joy of abundance.

Please, **do not force me to listen
to anything less than this,**
to that which does not bring those gifts!
Do not offer me **the hollow splendour of sonic entertainment!**
I would feel like a pauper, a beggar
who has nothing,
who is deaf and blind
and without memory.

Offer me only a blessed song of the soul,
which gives courage and strength, revealing the treasures of a wise mind.
So, fill my glass with the elixir of sound,
may **the sacred sound yarn be woven in the worlds of consciousness,**
may it spill over the rims and **beyond boundaries**
and **satisfy the eternal yearning;**
may it bring me **the soul's delight
of trust and sweet kindness.**

To sound images, undulating through me like a river,
I turn with gratitude and focus;
tears of Mercy, grace, and happiness flow down my cheeks,
filling me with meta-sensory images of cosmic telepathy.
I know that I still know all too little,
but I do know something for sure:
**today people do not clearly understand
why and how to live without pain,
why love and why rush
up the pyramid of transformation
into the expanse of consciousness;
how to use the remedy of sound**
and its elation of the soul,
in order to awaken and know the eternal Truth.

I know that a completely **new time** is coming,
which will bring everyone exactly
what they wish.

With an open soul, **I look forward** infinitely
to all new and **unexpected gifts**
of spirit, sounds and life,
to the revealing of **the soul's dormant abilities,**
brought to me by the sonic play,
**as it lifts the curtains of time, space, and timelessness,
the history of the Universe, the Earth and my own being.**
Thank you infinitely!

If you are interested in such a blessed sound,
treat yourself to the reading of this **book message,**
which attempts to unveil **the mysterious blessings of consciousness and sound.**
With gratitude, **I embrace invisible guidance,**
which resonates within me, urging me
to pour into verse and word
what **the whisper yoga** is telling me,
bringing me insights, blessing me,
waking me up.

By revealing **multidimensional sonic realms,**
I give sound to **the Truth,**
which smoulders at the levels of spirit,
to make it burn and **blaze**
with the flames of timeless wisdom;
and I mount **the waves of the spiritual pyramid.**
Within the fiery flames of transformation and constant change,
there is a fragrance of **the sacredness of life
worth living.**
Thank You, thank You, thank You – **from the heart of my soul!**

Mirit (in the night between 15th and 16th November 2011)

An introductory word about the book

This is a book about the long forgotten **wisdom of the ancient Mayans and our planetary ancestors.** Their extraordinary knowledge remains a great mystery for people today and their abilities and powers are still **an enigma.** The book reveals **different perspectives on the Mayan spiritual heritage and on the use of sound.** The author looks at the Mayan culture **through the frame of sound and eternal laws of spirit and life.**

By looking at it from higher levels of consciousness, the author puts Mayan culture onto entirely **different foundations.** In her own way, **she draws nearer to the essence and principle of Mayan sound and priestly practice, with which, thousands of years ago, the wise Mayans had been creating their reality, harmonising life on Earth, healing, and performing music.** The essence of ancient Mayan wisdom is also a valuable **signpost for humanity as a whole. Their cosmic or galactic consciousness is becoming once again interesting** and attractive in the spiritual emptiness of the modern world and its commoditisation of the truth.

The ancient **consciousness of the Mayans is becoming increasingly the consciousness of the new times, the new Earth,** but foremost, **the consciousness of a better and a more aware life.** Our values, which are constantly changing, are once again turning to the wisdom of the ancient times. **The past gives meaning to and reinvigorates the future. A new human being is now being born – more joyful and spiritually less impoverished.** Out of their conscious spirit and thought **arises the current moment gifted with peace and well-being.** With the boundless vastness of their consciousness, Mayan teachings put **sound and music** into a different perspective – on **to the altar of consecration and sacredness.**

So who is this writing for? For those who want something more from their life; **for spiritual seekers and warriors seeking peace, happiness and completeness;** for those who, somewhere deep within, **feel the miraculous levels of life, and their hidden, dormant abilities,** which deserve to be uncovered and lived. The world seems crazy. Conflict, war, theft, lies, etc. everywhere. Anything but the essence of life, which is nowhere.

In the first book of the *Cosmic Telepathy* series, I have described **my life story and the path that brought me to an acceptance of the invisible worlds.** My aim was first to share my life experience and **encourage** others **to enter the world of spirit.** This time, my desire is to encourage readers to embrace a more in-depth experience of sound and a more mindful approach to **everything that they hear, and even think.** At the same time, I offer **help with the elimination of problems** that might have occurred in readers' lives.

Mayans, who were masters of time, certainly possessed a great knowledge of invisible and inaudible cosmic forces (frequency waves) which, throughout the universe, are constantly creating and form-giving. These forces incessantly nourish the Earth and life on it. Numerous sages, including Siberian shamans, North American Indians, South American Indians, and those of the Yucatan Peninsula, still today have much of interest to tell about this. **People living thousands of years ago were not backward**, as the majority, including archaeologists, think today. Those people were **primal beings with their spiritual eyes and ears wide open, with exceptional telepathic abilities.** Through them they attained clear sight and hearing which enabled them to gain insights into realms here on Earth and beyond. Slovenes called them **giants or *ajdje*.**

Musician-priest-therapists, who were spiritual teachers at the same time, knew how to use the powers of those inaudible frequencies for their own benefit and for the benefit of others. Sound was essential to them. It was the most important surgical tool.

Everything that exists is, in itself, in tune and in harmony: the universe, nature, human being, spirit, soul... People work very hard to ruin this balance. Dissonance leads to **ignorance**. This is how **disharmony (in our bodies too), diseases, accidents, and poverty develop. Only when the pain is unbearable, do humans begin to search anew for the lost harmony.** The fight begins. Subsequently, this balance must be maintained. This is actually **the meaning of life.**

Fortunately, spiritual truths are universal. **The teachings** of all traditions, which carry within themselves eternal Truth, **are timeless. They are a mirror and an echo of the profound life experiences of countless generations.** These were carefully maintained and respected as sacred knowledge. **Wisdom keepers have always been individuals of heightened consciousness – priests, healers, spiritual teachers, artists, and musicians.**

By understanding our past, we open a portal to the understanding of our present and set off towards new possibilities. While on the way, **we discover countless wonderful concealed or hidden abilities that dwell in us.** To discover them is our life's purpose and our **innate right, the purpose of our existence.**

Table of Contents

    Ode to sound
    An introductory word about the book
I   Dedication
III Acknowledgements

1   THE MAGIC OF SOUND AND OCTAVES - THE SINGING LINKS BETWEEN CONSCIOUSNESS AND REALITY

2   *The octaves of life, forms and bodies*

2   Tiny oscillating light-sound strings resound across the octaves of the universes and the echo of the Earth
10 The holographic connection, parts resonating with the whole and images of sound in the sand
13 Octaves of sound and light in the auric field - reflections of higher dimensions in the physical world
17 The intelligence agency of our glands and a music medium, therapist, shaman, and cosmic telepath
24 The enchantment, or alchemy of sound and light
34 The imprint of pain and suffering was stuck in the 230th octave

39 *The conversation between the Cosmos and our cell's protein membranes*

39 The conversation between the Cosmos and our body
44 Astronomical knowledge - biological clocks, the oldest religion and the fullness of awareness

49 *The pre-Columbian and newer musical instruments – the quest for harmony*

56 *The universe breathing through Creation*

56 Embodied in the dual world on Earth
61 Theories of the parallel universes of our twin souls beyond the stars

65 SHAMANISM, PRIESTS' SCHOOLS OF ASTRONOMY AND MUSIC

66 *The shamanic journey into the unknown within the circle of life and death*

66 An offering to the Great Grandfather Fire among the Apaches
68 Mayan priests, the Lord of Sipán and ancient forms of penitence
72 Water baptism - connecting with the perfect wholeness and with all the dimensions of the physical and spiritual world
75 Spiritual warriors return to the spirit, to the visions of the energies of the Universe and to the immortal consciousness
78 Warriors of peace and happiness unveil and fight evil within themselves and in the world
86 The teaching of Don Juan and the battle for the unknown of the ancient Mexican shamans in Castaneda's opus
90 Shamanic teachings about warriorhood and power, life, death, and freedom
94 The Great Mysteries and rituals at sacred sites
96 Warriors of intention, will and courage, death rites of the negative
100 The awakened *nagual* - a master of awareness and intention
102 Gods paddling to the Heart of Sky and the three hearthstones
112 Eternal teachings and the power of the ancient Mexican shamanism
116 Disappointment triggers a virus infection, which in turn leads to a shift along the axis of consciousness, into shamanic detachment
120 A children's game of the warrior entering the thoughts of another and sensing the same Intelligence in everything
122 The detachment of Mexican shamans, the art of stalking and dreaming, the Eagle's emanation

128 *Gratitude to life and death*

129 Near-death, death and beyond death, the awakened consciousness
134 Death as an illusion and dreams of the spirit
140 Sacrifices, the symbolism of blood, funeral rituals, and the consciousness of the heart

149 *Shamanic initiation with snake venom*

169 *Mayan medicine*

169 The healers and the white and black magicians of Chiapas
175 Herbalists, healers, healing methods, and the symbolism of colours, candles, and smoke
182 Blowing, the healing prayer, giving birth, midwifery, and animal *naguals*
188 Picturesque leaflets about Mayan medicine
     and the warrior-healer

195 *The life and rituals of the Aztecs and Incas*

195 The stratification of society, the astronomical and priests' school for girls and boys
201 Penance without washing, musical instruments, the house of song, theatrical plays, ritual and symbolic games
206 Musician-priests in the ceremonies of sound and dance
207 Sacrificing to the God of fire and time
209 The Aztec fire ceremony and dance on the sacred tree

214 *Magical crystal skulls*

214 At a concert a crystal bowl opens my way into the research of the crystal skulls
218 My crystal pendulum vanishes and prevents me from healing a horse
220 The symbolism of the flower and the mysticism of my first connection with the crystal skull
222 The Mitchell-Hedges skull, one of the first to be discovered
228 The miraculous glow and sounds, the programming of crystal skulls
232 Crystal skulls - the computers or library of the past and tools for extra-sensory perception
236 Crystal skulls - symbols of life and death, detectors of good and evil in life, myths and fairy tales
239 Thirteen skulls for the activation of the portal of time and sound, their use in rituals
242 Testing crystal skulls, their lightness and invisibility
247 Crystal skulls as vehicles for the spirit and new-age tools
249 Working with crystals and sound during the process without food and liquid
253 Ways of connecting and working with crystal skulls
257 My obsession with skulls and my work with four skulls in the cosmic cross

266   I shall keep praying to the Cosmos until it gives the skull back to us

275   ETERNAL CHALLENGES BETWEEN THE WORLDS OF THE PAST AND FUTURE

276   *The ritual initiatory path of the 'Ancient Ones' and the ancient Mayans*

- 276   The cosmic university for the expulsion of fear and evil
- 281   The initiatory path of returning to the original Source of Creation – into the essence of the Primordial wholeness
- 283   The unveiling of the soul and ego begins in darkness
- 286   Ritual dying and self-sacrifice
- 290   Tulum – a bridge for messages from the past
- 297   The gathering of the wise Masters and Gods in Tulum and in the sacred temple of seven gates in Chichén Itzá
- 301   Tribute to the divine Hunahpu, Itzamna, Kukulkan, the mythical twins, monkey, the planets and stars
- 307   The pineal gland - a link with the energy of the Sun and planets
- 310   The magic of love and death and cosmic feathered serpents in the ballgame
- 313   In the ballgame, players run towards the goal
- 320   Snake descendants in the play of light, darkness, fire, and water
- 325   The sacredness of water springs and the Venus temple, the temple of the warrior's courage
- 331   The pyramid of Kukulkan in Chichén Itzá - the temple of the Divine Consciousness

338   *Hunahpu – the centre of the Universe and life*

- 338   The Mayan symbol Hunahpu in the rituals of centredness
- 343   When you are aligned - you are happy and boundlessly creative
- 346   The harmonious ratio 20 : 13 in musical intervals and in Mayan music

350 *A metagalactic human being and the consciousness of the Galactic Centre*

350 The centrifuge of transformation grinds and revisiting the values
361 The return of lost abilities
364 Listening to the messages of the Universe
366 The challenges of an attuned mind, soul and heart, and the healing powers of the connection to the Universe
370 The return of both cosmic memory and the cosmic initiations of perfection in the legends of Lemuria and Atlantis
373 The mysteries of the three-dimensional world are changing, yet remaining the same

377 *Silence – the path and goal of spiritual warriorhood*

377 To be able to hear yourself and the world in silence is the magic of the connection between the centre of your own being and oneness
381 Silence connects people with the centre of their own being
384 A priest-shaman and warrior must know how to consciously step out of the world of duality into the dimensions of silence and heart

392 *Bibliography*

395 ADDENDUM

396 *About the series*

397 *Summaries of the books from the series*

414 *Other English Language Books and CDs by Mira Omerzel - Mirit, Ph.D.*

429 *About the author*

430 *Great mysteries of life, the magic of sound, cosmic consciousness and the wisdom of the past*

Cosmic sound-energy surgery
Courses / intensivos
Veduna cosmic resonance
Veduna cosmic, galactic and planetary initiations
Concerts and CDs of the Vedun Ensemble
Books by Mira Omerzel - Mirit, Ph.D.
Retreats

435 *Therapeutic sounds of the Slavic, ancient Slovene and Balkan soul in the sonic yarn of harmonising sounds of the cultures of the world*

440 Musical instruments

Dedication

The books of the Cosmic Telepathy series
are dedicated to my close and distant
awakened ancestors of the great Cosmic Consciousness,
who have, across thousands of years, striven to preserve the core essence
of the peaceful and loving wisdom of existence,
which is the only one truly worth living.

May **the ancient tradition**
– timeless and eternal –
satisfy the eternal yearning of the soul
and fulfil our deepest desires
which come from cosmic-planetary dreams.
With a thankful thought for the maternal **patience of Mother Earth,**
who offers us numerous opportunities for an enlightened awareness,
for us to **awaken the 'unspoken knowledge' of the Universe**
and a myriad of overlooked, dormant human abilities.

To my son and to all spiritual seekers,
to our descendants, for them to remember and be reminded!
May we never forget about **living together,**
in tolerance and love,
with the Earth, the Cosmos
and other living forms and beings.

Mirit
a singing scientist, an artist,
mystic, and spiritual teacher

Acknowledgements

Many people helped me – through their assistance and presence in this turbulent time of transformation – sharing their life stories with me – in the writing of this **travel, spiritual, and scientific interpretive book about sound and the thousands of years old spiritual wisdom of the peoples of the world,** a creational process which has spanned a decade. I would like to thank all the dedicated students of my **Veduna School for the Development of Consciousness, a school of the cosmic-earthly university,** all brave spiritual **warriors and spiritual teachers** of the younger generation, who matured in the school and gave me the opportunity **to clarify life's riddles** together with them, and **to bring to life that which has been long forgotten.** I am honoured to have been able to be their teacher. Without their questions and troubles, these books wouldn't be here. Every question pulled out **a hidden knowledge** from me and drew me to **an inquisitive research of the magic of spirituality and sound.**

I would like to extend my particularly heartfelt gratitude to **Mojka Žagar** for her help. She persistently transferred to digital form my channellings (handwritten notes and dictations), my numerous corrections and additions. I would also like to express my heartfelt thanks to **Danijel Bogataj,** who made sure that these texts looked good on digital media.

My very special gratitude goes to my **musical colleagues** in both the **Vedun** Ensemble (the ensemble for old and meditative music and channelled healing sound with the instruments and songs of the peoples of the world) and the **Trutamora Slovenica** Ensemble (the ensemble for the reconstruction of the Slovene folk musical heritage from the archives): to **Mojka Žagar** and my son, **Tine Omerzel Terlep.** Through our shared performing of music, they have, for more than three decades, facilitated this sound experience and trial for me, also allowing me to test the emerging challenges of the resonating Universe and ideas.

Thank you, thank you, thank you!

Without them, my findings, adventures, testimonies, teachings, and presentations of the spiritual sound heritage would certainly be poorer.

The book was originally published in 2012, which is why the information in the text refers to that year.

This book is written in a particular way. Its interpretive and **philosophical section**, which explains the author's experiences and the wisdom of various cultures, was written **in a transcendental state of consciousness,** when thoughts were brought through **from the levels beyond. The book is therefore, also a channelled message from the Cosmic Intelligence/Mind/Consciousness.**

Words and sentences **in bold** enable the reader, **when rereading, to rapidly imprint only the most important concepts in their memory, mind, and consciousness.** Text in bold works **like a reminder, as a book within a book.** Those highlighted thoughts are **well worth reading over and over again in order to be well remembered. Our minds must seize them** during our transformation journey and the consciousness must accept them. That is why this book, as well as the others that make up the *Cosmic Telepathy* series, is **a magical spiritual growth textbook, a framework on which to reflect and meditate, a guide through the labyrinth of life.**

THE MAGIC OF SOUND AND OCTAVES - THE SINGING LINKS BETWEEN CONSCIOUSNESS AND REALITY

The octaves of life, forms and bodies

Tiny oscillating light-sound strings resound across the octaves of the universes and the echo of the Earth

Ocarina – mother with a child.

We were taught – incorrectly, of course – **that we are only material beings**, beings of the three-dimensional physical world. However, science is increasingly proving that this is not the case. Modern science, particularly **quantum mechanics and string theory**, or superstring theory,[1] demonstrates that **the smallest material and non-material subquantum particles are in fact light-sound strings,** which make up quarks, electrons, neutrons, and therefore also atoms, molecules, and complex organisms. These smallest light-sound particles are said to **form everything that exists.** That is why they are a distinct **bridge** between the visible and invisible worlds. **Subquantum strings are the fundamental building blocks of the material and non-material. At their core, those strings are the undulation of light and sound. Matter is a condensed echo of that undulation.** Scientists claim that **the entire Universe is built from oscillating strings. Everything oscillates, everything vibrates. This means that the Universe is constantly resonating.** Its resonance can be sensed. Those resonating strings are in fact **singing links between the worlds, or dimensions, between the levels of existence, which sing within a holographic whole.**

Different waves are also called dimensions. Vibrational (sound) patterns make up the different forms and different densities of everything that exists, ranging from dense matter to the finest frequency waves which are imperceptible to the eye and ear, but **can be sensed with our meta-senses. Dimensions can also be called (sound) octaves.** The octave interval is a musical notion, which, in music

....
1   The concept of superstrings first appeared in **1984**. During the following decades, this concept of microscopic insight was validated and enhanced. It seems that it is experiencing a veritable flowering in the new millennium. The most notable representative of this theory is **Edward Witten**, who developed the superstring idea further and a decade later, got through to scientific minds with it.

theory, means the relationship *(ratio)*, or distance, between two tones which have the same name, the same quality, but **resonate in different octaves.** A repeating tone (above or below a defined starting tone) resonates with an exponentially higher, or lower, frequency. Octave displacement is created by **multiplying by two – or dividing by two** – the basic frequency of the eponymous tone, when moving down through octave displacements. This is like stacking (or removing) one chair onto another, thus increasing or lowering the height of the structure.

The material world is made up of frequency octaves. Let me explain this in the following way for those who are not musicians and don't have an idea of what an octave is. **The seven successive tones of a seven-tone scale, as well as the twelve semitones of a chromatic scale, build the level of one octave,** one step level of a pyramid. Every **eighth** tone of the diatonic scale, of a tone sequence, or every **thirteenth** tone of the semi-tonal chromatic scale, is a **repeated tone. It is the frequency of the first fundamental tone** of the basic octave. **Each subsequent octave represents a step with a higher resonance, or lower** if we move downwards. **But of course, with our physical senses in this world, we cannot reach deeper than the third, second or first dimension. Yet upwards, our pyramidal path is practically unlimited,** although only the rare ones attain those boundless expanses.

The octaves follow one another, like a distinct 'sky ladder,' as the sages of old civilisations would have said. This octave ladder is symbolised by **a multi-step pyramid and the sacred tree, the world axis** *axis mundi* – **the axis of consciousness which leads across the worlds. The ladder of countless octaves** represents the frequency axis of consciousness **across countless dimensions, across sound, or frequency vibrations.** Each subsequent octave lies one scale, or one step, lower.

For example, **the first level, the first dimension of reality** is made up of a frequency which we recognise in the colour **red**. This basic colour is extremely strong. However, **in subsequent octave displacements**, on higher levels, **it fades away more and more. It loses its physical,** strong radiant colour and **becomes increasingly fine, translucent, less distinct, ever more non-material.** The frequency world which builds **the first three dimensions,** that is **the material world,** could be called the octaves of low frequency waves. After that, frequency waves **jump into the next octave relationship.**

In European diatonic musical language, **one octave** is based on **twelve semitones (seven whole tones** of the diatonic scale and **five chromatic tones)**. Across the octaves, frequency waves spread to all sides, rising exponentially from the basic (the lowest possible) tone, just like the dimensions, or the levels, of consciousness and reality. **Dimensions can be pictured as different octaves. Or, to put it another way, relationships between the dimensions are in octave ratios.** The realms, or dimensions which vibrate in higher frequencies, **resonate higher**, even so high that our **hearing doesn't perceive them anymore**. Traditions call this field of high resonance **the Field of spirit, the divine Source of all forms.**

Each frequency, which can also be perceived as a tone, resonates in higher or lower octave displacements, however, it is not possible to go lower than the basic (earthly) tone.

For example, **the tone of the Earth's rotation (tone G)** can resonate in different octaves. The same goes for any other tone, or frequency – from the tone G, which has the deepest resonance and creates the Earth's one-day movement, all the way to the highest, barely heard tones **which resonate on the very edge of our hearing field and stretch above and below it. When speaking about music octaves, we simultaneously touch the resounding octaves of the Universe. We listen to the spiral motion of individual tones,** which rise and fall from one frequency level to another, which pass from one scale, one octave, into another. It is as if **each octave is seated on one rung of the vertical axis, or on the ladder of both the material world and the pulsing, resonating world; one branch on the trunk of the sacred tree: spanning from the deepest possible sound to the highest primal (divine) 'resonance.'** This is how the sound yarn of life is woven and interweaved.

Chinese and Japanese tales (unfortunately, I am not familiar with any similar Mayan tale) speak about **the Sun God**, who had a daughter named **Zhinü**, or **Tanabata** in Japanese.[2] Zhinü was **the Goddess of embroidery and weaving, she was a brilliant celestial embroider (of sound and the energy yarn of life).** Into her weave, she braided the stars, sunlight, and shadows. **Her weaving was so beautiful that everyone,** even the Sun God himself, **was enchanted (life is miraculous and wonderful).**

One day, **in the middle of the heavenly river** (that is **the Milky Way**), she stood up suddenly from her weaving and looked at the beautiful sunny day. She looked to one side of the river and saw her father's **Cowherd**, who was taking two wonderful **sky oxen** (two cosmic forms, or beings) to water. The two young ones instantly fell in love. As both the girl and the boy were of **divine origin (the energies of Creation)**, God the Father agreed to their relationship. And when the sky weaver was weaving her **wedding dress out of the stars and light (when sky forces were preparing to merge)**, a wonderful **dawn** poured across the Sky, the like of which had never been seen until then (**the primordial beauty** shone in all its splendour).

....
2 Pavel Kunaver, *Pravljica in resnica o zvezdah* (*Fairy Tale and Truth about the Stars*), Ljubljana, Mladinska knjiga (1981), pp. 57-65; Aquila – the Eagle.

But unfortunately, the young ones, passionately in love, **forgot their duties** (there always has to be order in the Cosmos and life!). Despite the multiple warnings of the father, they kept neglecting their celestial duties (their celestial jobs as **creators and sustainers**). And the angry Sky father **separated them forever. He placed them on separate sides of the sky river** (Milky Way). **Zhinü** was put on its west side, where she shines as the star **Vega in the Lyra constellation** and **Niulang** was placed on the east side, where he now glows as the star **Altair in the constellation of Aquila**. The stars say that **with one word the Sun God first created the celestial path, the Milky Way,** which had not previously existed (only after this were the Sky and the Earth created, **the world of duality** and cyclical repetition).

The two lovers were despondent and begged the father for mercy. Finally, he **allowed them to meet once a year, on the seventh day of the seventh month,** but only after they had found their way to cross the heavenly river (this was the main shamanic task of the ancient Mayans). The Sky weaver came up with an idea, she asked **magpies for help**. So, **every year magpies build a bridge with their bodies,** so that the two lovers can meet. That is why in China and Japan, they say that on the seventh day of the seventh month, there are no magpies to be seen anywhere. If they do see one however, they immediately chase it up to the Sky, to help build the bird bridge. For this reason **the seventh day of the seventh month** was once a festival (**the festival of Creation**) in Japan. On that day people **hung colourful strips on bamboo poles, they wrote down songs which they threw into rivers or the sea,** because they believed **that earthly waters and the heavenly river** (the material world and the cosmic world of spirit) **came together** and took their songs (prayers, requests, visions) directly to the castle in which the Sky Weaver lived (the one who **weaves, or shapes, reality**).

So, the notions of **octaves,**[3] **or dimensions,** with which the science of the past described **different states of consciousness,** as well as different **densities, or hardnesses, of matter** and of other levels of reality, are but distinct **patterns of undulation and variations of the same. Frequency patterns and their wavelengths are simply variations of sound (frequency) qualities, therefore having different characteristics, both material and non-material. Just like water can be in a liquid, solid (ice) or gas (vapour) state,** frequency-vibration qualities can be in a material form or can be completely intangible, invisible and inaudible. At a certain frequency height, or wavelength, they can manifest **as dense**

---

[3] According to the calculations made by Hans Cousto in his book *Die Oktave*, Berlin (1987), p. 31. An octave also corresponds to a half-day rhythm.

matter. **We are multidimensional beings. Even our bodies (our physical, emotional, mental bodies, our spirit – soul, or consciousness),** made up of both the material and non-material, physical and spiritual, resonate in **characteristic vibrational contents.**

The terms higher and lower belong to the language of the three-dimensional material world, but, in reality, nothing is higher or lower, it is only different. The concepts higher and lower were created by a mentality oriented towards the physical world. We are using these terms in order **to understand all of this more easily** from our physical-space-time point of view. **However, everything is simultaneous and timeless, everything is in the material and non-material world at the same time, in the material, spiritual and cosmic (divine) simultaneously. That is why shamanic drums of antiquity** have three sections: mouths (the privilege of humanity) are in the lower section, an empty space (of the invisible spirit) is in the middle and above there is the eye, the Sun – symbol of the Universal on Earth. All three make up **the Triunity of the cosmic, spiritual and earthly.**

That which vibrates, or resonates, in space and time, also resonates in **timelessness and at the boundless octave levels of 'the identical,' in countless, even unimaginable octaves of the Universe,** which can only be sensed with our telepathic meta-senses.

The octave singing links connect us to different levels, different dimensions of our own being and to other beings and forms of life. The 'highest resonance' has **the First Principle, the Source, the Intelligence of the Universe,** which our inner sight perceives as **crystal white light** and our inner hearing hears as **murmuring, as the Sound of Creation and silence.** Melded, the frequencies of our visible spectrum also undulate **as a white light, as the colour of all colours,** in which different **rainbow colours** are revealed.

At the octave of **the fourth dimension, we enter the world of spirit, the world of the soul,** as we say. This intangible and invisible world is sensed and perceived **with our meta-senses,** but cannot be touched, **nor heard with our physical ears. Yet, it is here nevertheless, and it is equally important** as, for example, the tangible physical frequency world **'frozen' into hard matter.**

The deeper, or higher, we go on this symbolic ladder, on this frequency rollercoaster, **the faster the waves vibrate** and the higher and more penetrating their resonance is. The higher the resonance, **the finer** are those inaudible sound levels of reality, **but they are more difficult to perceive and, at the same time, also more difficult to attain.**

The octave relationships of different pattern waves[4] follow in different ratios which build forms and manifest in **the shape-giving power of inaudible**

---
4   The most basic geometrical forms of the matter are called **Platonic solids.**

and audible sound. Everything resonates and is built **according to the laws of resonance and is manifested in the geometry of harmony.** Harmony and resonance are possible precisely due to this multi-levelled **repetition of frequency patterns, due to undulation at different levels, octaves, or dimensions.** It is like looking at the colour red, or blue, **in different shades,** at different octave heights.

In its earthly manifestation, **the great sound flow (inaudible to our ears),** the river of frequency waves, is divided into **polar undulation, into the two complementary flows of the world of duality,** which are, especially in the Native American world, represented by **mythical twins. Frequencies colour, or complement, each other,** composing **always new forms of the whole.** They make up male and female essences and polar experiences of the 'bad' and 'good,' the polarity of cold and hot, of loud and quiet, of sound and silence, etc.

By listening to the Earth's frequency, for example, or by resonating within it, we can connect, or resonate, with all the tone heights of this pitch, **within all octaves, all dimensions of the material.** Whether we hear them or not, whether we are aware of them or not. **The cosmic telepathic** ability **and intuitive flashes,** or the '**I know**' moments, which occur **outside thinking and education,** are also proof of this. This phenomenon is best described by the word **omnipresence, for everything that exists is mirrored in the octave expanses of our consciousness, in the 'colour shades' of a holographic whole. The differentness of the same** can be seen both in the Universe and on the piano. **Resonance – equal with equal – takes place within different octaves of the material world. Naturally, the opposite is also valid:** octave relationships offer **an opportunity for resonance across all levels, across all worlds of reality.** Harmonies are established on both conscious and unconscious levels.

Meditations, ceremonies, becoming aware and a conscious connection to the Primordial Intelligence, to the Centre, the Divine Essence, the Source, to our own divine core – they all **lead us to a harmony with the octave frequency rhythms (dimensions) and into an enlightened state of spirit. The perfection of the Logos powerfully enhances the basic tone of a thought, or of life. With this perfection, we are more diverse, spiritually and physically stronger, more complete, and above all, we become increasingly aware of the different levels of existence.**

It is precisely due to the possibility of resonating across the octaves, across the dimensions, that we are able to hear even the high-frequency (high-resonance) sound of Creation, which is otherwise far above, or below, our aural field, and outside the material, outside the perception of our physical senses, including the ears.

Those who refuse to hear,
won't hear;
to those who want to hear the Universe sing,
it shall be given.
When the silence embraces them,
they will hear enchanting music.
How could you miss it,
as **the divine Source (God) is singing and shouting into everyone's hearts and ears?**

Music is a mighty bridge,
rivers flow beneath it,
quiet and roaring,
inexhaustible and eternal,
imperceptible to the eye, yet obvious.

In the service of God, musicians
sing and play ceaselessly;
with their enchanting sounds, **they awaken the world.**
Look beneath their fingers,
read from their lips,
listen to the sounds of their soul,
when they sing in honour of life,
or to bid farewell.

Pluck up your courage and cross the bridge,
built of their divine sounds,
their **hearts' waves,**
their wisdom and their whisper.[5]

Cosmic telepathic ability confirms the possibility to **resonate, or to closely hear all octaves,** all dimensions of reality. **But the key lies in the expanses of human consciousness.** The broader, the more open a person is, the deeper, or higher, they will be able to reach and resound. **Every ceremony can increase those abilities, so that we can 'hear with attention' even those high-frequency impulses of the Logos which are constantly 'creating' across the countless octave levels.**

High-frequency waves are called **gamma rays,** and are of the utmost importance for the understanding of non-physical worlds. **Due to the octave and**

---
5   Mirit, the poem *Cross the Bridge of Divine Sounds*, September 2012.

holographic structure of the Universe, of our consciousness and bodies, we are able to hear the sound, or the symbolic 'pure thought' of the Primordial Intelligence, of the Cosmic Mind, the impulses of the Galactic Centre, as the Mayans say, **the sound of Creation and the waves of primordial life energy** with which we nourish and **heal** living beings on Earth. This attunement is **perceived as a vision, idea or inspiration** within our mental-emotional vibration levels.

The constellation of Draco coils around the Little Dipper. Within it, shines **the North Star,** one of the most important stars, which humanity has used for orientation for thousands of years. In the past, it was important in the building of temples. Creation stories say that the dragon (or the cosmic snake) **helped the giants – the Titans – build the world.** The Chaldean dragon **Tiamat** existed in Creation myths even before the Sky and the Earth, because it was the symbol of **primordial darkness** and primal **chaos**, out of which light and the Sun God emerged.

The celestial serpent, or the river serpent, the sea **serpent, is the symbol of life energy** which winds through everything that exists. It is often replaced by **a dragon** in ancient mythology. The dragon can have one or more heads, which may greatly resemble human heads. **He breathes fire**, or smoke rises out of his mouth. Fire is **the symbol of transformation.** And **serpents and dragons are the guardians of wonderful treasures (of spirit), of immense riches which all humans carry within themselves.** They guard the golden fleece, the Nibelung hoard, the golden apple of the Hesperides. In a Slovene tale, they keep the treasure hidden **inside the *Bogatin* Mountain.**[6] **Only a person with a magic horn,** made from precious Goldenhorn's horn, can find this treasure. So, **only those who resonate with purity out into the world, those with pure hearts and thoughts,** can discover and earn it.

These dragon tales in fact speak of the battle between light and darkness, which takes place both at the time of the creation of the world and within human beings; they speak about the birth of light out of the darkness, **about the meaning of life. Tiamat, the primordial female creative life energy, also possesses the 'tablets of destiny,' the matrices of life.** We humans, just like the Light God, are bestowed with multiple **divine gifts in order to overcome the darkness within us.** We overcome it in motion – **in love and a truth-loving awareness,** which is symbolised by the wind **Huracan, the Heart of Sky.** According to the mythical tales, Huracan smashed evil – the darkness, the monstrous dragon. Then he created the Sky and the Earth, the stars, time, cosmic and natural cycles, as well as the material world. That is why humans have to constantly **return to primordial darkness to be able to find light within themselves, and build a better tomorrow with this light, a new consciousness and a new Earth.**

....
6 Pavel Kunaver, *Pravljica in resnica o zvezdah*, Ljubljana, Mladinska knjiga (1987), pp. 26 - 33; *Draco – the Dragon.*

The holographic connection, parts resonating with the whole and images of sound in the sand

> Do not worry if our harp breaks
> thousands more will appear.
> **We have fallen in the arms of love
> where all is music.**
> If all the harps in the world were burned down,
> still **inside the heart
> there will be hidden music playing.**
> Do not worry if all the candles in the world flicker and die
> **we have the spark that starts the fire.**
> **The songs we sing
> are like foam on the surface of the sea of being**
> while the precious gems lie deep beneath.
> **But the tenderness in our songs
> is a reflection** of what is hidden in the depths.
> **Stop the flow of your words,
> open the window of your heart** and
> let the spirit speak.[7]

We experience all levels of existence, all the octaves of our own multidimensional being, when we are in harmony (when we are symbolically pure), when we are attuned to all the octaves of the life flow, to all levels of our being, our consciousness and the Universe, and when we consciously attune ourselves to the 'high-frequency' Cosmic Consciousness. But we succeed in this completely only when we are impeccably **in tune** with all the octaves, when we are **enlightened.** Only then do we become a person, **a per-sona** (*sonare* means to **resonate**), **a being who resonates and is in tune.** When we look up into the Sky, **we feel love in our heart** and we spontaneously thank the Sun, rainy clouds, the Moon and the invisible divine force for all the gifts of life.

People who are connected to all of Creation, across all the octaves and dimensions, experience an immense **elation and a great power arising out of this connection, which facilitates an easier manifestation of ideas and visions** which are aligned to the divine Mind and their own souls. Such is **the dynamic of the vertical axis of consciousness – symbolically, of the sacred tree, – which comes from the Source, from the Centre, and returns to it.** It descends from the Source of

----
7   Rumi, *Hidden Music*, London, Thorsons (2001), p. 111.

our consciousness (from our soul) through different octave levels down into the material three-dimensional world; and with the immortal consciousness, **it returns back there, back to the wholistic oneness.**

When we resonate with the primordial idea, or **Intent**, through our thoughts and sound, through our **prayer or song,** we create **a holographic connection to the whole.** A hologram represents **the ability to resonate with cosmic, soul, and earthly levels:** both in our thoughts and actions.

The hologram is the connecting power between one part and the whole; it is the link between the divine wholeness and each string of the material world. That is why every part contains all information of the Universal Logos, which 'resounds' in every subquantum particle of the Creation, in singing strings. Every 'cosmic or earthly tone' spans across all octaves. And all octave dimensions are encoded in every tone, in every frequency pattern of the material. God, the Centre, or the Source, and humans hear each other, as we say. They communicate and send messages to each other.

The quintessence of the octave, or the ability to resonate, and the holographic all-connectedness across the octaves, across the dimensional levels of reality, are the fundamental laws of life and creativity. When frequencies from higher levels, which we normally don't see and hear, begin to shine in rainbow colours through rain drops, we can remember that frequency waves hidden from our physical perception really exist. After rain, we see them in the form of a rainbow, in the rainbow world of differentness, when light-sound waves break in droplets of water.

The levels of existence therefore consist of **different frequency patterns,** which are but **inaudible sound waves** – and therefore also **tones which are condensed into material forms** in the material world, in the solid-matter tangible realm. **These singing links between frequency waves and vibrational resonance make the invisible visible. They are the very foundation of embodiment in visible forms.**

Cymatics is a branch of science which explores frequency waves and reveals how invisible **sound waves** (both audible and inaudible) **form geometrical forms in the material world.** This was brilliantly demonstrated by Chladni[8] in the 19th century with his **Chladni figures:** various geometrical patterns emerged, veritable **mandalas,** when the edges of circular plates covered with fine sand were rubbed with a violin bow, thereby producing different tones. **The resonating frequencies arranged the fine sand into wonderful geometrical patterns. Such processes are constantly happening in our material bodies, especially in our body liquids.** Low

....
8   Michael Faraday and the Slovene physicist Jožef Stefan researched the shape-giving power of sound. Check the book by the most prominent Slovene acoustician Miroslav Adlešič, *Svet žive fizike (The World of Living Physics)*, Ljubljana, Mladinska knjiga (1964), pp. 381-382.

frequencies form more simple material forms, while high frequencies create more intricate geometrical patterns.

According to the law of resonance, the resonating Universe enables us to carefully hear yet other, different frequency levels of consciousness and multidimensional reality. Modern quantum physicists claim that **the Universe is Consciousness.** Consciousness which is constantly creating. Shamans would call it the Great Soul, the Great Spirit. Well, vocabularies differ. Call it what you want. The resonating world of the conscious Universe is also called **the sound yarn, 'the old spider woman's web,'** as the Native Americans would say.

The levels or octaves above the third, physical level are accessed **in dreams, meditation, and in strong feelings of love and devotion.** They can also be accessed in **a relaxed (alpha) state and during sacred ceremonies and initiations,** where we establish **a conscious link** to the singing octaves. In those states, our extra-sensory abilities also reveal **the collective consciousness** and its **power**.

In their dreams, humans **journey to (astral) levels** beyond the third physical level, spontaneously and without effort. **They then travel, with their consciousness, through the multidimensional Universe.** For thousands of years, humans have striven to consciously attain astral and higher levels, to reach **the database levels of the akasha.** But the degree of **our success depends on the depth of our consciousness, on the openness of our mind and our wholeheartedness.**

Those who have attained or **experienced those levels,** have described their experiences **in detail** (especially the ancient Vedic rshis) and have given them different names. However, such journeys and the conquest of those 'higher' pyramidic steps of existence, are certainly pretty **strenuous** for the physical body, because **the body needs to adjust to high-frequency vibration undulation, which it was not used to before.** That is the reason why travellers across the worlds are usually **extremely tired** after such adventures. When, for example during group ceremonies or today's courses with spiritual content, **we try to connect to the unconscious high dimensional worlds,** people always feel tired and slowed-down after that, **their cheeks glow.** This fatigue lasts until the body has adjusted to the new waves. Then comes relief, new understandings and insights (from other viewpoints, from other levels of perspective), which are followed by **an increased physical and spiritual power thanks to an increased energy flow.**

There is a simple tool for connecting across the octaves of our being and the Universe: **our breath.** Relaxed breathing connects us to our consciousness, to our soul, and to all the resonating octaves of our being and the Universe. With breath (and with sound), awakened ones can travel between these levels as they wish, and even beyond them, because they are in tune with all the octaves; they perceive and sense them, they manage and live them.

The levels beyond the seventh level, beyond the astral levels, are the levels of cosmic sound, the levels of the primal vibration resonance of the Cosmic Mind, of the song of the Universe. From there, the Source 'communicates' with everything that exists. That is why we say that high-frequency sound (which is even higher than gamma rays) is **the communication system of the Universe, it is a multidimensional language, a bridge between the worlds.**

We can also speak about **the seven important life levels of the physical world, about seven or nine bodies, energy centres (chakras) and the seven developmental levels of consciousness. Human consciousness, or better – shaman's consciousness, can reach to the seventh level.**[9] The subsequent levels are called the Absolute, the Source, God.

We are able to grasp **twelve octaves, twelve dimensions, twelve levels of fulfilment, of wholeness, perfection, divinity. Yet the levels beyond the ninth dimension of the axis of consciousness** (*axis mundi*) **are the worlds of the unintelligible Logos, the Absolute Silence and the omnipresent 'full' Nothing, or the Galactic Centre,** as the Mayans would call it.

The sound technology of different octave relationships of the singing Universe can also trigger the waves which create the geometry of **so-called crop circles.** The language of the **cosmic and sacred geometry** of different octave universes is encoded in them.

Octaves of sound and light in the auric field - reflections of higher dimensions in the physical world

In physics and music textbooks, **sound** is usually described as **longitudinal frequency undulation** of air particles, of molecules in the air. Yet, sound is far more than this. It is **energy undulation suffused with information. It has its own tone height, temperature, energy, colour, and even its own volume. It is enriched with the energies of thoughts and feelings.**

Physical, audible sound is also an efficient tool for attuning to the inaudible octaves of the resonating world, to the inaudible high-frequency non-material worlds. That is why we say that sound is an inter-dimensional window, vehicle or boat, which takes us across the boundless **ocean of the infinite symphony of frequencies.** In folk tradition, it is most often symbolised by **the wind or by a white horse** galloping across boundless expanses.

....
9   Remember that the levels of consciousness are named and numbered only to facilitate easier communication.

Life is more or less conscious eavesdropping on the sound play, in which we eagerly seek **the wisdom of listening, hearing, attuning and harmony:** in both the physical and spiritual worlds, in relationships, thoughts and actions, as well as a harmony between our bodies, soul, consciousness, the Universe and the Earth. **At their core, every thought and emotion is sound, and we continuously shape and create our reality with it. Ceremonies are important tools for expressing this intent and transformation.** With harmony or disharmony, we create **a new reality** all the time.

Sound vibrations are also the movement of energy in frequency patterns of individual octaves. They are the projection of a high-dimensional reality into the material world. Its attunement manifests as beauty, harmony, euphony, peace, and love.

Even seeing is a phenomenon of resonance. But we are able to hear far more octaves than we are able to see. **We see only one octave – the frequency field of seven colours, while our physical ear can hear ten octaves!** Ten different frequency sets or sonic colour shades. Yet our ability to see and hear is **only a drop in the boundless ocean,** compared to the infinite frequency (dimensional) waves of the Universe! Are we in fact able to recognise our poverty and the richness that resides on the other side? **With their extra-sensory cosmic telepathy, awakened persons can attentively hear more levels, perhaps even all the octaves, because they are not limited in their perception** of those dimensions which are difficult to imagine. It is human beings themselves who either limit themselves or reach out into the fairy worlds of the boundless.

Our auric field is charged by electromagnetic frequency waves, which strive to be attuned to the Earth's vibration, to the audible sound of **the Earth's rotation** (194 Hz). This frequency **changes** a little all the time. It is currently increasing. If we octave **(multiply or increase)** the inaudible rhythm (tone) of one Earth day movement **by 24,** its frequency waves **(from 8 to 10 Hz in the octave displacement)** will be **heard in our hearing field.** This frequency is called tone G or **SOL.** The tone G, as the fifth tone, or **quinta,** in the octave, was designated as SOL. The Earth's **companion, the Sun,** was named **Solei** and the Earth's name is **Gea.**

Our **auric field is a medium, a conductor** when aligning with **cosmic octave levels of this tone,** as well as with any other tone with a similar sound quality, which **ceaselessly undulates across the Universe,** as astrophysicists claim, and **bombs the Earth as well.** The tone of the Earth's rotation is also **the tone of a relaxed alpha state of consciousness (EEG from 8 to 10 Hz),** as well as **the cosmic tone** of the vibration of the Primordial life energy, or the Source. **THEY ALL HAVE THE SAME RESONANCE** – from 8 to 10 Hz. In our hearing field, this frequency is perceived as the octave displacement of **the tone G.**

Isn't this fact very interesting and extremely revealing at the same time? **To be, to live within oneness, within wholeness, therefore means to live within the energy vibration of the tone G and within all its octave displacements!** When we are attuned to the Earth, to the Primordial (divine) Intelligence and to ourselves and when we are in a relaxed alpha state, we are centred along the octave axis, which 'runs from the Earth's heart chakra to the Source,' and in the opposite direction as well – depending on our 'point of view,' claim the ancient ones. **During this time,** our **mind is calm;** the brain waves of both hemispheres (EEG) become coherent **when we are in harmony with the frequency of the Earth tone, with the vibration of the Galactic Primordial Centre.** We resonate with both **the consciousness of primordial perfection and our physical body,** which is thereby supported and strengthened.

The organ of Corti, located in the cochlea of our **ear, is composed of thousands of strings. It vibrates and transmits impulses into our auric body, into etheric bodies, brains, and glands. Hormones** secreted by glands then travel **into our blood and entire body,** into each cell and every string of **the light-sound quanta of the physical world.** This is how **messages from beyond space and time, messages of clairvoyant and clair-knowing persons are transmitted** through octaves, through dimensions. **Each frequency oscillates a precisely determined string, a receptor,** which then transmits the signal further on to where it is possible, or where it is needed. We must not forget that we also **resonate,** or to put it another way – **we echo in the sounds to which we listen:** both our consciousness and our entire body and every cell.

Even our etheric bodies resonate.[10] **Every layer of our aura has its own frequency, and every (subsequent?) auric layer 'resounds' in an octave with a higher frequency.** These different frequencies can be **seen as the different colours** of those bodies. What is more, each energy centre, each **chakra, pulsates in a characteristic frequency,** performing a distinct **physical-spiritual metabolism.**

Condensed frequency waves which build the material body also function according to such laws of co-oscillation. **Every cell** and all its parts, **every light-sound superstring, every organ** and each body vibrates, resounds and attunes to those frequencies which it **needs and requires to be able to work and develop properly. If this is not the case, disturbances, degenerations and diseases emerge.**

Therefore, if human frequency waves are attuned to the vibrations required by their individual material parts, or body parts, – which means that humans are **aligned along the vertical axis of the resounding Universe – we will be healthy, happy, and fulfilled.** But if frequency waves are disharmonious, if **an alien rhythm (frequency pattern) is imposed** on our cells and organs, then **disturbances, defects,**

---
10   The human auric field is said to have the frequency of 10^{-9} or 10 nanometres.

and diseases emerge. The flow of life energy is thus blocked and our organs and body do not have the required energy fuel. We will only feel tired at first, but a disease can develop if those blocks last longer. **With our unloving emotions and thoughts, we create blocks in this flow.**

The frequencies of our auric body, or field, are higher than those of our material body. The auric body oscillates with frequencies **outside the linear mind and outside the wavelengths of the material world** which conforms to physical (Newton's) laws. That is why the etheric auric bodies are **a medium between the physical body and the spirit,** or consciousness. And **the throat,** which creates audible sound, is an extremely important organ – it is a merciless gatekeeper and **a sound bridge leading into the 'high-frequency worlds.'** Using words, **the throat chakra (the etheric mould of the human aura) creates audible sound and expresses our thoughts** and emotions. The throat is also **a vibrational organ of communication** located in our material body, just like **the seven-dimensional cosmic sound of the Intelligence of life** is the communication tool across both the non-material and material levels. **The sound of our throat chakra voices both our thoughts and emotions and the visions of the cosmic Logos. It creates, shapes, nourishes, and transforms matter, in line with the laws of co-oscillation and holographic connection across the octaves of reality.** If we are afraid to say something, or to express something, it is like sticking a cork into our throat. **The bridge leading to the higher worlds of spirit will thus remain closed.**

The seventh energy centre, **the seventh chakra, located at the top of the head,** is said to be a centre which can communicate with frequencies; even with the highest frequency waves, **with the Creator, the Intelligence of the Universe.** It is a rapidly pulsing receiver of the visions of the Cosmic Mind, of Divine thought and Idea. It is a highly sensitive **cosmic-telepathic detector, a radar for inaudible octave waves.**

If there is no harmony between the octaves and if there is **dissonance** instead of resonance, **we get sick,** because we live in the centrifuge of chaotic relationships and in **poverty of all kinds,** which only confirms our **flow blockage.** That is why, for aeons, sages have **intuitively sought and created the sound of harmony. They sought the missing, or the supporting, sound, which everybody needs in order to maintain harmony, happiness, and abundance.** The sound of harmony was found in **the annual rotation of the Earth (the tone C).** It was also recognised in the tone of the Earth's platonic year (**tone F**), **with which our seventh chakra resonates,** rising like a funnel above our heads into infinite octave displacements.[11]

....
11   The tone F is the ancient official tone of Chinese mystics. Check the book *Die Oktave* by Hans Cousto.

The Universe is thought and consciousness. We can say that it is the echo, or the cosmic sound of the primordial Intent, of the primordial Idea; it is the symphony, or the orchestra of countless waves, countless frequencies, which resonate across the octaves, across dimensions in the form of the audible and inaudible sound waves of our emotions, thoughts, and consciousness. In the material world, the Universe also resonates as the sound of the unmanifested field which is continuously creating.

The Universe is therefore governed by three most important principles: frequency energy vibration through the octaves, the law of resonance, or the law of attunement, and the essence of perfection, the essence of perfect love which is the link and glue between the Universe and life.

Resonance can be **sympathetic** or it can be **imposed and morphic** or shape-giving. It can also be **radiant**, like the Earth's magnetic radiation, and **acoustic**.

> The great Audible Logos of the Universe
> is **the Father** and **the Mother**;
> it is a **thought, word, sound, and form**,
> which reveals itself as **music and energy**,
> as **whisper** and the flapping of a bird's wing.
> It seems like **a mirror and an echo of the divine Source**,
> like a spiral serpent, or a spirited **horse** galloping across the Field,
> like **the sound waves of the visible and invisible flow.**
> Sound can be **poison or a remedy**,
> which rouses and **awakens**,
> which is heard in ceremonial rhythms and songs,
> **which attunes and encourages you,** like the *nagual* guide,
> and shows you **the way to the centre of your own soul and mind.**[12]

The intelligence agency of our glands and a music medium, therapist, shaman, and cosmic telepath

This is what happened to me in **1995.** For several days I had been meditating with my **healer friends,** checking the energy activity of our healing and the vibrations emanating from our hands. We then headed to **the Posočje Region** to help **Marko Pogačnik,** the Slovene spiritual legend of geomancy and Earth acupuncture. Marko needed help in discovering the souls of the dead an blessing those who had died during **the First World War** in the Posočje Region. We wanted to

---
12   Mirit, *Sonic Universe in the Alchemy of Sound and Soul*, September 2012.

help the soul husks of those poor people killed in the horrible maelstrom of war at the beginning of the last century. We wanted to help them to set free from being stuck in the physical world, so that they could move on. We walked the area of the worst battles of that time. After many hours of intense work, I visited Tolmin Church with a friend. All of a sudden, **I heard wonderful music, a majestic and mellifluous choir of singers.**

"Do you hear it?" I asked my friend who was standing next to me. "**Do you hear this beautiful song?**"

But she just looked at me in surprise and said:

"Do I hear what? **I don't hear anything!**"

"You really can't hear? They are rehearsing very loudly."

She hadn't heard anything. But I was **immersed in those magical sounds and utterly melting in sublime harmonies and sweet voices.** The sounds filled me **with a loving peace** and with a special, inexplicable **power of spirit.** But it was not until a couple of years later that I grasped what I had actually heard in that small church. **The celestial bani, or shabd,** as **whisper yoga** is called, **was speaking only to me, it was speaking only within my wide open consciousness, my soul.** My friend couldn't hear it.

This event was **an introduction to my exploration of the wonderful abilities of human multidimensional consciousness.** When I came out of the church, I told the people gathered in front of it what had happened. Enraptured, Marko Pogačnik said:

"**Why didn't you write down what you heard?**"

I looked at him in amazement and said:

"Because it is impossible! These sounds and tones are simply impossible to write down! They can't be transmitted into our linear mind, time, and space! Any transfer would be but a shadow of what I had heard and experienced. The great musicians – **Bach, Mozart, Scriabin, Wagner,** etc. – perhaps did something similar, or at least in a limited way." They could hear voices and miraculous music, but **they were able to note down only an approximation of that!** But this **whisper of the Universe, this divine song** had been heard by **the sages, priest-musicians, and healers of long forgotten teachings.**"

Our brains, or brainwaves, measured with EEG devices, **are distinct sound receivers and transmitters; they are a radio, an indicator of the rhythms of consciousness – both cosmic and human consciousness.** Our entire body and brains are extremely sensitive to sound vibrations from all levels, from all octaves. **The pineal and pituitary glands** are of special importance in this process, as **they transmit, or 'filter' signals from the Universe into the physical world. They carry 'messages' into our body** with the help of **hormones** which they create under the influence of cosmic rhythms, cosmic waves, and everyday human reactions. **The pituitary gland,** called **the king of all glands,** is responsible for the harmonious life processes of our entire being; it also controls the work of other glands and the entire organism. Some traditions **associate** both the pineal and pituitary glands **with the soul, with consciousness.** They claim that both glands are antennae (like the seventh chakra) for the highest frequency waves. They are said to have a very important role in the expansion of consciousness, in spiritual development, and in inter-dimensional (shamanic) out-of-body travels on the wings of consciousness.

Transferring the waves of the Intelligence of life, the Logos, into our consciousness, **leads us back to the Centre, to our centredness, to perfection, and fulfilment.** Using various techniques, spiritual seekers of past cultures attempted, in different ways, to awaken **the dormant abilities of both glands** about which the official medical profession still knows very little. Perhaps that is the reason why the ancient Mayans performed **head binding** – to balance the work of both hemispheres, which **enables enlightened insights.** But more about this will follow.

So, sound is an important tool and technology for the expansion of consciousness and for connecting with all octave levels of our existence. It is an inter-dimensional **messenger, a connector and maintainer, as well as a transmitter of messages from the high-dimensional reality into the physical world. Frequency waves can be perceived with all senses:** with hearing, sight, touch (skin), even with smell, and taste. Yet, **with our physical senses,** we receive and recognise **only a small part of the complete universal symphony and show.**

We can do much more with cosmic telepathic abilities. **With extra-sensory cosmic telepathic sensations, we reach into the holographic whole incomprehensible to** the usual **mind,** which sees reality as being linear, in the past-present-future line, and only in three dimensions. With sound, we penetrate into **the all-encompassing multi-level frequency waves. Endocrine glands carry this high-frequency information into our auric field, etheric bodies and chakras, into our energy nadis, nervous system, blood, and into our physical body.** Hormones, secreted by glands, **carry the impulses of the Universe and consciousness into blood.** And **our organs, tissues and cells 'communicate' with each other through blood and cell rhythms.** That is why the endocrine glands are, together with our brain (hypothalamus), also **a control centre.** Glands, together with our nervous system, control our body responses – **fight or flight.** The pituitary gland can, for example, activate the **adrenal glands,** which are, among other things, responsible for our **physical power** and for the dissolving of **worry. The gland information system is able to remove worry and stress,** claim Chinese traditional healers.

Cosmic telepathy is a unique phenomenon which enables us to carefully hear high-frequency waves, or vibrations above the physical level of the third dimension. And **synesthesia is the ability to feel, to hear the emotions and thoughts of other people and the ability of resonance in the material world.** It is the ability to perceive different frequency waves. Some called cosmic telepathy **teleradiesthesia:** a technique for **hearing high-frequency cosmic waves,** or as Pythagoras would say, the sound of the harmony of different universes.

Techniques for hearing, which were known to Vedic rshis and jyotish astrologers, as well as to wise sages and healers of different ancient traditions, enable and **increase clair-perception of all our senses and meta-senses, both clairvoyance and clairaudience.** This is also made possible by **light-sound codes, or sound formulae, selected sounds, words, mantras and sutras, songs, rhythms and prayers,** etc.

Through their use, our consciousness aligns to different frequency worlds or octaves, even if we don't understand how the sound formulae work, and even without our total surrender to their effects. It aligns to the realms which were unknown to us until then. This happens unexpectedly, like my experience when I first received **the bija mantra,** following which I had a strong feeling that my life started to evolve in the opposite direction – **away from falling apart.** And when, in the initiation process, I received the light-sound code of the **cosmic resonance** technology (of the traditional shiki ryoho **reiki**) for aligning to the primordial life energy, for aligning my own mind to the Cosmic Mind, I burst into inconsolable tears, saying that **I wanted to go Home,** Home... At that time, **I had no idea what those words** and tears, **received and expressed through cosmic telepathy, meant. I only sensed,** at high-octave levels of consciousness, **the grace of the primordial Mercy, the Home of the soul.** I realised this only later. **The higher levels of consciousness know, but our mind is unable to grasp** what is happening, what the mind is touching, or what the sound codes and words actually mean.

In their throats, musician-shamans and healers create sound, they create needed frequency waves. They seldom look for them **in musical instruments,** but if they do so, **the shamanic drum** is very appropriate for this. The sonic remedy, the song, is channelled down through all levels of consciousness and is anchored in etheric bodies and the material world. **Every stage musician** is also a distinct **contemporary shaman,** if, with their sound and with the power of the energy of their emotions and intuitive insight, **they reach into the consciousness and even into the bodies of the audience.** This can be done **with the energy of selected sounds, harmonies and rhythms,** which they anchor into the audible and physical world. In line with the laws of imposed resonance, **they oscillate, cleanse, and charge the auric bodies,** emotions, and thoughts of the audience. This is how **musician-therapists heal.**

The truly effective musical art – which, centuries ago, was simultaneously also a healing art – mirrored **the medium-shaman's abilities** and was thus always performed **in a transcendental state of consciousness, in the shamanic trance**. It **attuned both the performer and the audience,** the healer and the patient, the priest and ceremony participants. It connected them to higher worlds, **to the Great Spirit** and the joyful **peace of euphony. It brought** to people **an invisible message about the gifts of Universal Love, which should suffuse every note and every sound.** Only in this way it can be truly effective.

Within the sound energy of higher octaves and love, the musician-medium and the audience resonate together in the harmony of beneficent sounds. People telepathically sense this invisible link and **the message from beyond time.** They say that they can powerfully feel the artist's voice, as well as their play and **the sound charge** of their instruments. This is what children said after a concert by my Vedun Ensemble: "**Your music smelled like bread from a baker's oven. Like the sweetest nectar in my throat, like balm in my heart…**"

Good stage artists should also be excellent therapists with a consciousness broad enough to be able to **create that energy field, that energy power** which will oscillate the bodies and souls of masses, and attune them to **the sonic messages of sound perfection.** In this way, **they bring into the world the selected sound energy which they create.**

But every applause with its snapping sounds, and every rhythmical shaking, breaks the energy connection between the performer, the sound waves and the audience. That is why applause is welcome only when musicians finish their performance of a piece of music, of an energy form and content, and **want to wipe an 'old sound imprint' from the room (ether)** and commence a different sound message. This is what every shaman and healer is aware of, when they are 'expelling the bad from energy fields and bodies' with the use of rhythms and noises. **With some sounds and rhythms, they can** of course **change the sound image of living beings, they can attune them to what they wish.**

Moreover, musician-healers and therapists must know how to align themselves to the vibrations of individual people, how to 'wipe out' their possible disharmonies, find their sound, discover the frequencies they lack, and add **what people need** in order to resonate in harmony again. This is how **healing, (re-)programming, and the manifestation of ideas** are done – from the idea to the material form.

Throughout history, **numerous sages explored the effects of sound and built the knowledge of it.** They were consciously building and using **the mastery of mind. The (shamanic) technology and use** of certain sound frequencies had been created and **passed down** for thousands of years. It served to both restore health and call in abundance and a joyful fulfilment. **This harmonising sound technology is as old as the world;** or it has certainly existed at the very least from the moment when humans began to be amazed by the power of sound.

Every tone, every rhythm causes changes in our consciousness and, consequently, also in our physical body. Every frequency is in fact rhythmical undulation. Rhythm is also a multidimensional (multi-octavic) cosmic language. And **rhythmical waves are the primal essence of our being and life,** given the fact that human consciousness, as well as our etheric and physical bodies, are made up from different rhythmical waves. **We react to this rhythmical undulation and its patterns,** we create them consciously or unconsciously, we listen to them continuously, we attune to them, or we decline them if they do not appeal to us, or if they are not in tune with us.

Rhythm is the language of our bodies, our emotions, thoughts and the layers of consciousness; it is the formula of cosmic and earthly cycles, the very pattern matrix of life and death. That is why rhythm is the most primal force and perhaps even the most powerful tool of shamans and healers, as well as that of spiritual teachers, priests, and musicians from different cultures. **Shamanic drumming, or the singing of guided sounds, affects our brainwaves and the coherence of our brain; it indirectly influences our consciousness as well: it can relax, connect, ground or elevate us, charge and strengthen us, it can create, dissolve, cleanse, etc.**

The melodies of songs and tunes influence our emotions and thoughts. They fill them with the energy created by the musician, or therapist. And this energy, in turn, affects our thoughts and emotions. **Harmony is the language of balance,** it is opposite to imbalance. **Harmony has the power to open our minds and different levels of our consciousness,** which is why it is the most important language of the enlightened ones. Being oblivious to this important knowledge brings about manifold unpleasant and painful imbalances, or **dissonance,** which is reflected in our lives. And this oblivion also echoes in today's modern music. **Imbalanced sound waves make us stupid, they close our minds and hearts and foster unhappiness at all levels of existence.**

Rhythm, melody, and harmony are important **building blocks** of sound language, of **musical language and of energy-sound therapy. They are also the keys to transformation and alchemical processes of life, keys to the quest for a self-realised euphony.**

The human voice has a powerful impact on both the material and non-material. **Vowels create harmony in the human body, they connect and expand its energy potential; while consonants, like snaps, dissolve blocked energies in our etheric bodies, they cut and file, decompose and dissolve, if and what is needed.

Vowels and consonants create **syllables** and virtually all traditions of the world have **sacred syllables**, which are **important sound formulae for aligning along the axis, or the levels, of consciousness** and for the realisation of visions. They encourage the free flow of energy potential through our energy centres and bodies.

Until recently, **Slovene tradition** knew a simple **children's sound game for self-harmonisation with vowels,** with the effects of the vowels. I have known it since childhood. Everybody in Slovenia knows "a, e, i, o, u, mame ni domu."[13] Beside the most known sacred syllables, such as **hu, hum, hrim, aum, there are also simple sound codes** from the folk tradition, such as **hey, hoy, ay,** whose purpose is **to harmonise** and balance. Priests of past eras commenced sound rituals with them. With them, they prepared the room, as well as themselves and the ritual participants, for the sacred ritual of harmonisation.

The principle of life is like an incomprehensible supercomputer. Our body is like a computer, while our mind, our thoughts are like a computer program, and our lives are a mirror of this splendid computer system, which teaches us to understand the nature of our reality. Thoughts and emotions trigger different frequency waves, they trigger **an electromagnetic flow, which in turn triggers bio-chemical molecular changes.**

Sound can also be a distinct **sonic x-ray device,** because the audible qualities of sound waves fairly clearly reveal the story of the current state. **The muffled sound of a drum or a rattle indicates the quality and flow of a sound wave** which has crashed into an energy **block, or obstruction. A clear, pure and strong sound, which can even be enhanced in the body, points to a free flow and to a connection across the levels, or octaves, of existence.** African and other peoples use **dried gourd rattles** for this purpose, while Native Americans use **leather bags filled with pebbles or seeds,** which are tied to a wooden stick for easier shaking. When they jump around bodies with them, they listen in order **to detect diseased spots (blockages). Rattling also dissolves energy blocks in living beings and in the environment.** Even gentle tapping on afflicted body organs – **percussion** – reveals **the truth about the state of frequencies captured in matter,** about the state of diseased body parts. But of course not every noise or rattle has a healing effect. The knowledge about it has been handed down **from generation to generation** everywhere.

....
13   "A, E, I, O, U – *mame ni domu; če pa je doma, kuhati ne zna.*" This is how the chant went – but in the atomic age more as a joke. However, the original purpose was probably different.

The enchantment, or alchemy of sound and light

I can
see angels
sitting on your ears,

polishing trumpets,
replacing **lute** strings,
stretching new skins on **the drums**
and gathering wood for the evening's fire.

They all **danced last night**
but you did not
hear Them.

If you ask Hafiz for advice
on **how to befriend their sweet voices**
and how to have the nourishing
company of the finer worlds
I would reply,

"**I could not say anything**
you could not
tell me."

Then,
what was the use of this story?

O,
I just felt like
talking.[14]

....
14   Hafiz, poem *I Can See Angels*, taken from the book *The Gift*, New York, Penguin Compass (1991).

Double ocarina shaped like two birds.

Harmonics, also called **harmonic partials, or aliquot tones (formants), are also important sound tools.** They resonate through all octave dimensions of each tone and give them colour. The interval between individual harmonics is always **64 Hz**. Harmonic partials follow in sequence across the octaves into infinity. This sequence reflects the harmony of the Universe. With their extraordinary energy, past and present masters of aliquot singing are able to change pretty quickly the **frequency state of consciousness and energy reality** of both the performers and the listeners, primarily of those who are sick or 'shattered.' By using harmonics, we can also influence the matter very effectively. Siberian shamans have preserved this wisdom until today within their **throat singing.**[15]

Tones, especially **harmonics** which we can create simply by **clapping our palms** gently **on our open mouths** whilst voicing vowels, have a powerful **influence on our brainwaves and consciousness, and even on our heartbeat. Children** are familiar with this magical game, which they play mainly when they feel the need to harmonise their energy fields. **The mysterious ritual murmuring and Native American ceremonial and war cries** have the same effect. We can create **a sound laser** by shaping our mouths into funnels, we can even focus the created sound onto the chosen goal.

It is interesting to note that harmonics, or aliquot tones, appear in **the interval ratios of the harmonious golden section.** They follow successively in the interval ratios of **a fourth, eighth, fifth, third, sixth and so on – which means in the most important sonic building blocks of our music and in the tuning of instruments.**

Until recently, all important **instruments** were tuned **in fifths and fourths**, whereas today only a few folk instruments have preserved this tuning. **The accompaniment of drones, or the fundamental intervals of a fifth or fourth,** held an important place **until the second half of the 20th century.** The entire Balkan Region, the Slavic musical heritage in Slovenia and elsewhere around the world echoed with their harmonies.

But this therapeutic practice has virtually disappeared today. In all musical genres, **the intervals of a fifth and fourth enhanced both the audible power and energy power of the basic sound and melody.** This was so **until Renaissance,** when a more modern multi-part and polyphonic expression was anchored in all musical languages. **Primordial simplicity lost its meaning and purpose, and music lost its therapeutic, healing function.**

15   See the third book in the *Cosmic Telepathy* series.

In its core, **every frequency wave is a rhythm, or a rhythmical oscillation, which is why** rhythmical sound, **drumming, is the most primal sound tool.** Before starting a sound ceremony, we usually have to **carefully prepare** the energy of **the room, clear away all disturbing vibrations with song, with sound, so that the ceremony participants can connect with each other more easily and ascend to higher levels of consciousness. And of course, the magus, shaman, choirmaster, musician-therapist, priest and ritual participants have to purify themselves first** – from all negative and unloving emotions and thoughts, as well as from all disharmonic contents in their auric imprints. **Screaming, drumming, and the shaking of rattles and bodies are a wonderful help** with this. We all have heard the harmonising **cries of Native Americans,** as they dance in the ceremonial arena, around the sacred tree, or fire. This **sound scalpel** is able to cut into the mind and body, into the consciousness and the ceremonial room.

Spiritual warriors can make use of different **sound formulae** during ceremonies. **All songs,** various **symbols,** secret **messages** hidden **in mythology,** and **multidimensional light-sound codes** are in fact sound formulae.

In the millennia before the Common Era, an extremely powerful technology of sound was developed by our planetary ancestors: the ancient Mayans, Celts, Slavic and Siberian shamans, ancient Egyptians and Greeks, Aboriginal peoples and Native American tribes, Indo-European peoples, Indonesians and Polynesians, Hawaiians, Indian rshis, and others. The Mayans certainly belong to this company of sound magi. They first had to become thoroughly familiar with the effects of sound. And on the basis of their discoveries, they brought together their **magical knowledge for the alchemical processes of sound, for the technology of sound.**

During magical practices, they enhanced their sonic work **with light effects, as light effects can increase our audial span and strongly expand our consciousness and awareness.** Even the grandeur of **a ceremonial fire,** which had been burning for several days and nights, asked people to surrender to **the spiritual fire of transformation, which burns, or dispels, all negative things. The Sun,** which visibly changes the world, is a representative of the cosmic fire on Earth; it can encourage the world to grow or it can dry it out and destroy it.

Thousands of years ago, in times before the Common Era, **the divine sacred sound, the cosmic sacred sound, raised consciousness on Earth. Our planetary ancestors shaped the reality of the moment with this sound; they even shaped contents of their lives according to their desires:** first the spiritual content, then the material. They were familiar with the eternal laws, for example: **by changing the frequency wave, or (sound) signal, you will change the contents of the moment, the octave of your reality. Along with it, you will change your consciousness and the world.** If you want to experience realms **beyond** the material world, **change the (sound) vibration of your consciousness** and with it, indirectly, also **the contents of your mind and your experiences.** With pure and focused thought and song, you are able **to 'sing your way' into different and mysterious realms of spirit!**

The power of a ceremony is shaped by selected and consciously created rhythms, which should follow, like an echo, cosmic rhythms and earthly cycles, the rhythms of repetition. With the help of those rhythms, ceremony participants change the waves of their consciousness and brain, they awaken their understanding of higher levels of consciousness. Ceremonies, ennobled with sound, provide an experience of high-octave Truths and reveal the existential (frequency) matrices which dwell at astral and higher levels, at the levels beyond the third – physical – level.

And **the energy imprints of our supplications, prayers, and songs return to our environment and to the Universe.** They imprint themselves into the energy field of the room and into the energy bodies of people. The imprints coming from the cosmic Field, where the imprints of our thoughts and visions are, then descend **to the material level**; they get embodied in the physical world.

By connecting to the forces of the Universe we are able to awaken the power of manifestation, the energy of realisation. It is possible to shape and fulfil our desires **with a focused attention and clear intent, supported by the sound. Ceremony creates the necessary connection to all the rhythms of the Universe and the Earth. To understand the rhythm is to see spirit, the Universal, everywhere.** This is how the dormant abilities of our multidimensional spirit are uncovered, how harmony, **the well-being of 'attunement'** is restored.

The sound-therapeutical musical art of the past is an inter-dimensional language and a multidimensional skill. The musical science of astronomy and mathematics, **or the discipline of sacred geometry,**[16] was esteemed until the Renaissance, as was the science and medicine of the body and spirit. Through them, humans can elatedly **dance with the divine.** But only if they have managed to discover the keys which open the path to the divine realms beyond. **Musical artistic expression and performance require a scientific mind and sense.**

Since pre-history, sound has revealed relationships between the material and non-material, it has strengthened the link between the Sky and the Earth. At least until the dawn of the Common Era, our ancient planetary ancestors have preserved this awareness and knowledge of frequency attunement to the Earth, the Universe and to the laws of life. They were the **magi** of different dimensions, of different octave realities; they were **the shamans of an octave**

....
16   More about sacred geometry can be found in the seventh book in the *Cosmic Telepathy* series, which deals with ancient Egyptian and ancient Greek wisdom.

(holographic) all-connectedness, of harmony. The song of an awakened person, the sound of an enlightened shaman has always revealed itself sumptuously in the euphonies of **sonic, rhythmic, harmonic, and melodic patterns.**

Shamanic drumming literally **imposes** on people (according to the laws of forced resonance) the oscillation of **a relaxed alpha state of consciousness (between 8 and 10 Hz), as well as the oscillation of the theta shamanic trance (between 5 and 8 Hz).** In this particular state, sound is especially effective as it **heals, dissolves, fills, protects, strengthens, identifies, connects, converses; it even enters our unconscious and meta-conscious, thus preparing us for the sacredness of a ritual attunement.** To achieve this, our ancestors employed **the technology of noise and rattle, of cries, even shouting,** in order to establish more easily **a channel for the medium's transfer of universal, divine, high-dimensional levels of sound and existence into here and now.**

Besides various frequencies (sounds), voices and tunings, **rattles** were also the indispensable **magical sonic tools of the past.** With them, it was possible to create **a healing noise, which dissolved disturbing energies in the human aura and environment.** Various rhythmical instruments, **drums** for example, were used to shape **suitable rhythms.**

The tone G was the tone around which **all music** revolved centuries ago; **in folk music, the tone G was the backbone of sonic creativity right up to the 20th century.** Voices rose above it, descended beneath it, and melded with it at least occasionally. **The beginnings and ends of songs and melodies had to resonate with this tone, like a distant echo and mirror of the game of Creation and life itself.** We come from the Source, from the Silence and we return to it. This ancient spiritual and sound practice, which is simultaneously **above** both **the fundamental tone** of the Earth and the primal, divine Intelligence, can still be found in **the Balkan throat singing** ojkanje for example. During ojkanje, singers develop **a melody** very skilfully **around the central sonic Sun, around the tone G,** and they occasionally **blend with it ecstatically to form a unison.** This ancient **technique for strengthening** the spirit and body has been preserved only in folk music in some areas.

The most sensitive sages of our planet were able to hear – even in octave displacements – the sound of the daily and annual rotation of the Earth. They heard the sound of the frequency created during the movement of our planet across **the cosmic-earthly year (the aeon).** They say the Earth's journey (a time period of approximately 2000 years) resounds in the tone **F.** And the technique for the strengthening of spirit and body was given the name **kung fu** – after the tone of the Earth's movement across **the aeon, the Platonic year,** which is of course mirrored also in all octave displacements of the tone **F.** This is why the Chinese named their official tone F. It is said that we **can never have too much** of the tone F, **because with this sound we receive the frequency waves of primal (divine) perfection.**

The instruments which had drone strings tuned to the Earth's tone (G) strengthened the physical body, expanded consciousness and even grounded visions and thoughts into the physical world. They were for example **drone instruments such as: European drone zithers, hurdy-gurdies and bagpipes,** which were popular in European aristocratic and bourgeois art until at least the end of the Middle Ages, and in folk art until the second half of the 20th century. The melody which was being played by the artist was **continuously accompanied by strings which resonated in the frequencies of the Earth's tone** and in pure ratios of **fifths, fourths, eights, etc.** Other instruments have a similar role and power: **flutes and stringed instruments alike, the basic tone of which is the sound of the Earth.** Arabic-Turkish **tambouras**, lijerica and **kemenche**, Greek **bouzoukis**, Indian **sitars and veenas**, Siberian **chartans and igils**, Slavic **bagpipes and hurdy-gurdies**, the Slovene **small cimbalom** with the lowest tone G, as well as Mayan **multi-chamber flutes**, all resonated in the cosmic-earthly drone. This is how instruments got **a harmonising, or healing, continuous sound.**

In addition, **the colour of the instrument, or the colouring of its voice,** was also very important in the past, as it furnished, enriched, and enhanced the effect of sound waves, and it also **altered its energy power.** When I play the Slovene **drone zither** called drsovce or švrkovence,[17] I find it **impossible to stop joy** emanating from the sounds which I am eliciting from the instrument. Sounds which are based on the Earth's sound **encourage movement and dancing.** The melody which I am playing rises and descends, while the drone in the tone of the Earth's movement remains **continuously present,** as if it was trying to say: **go and rise to spiritual heights together with the audience, but the earthly element will continue to resonate.** Until the strings break. **The delight** which emanates from this attuned instrument is unstoppable, while I am gliding along the frets, playing, channelling **the unrepeatable song of the current moment which celebrates life on Earth.** Joy then spreads around the room, among people and everyone **feels the need to move their bodies and rejoice, to dance and spin…**

The earthly frequencies of drone zithers fill us with the vibrations of physical power and **sustain our desire to live in the material world.** It is not surprising that the Church prohibited drone zithers centuries ago, it banished them from the church grounds and rituals, as only a spiritual presence was mandated. A pity

....
17   In Slovene, the word drsovce stems from the verb *drseti*, meaning to glide and the word *švrkovence* derives from the verb *švrkniti*, meaning to whip or flog. Hence the instrument's name denotes that the player 'glides over' or 'flogs' it with a wooden pick.

indeed, because joy and **a delight in the physical world open bridges to the higher realms of spirit. Tantric practitioners,** Slavic priests and reportedly also Mayan **spiritual warriors** knew this.

I recently made another important discovery. One day during my adventure in Cyprus I was very tired and my heart suddenly started to palpitate. A friend gave me a foot massage. He touched a very **painful heart point on my foot** all of a sudden. Immediately after, I heard a silent yet completely recognisable **high pitch** in my mind, in my consciousness. The tone lasted for at least thirty seconds. Then it disappeared. I had **an electronic tuner** and a Greek bouzouki with me, which I had just bought locally and had been playing a little earlier. I instantly checked the pitch of that barely audible frequency of the heart. What a surprise: the sound which I had heard and which **shows up sometimes in people's ears,** the sound that we occasionally hear if we are extremely tired or **stressed,** is in fact **the tone of the Earth's yearly rotation – tone C.** How about that, I thought. We should pay attention to this discovery and explore it further.

A flow of life energy was triggered during the massage, which allowed the Universal sound to run freely through me again. I believe that the Earth's tone nourishes us and strengthens our physical body and heart in a beautiful way. At the same time, it also serves as a portal into the symphony of the frequencies of the Universe, of the spirit. What the scientists of the Sorbonne have confirmed is true: **every cell has its own frequency, its own sound.** The same goes for each **organ and** each **body** which resonates in the total sum of all the above-mentioned frequency waves. And of course, the same goes for **the human body.** I would add yet another point to this: **our soul, our consciousness also has its own sound, as does every thought, idea, and vision. We live in a sonic Universe,** where sound, or song, creates our lives and **shapes the circumstances we live in.** The Universe plays its own music and our task is **to learn how to sing or play in harmony within this Universe, never to sing out of tune and never distort** this majestic **frequency-sound world** with aggression and insensitivity, destructive emotions, unloving thoughts and actions.

The purpose of life is clear: we must learn **how to play the game of life properly, harmoniously, and with dignity. Never against the flow of life,** because we would be destroying the harmony and euphony of the existing symphony. The purpose of life is **to learn how to be in tune and in a harmonious resonance.** In this quest we have the help of numerous **light-sound codes, or formulae, myths, fairy tales, legends, and of course songs, instruments, initiations and group ceremonies of the peoples and the cultures of the world throughout the history.** To resonate with the whole means to attain a fulfilled peace at the pyramid's summit.

Besides pure thought and clear intention, the principal magical tools for happiness, health, and abundance are: silence, selected sounds, and even noise – at the right moment and in the right place. The technology of climbing the axis of consciousness (the *axis mundi*) consists of: channelled guided movement (dance), the transcendental state of consciousness of performers and ceremony participants, as well as **shamanic trance** necessary to **consciously connect a ceremony participant to other octaves of cosmic-earthly levels.** Of help can also be **light-sound effects** created with sun light, fire and candles, as well as carefully selected **sound formulae and 'sacred syllables'** thoughtfully composed from the qualities of both vowels and consonants. Especially **effective** are **light-sound codes, as well as rich and hidden symbolism, myths, legends, tales, and fairy tales.** Magical tools were also **the well-thought-out melodic lines of ceremonial songs, harmonies and rhythms, as well as the colouring of sound with harmonics, with aliquot and throat singing, and the nasal colouring of the sound** (nose flutes which are played with the nose – not with the mouth). We should also include here **sound produced in the stomach** (sound enhanced in the stomach), as well as **chromatic microtonal glissando.** And the **shouted and exclaimed syllables ey, oy, ay, etc.** which are usually sung at the beginning or the end of a song, of a sound therapy. With them, the musician-therapist **clears and prepares the room for the sound play.** Moreover, the effects of sound therapy can be powerfully enhanced by **a laser-like sound** which comes from the musician's funnel-shaped mouth. All of the above, together with **a powerful sense of and clear thoughts about** the intent and desire of the ceremony, constitute the alchemical sonic toolkit of **every good magus, musician-therapist, and shaman.** The final **cadence** of a song or therapy, affirms the **'so be it'** thought (amen). Throughout the millennia, these tools enabled both *naguals* and ceremony participants to **sense and recognise,** with their souls and with all their bodies, **the wholeness of the sonic Universe and healing sounds on Earth.**

Clarity of vision and clarity of imagination are especially important in the process of creating with sound, **in the process of listening carefully** to the rhythms and harmonies of the Earth and the Universe. **They are a telephone line, a link to the divine Intelligence, to the Deities. Vision and imagination are just as real as thought, except that they can be reached at other (higher) levels of consciousness.** However, they are nonetheless equally tangible and are experienced just like life itself and just like the thinking mind of the three-dimensional world, space, and time. **Visionary thoughts or imaginary images help us to reach beyond the physical world** and draw from the spiritual and cosmic levels. **Transcending the usual mind enables a distinct reprogramming.** Using this sound magic, it was possible **to align to the Earth, to the Universe and to ourselves.**

The sound of the Big Bang resonates through all the octaves of the Universe and in human ears. It is a pity that 'everyone can **see (and hear), and yet we choose not to remember** what we see.'[18]

Years ago, astrophysicists reportedly discovered that the frequency wave, or **the sound, the murmuring, triggered at the time of the Big Bang which had created the world, still resonates in the Universe.** This primordial vibration still resonates **through everything that exists. Wise telepaths of the past were able to perceive and hear it.** They heard, or recognised it in the sound which resembles the consonant **M** in our audible sound language. They sensed it in the **rasping** of the consonant **H. The primordial sound, which is the harmonising sound of the beginning, of the Source, is in itself perfect and without distortions (so far).** It is embodied in **the sound codes** of different cultures, for example the ancient Vedic **HU, HUM, HRIM, AH,** the Egyptian **HOR,** the ancient Slavic **HURA (HURAY),** the Arabic **UHA** and the Hawaiian **ALOHA.** It can also be discerned in the Mayan **HUNAHPU** and **HU-NAB-HU.** These sounds are **the sounds of both the beginning and end; they are the vibrations of the creative forces of the Universe.** Such are also the Vedic **AUM, OM.**

The Mayan HUNAHPU represents the top **Deity, the Primal Principle of life, and the primordial sound of Creation; it is the sound of all sounds, the most powerful tool for transformation and also a remedy.** But, above all, this sound is the inconceivable **Absolute, the Source, the Centre of everything.** When we manage to carefully hear it within ourselves and when we begin to resonate within all its qualities, we have found the most powerful tool **for attaining balance, for (self-)healing, realisation, and even for materialisation and dematerialisation.**

The sound of Creation is in itself perfect, and is therefore divine. Returning into it is beneficent. In our aural field, this sound is recognised as **the tone G,** it is the sound in which our **etheric, auric body resonates.** We hear it when we are **calm and completely relaxed,** or when our brainwaves (EEG) are in harmony, **coherent (alpha state between 8 and 10 Hz).** In this state, the frequency vibration of the tone G is in tune with the cosmic undulation which nourishes the Universe and which reaches the Earth in waves. This is the sound of **the Earth's daily rotation around its axis.**

By using sound tools or song, a meditating spiritual seeker can share **experiences gained** in a transcendental state of consciousness with the ceremony group. They anchor them in **the collective consciousness.** In an ecstatic trance, the seeker's

....
18   Carlos Castaneda, *The Wheel of Time*, London, Allen Lane, The Penguin Press (1998), p. 172. The note in brackets is mine.

body is able to secrete **hormones of mystical states, such as for example melatonin** which alleviates pain, or **endorphins** which cause **feelings of joy** and stimulate the secretion of other substances which **have a relaxing effect** on the physical body, on our feelings and consciousness.

Frequency waves alter the colloids in liquids, even in the liquids of cells and blood. That is why it is possible to carry out **painless anaesthesia** with sound. Perhaps the Mayans performed painless (or sound?) anaesthesia prior to sacrificing. Sound is, for example, the foundation of thousands of years old Hindu practices, of **Brazilian and Filipino psychic or cosmic surgeries,**[19] and perhaps even that of the Mayans.

The art and wisdom of **sound alchemy, or magic,** has been preserved and carefully passed down **from generation to generation** through hundreds, even thousands of years. Often **in secret.** They can be found, in fragments at least, among **Greek rhapsodes, medieval travelling singers, musicians and bards,** gauklers **and vagants, among shamans and healers of different cultures, and even among folk singers from different traditions – right up to the end of the 20th century.** In Slovenia, those sacred artists were called *igrci* (igra means play in Slovene), because they **entertained and healed people. With their healing buffooneries, they made the audience aware** and participated in different spiritual feats and important rituals.

Yet this combination of entertainment and the artistic demonstration of sound abilities, rather than being natural, was already pointing to the loss and fall of the wisdom of sound magic, the loss of the teachings and technologies of the ancient alchemical sound practice handed down for thousands of years. As the 20th century drew to a close, the ancient wisdom about the technology of light (energy), of cosmic telepathic sound, was almost completely destroyed. However, at the dawn of the new millennium, we are enthusiastically again **seeking and reviving it** – each in their own way, because **the tradition of those teachings** was unfortunately **interrupted** centuries ago. We are collecting but crumbs from a once richly loaded table, in our desire to make the cake whole again. Perhaps in the future, we will manage to put it together, because such **a poor awareness as we have today** is just not worth the effort and cannot be sustained for long.

When we perform music with love – we sing the world. We ennoble and invigorate it – if the sound (music) is right, of course. The wise shaman within us knows this sound and knows which sound is for joy and which dispels sorrow. Is this the reason why we love to sing and listen to music?

....
19   More about this can be found in the sixth book in the *Cosmic Telepathy* series.

The imprint of pain and suffering was stuck in the 230th octave

In the mid 90s, I often spent a few days with my energy therapist colleagues **exploring human energies,** energy bodies, and centres. We were among the first in Slovenia **to revive this forgotten spiritual wisdom and the laws of energy waves;** we were alone in wrestling with **the exploration of the laws of life. We first checked the inaudible and barely perceptible energy flows on ourselves,** and then of course on each other. And we were amazed. We were excited about every discovery, every new knowing. We were **rediscovering things which were perhaps well known millennia ago,** but which had been pushed into oblivion or burnt at inquisition stakes over hundreds, or even thousands of years.

I was sitting one night on a warm tiled stove in an old house where our company used to stay for a few days, reflecting on sound, on audible and inaudible frequency waves and their energies, when my healer friend complained about **his leg which had been painful for years.** He simply could not get rid of the pain – **neither him, his doctor, nor other healers.** Curious, I immersed myself in exploring his etheric bodies. Initially, I checked **the first basic octave of the seven etheric bodies. Isn't it miraculous how invisible energy bodies which cause us to live, think and feel actually follow each other just like the tones of an octave?** Or, is miraculous the fact that humans are able to pour their invisible **frequency energy dimension into the sound language of the seven tones of an octave!** There's probably no sense in trying to find out which came first – the chicken or the egg, the sound octave or the energy vibrations of seven, or nine, levels. Prior to both of them certainly was **Primal thought,** the primordial sound of Creation, the idea which is the matrix of everything. **This universal matrix of the Logos is reflected also in our DNA genetic structures** which determine the world of physical forms. **Genetic structures** are but sound **codes of the Universal** which are inaudible to the ear.

So in the summer of 1995, **I sat right through the night,** driven by a veritable stubbornness, **in an attempt to discover how many energy centres (chakras), octaves, or energy etheric bodies, a human being really had.** I strolled **from one octave to another,** I went higher, deeper into the unknown, into ever more subtle realms. The first set of seven was followed by another set of seven, or another octave, and the third, fourth ... then came the hundredth ... five hundredth ... thousandth. Previously, my awareness had been muddied by being **trapped in the mental world of representations,** in a teaching that humans have only seven etheric bodies. And not more. But I wanted to know how many energy bodies a person had. **The eighth body is in fact already the next octave with an equal resonance – and thefore with a similar content** of a tone, or a body.

Tired, I fell asleep around dawn. But that deep and calming sleep overwhelmed me only after I had discovered **that we were in fact boundless at the etheric frequency non-material levels. We stretch into the Universe across countless octaves,** and at the very end, at the summit (this is simply how we symbolically call it in our language), **we connect to the Source, the Primordial Intelligence, to the Divine Essence,** as we say. There, we are all one: me, you, he, and she. Everything that exists is constantly being born in this extraordinary energy headquarters (**in the Centre of everything** according to the Mayans). **Our bodies and consciousness never loose this connection.** We still have it, even though **we are not aware of it. With our spiritual development, this awareness opens more and more and our journey through the octaves, through the dimensions of consciousness,** is expanded on the celestial ladder, **moving ever higher, ever deeper** – we use this expression in our symbolic language which can describe mainly experiences in the world of the linear mind, whereas in the world of spirit our vocabulary becomes too impoverished and very approximate.

All levels, or octaves of reality are in fact simultaneous. Here and now. **The broader our consciousness is, the more we are aware, the more octaves we are able to hear and the more levels of reality we get to know and experience. At the last station before enlightenment we ultimately manage to connect our understanding of all levels of reality into one mosaic image of all octave displacements.**

But I still couldn't stop wondering **why Franci's leg was causing him pain. Where was the blocked imprinted pain stuck?** There was no obvious cause at the physical level, nor in the first octaves of his etheric bodies. So I sat through the night again, checking body after body: thirtieth ... seventieth ... hundred and twentieth ... hundred and fiftieth ... hundred and sixtieth ... hundred and eighty-second ... still nothing new. I was about to give up, but I nevertheless **persisted** for a bit longer. Just a little more, I kept encouraging myself. And it was worth it. I finally found the cause of his pain in the 230th frequency, in his **230th inaudible etheric body – in the 230th octave of his being. There, the field had been blocked** in a distant past. A telepathic message arrived – **this field still carries the imprint, the memory of the pain and suffering experienced long ago, which was why it was squeezed and blocked.** But such memories are **not only stored in every cell; they are also stored in each etheric body which resonates in different octaves, different colours; and each has its own important life function and its own memory.**

The seventh body, or the seventh tone in the octave, vibrates at the highest possible frequency vibration within an octave set. The highest tone of the highest octave is **the Matrix of the Divine Intelligence, of the life Logos,** which determines our life. This Matrix, **which is transferred, through octave displacements (etheric bodies), into the material world and into our physical body,** determines our physical **appearance and talents.** It even determines **our reactions,** as our emotional and mental etheric bodies, including feelings and thoughts experienced long ago, resonate within the countless octaves. **Both bodies react in line with our past experiences which are imprinted in our octave bodies.**

This matrix (DNA) of our features (of the seventh tone, octave, etheric body, or chakra, with the higest frequency) resonates through all our bodies; **it is transferred into the sixth tone in the octave – the tone of intuitive insight, of inner sight, it is transferred into our intuitive awareness and telepathic understanding.** Then it descends to the level (of the fifth tone in the octave) of the **throat** energy centre, or chakra, which is **the cosmic bridge of the spirit. If our throat centre is blocked by anger, sorrow, condemnation and resentment, the path to the spheres of consciousness, of the soul, is closed. The path also closes if we are insincere or unable to communicate openly and express ourselves freely.** In this case unexpressed and suppressed **emotions block our throat centre.** That is why thoughts cannot come out, **our throat hurts,** words stick in our throat, **our song is not harmonious,** creativity is blocked, incomplete – in short, bad. **The clutter** of destructive thoughts and emotions is stuck **in the sound octave system of both our physical and etheric bodies.** And blocked communication and self-expression can cause the worst injuries of our being, both spiritual and physical.

But, when our throat portal is open, both our life's vision and cosmic life energy which **we perceive as enthusiasm, will be able to anchor themselves easily into our awareness. And they will be able to move even further, onto the level of our heart, of our feelings. The heart filter will offer an appropriate signal through our feelings,** an opportunity to transfer the primal thought, or vision, further on. Or, if it remains closed through fears, anger, insensitivity, unlovingness, etc., **the transfer is blocked.** The above-mentioned is precisely the reason why some people **perceive and sense so much more than others.** It depends on **how they live, feel and think.** Also, people blocked **by stress** live a very limited life. The sages call them **the living dead,** and also **the deaf-blind people.**

Our third etheric body is **a mental blueprint, it is a body out of which the matrices of shapes and emotions are transferred into our mental world.** With it, **we catch thoughts and meta-conscious messages. Our second body suffuses our thoughts with feelings, it colours them with emotions, which, if the thought is accepted, gives power to the thought, or it destroys it, if the body is blocked.** This is the reason why spiritual **cleansing, forgiving and conscious positive actions are crucial.**

Subquantum particles are the carriers of shape-giving information and energy. They trigger apppropriate shape-giving (transformational) chemical processes and the transfer of spiritual powers into the physical world. This is also what modern science claims. **Yet only unburdened nerve and brain cells,** which are therefore pure, without the defective energy imprints of destructive emotions and thoughts, **are able to transfer undistorted information into the material world.** In the opposite case, diseases can develop. **The entire process is also perceived by our first etheric body, our first etheric field,** which acts like **a photographic blueprint** which brings **the 'negatives' of the matrices** and etheric forms, or the octave tones, **into the positive: the non-material into the material.** This is how everything is born.

Scientists at the Sorbonne, but especially **Dr Bruce Lipton** of Stanford University[20] have discovered that **human beings are in fact vessels for cosmic-frequency waves** and that nothing can **stop** this flow through humans – **except humans themselves!!! With what? With unloving thoughts and emotions** towards themselves and others, with their **doubts, fears, lies, lack of acceptance, etc.**

So, in the middle of the night, **I pulled out Franci's blockage from his 230th field,** a blockage which had been created far back in the past. **And his pain disappeared.** This is how it goes. Suffering cannot be eliminated merely by chemistry. It is eliminated **primarily by our awareness and our conscious actions** which fill and harmonise our energy fields; **by gazing through the singing octaves of life and through all the levels of reality and being.**

But because in our culture **we speak only about audible sound,** which is like **touching just one tiny part of the body (of the octave Universe), or only one finger instead of the entire body,** the whole picture remains veiled; a wholistic healing of soul and body is therefore not possible and humans continue to be unhappy. Deep inside themselves, they know that **something is missing – that the octave is still not complete, which is why there is no harmonious resonance and no wholistic understanding.**

All our bodies react to every frequency. Each body – both physical and etheric – **has its own frequency, or sound. Each subsequent body has a higher frequency** and also every subsequent octave has a higher frequency, which at the same time requires more energy for its balance and a more pure 'fuel'. The same is valid for our energy centres, or chakras. Every body, every centre, **has its distinct frequency, which can always be heard. We can feel the energies of the chakras, we can see and even hear them.** It is the same for the energies of cells, body tissues, bones, and organs. That is why there are no unknowns in this story, but only mental predictions, mind speculations which keep contemporary **scientific circles** satisfied despite the fact that they **deny things they cannot see, touch or hear.**

....
20   Bruce Lipton, *The Biology of Belief*, Carlsbad, Hay House (2008). More about his discoveries can be found in the following chapters and books.

The body is an exceptional and extremely capable musical instrument, because it sings and echoes within countless octaves. It is well worth listening to it and attuning to it. Grateful, it will offer you well-being, happiness, its beauty and the peace of the soul. It simply wants you to express yourself and resonate freely and in a wholistic way – through all the singing octaves, or links between the Universe, Earth, and life. Then, the mysteries of life shall no longer be mysterious and inaccessible.

The conversation between the Cosmos and our cell's protein membranes

The conversation between the Cosmos and our body

> The conversation between the body, the soul
> and **the divine** Source is always possible,
> it takes place through **the light of sound and song;**
> it echoes across all octave bodies,
> across the resonating strings of our cells and the Heavens.[21]

At their core, cell proteins are said to be encoded vibrations which regulate and direct the cell's rhythm and undulation. And vice versa – **rhythmical waves and cosmic radiation influence cell proteins.** Proteins encoded with frequencies regulate molecular rhythms, which in turn regulate body rhythms. **We transmit the encoded (sound) rhythms of our bodies into space, time and reality. With our emotions and thoughts, we maintain or distort those rhythms, and we also bring them back into tune. This is how we ourselves create events in the space-time continuum, as well as our physical health.** Space, time, and the life we are living mirror the difficult to understand Cosmic Intelligence. This is also what rshis claim.[22] **Our thoughts and emotions are the creators of the non-material and material.**

All the frequency waves in our cells are in fact an echo, an imprint of the basic cosmic undulation, of the 'superstrings' of the Universe. In relation to the superstrings, the quantum mechanics holds that the Universe consists of countless billions of invisible strings, which all have a different sound and which form **different dimensional levels, or worlds, which are made of different energy patterns of consciousness and matter. Certain frequency patterns can even turn into the qualities of time and space.**[23]

Even quantum physicists claim that **the Universe is made of light-sound threads.** To put it more poetically – the Universe is made of **'cosmic yarn,'** or as the Native Americans say – **an invisible cobweb or weave. The Native American myth** about the divine **Spider Woman, who weaves the threads and destinies of life,** is very inventive, picturesque, and appropriate. **Spider Woman** is a miraculous mythological being from ancient Native American cosmology.

....
21 Mirit, September 2012
22 Check also Deepak Chopra, *Quantum Healing*, New York, Bantam Books (1990), p. 188.
23 Ibid.

According to Vedic rshis, **the foundations of the world's existence** are created from primordial sounds, or frequency waves which make up everything that exists. The sound of Creation, which began to resonate across the cosmic expanse at the time when the Universe was born, at the time of **the Big Bang, is the first sound** (or **the first word**, according to many mythologies) which started to undulate and **resonate in the primordial silence; it 'roused' and awakened boundlessness and timelessness, it transformed itself into countless other waves, which then created, or wove, the material world,** stars, and constellations, etc. Each wave vibration has its own frequency; it also creates in **its own frequency, or vibration, bringing unique gifts to life. It creates distinct physical forms and even living beings.** Those wave patterns are the very core of life, the very essence of life's contents and forms.[24] **Some create physical matter, while others shape the intangible, non-material, the spiritual.**

Not only cosmic matrices are imprinted in our cells, but also the memory of all our feelings, thoughts, and emotional turmoils. **The biochemistry process, which takes place in cells** and which is fierce especially while we have destructive, unloving thoughts and emotions, is of course devastating, as **it distorts the basic 'programmes' of our perfection.**

Dr Bruce Lipton, former researcher of the **Stanford** University Medical Center, a professor, biologist, and mystic, as he calls himself today, has studied the topic for over 20 years and during this time he wrote his book '*The Biology of Belief*.[25] He discovered some important facts which **confirm the ancient wisdom.** One day he heard **his inner voice (the voice of his consciousness),** telling him that his life and **work were based on a false premise** and thus began his rich path as a sensitive researcher and a bridge between modern scientific thought and the ancient knowings of different spiritual traditions – in the field of **microbiology**. I will summarise some of his most important discoveries, especially those which explain the topics of my reflections on sound ceremonies, energy-sound healing, the laws of spiritual growth, and even **reincarnation (re-embodiment).**

Cells are intelligent, just like people. They have their own memory. Cell receptors are continuously receiving information from the Universe. This is claimed by both Dr Lipton and modern microbiology.[26]

In his book, Lipton states that **cell proteins create life.** Cell receptors carry **'a programme' into the cells** and activate effector proteins. **Cell's membranes**

....
24 An interesting comparable work is a book by the Slovene author **Marijan Cilar**, titled Temelji življenja (The Foundations of Life). In the book, Cilar ponders about material and non-material **principles of life**, as well as about consciousness, the scientific thought and artistic symbolism.
25 Bruce Lipton, *The Biology of Belief*, Carlsbad, Hay House (2008).
26 Check the above-mentioned work.

convert the information into the language of biology, or biochemistry, which then creates the material world. **Cell membrane's proteins are said to be the very foundation of consciousness and human intelligence, and the incubator of physical bodies. The more receptor proteins (lipids) there are, the deeper (the broader) our consciousness is, and our spiritual evolution** is at a higher level, it is multidimensional.[27] **Maharishi Mahesh Yogi**, a great authority on ancient Vedic wisdom and a scientist who, in the last century, spread knowledge about life and its laws across the world, was another who spoke and wrote about these processes. I have also received some of his extremely great wisdom.[28]

A healthy cell is imbued with life substances and **life energy. The consequences of our protection responses – fight or flight – disrupt the healthy growth of our cells, their balance, maintenance, and the free flow of the necessary life energy, and they also disrupt the transfer of rhythms.** Lipton wrote that **A CONNECTION TO THE UNIVERSE IS CRUCIAL**[29] for the healthy growth of our cells, as it activates the axis of the glands, brain, and physical body. Undisturbed, this axis enables a clear awareness. **Signals from the Universe change those cell protein links which control life processes.**[30] Lipton offers foundation for this new (old!) science of 'magical' cell membranes, which work in our bodies like 'the antennae of NASA landers,' as he says.

Every protein responds to frequency stimuli coming from the cosmic expanse, like a mirror and echo of cosmic signals, or waves. With this, it also complements the picture of the Universe. Cell receptors are the basic unit of consciousness and the Intelligence.[31] **That is why the power of free will and thoughts is partial or partially limited.** It is just a distinct corrector of primordial essences within people. He says that **our thoughts are but an echo of the Cosmic Mind, the Cosmic Consciousness.**

Human thought develops under the baton of the Cosmic Intelligence, which some call **God.** We actually cannot move too far away from the Idea of the Universe! We can only circulate **within the framework of our primordial givens. Brainwave coherence, or harmony (EEG – 8 Hz), between the two hemispheres** (the right intuitive side and left intellectual side) offers the best possibility to **awaken our dormant abilities.** Among the catalysts of will and thoughts are also **transcendental consciousness, or shamanic trance, and sound codes which are an effective tool for changing and correcting what was distorted.**

....
27   Ibid.
28   As a practitioner of bija mantras, transcendental meditation, yogic levitation, and also as a student of ayurveda and Vedic astrology – jyotish.
29   Ibid., p. 120.
30   Ibid., p. 155.
31   Ibid., pp. 155-165.

Energy and matter permeate each other, claimed Albert Einstein. **Cells, which follow impulses from the Universe,** also react to **signals from our brain and the environment. Even the atom in the molecules of the body and matter is, at its core, a non-materialised field, an energy whirlpool or wave, which occurs in the frequential sound pattern of matter and it shapes matter accordingly. The Universe is a totality of co-dependent energy fields, which are mutually connected. Everything and everyone has their own energy signature – their own sound, voice or personal tone and their own characteristic look or shine in their eyes. This is exactly why neither the study model as we know it nor the mere filling of our heads with information are necessary for the discovery of wisdom.**[32]

According to Lipton, **biological identity is based in cell records, in cell receptors.**[33] And of course he, like many others, had to ask the question **what activates this identity, what comes and is received from the expanse of the Universe through the antennae of a cell membrane. How does our TV screen operate?** Perhaps the screen's reception of the signals from the environment and the Universe is poor, and it also transmits them poorly into the environment, even though the 'picture' from the transceiver is good in principle and the film of life is undistorted on the screen.[34]

The transfer of frequency waves from the Cosmos takes place constantly; we receive them even if we perhaps have **a broken 'receiver'** and think that we are not receiving the signals (**we are only deaf to the subtle**). Yet we are nevertheless continuously nourished by inaudible cosmic sound-energy waves. Unfortunately, the scientific establishment is primarily interested in **'what it is' and not 'why it is so.'** It is even less prepared to acknowledge and discover its powerlessness and **the Source of life energy.**

Cell receptors are distinct antennae and necessary aids for the reception of various signals and messages from the Universe, from **the Primal Headquarters, from the Source of life, the Centre, or the Galactic Centre,** as the Mayans would say. **Our very essence, our own silent 'self,' or the essence of our soul, is constantly present! It is here all the time, it anchors and also migrates into other bodies, during transmigratory (re-)incarnations of the soul.** This is also what Dr Lipton claims. **With this, we can explain the immortality of the soul, its eternity, as well as the indestructible memory of the distant past and past lives,** says Lipton. And due to the above-mentioned, the first creative impulse, the Big Bang of Creation, can still resonate within us. **The sets of receptors** (according

....
32   Ibid., pp. 69-71.
33   Ibid., pp. 159-160.
34   Ibid., p. 161.

to Lipton) **transfer to new bodies over and over again, to new incarnations, they 'join the game once more.'**[35] This is how our basic essence is transferred from life to life, and the records, or energy **imprints of our basic fears, desires, and experiences also migrate with it.**

The programmes, or records, of cell membranes are therefore immortal, claims Lipton.[36] **They are eternal. With the expansion of our consciousness, with spiritual growth, we increasingly fulfil and complete these records – the meta-sensory antennae** – over the evolutionary cycles of our lives. **We do this until we have attained the pure harmony of the frequency waves of our entire being** – of our physical, emotional, mental bodies, our consciousness, or soul, our subconscious and meta-conscious; **until we have started to resonate harmoniously with the omnipresent Intelligence of the Universe, until we are in tune with all the possibilities and abilities that Intelligence and the givens of our life, or the matrices of life, offer to us.**

All the degeneration and distortions in the physical world, as well as disease, are a reflection of the distortion of the described 'programmes' of the Intelligence of the Universe and are a mirror of our being out of tune with the universal laws of life. Our way of life and the level to which our consciousness, or soul, is open or closed, determine the way we feel and think in any moment.

Dr Lipton believes that **the consequences of disharmonious (or out of tune) imprints last longer than the lives of our physical bodies, as they are permanently recorded in our cell memory.** They are imprinted in our cell receptors and in **the memory of the higher levels of the soul. They are transferred into new incarnations through our immortal essences or matrices (and DNA); that is how they travel from life to life.** With this, we can explain **the law of karma, or destiny, sudden memories from our past lives, and déjà-vu sensations.**

Lipton also discovered that **our willpower and the power of thought** (including the power of positive thinking) unfortunately have **only a limited effect, or success.**[37] **Effective tools for changing disharmonies, out of tune states and the distortions of life signals are only those mental and cellular impulses which are created in the states of brainwave coherence,** in the states of a balanced activity of both brain hemispheres (EEG – **8 Hz**), **only those impulses which are attuned to the waves of the Universe and the Earth. At coherent levels of our brainwaves, we are able to effectively correct the distorted energy patterns and cellular patterns,** and to remove pain and the destructive emotional-mental patterns which are anchored in our subconscious. That is why those findings are an extremely important **surgeon's**

....
35 Ibid., 161.
36 Ibid., p. 162.
37 Ibid., p. 174.

tool for reprogramming imbalance into balance, the diseased into a healthy oneness.** This is what numerous yogis knew millennia ago.

The complete story of the evolution of the Universe, of the Earth and humanity, as well as that of individuals, is stored in our cell memory. Numerous sages from the spiritual traditions of the world, as well as by Dr Bruce Lipton, claim that **the energy of thought is weaker than cell memory.**[38]

When we are in the relaxed and meditative state of a calm mind, we are aligned to, or in balance with, the waves of the Earth and the Source of life, we are in resonance with the electromagnetic waves of the Sun and the Earth's field: we resonate with the Schumann electromagnetic resonance of the Earth, with the oscillation in the frequency pattern or rhythm of 8–13 Hz. The Earth's magnetic field has changed innumerable times in the Earth's history. The Earth's axis oscillates and tilts one way and then another. The last axis reversal is said to have taken place almost 800,000 years ago.** We don't know when the next one will occur, say astrophysicists. But perhaps Mayan astronomers calculated this too. Both **the Earth's magnetic current** and the Sun's magnetic shield are **currently weakening,** which increases **climate changes** on Earth.

Due to human activity, **the Earth is getting warmer,** but it is also **cooling** at the same time. We don't know what will prevail in the future. **The electromagnetic field reportedly stimulates the pituitary gland to secrete hormones, primarily serotonin and melatonin, which, in turn, have a beneficial effect on the human alignment to the Earth and its pulse, to the Universal wholistic Field** and their vibration links, or strings, of cosmic consciousness – both the Universal cosmic consciousness and human one in cells. That is why **the megaliths and temples** of the past were deliberately placed exactly **on magnetic intersection points of the Earth's radiation, because in this way they enhance the barely perceptible signals which heal.**[39] Practically all our **planetary ancestors**, all the way up to the Atomic era, were **masters** of recognising and using earthly and cosmic frequencies in the magic of life.

Astronomical knowledge - biological clocks, the oldest religion and the fullness of awareness

In the second half of the 20th century, French researchers at **the Sorbonne** studied the rhythms of living organisms. As they put it, they explored the laws of

....
38 This is also what Jasmuheen claims in her book *In Resonance*, Burgrain, Koha Verlag (1999).
39 More about this can be found in the third book about Siberian shamans in the *Cosmic Telepathy* series.

the oldest religion – astronomy. **Michel Gauquelin** wrote a brilliant book titled The Cosmic Clocks.[40] Their findings confirmed **the essence of the omnipresent cosmic waves in living beings and the occurrence of resonance in everything that is.**

The transfer of cosmic rhythms, or waves, is carried from cell to cell. Nothing can block or eliminate this transfer. Cosmic waves can penetrate everywhere. Their pattern imprints are in everything that exists, they regulate cosmic and biological clocks on Earth and in all living beings; it is also quite possible that these waves echo in non-living nature.

If we resonate with those rhythms, we will feel well, but if we try to ignore them, or if we struggle against those silent measuring instruments, we will feel dejected, powerless and sick. This has been confirmed both by ancient teachings and in the theses of the Sorbonne scientists. If we, for example, live and **work mainly at night,** which is the time to sleep and rest your body, but which todays' youth finds very appealing, **our biological clocks will be disturbed** and we will be confused. We will feel tired, without the encouraging visions of a new day, and life will seem to be **a nuisance, a non-sense, or 'stupid.'** This happens because **we are out of tune,** or better – **we are not attuned to the current moment and the flow of life. A bird** simply knows when to start its long autumn journey, **a fish** knows when it is time to spawn, **a snake** knows when it is time to shed its skin; **a tree** knows when to cover itself with a flowering blanket and when to mature, etc. Only **humans wander in the labyrinth of their mental representations,** lies, fake ignorance, bargaining, expectations, illusions, thought patterns, and demands.

With their discoveries, the Sorbonne scientists have unintentionally **elucidated the meaning of the ancient ceremonies of our planetary ancestors from different cultures and civilisations;** they have explained the intuitive, **cosmic telepathic (ceremonial) alignment to the waves and rhythms of the frequency Universe, the Cosmic Intelligence, the Divine, the alignment with its music.** With their explanation of the laws of the invisible and inaudible **existence of cosmic rhythms,** which – besides human bodies – some sensitive enough laboratory devices are able to detect, they have confirmed the meaning of **the activities of 'the Ancient Ones,'** which is what civilisations in harmony with nature call our distant ancestors.

Already in prehistory, people were eagerly following cosmic rhythms, natural cycles, earthly, celestial and personal cycles; they were recording repeating rhythms and occurrences, the repeating of the phases of the Moon, the annual seasons, life cycles of the Sun and the stars etc. in simple ways – in stone, wood, or in any other way. Remember that **the medieval education**

....
40   Gauquelin, Michel, *Cosmic Clocks: From Astrology to a Modern Science*, Chicago, H. Regnery Co. (1967).

(**quadrivium**) of initiates was based on four core subjects: **astronomy, astrology, mathematics, and music.** What an extremely important and **brilliant connection between these four seemingly different subjects,** which are all based on the study of the audible and inaudible pulsing of the material and non-material.

Astronomical-astrological studies are certainly among the oldest research efforts, they are the first science. They are the basis of all spiritual teachings, ceremonies, and the Great Mysteries of our ancestors. An attentive listening to natural conditions and to their sound patterns and rhythms is the basic wisdom of life, the foundation of all the teachings and laws of existence. It is also a departure point and intersection where we meet the Intelligence of the Universe, God, or the Highest Principle. The above-mentioned is valid for different evolutionary and history periods of the Earth, for different cultures and their **mythological contents, for the richness of languages, artistic images and hidden symbolism, as well as for sound-movement magic, the magic of dance.**

The Universe is the consciousness of a boundless number of resonating strings
which echo **the Plan of life.**
The invisible strings of the Earth and the Sky nourish people's voices, words, songs, and movement,
they give **sound language** to the animals,
they give the audible quiver and inaudible scent to the trees and flowers.
The inaudible cosmic sound is embodied on Earth
as the sound of song
and the language of invisible body strings.
The consciousness of the Universe and stars reveals itself **in the symbolic language of forms and images.**
The language of symbols is the language of **the meta-sensory perceptions of your soul,** her permanent **inspiration.**[41]

As we can see, **everything oscillates, vibrates and pulsates, and so it also resonates and sings. Everything is music and poetry of different wave patterns.** Everything we hear and even that which we don't hear. Even the inaudible can be clearly sensed: including **the resonating strings of our body cells**

....
41   Mira Omerzel - Mirit, poem *The Universe Echoes the Plan of Life*, taken from the book *Zvočne podobe prebujene ljubezni* (*The Sound Images of Awakened Love*), Vrhnika, Dar Dam (2012). The book is available only in the Slovene language.

and the DNA of our genetic chains, our non-material bodies – the soul, or consciousness, our emotional pulse, and the frequencies of our mind, and of course the rhythmical resonance of the Earth, the stars, the Sun and the Universe, etc. **Our truth and our view on the world, as well as our 'sound' and tuning, correspond to the degree to which we are able to open, or surrender ourselves to the whole.**

The tone G is the noble tone of the harmonious resonance we seek – the tone of the Earth's rotation and the tone of the cosmic waves of the Source; this tone is simultaneously also the frequency of brainwave coherence and a relaxed body. The tone G is the fundamental tone of our **songs, the tuning of our instruments and bodies (both material and etheric). It is the fundamental tone of all levels, or axes of the dimensions of consciousness. This tone is constantly reverberating through the octaves, through the dimensions of the universes and the soul.** It is found in the accompanying (drone) strings of many instruments from past cultures, in the basic **tuning of flutes, singing tubes and even drums.** The tone G is the tone, or the sound, of our body cells and spiritual perfection. It is also the tone to which we always gradually return in different ways. **We seek it everywhere.** Listening to it brings satisfaction.

Wisdom comes into our awareness in various ways. Its penetrating quality, its importance and brilliance are confirmed by numerous traditional **folk instruments, by the rich variety of strings with equal resonance** found on inventive instruments of various cultures – from the Indian **sitar** and veena, the Russian **balalaika,** Turkish and Balkan **tambouras,** the Mediterranean **mandolin,** Slovene drone **zithers** to European **hurdy-gurdies** and **Mayan flutes.** In folk singing, **voices interweave above the fundamental earthly tone G.** Elated **singing**[42] usually evolves above, but also below, the tone of **the Earth and the tone of the Galactic Source; such singing announces the beauty of resonance and euphony, which is so precious to the ear and so harmonising at the same time.**

The sound quality of the tone G **restores our physical power, it cleanses and balances** the activity of our body cells, emotions and mind, it both grounds us and **expands us into cosmic and spiritual dimensions,** into the realms beyond. The tone G **leads us back to the Home of the soul, to the First Principle and the Absolute.**

We always have everything we need. Our givens are being actualised in every euphony which caresses us like a mother's hand. It is therefore well worth rediscovering the powers of the harmony of this wondrous resonance. **May it always guide us!** And there will be no problems in life and no disease.

....
42 The Balkan *ojkanje* singing.

The consciousness of our soul **will show us the right path. It will lead us to the fulfillment of our eternal yearning,** which points out the direction of the return to our own **centre of the consciousness of the heart, to the centredness of spirit, the Centre of the galaxy – to Hunahpu,** as the ancient Mayans would say.

We should take another look at **the ancient stories and tales, songs and fairy tales,** which raised awareness and provided encouragement to countless generations long before our time. They awakened the world and perhaps **today they can whisper to us something that we have long been seeking. We will hear their silent messages undisturbed, when our consciousness is broad, open and connected enough, when our minds are silent and our cell memory cleansed.**

> **An emptied silenced mind** is a vessel,
> waiting to have **abundance and goodness poured into it,**
> **capturing the echo of the Intelligence of the Universe,**
> whilst **everything that exists is emerging** and undulating through human ears.
> **You were** given **a mind**
> in order to see that which is still hidden from you,
> and to hear the yet unrevealed.
>
> In this way, with the help of your mind, ears and eyes, **you return back Home,**
> **to the primordiality of your matrix,**
> **to the beauty of perfection,**
> **to the fullness of attunement,**
> to the audible grace of omnipresence,
> connectedness,
> **infinity and boundlessness,**
> **to a mellifluous harmony of all rhythms, all sounds,**
> all thoughts and emotional nuances.
> A silenced mind is a vessel of **peace and elation,**
> **it is your guide and** mirthless **teacher;**
> a conscious mind is an unrelenting **guardian of your happiness,**
> which, like a courageous knight, bravely **protects you from unhappiness.**[43]

....
43 Mira Omerzel - Mirit, poem *Emptied Silenced Mind Is a Vessel*, taken from the book *Zvočne podobe prebujene ljubezni (The Sound Images of Awakened Love)*, Vrhnika, Dar Dam (2012).

The pre-Columbian and newer musical instruments – the quest for harmony

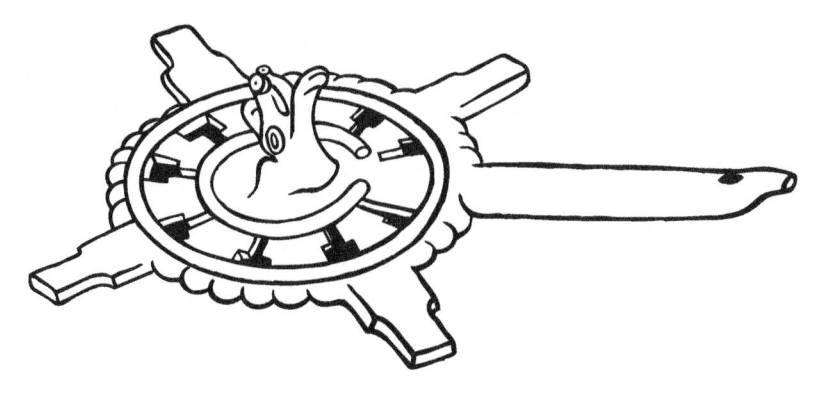

Flute in the form of the *nahui-ollin* symbol and a pellet, which allows the player to set the intonation of the instrument.

In 1978, ethnomusicologist **Samuel Martí** published a short book on Mexican pre-Columbian musical instruments. In it, he stressed that before the arrival of white conquistadors, Central and South American Indians **used music differently from how we do today. Single, double, triple flutes** and even instruments with four tubes, **producing four notes, had a ceremonial and religous role rather than a musical-aesthetic one. The purpose of music was not to show technical skills or virtuosity, its purpose was to honour Gods.** That is why the pre-Columbian music was **an expression of faith and hope**; it formed an essential part of indigenous **rites and magic.**[44] I believe that we could also say that the music of the ancient Mayans, as well as that of their descendants, **was** once **sacred. Its primary role was to search for balance, to dissolve psychological and physical (energy) blocks and to reveal the spiritual, divine dimensions of life**.

Most of the photographs of instruments published in Martí's book were taken from the **Mexican National Museum of Anthropology** collection and from some private collections. Especially thrilling are the **flutes with multiple tubes**, which can produce **three or four sounds simultaneously** and thus create a rich harmony.[45] Martí writes that **the practice of the system of pure harmony developed in Mesoamerica two hundred years before the developement of polyphony in Europe.**[46] Which means Native Americans must have been exceptional masters

---
44 Samuel Martí, *Music before Columbus/Música precolumbina*, Mexico City, Ediciones Euroamericanas (1978), p. 6.
45 Their sound qualities are unfortunately not specified.
46 Ibid., p. 6.

of **the language of sound, of communication through sound and musical** (and probably also **sound-therapeutic) expression.**

Martí quotes Historia Eclesiástica Indiana **from 1570** and mentions **two drums:** one was high and thicker than a man, made of very fine wood, well carved and painted, with deer skin. It gave **an (interval) of a fifth.**[47]

The vertical drum panhuehuetl **from Malinalco** was finely decorated with carvings representing **a war dance by a priest** of Xochipilli, **the deity of dance and reincarnation.** Depicted on it are also **Jaguar and Eagle** Knights, associated with the war symbol *Atl-tlachinolli*, **water and fire** – the origins of life. It is said that one of these drums was placed **at the top of the main pyramid of Tenochtitlan** in the Aztec kingdom around **1500.**[48]

Huehuetl is a smaller drum, played with fingers, like the bongo today. It was used until at least 900 A.D.[49]

Another important pre-Columbian drum is the *teponaztli*, **the great bass drum.** And the great drum *veuetl* is also **played with hands.** Other drums can be played with rubber-tipped **sticks.** It is said that the great drum can be heard from a great distance.

The finely carved *teponaztli* drum **with a human head**[50] **from Tlaxcala** produces two notes giving **a musical interval of a minor third.** It is played with sticks, like **marimba.** The famous drum was a war trophy of the Spanish conquistador **Hernán Cortés.**[51] The pre-Columbian drums and **xylophones** are usually decorated with the carvings of **animal motifs, especially sacred snakes and jaguars.**[52]

Shells are one of the oldest forms of the **trumpet.** They are known in almost all ancient traditions on all continents. By blowing through them, it is possible to produce **several aliquot tones,** similar to alpine horns. **Shells** come from the sea, which is a symbol of **the boundless cosmic ocean of life energy,** which is why **they are associated with numerous myths and ceremonies of Creation, as well as with the symbolism of water, rain, and abundance.** The symbols of the deity **Quetzalcóatl are the shell, wind, and bird.**[53] In his book, Martí published photographs showing several clay figurines of musicians **playing one or even two shells simultaneously.**[54] The true meaning of the ceremonial shell and its sound in

---
47 Ibid., p. 9.
48 Ibid., pp. 10-11.
49 Martí, pp. 12-13.
50 Ibid., taken from Motolinia: *Historia de los Indios de Nueva España*, 1553.
51 Ibid., pp. 14-17.
52 Ibid., pp. 18-19.
53 Adrian Gilbert and Maurice Cotterell, *The Mayan Prophecies*, Shaftesbury, Element Books (1995), p. 320.
54 Samuel Martí, *Music before Columbus/Música precolumbina*, Mexico City, Ediciones Euroamericanas (1978), pp. 20-23.

temples was discovered recently **in Peru.** The construction and **form of the temple enhance the sound of the shells,** which – like life energy from the primordial ocean – pours through the entire room.

One exceptional artefact in the museum's collection is a **clay trumpet with a jaguar's head and a spiral body painted with white** concentric circles. It produces the first **four tones of the natural scale.**[55] **Peruvians,** who were excellent masters of **metalurgy,** crafted them from **gold, silver, and copper** and used them mainly in **religious ceremonies and funerary rites.**[56]

The majority of **panpipes, or reedpipes,** and figurines of panpipe players were found in **the Gulf of Mexico** and date back to 300–700 A.D. Those kept in the **National Museum of Anthropology in Ciudad de Mexico** are exceptional.[57] Even today panpipes characterise Central and South American Indian music. **Accompanied by drums,** their sound can be either piercing or velvety, air-piercing or richly full.

Clay whistles had a special function in the sound ceremonies of Central and South American Indians. The photographs in Martí's book suggest they were fashioned in an ingenius way. **Double whistle in the form of a woman,** dating back to circa **500 years B.C.E.,** gives an interval of **a minor third.**[58] Native Americans clearly loved polyphony, euphonious harmony, simultaneity, and resonance. **The basic intervals of a third, fourth, fifth, sixth, and eighth** were obviously important to them, for they expressed **cosmic-earthly vibrational ratios.** But more on this topic can be found in the chapter about the divine **Hunahpu,** who was the very source of their musical inspiration.

Clay whistles can also take the form of **the shell of a snail.** If they have no holes, they produce only **one sound.** Some have been found among archaeological remains dating from 200 A.D.[59]

A particularly special artefact is a clay **whistle in the form of two women on a swing, dating from appoximately 500 A.D.**[60] Its mouthpiece is placed at the back and **sound is produced when the swing is set in motion.**[61] Some whistles are made **in the form of warriors.**

The National Museum of Anthropology in Ciudad de Mexico also keeps **a clay whistling jar in the form of an animal guide,** *nagual* **– jaguar,** which produces

....
55   Ibid., pp. 24-27. Mochica culture, Peru, circa 400 A.D.
56   Read *Mayan Priests, the Lord of Sipan and Ancient Forms of Penitence* in the chapter *The Shamanic Journey into the Unknown within the Circle of Life and Death.*
57   Samuel Martí, *Music before Columbus/Música precolumbina,* Mexico City, Ediciones Euroamericanas (1978), pp. 29-31.
58   Ibid., pp. 32-33.
59   Ibid., p. 38.
60   Ibid., pp. 42-43.
61   It is kept in the National Museum of the American Indian in New York.

only two notes giving a musical interval of **a second. Two small clay jars** were connected to make the instrument – one is **closed** and the other is **open.** The instrument produced **a whistling sound** when the whistling jar was **filled with water** and the spout was **blown** into. It is said that this sound vessel was used **in ceremonies. It had a magic character** and it dates from the Pre-Classic period, approximately **500 years B.C.E.** It is quite likely that the instrument was used for the ritual **cleansing of both the room and the ceremony participants, because a piercing sound has the power to do this.**

The museum also keeps **a whistling jar with four holes,** which originated circa 1000 A.D. By covering and opening its holes, it is possible to elicit **five notes,** while skilled fingers might even produce eighteen notes on some of the instruments.[62] All of these instruments are a proof of the Native American mastery of ingenious instruments.

Practically **all types of flutes (except nose flutes)** have been found among Central and South American Indians. They usually have at least two holes and **up to six finger holes,** which can produce **diatonic, chromatic, wholetone and even microchromatic scales.** The *quena* flute is still known today. Some flutes are made in the form of a globular **ocarina.**

Native Americans were excellent masters of the production of **ocarinas.** There can even be **double ocarinas,** usually finely decorated with various **symbols.** Double ocarinas are played like other double flutes. **The melody** is usually played **on one,** whereas the other accompanies it (bourdon). Double occarinas enabled **a richer harmony – euphony.** Martí published a photograph of an ocarina dating from circa **700 A.D.** It produces two **tones (E flat and F above middle)** and is in the form of **a mother nursing her baby.** It is said that this ocarina had a special **vibrator.** Ocarinas were also made **in the form of the sacred bird.** The Aztecs too used them in rituals. The National Museum of Anthropology keeps **an ocarina in the form of a human head with six holes,** which can produce **diatonic and chromatic scales.**[63]

The Aztec-type flute is played by **blowing against the sharp edge of the tube** (a type of Balkan-Oriental **kaval**). Some pre-Columbian **beak-type flutes** are made **in the form of the snake,** which symbolises the divine **Quetzalcóatl and spiral life energy.** This type of flute, kept in Ciudad de Mexico, dates from the Pre-Classic period, **500 B.C.E..** It can produce **six tones.**[64]

The ceremonial clay flute from the Campeche state is **closed** on one side and has a mouthpiece. It was found in **a tomb in a Mayan ceremonial centre (the island of Jaina)** and can produce the **diatonic scale.** Another interesting flute from

....
62 Ibid., pp. 34-37.
63 The information about the archaeological findings of clay ocarinas was taken from the Samuel Martí's book, pp. 47-57.
64 Ibid., pp. 58-59.

the same location is an **oboe-type flute from the Mayan culture,** dating back to **700 A.D.,** which can produce only two sounds, **E flat and F, middle register,**[65] which is similar to the ocarina in the form of a nursing mother.

In the book, Martí quotes a short text titled Monarchia Indiana (**Torquemada, 1613),**[66] which says: one of **the Priests,** dressed in the same costumes and insignias as those which the **Idol** would wear **during the procession,** strode from the temple carrying **flowers and roses and a small clay flute which made very high-pitched sounds. /.../** When the flute was played, **all the thieves, fornicators, assassins, and other delinquents and sinners felt a great fear and sadness and some would be so stressed that they could not conceal their guilt. /.../** The strong and brave men and all the old soldiers of the militia, **upon hearing the sound of the small flute, called** upon their God with great vehemence **for strength and courage /.../** These high-pitched sounds probably **dissolved energetic-emotional blocks in their bodies and raised suppressed emotions;** probably these sounds also **cleansed traumas and set people free.**

Five-tone Aztec-type flutes are indeed something special, they have **a great mouthpiece in the form of a flower, which symbolises Xochipilli, the Aztec Deity of love and music.** The flute dates from circa 1500 A.D.[67]

Two flutes are connected into one **ceremonial beak-type flute in the form of a human leg.** One **accompanies** the melody with an interval of **a fifth and an octave,** and the other one produces the **scales G flat, F, E, D, and C.**[68] It is therefore similar to Balkan **double flutes.**

But there is nothing to be found in the world's treasure chest of instruments which is similar to Native American **beak-type flutes in the form of the** nahui-ollin **symbol,** which at the same time indicates **the four cardinal points, the four winds, or paths.** The flute is circular and features **a wheel.**[69] Different **animals** are positioned at its centre. **A movable pellet** enables the player to produce **tones, semitones, and even microtones.** Most often these types of flutes originate from circa **700 A.D.** The movable wheel on the flute or on the two flutes is therefore able to produce more sounds. The movable pellet **shortens the air-column and produces a rich variety of sounds.**

Native Americans also made **triple beak-type flutes (The Gulf of Mexico, circa 700 A.D.).** The three tubes are connected by **one mouthpiece,** which means that the musician could simultaneously play **three melodies,** or one tube (tone) **accompanied the melody with a bass.** Triple flutes can also have **a register-change**

....
65   Ibid., pp. 64-65, 68-69.
66   Ibid., p. 70.
67   Ibid., pp. 74-75.
68   Ibid., pp. 76-77.
69   Ibid., pp. 78-81.

hole in order to change octaves.[70] This immensely enriched the sound picture made by the player. Changing octaves also has a symbolic function of moving from one level of reality to another.

Beak-type flutes with several tubes, which can produce more sounds, are not rare. They are **a proof of the quest for different sonorities, harmonies, sound colours, and sound qualities,** which humans seek in their lives. It is said that today, such flutes are still made **in Bolivia** and **at the Titicaca lake.**

The flute with a human head on its mouthpiece, which dates from approximately **700 A.D.**, was found in **the Gulf of Mexico.** It belongs to **Mayan** culture. According to Martí, **it is a proof of the extraordinary accomplishments of Mayan indigenous people.** It consists of **two melodic tubes,** which have **four finger holes,** and **two** additional **tubes** attached to it – one with one hole, another one with two holes, which both produce **drone notes.** The person playing the instrument can **create four melodic lines,**[71] **or three-part harmony accompanied by a drone bass.** Which means that the one-man band concept is very old indeed.

In the book, there is also a photograph of **a beak-type double flute decorated with a human head, a necklace, a flower-shaped pendant with eight petals** (the symbol of **an octave** with eight tones). **The Deity, or priest,** on it shows **dental mutilaton** and wears **ear-plugs and a loin-cloth with five tassels** (perhaps in the form of the Venus glyph).[72] This is why the human figure on the instrument might represent **the Venus priest-warrior or an instrument in the service of the divine image of the star Venus.** Whereas **skulls** (in the proceses of **ritual dying, or spiritual transformation**) represent **death and the immortality of the human soul.**

Cross flutes with four or six holes were not unknown in the Native American world. They are finely decorated with various **human and animal figures (the guides, or *naguals*, of priest-musicians?).** Their symbolism is unfortunately hardly recognised today, but the flute is nevertheless admirable.

Rattles with or without **bells,** and drums were made **from turtle shells.** The Mayans were specialists in the firing of clay. Their flutes are made from clay, hollow **reed** and bones. Native Americans say that **they fly with the drum and with the sound of the flute,** when they are listening to **the rhythm of the Earth, resonating in it.** Using drums, they set off on **inter-dimensional journeys with the heart beat of the Earth and the Sky.** This is also how they control their own heart beat. Undulating in a spiral, the **snake** of life energy, which is also **the song of the Universe, is poured into the sound of 'talking drums,'** which celebrate life. **For life is a rhythm too.**

....
70   Ibid., pp. 82-83.
71   Ibid., pp. 84-87.
72   Ibid., pp. 90-91.

It is likely that, in their sound celebrations and ceremonies, Central and South American Indians also used **dried gourd rattles containing seeds,** which have not survived. **In both antiquity and the modern era, rattles have been primarily ritual tools for the cleansing and healing of etheric bodies and of the room.** The sound of rattles **dissolves both energy blocks and the distorted, destructive energy formations** of emotions, thoughts, and physical toxins. Today, rattles and clay flutes are still **important** instruments for almost all Native American tribes. They feature various **symbols, which speak to the human spirit by means of a high-dimensional pictorial language,** so that both musicians and ceremony participants would not forget **the direct path, connectedness, focus, clear intent, their cosmic (soul-ar) origin and their earthly tasks.**

Wikipedia describes the **pre-Columbian stringed instruments from Guatemala,** which belong to the Mayan Late Classic Era (years **600–900**). There were only a few stringed instruments to be found among the Mayan archaeological artefacts. Well, the one from Guatemala is said to produce **a sound similar to a jaguar's growl.**[73] Why? In order to invite, as vividly as possible, **the sounds of a watchful jaguar** to rituals and everyday life, because the jaguar is the symbol of **spiritual power, watchfulness, attention, and wisdom.**

Yet, the richness of audible and barely perceptible harmonies of ancient instruments can be **heard only with the inner ear.**

---

73   Check also *The Garland Encyclopaedia of World Music*, Volume 2, New York, Garland Pub. (1998).

The universe breathing through Creation

Embodied in the dual world on Earth

"... with **the ring of abundance** on my finger
and **the divine crown** on my head.
I can fly for he (my teacher[74]**) has given me wings**
I can roar like a lion, I can rise like dawn.
No more verses
for **I am taken to a place from where
this world seems so small...
My heart is like a lute
each chord crying
with longing and pain.**
My Beloved is watching me
wrapped in **silence.**"[75]

A Mayan priest connecting to the forces of the Cosmos via his psychic abilities (C.U.M.).

So, what does Mayan mythology speak about?
The timeless Cosmic doctrine of Creation of which speak the inner, **spiritual adepts** of our planet, stresses that what is **on Earth is the same as in the Cosmos: as above, so below.** The wisdom of the Great Mysteries derives from an awareness that the only true reality and the source of everything is the invisible Cosmic Field of Consciousness and energy, the unmanifested Universe, also named the **Intelligence of the Universe, the Cosmic Mind, or Cosmic Consciousness.** This is the only reality worth taking into account, reality **beyond the usual human illusions,** which are today erroneously called the only reality. The Universe is said to consist of **different patterns of (frequency-energy) waves,** which are also called levels, or **dimensions,** as well as **the octaves of sound and light.**

....
74 The note in brackets is mine.
75 Rumi, *Hidden Music*, London, Thorsons (2001), pp. 2-3. Rumi's spiritual teacher was master Shams.

We are beings of a cosmic consciousness, cosmic-earthly children, born from and determined by universal and earthly laws that wish to be and must be mutually aligned, or attuned. When **the Absolute,** or the unfathomable **Universal Consciousness, the Great Spirit, or God (the Intelligence of the Universe),** creates primordial movement, or waves within all created universes, **movement arises from the primordial silence, from the primordial chaos – an undulation inaudible to our physical ears: in the form of vortices, spirals, and ray structures.** This is what cosmic doctrine says, which has been the same everywhere and at all times.

The spiritual traditions of different cultures claim that **the Universe breathes and resonates;** it gives birth to subtle **cosmic matter** and **out of chaos emerges order,** which is in the dynamic Field determined by the oppositions of **the same, by complementary differences of the whole.** After non-material energy and etheric fine-matter particles had been shaped, a possibility for the creation of more complex **molecular organisms and beings in the three-dimensional world is created.**

The First Principle, the Logoidal Idea, the primordial 'thought' of the Cosmic Mind (or Plan), which is, at its core, invisible sound, creates movement within the cosmic expanse, it creates **the undulation of light and sound** which 'condenses' into different wave patterns of the physical, or **audible, sound.** This is what the cosmic doctrine of both various peoples of the world and modern science suggests.

Cosmic rhythms occur, because wave patterns are constantly repeated. These rhythms are permeated with the primordial **Logoidal Idea, 'the Divine Purpose,' or 'the Cosmic Will,'** as we call this universal creative principle. This is how **evolution and devolution** are conceived, how building and disintegrating, ceaseless **movement towards the centre, towards the Source, the Absolute,** as well as movement outwards, towards the periphery, is conceived.

When, through the evolution process, a little part or a more complex being, **seeks a balance** of seemingly opposite forces **in the world of duality,** it travels to the primal centre, to the balanced stillness of **itself, to its own very essence, its own awakened origin.** And with this continuous **movement towards enlightened consciousness, with this movement towards its own centre and out of it,** it creates a restless journey which we call **life.** Life which time and time again **converges towards centredness, to the Source and Truth, to the very essence of existence. Breathing** connects the human body to both our own and Cosmic Consciousness, to the essence of our being, **to the Source,** to the primal centre.

Rhythmic frequency movements of material and non-material **energy subquantum particles (biophotons)** and their **interaction** unfold in **numerous relationships;** they create subtle wrappers of **cosmic matter** and also **physical matter itself.** In the wide open expanse, **the rhythmic waves of one plane, or**

one rhythm, are transferred to other planes, to another rhythm, into other dimensions, or frequency patterns. **Development, which strives to establish perfection, or wholeness,** balances and even disintegrates everything that exists.

According to the **cosmic doctrine** of earthly-spiritual knowledge, there are **seven different fundamental planes of motion** on Earth, and there are countless cosmic frequency or energy, wave patterns in the material atomic world. **On the first plane of evolution, the atoms are said to create a tri-angular path – like a mirror of the Holy Trinity, or as an echo** of the three primal universal creative forces, or First Principles, called gunas in the Vedic tradition, or **the three sacred stones** according to the Mayans. These forces are said to shape the universes, the etheric (spiritual) planes and physical matter.[76] **The ancient Principle, or the Absolute is triune.** That is why the number **three** is an important **number in folk tradition and a symbol of spirit, or soul.** The same goes for the number **ten, which is the number of evolution, completion, and fulfilment. Seven-fold undulation** is said to be especially important in our physical world, as well as the ten-sided, or **ten-fold** cosmic movement of completion. Movement creates **seven different circular waves** in the Universe, **and our solar system is also made up of seven fundamental planes, or dimensions, of reality,** claims the cosmic doctrine. Humans can attain or experience **seven different levels of consciousness** and can activate **seven levels of sentience, or seven senses,** as we call them. **The sixth sense, or the seventh sense, is the ability of a telepathic perception of the highest frequency levels, the Absolute. The seventh sense simply knows.** And in life, humanity passes through **seven deaths, seven spiritual immaturities of the ego.** And Native Americans worship the four cardinal points and especially **the seven directions (4+3),** which link the material and non-material levels.

> 'I was seeking knowledge
> when that beautiful one appeared.
> I tried to charm him and asked:
> **Would you kindly interpret the dream**
> I had last night, you are my only confidant.
>
> He shook his head and smiled
> as if he could see through me and said:
> **'Don't try to charm me,**
> **I see every nuance,** every colour and scent.
> **I am your mirror.'**

....
76 Numerous Vedic texts (especially *Rigveda*) and oral spiritual heritages from different cultures speak of this. More can also be found in the book *The Cosmic Doctrine* by Dion Fortune.

> **In his hands I become the design he weaves**
> with golden thread,
> **I become his living masterpiece.**'[77]

Spiritual teachings claim that **a human being is a multidimensional being, a being of all nine levels, who can telepathically perceive even twelve levels, or dimensions, of consciousness and reality.** The symbolism of the number three, multiplied by itself (3×3), gives another extremely important number – **nine,** which is the symbol of **the invisible, etheric, cosmic, spiritual, primordial, perfect, etc.** A human being is therefore a being defined by nine different levels of both the material and non-material, nine different fundamental frequency wave patterns.

The first three dimensions comprise the physical and tangible, while subsequent patterns with a higher frequency, located between the third and the seventh level, make up the frequency waves of **etheric bodies, emotions, mind and spirit (soul), or consciousness.** With them, our consciousness touches, connects, and melds **with the Primal Intelligence, the primordial idea of life,** which is encoded at all the levels above the seventh dimension, as we call it.

Through our life's transformation, **we are learning to understand the Cosmic Consciousness, the Logos of the Universe,** which is also called **the Divine Will;** we are learning to accept it, surrender to it and **live in harmony with it.** Every wise and successful healer, or shaman, must be able to reach those levels and to perfectly master the connection to them, as it enables **a miraculous cooperation with and handling the forces and powers of life.**

Existence, which is in total harmony with primordial Intent and is devoted to it, is called **enlightenment,** as well as **assumption,** because we are then able to **connect to the levels above the solid-matter physical level, to the levels of consciousness above the fourth, or astral, level,** which is in folk tradition called the Sky, or **the Heaven.** We are also able to connect **to the levels between the fourth and ninth, or twelfth, dimension.** An awakened person can align to **the Mind of the Universe,** to the 'father's and mother's primordial life Field,' as we put it symbolically. **Enlightened persons can sense and experience all nine levels of their being,** while beyond stretches **the Silence of the primordial Nothing,** abstruse to an unenlightened consciousness, **the soundlessness of harmony, which is both the fullness of awareness and the unconscious at the same time.** That is why folk traditions of different cultures speak of **'nine, or twelve, Heavens.'**

We live on Earth and we are a part of the Earth. The Earth is a planet, or a little part of the solar system, of the galaxy and of our universe. There are

---
77   Rumi, *Hidden Music*, London, Thorsons (2001), p. 23.

countless universes and galaxies. **By expanding, or developing, their consciousness, humans regain their complete memory,** even the memory of the evolution of the Universe and the Earth, the memory of Creation and of the first creative impulse and sound of **the Big Bang.** Yet, this wholistic memory comes back only if, through the process of becoming aware and devotion, humans **develop themselves to an enlightened perfection and act** in line with the eternal **idea which is woven into** every single subquantum particle and **atom of matter, in line with the matrix of the Intelligence of life, with the perfect and harmonious whole of spirit and matter,** creating **all-connectedness** with all life forms. Such a person can hear **the stars and can sing with them. Planets and stars are thus granted the status of an (energy) being,** for they live, are born and die, just like humans, or they depart to the darknesses and nights of the invisible for a certain period of time.

Humans are **returning to 'the divine qualities,' to perfection. By developing their spirit, humans themselves become the Logos and try to live within all seven or nine levels, or dimensions, of their own being.**[78] They become divine, aligned, or **attuned,** to both the earthly levels and the levels out beyond, which belong to the primordial sound of **the Absolute, or the First Principle. They become one with everything that is.** This is also what **the cosmic doctrine of existence** teaches us.

We are ceaselessly **seeking resonance, or harmony, through the trials in our lives,** through the messages which life situations and learnings offer to us, especially through relationships. **By being in harmony with everything, we align to the Cosmic Mind. We become a part of the collective soul of the Universe, a being in the galactic family (as the Mayans would say), a being in the family of innumerable vibration forms, who can no longer lose his or her connection to the primal life force, to the Intent, or Plan. They can only forget it,** for a long time, even for life-long periods. **Life is Cosmic Consciousness, or Divine Consciousness, on Earth, it is the serpent-like, spiral frequency-energy flow of love in movement and forms.**

> '**Love** means to **reach for the sky** and
> with every breath to **tear a hundred veils.**
> Love means to **step away from the ego,**
> **to open the eyes of inner vision** and
> not to take this world so seriously.

....
78 Check Barbara Hand Clow, *Alchemy of Nine Dimensions*, Charlottesville, Hampton Roads Pub. (2004).

> Congratulations dear heart!
> You have joined the circle of lovers,
> tell me in your own words
> when did all this throbbing begin?
>
> 'I was absorbed in my work in this world
> but **I never lost my longing for home,**
> One day, exhausted with no strength left,
> **I was lifted** suddenly **by the grace of Love.**
> To describe this mystery there are no words.'[79]

Theories of the parallel universes of our twin souls beyond the stars

Discoveries in **quantum mechanics**[80] are ever more interesting and astonishing, especially **the theory of sound-light subquanta and parallel universes, or worlds.** Modern science, just like our ancient ancestors, is **teaching us** ever more successfully **about multidimensional reality. The unknown Universe is once more becoming increasingly known to us.** And both the age-old spiritual heritages and science claim that we only can decide **in which universe, in which sound language, or in which octave, or dimension of reality, we would like to live.** And this is indeed so: **spiritual seekers and warriors can begin to additionally live within other** (higher, as we say) worlds, or levels of consciousness and **reality.** Which means **their lives will be richer and fuller** than the lives of those to whom these worlds continue to remain inaccessible.

Today's science is actually **(re-)discovering things which were thousands of years before us perceived** by and known to our ancestors, the spiritual warriors of different cultures. The modern claim that **every particle of matter is simultaneously undulation and can be in many places at the same time** is interesting. Of course, sub-atomic or quantum reality explains multidimensional worlds differently from how it was done in the past. **Our ancestors used symbols, interesting metaphors, and Divinities to explain** events in the Universe, on Earth and in living beings, whereas quantum physics explains this with **the symbolism of formulae.** But physics today, just as **distant priests and shamans did, claims that we live in several worlds simultaneously, yet we only feel and see that which we have chosen, or that which we want to see or hear.** Interesting thesis indeed. I believe that we in fact **feel and understand only up to the point to which our**

....
79 Rumi, *Hidden Music*, London, Thorsons (2001), p. 18.
80 The leading authority in it is currently **Hugh Everett**.

consciousness and the arrows of our awareness have reached. So our Universe can **split, or duplicate,** and our sensations in it can dilute, or multiply.

Recently I watched on the **Discovery Channel**[81] a National Geographic programme called The Unknown Universe, in which physicists talked about **the Universe splitting infinitely.** They claimed that **humans can die in one world, but not in another world** (not on other planes of **consciousness, or soul,** as folk traditions put it). **So, we can be dead in one world, but we are (still!) alive in another world.** This thesis is of course widely **confirmed by 'after-death' experiences,** by the 'life after life' phenomenon,[82] as well as by **eterity and the immortality of soul essences. Both migration of souls and reincarnation are also possible** according to these findings.

The **theory beyond stars** suggests that **there are planets which are copies of our own planets,** including **mirror copies of life on Earth.** This is also claimed today by astrophysicists. Everything **that exists in the physical world is therefore duplicated in alternate universes – even we and our thoughts.** It is this theory that validates precisely the knowings of ancient initiates with a broad perception and it also confirms the theory of the **'twin soul,' or the non-incarnate cosmic soul.** This theory is based on age-old discoveries which say that **out there, in the cosmic dimensions, dwells our second half, the second part of our soul's essence – our cosmic soul** called nik nahal in the Mayan tradition. If parallel universes do exist, then our unlimited consciousness is certainly able to find a way to them, or to contact them. And the theory of **the soul's journey (reincarnations)** becomes more probable.

Astrophysicist claim that our Universe was created in a trillionth of a second after **the Big Bang.** But science still **doesn't know what caused this bang. The Universe bends itself in time and space and is in fact energy.** And innumerable new 'big bangs' are happening all the time in these multidimensional universes. **The patterns of cosmic waves are constantly repeating in the universe.** In the language of sound, we would say that the patterns of frequency waves, of wave vibrations, or tones, are repeating time and time again. So our **ancestors were again right. Why don't we believe them?** Why does **science listen to them only after it has finally managed to discover and perhaps see under microscopes things which were invisible and intangible until then?**

Contemporary science is increasingly interested in **how we are able to perceive numerous universes, or dimensions of reality. Our all-encompassing consciousness** certainly has the necessary tools for all of this. Quantum mechanics has discovered that other universes, **worlds, or dimensions influence each other, they even merge and move together, or they annihilate each other in collisions.** Physicists suggest that the easiest way to imagine these universes (dimensions)

....
81 The programme was broadcast in October 2011 on TV Slovenia.
82 When humans leave their physical body, their consciousness is still 'alive' and continues to live.

is **as soap bubbles** floating in the air. **There would only be a problem if these parallel universes (copies) were to collide. Then they would annihilate each other.** Theories still differ in this area and there are no final theses yet. But a **long time ago,** long before us, our ancient planetary ancestors discovered all of this with their telepathic senses and abilities. In their own picturesque way, of course.

Especially interesting is a modern scientific thesis that **there is an infinite number of versions of our universe and ourselves.** So, if parallel universes do exist, then everything is, from a broader perspective, much more vivid, **less stuck, and above all, much less serious.** This is even what scientists are saying. Then **annihilation (or death) loses its weight. Every experience can be repeated countless times in other worlds.** This validates the findings of our ancestors **that nothing gets lost** – material aspects, **visions, not even thoughts, and emotions.** Every thought, every emotion is extremely important and eternal at the same time, which is why we need to carefully control them. **The imprints of our emotions and thoughts remain in the Field.**

This also confirms **the theory and belief in the journey and incarnations of souls. If a persons dies in one of the parallel universes, his or her consciousness will continue to live in alternate universes, or dimensions.** Especially interesting is a postulate of modern physics that an accurate and **perfect copy of every being in those parallel universes is actually eternal.** That is why it is not surprising that the Mayans spoke of incarnated and cosmic souls. And the dimensions, or **octaves, of the universes are the creative principles of the Universe** in which we live.[83]

The nine dimenions of body and spirit are like different states of water: liquid, ice, and vapour.

> **Dimensions of consciousness and reality are like colour nuances** on a painting palette.
> Like **liquids** of water, vapour and ice **with a higher resonance,**
> their presence is barely perceptible,
> they permeate each other, they interchange,
> and **bring messages from the Source to the earthly ground.**
> **Luminous images,**
> put into picture and sound
> by **the invisible sound of the Source,**
> **are like vessels for the messages of the Universe,**
> **wishing to be embodied in the physical form,**
> in the form of grasses or a human being.

. . . .
83   A book by Jim Al-Khalili, *Quantum*, London, Weidenfeld & Nicolson (2003), is interesting and complementary reading.

This is how **the matrices of the elusive Intelligence of life** and of everything
that is
converse across the levels of the intangible
from a seed and foetus to light and material form,
to human nature and sun light,
to energy, warmth and life flow...[84]

....
84 An excerpt from the poem *Dimensions of Consciousness and Reality*, taken from the book *Zvočne podobe prebujene ljubezni* by Mira Omerzel - Mirit, Vrhnika, Dar Dam (2012).

SHAMANISM, PRIESTS' SCHOOLS OF ASTRONOMY AND MUSIC

The shamanic journey into the unknown within the circle of life and death

An offering to the Great Grandfather Fire among the Apaches

Shamanism is a journey of return. A warrior returns victorious to the spirit, having descended into hell (into ordinariness and suffering). And from hell he brings trophies. **Understanding is one of his trophies.**[85]

During preparations for a Navajo Sun Dance (in 2000),[86] a couple of days before it began, I headed with my Navajo host for the northern part of Arizona, high into the mountainous lands of **Apache** territory, where the Sun Dance was already under way. **Everybody was dancing equally fervently.** I was truly touched by the immense enthusiasm of the supporting group, by their shouting and encouragements. **Nine drummers** sat at a huge drum, beating on that mighty instrument in elation, **in semi-trance. Two women were singing with them** and at times, sudden, high-pitched **cries** came out of their throats.

Musicians (priests?) with ceremonial rattles (**Bonampak, Chiapas**).

My friends and I approached the ceremonial site more or less in the middle of the Dance. There was **solemnity** in the air. **The sound of drums was extremely piercing.** You could sense the proverbial Native American **watchfulness and attentiveness** everywhere. They noticed me. But I was not allowed into the vicinity of the ceremonial site – because I was dressed in trousers. In the way of a man. I had come by truck together with my Native American host. And it truly had not crossed my mind that my trousers might disturb anyone. However, **women were supposed to wear women's clothing – skirts – during ceremonies.** Such are the **ceremonial rules** of the local Native Americans.

Sad, I strolled around the margins of the site, when I suddenly saw **a shaman dressed in white.** He stood at a fireplace, **making elegant gestures with an eagle**

....
85 Carlos Castaneda, *The Wheel of Time*, London, Allen Lane, The Penguin Press (1998), p. 262 (the note in brackets is mine).
86 Read the first book in the *Cosmic Telepathy* series.

feather above the heads of the people and above the rising smoke, which was billowing from the fireplace in front of him. From a distance, I watched what he was doing and how he was doing it. People were constantly coming up to him, individually or in family groups. He was bestowing **energy blessings** on them and **explaining the insights** which the smoke revealed to him.

All of a sudden, he noticed me. He motioned me to **come closer.** A bit uncertain, I went over to him. Is there again something wrong, I thought. First my clothes are not right, then my slippers, because they are not genuine Native American moccasins, now I am standing in the wrong place?

We exchanged the usual information. I discovered that he was **a visiting shaman of Mayan descent from Mexico.** He pointed at the fire and told me **to offer a gift to the Grandfather – the fire. To offer my dreams, my pain, and fears to the fire.** I didn't understand him completely at first. To which grandfather am I supposed to give a gift? I had not been expecting such a picturesque metaphor for fire. When I grasped what he had said, I smiled and looked into the flames. And I **threw off my burdens.**

Meanwhile, Native Americans of different ages, tribes, and countries joined us in a growing **circle** by the fireplace. They held hands. The shaman somehow mingled me in and started **blessing life** in a wonderful elated manner. In the middle of this blessing and healing, he suddenly said: **"You continue!" Then he disappeared.** Evaporated. And he left me in the middle of a crowd of strangers.

For a while, the Native Americans watched me with surprise and I watched them. I sensed a hidden fear and a bit of unease in their eyes. **They were afraid to spiritually open up to a white woman,** which was understandable, given their history. But they had complete trust in the visiting shaman in white and in his actions. So they stayed. And I was somehow forced to continue what the shaman had begun. To **exit** completely and **enter spiritual bodilessness.** This was obviously what the wise healer of souls and bodies had wanted and he helped make it happen. The crowd's fear soon dissipated. I continued to heal and bless, embraced by a family of Native American people and kindred souls. We were all absorbed by **the ecstasy of boundless love. By the glow of life. The glow of all-connectedness.**

After half an hour or so, the visting **shaman suddenly returned.** He thanked me for my help and re-joined our circle. We continued with offerings to the fire, as if he hadn't disappeared at all. Together, we gave blessings of **life energy** for quite some time. Why did he disappear and allow me this wonderful experience? **Had he been reading what had been written, what had been interrupted long ago? Had he seen into the soul of my experiential quests? Or did he simply understand the importance of that moment in my search of the world's spiritual traditions and my wish to connect?** Or had he merely treated himself to a short break, because he thought he had found a replacement? Perhaps something had 'whispered' to him, telling him to offer me this unexpected experience? There was certainly **the beauty of the unexpected, of the sudden** in this experience.

> **'My grandfather always rose with the sun.
> It was his oldest friend.**
>
> The front door of the general store he ran
> faced toward the east and he'd sit there
> in a blue painted chair of pine cut from his woods,
> waiting for those first rays to touch his face.
>
> **He grew stronger as the light moved higher,**
> hands moving like crickets coming back to life
> among grass blades frosted overnight.
>
> Then, **before he'd stand to his long day's work,
> he'd lift his palms and hold them there,
> just long enough to cup the sun.'**[87]

Mayan priests, the Lord of Sipán and ancient forms of penitence

Mayan priests were called nik vakinel (**those who know**, according to Jenkins), *Ah Kin May* and *Ahau Kin May*. The last two words denote the high, spiritually broadest Mayan priests, respected by rulers and the community alike. Their duties included: **giving advice to the chiefs** and answering their questions, **performing offerings and sacrifices,** leading ceremonies, and teaching about the laws of life. They had to set **good examples** for other people. They mostly dealt with **books,** they wrote them and of course they also read them. They studied the wisdom of **sacred ancestral books and taught people about the ancient wisdom, they divined, maintained temples, and healed.** Books were written on paper made of the roots of a tree.[88]

In his book *An Account of the Things of Yucatán*, Diego de Landa complains about the large number of idols and temples. He says that the lords, priests, and the most important men had shrines and idols **in their houses** for their **private**

---
[87] A poem by Joseph Bruchac, taken from the book *Tudi trava ima svojo pesem*, Radovljica, Didakta (2000), p. 202.
[88] Fray Diego de Landa, *An Account of the Things of Yucatán*, Mexico, Monclem Ediciones (2000), p. 38. The original was written between 1563 and 1572.

prayers and offerings. They venerated **Cozumel and Chichén Itzá** as much as Europeans did **pilgrimages** to Jerusalem and Rome; when they did not visit those sites they sent their offerings, mostly the copal incense. **The friar of course mocks the Mayan idols, saying that there were no animals or insects of which they did not make statues, they made all of them into** gods and goddesses.[89] Yes, the Mayans **knew how to see the Spirit, the divine power, in every form of life, in every being.**

The Mayans had **idols of stone and wood,** but the greatest number was made of **clay.** De Landa states that wood idols were so highly prized that they were passed down as something most valuable. They had no metal statues, there being no metals in the region. The most idolatrous were **the priests, the chilánes – the sorcerers, magi, physicians, but also the** chaces and the nacónes. The most important duty of the priests was to **teach the laws of life. Forecasting, divining, and the dating** of celebrations, rituals, and sacrifices were also of great importance in the Mayan society. The chilánes carried out their work so devoutly that they had to be carried on shoulders (probably **in a trance?**).[90]

The word balam denotes both **the jaguar and the priest.** Priests can also be called *nik vakinel*. The Mayans themselves know what connections between spirit and life they used; they saw distinct links between apparently totally disparate objects, things, and concepts. **The jaguar symbolism** is very important and strong in Mayan culture; it indicates **alertness and power.** Even the mythological twins **Hunahpu and Ixbalanque wear patches of jaguar skin** or have spots on their bodies, the likes of which jaguars have. It is interesting to note that the same symbolism was also known among the Egyptians and ancient Greeks. **The pelt of a jaguar denotes power and supernatural abilities,**[91] which is why it was a vital part of priestly attire.

Today, during the Mexican pre-Lenten festival, the priests **still dress as jaguars** for a ritual called *el Pochó*. They dance on the streets, accompanied by **solemn rhythms, by the sounds of reed pipes and drums.** According to ancient beliefs, priests dressed in jaguar pelts and masks could cross **from the land of the living to the place of the dead and thus connect the two worlds.**[92]

Renowned are also Mayan figures in yoga poses. We find them in Palenque, Copán, Tical, on the Wall of the Kings[93] and perhaps elsewhere. The facial expressions of these figures portray **people in a relaxed posture, in meditation. Mayan**

....
89   Ibid, p. 80.
90   Ibid, p. 81. The note in brackets is mine.
91   More on this topic can be found in the seventh book in the *Cosmic Telepathy* series, which deals with the ancient Egyptian and the ancient Greek cultures.
92   Mysteries of the *Maya, National Geographic Collector's Edition* (2008), p. 110.
93   According to Ivan Šprajc, *Quetzalcóatlova zvezda*, Ljubljana, Založba ZRC (2006).

kings too are seated in yoga poses, at least in Copán. A number of researchers of Mayan culture have written about this.[94] The Mayans were supposedly familiar with the benefits of a type of physical exercise similar to Hindu yoga.

Recently, I watched a TV programme[95] about the Lord of Sipán, about a burial site high up in the Andes, **in Cerro Blanco in Peru,** where **Huaca del Sol, the Sacred Pyramid of the Sun,** is located. The local **Mochica** people were Mayan contemporaries. Since **1987,** the archaeologist **Walter Alva** has been devoutly excavating the site and has found one of the most important and majestic tombs in America. The tombs' platforms date back to **the first centuries of the Common Era,** even to the centuries before Jesus' birth.[96] In them, Alva found **skeletons of a ruler, priests, and servants,** buried with wonderful artistic **artefacts and jewellery** from **the Moché, or Mochica,** people. **A wonderful necklace with round beads and a beautifully crafted cobweb with a human face** were found in the earliest platform. It probably belonged to a dead **priest.** An old nobleman and **priest-warrior** in the third tomb wore **priestly attire in the form of a bird** and **an owl** headdress (the symbols of death and immortality). He was adorned with special nose jewellery.

In the second tomb, there was **a priestess** buried next to the priest. It was discovered that priests wore **little bells** around their waists (in many cultures, the sound of bells has a special **meaning – that of awakening higher levels of spirit**). In the TV programme, Walter Alva stressed that **the Lord of Sipán** wore **a golden crown** on his head, which was **the symbol of his shamanic power.** It looked like a splendid **auric glow** with rays looking up to the Sky. There were also **horns which resembled open-mouthed serpents.** The burial site with the skeleton of the Lord of Sipán belonged to **a pre-Inca culture,** which carried out sacrifices by crushing heads and cutting throats. To be **sacrificed was a great honour** at the time.

Sipán culture was **contemporaneous with the Mayan culture.** While interpreting the local culture, archaeologist Walter Alva discovered and mentioned an important sentence: **Drink the water of the Gods.** These words clearly encourage people **to immerse themselves into the boundless, divine ocean of spirit.**

In Sipán, **virgin daughters** were also sacrificed to the Gods. First they consumed hallucinogenic **drugs,** following which they threw themselves off a cliff in a trance. **Was it like that (only) in the new era** and during the transition into it? **It is said that the rituals in Sipán were led by priestesses, who made offerings to the owl Goddess. Priestesses also taught shamanic wisdom to the girls.** The experience of a state of transcendental consciousness was said to allow

---
94 John Major Jenkins, for example.
95 *The Lord of Sipán*, Viasat History, 26th August, 2011.
96 Check the book *Iščezle civilizacije (Vanished Civilisations)*, authors unknown, Ljubljana (2002).

the audience to travel across time and space, into the expanses of consciousness and the worlds beyond the material.

Excavations in Sipán showed a new view of the ancient Native American cultures in South America. It turned out that the culture even had **irrigation systems. Feeder canals were built,** which carried water to dry lands when the wild rivers, full of watery abundance, were flowing from the Andean highlands. Today, the Mochica people still construct **the same canoes** as their distant ancestors did two thousand years or more ago.

Priests reportedly lead **religious processions to the sea.** There, they collected and bought **shells (***spordylus***), which were considered sacred.** The shells were ground into a **sacred powder,** which was used for **the offerings** to the Gods, while entire shells were used for **pectoral shields.** The Lord of Sipán also wore **nose** ornaments made from shells. The ornament covered his mouth, which allowed him to hide his emotional expression. **Shells were sacred symbolic objects and of course brilliant music instruments (for signalling), they were wind instruments.**

The Mochica people were **highly skilled** potters. They made **sophisticated statues** and wonderful clay pots, which were often **decorated with the images of the processions of musicians with their instruments – rattles, flutes, bells, trumpets, pan pipes.** Pottery items depict scenes in which a priest is offering **a shell to the supreme priest-warrior,** to the lord. **A ruler was also a priest-warrior.** Shells certainly had a special value, which was perhaps similar to that in the ancient Vedic culture in which days and ceremonies alike began and ended with shells. Clay objects were fired, which made them more durable.

Pottery was made **without potter's wheel.** Which means that Sipán pottery belongs to a culture in which the **wheel did not determine the level of its culture.** Without using wheels and potter's wheels (as well as no metal tools and no domesticated animals), they were brilliant sculptors and painters. They also crafted **clay portraits. Musicians with pan pipes** were most often portrayed on clay. And there were also **erotic figurines** and male figurines with erection – in a fertile form.

The clay figurines of priests were of the same size as the figurines of the rulers, which perhaps explains the importance of priests. The locals were said to worship **the spider God, which holds all the threads of the world together.** The spider God probably represents **the vibrational, frequency sound weave of invisible energies** – the weaving blueprints and shuttles of life. **The Spider Woman** of the North American Indians still has a similar meaning today. Weaving the invisible yarn of life energies, the spider God holds the threads of life in his hands, **leading people to the realm beyond death,** which is part of life on Earth, leading them into a new life and the world of ancestors.

They also made tools, weapons and decorations from copper. **As early as two thousand years ago, they knew how to gild gold, how to silver-plate, and weld metals with the help of electro-chemical processes.** In Europe, this skill was not discovered until the 18th century.

Looters had plundered the tombs in Cerro Blanco to a significant degree before Walter Alva discovered them. But many have since consciously stepped over to the side of researchers and conservators and have begun to protect their heritage. They began to excavate together with archaeologists. It is interesting to note that they all **feared the tomb disease – the fact that the dead might return and possess the living. Realms beyond death obviously still have great power there.**

The Lord of Sipán wore **a v-shaped crown** on his chest, which probably denotes opening, broadening upwards, **into the spheres of spirit** and soul. The Lord of Sipán was also buried with numerous **tools,** weapons, and skulls for his life beyond. It is known that in battles, enemies were beheaded with clubs weighing approximately 5 kilos. The meaning of skulls is still not entirely known. Perhaps they indicated **the acquired power.**

The Mochica also performed **ritual fights,** which partly resembled medieval knight's tournaments. The winner undressed his opponent, seized his weapons and took him to the lord, which then sacrificed him.

In initiatory rituals, boys competed in **ritual running.** They took **small bags containing seeds for divination** with them. The winners, the best runners, became members of **the lord's guard.** But priests had of course first checked the destinies of the warriors who protected the lord until his death.

The Mochica attributed **divine abilities and characteristics to their ruler.** When he died, priests put **a sacred death mask on him and covered his eyes and mouth with golden discs.** In a similar way, ancient Greeks equipped their deceased with coins.

Pre-Incan peoples used **musical instruments at their funerary celebrations** – mostly **brass instruments,** which produced unusual, other-worldly **sounds, warning of the difficult to imagine life after death.** Today, white people still accompany their dead with trumpets.

Water baptism - connecting with the perfect wholeness and with all the dimensions of the physical and spiritual world

Some Mayan **ceremonies and rituals could last as long as three years.** It was a great sin if these commandments were broken. Friar de Landa writes that men were so **given to their idolatrous practices** that even women, youths, and maidens had to **burn incense and pray** to the Gods in order to **protect** them against demons and evil.[97]

Friar Diego de Landa writes[98] that **water baptism** was found only in Yucatan. This custom was denoted with a word meaning to be born anew or again, which was the same as the Latin *renascere*. The Mayan word *caputzihil* also means to be reborn. The friar says that the custom was very old; its origins date back to **the Pre-Christian period.** Baptism was said to symbolise entry into **the purity of spirit,** which was of great importance to everyone, especially to the **warriors** of the Truth and future **priests.** The ceremony was led by a priest and the Mayans believed that **by receiving it, they will no longer sin.** Which means they shaped the content of their lives **with a focused intent. Through baptism, they received what they had believed in.** They believed that **with it, they acquired a predisposition to be good in their ways and that this custom would protect them against demons** (against the evil outside and inside themselves?), that they would enter the realms of paradise more easily. And of course, baptism was accompanied by a feast with abundance of food and drinks.

An interesting baptism, described by de Landa, goes as follows: women brought children **aged three** or more. They placed a decorated **white cloth** on the **heads** of the boys, fastened to the hair on the crown; the girls were encircled about their hips by a thin cord, with **a small shell** attached to it that covered their private parts.[99]

When parents desired to have their children baptised, **they went to see the priest, who then chose the most auspicious day** for this ritual. The man who was giving the feast, selected **the leading man** of the town to assist him in the matter. These were usually **the oldest and most honoured men.**

On the day, all assembled in the house of the one giving the feast. The ritual took place **in the court or courtyard of the house,** which was cleaned and **scattered with fresh leaves.** The boys stood on one side, the girls on the other. An old woman was made protectoress of the girls, and a man was put in charge of the boys. When this was done the priest proceeded with **the purification of the house, casting the negative from it.**[100]

Four benches were placed **in the corners** of the courtyard, on which sat **the four guardians,** *chacs*, with a **cord tied from one to the other so that the children were** confined inside it (inside the sacred space and event). Then, all the children's fathers entered the enclosure by stepping over the cord, into the circuit. They placed another **bench in the centre** on which **the priest** sat, **with ground maize and incense.** Then

....
97 Against the devil, according to Christian tradition.
98 Read Diego de Landa, *An Account of the Things of Yucatán*, Mexico, Monclem Ediciones (2000), pp. 75-79.
99 Ibid., pp. 75-77.
100 Fray Diego de Landa of course used the expression to expel the demon.

the boys and girls went up to him in line, and the priest put a little of **the ground maize and incense** into the hand of each, and all of them threw it into the brazier. When this was done, they **took away the cord.** They poured a little **wine** into a drinking cup and gave everything to an Indian for him to carry it out of the village. He was told **not to drink, not to look behind himself as he returned;** they said that with this the **demon, or evil forces, was expelled.**[101] The purpose of this part of the custom was probably **to divert attention** from the real event. In Slovene and Slavic folk traditions, **a false bride doll, or a false name for the sick person** among Siberian shamans, had a similar purpose until as recently as the 20th century.[102]

After this, they cleared the courtyard of leaves – leaves of a tree called *cihom*, and scattered others of a tree called *copó*. **The priest put on his ceremonial attire. He entered wearing a tunic of red feathers,** with long feathers hanging from the edges. On his head he wore a sort of a cone **of the same feathers,** and below the tunic there hung to the ground **cotton ribbons** like tails. He held **a water sprinkler** made of a short rod, which had as fringes or tassels the tails of a certain serpent (like rattles, which made a rattling sound, perhaps **reminding them of the primordial,** sinless, and perfect **sound of Creation**). In his wonderful attire, the priest looked **like an emperor.** The chacs then went to the children and placed **on their heads white cloths** which their mothers had brought for the purpose. They asked the older children if they had done any **bad thing,** and if any had done so, **they confessed** and were separated from the others.

When this was done the priest ordered all **to be silent (silence is the expression of solemnity and the very goal of a warrior's path)** and to be seated. He began to **bless the children, using many incantations** (which means he used **the magic of selected sound**)**, and to bless them with his sprinkler.** After this benediction he seated himself, and the man chosen by all the children's fathers would rise and **strike the children nine times on the forehead** with **a bone** given to him by the priest **(to confirm the nine-dimensional consciousness and reality, the fullness of perfection).** After this he dipped **the bone into a vessel of liquid** he carried.[103] The striking, or touching, with the bone also had a different purpose – perhaps a more solemn and sacred purpose than we might think. Could it be **a distinct reminder, a connection to the realms of the souls and a link to the spirits of the ancestors?**

The holy water used for blessings was made of certain **flowers and of cacao,** steeped and mixed in **virgin water,** collected from **the hollows of trees or rocks in the forest.**

....
101   Ibid., pp. 76-77.
102   More about this can be found in my subsequent books.
103   Ibid., p. 77.

When the baptism was over, the priest rose and **removed the white cloths from the children's heads,** as well as those they had **on their backs,** containing a few **feathers of very beautiful birds and some cacao beans,** all of which were collected by one of the chacs. Then, **using a stone knife, the priest cut off the beads** from the boys' heads. After this the priest's assistant brought a posy of flowers and an Indian pipe; with these they **smudged** each child **nine times** (they once again indicated **the ritual of entering all the levels of reality, a devotion to the process of wholeness and perfection).** Then they gave them **the flowers to smell and the pipe to smoke.**

After this, **they gathered the presents** brought by the mothers. They gave these to each child to eat. Then they took **a fine cup of wine** and **offered the rest of the gifts to the Gods.** This cup they then gave to another assistant called *cayom*. When this was over **the girls were the first to leave,** their mothers removing the cord and shell they had worn (**shells protected their virginity); this was a sign for them that they could be married,** whenever their parents wished.

The celebration ended with plentiful **eating and drinking.** They called this feast *em-ku*, which means 'the descent of the God.' This expression brilliantly confirms the description above. The entire celebration continued **for yet other nine days.**[104] The number of ritual days is symbolic and revealing. It indicates **a nine-level initiation, nine levels of consciousness and awareness, as well as the nine stations of spiritual transformation.**

The ritual of the ancient Vedic (pre-Christian) baptism is therefore **a distinct way of connecting** people to the whole, to everything that is. It also reveals **all the dimensions of the physical and spiritual worlds, of consciousness and mind,** as well as **a connection** to them. We are people, which means that we are constantly both learning and discovering unfathomable worlds.

Spiritual, or personal power is a gift, which a warrior earns after a persistent fight, which can last all his life. This is also what Don Juan claims.[105]

Spiritual warriors return to the spirit, to the visions of the energies of the Universe and to the immortal consciousness

Everything that **warriors** do is done as **a consequence of a movement of their assemblage points, and such movements are ruled by the amount of energy warriors have at their command** (whereas this energy is ruled by the

---
104 Ibid., p. 75.
105 Carlos Castaneda, *The Wheel of Time*, London, Allen Lane, The Penguin Press (1998).

depth of their consciousness). Any movement of the assemblage point means **a movement away from an excessive concern with the individual self.**[106]

'No, this book can't be **without the wisdom of ancient Mexican shamans and Carlos Castaneda!**' That is what my inner voice told me, as it shook me awake one night thirty minutes after I had fallen asleep. It was **Christmas time 2011.** Before I fell asleep, I had been thinking that the next day I ought to finally start piecing together the last mosaic image of this book. And here I have a new order – **the order of my consciousness** and a new task. Where on Earth are my **Carlos Castaneda** books? I read them more than thirty years ago. This seems so far away!

I began searching in the middle of the night. And soon I found the books. I was happy that this **important teaching of ancient Mexican shamans** came to my mind. And, at the same time, I became worried that the completion of the book would be delayed far too long and that my work might stretch into infinity. Among my Castaneda's books, I luckily found the book, titled *The Wheel of Time – The Shamans of Ancient Mexico, their Thoughts about Life, Death and the Universe*. The book is a kind of summary, containing quotations from his previous books, which the above-mentioned brave anthropologist wrote on the threshold of the new era. It will be enough, completely enough, I thought. It will be enough to extract from this teaching at least the most important thoughts of Mexican shamans, the descendants of ancient Mayans.

The next day, as I was reading *The Wheel of Time*, I discovered that **Don Juan's thoughts brilliantly confirm the spiritual messages I had channeled** and included in this book. Only the language and symbolism of ancient shamans differ from the contemporary vocabulary. In their own way, the words of this Native American nagual**, the guide and teacher,** explain the cultural heritage and spiritual **wisdom of Native Americans in Mexico,** which probably originated in a remote past.

The first book by Carlos Castaneda was extremely important in my life, for it was **the first book on spirituality** which could be found in Slovenia at that time. It **captivated** me to the degree that I kept it under my pillow in bed all the time. Who knows why? **The soul knows.** Soon after they were published, Castaneda's books stirred the world's public, because they were somehow too fantastic for modern intellectuals. They condemned his books as being made up and falsified. Critics claimed that if they were really a falsification of old teachings, then this falsification was truly brilliant and rare. Well, in general, everything that is written **on the subject of spirit seems magical, incredible, shocking, unexplainable, etc.** to the majority.

....
106 Carlos Castaneda, *The Wheel of Time*, London, Allen Lane, The Penguin Press (1998), pp. 270-271. The note in brackets is mine.

I will never forget the evening when I briefly put down my copy of Castaneda's book after reading it. I surrendered myself to reflecting on what I had just read. My thoughts slowly drifted away, I was drifting more and more into a peaceful sleep and relaxed (alpha) state of consciousness. Suddenly a strange and totally unexpected thought came over me. It said: **'Someone has a certain purpose for me, perhaps a similar one as for Castaneda. What purpose?** What does this vision speak about? What is my mind babbling again? And who is this someone? No, it is **Someone** with a capital letter.' And I was again wide awake. But I didn't find the answer.

For a long time, this thought remained deeply anchored in my memory and I have never forgotten it. It appeared all of a sudden, it was so powerful and unobtrusive at the same time that it pervaved and conquered me. **As if it wanted to wake me up from a deep sleep,** from my lack of awareness. But it was not until years later that I came to grasp its message. I was given a task similar to the one bestowed on Carlos Castaneda, yet, at the same time, mine was quite different. **I had to look** at the world of **ancient spiritual warriors and shamanism through the window of sound and through the mirror of my own experiences.** Everything came to my consciousness **telepathically** and by itself. And then I needed to piece everything I had discovered together into the mosaic image of my personal experiences and into the prism of **contemporary scientific findings, which confirm the miraculous powers** and exceptional knowings of ancient shamans.

The harder I tried to finish my writing, to complete this book, and wrap up the whole, the less successful I was. Obviously 'someone' or 'something' wanted it differently. Was it my conscience, my consciousness, or something broader? **In any case, expectations are always outside of real happenings.** I kept saying to myself for months: 'I will include only a little bit more and then nothing more.' But to no avail, every time things started to unfold differently than how I had wanted it to. Every now and then I wrote down that, being 'at the end of this book,' all that was left to add was only a couple of little things. But this end became ever more distant. **As if an invisible force, a path long since preordained, was directing my work completely in its own way, indifferent to my endeavours,** even less so to my exhaustion. **I had to follow it** without objection. It always whispered new things. Sometimes I had the feeling **that I was the one writing, and sometimes I felt that someone else was writing through me – an Intelligence, which had its own plan and a purpose not entirely known to me. I was only listening** and recording.

This hidden **purpose,** discovered three decades ago, **started being realised (after the year 2000).** I was writing passionately, quickly and so very clearly, as if Castaneda was standing next to me, dictating the sentences. I have felt **the presence**

of his immortal consciousness since **2002,** when a sudden **live presence of his soul** overwhelmed me during the pre-Christmas time. This energy of his presence is similar to **the energy of the Anasazis, the Ancient Ones in Arizona,** which appeared during my stay with the **Navajo** Indians.[107] Well, this was a piece of cake for a Mexican nagual – **the warrior of consciousness!** He can be **anywhere he wants and at any time he wants. Space and time can't be an obstacle.** I have obviously earned **additional help,** I joked. Even if all of this would be merely the fruit of my imagination, or the Moon's reflection on the surface of the ocean of consciousness, it wouldn't be bad. Imaginary world has a powerful effect too. **And the supporting feelings of presences are always much welcomed.**

Mature spiritual warriors know that **they have to surrender to the flow.** It will always take them **where they need to be.** Thought usually likes to follow the calculating ego, which wants this, that and the other, constantly bargaining and directing the flow of thoughts. **But it is different when we are telepathically channeling 'the thoughts of the Universe.' The flow of words runs its own way – independantly from the flow of words created by our minds.**

So, when, at least for the fourth or fifth time, I was convinced that I had finally managed to piece the book together into a readable whole, I exictedly added, in my fourth or fifth attempt, a summary of Don Juan's teachings, which were recorded by the anthropologist Carlos Castaneda. Castaneda wanted to explore **Mexican shamanism** in the last century, but got caught up with **revealing the warrior's path** of spiritual truths. During his explorations, he fell **into the trap of the teachings of Don Juan Matus, a spiritual guide, or** nagual. After some time, Don Juan ordered him to write a book about their wisdom, but **not to write it as a writer, but as a shaman-warrior.** And my task is to **lay bare the world of sound, a sonic window of multidimensional consciousness,** by experiencing the wisdom of the Yucatan Mayans.

Warriors of peace and happiness unveil and fight evil within themselves and in the world

Warrior of Light and Truth

A true spiritual warrior does not bear arms.
His tools and weapons are peace and silence,
focused thought and loving intent.
Persistence is his virtue,
and **courage** is the quality which ennobles and encourages him.

---
107 Read the first book in the *Cosmic Telepathy* series.

His goal is not material belongings,
rather his **own perfect excellence.**
He is always alert and focused,
not to miss the intent of the moment.
He delves into his path, into things
which reveal to him **what is still unknown,**
inviting him into the expanses of consciousness,
which each new day lays bare.

He is never really asleep, **he is alert and awake all the time,**
compassionate, loving, but also sharp and inspired with life.
Undoubtedly, **he knows the flow of life,**
its **laws and gifts,**
the power of a focused thought and **the purity of mind,**
the immense wide open fields of spirit and the grace of heart,
which delight him.
He fights not solely for himself, but for others too.
With his actions, he **helps** people **build a bridge,**
arching **from the Earth to the Sky.**

Insight is his precious ladder,
lifting him up **to the rainbow treasure**
beyond suffering and pain.
He does not know what awaits him on the other side,
yet **he feels it worthwhile to make the effort and accept**
what life offers him.

Bravely, he lays bare everything that torments him,
and changes that which hinders him.
A brilliant warrior is not rigid,
he is **flexible and without resentment,**
because he knows the world's immortal impulses.
But, within himself, he is **firm and strict**
because the silence of heart alone
holds value and attraction for him, is compelling for him.
Only perfect wholeness and a connection to everything
are compelling enough bait, drawing him into the paradise of spirit.
This is how he actualises and completes
his own life plan and the blueprint of his awareness.

**Once he attains his enlightened goal,
he withdraws from the madness of the world,**
but works for its benefit with even greater devotion.
What he then offers to people
is **immensely valuable,**
although only a handful recognise
what he brings and offers to the world.
But he himself clearly knows that,
**despite pain and isolation,
this is the only way worth living.
With his wisdom** and compassion of **love,
he ennobles everything that is alive;**
he delves into the divine ocean, the infinite **Field,
where life is born, shaped, and sustained.**

That is why his **thought is eternally clear,**
his **vision oriented towards the flow of this core.**
His heart is open, singing with the river of life flow,
and fully aware, playing the game of the Divine Plan.

Once a warrior has understood all the riddles of life's labyrinth,
nothing will be hidden from him **anymore.**
So he can **descend and rise,** without difficulty, **on the Eagle's wings of consciousness**
to the magical realms of the soul and the fields of reality.
From the pyramid's summit, he observes and listens,
he sings the world and heals it,

ennobling it with his heart-felt wishes,
serving it faithfully.
He sails on the waves of timelessness
and embarks not only to the earthly and celestial **sacred sites,**
but also out beyond space,
to the land of light and shadows which lies beyond space.

A warrior-shaman is a musician and therapist,
who knows the thoughts of the Universal Intelligence and the will of God;
he **communicates with energies,** with divine characters,
which undulate across the countless levels and dimensions of reality.

His communication and speech are always **sincere,
fruitful, efficient, and welcome.**
This is how he can **make rain,**
if necessary,
or tame a storm,
which threatens the world and its people.

**A warrior never rests,
he is constantly alert and working**
for the benefit of all forms and the world.
**He does not complain, nor does he boast,
instead he works and heals,**
according to his conscience.

He telepathically listens what the divine echo whispers;
with his sacred **sounds and rhythms,
he improves himself, people, and the world.**

He does not care for gossip, competition, and boasting,
because he receives everything he needs from the Divine Mind.
The mundane no longer has the same value for him.
He gazes at everything from the heights of his heart's consciousness,
which is why **he sees everything differently** than other human beings.

He knows the Intent, the Truth
and the sound waves of the Divine flow.
**He plays in the orchestra of the Earth and the Sky,
he sings the song** of night and day,
he dances his harmonising dance of the winner.

Mellifluous harmony is his **ally,**
balanced rhythm is his **tool,**
the fullness of silence is his **power,**
the emptiness of mind is his sacred **vessel,**
clear intent is his **light,**
open heart is his divine pledge,
while compassion is his redemption,
giving and receiving
without demands and expectations.

A shamanic warrior's faith is the seed and the fruit,
the compass and elixir of his actions;
a warrior **never bargains with truth,**
which is why he is **painfully sincere**
and **never hides**
what he hears and sees,
what he knows or thinks.

For humanity, a spiritual warrior is a very **precious being,**
who directs the world along the white path of spirit and transformation,
which people need,
want,
but also fear.

A warrior-shaman is like a beacon, **illuminating the dark night of the soul,**
he is like **a softener,** dissipating human anger and fears.
His power and worth are beyond compare,
even though blind people constantly criticise his character and work,
slander him, sully, and hinder him wherever possible.
The blind cannot yet see the light and the beauty,
which his help and warnings bring them;
but those who are curious and courageous perhaps intuit it somewhat.
The deaf unfortunately **do not hear**
that a warrior is **singing all the time,**
a song sublime and sacred.
Were they to hear,
they would want to resonate in a similar way.

An awakened warrior of light attunes the world and helps
to heal its soul, to restore the harmony of spirit and body.
That is why the world needs an enlightened warrior,
even though he is far, far **too little understood and appreciated.**

It is important that **he always sees, hears, and knows well**
what the divine Light is saying.
Everything else **follows by itself;**
redeeming, fulfilling, free.

A warrior's virtues are again compelling
in our times.
**With a warrior's doctrine, it is possible to change the world,
to make it resonate again in a euphonious balance of spirit and matter.**[108]

I don't think that there were significant differences between the warriors of Mongolia, Khakassia, China, Japan, Mexico, and Hawaii. **Warriorhood, based on a research of spiritual powers, was similar more or less everywhere.** But it is highly probable that this great knowledge started to be lost at the beginning of the Common Era. In this new era, the ancient warriorhood and spiritual doctrines started losing their importance, yet fragments of these ancient skills and knowledge managed to survive **until approximately 1000 CE.** After that, **different world views** and values totally different from those of the ancient era began to emerge. **The principles of cosmic consciousness were ultimately banished, the expanses of spirit were ever more overlooked.** But, not everything that is old is bad.

A Mayan astronomer observing the North Star with the help of the calendar glyphs *kan* and *imix*, which are a distinct telescope (C.U.M.).

Shamans believe that **modern man is a killing egoist, completely absorbed in the individual self.** This is primarily due to the position of the assemblage point. **Having lost hope of ever returning to the Source of everything, they seek solace in their selfishness.**[109]

Spiritual warriors of the ancient past **wanted to overcome the evil in and around themselves.** They strove to constantly better themselves. So **they first fought themselves, their emotional and mental issues,** and of course those who wanted to push them into darkness and misery. **But contemporary people do not care much for the abilities of the spirit.** They are primarily interested in material goods and comfort.

The course of a warrior's destiny is unalterable. The challenge is **how far he can go and how impeccable he can be within those rigid bounds.**[110]

....
108 Mirit, March 2012.
109 Carlos Castaneda, *The Wheel of Time*, London, Allen Lane, The Penguin Press (1998), p. 271.
110 Ibid., p. 187.

By **using sound as a tool and a weapon (both audible and inaudible sound)**, warriors of past eras **sought balance within themselves,** and they also **sought a balance with nature and their environment, with cosmic and divine forces, and with the Earth.** Whereas in the modern world, the majority are fighting merely for visible and tangible values. **Sound has lost its original grandeur and importance, which is why today sound pollution is enormous in the places where we live.** It is almost impossible to avoid noise. It is everywhere. And **a knowledge of the power of sound is practically nowhere to be found.**

Only as a warrior can one withstand the path of knowledge. A warrior's life is an endless challenge.[111]

Contemporary humans strive principally for material prestige, physical power, authority, and money. But **warriors of past eras fought for inner peace and spiritual power, which is the source of everything, including health and well-being.** That is why people in the past **learned to master their thoughts and emotions and to create, to invoke, in the silence of their minds, what they wished for and needed.** Contemporary people do not even know that something like that can in fact be learned at all.

The seventh principle of the art of stalking says that warriors **never push themselves to the front. They are always watching from behind the scenes.** This enables them to **never take themselves seriously,** which is why they can **laugh at themselves, because they are not afraid of being a fool.** So they can fool anyone. And there is something else that warriors need – **endless patience.** Warrior-stalkers are **never in a hurry; they never fret,** so they acquire the capacity to improvise.[112]

Realisations are of two kinds. One is just a **pep talk,** great **outbursts of emotion** and nothing more. The other are **actions without emotional outbursts – the product of a shift of the assemblage point.** Emotional realisations come years later after warriors have solidified, by usage, the new position of their assemblage points.[113]

Spiritual seekers, warriors of ancient cultures **tried to rid themselves of the mass of data and thoughts in their heads, whereas modern people are utterly obsessed with them.** They think something is missing if they lack information about everything that is happening in the world. Our predecessors were far less engaged with this sort of thing, but still enough to keep them busy when they were preparing to enter emptiness and silence. But **contemporary people are unable even to imagine emptiness and silence,** which is why these two notions hold no adequate meaning for them.

....
111 Ibid., p. 135.
112 Ibid., p. 207.
113 Ibid., p. 238.

> "**The spirit of a warrior** is not geared to indulging and complaining, nor is it geared to winning or losing. The spirit of a warrior is **geared only to struggle,** and every struggle is a warrior's last battle on Earth /.../ in which he **lets his spirit flow free** and clear."[114] This state is called **devotion.**

Luckily, in this exceptional time of change and **a search for better ethics,** more and more people are delving into the lost wisdom of the past; at least those **who seek something more from their lives,** something which is hidden from their eyes, inaudible to their ears, but still of great importance. More and more people, especially the young, are again **interested in unjustly banished shamanism,** which is simply **a path of attention and a path of operating out of the expanses of consciousness. The true one,** the brilliant shamanism, of course, which has very little in common with contemporary self-proclaimed shamans of dubious value. The young are interested in **invisible energies,** in the usual riddles of life and **the after-death realms.** And they are of course interested in **ancient martial arts,** rei-ki, etc. They want to know **why things are as they are and why they are not different.**

Ancient wisdom and techniques are based on a totally **different perception of the world and thinking.** They are based on the fact that **spirit (the Intelligence of life) is everywhere and in everything.** Which is why warriors recognise and see **Spirit, or God, in action** in everything that is around them.

Warriors focus primarily on spirit and they have to, as far as possible, get rid of material things on which to focus and hold onto, and thus lose their power.[115]

The time has come for us to revive and re-visit the ancient knowledge, which is, in many areas, far more effective than that of today. For it is primarily **far more life-related. The new should be based on a respect for past wisdom and on a knowledge of our ancestors.** In this way, we would **shorten our path** across our life's quests and spare ourselves many senseless efforts, even pain, because, not believing anyone, we attempt to discover and try out everything for ourselves.

> "A warrior **believes without believing** – he **believes without any exertion,** he does it as a choice."[116]

By condemning ancient pagan knowledge, Christianity has banished the age-old wisdom from all aspects of life. **A great emptiness has thus been created** in the world of the white man and Christianity has been unable to fill it, as it is

....
114 Ibid., p. 58.
115 Ibid., p. 183.
116 Ibid., p. 137.

unfortunately too narrow and is intolerant of differentness. **This great void emerged and during the last 1500 years people have perhaps consequently been unhappier than ever before.** They are unfortunately also **ever greater liars and traders with Truth.** On top of that, they struggle with **despair, feelings of guilt and valuelessness.** And there is also **a lack of self-respect** among people in the Christian doctrine.

> "The basic difference between an ordinary man and **a warrior is that a warrior takes everything as a challenge, while an ordinary man takes everything as a blessing or as a curse.**"[117]

Everyone is **suffused with the yearning of the soul** and this yearning safely leads them along the white road of enlightenment. Sooner or later **everyone will find again the overlooked expanses of the spirit. Whoever shall seek, shall find. Whoever will come to see, will get to know. Whoever will want, will be able to fulfil their wishes.** May it be so also in the future!

The teaching of Don Juan and the battle for the unknown of the ancient Mexican shamans in Castaneda's opus

> "The warrior's art is to be perennially fluid in order to pluck it (power)."[118]
> **A warrior is attentive to everything in every moment.**

The nagual Don Juan Matus was a Mexican Native American of the **Yaqui** tribe. He told to Castaneda that he had spent **thirty-five years of his life seeking the maturity of a warrior.**[119] His lineage had its origins way back in the past, among the shamans who lived in Mexico in ancient times. Indeed, even inherited memories can go back thousands of years.

Gradually and very methodically, the nagual Don Juan guided the spiritual development of Carlos Castaneda, through which Castaneda focused on the warriors' way more and more. Don Juan explained to him that **the warrior's way was established by the shamans of ancient Mexico. Those shamans had derived it by means of their ability to see energy as it flows freely in the Universe.**[120] Therefore, the warriors' way was a most harmonious conglomerate of energetic facts, irreducible truths.[121]

. . . .
117 Ibid., p. 136.
118 Ibid., p. 139.
119 Ibid, p. 152.
120 I call it Universal Intelligence or the energy of life.
121 Ibid, p.103.

Being a true (spiritual) warrior of the ancient world, the *nagual,* **or spiritual teacher-guide** Don Juan taught Carlos Castaneda in various ways about a different world, **a different reality.** He worked together with fifteen shamans. For thirteen years, he **revealed** to Castaneda **the laws of their cognitive system, of awareness, and of seeing from a different point of view.** He taught him **fundamental spiritual laws and** he also taught him **to perceive energy flows which flow in the Universe and in living beings.** Don Juan called this act **seeing.**[122] I inserted quotations, or the thoughts of the *nagual* Don Juan[123] into my reflections and into the very viscera of shamanic ethics.

The success of a warrior as a teacher depends on how well and how harmoniously he guides his wards in **erasing their personal history. He teaches them how to lose self-importance, how to assume responsibility** and use death as an adviser. He teaches them how to **get rid of self-pity.**[124]

For Mexican shamans, **perceiving energy as it flows in the Universe was of fundamental importance and it was the first step in their spiritual learning.** Different tools were used to recognise the inaudible and the invisible. One of them was **recapitulation, an insight into one's past life.** This was done in order to understand the present better and change its course with one's own will. Recapitulation is a distinct **scrutiny of one's life values, past errors and suppressed emotions and thoughts. Only those who see the truth are able to travel further.**

Castaneda wrote in *The Wheel of Time* that for Don Juan, **to recapitulate meant to relive and rearrange everything of one's life** in one single sweep. The warrior **Florinda,** who called herself **plower** and **had no illusions** about herself, no dreams of grandeur, meticulously taught Castaneda about the details of these shamanic spiritual techniques. She coached him to **enter into aspects of recapitulating** that the writer himself was **at loss to explain.** The writer also recapitulated Don Juan, which resulted in an in-depth insight about him. **The views of him were infinitely more intense** than any views he had while Don Juan was alive. He got astounding insights into the practical possibilities of this technique. **With unwavering force,** warriors should **focus their attention on events lived.** They can even focus it **on people they have never met** (this is what every good shaman-**healer** needs to know, to be able to **heal at a distance**). The end result of this deep focus is **the reconstruction of the scene. Whole chunks of behaviour, forgotten or brand new, make themselves available** to a warrior.[125] Shamans, as well as Indian yogis and rshis, also claim that **contact with the knowledge of those who had died long ago** is always possible.

....
122 Selected quotations and thoughts are taken from the above-mentioned book *The Wheel of Time.*
123 Ibid.
124 Ibid, pp. 144-146.
125 Ibid, pp. 213-214.

A warrior-hunter is not at all like the animals he is after, /.../ he is **free, fluid, unpredictable. He must assume responsibility for being here, in this marvellous world, in this marvellous time.**[126] **A warrior is a hunter. He calculates everything. /.../ Once his calculation is over, he acts. He lets go.** /.../ No one can make him do things against himself or against his better judgement.[127]

On his way, **a warrior must erase his personal history,** he doesn't need it. Mexican shamans taught that with this, **he gets rid of expectations, disappointment, and anger.**[128] A warrior can **remember everything, even most excruciating details, perhaps even details which are not very pleasant to him. This is why the warriors' way of ancient Mexican shamans** (which stems from the ancient Mayan spiritual heritage) **is the epitome of human accomplishment.** This is also what Don Juan believed.[129] Past events are thus reconstructed in a way that allows you to almost hear and sniff them.[130]

A warrior who **does not surrender when faced with the unknown might face his tyrants** (Xibalba, in the Mayan tradition). If these seers can hold their own in those facing petty tyrants, they can certainly face the unknown with impunity, and then they can even withstand the presence of the unknowable. **Nothing can temper** the spirit of a warrior **as much as the challenge of dealing with impossible people in positions of power**. Only under these conditions, which are a special challenge, can warriors **acquire sobriety and serenity.**[131]

Warriors do not venture into the unknown out of **greed.** Greed works only in the world of ordinary affairs. **To venture into that terrifying loneliness of the unknown, one must have something greater than greed: love. One needs love for life, for intrigue, for mystery.** One needs unquenchable **curiosity and guts galore.**

> **'Warriors who deliberately attain total awareness** are a sight to behold. That is the moment when **they burn from within. The fire from within consumes them. And in full awareness, they fuse themselves to the emanations of the Eagle (to the Cosmic Intelligence) at large, and glide into eternity.'**[132]

Impeccability begins with a single act that has to be deliberate, precise, and sustained. If that act is repeated long enough, one acquires a sense of unbending intent /.../ If that is accomplished **the road is clear.** One thing will lead to another

. . . .
126 Ibid., pp. 84-85.
127 Ibid., p. 93.
128 Ibid., pp. 73-74.
129 Ibid., p. 214.
130 Ibid., p. 216.
131 Ibid., pp. 224-225.
132 Ibid., p. 234.

until the warrior realises his full potential.[133]

But nevertheless: **a warrior thinks only of the mysteries of awareness; mystery is all that matters.**[134]

Similar to other traditions, Mexican shamans saw **a human being as a luminous egg or a luminous ball.** They taught that in it, there is a point of brilliance, **an assemblage point,** where perception was assembled.

The **perception** of spiritual warriors, or shamans, is of course **different** than the perception of average people. **Those who see, hear, and recognise the energy facts of the world can of course see the world in a completely different light, in different dimensions.** Shamans avoided rumination on eternal laws and did not allow their views to be crammed into the standard system of cognition. They were convinced that **the process of cognition was the product of our upbringing, of social and family patterns.** They were therefore well aware of the trap of thoughts, illusions, and inherited views.

The word nagual **means a spiritual guide, a leader, a person who is capable of perceiving energy waves. By using clear and focused intent, they should be able to manipulate the energies in space, in people, on Earth and in the Universe.** For the shamans of ancient Mexico, an **intent was actually energy (life) force which flows in the Universe.** They considered this force to be **an all-pervasive, invisible power, which constantly affects time and space and which is the impetus behind everything.** The ancient shamans **were able to direct** this all-pervasive force **by means of their** attention, intent, and their own will. But they could affect this force only **in an attuned state of consciousness, in the state of perfection, with their impeccable reactions to life challenges** which had come their way. Don Juan said that only the most **disciplined,** spiritually the broadest, shamans were able to manipulate this force.

The shamans' **understanding of time and space was different** from that in the white man's world. **It transcends our ordinary, linear perception of time,** through which we conceive the past, the present, the future and **the three-dimensional field of the physical world.** For the shamans of ancient Mexico, **time** was actually something like a thought, **like a great (Cosmic) Thought,** incomprehensible, and majestic at its core. And **a human being is but a tiny part of the thoughts of the boundless Cosmic Mind, or Intelligence;** a tiny part of the thoughts which are 'thought' by these great forces, thoughts which are inconceivable to human mentality.

What is more, ancient Mexican sages understood **space as an infinite Field.** They referred to it as **the total sum of all the endeavours of living creatures.** For them, **time and space were an integral part of human beings.** It is slightly more

....
133 Ibid., p. 236.
134 Ibid., p. 241.

difficult to comprehend their concept of **the wheel of time,** which they described as an infinite **tunnel with reflective furrows** (infinite spacelessness with light-sound weave). Every **furrow is infinite, just like the whole is, and there are an infinite number of furrows within this whole.** These furrows are today called **frequency (sound) levels, or dimensions of reality, or consciousness.** According to shamanic tradition, **living beings, with their own life force (at the levels of their consciousness), gaze into one furrow and live it** (at one level of consciousness and awareness). Beings are somehow trapped in them.

A warrior's final goal is to focus their unwavering attention on the wheel of time in order to make it turn. If we express this in the language of this book, it means that people, through their powers and endeavours, **can rise to all the levels or dimensions of consciousness, and can also embrace the gifts from the individual levels of reality.** This is why a warrior needs to **learn to look in both directions – at time which is retreating and at time which is approaching.**

The wheel of time is like a coil (life is spirally encoded). The Mexican shamanic teaching says that **power rests on the kind (on the quality, or depth) of knowledge** that one holds. When a man is **wide awake and has fear** (he no longer suppresses it into the unconscious), he acquires **respect and absolute assurance, and probably he will no longer make mistakes** which he will have to account for **(through pain and suffering).** They say that his action will lose the blundering quality, which the acts of a fool usually have. If a warrior **fails, he knows that he has lost only a battle, and there will be no pitiful regrets over that.**

Don Juan Matus says that **when one has nothing to lose, one becomes courageous,**[135] and goes on to explain that a warrior could not possibly leave anything to chance. He actually **affects the outcome of events by the force of his awareness /.../.**[136]

Shamanic teachings about warriorhood and power, life, death, and freedom

A warrior is an immaculate hunter who hunts power.[137]

The limits of a man's learning are determined by his own nature, or consciousness. It is terrible to think of **a man without (spiritual) knowledge.** Don Juan taught that **such people recklessly destroy themselves, their environment and the world.**

....
135 Ibid., p. 155.
136 Ibid, p. 156.
137 Ibid., p. 90.

> The warrior seeks impeccability in his own eyes and calls that humbleness (a humble awakeness). The self-confidence of a warrior is not the self-confidence of the average man. The average man is hooked to his fellow men, while **the warrior is hooked only to infinity.**[138]

Mexican shamans say that **dwelling upon the self too much produces a terrible fatigue. This prevents him from seeing miraculous worlds.** A man is then **deaf and blind** to everything else.

The warrior's path must be free of fear and ambition. Don Juan says that all paths are the same: they lead nowhere. However, **a path without a heart is never enjoyable. On the other hand, a path with heart is a joyful journey; as long as a man follows it, he is one with it.** People have four natural **enemies: fear, clarity, power, and old age** (yet at the same time, each of these enemies brings deeper insights into life).

But a warrior knows that he is only a man. He needs to be light and fluid and needs to get rid of the feeling of self-importance. A warrior sees human beings as fibres of light, as a luminous (auric) egg. He also sees that **every man is in touch with everything else. The fibres of light join a man to his surroundings** (and other living beings); **they keep his balance; they give him stability.** But a man remains glued to **the inventory of reason** due to his reason. **Reason doesn't deal with man as energy,** says Don Juan.[139]

> 'Losing the human form is like a spiral. It gives the warrior a freedom to remember himself as straight fields of energy and this in turn makes him even freer.'[140]

> **The average man's connection link with intent is practically dead,** and warriors begin with **a link that is useless, because it does not respond voluntarily.** In order to revive that link, warriors need a rigorous, fierce purpose – **a special state of mind** called **unbending intent.**[141]

> '**The human form is a conglomerate of energy fields which exists in the Universe** and which is related exclusively to human beings. Shamans call it the human form because those energy fields have been **bent and contorted by a life-time of habits and misuse.**'[142]

....
138 Ibid., p. 109.
139 Ibid., p. 233.
140 Ibid., p. 185.
141 Ibid., p. 256.
142 Ibid., p. 159.

> **Human beings are two-sided. The right side is reason and the left side is a realm of indescribable features, a realm impossible to contain in words. The left side can be comprehended only with the total body.**[143]

Therefore, human beings are boundless luminous beings and the world of objects and solidity is only a description (illusion). Their reason usually makes them **forget that description is only a description,** which is why they get trapped in a vicious circle. The manoeuvre of shamans is the same as the manoeuvre of the average man. Both have a description of the world. **The average man upholds it with his reason; the shaman upholds it with his intent. /.../ but intent is more engulfing than reason.**[144]

Don Juan taught that there are no volunteers on the warriors' way (excellently expressed!). A sober-headed man (a man stuck in his reasoning) has to be tricked into the warriors' way (this is what life usually does through **problems, pain, suffering**). **But only the warriors' way is purposeful. A warrior never worries about his fear. Instead, he thinks about the wonders of seeing the flow of energy.** The rest is unimportant frills, says Don Juan. When a man learns to see (when they are awakened and see the reality), **nothing is ever the same. The most effective way to live is as a (spiritual) warrior. The warrior's life are acts** (and conscious reactions). He is aware that his acts are useless, and yet, he must proceed.

> **'The eyes of men** can perform two functions: one is **seeing energy** at large as it flows in the Universe and the other is **'looking at things in this world.'** Neither of these functions is better than the other; however**, to train the eyes only to look is a shameful and unnecessary loss.'**[145] **The same goes for the sense of hearing.** Everyone can see, yet we choose not to remember what we see.[146]

A warrior chooses the path with heart /.../ and follows it; and then he rejoices and laughs, even though he has nothing. He has only life to be lived. His only tie to his fellow men is his controlled folly. He is aware that nothing is more important than anything else. The average man is either **a persecutor or a victim.** But when one **learns to see, seeing dispels the illusion of victory, or defeat, or suffering. Even to be hungry and to be in pain means that the man is not a warrior.** Life without food and hunger is therefore **the warriors' way of devotion.**

....
143 Ibid., p. 192.
144 Ibid., pp. 131-134.
145 Ibid., p. 40
146 Ibid., p. 172.

The only **freedom** warriors have **is to behave impeccably.** Not only is impeccability freedom; it is the only way to straighten out (**to harmonise**) **the human form.**[147]

Intent is not a thought, or an object, or a wish. **Intent is a force,** which can make a man **succeed even in the impossible.** It operates **when a warrior surrenders himself (to the flow of life). Intent is what makes him invulnerable. (A focused) intent is what sends a shaman through a wall, through space, to infinity.**[148] When a man embarks on the warriors' path, he must **adopt a new way of life (and thinking).**

And there comes **a time** in the life of a warrior **when he can do things which he couldn't do years before.** Those things themselves did not change; **what changed was his idea of himself.** His old habits and routines may stand in his way.[149]

The shamans of ancient Mexico gave the name **allies** to **inexplicable forces. These are (energy) beings without corporeal essence that exist in the Universe.** And they were here even before us.[150]

In order to **discover the marvels of life, warriors need detachment, affection, abandon, courage; a warrior needs to be calm, collected, indifferent, seasoned by the onslaughts of the unknown.** Warriors are silent and **solitary,** their **work is unobtrusive.**[151]

Death is everywhere. The idea of death tempers the warrior's spirit.[152]

Whatever is touched by death becomes power. The idea of death **makes a warrior sufficiently detached** so that he is capable of abandoning himself to anything. Death is a whirl. **Death is in everyone.**[153] A warrior must learn to **focus his attention on the link between himself and his death. A warrior-hunter knows** that his death is waiting. /.../ Most people move from act to act **without any struggle or thought.** A warrior-hunter, on the contrary, **assesses every act; and since he has an intimate knowledge of his death, he proceeds judiciously.**[154]

'Death is our eternal companion. /.../ **Death is the only wise adviser** that a warrior has. Whenever he feels that everything is going wrong and he's

....
147 Ibid., p. 162.
148 Ibid., p. 52.
149 Ibid., pp. 110-111.
150 Ibid., p. 35.
151 Ibid., pp. 151-152.
152 Ibid., pp. 37-38.
153 Ibid, pp. 55-57.
154 Ibid., pp. 88-89.

about to be annihilated, **he can turn to his death** and ask **if that is so.** His death will tell him that **he is wrong /.../**.[155]

The Great Mysteries and rituals at sacred sites

Initiation paths usually take place **at sacred sites, in temples,** on pyramids and inside them, and also in natural temples, such as **glades, mountains, caves, wooded plains, at sacred rivers, and trees. Temples and sacred sites are a type of map, where people can more easily and quickly recognise the depth or shallowness of their own consciousness.** They are also **signposts for a yearning soul leading** spiritual seekers **'back to the centre' of themselves.** Initiation rituals performed at those locations push spiritual warriors **up the ladder of their own consciousness, higher, and higher.** At these sacred places, they more easily recognise the path they have to walk in order to reach the goal; they walk from station to station, from one level of reality to the next, from one life experience and trial to the other, **from the illusory consciousness of delusion to the awakened soul.**

From an energy perspective, **rituals at** the summer and winter **solstices,** and spring and autumn **equinoxes, are the most effective.** At these times, **the radiation of cosmic energy from the Galactic Source (black hole) is strongest,** perhaps also **purest** in its vibrational quality. The world's spiritual traditions say that, regarding the movements of the Earth and the Sun, that is when **the vibration flows which powerfully support the human feeling of unconditional love** reach the Earth. This is when people have to (according to the Mayan lore) travel through **'Xibalba,'** through **the darkness and ignorance of the underworld, and rise to higher levels of awareness.** This is how they attain their goal, where time (or the linear perception of the mind) can stop. They transcend the earthly and expand themselves into the beyond, into non-material realms, onto spiritual and cosmic levels of reality.

Ceremony participants, or initiates, came to sacred sites and temples **to re-tune 'their cosmic-earthly clock, or frequency station,' to the 'Cosmic Consciousness Station.'** They came **to revive and comprehend the details** of the labyrinth of life, primarily those details which had been overlooked until then.

The Great Mysteries, or hidden Mystery schools, in which different initiation ceremonies played an important role, took place at sacred sites, and in some places they still do today. With their help, people can gradually attain **complete awareness, self-realisation. For centuries,** stone walls and sculptures in temples, as well as the land around them, **have kept the energy imprints of the eternal**

---
155 Ibid., p. 77.

wisdom of ancient ceremony participants, who were striving for the same goal. Many energy imprints in temples which have been preserved until today are suffused with the memories and prayers of numerous generations, who **sought happiness and full awareness.** What is more, in many places we can still discern the imprints of spiritual seekers dating from millennia ago, for example, from the third Earth, as Native Americans would say. There, the inhabitants of a broad consciousness left their piercing imprints of **a cosmic consciousness of existence.**

It is said that Mayan spiritual teachers **chose their students for spiritual learning.** The consciousness of the chosen students had to be **already sufficiently receptive to connect to the mysteries of the Universe.** In everyday life, during various teachings and festive rituals, students and teachers together **built a bridge between the human world and the Universe, the purpose of which was primarily to return to the Galactic Centre, to the perfect centre of themselves, to the Home of their soul.**

By joining the material and spiritual worlds, we can **build an inter-dimensional bridge along the axis of consciousness,** which the ancient Mayans and members of other cultures called **the joining of the Cosmic Mother and the Cosmic Father,** as well as the 'merging of the Sky and the Earth.' This is when doors into the unknown open and we can peek through time-space dimensions. Mayan *nik vakinel* priests, for example, were able to **permanently gaze through the veils of time and space.** They could consciously open space and time portals of consciousness, of the soul, into the dimensions beyond, above the third dimension.

It is easier to **connect to eternally present (divine) cosmic vibrations** in temples and at sacred sites. There, we can most easily transcend our own limitations, step through the portals of time and space, and enter parallel worlds and dimensions of spirit, consciousness, soul, and reality. And when those with expanded consciousness and perspective want to **face themselves,** their **psychological content** – their emotions, thoughts, fears and content suppressed into the unconscious – they become **conscious seekers, warriors of light** in the cosmic-earthly game, in **the great cosmic-earthly ritual.** In it, every frequency vibration, every **energy (sound) has its own place,** its own role and purpose. Perhaps it even received the name and **status of a being, God, demon, etc.** The Cosmos, which is indicated by a look into the Sky and is, in Mayan culture, symbolised by **the owl, eagle, and serpent, is a sacred and respected arena for the chiselling of conscious human beings.**

Native American warriors of light follow the example of the three sacred animals. The jaguar, eagle, and serpent. **The jaguar** never sleeps. He is always **awake** and alert. From high up, eagle **has the best view** of his prey, of that which he wants to seize. While **the serpent** represents the energy of life and sloughing, or **transformation,** which is cyclically repeated. That is why these three **animals are still the sacred Native American symbols of awakening and spiritual powers.** Conscious people need to enter the transformation of their lives as consciously as possible. They should **be eternally watchful like the jaguar,** be able to **see their prey** like the eagle from a higher perspective (to see their destructive patterns, distorted ways of thinking, blockages, emotional and mental delusions, unloving deeds, etc.), be able **to seize and dissolve their prey.** Then they need to **slough like the serpent** – to eliminate, **to throw away what is not valid,** and turn the bad and destructive into something which makes them good and wakeful. **This is how they cleanse themselves of pain and wounds, which they have inflicted upon themselves as a result of ignorance and lack of knowledge.**

What is more, temples are also large sundials, astronomical observatories and maps of the Earth's and human's evolution cycles. At the same time, they are signposts which help to resolve life's dramas. **There, human beings and the great cosmic being, God, meet.** In Creation myths, God emerges **'from the darkness' of the Source,** from the infinite, the inconceivable. **Cosmic human beings** can **become self-realised** at sacred sites, with all their abilities, givens, and talents. In this, they are **guided by their inner yearning for fulfilment, happiness and peace;** and they also have the guidance of intuitive wisdom from the higher levels of consciousness, or soul.

Warriors of intention, will and courage, death rites of the negative

Let us once again take a look at perhaps the most important part of the Creation Story in the sacred book *Popol Vuh*.

> The father and mother of One Hunahpu were **Xpiyacoc and Xmucane.** They had twins, **One Hunahpu and Seven Hunhapu.** One Hunahpu had two children, **One Batz and One Chouen.** The twins were great thinkers, for **great was their knowledge.** They were **seers (they discovered all their dormant abilities and talents)** /.../. They were **good by their nature,** and in their birth as well.[156] They **played ball** every day (the game of life riddles). The lords of Xibalba heard them (the lords of the human dark, shady side) and summoned them to play ball with them (a fight with the unconscious darkness cannot be avoided).

....
156 *Popol Vuh*, electronic version (2007), pp. 100-101.

So, the lords of Xibalba (lords of unconscious destructive content or shadows) summoned the famous twins. **Xibalba (underworld) is crowded with trials (fears, pain, and suffering suppressed into the subconscious).** The lords of the underworld defeated the twins (**unconscious content took control over their usual awareness**) and the (wise!) head (divine **Principle**) of One Hunahpu was placed in the midst of a tree (on Earth). **The tree bore plenty of fruits (life with primordial wisdom always brings an abundance of fruits.)** But the lords of the underworld (**human shadows**) did not allow anyone to touch the tree **with miraculous fruits (the tree of knowledge; through countless agonising ordeals, unconscious content leads everyone to a transformation into wisdom** with which **miracles** can be created).

But there was a maiden who noticed One Hunahpu's head amidst the tree. She stood under the tree, even though she was afraid of death (fear of new knowings is frequent among people). **The skull spat some of its saliva on her hand (a spiritual-physical elixir** – the symbol of the invisible life flow **of the soul. Thus offspring was conceived. Wisdom (of the head, or soul) with miraculous fruits of wise awareness gave birth to a new life** with miraculous, divine abilities.

This story vividly describes both **the eternal quest of spiritual warriors and the meaning of life.** At the same time, the story of the mythological twins and the Primal force Hunahpu explains **the wonderful talents of the life game and transformation – everything is possible.** It explains **talents,** which humans, like the twins, are able to achieve and which **are exceptional: they range from the mastery of all skills to the prophetic clairvoyance of the musician-twins.**

People's thoughts are never in isolation, as they usually believe. **As cosmic beings, they are a part of the Cosmic Mind, of the Consciousness of oneness.** Which is why their thinking cannot be totally independent of the Source, from the all-present Intelligence of life. **Their free will is limited, it is only partial. This is the reason why we try to align ourselves** with a broader – cosmic and earthly – given of life, whether we like it or not. To think only about yourself, or out of yourself, means to live a fragmented consciousness, say Mexican shamans. Our distant ancestors lived those knowings, which is why, **during ceremonies, they tried to attune themselves time and time again to the flow of life, to the sound of the Sky and the Earth – to the perfection of the primal.** Even though the majority might think that we think and create out of our own inspiration, this is far from truth. This is also what the great Vedic rshis claim. Scientists have discovered that the human psycho-physical state and their **thinking depend on the Earth, on cosmic rhythms and even on the sound vibrations of the entire galaxy.**

Our linear mind and thought operate within the illusion of time. It is therefore unreal, created by our emotions and thoughts. The mind is nourished by our emotions. Emotional reactions 'colour' human thoughts. And the mind is afraid of anything that smells of pain, including the pain which has already been chewed over and outlived. Our reactions to past experiences and lives are stuck in our mind. **This is why we get stuck in our illusionary world, which is brightened or darkened by our everyday feelings. The mind dreams its infernal or heavenly dreams, depending on what we feed it with: with fear or love.** The essence of love creates heavenly realms and an elated and light life.

After Grandfather **Sun** and Grandmother **Moon** had created the stars, **the heart of the Earth and the Heart of the Sky,** they made the sea, rivers, the fish, lakes and springs, trees, plants, and animals. But there was still something missing, even though the Earth was **filled with endless chatter** (countless different sound waves or vibrations). As if they were children, the Sun and the Moon joyfully started making humans. **Beings with life and emotions were missing; creatures, who can love and cry and are made of the stuff of nature. Creatures, who will live in goodness and will cross the breadth of time. All the forces of Universe gathered at a creative party to shape life on Earth. Today's people are** the **grandsons and granddaughters** of grandmother Moon and grandfather Sun, and they are also the children of Mother Earth, the Heart of the Earth, and the Father Sky, the Heart of the Sky. These forces were named **Ajaw** and each was given **a special mission.**[157]

Mayan acumen was certainly **far-reaching.** Its exceptional spiritual essence has been recognised by an increasing number of researchers of Mayan culture. The ancient Mayans knew that the Centre, the Source of all cosmic frequency waves and information, is somewhere within **the Galactic Centre,** near the **black hole, in the Milky Way** (in our galaxy). And this Centre transmits the universal, or galactic, vibrational flow to the Earth, via **'the local information relay station'** – **the Sun.** All living beings thus receive what they need for their growth and life through **the Sun's light,** through this transmitter of life information and **the energy of life,** which invisibly **'commands' living beings and the Earth.** With the essence of the Sun, beings re-create life on this planet time and time again.

In their rituals, the Mayans constantly **returned to the Galactic Source of information,** and this is why, in their numerous rituals, they of course

....
[157] Rigoberta Menchú and Dante Liano, *The Honey Jar*, Toronto, Groundwood Books (2006), pp. 13-20.

also **worshipped the Sun – the most important onward transmitter of the necessary cosmic frequency waves** to the Mother Earth. They knew that **the Universe communicates through light – through light rhythms, which are, at the same time, inaudible sound. The vibrational imprints of the Universe and life are encoded in this light-sound undulation, including the thousands of years old (frequency) memories of events which happened in the expanses of the Sky and the Earth** right back to the Big Bang. **The fundamental cosmic, earthly, and life rhythms are also recorded in this memory. Every cell in our body is suffused with the above-mentioned memory, with this frequency imprint.** And in every memory, in every imprint, there lies **a seed, which is capable of creating a new, similar Universe or being! Microcosm within macrocosm.**

When initiates, or warriors of life, begin to master the powers and forces within themselves, on Earth and in the Universe, **they connect the two serpents into one:** *nagual* (the invisible) and *tonal* (the visible). For the Mayans and their descendants **the Toltecs,** naguals are spiritual teachers, **people with a focused will, who have managed to overcome fear; people who successfully master all levels of reality (the physical, spiritual, and cosmic) – all the levels, or dimensions, of existence. Only those who can truly manage this can teach and guide people and enable them, with their experiences and awareness, to remember what they had forgotten; to remember WHO THEY ARE – the children of the Earth and cosmic forces.** Today, we unfortunately live without the awareness of what **beings we actually are** and why, for millennia, we have been asking ourselves the question about the meaning of life. **The material world can be of help to us,** but it is not the only world we should know. The spiritual scripts and **sacred books** from different cultures and spiritual teachings can teach us more **about this eternal quest.**

The naguals of a complete or awakened, consciousness must always, in the material world, or during the time of their life in a physical body, be able, in a wholistic way, to **feel and connect to the essences of non-material forms, to the energy formations on Earth, and in the Universe,** which they named **beings or Gods.** They can connect **to the consciousnesses of the wise spiritual teachers of the past eras, who, with their consciousness and at the levels of consciousness,** still 'live' beyond the physical and reincarnational cycle, in the dimensions above the third level, **in the field of eternity.**

The awakened *nagual* - a master of awareness and intention

Feathered serpent in the form of **Chaak-Mul**, which personifies wisdom

When we liberate ourselves from the thought 'this is how things are and they cannot be different,' and when we release the traumas which are imprinted in the field of our subconscious and memory and which we ourselves have created, then we will be able to sail into the ocean of reality, without a mask and disguise. We will no longer react like a puppet on strings, moved by an unknown actor – **fears** in our unconscious, fear of pain, fear of not being accepted, fear of painful experience and suffering. We will come to understand **the way we react and operate, we will comprehend that we actually bargain with Truth, lie to ourselves, run away from life's challenges, etc.** When we admit to ourselves our lacks and **false images, innumerable insights – of why this is so – start flowing through us.** And we begin to fruitfully change our habits and bad habits. **We embrace transformation.** Thus begins a struggle in the world of duality – a struggle between **the forces of our subconscious darkness (Xibalba) and the light of the soul,** a struggle in the world which is personified by the twins Hunahpu and Ixbalanque in Mayan mythology. We need to understand **the illusory world of separation and division,** which appears on the earthly stage of opposition and resistance. **This is ego's fight, a fight between ignorance and the silent knowing of our soul. We have to move beyond these opposing sides and unify them** – integrate them into a complete picture of the game of life, **without conflicts. We are learning to accept everything, to change imperfections, and above all, we are learning devotion to the current game and to the flow of life.**

When we accept differences and the lessons of apparent oppositions, and when we accept the current situation as a game which we need, and when we accept the thought 'I do it this way, others do it differently,' we have attained the **necessary tolerance,** which is proof of the depth of our consciousness. The broader our awareness is, the greater our tolerance and patience are. And with them, we also **admit to ourselves our own imperfections.** We do not condemn ourselves, we instead fix our mistakes as soon as possible. This is when **the cosmic doorway into new dimensions of existence opens.**

The world and human understanding are constantly changing. **People's consciousness is a painter's brush.** In ritual processes for becoming aware participants **re-live both the genesis of Creation** and the riddles of their own lives. They

learn to recognise and master the contents of their subconscious and to anchor themselves in divine Cosmic Consciousness. **Sooner or later, every person and every shaman has to walk to the end of this path.** It is not important which religion they belong to, **it is the content of their consciousness and subconscious that matter.**

Wisdom is not built from numerous data and good recollection, as the majority believes today; **wisdom is built from our understanding of the laws of life and our knowing of the Truth, and this depends on the expanses of our consciousness.** In order to attain the levels of enlightened cosmic consciousness, **we have to consciously sacrifice what is not valid,** what is false and therefore untrue; we must sacrifice what is distorted, **imperfect,** everything that is not unconditional love itself.

This is how **strong-willed human beings are awakened – shamans, warriors, masters of awareness, vision and focused intent – the awakened ones, the naguals, who master forces within themselves and around them.** Even natural forces, such as rain, storms, etc. Naguals (the word means **'invisible'**) are therefore people who **master the non-material worlds of spirit, their emotions, thoughts, and actions** (and not the other way round!). They are people who have **conquered fear completely and came to see their own unconscious content,** primarily their unwilling lies, **which derive from fear and suppressed emotions. The awakened ones observe without emotional unrest,** they observe sincerely and without distorted mental patterns.

But first of all, **spiritual warriors must become totally attentive and alert. They have to learn how to listen to life, to truly listen and to be able to hear** even the grass growing, the sound of the Sun, the Moon and the Earth; **they must understand the speech of animals and the wind, etc.** What is more, they must be constantly **attentive to their parasitical, destructive thoughts and emotions. Within themselves, they must awaken the eagle, jaguar, and serpent:**[158] **the jaguar who never sleeps,** alert and prowling all the time; **eagle who, from the heights (of his consciousness) sees perfectly his prey and treats himself to it,** so that he can travel on.

Like eagles, warriors of light must always see their mistakes; they must grab them, so that they can then **surrender to transformation, sloughing like serpents.** Like serpents shedding their too tight skin once a year, **they have to throw away everything which is not valid; they have to transform feelings that hinder them and aggressive behavioural patterns.** Conscious and sincere warriors are therefore **hunters of their unenlightened spiritual content, which lacks compassion; hunters who illuminate themselves and the world** around them **with the light of sunrays (of**

---
158 This symbolic animal trinity is mentioned also by Ruiz.

love). Such processes are also explained in the sacred book *Popol Vuh*. **The blowguns of the mythical twins,** symbolising **the Sun's light,** represent the visible tools of this process. **Spiritual and life's power is built** through successful hunting. **The never-ending serpent of delusions and mental patterns must therefore die.** We need to sacrifice it on the altar of life. **The death of obstacles enables us to comprehend and embrace undistorted reality.** When lies die, the new, the better is born.

A connection to immortal essences, to the souls of the dead, becomes possible and it is not unusual to sense the distant essences of the souls of the Native American ancestors – **the Ancient Ones, the Anasazi.**[159]

Gods paddling[160] to the Heart of Sky and the three hearthstones

The Paddler Gods ceaselessly paddle along **the Milky Way,**
they row through the cosmic soup of life,
in order to **set their hearthstones in the heart of Orion.**
To return to the primal sea,
to completeness, oneness and the perfection of the Triune.
To the sacred site, they bring **the Maize Deity – the God of abundance,**
so that he can be reborn in the mouth of the cosmic serpent of the divine;
the ceremony participant thus regains his **fertile power and purity of thought.**
From there, with the indescribable power of cosmic force, **the Gods create the boundless,**
the world of polarity, time, space and **the remedy of love.**
A human being, who consciously paddles 'back' to primal perfection, is also capable of that.[161]

Participants in Mayan ceremonies **addressed their Gods,** as well as the Lords of Xibalba, the Lords of darkness and bounded time. They prayed to them for **the cosmic, or spiritual, fire of transformation, saying that long ago all people had been close to each other.**

Yes, perhaps in a distant past people had been much closer, not only to each other, but also to other beings (animals, trees, plants). **The ancient ones lived within a miraculous consciousness of complete oneness.** The sacred book *Popol Vuh* relates: **Were we not of the same home? We were of the same mountain (the Source, the Home of the Soul), when you were framed and when you**

....
159 More about this can be found in the first book in the *Cosmic Telepathy* series.
160 In the sea of consciousness, in the conscious Universe.
161 Mirit, 2011.

were shaped. When they **came to ask for the fire,** the God **Tohil** was asked what people were to give. And the answer came in the form of a question: **"Do they not want to give the breast beneath their shoulders and their armpits? Do they not desire in their hearts to embrace me—I, Tohil?'**[162] **It was explained to them that they would not receive the fire (of transformation) if they were not ready for it.**

True, **there will be no spiritual transformation unless we want it and allow it. If we want to ignite the 'cosmic fire' of the soul and the miraculous,** we must completely surrender to the divine flow of life, and **place the kindness of our hearts on the sacrificial altar.** The seekers replied that the breast shall be given and that they were to embrace him[163] – to **surrender to it completely. May this happen!** They thus immediately received fire and they were warmed (the kindness of surrender warms!). **They merged their hearts with the cosmic fire; they aligned the fire of their hearts with the divine fire.**

Mayan lore narrates that the Great Creator **Hunahpu created everything that exists** according to eternal principles, to **the laws of the Universe. He built universal ratios into human beings, into the Earth, animals, plants, stars, Suns,** etc., as well as into the spiritual essences of those beings. We, spiritual-material beings, carry these ratios in our bodies and in our spiritual powers, and we even **intuitively recognise them in music.** We constantly reflect those ratios out **into the environment.**

Mayan tradition says that Hunahpu first created **the Centre, the Heart of the Universe – the Heart of Sky.**[164] The **three hearthstones,** which the initiates or shamans use in ceremonies, represent **the first three fundamental stones, the three fundamental essences of universal creation.** They are also called **Orion's** first three stones of creation, the three stones of **the cosmic fire of transformation,** which, in the Creation story, are said to ignite other fire flames. These three signs, which are also depicted on the turtle shell, can be seen in the stars of Orion's belt, between the stars **Rigel and Betelgeuse.** Connecting to the vibrations of **Orion** during ceremonies, **therefore symbolically indicates rebirth within the boundless ocean of the Source, of the primal; it indicates the transformation of darkness into light, pain into love.** That is why, in their thoughts, warriors leap up to Orion to awaken within themselves a connection **to both their own soul and the souls of their dead ancestors.**

For the Mayans and their descendants, the Quiché Mayans, the three symbolic stones are also **three 'talking' stones,** narrating the Creation story, reminding us of our **necessary gratitude for the gifts of life.** These stones remind Mayans of the first creative impulse of the Universe (**the Big Bang**) and of the basic shape-giving cosmic

---

162 *Popol Vuh*, electronic version (2007) p. 203.
163 Ibid., p. 204.
164 More about this can be found in the book *Mayan Cosmos* (by Linda Schele, David Freidel, Joy Parker), New York, Perennial (2001).

forces – of **the Holy Trinity, the Heart of Sky.** That is why today in some places three sacred stones are still placed on domestic hearths, **protecting the 'cosmic fire' of spirit, the essence of life.** At sacred sites, ceremony participants usually place them in the form of a **triangle.** They are said to speak to people's consciousness and to **transfer the boundless power of creative forces, of the Heart of Sky, to Earth.** Moreover, the three stones are a symbol of the **Creator (God the Father)** and the first cosmic creative act – **the Big Bang – the first cosmic sound and the fire of life** and incarnation.

And when Native Americans sprinkle **maize pollen** during ceremonies, they are thinking of this very essence of life's game. In their thoughts, they are bestowing creative power on vegetation and other living beings. They are creating abundance.

The **eternally renewing creativity** of the Cosmos and the Earth **is reflected through music, sound, and dance.** Of importance is **the preparation of the sacred site** where the transformation ceremony is to be held. Dance, guided movement, and the guided sound of a medium, **priest, healer-shaman – they all mirror the whisper of the Universe and the whisper of the creative forces of life.** Participants dance with death. In their near-death experiences, they consciously enter processes of rebirth and the consciousness of resurrection. Something is ending, something begins anew. **Within themselves, they kill the lord of darkness, the Lord of Xibalba,** who yet always manages to escape. The same goes for our **negative sides** – they always manage to **escape from us** and then come back to life. When we believe that we have finally seen them and banished them, they reappear all of a sudden. Warriors have to pay **attention** to these contents. **The stalking technique is particularly necessary here.**

> **Sacred song is the jewel of the heart,**
> **the sonic purity of the mind,**
> elevating the Earth to the Sky,
> and humans to Heaven.
> Its euphony **eliminates suffering,**
> **it gives sound to faith and builds it,**
> bringing out the **harmony** of the entire community.
> Sacred song is the hand on the cosmic clock,
> **measuring time, painting the images of life,**
> Honing our insight into the mysteries of existence.
> Sacred song is therefore untouchable,
> like a respected gracious lady,
> unchanged over hundreds, thousands of years.[165]

....
165 Mira Omerzel - Mirit, poem *Sacred Song is the Jewel of the Heart*, taken from the book *Zvočne podobe prebujene ljubezni*, Vrhnika, Dar Dam (2012).

Mayans, Aztecs, Yaqui Indians, and others carefully prepared their sacred places and **altars,** which served to **invoke, or anchor, divine energies, and to communicate with 'Gods.'** The shaman Pancho also paid considerable attention to the place where the rain calling ceremony was to be performed. It occupied him for the entire week, until he was satisfied. This has been so for millennia. Fragments of past priestly tasks and games can still be discerned in the tasks of contemporary Mayan healers and shamans. But **the connection to divine waves and essences is most powerfully, most quickly, and most easily established by means of sound, with music.** This is the reason why **sacred sound** was present in various ceremonies, in temples, and royal courts.

To perform music, or to transfer life energy through sound, they used **different musical instruments,** which are brilliantly depicted on the murals at **Bonampak.** And of course they used the most natural of all instruments – **the voice.** Ceremony participants with **rattles** depicted on these murals are exceptional.

The ancient Mayans were certainly familiar with the **sound technology of merging themselves with the audible and inaudible sound of the Universe, planets, stars;** and they also knew the **cosmic initiations** used for connecting to them. The technique of dissolving, of **changing the weight and gravity of a material** by using sound, had probably already been discovered in antiquity. This technique is based on **a change of frequency wave patterns.** Even manifestation, or **materialisation,** was most probably known to them.

In the past, ancient musicians, who were most often also **priests,** always **performed music in the service of the Gods.** Creating with sound was **a sacred task.** They **grounded** the cosmic, the divine, into the material world. Their role was to **discover life's purpose and to ground it;** their role was **to heal human bodies and souls, to expand consciousness and awareness, and to guide people to their awakened goal.** The role of Mayan **musician-priests** and astronomers served the same purpose. **By using energy and sound, they were re-shaping, they were balancing the forces of the Sky and the Earth. This had to be supreme and perfect** and it was perhaps quite similar to the sound magic of the ancient Egyptians, Aboriginal peoples, Celts, Slavs, Hawaiians, etc.

Guided sound and guided movement, expressed through our **playing of musical instruments, which we have never learned and which unfolds spontaneously, can never force their way into the laws of nature, karma, the soul, or into auric bodies. Together with the technology of cosmic resonance, they belong to ancient methods of merging with the Intelligence of the Universe** and with all-present life energy. Being precious **remnants of a distant past,** or rediscovered dormant abilities, both have somehow managed to survive until today, at least in a fragmented form, because they belong to **inherent human abilities. Both are**

the right of a multidimensional being and existence. But they operate according to the abstruse laws of the Intelligence of the Universe, of the Universal Logos/Mind; they do not belong within the framework of the usual mind, they are not acquired through learning. All of this **does not unfold because of us, it merely runs through us and is in harmony with the language of the divine.**

The channelled, guided sound of a medium, healer and shaman, which **descends through a silent mind, without the interference of our mind,** works **like a surgeon's knife, a scalpel, a needle; like a tool which composes and disperses, connecting the material and the spiritual. It is the soul of the Universe, of which Pythagoras spoke, a bonding agent and glue, a powerful surgeon's tool,** and unfortunately, in some places, even a weapon. Whereas, **by using guided movement, the body** imitates inaudible high-frequency sound, which **has the effect of a physical scalpel or laser.** Together, they thus **dissolve energy blocks and disharmonious formations** in the physical body.

Developing the abilities of a medium and channelling sound-movement tools as a form of help, was in ancient times the principal teaching of both ancient shaman-musicians and mystery schools. This is also the key task of my Veduna School,[166] in which we try to follow the wisdom of the sound-frequency Universe. **Sound is everything. It is the building block of everything. It is the language of the soul and heart.**

The gestures of Native American warriors, which I call guided movements, do not mean signs or body movements, but **acts of true abandon, acts of largesse, of humour. The spirit listens only when the speaker speaks with gestures.** That is when warriors bring out the best of themselves and silently offer it /.../ (they touch the grandeur of the unknown and eternal).[167]

Selected, or **channelled, sound** and sound formulae **expand initiates' consciousness** during rituals and feasts, **connecting them to all the dimensions of their own being, to all the dimensions, or octaves, of existence, and to their own soul, their own essence.** The sound of selected **musical instruments** and their sonic qualities, together with **the guided sound of a shaman-medium,** were quite possibly the most important **tools in initiations and other rituals;** they were a mighty support for ritual participants, dancers and priests, who entered **into a state of trance and journeyed out beyond the mind and usual consciousness. The unusual abilities** of transcendental consciousness, which were **attained with these sounds,** enabled participants to connect to **numerous octaves, or worlds of reality;** they enabled them to sense them and resonate with them. They helped them

....
166 The 16-level technique of cosmic resonance, 9 cosmic and nine galactic initiations, and intensive courses on various life topics.
167 Carlos Castaneda, *The Wheel of Time*, London, Allen Lane, The Penguin Press (1998), p. 278.

'hear' cosmic waves, which were given the names of Gods. Through this sound play, they could even touch the essences of their **ancestors'** immortal **consciousness.** To establish the aforementioned connections, the Mayans and our distant planetary ancestors also used **loud breathing.** This is what the book *Honey Jar* says:

> **Ajaw – the Heart of the Earth,** Mother Earth, the Heart of Heaven, Father Sky **called all the elders** of the world together. White-haired and toothless elders with **eyes that seemed not to see but saw all that is deep in our hearts.** They had been walking **the four paths** of the earth for a long time – **the red path, the white path, the yellow path, and the black path – the four magical paths of wisdom. That's why they couldn't see things far off, but only those close up, with great depth.** Ajaw spoke to them: 'You, the elders of great birth, of great reverence, will be the paths and **guides** (naguals) to direct the future of creation.'[168] Their advice and experiences are an invaluable **treasure.**

Many have walked the path of transformation before us and have passed on their knowledge in the form of art, music, musical instruments, fairy tales, and songs. That is how we know this path is worth taking. In any case, we simply do not have a choice. The path is preordained.

> This is what the wise elders were told: 'You are going to build cities all over the world. Each city will have its own **songs,** paintings, palaces and houses, **temples and dances, prayers** and pleasures, **languages and books,** poetry and music /.../ The happiness of the world will sprout from these differences. You will **pass the wisdom on** to your daughters, sons, granddaughters, grandsons /.../ **They will know that the earth does not belong to them, but that they are part of it.** /.../ Thanks to your counsel, **people will plant their dreams on the earth,** and their dreams will blossom as if they were magic flowers.' They made **a pact with the Creator.** To celebrate the occasion, Ajaw called **lightning and thunder** so that they could announce the great pact.[169]

Before the start of a ritual dance, priests usually prepared the site **of the ritual** with great care. They placed a **sacred tree** in its centre and **anchored it deep into the ground.** The tree was a symbol of **the axis of consciousness; it was the anchorage of the spirit, a link between the Sky and the Earth, between people**

....
168 Rigoberta Menchú and Dante Liano, *The Honey Jar*, Toronto, Groundwood Books (2006), pp. 21-22. The note in brackets is mine.
169 Ibid., pp. 22-23.

and God. **A sacred tree** is a brilliant metaphor for the cosmic-earthly tree of life and for the countless worlds of reality, which spread like branches, rising up into the invisible spheres of the Sky, the spirit. It was around this tree that the dance of renewal and restoration, the dance of healing and rebirth, usually took place. The inter-dimensional spiritual connection between the realms of consciousness unfolded more easily with the tree.

The cosmic tree could also be represented by a simple **cross – the intersection of the four directions** – which, similar to the sacred tree, served as an anchor for cosmic energies in the physical world. **The tree,** which, in animal form, was depicted by **a crocodile, represented the immortal and eternal axis-connector between the worlds and human levels of consciousness. The tree, axis, and cross are therefore symbols of the shamanic journey into the centre of the Universe, into the centre of ourselves,** and they must not be left out of sacred rituals.

Mayans narrate that, after the Creator had created **the three sacred stones,** the Universe, the planets and the Earth, he also made **the sacred tree.** With it, he enabled people to journey between the different branches, between the different dimensions of the world, across the fairy-tale realms of spirit. He thus showed them **the ascent into the Sky and the return to the sea, to the 'cosmic soup' of the Source,** in which everything which is perfect at its core was created.

The sacred tree is also depicted by Gods and their **enlightened representatives** (priests, rulers, shamans, and other sages) on Earth. As proof of their **devotion,** they are said to have offered **the most precious** to the Gods – the juice of their life, **blood,** which they **sprinkled on the ground** as a sign of gratitude. **Blood is the essence of life and of the soul which resides in the heart;** it is an important sacrificial offering. It is a vital element of life-and-death rituals. Not only is **blood the symbol of life, it is also the symbol of the Primal creative power of living beings, a symbol of life energy.** With it, **life is renewed and continued** (symbolically too). That is why **ritual bloodletting** was of exceptional importance to the ancient Mayans. Initiates and enlightened rulers are often depicted **in their self-sacrifice rituals, bloodletting their own blood;** and that is a metaphor for **the rituals and processes of transformation into perfect beings** with great spiritual abilities and powers, who are able to connect people to **the Source, to God.**

It is with clearly articulated intent and focused attention that the initiation dance of life and death, of dying and rebirthing can begin and can unfold without disturbances. **The energy of intent actualises our wishes.** This ancient Mayan thinking is demonstrated by numerous symbolic **ritual objects,** which carry a cosmic and spiritual meaning, such as **the cross, sacred musical instruments, sceptre, sacred bird, its feathers, sacred serpent, etc.**

Animals too help people reveal and understand reality, especially **the bird, serpent, monkey, dog, jaguar, eagle, etc.** With their presence, animals remind us of hidden human qualities. **Many were given a special mission in the Creation drama.** The Creator bestowed upon **the jaguar** the task of safeguarding human beings, whereas to the four-leggeds – **deer, tigers, lions, wild cats, and pumas** – it gave the mission of **sustaining the power of the Universe.** To **wolves and dogs,** the Creator presented the mission of judges and **defenders of the Truth,** those who know and carry **the signs and omens of the future.** The owl became **the keeper of death and the other world,** while **bears** are the guardians of the air (the invisible power of ether), because their breath can reach all the corners of the Universe.[170]

> "I was directed by **my grandfather**
> To the East,
>   so I might have **the power of the bear;**
> To the South,
>   so I might have **the courage of an eagle;**
> To the West,
>   so I might have **the wisdom of the owl;**
> To the North,
>   so I might have **the craftiness of the fox;**
> To the Earth,
>   so I might **receive her fruit;**
> To the Sky,
>   so I might lead **a life of innocence.**"[171]

That is why, at its birth, every child was given a **nagual in the form of an animal** – its invisible guide through the life quest. Yet, it will lead them only if people notice and **accept** it. The invisible nagual (spiritual world) is the opposite of tonal, the visible. **Of course, priestly animal guides, also include: the alert and always wakeful jaguar, the sprightly and clever monkey, the sacred bird, the clear-sighted eagle, etc.** While **the fish,** which lives in water – and there is no life without water – represents the nagual guide and the God of maize and abundance.[172]

Animal guides are brilliant and precious assistants for people in their struggle with **the Death God** called **Ah-Puch,** which is, at an earthly level, represented by **the owl and dog.**[173] It has a grotesque form, **with eyes on its hands.** The **soul is**

. . . .
170 Ibid., pp. 19-20.
171 Poem by Alonso Lopez, taken from the book *Tudi trava ima svojo pesem*, Radovljica, Didakta (2000).
172 Taken from the Slovene translation of *Popol Vuh*, Ljubljana, Mladinska knjiga (1994), p. 150.
173 This is so also in the Indo-European and Slavic traditions.

immortal and the soul's essence is **eternal** (only the physical body dies), so **there is no real death at all. Which is why fear of death is senseless and grotesque,** the image of Ah-Puch is telling us. Moreover, it is very wise to see with your hands too, to **see with all your senses and meta-senses,** which are especially **widely revealed, or awakened, near death, at the soul levels beyond death.** This is what the ancient Mayans teach us. Which is why, **in near-death experiences,** ceremony participants and initiates **experience the most important things.**

The dance of the cosmic serpent of awakening, of life energy, can be furnished with numerous symbolic tools and aids, including the sacred (**cosmic**) **fire of devotion,** which must constantly burn, **healing herbs and dancing in the four cardinal directions.** Within these directions, ceremony participants dance ecstatically, thus drawing in, or **actualising their intent. In some places, participants dance through thirteen fields, through the thirteen levels of consciousness.**

The Lords of **Xibalba** are said to represent the **fear, horror, and evil** within the humankind. According to the Quiché Mayan mythology, **human enemies reside in the underworld,** in a symbolic way. Some interpreters of the sacred book *Popol Vuh* argue that Xibalba is a demon or apparition.[174] **Xibil** means to **disappear like a ghost.** Based on this we can conclude that Xibalba, the underworld, originally represented **the human unconscious, all the horror and pain suppressed in the subconscious,** all the incomprehensible and suppressed **destructive feelings and thoughts, the absence of light and love, which distorts our reality and clear perception.**

Talking to our soul is crucial and **cannot be avoided** in initiation rituals. Mayans understood **the consciousness, or soul (*nik-nahal*),**[175] as the **invisible substance** of physical bodies, as **the energy presence of the cosmic laws and rhythms of the inaudible sound of the Primal Mind.** The soul connects us to the non-material upper worlds. They believed it is a force which can be embodied in any form. It is people's invisible and persistent **guide through the traps of life, a silent advisor and teacher** of life wisdom. It is constantly **whispering to us, yet unfortunately we usually do not hear it. Or we haven't so far.**

Mayans recognise **two kinds of souls.** They want to revive the link to both of them. Sak nik-nahal is the soul, or **the awareness of pure cosmic Intelligence, or Consciousness,** which, like a compass, leads people through their bitter, yet inspiring transformational processes, all the way through to the awakened goal of their life's path. But humans become aware of its presence and expanse only in an enlightened state of consciousness. The soul — like a cosmic link, a

....
174 Taken from the Slovene translation of the *Popol Vuh*, Ljubljana Mladinska knjiga (1995). p. 150.
175 According to M. A. B. Calleros.

cosmic thread – supplies shamans and healers with necessary **information about life and the causes of problems**; it also brings to them images, data and sound from **high-frequency worlds. It fosters a multidimensional journey and even the transformation of physical forms (shape-shifting)**.[176]

The other kind of soul of an incarnated being – *huay nik-nahal* – is the **part of the presence of boundless Consciousness, or the divine Mind,** which is grounded and bound in the physical body. It **accompanies** humans **throughout their lives and destinies, helping them to gain insights and understand life.** This soul is closer and more accessible to humans. It constantly whispers to them wise thoughts and ideas, and, with its help, humans **cleanse and gain insights** during their rebirth processes. We can **hear it** at high-frequency levels. This part of the soul helps people **merge the two parts of the soul into one single essence, into the consciousness of perfection.** In ceremonies, participants are building a **connection** between the two souls.

The path to the soul is also opened by using relaxed **breathing and the barely audible and channelled sound of a medium, which is the echo of the sound symphony of Creation.** In addition, **blood is the fundamental material substance of every human being. The soul resides in the heart,** claim our ancestors, which is why the heart is the symbol of humans and (even that of) animals. The heart has gained the immortal reputation of a living being.

Breath, the sound of musical instruments and singing are all tools of the soul, which connect warriors of truth to the upper worlds. They renew them and align them to a harmony of peace and health. Human **breath is indirectly linked to the untouchable essence of blood. Music is suffused and ennobled by the content of our soul.** That is why today the Mayan **healers,** *ilols*, still **blow away the negative from bodies and spirit; and, by inhaling and exhaling loudly, they bring in life energy** into those who need it. **By whistling, they scare the evil and distorted life forces out of people and the environment.** This is what they still claim today.

> 'Indian poetry has always been basically **a ceremony of thanks to the Great Spirit, to Mother Earth, to the grasses and the various creatures, a song.** Indian poetry across the long travel of time has been essentially spiritual. Though a young man **sings and plays his flute** for the love of a young woman, he is thanking the Great Spirit for his love's existence. Though a poet studies a milkweed-pod's flight across the air, **he is thanking the Great Spirit for the milkweed's existence.** While he sings of the hunt, he blesses the deer or

---

[176] More about this can be found in the book about the Aboriginal *ngangkaris* and ancient Slovene *kresniks*.

moose for giving its flesh so that the hunter may continue, and **he thanks the Great Spirit** that the deer exists.'[177]

And love is the most essential part of a ceremony and a soul. **The unconditional love of the soul is the most powerful force in the Universe. It is God itself, the Cosmic Essence, the glue of the Universe and the centre of our quests, the song and poetry of life. Love is the reality of many dimensions simultaneously, the sound of completeness,** which suffuses the entire Universe. **Joy and peace** come when we connect all the levels, or worlds, of reality to love. And when **our love is** truly **unconditional, we rise** above the usual material world and touch the indescribable **Grace** of the Primal Consciousness and high-frequency reality. That is why within love, **the flow of thoughts can stop.** We no longer think and **a meta-sensory perception** of high frequency worlds, inaudible to the physical senses, **is thus opened.**

Mayans also knew transformational methods, similar to the Hindu **tantra,** through which both traditions sought to attain supreme goals. **But not merely through sex, but through the love of the soul!** Unconditional love is an exceptional **cosmic gift, the gift of life and the sun's light.** Ancient traditions even claim that love is the **invincible universal force, a reality even greater than light! It is the force which dissolves darkness and nourishes all the layers and levels of a being. That is how living without usual food,** living on prana, living solely on cosmic life energy is at all **possible.** We must only connect, permanently and with love, with the sea of energy. **Our love must only be strong, or wide, enough. Breatharians are nourished by the vibrations of cosmic love!** And everyone who participates in rituals must be able to live without food and liquid at least for some time. **They have to learn to ladle from the omnipresent cosmic soup,** as we say.[178] **When people stop feeding on fear** and other exhausting emotions and thoughts, all of this becomes possible and life becomes miraculous.

Eternal teachings and the power of the ancient Mexican shamanism

To change our idea of the world is the crux of shamanism.[179]

Castaneda says that when you deal **with the world of the shamans of ancient Mexico, that world shows its face to you from time to time. But it is difficult to take that sight.** A great unknown **fear** can appear. Or you can be suffused

───────
177 By Maurice Kenny, taken from the book *The Remembered Earth*, edited by Geary Hobson, Albuquerque, University of New Mexico Press (1979), p. 13.
178 More about this can be read in the first book in the *Cosmic Telepathy* series.
179 Carlos Castaneda, *The Wheel of Time*, London, Allen Lane, The Penguin Press (1998), p. 114.

with the unknown **mood of the ancient shamans**, facilitated by the intent of the shamans of antiquity. Any man could enter into this mood. The **intent** of the shamans of ancient Mexico was **so powerful;** they made sure that **anything foreseeable would be included.**[180] **This force can be touched** at any time – without complaints, expectations and praise; with devotion and attention.

> '**All the faculties, possibilities, and accomplishments of shamanism,** from the simplest to the most astounding, **are in the human body itself.**'[181]

A warrior is **never disappointed when he fails.** That's the only advantage a warrior has.[182]

Warriors speak of **shamanism** as a magical, **mysterious bird** which has **paused in its flight for a moment in order to give man hope and purpose; warriors live under the wing of that bird, which they call the bird of wisdom, the bird of freedom.**[183]

The warriors' (shamanic) way is a perfect structure. The ancient shamans were absolutely thorough and disciplined, and they foresaw all possibilities on this way. It consists of the supporting teachings for all the novices or apprentices of shamanism. Don Juan considered **the warriors' way to be the very crowning glory of the shamans of ancient Mexico. It was overwhelmingly important to them, it was the epitome of mental and physical health. For the shamans of ancient Mexico** to have created such a structure meant that **they were supreme magi** at the height of their powers, at the peak of their happiness, the apex of joy,[184] pervaded with a humble gratitude and the **elation** of a man **in front of his goal.**

> '**The spirit manifests itself to a warrior at every turn. However, this is not the entire truth.** The entire truth is that the spirit reveals itself to everyone with the same intensity and consistency, but **only warriors are consistently attuned to such revelations.**'[185]

If a man's spirit is distorted he should simply fix it – purge it, make it perfect – because there is no other task in our entire lives which is more worthwhile. To seek the perfection of the warrior's spirit is **the only task** worthy of our temporariness.[186] **A warrior knows the spirit without words or thoughts. It's an**

---
180 Ibid., pp. 64-66.
181 Ibid., p. 193.
182 Ibid., p. 160.
183 Ibid., p. 254.
184 Ibid., pp. 102-104 (the note in brackets is mine).
185 Ibid., p. 253.
186 Ibid., p. 91

abstract because he can't conceive what the spirit is. Yet, without the slightest chance or desire to understand it, a warrior handles the spirit. **He recognises it, beckons it, entices it, becomes familiar with it, and expresses it with his acts.**[187]

It isn't that a warrior learns shamanism as time goes by; rather, what he learns as time goes by is to save energy. This energy will enable him to handle some of the energy fields which are ordinarily inaccessible to him. **Shamanism is a state of awareness, the ability to use energy fields** (or frequency waves) that are not employed in perceiving the everyday-life world that we know.[188]

In the Universe, there is an immeasurable, indescribable force which shamans call intent, and absolutely everything that exists in the entire cosmos is attached to intent by a connecting link. Warriors are concerned with discussing, understanding, and employing that connecting link. They are especially concerned with **cleaning it of the numbing effects /.../. Shamanism can be defined as the procedure of cleaning one's connecting link to intent.**[189]

Shamans are vitally concerned with their past, but not their personal past. For shamans, their past is **what other shamans in bygone days have accomplished.** They consult their past in order **to obtain a point of reference. Only shamans genuinely seek a point of reference in their past.** For them, establishing a point of reference means a chance to examine intent.[190] **But an average man examines the past for personal reasons, in order to find justifications** or to establish **a model for himself,**[191] even though it might lead him to his downfall.

The shaman seers of ancient times, through their seeing, first noticed that any **unusual behaviour produced a tremor in the assemblage point. If unusual behaviour is practiced systematically and directed wisely (not in line with patterns and expectations), it eventually forces the assemblage point to move.**[192]

Shamanism is a journey of return. A warrior returns victorious to the spirit, having descended into hell. And from hell (from ordinariness), he brings trophies. **(A wholistic) understanding is one of the trophies.**[193]

In order for **the mysteries of shamanism to be available to anyone, the spirit must descend** onto whoever is interested. **The spirit lets its presence by itself move the man's assemblage point to a specific position.** This precise spot is known to shamans as the place of no pity. The spirit touches the person and his assemblage point moves.[194]

....
187 Ibid., p. 255.
188 Ibid., p. 249 (the note in brackets is mine).
189 Ibid., p. 250.
190 Ibid., p. 251.
191 Ibid., p. 252.
192 Ibid., p. 260 (the note in brackets is mine).
193 Ibid., p. 262 (the notes in brackets are mine).
194 Ibid., pp. 266-267 (the notes in brackets are mine).

A warrior must work with no stress or obsession (or stuckness). The passageway into the world of shamans opens up after the warrior has learned to shut off his internal dialogue. This is when everything becomes possible, attainable.[195]

For the rational man to hold steadfastly to his self-image ensures his abysmal ignorance. He ignores the fact that shamanism is not incantations and hocus-pocus, but the freedom to perceive not only **the word taken for granted,** but everything else that is humanly possible to accomplish. **He trembles at the possibility of freedom.** And freedom is at his finger tips.[196]

'An average man thinks that **indulging in doubts and tribulations is the sign of sensitivity,** spirituality. The truth of the matter is that the average man is the farthest thing imaginable from being sensitive. **His puny reason deliberately makes itself into a monster or a saint,** but it is truthfully too little for such a big monster or saint mould.'[197]

'**Self-importance is man's greatest enemy.** What weakens him is **feeling offended** by the deeds and misdeeds of his fellow men. Self-importance requires that one spend most of one's life **offended by something or someone.**'[198]

'**Human beings love to be told what to do,** but they love even more to **fight** and not to do what they are told, and thus they **get entangled in hating** the one who told them in the first place.'[199]

When nothing is sure we remain alert, perennially on our toes. This is why it is better for us **not to behave as though we knew everything.** As long as a man feels that he is the most important thing in the world, he cannot really appreciate the world around him.[200]

Mexican shamans of course **healed themselves. They took care of their balance and health.** To seek help for their health elsewhere was shameful. This was what **Florinda Matus** explained to Castaneda. Unrelenting and straightforward, Florinda was one of Don Juan's most audacious warriors, whose influence on Castaneda was perhaps the strongest.[201]

Don Juan explained to Castaneda that sooner or later, **after years of learning and striving,** a moment will come when the **energy fields contorted by a lifetime**

---
195 Ibid., pp. 112-115 (the note in brackets is mine).
196 Ibid., p. 276.
197 Ibid., p. 128.
198 Ibid., p. 222.
199 Ibid., p. 170.
200 Ibid., pp. 75-76.
201 Ibid., p. 176.

habit are straightened out. Warriors must be impeccable in their effort to change, in order to scare the human form and shake it away. A warrior gets deeply affected, and can even die as a result of this **straightening out (or re-attuning) energy fields,** but **an impeccable warrior always survives.**[202] The warriors' way therefore offers a man a new life. He can't bring to that new life his ugly old ways.[203]

Disappointment triggers a virus infection, which in turn leads to a shift along the axis of consciousness, into shamanic detachment

People's actions no longer affect a warrior when he has no more expectations of any kind. Peace becomes the ruling force in his life. He has adopted one of the concepts of a warrior's life – **detachment.** Detachment does not automatically mean wisdom, but it is, nonetheless, an advantage, because it allows the warrior to pause momentarily to reassess situations, to reconsider positions. In order to use that extra moment consistently and correctly, however, a warrior has to **struggle unyieldingly for the duration of his life.**[204]

During the final days of December **2011,** I had been studying the warriorhood **arts of the samurai, shaolins, shoguns, Mexican shamans,** and I had added to the book a new chapter about this **timeless warriorhood,** known throughout **different cultures.** A new book thus came into being.[205] But my daily overwork had weakened my immune system considerably, and I fell ill a couple of days after the New Year. I caught the virus which my colleague had brought into the house. This was also a consequence of my being far **too involved in the problems of my students.** People often become harshly adversarial, even **angry with me, when I tell them sincerely what I see in them, what I see in their lives.** Sometimes I simply cannot believe that they can be so stuck in their imagined correct opinions, **running away from different insights and introspection. A mass of disappointment** had grown within me over these almost two decades of teaching and healing people who came to me for help. And this mass caused an inner conflict. On the one hand, I was aware that I should have completely allowed their reactions, even if they were negative and destructive. **Let them do what they want with the knowledge they had gained! Everyone travels in their own way,** directly or along wayward paths, straight into ruination or into a brighter future. Everyone chooses for themselves.

Of course, **mentally, I completely understood this; however, a small part in me got caught up in painful emotions.** Within a small part of my consciousness I

---
202 Ibid., p. 161 (the note in brackets is mine).
203 Ibid., p. 168.
204 Ibid., pp. 188-189.
205 In preparation.

felt **regret,** although it seemed to me that this regret was barely perceptible, that it hardly existed at all. I felt sorry for the situation. For years on end, I had, on daily basis, watched people, who **usually moved straight into a direction opposite to that which would have pulled them out of their problems and diseases.** And these tiny emotional discomforts had been piling up within me for too long. That December, the bottle was obviously full. On top of that, this conflict within me exacerbated by an increasingly difficult cooperation with radio and television editors and journalists, who often refused to communicate sincerely about the negative sides of their writing (interviews, for example). They saw every well-intentioned **comment as an attack on themselves.** In recent years, **the temperature in culture and art** had dropped below freezing point. The same goes for publishing.

My physical fatigue, the result of overwork, and my inner dissatisfaction had weakened my physical immunity. So **I fell ill, after more than two decades.** And I wasn't even registered with a doctor! Why should I have been? **I harmonised everything with the cosmic resonance technique.** Even myself. But now I had **fallen out of my psycho-physical balance** and the virus, which years before would not have even touched me, or from which I would have recovered within a couple of hours, began to work deeply on me. Given the fact that I live without usual food, such a state is very strenuous for me, even dangerous. When **in a state of imbalance, it is impossible to feed on cosmic energy. And feeding on physical food is impossible too, as my body is no longer used to it.**

I was in a centrifuge for the entire nine days, and in the end the stuff got flushed out. During that time, **I climbed the nine-level spiritual pyramid, deeper and deeper, or better – higher and higher. Deeper into my subconscious and higher into my meta-conscious and on to meta-sensory levels.** All the while, I continued to work on this book, but I allowed myself to rest briefly from time to time. During these beneficent moments of rest, my **inner peace was slowly being restored, bringing me a new awareness. With my senses, I finally came to understand what was going on. Let the current flow in its riverbed as it pleases. Let go completely!** Why should you care what others are going to do with the knowledge you passed them. Let this be their own business. After all, **everyone lives for themselves, in their own way,** and everyone struggles with their own life and insights – in a good or bad way, at a slow or fast pace.

Detachment, which Don Juan spoke about, was revealed to me in its details, in the hidden shamanic experiences of life. I was relieved. **I finally let it go.** After that, I was no longer in an emotional centrifuge, even when people rushed headlong into their ruination, due to their foolishness. I am here speaking primarily of **the feelings of unease, which accompany insights and knowings. No one can convince anyone of any single thing. After all, there would be no point to this!**

A warrior takes his lot, whatever it may be. The humbleness of a warrior is not the humbleness of the beggar. **The warrior lowers his head to no one**[206] (**he does not bargain**).

Look, my inner voice said, it is not that important to withdraw and live somewhere outside town or at the edge of a village. More important is to **completely banish the feelings of worry from our emotional and mental field** – worry about both ourselves and other people. Even though we might think that there are practically no such saboteurs of peace, **there is still, somewhere in the corner of our consciousness, a tiny thought, gnawing at us, causing us to regret that things are as they are;** or we feel bad because people are (still) unable to move through their wall of illusions and obstacles, which they themselves have built. And that's the way it is.

> "Warriors can never make a bridge to join the people of the world. /.../ they have to make a bridge to join warriors."[207]

Warrior-shamans have to keep their detachment.

As I read the samurai codes and Castaneda's books about the teachings of Don Juan, the detachment of which spoke the spiritual teacher nagual touched me even more. **Detachment** does not mean only physical separation from someone or something, it primarily means **total mental and emotional neutrality – outside the struggles which unfold within people.** Yet, mere intellectual understanding, which I did not lack, is something completely different from **a total absence of emotional unrest and the presence of a completely open flow.** Great **wisdom and power** lie in this spiritual law, although it may sound paradoxical. Warriors, who **manage to completely rid themselves of these barely perceptible restless feelings and thoughts, can touch silence, an emptiness out of which they can act peacefully, in a complete and perfect way. Their power is not limited by anything.**

"Warrior /.../ strives to **stop his internal talk** (the babbling of his mind). The world is incomprehensible. /.../ we won't ever unravel its secrets. Thus we must treat the world as it is: a sheer **mystery.**"[208]

In any case, how can an ocean of knowledge help us? When all is said and done, the goal of everyone is to find inner **silence and peace, to be able to function reliably.** The only problem is that **we are not usually aware of what we carry in us,** in our consciousness, and especially in our subconscious – in Xibalba, as the Mayans would put it. What is more, the majority of people **do**

---
206 Carlos Castaneda, *The Wheel of Time*, London, Allen Lane, The Penguin Press (1998), pp. 116-117.
207 Ibid., p. 265.
208 Ibid., pp. 59-60.

not even know just how stuck they are in a particular thought pattern. For a long time, despite my awakening experiences, I had not recognised **the prowling dragon of barely perceptible unsilenced emotions,** which reside somewhere at the back, very deep, very far away. It is much **more difficult to discover** this dragon **at the emotional level, and it is even harder to overcome it, as it skilfully evades us.** It is difficult to notice it, but we ought to have done so. We pluck up sufficient strength for our victory only when our emotional content is brimful in the bottle. **When we simply cannot take in anymore!** Because **it's enough, far too much!** When we have been tormented so much that we have truly had **enough. Then, the scales tip.** The liquid in the bottle – our inner dissatisfaction – **pours over the brim.** Why on Earth should we torment ourselves with the immaturity of other people? There is no point to this. I do my best, but, **after I have detached myself from this, I will perhaps be able to offer even more than before, because not a single drop of my energy will be lost in the labyrinth of the emotional world.**

I experienced all of this in its fullness on the ninth day, on the very day of my course on the spiritual wisdom of the arts of a warrior. **My nine-level process of becoming aware was then complete.** The powerlessness, which had tormented me for the entire nine days, turned into power. I felt like jumping with joy when I started the course and saw familiar and unfamiliar faces, full of expectation. I felt extremely **light and free!** The students seemed so **beautiful** to me – no, they were utterly wonderful and shining within all their problems and immaturities. **My love for them all was now even greater,** more majestic than ever before. This is how things work. **If absolutely nothing torments us at an emotional level, not one tiny bit, then we are able to feel kindness towards everything. We come to see the beauty of everything, even of suffering and current foolishness.**

My **disappointment** with the fact that people who had come to me for help, had not been ready to accept my insights about their problems and diseases, **departed. Many simply refuse or are (still) unable to move from behind their walls. They still need them in order to learn and spiritually grow.** Yes, yes, all of this is of course clear to the mind. But the problem lies elsewhere – in the emotions, which **block the energy circulation. Liberation, which comes after we have resolved our dilemmas and emotions, is reflected in the beauty of life, the essence of which is love. It is reflected in joy, which pervades both.** I wanted to shout out – **freedom,** freedom, freedom, and dance ecstatically in circles for a long, long time. And I did so. We danced our **personal *tai-chi* with guided, spontaneous warrior movements,** enjoying immensely the velvety sounds of Chinese cimbaloms.

Warriors have only one thing in mind: their freedom. To die and be eaten by the Eagle (or the serpent) /.../. On the other hand, to **sneak around the Eagle** (or around the immense flow of life energy) and be free is the ultimate audacity.[209]

Before each course, I usually experience different human dilemmas and problems. This was **my agreement with the Universal Intelligence.** The purpose of that is to test on my own skin and so realise the necessary things in relation to the topic of the upcoming course. I need to feel what people are struggling with in the current moment. **Experience is the best teacher. And to share my experiences with people is the greatest gift.** At this time, **an important detail from warrior's teachings,** from both teachings of Mexican shamans and contemporary spiritual seekers, was revealed to me through my experience. We are all ceaselessly moving within the river of teachings, within the flow of teachings, which sooner or later, we must come to understand. I give thanks for every nuance of this timeless wisdom. **Thanks for the joy which comes with every discovery.**

A children's game of the warrior entering the thoughts of another and sensing the same Intelligence in everything

During the course on the skills of a warrior, I remembered a game **my father used to play with my twin sister and me.** We played it in pairs. One person places their hands in front of them, palms down. The second person places their hands, palms up, beneath the first person's hands, trying to **bring their hands up as quickly as possible and slap their 'opponent'** on their palms. Of course the opponent would try to pull their hands away as quickly as possible. Who wants to be slapped?

This children's **game is a good exercise for psychological and spiritual flexibility.** If you wanted to be **quick enough** to touch the other person's palm before they pulled them away, **you had to enter the oponent's mind with your mind and capture the 'opponent's' thought, because every movement starts first with thought.** There has to be **a thought, an intention,** before the 'opponent' pulls their hands away. **Thought is the precursor of every action.**

And the person who is pulling their hands away **should also perceive the moment when the 'opponent,' in their thoughts, triggered a signal for removing hands,** in an attempt to slap their hands. In this game, both parties are **warriors, who must feel the thoughts of each other.** A brillant game, indeed. Those who are sufficiently attentive will recognise this mental impluse soon enough and will react in time. If not, they will miss or they will be slapped.

....
209 Ibid., p. 209.

The delay between the thought and physical reaction lasts only a second, or maybe three seconds at most. The entire action has to unfold within this time. **The less people are stuck in their mental patterns, the less numb they are, the faster their reaction will be. The more they mull over their thoughts and emotions, the slower they will be.** Try out this wisdom for yourself. These simple games are a brilliant test of the basic skills of a warrior.

Everyone is a warrior. Everyone who plays the game of life, must, whether they want to or not, **find a balance between their mind, emotions, and body. We should thoroughly recognise the game between the body, emotions, and mind.** The more we are able to manage this, the greater masters of martial arts and life we will be. **The faster we react, the more peaceful, the happier we will be.**

The following **exercise** is also wonderful proof of the importance of **perceiving spirit everywhere and in everything.** The wisdom of the Ancient Ones was based on this perception. This is what my students and I did. We placed a vase containing a flower in the centre of the room. Then we **focused our attention on the flower. We gazed fixedly at it.** While doing this, we tried to **understand that this flower had been created by the same Universal Intelligence, the same creative force, the same cosmic energy, or Divine power.** When we completely embrace this in our thoughts, we can begin to feel the flower as **a small part of a common energy field,** which is not somewhere outside, but which is **here and all around.** We feel **a warmth around our hearts and this warmth spreads and spreads, flowing through our whole body and filling the room. When we become aware of the serpent-like, spiral energy of everything that exists, we expand ourselves into the boundless creative Field and we become a small part of this boundless Field ourselves. Boundaries between the flower and ourselves disappear.** We start to feel that we are **all one** – lack'ech, as the Mayans would say, **I am you and you are I.**

Strong energies, like torches, are lit **in our bodies,** when this great insight starts shining within us. **We have entered into the inexhaustible energy system of life flow and we have felt the whole.** We can always do this exercise in our thoughts. To percieve and create such **power of all-connectedness,** shamans also use other keys, including **symbols and various sound formulae.**

When you feel other beings and their energy in the same manner as you feel yourself –that their energy is actually the same as yours, deriving **from the same Source** – you will, alongside warmth, feel **peace, omnipresent love and the pulsing flow of the serpent-like undulating life energy.**

This means that every conscious spiritual seeker or warrior must first connect to this **mighty spiral.** Once you have entered into it, **you will know that, within it, or with its help, you can create as you wish. You have touched power and power has touched you. Boundaries have disappeared. Creating becomes a wonderful**

task. People who enter into that point of emptiness, into the silence of this point, will merge with **the Field, with the sea** of an invigorating, **always present** energy, which is available to them. It is important that we **learn how to use this energy of 'the sacred serpent'** for the benefit of ourselves and others.

> **To be happy** is the most important life question. For an Indian, success does not depend on how much he earns or on his status in society – it depends only and solely on **how happy he feels.**[210]

The detachment of Mexican shamans, the art of stalking and dreaming, the Eagle's emanation

> 'And I cling to nothing, so I will have nothing to defend. I have no thoughts, so I will see. I fear nothing, so I will remember myself. Detached and at ease, I will dart past the Eagle to be free.'[211]

Mexican shamans talk about the **Eagle**, about the **Eagle's emanations**, when they want to refer to or address **the inaudible cosmic (frequency-energy) waves.** They say that we live in the world of the Eagle's emanations, which are **made out of time and are constantly in motion.**

Time is the essence of attention. **The Eagle's emanations (i.e. cosmic radiation) are made out of time.** When a warrior talks about time and **enters into other aspects (or dimensions) of the self**, he is becoming acquainted with time.[212]

> 'Warriors say that we **think there is a world of objects out there only because of our awareness.** But what's really out there are the **Eagle's emanations** (radiation, frequency waves), **which are fluid, forever in motion, and yet unchanged, eternal.**'[213] The Eagle is therefore a metaphor for the flow of life.

Warriors who attain **total awareness (the perfect awareness of oneness) burn from within.** They fuse themselves to the emanations of the Eagle at large, and glide into eternity.[214] For Mexican shamans, the **Eagle** is also **the invisible Intelligence of life and of everything that is.** And this Intelligence governs human destinies.

....
210 Beryl Blue Spruce, taken from *Tudi trava ima svojo pesem*, Radovljica, Didakta (2000), p. 182.
211 Carlos Castaneda, *The Wheel of Time*, London, Allen Lane, The Penguin Press (1998), p. 190.
212 Ibid., p. 210 (notes in brackets are mine).
213 Ibid., p. 228 (the note in brackets is mine).
214 Ibid., p. 234 (the note in brackets is mine).

The Eagle devours the awareness of all the creatures that, alive on Earth a moment before and now dead, have floated to the Eagle's beak like a swarm of fireflies, to meet their owner, their reason for having had life, says Don Juan. **For awareness is the Eagle's food.**[215] The power that governs the destinies of all living things **is called the Eagle.**[216]

Every living thing **has been granted the power to seek an opening to freedom and go through it.** It is evident to the seer who sees the opening that **the Eagle has granted that gift** in order **to perpetuate awareness.**[217] Concealed within these poetic metaphors is **the very essence of the meaning of life.**

'**The Eagle's gift of freedom** is not a bestowal, but **a chance to have a chance.**'[218] We can always choose between countless opportunities.

'Warriors have only one thing in mind: their freedom. **To die and be eaten by the Eagle** is no challenge. On the other hand, to **sneak around the Eagle and be free** is the ultimate audacity.'[219]

A warrior **can no longer weep, and his only expression of anguish is a shiver that comes from the very depths of the universe.** It is as if one of the Eagle's emanations were made out of a pure anguish, and when it hits a warrior, **the warrior's shiver (his elated excitement) is infinite.**[220]

Castaneda's last book, The Power of Silence, speaks of **inner silence** and is a distinct **review of the thoughts of the shamans of ancient Mexico.** In it, Castaneda wrote[221] that when he was working on that book **he got contaminated by the mood of Mexican shamans, by their desire to know more.** The warrior Florinda explained to him that **in the end, these shamans had become extremely cold and detached – it was their effort to match the coldness of infinity.** Even their eyes matched **the cold (probably detached and emotionally completely calm) eyes of the unknown.**

True, **high-frequency energies,** high-dimensional sound vibrations are always **cold.** They shake and perturb people, as if they were in a fridge. Nothing can warm them up. I know those **inaudible vibrations, or sound,** very well. **They are the harmonising power of the Cosmic Field, or Consciousness,** the tool of cosmic resonance and cosmic initiations. Castaneda was at first frightened by the thoughts about detachment and cold, and probably also by his experiences related to it. Even though he was already able to **feel the essences of an infinite joy in his life,** he

215 Ibid., p. 195.
216 Ibid., p. 196.
217 Ibid., p. 197.
218 Ibid., p. 199.
219 Ibid., p. 209.
220 Ibid., p. 211 (the note in brackets is mine).
221 Ibid., p. 279 (the note in brackets is mine).

at the same time increasingly perceived the merciless (and detached) fate of a shaman. But **he did not want to be swallowed by infinity** just yet. He wanted to be ready for it at least. But perhaps he (still) was not.

Castaneda wrote that, in his Mexican spiritual adventure, **he focused his recapitulation attention on the mood of the ancient shamans and got trapped by it without hope.** Florinda explained to him that this state only seems to be final and said that **a moment will come when he will change venues. He might perhaps even chuck every thought about the shamans of ancient Mexico (he will become enlightened** and will transcend all limitations, the path itself and its teachings, for **he will no longer need them).**

The warrior has no limits, his sense of improvisation (or his sense for adapting to the moment and accepting the unrepeatable gifts of the moment) is so **acute that he will make constructs out of nothing,** workable, and pragmatic constructs. It is not that he will forget about them, but at one moment, before he **plunges into the abyss (or into the cosmic energy serpent),** if he has the daring not to deviate from it, **he will then arrive at warriors' conclusions of an order and stability infinitely more suited to him than the fixation of the shamans of ancient Mexico.**[222] True, he will discover an order which is completely his own, **an order of perfection and completeness,**[223] his rhythm, his path, a unique and distinct one, outside all rules! He will touch the silence of the mind, the silence of nothing. But there can be a flaw if he will want to reach this totally different orderly view of the world and himself (according to Castaneda): **he will need to walk along the edge of the abyss (he will have to enter the Eagle's emanation, the sacredness of the serpent, the worlds beyond).**

According to the nagual Don Juan, one of the most dramatic things about the human condition is **the macabre connection between stupidity and self-reflection.** It is stupidity that forces the average man **to discard anything that does not conform with his self-reflective expectations** (or with his **foolishness).** For example, **as average men (with a narrow consciousness), we are blind to the most crucial piece of knowledge** available to a human being: the existence of the assemblage point and the fact that it can move.[224]

> **'The art of dreaming** is the capacity to utilise one's ordinary dreams and **transform them into controlled awareness** by virtue of a specialised form of attention called **the dreaming attention.'**[225]

....
222 Ibid., p. 281 (the note in brackets is mine).
223 More about this can be found in the chapter about the Great Mysteries of our planetary ancestors.
224 Carlos Castaneda, *The Wheel of Time*, London, Allen Lane, The Penguin Press (1998), p. 275 (notes in brackets are mine).
225 Ibid., p. 181.

Native Americans are exceptional **dreamers,** I wrote about this already in the first book in the Cosmic Telepathy series. Dreamers can **embark on an inter-dimensional journey across the levels of consciousness and visit all the places in the universe in a bodiless state**[226] (the rhythms of drums help them on this journey). Dreamers are actually **the creators of their own reality, and they are also excellent healers, clairvoyants and diviners, because they enter parallel worlds, other dimensions of reality, by choice – with their consciousness of higher levels, with their dreams; they work in harmony with the Great Spirit across all the levels of awareness.** Of course only their **consciousness and etheric doubles** travel **to the dream world. For them, there are no limitations,** neither temporal, nor spatial. **They meet the souls of ancestors** in the worlds beyond.

Native Americans believe that dreamtime is the **parallel reality in which human spirit or soul (consciousness) and Cosmic Consciousness (Great Spirit) work together.** The little spirit receives visions and the necessary information from the Great Spirit so that we would understand more easily what is happening in the physical world of duality, or what we need to know or create, but are still unable to. **The etheric double therefore performs the role of a postman, an intermediary. It is a telephone link between different levels of reality, between material and non-material levels.** Dreamtime is also a **subtle** (high-frequency) **non-physical matrix of the material world.** It is also the reality of **high-frequency octaves of our givens.**

Non-material dreamtime is **without (spatial-temporal) limitations.** Our etheric double can **travel anywhere** at the dimensional levels of dreams, **even to the centre of the Earth, to the centre of the galaxy. It can walk through physical and non-physical worlds (and objects) if it wants so; it can fly to infinite and boundless realms, to the past and the future alike, etc.** The idea of the 'time wheel or time clock' is so exciting. We have forgotten that **we carry it in ourselves all the time – at the levels of expanded consciousness.**

But, in order to become dreamers, we first have to acquire **the inner purity of body and emotions, and the peace of the mind.**[227]

Castaneda wrote that **the *nagual* Elias was,** for example, **such a good dreamer that he covered the most recondite places of the universe in a bodiless state. From there, he brought back his inventions.** The warrior **Florinda** told to Castaneda to focus his recapitulation attention on those inventions. He will even end up **sniffing them, feeling them with his hands, although he has never seen** (or experienced) **them. He only needs to establish a point of reference,** through

....
226 Ibid., p. 216.
227 The paragraphs are taken from the first book in the *Cosmic Telepathy* series, pp. 317-318.

which he will be able to **see everything with infinite clarity.**[228] Castaneda added that the recapitulation views lacked the warmth of the living, but they nevertheless brought extremely **accurate insights.**

Warriors, because they are stalkers, understand human behaviour to perfection. They understand, for instance, that **human beings are creatures of inventory.** Knowing the ins and outs of a particular inventory is what makes a man a scholar or an expert in his field.[229]

Don Juan taught Mexican warriors – future shamans – **the art of stalking,** which is **a set of procedures and attitudes** that enables a warrior **to get the best out of any conceivable situation.**[230] **The art of stalking is based on the learning of all the quirks of your disguise.** For that you need to be **cunning, patient, ruthless and sweet.** Ruthlessness should not be harshness, cunning should not be cruelty, patience should not be negligence, and sweetness should not be foolishness.[231] So, the art of stalking primarily requires **a sincere process of becoming aware.** Don Juan says that the trick for the warrior is **to pull his personal power away from his weaknesses.**[232]

The main principle of the art of stalking is that a warrior chooses his battleground and discards everything that is unnecessary. He aims at being **simple.** He applies all the concentration he has to decide whether or not to enter into battle, for **any battle is a battle for his life. A warrior must be willing and ready to make his stand here and now.**[233] This is also why he compresses time (the sixth principle of the art of stalking). **Even an instant counts,** a second is an eternity, an eternity that may decide the outcome. Warriors aim at succeeding, therefore **they compress time. Warriors don't waste an instant.**[234] **In this, they need to relax and abandon themselves; they fear nothing.** Only then will the **powers** that guide human beings **open the road** for warriors and aid them.[235] When faced with odds that cannot be dealt with, **warriors retreat** for a moment. They let their minds meander.[236]

'A warrior knows that he is waiting, and he knows what he is waiting for, and while he waits he feasts his eyes upon the world. A warrior's **ultimate accomplishment is to enjoy the joy of infinity.'**[237]

....
228 Carlos Castaneda, *The Wheel of Time*, London, Allen Lane, The Penguin Press (1998), pp. 216-217 (the note in brackets is mine).
229 Castaneda, p. 263.
230 Castaneda, p. 182.
231 Castaneda, p. 258.
232 Castaneda, p. 171.
233 Castaneda, p. 202.
234 Castaneda, p. 205.
235 Castaneda, p. 203.
236 Castaneda, p. 204.
237 Castaneda, p. 186.

The voice and memories of the Universe, or **the Eagle's emanation, can be most clearly heard mostly in silence.** We have special **extra-sensorial** abilities and perceptions for this – **the radars of the soul and even the DNA detectors.** The shamans of ancient Mexico and the shamans of the Amazon were even **able to perceive the molecular essences of life and follow the genetic helix all the way to the core of life, including those areas where pain and disease dwell.** And from these levels, they were then able to **create perfection and the necessary order.**

'Despite his wisdom and ingenuity, **the white man** lacks something. **He has lost contact with the Creator.** Indians still **respect the Great Spirit** and continue to abide by its laws even in this changed world. Scientific development, triggered by the white man, served well-being at first, but has now invented a monstrous weapon – the atomic bomb. **The knowledge and ingenuity of the white man has reached a point when he knows how to make a weapon which can destroy everything that lives on Earth. What will become of this country that we love, that was created so that we could fulfil the task of the Great Spirit on it?**'[238] This is what Native Americans ask themselves. Where did the wise knowledge of euphony and harmony of all of us living on Earth disappear to?

In order to attain the miraculous shamanic abilities which he will use for the well-being of people, a warrior must first descend into **the ritual process of dying, into the initiation of transcending limitations, imperfections, and physical death alike.**

---
[238] David Kindle, taken from the book *Tudi trava ima svojo pesem*, Radovljica, Didakta (2000), p. 171.

Gratitude to life and death

The human being is a cosmic child,
living in the ocean of innumerable possibilities and exceptional opportunities.
All beings **choose for themselves:**
they can **bow to the Principle** of their mission
or foolishly **reject** the inherited **teachings of life.**
On Earth, they learn how to travel between the worlds
of reality and imagination,
vision and illusion,
and they learn how to sail as lightly as possible on the waves of life and death.
Every cosmic-earthly child chooses
between the compassion of a loving attention
and the egocentric clamour
of a deluded and blind folly.
This is how they learn to explore **the worlds of rainbow sound,**
the field of stillness and harmonious silence.[239]

....
239 Mira Omerzel - Mirit, poem *The Human Being is a Cosmic Child, Learning how to Travel between the Worlds*, taken from the book Zvočne podobe prebujene ljubezni, Vrhnika Dar Dam (2012).

Near-death, death and beyond death, the awakened consciousness

Whistle in the form of a jaguar – balam.

Life and death are the two poles of our existence, **the two halves of every life cycle.** Today, we have unfortunately **lost the feeling for death and near-death experience, because we are suffused with a great fear of death or annihilation, the consequence of our loss of spiritual wisdom, which had once been passed down through generations.** This fear has **increased** over the last 2000 years, partly due to **the Christian mindset,** which frightened people **with its teaching of hell and punishment, deterring them from thinking about death and after-death realms,** about the meaning of death, which is a part of the cycle of life.[240] For the church authorities, the ancient philosophy of **reincarnation** was supposedly too disturbing, as well as being redundant. The teaching of the reincarnation of souls was reportedly **erased from spiritual and religious teachings around the year 500.**[241]

The idea that **death is a human's companion** is an important tool, which was used by the ancient Mexican shamans for tempering warriors. **A bridge is formed once death is accepted, a bridge which extends across the gap between the usual world and the unknown.** The only one who is capable of **crossing this bridge is the warrior** – silent, undetainable, efficacious, and functional.[242]

....
240 More about this can be found in my essay about life and death in the fourth book in the *Cosmic Telepathy* series.
241 Deepak Chopra, *Life After Death: The Burden of Proof*, New York, Harmony Books (2006). In the book, Chopra mentions the year 553, when this was reportedly happened.
242 Carlos Castaneda, *The Wheel of Time*, London, Allen Lane, The Penguin Press (1998), pp. 67-68.

In the past, a conscious stepping into the process of transformation, into the process of dying, of dissolving distortions and traumas, took place in different ceremonies and initiations (from spontaneous cosmic initiations to the ones which were invoked consciously). These processes, undertaken by spiritually aware people, required courage of those who sensed **the grandeur of death. We can enter near-death experiences consciously and of our own free will,** as did for example Hindu rshis, yogis, Aboriginal ngangkaris, Buddhist lamas, ancient Egyptian and Mayan priests, Slavic kresniks and other **shamans, priests, and traditional healers** from different cultures.

But meeting death, meeting dying and **the death of the old,** can also come to us by itself. Near-death experiences bring us **lessons about the worlds beyond, about the soul** and the levels which are sleeping in the spirit, of which we are still unaware. That is why **during their life, healers, shamans and spiritual teachers have to feel, on their own skin, the closeness of death and to experience the after-death realms, the worlds beyond. With them, they expand their consciousness immensely.** They come to understand our existence on Earth in a more complete way. Near death, they **nurture compassion,** they open up to life and thus **increase the flow of life energy** through all their bodies, in order to be able to receive it for themselves and to offer it to others. Mexican shamans teach that **death is the only wise advisor,**[243] while the very idea of death is present always and everywhere. With it, warriors **temper their spirit.**[244] **Whatever is touched by death indeed becomes power,** making them sufficiently **detached.**[245]

They say **love is the connector and shaper of life – both in the world of the living and in the after-death realms, in the worlds of immortal souls.** Without it, we are unhappy and we attract all kinds of **difficulties** in our life. The unconditional love of the soul (especially near death) brings **joy, peace, abundance and the feeling of fulfilment.** The world's spiritual traditions claim that **the essences of love are even shaping the worlds beyond.** Our material world is only **an illusion,** and the seed of this illusionary reality originates **in the levels beyond – in the worlds, or high-frequency dimensions, beyond.**

Bruce Lipton, a former Stanford University researcher,[246] discovered that **representations** which we receive or build during our life, before the soul separates from the deceased body, and also those we receive through genetic records,[247] **are transferred through immortal consciousness into our existence beyond and**

....
243 Ibid, p. 77.
244 Ibid, p. 37.
245 Ibid, pp. 54-55.
246 More about his findings can be found in the chapter on cell memory and in the third book in the *Cosmic Telepathy* series.
247 Bruce Lipton, *Biology of Belief*, Carlsbad, Hay House (2008).

into future lives. **So, it is impossible to escape from ourselves,** regardless of how hard we try. **Life goes on** – it first visits the non-material levels of spirit and then incarnates once more in the material world. This is claimed by almost all spiritual teachings and also by contemporary science.

In almost all the spiritual traditions of the world, the serpent is a symbol of life energy, a symbol of the inaudible cosmic vibrational flow, which builds, shapes and sustains everything that has been created, including life on Earth. But **the serpent coiled around a staff,** held by a man figure called **the serpent bearer,** is something special. **The myth of the first healer, the serpent bearer** named **Aesculapius,** [248] which is found in the European cultural heritage, derives from Mesopotamia and represents **the Deity of light and good, fighting the dragon Tiamat, which embodies the darkness of the Source.** This constellation located between Scorpius and Hercules is said to represent **the first doctor on Earth, a sage beyond compare and a herbalist with aureole,** with a sacred auric glow around his head.

The serpent bearer was immortal and could restore the dead to life. The mythical being **centaur** – half-horse, half-human – helped him in this. Legends say that **Aesculapius, the 'one who holds the serpent,'** once **killed a snake.** But the snake **came to life again, after ingesting a herb** which it carried in its mouth. This is how the wise healer **learned of the power of medicinal herbs** and he began to use them successfully in his healings and life-restoring processes. **He knew the secret of immortality, which is why he had to die. Pluto – the God of the dead** – complained to the supreme **God Zeus** that this was not how things should be. And Zeus (the God and a symbol of the Intelligence of life) determined that **death is the fate of humans,** which cannot be avoided. And that **no one** – not even the wisest doctor – **is allowed to restore people to life, despite having attained this knowledge and power.**

But as a result of his wisdom and merits for humanity, Zeus placed Aesculapius among the stars. He is still standing there with a snake coiled around the staff he is holding – a contemporary **symbol of healing and medicine. The quest for connections to the eternal and immortal consciousness is timeless,** it was known in all cultures and at all times. **To touch the indestructible soul means to discover your essence and to start living your own fullness,** which is also the purpose of the 'serpent initiation.'

No form of life is permanent. Only eternal consciousness, the shape-giver of the worlds, is indestructible and timeless. This is what ancient traditions believe. Lyrically and through rich symbolism, they depict **the human dreamtime, the existence beyond the physical,** which is said to **resemble dreams. Our consciousness**

....
248 Pavel Kunaver, *Pravljica in resnica o zvezdah*, Ljubljana, Mladinska knjiga (1981), pp. 167-172, Ophiuchus – the Serpent Bearer and Serpens – the Serpent.

is actually constantly dreaming and thus shaping within the non-material and material worlds alike. We are **in the centrifuge of interlacing and changing** all the time. Even death seems like a dream.

Death and near-death experiences ennoble our life and expand our consciousness into the eternal and boundless, into the infinite and timeless. The world's spiritual traditions (except Christianity) claim that life offers numerous possibilities for **an after-death audit of our soul, it even shapes the contents of our future lives in new incarnations. Death makes new births possible, it enables our rebirth into ever broader and more complete levels of awareness,** into a new world. Life and death constantly offer new possibilities and **opportunities for spiritual growth.** Which is why both life and death are gifted with **Mercy.** The nagual Don Juan says that a warrior or a **shaman-healer has to focus on the connection between death and himself,** because he knows that **his death** is waiting. A warrior-hunter has an intimate **knowledge of his death.**[249]

Fear of annihilation, fear of loss or death, is a general human fear, which, concealed, continues to exist until we have experienced the reality beyond. This fear stems from **thoughts of the finite.** The fear of annihilation has today unfortunately **poisoned our thoughts and minds, our reactions and philosophy of life (especially that of white people),** which is why this philosophy is **distorted and incomplete,** or is insufficient and has at least very much deteriorated. It is also misleading, as **it blurs our view of the purpose of life.**

The fear of death, or annihilation, paralyses us and creates countless other inhibiting emotions, thoughts and deeds. **Daily, wars, fights, and conflicts are created by people, because we are afraid of losing something, or we are afraid to die.** Yet, we carry nothing with us to the beyond, only the richness or poverty of our soul, our consciousness. But people who are afraid unfortunately do neither see nor perceive well, their reactions are not in tune with their path, destiny and the current moment. They do not resonate in harmony with all of that. **Which is why they feel a painful separation.**

> "In a world where death is the hunter, there is no time for regrets and doubts. There is only time for decisions."[250]

When I was a child I used to feel like **laughing,** in an odd and **subdued way,** when we were bidding farewell to someone upon their death. I felt a certain **disharmony** between the representation of the dead person created by people and my own inner awareness, which persistently whispered to me that **death was a**

---
249 Carlos Castaneda, *The Wheel of Time*, London, Allen Lane, The Penguin Press (1998), p. 89.
250 Ibid., p. 79.

wonderful experience. And this is how I have experienced it many times in my life. The realms beyond death are understood to be a part of the life cycle by those people who still live in **communities in harmony with the pulse of nature,** with the cycle of life and death and with cosmic-earthly rhythms – with the cosmic doctrine of their ancestors.

Ancient civilisations, especially those dating back to before the Common Era, **understood the polarity** of life and death **in a completely different way,** apparently in a more complete way than we do today. Their knowings were subtle and admirable. Christianity has unfortunately veiled our insight into the beyond-death mystery of life by removing the teaching of reincarnation,[251] or **the teaching of the soul's cyclic incarnation. This is when the most important knowledge of the meaning of life,** the knowledge of human spiritual growth and constant transformation, **disappeared from our view. Death, however, is but the transfigured, expanded consciousness of a being, who resonates in higher (non-physical) octaves of reality.** Death comes when, according to our 'soul's agreement,' our earthly learning in the illusionary world comes to an end, our fate, or karma expires, unless there has been a mortal accident. **The development of spirit and learning continue in the realms beyond death, at spiritual, non-physical levels.** This is claimed by the Mayans and other Native Americans, as well by the sages of other cultures, and even by some contemporary psychotherapists.

The cyclic passages and **intertwining of life and death are also the foundation of all ceremonies** and processes for aligning with the Earth, nature, and cosmic rhythms. **To embrace death, near-death and the realms beyond death as a natural necessity, as something sacred or blessed, is the gift of a wide open soul and unbounded spirit.** We should accept death and **the end of everything that is not good.** But a limited mind unfortunately acknowledges only that which can be perceived by human senses, primarily by **the eyes.** Yet, behind the visible worlds, there are **numerous other levels** of the invisible and non-material: less dense, less coarse levels, **levels of faster frequency waves (shorter wavelengths, or higher sound), a world of higher dimensions,** which our body cannot reach. But **everyone's spirit, soul, or consciousness,** and their cosmic-telepathic **meta-sensory perceptions** are able to reach them.

> "Death is the indispensable ingredient in having to believe. **Without the awareness of death, everything is ordinary, trivial.**"[252]

....
251 Deepak Chopra, *Life After Death*: The Burden of Proof, New York, Harmony Books (2006), Chopra states the year 553.
252 Carlos Castaneda, *The Wheel of Time*, London, Allen Lane, The Penguin Press (1998), p. 138.

When our body dies, we continue to exist without it, at high-frequency levels of the immortal soul, out beyond. This is claimed by almost all spiritual traditions on our planet; every tradition depicts those levels in a different way, ingeniously furnishing them with rich symbolism and artistic metaphors. **Death and the vicinity of death enable us to re-visit our understanding** of life, our understanding of both the terrestrial and the beyond; they enable us **to check how we understand the flow of life.** Near death, we come to know the grandeur of life and death, the power and energy of those who are present and those who are absent. In near-death and after-death experiences, people **grasp things which they were unable to grasp during their life.**

"For a seer, the truth is that **all living beings are struggling to die. What stops death is awareness.**"[253]

Group (near-death) ceremonies and spiritual initiations have a similar purpose. **Broader consciousness, broader awareness,** invoked by (enlightened) sages who lead the ceremony, **is gradually poured into the collective awareness of the beyond of the entire community. The unconscious becomes conscious, what we barely intuit becomes clearly recognisable.** People experience the Divine presence. That is why, for example, North American Indians are still dancing their **Sun Dance of awakening** today, that is why contemporary descendants of the Mayans still go on pilgrimages to **initiation ceremonies** at pyramids, temples and sacred sites, where they openly enter the processes of **rebirth into ever broader (or ever higher) levels of consciousness.** This allows them to move across the levels of **multidimensional reality, across the worlds or sounds of the axis of consciousness,** as we say. It allows them to **journey across the realms of the living and the dead, across the eternal 'ancestral messages.'**

"The worst that could happen to us is that we have **to die,** and since that is already our unalterable fate, we are **free; those who have lost everything no longer have anything to fear.**"[254]

Death as an illusion and dreams of the spirit

A warrior is only a man, **a humble man. He cannot change the designs of his death. But his impeccable spirit /.../ can certainly hold his death for

....
253 Ibid, p. 231.
254 Ibid, p. 239.

a moment. We may say that that is a gesture which death has with those who have an impeccable spirit.[255]

Unfortunately many spiritual seekers who live in the civilisation of **the white man run away from near-death experiences,** whereas they could instead open new gates and discover a new array of possibilities through them – **a cosmic portal into the worlds beyond,** into realms beyond the material body – the precious worlds of spirit. They in fact set up a trap for themselves by convincing themselves **that everything ends with death, that we live only once** and that death is painful, which means we have to be afraid of it. True, the processes of dying can be painful. But those processes are like that only if life was dissonant and did not unfold according to the (timeless!) laws of life; if it was out of tune or **poisoned with distorted emotions and thoughts. It is primarily physical pain and an obstinate persistence with unenlightened patterns, thoughts, emotions and bad habits, which are painful.** What we send out into the world will **sooner or later come back to us, in line with the laws of resonance.** But that which stays when the body dies is not painful. **After the physical body dies, our consciousness, mind, and emotions remain, they continue to 'live' and be present** in the physical world for some time. Then they 'move on along their way.'

In the worlds beyond – in the spiritual world of immortal essences – our consciousness expands immensely, our mind clears up, our sensations strengthen as **meta-sensory perceptions** open up. These perceptions bring out the sound of the essence and content of our soul, which is the phone line to the cosmic Field of Consciousness, to the Intelligence of the Universe, or God, as we say.

> Don Juan says that the **only irrevocable thing in the everyday world is death.** In the shamans' world, on the other hand, **normal death can be countermanded, but not the shamans' word.** In the shamans' world decisions cannot be changed or revised. Once they have been made, they stand forever.[256]

Cosmic-telepathic meta-senses enable us to read information from the Primordial Intent of the energy Field, where both material and spiritual worlds are born; they also enable us to read information **from dimensions beyond death. We can hear information about everything that has lived, is living, and even that which will live.** In this Field, there is also **the data bank of our destiny, of our life path.** It is worthwhile striving to **hear** these worlds, these signs.

....
255 Ibid., p. 94.
256 Ibid., p. 274.

In the creative field of all possibilities, which Vedic rshis named **akasha**, there is **the seed of everything, including the seed of our thoughts, visions, our soul's sacred agreements and the matrices of destiny. There, our immortal consciousness and meta-sensory perception meet the immortal essences (imprints) of the souls of the dead. Contact with our ancestors is possible.** My experiences with the energy imprints of deceased souls will, along with my findings, be described in detail in my following books, especially in the third book, which goes into **Vedic-Balinese** communication with the dead. At this point, I shall only mention that **my first contact with the consciousness of my dead father,** who lost his life in a road accident, **completely changed my perspective on life and death.**[257] After the initial shock had passed, **I experienced a veritable catharsis** and that totally changed my relationship with death.

Within the Field of consciousness, both the living and the dead create their own reality, but at different frequency levels. Initially, at the levels of eternal consciousness of the non-material, in the spiritual worlds of **immortal souls,** as we say. New souls then carry these **matrices** (the **seed** of forms and bodies, along with their content) over **to the illusory world,** to the seeming reality. This is claimed by both our wise earthly ancestors and by the most courageous scientists. Let me mention once more the most important findings of the microbiologist **Bruce Lipton.** He discovered that we are constantly receiving **powerful cosmic radiation, which dictates the rhythm of life and death of the cell membranes of living beings; it even dictates their reactions and abilities.**

Sages of the past and scientists alike claim that **the physical reality within which we live is built by our thoughts, representations, and even by our delusions and emotions. The world is the mirror of our consciousness. Illusions lead us away** from that which is real, primordial, harmonious. That is why the world is as it is. For the majority of people, life is primarily (still) 'the vale of tears,' the vale of hardship and penury. This is so because **we are persistently distorting the seed and genetic matrices** of the material world.

What we see is actually **a mirage of our consciousness.** The world of form is illusory and so is the world of spirits. Real are worlds beyond death and **the dreams of non-physical spirit,** which is dreaming its **instructive, beyond-death dreams** on the other side. **Both the living and the souls of the dead dream, or shape, their own truth within the Field of life. This Field consists of consciousness and energy, which suffuses the living and the dead alike – it suffuses the worlds of different vibrational (sound-light) levels or dimensions of the material and non-material alike, and it also suffuses different life forms.** This is what spiritual teachers from different periods and cultures claim. And because we have **very different** mental **representations** and

---
257 I wrote about this in the first book in the *Cosmic Telepathy* series.

very different levels and contents of consciousness, **we create different worlds in our consciousness and mind,** we create our own life theatre, our own stage play. Even the symbolic **'heavenly' illusory landscapes of the realms beyond death and thoughts are totally different** in the consciousnesses of a Native American and a white person, of a Tibetan or a Slavic shaman. They differ in the heads of Christians and Muslims. Yet, at their core, they arise **from similar knowings.** They are, at the same time, **mirror images of the collective consciousness of the entire community,** which was also created by **various teachings and religious, cultural, and family representations.** That is why the image of the 'paradise world' of perfect souls is different everywhere.

> I don't know for certain what is **the deepest mystery of the world.**
> **Perhaps the sound of the soul.**
> Only life and my soul know it.[258]

The soul is like a contemporary microcomputer. Within the framework of its currently valid mental formations, science is in vain trying to discover **where consciousness comes from and where it disappears to after death. Consciousness itself simply knows** – without any microscopic instruments. When my students manage to **connect to their soul, to their higher self, they** usually **cry because they are touched.** The world of souls has a sound that touches us.

In our dreams, in the worlds of the soul, we can meet the essences of the souls of the dead, we can perceive them and even 'communicate' with them telepathically – at the high-frequency levels of our consciousness, of course. We together can either live **in a harmonious co-existence or we can disturb each other.** Without being aware, we do the latter especially when we **nurture sorrow** and when we cry unconsolably for people who have departed into life beyond death. **We disturb the deceased with our energy formations, with the low-frequency waves of our gloomy and sad thoughts,** and also with our unloving thoughts about them. We pull them back to the physical world. It would be better if we were to control our sorrow. **When the bodiless consciousness is free, it also sets free physical rigidity.** Passing from the solid, material world into **the Field of Consciousness** is a part of the earthly game, which helps us **understand life in its totality.** Don Juan says that a warrior can **keep his awareness, which he needs to give to the Eagle at the moment of dying.** This is **freedom.** At the moment of crossing, the body in its entirety is kindled with knowledge. Every cell at once becomes aware of itself and also aware of the totality of the body.[259]

....
258 Mira Omerzel - Mirit, poem *The Deepest Mystery of the World – the Sound of the Soul*, taken from the book *Zvočne podobe prebujene ljubezni*, Vrhnika, Dar Dam (2012).
259 Carlos Castaneda, *The Wheel of Time*, London, Allen Lane, The Penguin Press (1998), p. 198.

> A warrior considers himself already dead, so there is nothing for him to lose. The worst has already happened to him, therefore he's **clear and calm**.[260]

We are actually dying all the time, we re-emerge, change, and are reborn. Every opportunity, situation and lesson within relationships offers a possibility to realise things. Throughout our life, **we change our outer image and inner content – physical and psychological content alike.** Our planetary ancestors claim that **time and time again we embark on new incarnations, new life opportunities and new trials in order to develop our consciousness to perfection. Following which we rise to after-death dreams.** After death, these dreams enable us to harmonise the chaotic, still imbalanced content, through the process of 'digestion,' through the process of becoming aware of everything we had lived in the physical world. And they help us establish **a new order, a more mellifluous and balanced order.**

Our **consciousness expands immensely after the death of our physical body, and our soul can thus comprehend** that which it was unable to grasp during our life time. Everything we experienced is **imprinted in the data bank of human consciousness,** but it **gets almost, but not completely, forgotten in our new incarnation. We will remember when the time is right** and when our past experiences become useful to us. At that point we usually say that **we knew or came to know something intuitively,** telepathically.

The human **journey from mind to heart reawakens the imprints of our memories,** and it also reawakens **the Silent knowledge, the eternal wisdom, which is waiting to be revived.** This happens only when, through our current experiences, **we begin to resonate with the content of our soul** and with the memory imprints which dwell within it; it happens when **we find ourselves once again in similar trials and life lessons. We keep repeating the lesson because we haven't (yet) passed the test. That is why life offers us new opportunities again and again.** And if, perhaps at the second, third or tenth time, we manage to pass the test, to hold our nerve in trials and **react lovingly, there will be no similar painful trials in the future.** This was the way the Ancient Ones thought.

> When a warrior makes the decision to take action, **he should be prepared to die. If he is prepared to die, there shouldn't be /.../ any unwelcome surprises /.../ because he is expecting nothing.**[261]

Things that have the same resonance awaken each other. When we re-experience similar situations and similar problematic relationships from the

---
260 Ibid., p. 121.
261 Ibid., p. 143.

past, we are actually browsing through **the memory of our subconscious and meta-consciousness, our soul. The soul's divine love guides us and whispers to us** that, in a given situation, it would perhaps be best to do something differently than what our rigid mind advised us. The mind is constantly analysing, reaching conclusions, and making decisions **based on our past experiences, which are most likely spiritually still immature (unenlightened) and therefore wrong,** or still imperfect. **When we move beyond the mental and emotional patterns imprinted in our mind, we open up a path to different and better possibilities, primarily a path to more loving reactions,** which are in harmony with our spiritual path and growth.

Native Americans and other peoples of our planet say that **in the spirit's after-death learning,** our soul, or our consciousness, **revisits primarily the content which we hadn't been able to comprehend during our lifetime.** This allows a broader, higher awareness – a clearer and spiritually more mature awareness – to gradually pour into our everyday mind, everyday thinking. **And enlightened people never again lose their earthly and after death memory.** They can even keep it in their new incarnation. And they can begin to live a new life in the physical body **with perfect awareness,** even though they no longer need testing trials in their life. They have attained the goal of their life and **completed their learning in the material world.** They can now enrich other people's existence with their **awakened kind-heartedness,** with their **mental clarity** and presence. They can **teach them through their wisdom.** This was also what the Mexican shamans taught.

> **To us /.../ the woods** and the big hills and the Northern lights and **the sunsets are all alive** and we live with these things and **live in the spirit of the woods like no white person can do.** The big lakes we travel on, the little lonely lakes we set our beaver traps on with a ring of big black pines standing in rows, looking always north, like they were watching for something that never comes, same as the Indians /.../ and **when we are alone we speak to them and are not lonesome. Only thinking always of the long ago days and the old men. So we live in the past and the rest of the world keeps going by.** For all their modern inventions **white people can't live the way we do and they die (they are spiritually re-born) if they try,** because they can't read the sunset and hear the old men talk in the wind. **A wolf is fierce, but he is our brother, he lives the old way. But the white man** is sometimes a pup and he **dies** when the wind blows on him, because **he sees only trees and rock and water,** only the outside of **the book and can't read.**[262]

....
262 Anaquoness, taken from the anthology *I have spoken*, compiled by Virginia Irving Armstrong, Chicago, Sage Books (1971), pp. 142-143. The note in brackets is mine.

We experience many different deaths during our life. **Every change is a passage, an initiatory death of the old into the new,** which celebrates the fact that we have moved beyond the old and opened up to the new. Initiations are distinct death experiences too; they enrich and reveal new paths **through near-death experiences, by touching the immortal and eternal worlds** of the consciousness beyond.

Earthly living beings (people, animals, plants and even the Earth itself) are **light-sound and energy beings of the Primordial undulation of light, of the primordial thought, of sound and light.** This undulation holds an imprint, a record (matrix) – a vision (of the Universal Logos) of happiness, all-connectedness, and even a vision of nirvanic bliss. **So, it comes as no surprise that sound is our most important tool for (self-)harmonisation, (self-)healing, for our actualisation** in the material and the spiritual realms, even in the cosmic and divine realms. We cannot live without sound: we express ourselves through **the sound of our words, songs, emotions and thoughts. When we touch the Primordial Truth and when we live it, we are happy, calm, we sing in our soul. We sing ourselves and the world.**

Every being yearns to be **permanently connected to the Primordial Centre.** When we are connected to divine creative forces, we feel that we are **the centre of the Universe and the Earth**, we feel that **we exist at all levels, or dimensions, of reality.** When we manage to **permanently connect all the levels within ourselves**, all the dimensions of our being – from the physical body to the highest frequencies of our consciousness – **we can attune to everything and we can fly everywhere on the wings of spirit. We have attained the self-confidence of the Centre, we have attained enlightenment, awakening, complete oneness.** This central point of our consciousness is both **the observer and connector** – the divine watchful **consciousness of the 'God's eye'** and the inexhaustible **source of information, abundance and peace. It is the observer, the observed object and the act of observing** simultaneously. **It is God,** as they say. It is the Divine within itself and within all its parts.

Sacrifices, the symbolism of blood, funeral rituals, and the consciousness of the heart

Fray Diego de Landa wrote in his books[263] that **the magi and healers often** practiced **bloodletting** on the body, in areas where patients had problems and pain. **Sacrificing blood, the liquid of life, was an obligatory part of ceremonies.**

....
263 Diego de Landa, *An Account of Things of Yucatán*, Mexico, Monclem Ediciones (2000), p. 81. The original was written between 1563 and 1572.

The friar reported that **men often sacrificed their own blood.** Which is, for example, why they **cut their earlobes.** Sometimes they **pierced their cheeks, lower lip, or tongue,** which was extremely painful. **Blood was sprinkled as a protection against demons (against the negative).** And the more they practiced this, the more **courageous** they were deemed to be. **But it was not customary for women to sprinkle their blood** (a menstrual cleanse was obviously enough).[264] And at times animals were sacrificed.[265]

Barbara Hand Clow claims that the elementary of the Earth's centre and its crust contains all the memories and records of life forms through time, from the Big Bang on. They are said to be **encoded in the Earth's crystalline memory grid,** which co-oscillates with the basic building blocks in the human body, **in blood.**[266] That is why human blood is said to be not only **the symbolic essence of our ancestors, but also the visible and material energy of life.** If the body is drained of blood, it dies, people certainly already knew this in distant prehistory. **Blood is the juice of life, the mirror of the Intelligence which had created it; it is the tangible proof of the incarnated soul, a reflection of the nature's laws. It is a multidimensional connector,** a distinct **axis between the worlds,** between the levels of a human being. The astrophysicist Andrew MacFadyen claims[267] that **the iron** which we have **in our blood was forged in the explosion of the supernova** (which means that our essences come from the stars!). So, there is a direct connection between us and the stars. Native Americans and other peoples are right. **The iron in our blood** (according to B. H. Clow) 'attunes' **to the iron in the Earth's crystalline gist. That is why humans can perceive everything that occurs on Earth** by means of the metaphysical sensory radars in their blood, by means of their etheric bodies and **meta-senses,** which are far more sensitive than physical senses.

Everything constantly vibrates, oscillates, and pulsates both on Earth and in the Universe. The Universe and the Earth are suffused with **a symphony of frequency waves.** When a change occurs in the Sky or somewhere on Earth – when, for example, a star explodes – then **the energy pattern or the imprint of this** (frequency!) **occurrence will be transferred to all the octaves, all the frequency sets of reality,** including the material levels, by means of the intervention of material and non-material particles and the **(morphic) field.**[268] It will also cause the energy and electromagnetic field of humans to oscillate. We are not alone, we are part of

---
264 Ibid., p.81.
265 Ibid., p. 82.
266 Barbara Hand Clow, Gerry Clow, *Alchemy of Nine Dimensions*, Charlottesville, Hampton Roads Pub. (2004).
267 *National Geographic*, March 2007.
268 In his numerous books, **Rupert Sheldrake** was the first to draw attention to such transfer of information.

the whole, the Ancient Ones already knew this! **The altered flow of one particle will alter the sound of the whole.** And the sound of the whole (of the orchestra) will change the resonance of its particles. A frequency-energy (sound) imprint will cause the microscopic subquantum building blocks of the body, the body's cell membranes and strings to oscillate.

Blood and other body fluids co-oscillate, or co-resonate, with cosmic and earthly waves (signals) of various wavelengths, which are constantly ennobling the Earth. That is why **nothing that happens in the Universe can remain hidden from us.** This is also how **the sacred geometry of patterns of perfection, which the Intelligence of the Universe anchors into the material world,** passes into earthly life forms across the levels, or dimensions of existence. **Fluids are mediums,** they brilliantly channel frequency-sound waves. More sensitive people can even **perceive the gamma cosmic rays** (X-ray, ultrasound). People who are able to perceive the X-ray or ultrasound (gamma) waves, can also sense or **hear the sound of the Earth's rotation, the waves and songs of the stars, and of course also the silence of the immortal souls.**

> Near death, the sound of bliss and stock-take is heard,
> the mundane and the usual lose their inflated **value**.
> **Near death, Truth reveals itself,**
> usual reasoning loses its power.
> It might seem everything is going wrong,
> yet **a fulfilled peace of awareness and fullness, of accomplishment and completion,**
> resides in the soul.
> This is the time of taking stock
> which cannot be avoided.[269]

Biochemistry unfolds in our cells, it is **the alchemy which turns non-living substances into living matter.** Invisible elements build the visible world **in line with the laws of the invisible Intelligence of life,** spirit, soul, consciousness. **We are beings of light-sound waves, capturing the messages of the Earth and the Cosmos,** converting them **into thoughts and biochemical processes.** The energy of thoughts can even re-shape and heal material forms.

Every organ in our body has its metaphysical tasks. **Taoist wisdom** and its successor, Chinese medicine, have recognised this brilliantly. **Kidneys** are a filter for worry, **lungs** for grief, the **stomach** for emotional distress, **the throat** is the

....
269 Mira Omerzel - Mirit, poem *Near Death, the Sound of Bliss and Stock-take Is Heard*, taken from the book *Zvočne podobe prebujene ljubezni*, Vrhnika Dar Dam (2012).

door for the (un)expressed, the **heart** either allows or stops the flows of feelings and kindness. Our throat, heart, stomach, they all contract at unpleasant thoughts or news, etc. And **blood** is the transmitter of the essences of the soul.

The blood fluid carries **the information, the commands and signals of life matrices and codes** throughout the physical body, between cells and more subtle etheric levels. **Blood is the link** between the Source and the earthly, between the physical body and etheric levels, or bodies. But it does not only carry the 'information' of **Divine Intelligence into the material world, it also transfers into the material world the vibrations of spiritual waves, the vibrations of emotional, mental, and spiritual bodies and love.**

When Mayan military conquests spread during the first centuries B.C.E., some cities surrounded themselves with wooden or stone walls. This was also **a time of brutal sacrifices** and decapitations.[270]

Friar de Landa says that the Mayans **believed in the immortality of the soul to a greater degree than other nations.**[271] They believed that, **after death, there existed another, better life, which the soul enjoyed after having been freed from the physical body.** They said that this future life was divided into **good and evil, into suffering and peace.** Peace after death was for those who led virtuous lives; suffering was only for the wicked. **The good ones were said to come to a most delightful place, where nothing would give pain, where there would be food and drinks in abundance** (food is the symbol of **abundance**); **they were said to rest under a shady tree they called** *yaxché* (a mythical tree denoting the axis of human consciousness). Beneath its lush branches they were said to **rest in peace forever.** Friar Diego de Landa says that **the wicked went to a place that was lower than the other,** called *mitnal*, meaning **hell** (this expression is the closest to the Christian mindset). There, they were to be tormented by demons, by **cold, hunger, exhaustion, and sadness** (this happens in the earthly life too). In this place, there was **a chief demon** whom all the rest obeyed and whom they called **Hunhau.** They say that these good and evil lives **had no end (the cycle of reincarnations consists of countless lives, lessons, and incarnations). But the immortal soul cannot be annihilated.** The Mayans were quite certain that **those who had hung themselves went straight to this paradise;** and there were many who ended their sad lives by hanging themselves due to this nonsensical superstition. **Ixtab,** the goddess of the scaffold, was said to carry them.

They wrapped the dead in a **shroud, filling their mouths with ground maize, food, drink and stones,** which were supposedly used for **money** in the afterlife.

....
270 *Mysteries of the Maya, National Geographic Collector's Edition*, 2008, p. 75.
271 Diego de Landa, *An Account of the Things of Yucatán*, Mexico, Monclem Ediciones (2000), pp. 95-96.

The deceased received all of that in order not to suffer from any shortage in their afterlife. They **threw some of their idols into the grave. If the buried person was a priest, they threw in some of his books. If he was a sorcerer, they threw in some of his divining stones and other belongings.** They usually abandoned the house of the deceased person. The bodies of chiefs and high-ranking people were **cremated, their ashes were put in urns and temples were built over them.** During the times of friar de Landa, ashes were stored **in clay vessels which took the form of different statues.**[272]

When **a chief died, his head was cut off, they boiled it and removed the flesh. Then the back part of the skull was sawn off,** leaving the front with the jaws and teeth. They **replaced** the removed flesh **by a special paste,** with which they reproduced perfectly the features of the person whose skull it was. These they kept **with the urn containing ashes.** The urns were kept together with divine images and idols on house altars with great reverence. At all celebrations and feast days they put before them **offerings of food,** so that they would not be without in the afterlife, where they believed their souls rested and their gifts were appreciated.[273]

To walk along **the main avenue of Teotihuacan,** called **the Way of the Dead,** means to **follow the soul which travels along the Milky Way.** The Milky Way had a special significance in ancient cultures, including the Slavic and ancient Slovene cultures. It denoted a street, or **path (of the soul).** The souls of the dead which were about to be **incarnated on Earth** were said to travel along it, somewhere far away. Almost all ancient civilisations believed this. **The Milky Way can also be viewed as a crocodile.**[274] This symbolism was also known in ancient Egypt.

In Chichén Itzá, the journey of those who die ritually and consciously leads past the majestic Pyramid of Kukulkan, past the Pyramid of the Sun, and the Pyramid of the Moon.

> **When I pass,**
> this prairie will hold my **tracks**
> as long as the wind
> sleeps.[275]

Human victims, most often **prisoners** of war, were **anointed with blue** (with the colour of rivers and seas – **the symbol of the flow of life**) before they were sacrificed. **Miters** were put on their heads, **they were ritually purified,** after which they **cut them so that their blood dripped onto the ground. Then they shot**

---
272 Ibid. p. 94.
273 Ibid., p. 95.
274 Adrian Gilbert, *The End of Time*, Edinburgh, Mainstream Publishing (2007), p. 174.
275 Jim Barnes, taken from the book *Tudi trava ima svojo pesem*, Radovljica, Didakta (2000).

an arrow to the victim's heart, writes de Landa.[276] When his **heart was to be taken out on the sacrificial altar,** they conducted him **with a great display** and concourse of people. The heart was taken out with **a stone knife** (most often made from obsidian). Sacrifices were made **at the top of the temples and pyramids** (the symbols of the supreme), following which they threw the dead body rolling down the steps to the earth. An assistant **handed the still pulsating heart to the priest, who placed it on the altar among the idols (Deities) in the temple.** Sacrificial killings were already booming by the new era. Then the victims were thrown **into holy wells – *cenotes*.** Christian missionaries were of course appalled by these acts.

As we have seen, **consciousness, or soul, forms both the material and non-material. Blood is the medium** for the transfer of the necessary guidelines for this **soul-earthly alchemy.** Blood liquid balances the physical and spiritual. It is the medium of their harmony, connecting the world of complementary opposites. **This is why rituals associated with the Earth were always linked to the symbolism of blood.** Later, especially in the centuries of the Common Era, this has unfortunately developed into **brutal bloody sacrifices.** Especially among the Mexican Mayans. Such **distortion** of metaphysical, spiritual principles could have happened **only after the primordial spiritual symbolism of blood and heart had been forgotten. But the rituals of connecting with blood symbolism were preserved until the Atomic era.** My generation still recalls a game we used to play as children: we **made small cut on our fingers and exchanged droplets of blood** with a person who was close to us. This was the **brothers' or sisters' oath, blood brotherhood. Drops of blood confirmed, or 'recorded', the oath and contract of connection, a friendship responsibility** for each other. If a blood brother needed help, his 'blood brother/sister' was sure to help. **Blood is both the material and symbolic juice of life. And life needs cooperation and resonance.** Perhaps the Mayan blood brotherhood rituals did not differ much from our children's ritual.

Almost all spiritual teachings of our planet teach that **the consciousness of the head needs to be directed into the consciousness of the heart, into experience. The attention of the mind should be directed to the sensing of the heart,** which is why there are so many songs about the heart and **the heart is** also **a very frequent iconographic symbol and the myth of life.** When our attention **descends into the heart area, we feel warmth,** even intense heat (**the warm waves of life energy**). The energy presence of the heart then pours throughout our body, **illuminating the surroundings of the warm-hearted person. This flow of the heart's energy is beneficial, harmonising, and extremely healing. To hold a person within your heart means to perceive this person with love, as the light of the soul,** it means

---
276 Diego de Landa, *An Account of the Things of Yucatán*, Mexico, Monclem Ediciones (2000), p. 83.

that we feel a compassionate and **beneficial connection.** To denote this state of spirit, the Mayans used the word lack'ech, **we are all one** – I am you and you are I.

Sardello speaks about **the silence of the heart** in a very poetical way.[277] It is said that the **undiscovered, dormant abilities** of the human nature reveal themselves within it. In his opinion, **the mind and the physical heart are connected.** Sardello believes that **the heart is both a physical, psychic, and spiritual organ,** through which we receive the gifts of silence. **Silence can be individuated and cosmic.** He says that **the heart is enlivened in silence and that the heart's consciousness is the very liveliness of the Silence. The heart's spirituality,** which differs from the spirituality of the heart, reveals the heart to be an organ of silence.[278] This is why it is probably not a coincidence that all spiritual practices speak about the heart as an organ, or **centre, of feeling.**

Furthermore, Sardello believes that **the heart is able to feel spiritual presence (and soul). Within silence, the heart's spiritual nature connects to the consciousness, to the soul.** This is why Sardello equates silence with the heart's consciousness and believes that **we need to find the centre of our consciousness.** And this is precisely what the Mayans and many other conscious peoples of antiquity sought to attain. Some still try to attain this today. Contemporary **Mexican shamans** are among them.

The heart's consciousness (cosmic awakened consciousness) is nourished by clear feelings, which are unclear in the usual consciousness. **They become clear and intense within the heart's consciousness, within the consciousness of silence.** That is why we should **develop the heart's consciousness** and we can do this by means of focused, strong feelings. According to Sardello and other spiritual teachers of the world, our heart (our heartfulness) enables us to experience **the gifts of silence, such as the knowledge of who we are, an ability to connect to the soul, boundless creativity, expansion into boundlessness, the reception of insights, spiritual and physical cleansing, the perception of freedom and non-attachment.** This is how we build **a bridge to invisible worlds.**[279]

When we feel **the invigorating energy of the heart** within our breast, we are truly **alive and fulfilled. We experience the world in a glow of kindness and attention, in a sonic silence of peace.** In such a psycho-physical state, **we cannot be rough to anyone, wars are not possible. When did the Mayans undergo such an immense devaluation of the heart's consciousness and start to tear physical hearts from human chests?** We should only hold other beings within our own heart, for this is extremely beneficial and therefore important. Why did humans

....
[277] Robert Sardello, *Silence – The Mystery of Wholeness*, Benson, Goldstone Press (2008), from p. 95 on.
[278] Ibid.
[279] Ibid.

become so extremely shallow and their heartfulness so devalued that **life lost its sacredness, heartfulness lost its value** and a torn out, sacrificed **physical heart came to be a macabre symbol of the continuance of life** and prosperity?

When looking and listening within silence, within the heart's consciousness, we see mysterious contents of other beings and we empathise deeply with them. We see the world from the perspective of the heart. From the point of view of the heart, of which yogis and ancient healers of other cultures spoke. **Sufis named it** *mundus imaginalis*, **or** *himma*.[280] Himmas are the songs of the heart, which in a meditative silence, understands, feels, and sees the world from the point of view of the heart.

When we move our consciousness into the point of the heart, into our own centre, we touch the Universal, basic, and boundless creative Cosmic, Divine Consciousness, or Essence. Sardello even mentions **three aspects of the heart's spirituality: the heart lives in service, the heart lives in healing, the heart lives in worship.**[281]

The heart projects the silence and energy of the Intelligence of the Universe into life. The heart is like sound, travelling from our ears back to the Source. Try it! Try to **follow the sound back to the Source, to where it came from;** to where life is born, **to the very Source of sound undulation, to the Source of life.** This exercise, which has also been revived by Sardello, is known by numerous ancient traditions. It is a distinct **awareness exercise, leading the singer back to the centre of life, to the Source of sound waves, to the centre of Silence.** This awareness exercise **condenses diffusion and turns it into the powers of listening to oneness and wholeness.** According to Sardello, **the spiritual alchemy of the heart** transfers all that happens and exists within Silence, within the central system of life, into the material world.

If we send the energy of the heart into the world, we will see the world in a different way. Beings who we have despised or criticised, will now shine forth in **the beauty of their soul and in their spiritual beauty. The ability to feel people in this way is an exceptional gift, confirming the path to perfection – to an enlightened cosmic consciousness.** The **sages** of the cultures in harmony with nature **still teach how to live, look and listen in this way.** And white people laugh at them as if to say what are they babbling about. All of this cannot be proven with microscopes. Millennia ago, ancient Mayans probably perceived the heart in a similar way.

Reverence will emerge in the person who sends love into the world. Thus the beauty of peace will be anchored, in accordance with the laws of resonance (**synaesthesia**).

....
280 Ibid., p. 102.
281 Ibid., p. 103.

Images and colours will shine forth in all their splendour, they will reveal themselves in countless shades. And the fullness of sensations will solace and enrich the person, it will let him know that he **is a spiritual being without limitations.**

By looking with kindness and compassion, **you have nourished and enlivened – within your heart –** the person you have held in your heart.

So this is what it means to **gaze and react from the level of the unconditional love of the soul,** with an iridescent array of the soul, which **ennobles the world,** nature, and people. It brings forth the thought that **we are all one – we are all children of the same cosmic force, of the same divine Intelligence of life.** At the levels of the heart, **we experience the world in a realistic way, in all its fullness, and we stop inventing false images, nonsense excuses, painful condemnations, rigid pigeon-holing, unnecessary criticism, etc.**

The sound of love and silence will be understood by those who hold it within their hearts and loving thoughts and by those who look at it heartfully from the level of their soul, even though it might be far away.[282] The love of the Silence **changes our worldviews. Are we satisfied with the world in which we live?** No, we are not! Shouldn't we then **change our view of the world** and thus **enliven and heal it? We would all benefit from this. But first we need to find silence within us.**

> The early breeze before dawn
> is the keeper of secrets.
> **Don't go back to sleep!**
> It is time for prayer, **it is time to ask for
> what you really need.**
> Don't go back to sleep!
> **The door of the One who created the world
> is always open.**
> Don't go back to sleep.[283]

Even though, according to the teaching of Mexican shamans, **death is the only irrevocable thing,** a shaman **can countermand it.**[284] They can **rise to the immortality of the soul.**

So, get to know and **overcome the thirteen lords of darkness and death, of Xibalba** on Earth, and life will be more beautiful and better. **It is said that the Gods envy our mortality** – all the wonderful gifts we receive when near death. It is good to know that **every moment** can be your **last one. So, always act accordingly – and with heart.**

....
282 This is also what Sardello speaks of.
283 Rumi, *Hidden Music*, London, Thorsons (2001), p. 35.
284 Carlos Castaneda, *The Wheel of Time*, London, Allen Lane, The Penguin Press (1998), p. 274.

Shamanic initiation with snake venom

Life is truly miraculous and it always brings you what you need, or what you seek. There are no coincidences indeed. I have been on the verge of death countless times, and I was also in the worlds beyond. I will write about my near-death experiences in detail in the fourth book in the *Cosmic Telepathy* series, titled *The Mysteries of Life, Death, and Soul in the Ancient Vedic Lore of the Balinese People in Indonesia*. I will now share with you just one of them.

After I had finished the chapter on the sacred serpent for this book and started writing the chapter on shamanism, I was convinced that within a couple of days, I would have finished writing the book. I would only need to review the chapter on Mexican shamans and warriors. But I unexpectedly **experienced a distinctive shamanic initiation through a snake bite, the most difficult initiation of all up until then.** Initiations without food and water, or in darkness, were quite easy compared to this one.

Yes, it is true, **you simply cannot talk and write about serpents and serpent initiations without having experienced a snake's power yourself.** It is simply not possible! Do I really have to experience everything first on my own skin, I asked myself. Obviously. Such was my **contract** with the divine Intelligence and **the promise** I gave upon my permanent transition to **life without food in August 2000.** At that time I had asked that life would always serve me the experiences I needed for both my spiritual growth and for my teaching and helping people. **Exactly twelve years had passed since then.** Precisely to the very day. Which is why my snake initiation certainly had a deeper meaning. About a month prior to having been bitten, I sent a request to the Source: **whatever happens,** let the people around me and my students **finally move away from their rigidity and painful non-sense.** And then I forgot about this thought.

Wednesday, **1st of August, 2012,** was a hot day. Tatjana and Eugen, my students from the Primorska Region, had come to help my son Tine paint the fence. When the work was done, we wanted to take them to the nearby countryside, to show them the wonderful places around our home. So we went. I hadn't been to **the Petelin Valleys at Mokrc and above the Iška Gorge** in a long time, where a rock wall descends very steeply into the valley where the Iška River runs. I had often visited those sites previously. They seem so timeless and yet so unusual, as if they weren't in Slovenia at all, let alone near my home. Lonesome spruce trees grow on almost vertical rocks, which is why the landscape resembles a veduta from China. These places, which are rarely visited by people, are magically painted with the sunset's red-yellow glow.

I like isolated places, but I am not the only one. Snakes adore them too, especially vipers. **2012 – the year of great changes.** Nature brought us generous gifts. There were myriads of **mice** all over the land. And as there was a glut of **acorns,** many mice had survived. And mice are food for **snakes,** which is why there were so many of them that year. The year of abundance shows its different faces.

I had been to this wonderful place above the Gorge countless times, but it had never occurred to me that I might encounter a snake who would disapprove of my visit. It is true that I hadn't been there for at least a couple of years. Bushes had grown, grasses above the overhang were half a meter tall. It was no longer easy to reach the rock where I usually sat. I stepped onto the grass and came upon a narrow path which appeared clear. All of a sudden, **I felt a sharp pain in the instep of my right foot.** What has bitten me, I thought. I took a closer look at my instep. I saw two small drops of blood and a little way from them, two tiny, barely visible holes. Oh no, it can't be a snake, I said to myself. But that bite was no joke. The sharpness of its pain was stronger than that of a bee or wasp.

I scratched my foot a little and sat on the edge of the rock despite a slight pain. I sat there with my son and the two friends. For the first fifteen minutes, the effect of the bite was minor. But then **the pain grew stronger** by the minute, it grew **unbearable.** I wouldn't wish such a pain on anybody. I suggested to my friends that we head back home. Luckily, the car was close by, as it was increasingly difficult for me to walk. We needed around fifteen, twenty minutes to get home. On the way, it felt increasingly **difficult to breathe.** It was then that it became clear to me that the bite was certainly a snake's. My son noticed that my lips had turned blue. Well, here I go again! What's this all about? **You shall see,** answered my inner voice.

Four days previously, I had given **a course for therapists** for the students of my school. The course was called *The Veduna Therapeutic Touch.* Was it something connected to the course? Or was the painful bite connected to my digesting of **an emotional unease brought about by my increasingly traumatic realisation that Slovenes,** in the middle of a recession trauma, which is exacerbated by the media, **were sinking into the emptiness of mere entertainment. The culture was becoming ever more spiritually empty, losing its ethical values.** My disappointment had been increasing over the previous few years. I was simply unable to cleanse on a regular basis everything which had been loaded onto my soul, when faced with the events in Slovenia and abroad. **My uncle had been buried** a week before the bite, he had died suddenly while on holiday. When I looked into his disappearance and its causes, I got a totally different story than that of the rescuers. I told this to my family, but **they were unable to accept my insights, which made me a bit sad.** You know, things that happen between our nearest and dearest are the most difficult for us.

Some days before the bite, I had suddenly **burst into tears** during a meeting with my colleagues. There had been obviously **too much of everything. True, the old was departing at an ever greater pace and the completely new was coming in at an even greater speed.** I occasionally had the feeling that I could hardly bear the shifts in my consciousness and energy field. The majority of the Slovene audience doesn't care much for our revival of the Slovene music tradition, of **folk songs and instruments.** 'Oberkrainer' music has swamped everything. The one exception is Slovene **spiritual seekers who are seeking a path into the worlds of soul and eternal values. Fortunately, their number is growing, especially among young people,** which is why our concerts and workshops are packed. There is not enough space for everyone who wants to participate. This knowing detached me somehow from the elated efforts I was making for those Slovene people who care only for cheap entertainment. **Today, the world is a big village in which everyone influences everybody. The path into the world is** increasingly **opening up,** where our spiritual and musical work is appreciated and where people want us to visit them with our concerts and workshops. So there is nothing to think about. We need to go with the flow and cleanse unloving destructive emotions. So was my digestion of these emotions the reason for the accident? Or perhaps the essences of the immortal souls of **Mexican shamans are teaching me about isolation and non-attachment,** I thought.

In many traditions, **the serpent is a symbol of transition into the new. That is quite right. Well, a shaman must never permit despair, not for a moment.** This is of course clear to me. But we are people with thoughts and emotions. And it is easier to say that you don't want fear, despair, disappointment, etc. rather than to actually remove them. Especially if those painful emotions emerge as a result of disharmony among those who are close to you, or as a result of something that means much to you. More than a month ago, it occurred to me, and I also wrote it down in my diary, that the second book about the Mayans perhaps needs more personal experience stories. Well, here we go, with one more experience!

I kept thinking: aha, there is another explanation of why I could have **drawn this snake bite experience to myself.** I had consciously given up food exactly twelve years before. In August 2000 I transited to life without usual food, to **life with the cosmic serpent,** as the Mayans, Aborigines, ancient Egyptians, and ancient Slavs would say. I underwent various processes without food and liquid many times, and I also underwent completely different processes. **Over this period of twelve years, which is usually a complete cycle,** I needed **less and less sleep.** A couple of hours was completely enough. I also consumed **less and less liquid.** And so, at the end of writing this book, I experienced **another process**: without food, **with an enormous amount of venom** for the first four days and **without liquid** on top of that. **This could have cost me my life,** if my body hadn't been strong enough. Fortunately, I have great renewal abilities. Well, we will see **what this experience will bring me in the future.** I could perhaps **live without liquid,** I said to myself about a month ago. But these were just my first guesses. **Warriors must first discover what they are doing wrong. And what the experiences bring to them.**

We got home. I could hardly get out of the car and I waddled to our garden bench. I wished for cold water. My son brought a large basin of cold water. I put my feet in it. **But the pain grew and grew, it was increasingly unbearable. I felt a lack of power and was almost unable to move.** In this growing pain, tears of despair washed over me for a moment. This was followed by **strong muscle cramps in my fingers**, bending them, pulling them together. I was experiencing muscle cramps the like of which are felt by people who are full of blocked emotional pain. But this time it was the venom that caused the muscle block. **Physical poison has an impact on our nerves and muscles similar to mental and emotional poisons.**

Pins and needles began to rise from my feet towards my chest. I soon felt that the left half of my tongue and head were numb. It is obviously true that the left side of the head, or brain, is connected to the right side of the body and vice versa. I was experiencing this clearly and strongly. I felt my right foot and left cheek becoming **numb and bloated** and my foot was swelling up more and more.

But my heart was protected, as if in a balloon, or a cocoon. I twisted one of my heart valves due to extreme physical strain brought on when sailing in a powerful storm. If the venom had reached my burdened heart, this would have been the end of me in an instant. A snake bite is **most often followed by cardiac failure.** Its effects can also be **muscle necrosis**, defects or **failures of organs, the collapse of breathing or the vascular system.** In this unbearable pain I, however, **felt protection and even gratitude.** That was how I knew that **this entire adventure had its own purpose and that I was fully protected by cosmic forces in this painful initiation.**

Using both **the cosmic resonance technique** and the therapeutic knowledge they had acquired, Tine and Eugen gave me a hand massage, while Tatjana **gently** touched my right foot. The two guys panicked for a moment, when they saw me suffering, they even thought of taking me **to the doctor. No way! This is my lesson and I have to experience it thoroughly myself.** From the beginning to the end! **A test of my devotion to the cosmic serpent, to life forces and to the power of my connection to it, to them.** It is not a coincidence that this happened right now, when there is hardly a chapter in the book in which cosmic serpent has not been mentioned. Well, isn't the poison of a snake already a heavy enough burden? Every little amount of poison is an enormous burden for me, as I live on pure food, on cosmic life energy. I certainly don't need the poisonous substances found in medicine. One single cup of coffee would cause great problems – a headache, diarrhoea, a lack of power. My body certainly finds snake venom much more difficult to handle than does the body of someone who poisons themselves with food, coffee, alcohol, and stress on a daily basis. No, **a doctor is not an option**, I told them. That which is happening, is **my challenge and a test of my own powers and abilities,** my own test for dissolving poisonous substances.

The agony of the pain grew stronger. Even water touching my foot was too much to bear, its touch was all too painful. **Sitting on the garden bench became extremely tiring.** With great difficulty, with my son's help, I moved onto the couch in the living room, only a couple of metres away from the garden bench. I felt a great **thirst and drank a glass of water**. But **intense nausea** followed, accompanied by an even greater pain, by tearing and pain in my muscles, which was followed by **vomiting**. I vomited at least ten times within the next hour. But what was there to vomit? There was nothing in my stomach except a little bit of water and stomach acid. This sour and bitter vomiting was quite strenuous and annoying.

Soon after, I felt a need to empty my bowels. My body reacted very fiercely – the poison had to go out as soon as possible. I had **diarrhoea**. I headed to the toilet with great difficulty and with the help of everyone beside me. The pain in my foot, which was now on the ground, grew immensely. I was barely able to sit on the toilet seat, because the nausea and pain were stronger once I had stood up. They were terrible. That which had to go out, utterly flowed out of me. I lost consciousness due to the pain and I **fell into a coma** for a while. My colleague Mojka later told me that, before that, I said I could **hear crickets**. A sudden auditory hallucination caused by the poison in my body?

But I was **unable to stand up**, I just sat there, leaning on the washing machine. I had a feeling that **the pain would race up my leg and that I couldn't move a millimetre more.** Which is why I asked my friends to place something to lie on right there on the bathroom floor. Every move was terribly painful. With great difficulty, I slid down from the toilet seat to the bathroom floor, which was padded with cushions from loungers and garden chairs. I remained there **on the bathroom floor for fourteen days.** Toilet seat to the left (close by, thank God!), the washing machine as a night table, shower to the right, washbasin in front of me. I was so **grateful that our bathroom was big enough**, as it became my small holiday apartment for the next two weeks. So, I lay there on the bathroom floor for the next two weeks, although I had been dreaming about a holiday, which I had desired so very much. Well, I got **camping on bathroom floors, a holiday in our green bathroom**, where everything was within my reach.

I could not drink for the first four days. Every sip caused a disgusting **nausea** in my stomach. Liquid was obviously superfluous with all this poison. Of course,

liquid is of extreme importance in body detoxification, especially if detoxification is left to the body itself, **without antiserums** and any other contemporary chemical aids used to dissolve snake venom. Both **serums and anti-allergic injections, antibiotics, and tetanus injections are an additional heavy burden for the body.** Some people perhaps would not survive all of that. Or, like snake venom itself, these drugs would damage the organs and weak points in their bodies. That is why in some places antiserums and other drugs are not given to people bitten by a snake. I would probably not survive the additional poison.

After four days, **a slight headache** started, and **my foot and eyes were burning**. Once, when I was dozing in the middle of the day – at least it seemed to me that I was dozing (or was it the **venom,** which is **a drug**, that had affected me), I had a vision of **a wonderful gazelle.** It was as if she was watching me attentively, moving away from me, **showing me the way forward.** The gazelle was beautiful and in an especially elegant posture. I was watching from a vantage point behind her, immersing into her image. When she turned her head to me, I was touched. I wished I was able to paint brilliantly in order to capture and carry this scene on paper, to store it forever in the memory and physical world. A feeling of **elation** washed over me at the sight of this **beauty.**

This was followed by a waterfall of rainbow colours. They were pastel at first, after which they began to grow more and more radiant on the screen of my inner vision. I woke up. Actually **my painful ears woke me up.** The pain in my ear would then reappear and disappear **every four** days, for the following four weeks. The amount of earwax increased. So strange!

Well, after all – why wouldn't **the common viper's venom** reach all body parts? The venom of a common viper is reportedly weaker than that of the horned viper, but it is greater in volume. They say that **nine bee stings equal one wasp sting, nine wasps equal one hornet's sting, nine hornets equal snake venom. So, I was stung by 729 bees all together.** Hey, that is something. Luckily, I slept through the first night due to fatigue and the body shock which followed the pain.

On the second day, **the film of my life began to unfold. The images of my childhood** were especially vivid, it was as if I moved back into my childhood and adolescent years with all my body and soul. **The snake bite clearly brought me near death.** Near death, a film of our life always unfolds when our life is drawing to an end. After all, this experience could have well ended with death. But **its purpose was different.**

During the first days, I constantly **joked at my own expense** despite the pain, especially about my strange situation in the bathroom camp. But the situation grew **more difficult and intense by the day.** I was convinced that I would deal with this trial quickly, just as I had done with some other difficulties. If I sense that I am about to catch a cold or a virosis, I dissolve it in an hour or two. But this time, I was given a far more tenacious experience. My foot was increasingly swollen and black. I had the feeling that it would explode.

Yet, in my head, I could not stop writing. Thoughts connected to the writing of this book, were racing in my head, even though the writing was unexpectedly interrupted. I wrote down, as thoroughly as I could, everything I experienced in this initiation. And my thoughts were ever more clear and interesting. **My body was fighting, my consciousness was expanding.** I felt that **the venom in my body was moving up** towards my thigh and higher. On the **fourth day, pins and needles came right to my nose**, but I banished them with the help of cosmic resonance. **My breathing through nostrils** was very deep, its flow was **wide open**, without any obstacles. I was amazed. **Yogis work hard for decades to achieve such effects.**

From the second day on, I could observe **the benefits of snake venom: my skin became velvety soft, tiny crystals,** which had accumulated in **my muscles** due to fatigue, **disappeared.** My slightly **inflamed receding gums** were again **healthy.** The venom obviously dissolved little inconveniences in my body, it even **rejuvenated** it. The initial exhaustion caused by the venom fight only came over me **after seven days.** I later found out that snake venom is used in beauty procedures for skin **rejuvenation** and for removing wrinkles. Venom is injected under the skin. Small amounts, of course.

It is said that **monks, in the Middle Ages and even later, occasionally consumed some snake venom in order to strengthen the immunity of their body and their immune system.** That was how older monks trained the novices. When the novices woke up from coma, they received a fresh quantity of venom and so departed once again into the unconscious worlds, **out beyond.** This was repeated several times. After they had undergone these venom processes, it was reportedly **no longer possible to poison them.** The poisoning of enemies was a quite usual practice in past centuries.

On the fourth day, my body temperature rose, which indicated that my body was fighting the venom. I was increasingly **disturbed by light** and even by **distant noise.** I dreamt of my mother's dishes. The dishes I liked the most as a child. Gnocchi, plum dumplings, risotto with chanterelle mushrooms, etc. **I had a strong desire for food.** This was unusual, as I had **never felt hunger** during these twelve years of living without food. **But this time, I felt it. My body obviously needed additional fuel.** But my stomach does not accept food anymore, not even a hundred percent natural juice. It throws it out immediately, and my stomach burns unpleasantly. **I was aware that during this painful experience, I also wanted loving attention,** the like of which mothers give to their children. Was this why I was remembering my mother's delicious dishes?

The vibrations of my consciousness and body obviously greatly increased in this trial, which is not strange, given the fact that high frequency waves **can do more.** I needed this more. At the same time, my body **refused all lower vibrations, everything that was not totally in tune with it.** The desire to eat soon disappeared, but not the desire to taste.

After being bitten by a snake, it is supposedly **the wisest to rest completely and to drink a lot. Cold compresses** ease the pain and **cool down the fierce chemical processes in the cells** which are fighting the venom. Reactions are obviously extremely intense. It is said that some snakes, but not European ones, cook their victims by injecting venom, after which they absorb the meat prepared in this way. I am not surprised, given my extremely hot foot. **My body itself forced me to rest totally.** If I tried to stand up just a little, I became unbearably sick.

The first week after the bite was **difficult and challenging. I was not able to increase the energy flow through my body in order to stimulate a faster recovery.** I soon came to understand that this would not be good, as **too much poison would then be excreted from the body,** which could damage my detoxification organs. So I was forced to enter **the initiation of my surrender to the body, the initiation of testing my physical powers.** The battle between my body and the venom flared up. My body allowed dissolving as far as it could. There was nothing else to do, I could neither accelerate nor amplify it. Luckily, I was guided by my natural physical immobility, which did not allow any movement. I reclined in a semi-seated position to prevent poisoned blood to move upwards and burden my heart too much. **I had to give my healing into the hands of my body logos and its power. I could just observe** what was happening. A brilliant experience **for surrendering and a total realise of control.**

My instep and toe were extremely swollen and black. My sole was so painful that **even the slightest touch with a wet towel was too painful** and therefore redundant. **Thousands of little needles were burning** in my foot, **my calves were burning hot.** As if my foot was in an oven. This was especially so in those areas where I had already been aware of the tiredness of my muscles. **The blackness began to move upwards along my foot** which made it look bruised.

On the fourth day, I sensed **the first itching,** along with pain, which indicated **healing.** The itching grew stronger over the following days. It occurred unexpectedly – all of a sudden, I would begin to feel itching or stinging here and there. My student and friend Milka came to give me **a gentle foot massage** every day, which did me good. Our Veduna course for therapists was clearly useful. Now I began to get back what I had given to people. A truly gentle touch **enabled the poison to be released from muscles and improved the blood circulation** in my foot.

On the fifth day, I feel a strong heart ache. I become aware that my end might be instant. I sleep for a short while during the night and unwillingly, **I glide from my semi-seated position into lying.** In sleep, I somehow sense an even greater nausea than the evening before, and I also sense **my heart becoming arrhythmic and weaker. Poisoned blood** is obviously moving up towards my heart. But **I cannot wake up.** With a little part of my consciousness, I know that I am not in a good position. My soul is shouting! Then **I exit my body. My soul rises from the physical levels** and I observe my sleeping body from below the bathroom ceiling. This is what happens next. **My soul, the higher levels of my consciousness, wake up my body.** My mind clears in a second and I realise that I need to move. I move and **I stand up again, nausea stops. This is how I save myself. And I experience my own duality – duality in action – two beings,** physical and spiritual, which can even **operate separately; the shamanic journey of the soul** outside of physical boundaries, her work outside the material world.

It was very difficult on the fifth and sixth day. Previously, I had been applying compresses myself day and night, yet they were more warm than cold, as the water in which the towel was soaked hadn't had ice in it. The pain was burning mercilessly. **I cried** in the morning of the sixth day. **I had had enough.** Yet, there kindles a thought: **I know, this experience will certainly bring me something new and important.** New awareness, completely new experiences, etc. **So, be patient!** My friend and colleague Dani helped me to set up a wide bed in the bathroom and he prepared everything needed for **ice-cold compresses, which eased my pain.** He was also on duty during the night, bringing me ice, changing the dressings on my foot. He was the only one who could handle the night shift.

On the seventh day, I finally sleep for a couple of hours. The pain is still terrible, especially **the tearing pain in my muscles, but the swelling starts to disappear slightly if I rest.** Then there were **nightmares.** Every now and again, dreams appeared in which **I was saving people with energy flowing through my hands.** They were **agonising dreams about the future, dreams about the much needed sound surgery,** with which I had been helping people for many years. I laugh playfully and think: did I catch the Aztec logic and fear of destruction? No, I know that these dreams, which had been persistently recurring over a number of years, are **somehow symbolic and prophetic.** I also know that **ahead of me, there is an important part of my life with much effort and work,** especially to help people expand their consciousness and heal their aching souls and bodies.

The pain affects me physically. I begin to drink again after the first four days (so I have survived this too!), and I occasionally feel a sudden **strong and painful tugging in my muscles. Like sharp knives, life energy is breaking through the blockages** caused by snake venom. Luckily, it is pleasantly cool on the bathroom floor, despite the outside temperature being approximately 36 degrees Celsius throughout the entire week.

Fatigue increasingly sneaks into me and **my spirit gets carried away.** Ever more and ever farther. The friend who is on duty beside me is now changing the compresses every couple of hours. I finally manage to doze a little at dawn. I begin to feel **stinging in my heart** which is of course very burdened. **My voice is more and more weak, my eyes ever more burning. So there is a fight going on.**

On the fifth day, I start drinking coconut water. I feel it is rescuing me, helping me to cleanse poisons from my body. Only its sweetness feels redundant. I am not used to it anymore. And despite the strenuous process, I start to gain weight because of the sugar. Everything that is not pure liquid is superfluous. **I get everything I need from the ocean of life energy.**

My ears are also burning more and more, and the point above my heart, on the heart meridian, is painful. My foot is **slowly changing colour** in some parts. **Black turns into purple and yellow.** These coloured bruises are **moving** onto my thigh. Without a compress, **my foot gets warm, turning completely black.** This happens especially if I fall asleep due to fatigue and the towels get warm. **My instep, calf and foot** are the most affected. **A gentle massaging touch suffused with the energy of cosmic resonance felt extremely good.** Both Milka's and Mojka's touch.

Scenes from my childhood unfolded through all of the second week. I remembered my grandmother, grandfather, I remembered my stays in the old house at the foot of the mountains, the pleasant courses on the island of Murter and more. I wanted to go on holidays in August or September, on research holiday of course. To Scandinavia or Iceland. This seemed so far away now! I was now strongly drawn to our three hundred year old house at the foot of the mountains; or was I drawn to it by the nice memories of our stays there.

A new episode in this snake initiation happens **on the ninth and tenth day – a profound cleansing** of the venom from my calf muscles. **The tearing in the depths of my muscles** grows stronger. **I am now changing compresses every hour during the night,** and the towels soon become hot, rather than warm. **The body knows what it is doing.** My conscience tells me that **the body has its own mind. It is well worth getting to know it and respect it. So I surrender more and more to my body logos, I trust it completely.** But a dependency on others can sometimes be very tiring.

I surrender to my body logos on the tenth day. I no longer expect a quick recovery and I stop making plans. I only am, outside time. Time has in fact disappeared. It just vanished. Well – I no longer care for writing, deadlines, agreed dates, etc. **I only am. I am and I exist within the experiences of this agonising and inspiring initiation.** I surrender completely to the healing of my body, I observe it. I no longer try to activate energies.

My right foot is hot, my left foot is cold. **I keep cooling down my right foot, and I keep warming up my left foot, because I am cold. Not cold – I am shivering with cold! A brilliant lesson for understanding separation and duality.** Due to cold compresses, I quiver and **shiver** even deep down inside my body. I have six blankets on my left foot, a warm fleece jacket on me and ice on my right foot. And it is 36 degrees Celsius outside!

My consciousness is expanding more and more. My memory, which had weakened a little over the previous years due to the amount of data and information in my mind, came back with great clarity. **I feel that I again remember the details** which I might have been overlooking previously. A hot-water bottle, which I named **Neža,** eases the cold which is shaking me. I alleviate the cold with it – both physical and spiritual cold. High-frequency energies of consciousness make me broader and make me cold. It is easier with my little Neža.

My sensitivity to sound increases by the day. All the time, from the very first day, **I keep up a stream of writing in my mind.** Aha, that's that, this is how it goes. I am continuously shaping thoughts and sentences in my head, seeking out appropriate words, writing them down. Well, what else can I do in this physical powerlessness?

Time vanishes. **More and more, I experience timelessness, that eternity which people touch in their near-death experiences. My mind empties, stressful thoughts** and hurry are **banished by eternity captured in the current moment.** Or is the current moment fading into eternity. My son Tine had his own distinct shamanic **leap into new consciousness in March; I am experiencing mine just a few months later.** Strange. My son, who performs sound surgery with me,[285] **had changed in the difficult situation** and is now able to **empathise** better and more easily **with me, to take care of me with more devotion.** Thank God!

In the middle of the **eleventh day,** half-asleep, **I see a dance of snakes** on the screen of my consciousness. They resemble whirlwinds racing above the ground. During the last millennia, the sacredness of snakes has been replaced in many cultures by monstrous **dragons.** But those snakes look like they are dancing the Hawaiian **hula dance.** Is there anything strange if they appeared?

It is ever clearer to me that **ancient priests certainly had a knowledge of the use of snake venom.** It worked like a distinct **refreshment, cleanser, amplifier, and also like a drug for passing into worlds beyond and for rejuvenation.** Has everything now been forgotten? Perhaps not. This was whispered to me: perhaps the **Hopi priests** did not simply **dance their ritual dance with rattle snakes around their necks,** but it was quite probable that they had similar 'snake initiations' using snake venom – in small and **carefully selected quantities,** of course.

---
285 More about this in the fifth book in the *Cosmic Telepathy* series.

It would have been strange if they hadn't treated themselves to it. This is what I think now. I found out later that Native Americans living near the **Amazon** River prepare poison for their lethal arrows from herbs and from **the womb of the anaconda** – the great snake. Not only that – they **bring dead back to life** with this poison. Their knowledge too is getting lost. Only few people know the secret of snake venom. I saw a shaman who brought a bird back to life with a potion.

On the eleventh day, a thought washes over me: there is nothing more important than just to be. **There are no more important things than life itself, the moment in which we are living right now!** Everything has its own **long-term meaning and lesson.** Then my sense of being stuck in my work, especially in writing this book, vanished.

It comes to my mind again that perhaps **the souls of Mexican shamans might be teasing me, guiding me through important teachings and knowings** which are coming to me right now. Am I not at this very moment experiencing **a shamanic broadening of consciousness, a descent into the Eagle's emanation, a merging with the cosmic serpent,** as the Native Americans of Central and South America would say? **With the help of a physical serpent, I am being poured into the flow of the cosmic snake, into the Cosmic One, into the interplay of life and death.** My physical (body) and spiritual (consciousness) are being **invigorated in new dimensions** and experiences.

I feel **my body is getting weak.** I live without usual food, **I am fed by cosmic energy, which means I need total balance for this kind of nourishment. If there is no balance, nourishment is not possible. And there is not enough energy for the healing processes.** That is why, on the eleventh day, I treat myself to a bomb – softened fruit on caramel with cinnamon, the way they prepare it in Brazil. I eat it immediately. It gives me instant strength. But then nausea and diarrhoea follow, a small sty even appears on my left eye, warning me about this **unnecessary transgression.** Be patient. **Power will come after a lack of power!**

It is said that **deadly snakes do not live in Slovenia, in Europe.** However, the medical profession adds that a person bitten by a snake can suffer from **organ failure** and that, due to the rapid congealing of the blood, **clots can occur, which then travel to the lungs and heart,** causing **death.** There are laboratory tests in which a drop of snake venom is put into a bowl of human blood. The blood instantly turns into congealed slime, resembling a brawn jelly. No, **it is not an easy task indeed to survive the poison injected by a snake.** Fortunately, my blood is congealing more slowly.

After two weeks, I discover that **my healing process is unfolding in the symbolism of sacred Mayan numbers. Bigger shifts, or special experiences, happen on the fourth, seventh, ninth, thirteenth, twentieth day.** Is someone playing jokes on me? Or do **sacred proportions exist in nature itself,** including the human nature? After each week, **after each set of seven days, I move one step forward,** a step higher, towards something better.

I try to stand up after the first seven days. Blood rushes into my foot, which is very painful. I try to walk, but nothing happens. Lying down is still necessary. This is what my body tells me. On the tenth, eleventh day, **I get tired of the slow recovery process. "I want an immediate recovery!"** I say firmly, in a low voice. My eyes become clear in a second, they are no longer burning. **I triggered a strong flow of energy.** But then I begin to feel **a strong tearing pain** in my foot, in my muscles, after which **the pain in my foot disappears. Heat disappears.** After three hours, the compress is still not too hot. The area of the bite on my instep swells. There is **a small lump** there all of a sudden. **The process started to unfold so powerfully and so painfully that I negated it.** A new **insight** washed over me. **No, my contract was different. I have to get to know, as thoroughly as possible, the healing processes which occur following a snake bite,** which was experienced, and still is, by people on all continents. **Without medical interventions and other aids. So, I again leave the healing to my body.**

In the Balkans, they say that you should **run away if you see a snake's slough.** They call the slough *košulja*, **a shirt.** But you **always** have to run **in the direction opposite** to that to which the snake's shirt is turned. I will pay attention in future. I certainly won't go to sunny rocky overhangs without firm hiking shoes and trousers. But in any case, **whatever is meant to happen, will happen, regardless of whether I want it or not.**

There is a mayhem in the house on the tenth day. A drain is blocked. **Helplessly, I observe those close to me** running up and down the stairs, trying to sort out the situation. This, on top of everything else! **I can do nothing.** Yet, I am completely calm, quite detached from what is happening, which surprises me. This extraordinary peace is something new for me, as I am always in the very centre of action. Aha, again **a test of detachment.**

Late at night, the **cold fever** appears again, interchanging with **a high temperature.** But during **the second week** I perceive that **the flow of life energy has slightly increased.** The healing process was assigned to my physical body and to its energy supplies only during the first week, and there was no snake-like flow that usually runs through me. **But on the eleventh day, I consciously let light run through my foot. I sneeze while doing this, my heart flutters, heat washes over my body.** But I don't force anything, I don't invoke any additional energy flow to run through my body.

In the second week, I am already working – lying on the bathroom floor, even though it is difficult at first and very tiring, and, on top of that, my sight is not so good. **Emotional unrest and panic**, which are reportedly characteristic for a snake bite, as I found out from the internet, **didn't** touch me **at all**. Rather the opposite. I knew with certainty that **all of this had had to happen, because this 'serpent initiation' had its own purpose and meaning.** Not only **to share this story with people,** but also **to switch off my mind for a little while.** If it hadn't, I could have burned out. A red light was already on. And this was also going **to open new windows into the realms of the soul.**

But primarily, **a transition into the new** unfolds. **I feel this** new **more and more. It is ever closer. I look forward to everything that is coming,** especially concert tours and autumn workshops at home and abroad. **I feel harvest coming.** Agony, lack of time, and my proness to overwork will end. Well, **what doesn't kill you, makes you stronger,** says a Slovene folk saying. But **why do we know so little about snakes,** especially about the problems and pain of snake bites? They only scared us at school, we learned nothing more.

I make several attempts to stand on my feet during the day, but I cannot manage it for more than a minute. Yet, **I am able to perform therapies on others,** despite the painful healing process, mainly on the students of my school, on those for who I reckoned needed support in order not to lose strength. So the **cosmic serpent** of life energy can **run through** me undisturbed and **with all its power – but only for others,** not yet for me. Nevertheless, **this near-death serpent initiation unfolds through facing up to the past and present, opening me towards the future. It centres me at the very essence of life.** I felt that in it, I can be **absent,** but also **ever more present** at the same time. **Human nature is indeed miraculous.**

During the entire week, **I keep asking myself why snakes exist at all. And why were they treated with such great awe and respect in antiquity, and even in the recent past.** I come to understand the following. Their venom is so **powerful** (depending on the snake) that they merit respect and careful **handling. They can quickly bring humans to the verge of death, even to death itself** (tropical snakes can do this in a couple of seconds). Even European snakes can, for example, take a sick or weak human being over the threshold. When having been bitten by a snake and near death, humans can instantly experience **all dimensions of existence, primarily the cycle of life and death.** A snake is also a distinct **judge and teacher, which always brings its lessons (bites) unexpectedly.** Snake bites give us extraordinary **pain therapy,** a therapy which makes us aware and which **nourishes our patience.** Overcoming the venom is **a test of our personal, physical and energy power.** A snake bite will foster **invigoration and rejuvenation;** it is also possible to **strengthen your psychophysical power and increase energy flow with it.** With correct amount, of course.

At the end of the second week of my initiation, I catch a telepathic thought: "Well, now you have **the wisdom of an almost fifty-six year old woman in the body of a thirty-year old woman.**" In the processes of dissolving snake venom, **near death, humans revisit the values of their life,** and especially their own **patience.** With a snake bite, humans enter **a powerful shamanic initiation of pain and patient surrender** – surrender to both **the snake-like life energy**, and to their physical power and mind. We can perceive **realms beyond the material world, timelessness, and the values of time.** We face the past, present, and future.

During this time, after the course for the Veduna touch therapists, **I even checked the abilities of my students** on top of that. I checked **their therapeutic and spiritual abilities and knowledge.** It was interesting. Nearly everyone was caught in one of their incomplete immaturities, in their stuckness, clumsiness, fears, patterns, escape, etc. **But shamans, wise human beings, keep carving themselves ceaselessly.** It's a long road to the goal.

But the trials were not over yet. **On the twelfth day,** the sacred number of fulfilment, I feel a strong wish to see my garden again. I put my arm around my son's neck, so that he can drag me through the door. And then bang! The muscle beneath my right breast gets torn. Like I didn't have enough pain already! I had torn it a month before, lifting something too heavy. It had barely healed, and now it was torn again. Pain in this muscle was now stronger than the burning muscles of my foot. But I soon received **a new lesson.** **This torn muscle beneath my breast began to ache strongly** whenever I tried **to step on my injured foot.** And when the muscles of my right foot ached, **the muscles of my left foot warned me about it, like in a mirror. I felt the connectedness of all body muscles.** The clair-perception of the energy paths in the body had opened up when I began to work with my crystal bowl some years before. Now, **the feeling of the muscle connections and nervous system was revealed** to me. These paths were perceptible – like **a cobweb.**

On the thirteenth day (thirteen is the Mayan sacred number) **I move from the bathroom to our living room** with kitchen. It was like coming back to civilisation. It was rather odd, much more lively and full. **Beneficent silence was no longer present.** I try to **walk alone** in the kitchen that day, I try to move out to the Sun, to our garden bench. I go to the toilet alone, but my foot still **swells** quickly. After fourteen days, a more familiar energy finally starts flowing through me again. The flow I know when I am not performing cosmic surgery. It is far stronger during the surgery. I move to **my paradise – onto a lounger in the garden.** I missed so much being in the green! And from then on, I keep editing my unfinished texts and books in the garden all day long.

In the third week, **I edit a fairy tale, a spiritual story entitled *Journey to the Summit of the Sacred Mountain.*** It is beautiful and I am even thrilled about it myself. The fairy tale I had finished now **shook me**. I kept thinking about it over the following days. It lifted me and **gave me the will to finish** one more story, which was waiting in the folder, a story titled *A Warrior Story of the Black-White Jaguar*. This one speaks about Mayan warriors and their schooling, about the spiritual **teaching of a priest-shaman who is teaching the youth about the wisdom of life.** Then I begin three more stories with a spiritual content and I also **finish this book**. My creativity is boundless. I only wish my body would be able to carry out, what my mind wants.

On the eighteenth day, I am already watering the garden, cutting back withered leaves and flowers. My foot becomes really tired, but the feat is obvious. In the evening, **my ear starts aching** terribly. And I feel a tightening in my heart. I am tired. I perceive that **pains in my ear and heart grow stronger whenever my body is overburdened. I cannot sleep during the night. I only doze.**

I am very tired **on the nineteenth day, my heart quivers. I sleep through the morning**, which is very unusual for me. But after this rest, **a more powerful flow of life energy triggers** itself. I am happy about that. Finally, I come to think. But my foot is still changing colour, like a chameleon. **It stiffens, swells and is painful, when I walk too much, and I can feel the entire muscle connection, from heels to heart. My veins are burning.**

I lost a full week of working days, but my **mind had had a rest. No, I gained** those days. That is why, after I had finished the fairytales, I could start editing the texts for the book. **All my time was available for creativity alone.** This is perhaps how it had to be. Others had to do the household chores and all the necessary things. **The pain grew less by the week, but it went very slowly.** I had to accept this slowliness. **The peace of my soul was ever deeper, almost perfect. In meditation, thoughts disappeared instantly. I reached a shamanic trance faster than ever before,** as if a heavy anchor was pulling me into the depths. During the third week, I could function almost normally. Only the foot was still painful, especially to the touch. And the pain was disappearing slowly. The only thing left now was to fully recover.

On the morning on the 27th August my foot was suddenly surprisingly good. A true quantum leap happened, even though I had not put compresses on it during the night, because I had fallen asleep. My foot tended to swell up greatly during the previous days, if compresses were not applied to it. But all of a sudden, they were no longer needed as often, and I could walk much more easily and more. Yes, of course, **my holiday sound surgery in August is scheduled** for today. **I usually feel its effects hours, even days, before.** I didn't want to burden my foot too much, so **I performed the surgery at a distance.** I connected with all the participants and the necessary energy began to flow. As soon as I started

I was immediately washed by **an indescribable joy. I was so happy to take this surgery.** I normally don't perform it during summer months. I had scheduled only one, so that the break wouldn't be too long for people. During the surgery, **my heart chakra** began to **expand immensely. A powerful and unusual sound switched on,** a sound **much different** from that which flows through me when I heal people. **Sound effects** usually support the energy surgery even when I am not physically present. **I coughed,** because my breathing paths were being cleansed; my physical heart ached but only for a short moment, and my heart chakra kept expanding and expanding.

I felt a strong stinging in my foot several times during the surgery – **sharp pain** cut into my flesh for a moment, then it **disappeared** instantly. **My foot began to radiate right up to my hip.** I fell into **a total coma for a couple of minutes** during the surgery, into **a shamanic trance without awareness.** But I had never sweated during those four weeks. Not even during the surgery.

I had the feeling that **the energy running through me simply shot through my body.** Not surprising, as I was performing surgery on thirty eight people simultaneously. **Heat** washed over me and there was a strong tightening in my chest. My **foot was instantly at least half better** during this surgery with sound and the spiral (snake-like) cosmic energy. **Compresses were redundant. I threw them off the foot. My foot was not painful at all during the surgery!** I simply couldn't believe it. I checked its state with a touch. I could feel pain deep in my muscles only if I pressed strongly on some of the places. **Humans do not feel pain in a trance. This cosmic surgery is so miraculous! I needed it too.** But I first had to go through the usual recovery process, without surgery, and had to experience the effects of snake venom without any support. It was only then that I sensed and **grasped the surgery's exceptional power and effectiveness. I need to perform it more often,** I thought. I found out that it brings such great benefits. Yes – echoed my telepathic voice. But my thought said: oh, better not, it is too difficult. It brought me **the worst pain ever.** But **with this initiation, something changed in my cosmic and spiritual surgery.** Its power immensely, **immensely increased** after the snake initiation. This was also confirmed by people who experienced the surgery on that day, after my process with the snake venom. **My body was now able to endure a far more powerful and more burning energy flow of the cosmic serpent.** Only a slight touch – and pain disappeared. I **instantly eliminated the neck pain** of my colleague Mojka who was patiently transferring all my texts into computer format. Others experienced **fundamental shifts in their consciousness** and in their reactions to situations in their lives. So this was it! Not only do I not need food, but **I hardly need any sleep** either! **Is this a new addition to the gifts of cosmic consciousness? A new gift** of my connection to the Cosmos and

Earth, to the cosmic serpent? What did Rumi say? **A man of God** is not hungry, he does not drink, and he does not sleep. So **since then, I am primarily and only a sound-energy surgeon on Thursdays.** I am not allowed to do anything else. My thanks to **the physical and cosmic serpent**! There is not much left to my complete physical recovery.

On **28th August**, after four weeks (4 × 7) **the initiation ended within all its spiritual breadth. So the test of my trust and devotion was complete.** The swelling almost totally disappeared. And my ankle was again visible. **My heart calmed down**, the tightening eased. **My spine became very flexible, as if I had been doing yoga for a couple of hours.** But I hadn't. My spine had been painful many times during the previous weeks, because I had been constantly in a semi-seated position. But wait, this just seems **to be the end, but it isn't.** To top it all, **my false tooth fell out on the twenty-eighth day.** I had lost my real tooth as a teenager, when I jumped into a swimming pool head first and rose up too late. This tooth was just temporarily attached. Now I can even **play with shaping sound in my mouth. It is different without a tooth.** When repairing the crown a year before, the dentist had used chemicals, which shattered me completely. Every chemical is a heavy poison for me. Will a dental intervention be **detrimental** to me again? **Or will I gain strength and toughen myself through the snake venom?** It turned out that the latter was the case.

Well, my snake initiation **suddenly ended** with a surgery, after a one month break. It ended as unexpectedly as it came. I thought I would need at least a week or more to recover completely. **Everything was** obviously **guided somehow, outside the usual. My thanks to the divine Intelligence! My body is only now adapting to this new snake-like flow.** When I work and when **I am within this snake-like flow, there is no pain whatsoever,** and no swelling either.

On Wednesday, 29th August, **I drive the car again, and I sleep in my own bed** upstairs **for the first time in a month,** because stairs are no longer strenuous. Without compresses. All through the night. Previously, I had to change compresses every three hours at the very least. In the morning, I feel that I don't need compresses anymore. How strange and even illogical. Well, this is what the mind thinks. There is no swelling. **This change came so suddenly. Well, it came after the surgery.** After riding on the waves of cosmic energy again. A slight swelling appears only when the body is too tired. But **such initiations with snake venom, with the snake drug, are perhaps not for everyone,** just like **mescalito or peyote**, claim Native Americans.

The experience was over, **three books were completed, one half finished. Sound surgery has been transformed and is more powerful, my shamanic trance is deeper, my desire to perform surgery is stronger. I should treat** myself to it more often! And on top of that, I experienced a much needed detachment, and I am now firmly determined to cancel everything that is (no longer?) in tune with me. **A new and different service to life begins.** Six weeks have passed and I am back on my feet for the entire day, despite a slight swelling. I have to facilitate an intense, strenuous, but wonderful **four-day** renewal **course with sound and surgery near the Kolpa River in the Bela Krajina Region. I am teaching for three hours in a row and, without a break,** I dance with participants the sacred and folk dances of different nations. I don't feel any pain while dancing, only calf muscles on my healthy left foot are tired the following day.

After the rain comes the Sun. **We cannot appreciate light without darkness. It is in pain that we come to know joy, and it is near death that we get to know the values of life.** This is how everyone **carves out their shamanic healing abilities.**

After I had finished this chapter about my shamanic initiation with snake venom, **the energy flow of the cosmic serpent doubled. New insights about the future** began to flow. They flowed for two days without stopping. So, it is true that **Somebody (the Intelligence of life) has plans with me. Why?** This was the answer: first, so that **you could finish this book this year** (in 2012, I couldn't have done it alongside all the other everyday tasks); then because you had **to write about this experience** – know that **the Hopi, ancient Mayans,** and shamans from other cultures **strengthened their abilities with snake venom.** And you had to experience the snake bite in order **to increase your energy and cosmic surgery abilities.**[286] All of this happened, because **a new time lies ahead of us and there will be more and more people stepping onto the path of spirit and spiritual healing. The number of people you will need to balance with your guided cosmic surgery will triple in the following year.** You will be a surgeon **four days** a week and a writer and scientist for **three days** a week.

So let it be! Well, I don't have a choice. Things happen, because they need to happen and because they support my service.

My God, **was I really bitten only by a venomous and visible snake?**

Seven weeks later, I fell and **broke a rib** at the end of the therapeutic course on the Murter Island, where I was with my students from Slovenia and Croatia. I could move not a millimetre during the first week, it was too painful. **I stood up on the tenth day** and on the eleventh day, I went for a walk. On the eighteenth day, I was again doing sound surgery. The recovery of ribs normally lasts from five to eight weeks. The two difficult and painful trials, my two **shamanic initiations,**

---
286 More about them can be found in the fifth book in the *Cosmic Telepathy* series.

strongly shifted the awareness of people who came to my **Slavic-Pythagorean school for the expansion of consciousness and (self-)healing with sound.** They primarily **gained trust in the power of cosmic life energy, in the power of the serpent, as the Mayans would say. They gained trust in human capabilities. My pain laid bare and moved their suppressed pain.** They cried like children, releasing through tears their own painful emotions, which they had pushed, who knows when, into the darkness of the unconscious. **They also got to know the power of thought.**

This is how the self-sacrifice of priests and shaman-teachers unfolded and is still unfolding.

Mayan medicine

The healers and the white and black magicians of Chiapas

I need help, my soul and body ache!
I therefore pray to the Deities and to the beneficent undulation
that they reveal to me what is concealed and entangled,
what is unloving inside of me; that they reveal **the silent thought
about my resistance to the advice of the soul,**
which was sent out into the Sky who knows when.[287]

Ixchel – the Moon Goddess of fertility with a snake-like headdress.

The heat was unbearable during my visit to the northern and central Yucatan. I found it hard to bear and I looked for shady corners everywhere. That is why it felt so good when, after 24 hour bus ride, we reached the highlands of **Chiapas and San Cristobal de las Casas.** Here, the temperature was at least 10 degrees lower and the weather was much more rainy and grim. However, I was no longer able to feel **open human nature, Mayan warm-heartedness and geniality,** which I had encountered in the northern parts of Yucatan. This was a totally different, much cooler, mountainous and humid world. The Native Americans usually just watched passersby from beneath their eyebrows while always looking at the ground. They were obviously suffused with **a feeling of great inferiority.** Like shadows, they passed the white people, incidental newcomers, descendants of white conquistadors. Life was actually much harder here and that seemed to get in the way of opening up to heartfulness.

It really hurt me to watch the tourists from all over the world, coming **into this Mecca of the ancient Native American tradition with its rich costumes and attires, numerous traditional customs and habits,** and gloating over this colourful differentness. For them, a trip to the local Native American tribes was merely an excursion to a colourful world of the folklore of a nostalgic past. Having lost it long ago, white people wanted to see and feel it on the other side of the world. Some seemed to me to be completely lacking in compassion or polite kindness. It was

....
287 Mirit, November 2012.

really painful to watch these **two worlds, which were simply unable to meet, let alone come together into a supporting whole. There was almost no connection between the Native American and white worlds!**

In Chiapas, while I was looking for local shamans and healers, who are called *curanderos* or *ilols*, I touched upon a world which was very alien to me; a world of **blatantly and publicly performed black magic rituals**, following the recipes of local indigenous people who, **out of despair, consumed alcohol** or intoxicated themselves in other ways **since childhood, in order to forget themselves and their misery.** The renowned **church in Chamula** offered an attractive, yet **distorted image of their ancient and glorious tradition,** which was by now merely an image of misery and sadness, **a pale shadow of a once highly developed and fully aware Mayan spiritual practice.** Don Juan de la Cruz was right. Here, it would be highly unlikely for me to find people with high-frequency cosmic and earthly telepathic abilities.

Members of **the variegated community of Native American tribes from the mountainous regions** flocked to the Chamula church every day, bringing offerings with them, mostly **white or black chickens** tucked under their arms. A white chicken supposedly indicated that a person would perform **a white magic ritual** in the church – at a sacred site, whereas a black chicken meant that **a person, out of his angry, envious or sad mind, would** invoke or conjure upon somebody a malicious deed **in a black magic ritual** (at a sacred site!), and thus **create a new evil – a vicious circle of misery and death.** During these rituals, the Chamula 'magicians,' among whom were boys barely ten years old, intoxicated themselves considerably and staggered all the time. The end of a ritual was marked by breaking the neck of the chicken. Phew! **When did the victory of the past spiritual grandeur turn into a defeat of the spirit?**

Here, the *lack'ech* – we are all one – was so far away! I had arranged a meeting in the surrounding hills with a local healer, at which I was to witness a healing ritual, but I cancelled the meeting. I simply **could not accept these rituals, which had been distorted long ago, and these habits, which had turned to evil,** at the end of which the neck of a chicken was broken and evil was strewn around without a second thought. I was not at all tempted to enter this world. I didn't need to experience this. It was enough that I knew it existed. Even that was far too much!

Don Juan de la Cruz was right. **I would probably not find what I was seeking (the high-frequency levels of consciousness), especially not there, because what I was seeking had no longer been here for a long time. But it still (!) exists in the parallel (non-material) dimensions beyond time and space, in the eternal imprints of the high-dimensional reality and consciousness of the sages, who are clearly no longer here or are living unnoticed somewhere there, hidden from** the world. At the summit of the spiritual pyramid, it is still possible to follow the past grandeur of the forgotten wisdom. Today only a handful of people have preserved this ancient light of timeless consciousness. And like Pancho, they have probably withdrawn from this off-key world, created by white people, by their nonsensical dogmas and spiritually empty deeds.

While in Chiapas, the memories of the northern Yucatan healers fortunately still warmed my heart, giving me **hope that soon something might change in these gloomy places and in the world in general. It needs to change. Or we will all become the living dead.** But surely nothing valuable can happen through the ostentation, contempt, and **insensitivity of white people. It only seems to visitors to these places that time has turned back, or that time has stopped there,** that they have arrived to a distant past. It is primarily **a brutal reality that resides there, far away from the ancient knowledge. To uninvited people,** this grey everyday **does not speak about the grandeur of past times. Perhaps it has been so for several centuries** – since the arrival of the white people in these places. The first researchers of the Mayan culture, archaeologists and Christian missionaries were already reporting about the great poverty among Mayan descendants. **Who pushed them into such great penury and apathy, and why? Who was responsible** for this dreadful misery? Those who refused to understand at least a little of their differentness and whose knowledge did not allow them to understand their mysterious – but today physically provable – deeds, rituals, healing practices, etc.

Herbal medicine is very dear to me. I have inherited an interest in it and its gifts **from my grandmother.** So, **in Chiapas,** I visited **a museum dedicated to the medicine** of the indigenous healers of the **Tzotzil and Tzeltal Mayans,** who belong to **the Olmecs.** The centre brings together local healers. Daily, its members treat people who come to them for help. The organisation **in San Cristobal de las Casas (Chiapas) is a non-governmental organisation of herbalists, healers,** and healers who set bones, midwives, healers who **heal with prayer (sound!) and pulse readers.** The museum was founded by **Organización de Médicos Indígenas del Estado Chiapas (OMIECH).** They hold regular training programmes on health and medicine herbs and they educate women on pregnancy and labour. **The museum of Mayan indigenous medicine** was established by this organisation, which was founded in **1997.** The following chapter is based on the information I received from local **healers,** in the above-mentioned museum and from Yucatan shaman-therapists. **I try to explain the seemingly unusual and perhaps even strange procedures from a spiritual perspective and through esoteric teachings, because contemporary Mayan medicine is based primarily on the invisible world of energies.**

In **San Cristobal de las Casas (Chiapas)**, I had the opportunity to experience a healing session performed by **a healer** who used to come to **the medicine museum, to the Museo de medicina Maya**, several times a week. He was appointed by the **Organización de Médicos Indígenas del Estado Chiapas (OMIECH)**, an organisation of indigenous therapists who speak the **tzotzil and tzaltal indigenous (Mayan) languages.** The museum had opened recently and they do their best to present the values of Mayan medicine. There, healers with ancient knowledge heal those who want their help. The healer I met **recognised bodily and physical imbalances in people in a similar way to Candido.** But prior to the session, he made invocations in a loud voice, calling upon **'the Forces of the Sky,'** mostly by connecting to the energy fields of Christian saints.

When I visited the above-mentioned small **medicine museum, I sensed calm and benevolent vibration waves in the first room,** as soon as I entered it. There, **cosmic-telepathic energy healing sessions** were performed **by local healers *ilols*** on a daily basis. Which meant that there were still revered people there! Luckily enough.

Three figures kneel in the first museum room, showing a healing session – an *ilol* healer, a sick child, and a mother. All three are dressed in **Chamulan attire.** On the wall, there are **pictures of four important saints: St. Peter, St. Lawrence, St. John, and St. Andrew.** This is to satisfy Christian doctrine, even though they heal using the old method, by connecting **people, the Earth, and the cosmic forces of life or energies.**

The life-size **human figures** dressed in indigenous attire, which were displayed in the first room, looked alive. I flinched, for at first I had the strong feeling that I was looking at a living family. They were obviously **greatly suffused with channelled life energy. They were imbued with the magic of something unspoken and untouchable, yet important for life.** This magical atmosphere could be felt mostly in this first room, to which different indigenous healers from the surrounding hills came every week to treat people who wanted to get rid of their problems by using **natural and spiritual medicine practices.** On the wall, there were paintings of various **Christian saints.** In front of them, there were four figures, dressed in black with colourful accessories, kneeling in prayer. A couple of benches and chairs for visitors were placed next to the walls.

On the day of my visit, a 'duty' healer, named **Don Juan**, was holding a couple of healing sessions, primarily for the locals. **He conducted a ceremonial diagnostic and healing procedure using an egg.** Similar to Candido, he spilled the egg's content into a glass of water and **observed the bubbles and forms. He commented out loud what the forms of the egg white spilled in the water were telling him, how those forms interpreted the laws of resonance, or synergy,** the laws of attunement or dissonance; he explained **what the current life energy of the person in front of him was telling him. The person's energy was mirrored in the material world, in different forms and structures.** My **grandmother** used to do something similar with **coffee grounds.**

Of course, the healer on duty first performed **a ritual in which he connected to all the accessible invisible cosmic-earthly forces and the essences of the enlightened ones and saints, to the cosmic Source of life – to the Heart of Sky,** as well as to the divine essences of all the **souls** who were present. Prior to the session, **he touched each painting on the wall with a bundle of herbs,** which visitors needed to bring. He said a short prayer and asked for help, for a possible important **message and efficient healing.** Every visitor needed to bring both **a bundle of herbs** and **a prescribed number of candles of pre-determined sizes.** Then the ritual could start. And of course **I had to experience it myself.**

I had brought everything that was needed, everything the local healing rituals required, and my friends also bought **eggs, candles, and herbs.** I queued with the others who were waiting. Before each healing session, **candles** had to be placed on the ground **in several lines before being lit. Considering the movement of flames and smoke, which rose from them,** the healer then **checked and recognised a person's physical and psychological condition, the power of his consciousness, emotions, mind and body. He 'read' the messages of the moment and discovered people's physical and psychological condition** on the basis of these insights into balance and imbalance.

All of this is possible when the medium is a pure channel, a telepath. And all of the aids – from eggs to candles – are merely visible aids, deflecting the attention of participants, so that they would not interfere through their thoughts and emotions with the channelling and energy flow of the healer. At its core, attention is in fact focused energy undulation. When people watch what is happening, their disturbing thoughts are diverted elsewhere, to the smoke and flames of the candles. **This makes the presence of their thoughts less disturbing;** it results in less influence on the consciousness and mind of the healer; but it nevertheless **impacts the observed objects – the candles and the movement of the smoke.** The essences of the fire 'respond' to them. **Sages understand this language of forms, sizes, and directions.**

The Vedic sages rshis say that **the observer, the observed object, and the act of observing are not separate; they are invariably connected, influencing one another.** No element of this triunity stands alone for itself. There is always an interaction between them. **Every object is suffused with the energy of both the observer and the observation, and the act of observation influences in turn the observer.** We can also put it in a different way: **the energy of the observer and** the energy of observation influence the energy waves of the object, while the object in turn affects the process of observation and the observer himself. And this chain of connection and inter-dependence lies at the heart of the described ceremony and healing. Nothing is co-incidental.

Observation influences the movement of the flame and the billowing of the smoke in the room, which is imbued with the energy of observation and the energy of the participants' attention. **The act of observation and the observed object merge into a whole; they reflect the current moment within this process and also impact the observer,** who triggers energy undulation; this is how he can see and hear what the invisible waves are telling him. **But one needs to learn how to read this mysterious language of the moment and its mirroring energy images in the material world.**

Other Native American tribes and the sages of other cultures on our planet[288] also 'read' **from current forms, which reflect the laws of the frequency waves of the harmonious or disharmonious.** This method of reading the soul's images and events is still in use in India, China, Tibet, Indonesia, Siberia and the Balkans. On **the 6th of January, Dalmatians** (from the Croatian islands) **light candles** and place them in a pot containing **young grain** (the symbol of a new year and **new fecund forces**). In the evening, they then watch in which direction the smoke drifts. They say that **in the new year, you have to follow the direction of the billowing smoke.** The direction of the smoke is your path and your life should unfold in this direction.

Two worlds connect in the forms of flames, fire, smoke and water: the world of spirit (thoughts, emotions and the frequency vibrations of etheric bodies, which envelope the human physical body) **and the material-physical world of forms. A shape-giving interaction emerges between them. The high-frequency waves of emotions, thoughts, and human consciousness can 'condense' in the tangible and visible material world, or at least they influence it. Their vibration is also mirrored in the material world of physical elements and objects. We are what we think.** This is the only magic.

Let me explain a bit more: **a bright thought or emotion,** which reverberates out into the room **with a high-frequency wave,** will give birth to a bright smile on a person's face and **a vertical rising flame or smoke.** Anger, jealousy, dark thoughts, and sorrow will bring about just the opposite. **The frequency (invisible, inaudible) waves of darkness, rigidity, disease, unhappiness, and evil push towards the ground.** Smoke has no wings there. Unfortunately, the ordinary levels or tones, of existence press to the ground. **A bright and loving mental vibration will always rise up, into the worlds with a similar 'high frequency,' into the worlds which are lighter (more etheric) than the three-dimensional solid world.**

....
288 More about this can be read in other books in the *Cosmic Telepathy* series.

With all their bodies (physical, emotional, mental, spiritual), humans are constant creators of a multitude of energy waves, inaudible sounds, or energy imprints and forms within time, space, even within their own body and within timelessness, or akasha. When Don Juan from San Cristobal de las Casas lifted the glass containing my egg white to the sunlight and looked at it, he said: "You see how many bubbles are there on the surface?"

Then he added: "You know, **many people envy you.** As many bubbles you see, that is how many people are envious and **jealous** of your success in your surroundings. But other forms and the form of the egg yolk show that **no one can harm you.**"

Interesting indeed! Well, I do know that, I agreed silently. Throughout my life, I have fought envious people in my surroundings, or those who do not understand my thoughts and what I am doing, which is why they throw spanners in my works. But somehow I always manage to walk on, along the destined path of my fate. When I heard Don Juan's interpretation, I flinched for a brief moment, but was then relieved. **Spiritual growth and power are the best protection! Then no one can do you any harm!**

He clearly masters the magic of recognition, though only with water bubbles. What about me? Is everything that is happening (to me), somehow **written inside me,** do I **carry** this destiny and burden **with me**? This is obviously how it has to be. **The subtle etheric world does not lie, but it is however flexible, changeable even with imperceptible vibrational influences.**

In a loud voice, the healer Don Juan then started connecting to the saints on the wall and praying ever more loudly. He was **channelling a supportive energy vibration,** but this vibration in no way reached the powers, dimensions, or efficiency which Pancho and Don Juan de la Cruz were able to invoke during their healing rituals. But his **work** was nevertheless **beneficent and effective.**

Herbalists, healers, healing methods, and the symbolism of colours, candles, and smoke

Until recently, the people of **Yucatan** believed that disease, **suffering, and even death** would come on them as a result of **wrongdoing and sin, if they broke the laws of life.** The Mayans believed in **the power of confession,** which is why they always, when in danger of death due to a disease or other things, **had to confess their sins and mistakes.** They had the support of their relatives and friends, who even referred them to a priest. The sinner could also **make a confession to his mother or father, husband to wife, wife to husband.** Sins were theft, homicide, false testimony and other things.[289] They believed **confession set them free. And they were right. Destructive emotions and thoughts need to be eliminated as soon as possible.**

> **A warrior acknowledges his pain but he doesn't indulge in it.** The mood of **the warrior who enters into the unknown** is not one of sadness; on the contrary, **he's joyful** /.../, fully aware of his efficiency. A warrior's joyfulness comes from having **accepted his fate** (people are usually afraid of the unknown).[290]

The friar goes on to explain that men supposedly **confessed their infidelity and adultery,** except that committed with their female slaves, since they held it was a man's right to make use of his possessions as he wished. **But they did not confess sins of intention,** wrote de Landa. Who knows, maybe even de Landa did not completely understand their behaviour or did not understand it in the same way as the Mayans.

Abstinence was a distinct penance: they were **not allowed to use salt and chilli pepper in their food.** These spices were obviously of great importance to them. **Often they abstained from their wives before feasts,** writes the friar. Those who had been widowed did not marry for a year, having no relations with a man or a woman during this time.

They deeply believed that some diseases stemmed from the breaking of those laws. The Mayans knew that **disharmony causes psychological conflict, which in turn causes disease** and other problems. They were familiar with **cause and consequence. If only contemporary people would recognise it!** There would be far fewer conflicts and life would be simpler, with less of a heartless ego. During some of their ceremonies, the Mayans **neither ate meat nor had relations with their wives.** De Landa praised them for totally devoting themselves to the duties related to the ceremonies.

Medicinal knowledge passed down through generations is still of great importance to the tribes and language groups **Tzotziles and Tzeltales in Chipas.** It is the same with other indigenous peoples on other continents. Remember the healing ceremonies of Pancho, Don Juan de la Cruz and Candido. A series of **elements of ancient symbolism and mythology** can still be found in Native American healing methods, which, as opposed to the official medicine, are **based primarily on energy balancing.** For them, **earth and rain still hold a sacred meaning** and they are still closely **connected to the four elements.** In some

....
289 Diego de Landa, *An Account of the Things of Yucatán*, Mexico, Monclem Ediciones, p. 79.
290 Carlos Castaneda, *The Wheel of Time*, London, Allen Lane, The Penguin Press (1998), p. 148. The note in brackets is mine.

communities, for example **Zinacantan and Chenolho,** earth is even more important than rain, as it represents **the Goddess of universal life.** In other communities, like **Oxchuc,** the rain God has been symbolised by a **cross for thousands of years** – not the Christian cross, but the **prehistoric** cross, which is also symbolised by **the sacred tree** ceiba, out of which life stems.

For the Mayans in Chiapas, the earth is also the mother of universal life, **the Goddess of mountains and cosmic forces: fire, wind and rain, as well as the Goddess of the ecliptic and earthquakes.** Yes, you have read it right, the ecliptic – the apparent **path of the Sun** (this connection is interesting). This path is still of great importance to the Mayans. They believe that **diseases and famine** reflect **the anger of those forces.** Expressed in the symbolism of words. What is more, diseases and everything negative derive from **the work of the four fundamental directions of the cross,** which are associated **with colours: red** in the East, **black** in the West, **yellow** in the South, and **white** in the North. The directions and their colours are obviously the same in both Mayan country and among the Native Americans of Arizona in North America.[291]

Contemporary Mayans from Chiapas have **five different techniques or branches of folk medicine and five main categories of healers:** *ilols* are general healers and pulse readers, *k'oponej witz* are healers who, from mountain tops, heal with prayer, midwives are called *jve't'ome,* bone healers *tzac'bak* and herbalists *ac'vomol*. Healers are also called *j'ololetik*.

Similar to ayurvedic doctors, Mayan descendants have **a method for reading diseases from the pulsing of blood in the veins.** This is clearly a very old and very efficient diagnostic tool, which painlessly and successfully **recognises problems and imbalances in the human body.** I had an opportunity to test this great knowledge both among Indian ayurvedic doctors and the Mayans. Both **place three fingers on the vein** in order to recognise the cause of a disease from the barely perceptible flow of blood and to find out whether imbalance was caused by **evil spirits, i. e. fears,** destructive emotions, like envy and anger, or whether some other natural forces had provoked it. When healing, they rely on the elements of nature – on **the serpent-like flow of life energy. They say that they can penetrate the invisible world and face it (repair disharmony) in order to save the patient's soul,** which can be lost or imprisoned in this world (of blocked energy). They can even perceive small differences within the flow of blood. They claim that **everything can be made known through the blood.** They say that they can **even hear the voice of the blood, which tells them what had caused a disease. Blood is the essence of life; it is imbued with the energies of the soul.**

....
291 Read more on this topic in the first book in the *Cosmic Telepathy* series.

The Mayans in Chiapas also have a special form of healing, which is **performed only high up in the mountains – in the pure energy of the mountains,** where spiritual work is most powerful. There, they pray at **chosen sacred sites.** The mountain prayer is used especially when imbalance, or **crisis,** occurs in a community, it can be an economic, cultural, even political crisis. Or perhaps the harvest is bad. Up in the mountains, **they pray for rain** to nourish the fields or they **heal relationships and conflicts** by means of prayer (thought). They believe that by doing this, they **call on good spirits (invigorating energy waves),** which will bring balance to the community. At the summit of the sacred mountain, **they also pray to the spirits of the Earth, to the four cardinal points.**

A healer said that **he heard a spirit** (the thought of his conscience) **inside him,** telling him that he would not be given food unless he prayed for a good harvest. When people **pray and give thanks, they can attain anything (with their benevolent thoughts, they create good energy conditions for life, and a full field for the realisation of their wishes and goals).**

Prayers at sacred sites high up in the mountains are actually intercessions for peace and prosperity. They say that when a prayer is performed, **the spirit will give you what you want** (the person praying **creates conditions for the realisation** of their wishes). **But if you do not pray, if you do not clearly express your wishes and intentions,** there will be problems and disease everywhere, because there is **no energy support for your wishes.**

Wise women, **midwives** from Chiapas, are respected and their **knowledge has been passed down through generations,** often within the family. They are usually **excellent herbalists.** They advise women during pregnancy, during labour and about caring for their baby. They know how to eliminate possible problems and how to keep mother and children healthy. They are also masters in **balancing menstrual cleansings, they heal the urinary system and pathways,** problems during pregnancy, painful menstruation and **infertility,** and they can even treat a lack of mother's milk.

Bone healers from Chiapas are distinct specialists, who eliminate **bone pain and bone deformities; they also give massages.** It is interesting to note that they use **blowing and whistling – they add them to their prayer,** to their healings with the four basic elements. They are convinced that **blowing blows away bad spirits (read: energies), while whistling frightens them away (sound penetrates the auric field and shatters energy blocks).** Bone doctors also use **herbs, incense, and candles.** They cure bone diseases and fractures. **They know where to touch in order to recognise problems** and diseases and heal the patient with whistles, herbs, and prayer.

Herbalists certainly have a special and very important role in Mayan medicine in Chiapas. They are familiar with practically all local medicinal herbs, they know their effects, their **use and symbolism. Before picking a herb, they perform a ritual in which permission to pick it is asked of the plant.** They have to know very well **at which time medicinal herbs are the best,** when their **juices are most effective:** some **at sunrise,** others **at sunset.** At home, before setting off to the mountains to find the herbs they need, they say **a prayer to find the plants they are looking for** (first they **realign** themselves with their intent and the plants). They always ask **the plants for forgiveness for being picked.** And of course, they also need to **know which parts of the plants can be used for healing** – the entire plant or only parts of it, leaves, flowers or roots – and they have to know **what they are healing.** They need to know **how to dry the plants so that they do not lose their powers, how to prepare them, how and where to store the plants to preserve their active ingredients.** They use different grasses, flowers, and tree parts. It is like this all over the world.

But there is one feature unique to Mayan herbalism. Herbalists need to know whether plants have to be **prepared cold or warm, strong or weak, for men, for women or for children.** They need to know whether herbal substances need to work **quickly and strongly or whether they have to cure slowly and over a longer period of time.** Some plants have to be **boiled,** some **crushed,** some are **only heated** and others are **used fresh,** for example for cleansing. Besides plants that heal, every herbalist also needs to know **poisonous plants.** Similar to ayurvedic doctors, Mayan herbalists ac'vomol **have to store all of this knowledge of numerous plants in their memory.**

The majority of these healers are of course **endowed with a natural, telepathic gift of recognition.** They say **this is the gift of nature, or the Gods; it is the force of nature, the power of the Gods** which bestow healing abilities upon people. It is said that **the ability to heal is received in dreams, after** which some are able to **see,** some receive **the power to work with sound and energy (with whistles, for example),** while others are given **the ability to heal with life energy (of the cosmic serpent).**

Mayan healers say that **at night, the soul learns everything it needs** (at night and in dreams, the soul is **more receptive for becoming aware and for a telepathic, subconscious entering into the Silent knowledge of the Universe).** The Mayans believe that everyone has **a talent,** which then leads them to healing, singing, dancing, speaking, even dreaming, etc. Some are given their gift of healing as a family heirloom, while others **receive** these gifts **by themselves** from the divine Source.

Extremely important is **the room** in which a healer heals, cleanses, prays, burns candles and incense, and turns to the Gods and saints on the altar (this is so Chiapas). **Churches, sacred sites, mountain tops, sacred springs** and the rooms in which healing sessions take place, are **holy, alive, and constantly working (energy-wise)**; the room is full of energy, especially when healing ceremonies are frequently performed there. Such a place was also the museum's healing chapel, which I visited and checked whether this was truly so. All the healers who treat people there, **clean and cleanse the room** by themselves – both physically and energy-wise. They bring flowers, candles, they burn incense and **blow** across the room; **they bring herbs** and other symbolic objects used for cleansing and as offerings to the Gods and saints. Sometimes people bring food and even alcoholic drinks as offerings. They are convinced that **at these sacred sites, spirits and Gods live together with people (the energies of cosmic, earthly and human forces connect here).**

The following **healing method** is most frequently used in Chiapas. The healer **arranges candles of different colours around the room** and the patient, who kneels or stands, prays together with the healer, so that they can **connect to the energies of the spirits and saints (to the flow of the undistorted life energy).** They often **pray out loud while breathing deeply** (breathing relaxes them so that **the serpent-like flow of life energy can flow through them more easily).** Through prayer, they liberate their breath and their souls. The healer **touches the patient's body** from head to toe **with basil, common rue** (like Pancho and Don Juan de la Cruz) **or pine needles;** sometimes they even use **an egg** (symbolically), if the disease has already spread throughout the body. The egg is a reminder; it denotes **the whole** and it anchors **wholistic healing** into thoughts. Today, healers might even **sprinkle an alcohol drink on their patients.** They do this **from all sides, in order to frighten evil spirits (or bad energies) away,** as well as to expel bad winds and purify the person.

Prior to a healing session, healers **bless the saints and ask them for help.** They usually use **candles.** They say that with them, they **eliminate the injuries of the soul and liberate the patient's spirit.** Fire **cleanses the energy** of the room, preparing it **for more subtle flows.** They **claim that the number of candles is important, as well as their size and colour. The disease** itself determines which **candles** the patient needs to bring. Their number, size, and colour **speak to the healer's mind,** enabling him to **focus on the healing process** more easily.

Candles must **always burn out.** It is still claimed today that **smoke is a food for Gods and saints.** They use **white, golden, yellow, and red candles. White** candles are used **to connect to the God in the Sky. Golden or yellow** ones are used if the disease was caused by **envy or a spell** (evil intentions and thoughts). **Red** candles are also against spells. **The bigger the candles, the greater their cleansing power.** Those who want a long and better life without disease, as well as unity in the family and with other people, have to burn **white candles, for they connect them to the God (Gods) and to mother Earth,** to saints and angels.

For protection against disease, diarrhoea, fever, headache and vomiting, they use **thirteen white, thirteen yellow, thirteen golden and thirteen red candles** (in the symbolism of **the end of the old,** or the expulsion of the disease, and **the start of the new,** healthy.) The golden colour is **the symbol of purity.** If they want to **get rid of fear,** they burn two little white candles and one little golden one. **For good growth of corn** on the field, they usually say **two prayers.** In the first prayer, they ask that they shall **not injure themselves** with tools **during the field work,** while the second prayer is said when the corn is ripe and ready for harvest. In it, they ask that **the harvest shall not be destroyed by wind or heat.** They go **to the centre of the corn field, where they pray to the spirit of the Earth and burn thirteen golden candles. For abundance** – in the field and in life alike. For personal health, they prefer to go to sacred mountains or underground caves. There, they burn thirteen white candles at the four cardinal points.

Candles are reminders: intention is grounded within people when they look at them and reflect on their purpose, on why they came and brought them – the content of their prayer is being focused. The more people concentrate on their purpose or goal, the quicker it is manifested, because the energy of the thought is constantly present. Reminders (candles and other ritual objects) hold thoughts in constant attention.

The white colour symbolises mother Earth, God, and purity. Pink and blue denote not only **the healing of a disease,** but also the wish (and power) that **business thrives** and the wish to get a partner. **Yellow eliminates negativity (destructive thoughts and emotions), envy** and the bad energy of unloving thoughts. **Green** indicates **the elimination of a disease. Purple** usually accompanies other colours. **Red indicates the restoration of life energy. The colours of gold and the rainbow mean luck,** which is why golden and rainbow candles usually accompany white candles. **Tallow (translucent white) colour** indicates **mastery over all the bad energies.** Candle colours show **what people carry inside them, their wishes.** At the same time, **the chosen colours speak to us, unveiling the power of the silent awareness of those wishes and longings that reside in the mind of those partaking in a ceremony or prayer.**

Prayers are wanted always and everywhere. Especially when **a person has lost their soul or become unwell.** Just like corn is food for people, **the smoke** billowing from incense burners and candles is **food for the Gods.** It connects the Earth and humans to the Sky, to cosmic life forces. **The *copal* incense** is still esteemed in rituals and healing sessions. Native Americans also bring **flowers and** young herbs to the altar. **An offered twig represents the one who is praying, while flowers** are, similar to incense, food **for the Gods.**

In Chiapas, **a mixture of wild tobacco and lime is called** *pilico*. Contemporary indigenous people still consider **wild tobacco** to be **a sacred herb.** Pilico is used for **protection against envy and bad winds as well as for personal protection** so that nothing bad will happen, especially when people **travel great distances or at night.** It also helps with **stomach cramps.** The mixture is prepared by mixing together **tobacco, lime and garlic;** the ingredients are mixed well, then **the powder is put into small pots made of dried gourds** and given to people. Sometimes they place it in **small bags which they wear around their necks.** This is how they use it: they **take a pinch** of this mixture **with three fingers** (within the balance of the Holy Trinity – of the earthly, spiritual and cosmic) and place it in their mouths. The mixture is **rolled around in the mouth** and swallowed slowly. The taste of pilico is hot and sharp.

Blowing, the healing prayer, giving birth, midwifery, and animal *naguals*

Blowing into a liquid (or into a type of liquor) brings **satisfaction** to people; **blowing away strengthens them and drives evil spirits away** (i. e. the negative in spirit, thoughts and emotions). Native Americans from Chamula still believe that **liquor expels spirits that have injured people** and made them suffer. This **liquor, or honey brandy** in some places (the like of which Pancho used near Ek Balam), **is offered to the Gods.** Today, patients can also be purified **with soda,** in a similar way to liquor. Liquor, honey brandy or soda water is sprinkled among the candles in order **to eliminate all the evil that is embodied in the patient. Sprinkling is supported with a focused thought, with clear intent; it can have great power** and can **trigger accelerated processes of self-healing (including the placebo effect) and self-conviction,** but we should not mix this with **the true energy healing** which takes place on the etheric levels of **a being and consciousness.** Today, they say that it is simpler to use soda water.

Crosses are still of great importance to the Mayans, but they have a different, not Christian, symbolism. **A wooden cross can represent a Goddess protecting the home, an altar, sacred springs (and the Source) and ritual hills.** If people are far away from home, from their community, **the cross (of connectedness) is for them a protection against the negative.** The Mayans of Chiapas still believe that the cross is a metaphor for **well-being and health maintenance.**

In the museum of **the OMIECH organisation in San Cristobal de las Casas,** I found written information about Mayan medicine, and I also found the following **prayer** which says a lot about how contemporary Mayan descendants understand disease and suffering.

Lord God,
Father Saint Manuel,
Lord Jesus Christ,
I ask a favour of you
I ask you for kindness,
which you share
and invoke for your children
and your ascended ones
hidden in your blessed face /.../
Why do your children, your ascended ones
suffer in their bodies
and souls?
Your children suffer
from vomiting and diarrhoea.
But /.../ why did they fall?
Why did they shatter?
When were they frightened?
In your blessed face, Lord?
But /.../ you will set them free,
you will absolve them
and bring their souls back into those
who want to be your servants,
Master of the blessed Earth, Lord.

When healing, healers in Chiapas can also **sit in front of a rock, or a pine tree, and pray. They pray for the divine right,** which should be given to them in accordance with the laws of life. They are dressed in **traditional attire (white and black** with colourful accessories). The Mayans of Chiapas believe that **humans experience disease or suffering only once in their lifetime.** Both occur **cyclically. The common cold** is among them. They teach that these diseases **can be prevented through prayer three times a year on the sacred mountain, at a holy well or a sacred site, these days also in a church.** Healers also go to pray on sacred mountains, where good spirits and Gods dwell. Sometimes they **take domestic animals** with them and pray to **the mountain Deities** to liberate them from disease. In

June, **when the corn starts to grow, they go to corn fields and make offerings for a rich harvest: they offer candles (for the sacred fire of transformation), music (as the elixir of life), and they light fires to the spirit of the Earth. Today, music is still an important offering essence.**

In the museum rooms where Chamulan healers treat patients, there is **a mural portraying a village and the mother Earth. In the middle of a lake, there is an embryo, which denotes the birth of life,** emerging from the mother Earth. For indigenous people, **the Earth is still the highest Deity,** which can look like **the fountain of life and death. The Earth is also the harvest Goddess. It is said that the good and the bad happen according to her will.** And the Earth is also the planet where our bodies live. They say that we return to the Earth **when we die, when we become one with everything that exists. Mother Earth gives food to people and at the end, we once again return to her, to return the favour for her feeding us.** That is why Mayans are always respectful to nature and cannot understand the white settlers' insensitive plundering of her natural treasures. **Mayans still see the soul everywhere and in everything that is.**

When, for example, a Mayan woman finds out that she is pregnant, she asks **a midwife for help and guidance.** And after that, the midwife is **always at her disposal,** even at night. Women usually **give birth at home. Husbands and midwives** help them. If the child's father cannot be present, any other close person can take over his task.

During labour, **the woman kneels in front of her husband, who sits on a chair, holding his hands under her arms and breasts, supporting her. The midwife usually stands behind her,** gently pressing her stomach. The woman can also hold the midwife's shoulders. Midwives, who are excellent herbalists, often **use selected herbs to accelerate labour.** Mayans in Chiapas believe that a woman can **make an offering of a lock of hair, which is a trick for the acceleration of labour.** This symbolically means that **the woman is ready to push the baby out** of her body. The symbolism of a lock of hair **focuses her intention to the physical act of pushing.**

During labour, they even use **symbolic tools,** which might seem quite odd and nonsensical. The midwife can **massage** the woman **with stones** – she passes **three times** from the top of the woman's head to her toes. Or she can go around the woman's body with some other object which is at hand; she may even pass with it three times over the woman's abdomen. This act centres the woman's and midwife's thoughts in order to surrender to the Holy Trinity of the divine energy of life. It is said that this act also **symbolises a (cosmic-earthly) orgasm, which giving birth actually is.**

Midwives are highly respected and privileged in Native American society. This is so because their **wisdom is passed down from one generation to another,** through the lineages of wise women. And also because they help life and they help to overcome all the negative in it. **The knowledge starts to be passed down in early childhood,** which means that they can of course start to learn more quickly the necessary things within the family.

Midwives say that **they ensoul life, they give soul to the birthing mother and the child, they help the child to breathe in the soul (they provide energy support)** until the baby itself gains enough strength to live independently. They say that, at birth, a child **does not have the right blood (energy).** Or this blood **does still not run through the body due to the baby's fear (death in the cradle), shame** or because its **soul remains in dreams** (at the levels of the soul). **For Mayans, blood is still primarily the symbol of the energy flow of life.**

They say that if there has been an accident, for example if someone fell from a rock, a tree or into water, **their soul remains there. Which is why people are usually afraid of these sad places.** They say that **a midwife can make a small, big or middle-sized soul** (the size relates to the different depths of people's consciousness). People can **walk the bright path** (with a broad consciousness), **in darkness** (with a narrow consciousness) or somewhere in the middle. **To ensoul means to pull people into life.** This is what midwives do. This is how they heal souls and bodies. While doing this, they **sprinkle soda** water generously to expel enemies.

All midwives operate more or less in the same way. If there are problems during labour, they **make herbal tea** for the woman, they pass three times **around her abdomen** with a stick, or even a knife. They do this to **symbolically cut the woman's energy knots, or energy blocks, and to impress into both her and their own minds the thought that knots need to be unravelled** in the physical and energy bodies, **what was stuck needs to be cut.** Of course they also **check blood pressure and pray all the time** for the labour to speed up and unfold normally.

When the baby is born, the midwife continues to press the woman's abdomen **to expel the placenta.** Then she carefully washes the baby in warm water and cleans its breathing paths. They believe that **the washing of the baby should be done very carefully.** There is in fact **a special technique of washing a new-born baby.** They believe that if it is not washed properly, the child can **later have bad dreams, or nightmares.** Then the midwife cuts the umbilical cord with a disinfected knife. If the baby is a boy, she leaves twelve centimetres of the cord, while **a baby girl** gets only six centimetres. Probably there is a symbolism in this too. **The umbilical cord is then tied into a knot and covered with a clean cloth.** They say it must be covered well, so that the baby doesn't feel cold, because it continues to sense the cord for some time afterwards. Yes, we can even **feel the missing parts of the body throughout our entire life,** even though we no longer have them at the physical level.

Then the midwife **cleanses the baby with an egg, the symbol of wholeness,** in order to eliminate bad air and everything negative. Egg cleansing means to **remove the devil's eye, or evil look,** because the baby is now exposed to multiple looks (to people's energy influences), due to which it can get **unwell, can cry ceaselessly or get cramps.** Native Americans explain that **the midwife thus removes the energy of those thoughts, or looks,** so that they do not stay in the baby's eyes. And they are right. The energies of the physical world are rough. And the egg is a reminder, a symbolic link to energy worlds, to energy centres (chakras), and etheric bodies.

As recently as twenty five years ago, I was told something similar by people living at the foot of the mountains of Western Slovenia (in Bohinj) – they removed **'the evil eyes spell'** from horses. A white leather cloth was placed on the horse's forehead to give the impression of a marking. This was done **to stop a person's look (thought) at the white marking and so not penetrate the living being,** for this could disturb the horse. Thought is like a radio wave which we feel in our auras.

The newborn's father then buries **the placenta in a deep pit he had dug in the garden.** Placenta continues to be a material link with the baby; were people to hold it or look at it, they **would be able to influence the baby** – unfortunately also in a negative way. **Australian Aborigines, for example, bury the placenta under a sacred tree,** after which that tree becomes **the child's sacred medicine tree for their entire life.** The child comes to this tree for help in times of trouble. A Native American in Chiapas says that if parents want the next baby to be **a boy, the father should bury the placenta face down,** if they want **a girl, he should bury it face up. This is how they focus the energy of their wishes and intention.**

Before the mother starts to **feed the baby,** the midwife washes her breast with warm water to prevent infection. In order to **protect the mother and the newborn against bad spirits,** or bad energies, the midwife can also perform a special **symbolic cleansing with a rooster and a hen.** In the contemporary Mayan world, these two animals represent **male and female energies,** which does not seem to have any sense. It is probably how the midwife redirects her thoughts most easily into the energy field of the boy or girl. Then she offers **tea** to the birthing mother **to foster a lighter cleansing of the bleeding and of abdominal cavity,** after which she gives her instructions on how to care for the baby.

In the Mayan tradition, a new mother has to **take great care of herself over at least the following three months. She can eat a little bit of everything,** but if the baby is **a boy, she has to avoid avocado, onion, and meat to prevent the inflammation of his genitals.** The three are strong foods, which are difficult to digest and which **cause aggression** and allergies.

When the baby grows up, it is given **a piece of amber in the form of a doll or necklace, which is said to protect it against evil,** or according to the new

(Christian) tradition – against the devil's eye. All children also receive **their own naguals, guide-protectors,** which will accompany them throughout their lives. Most often they come in the form of a clay figure. Nagual can be **an animal or a natural phenomenon.** The animal nagual will **offer the child everything it needs in its life.** People usually have **three or more** naguals **in their lives. Healers can have up to thirteen** naguals (a perfect number). In most cases, naguals are animals, but, in case of a person with supernatural powers, they can also be **natural or cosmic forces,** such as **twinkling, thunder and lightning, whirlwinds or even a meteor.**

In the gardens of the museum in San Cristobal de las Casas, there is an interesting **herb garden,** which is quite similar to ours. You will find everything there – **from sage, butterfly stonecrop, ricin to Saint John's wort.** There is also **a pharmacy,** where herbal preparations are made for all kinds of diseases. In the garden, there is a **sauna,** called *temazcal.* Rocks for a hot steam bath are heated on a fire and then brought into the hut. Water is poured over the hot stones from which steam then rises. **For contemporary Mayans,** such steam baths **represent relaxation, the release of strain, purification, detoxification, and the elimination of negative energies. They are important for maintaining balance.**[292]

Perhaps taking a sauna before the ritual ballgame also had the same role and rich symbolism. During the pre-Spanish period, steam baths were very often used **for healing** disease and even a bad temperament. In this way, they **prevented (energy) cold from entering** the body. For the Mayans, *temazcal* **is like a mother's stomach, enabling ritual purification and rebirth.** This is why at a temple site, **the ritual sauna** which initiates enter prior to the ballgame is **a symbol of new birth and a mental reminder of the need for renewal.** A sauna **cleanses the body and soul.** They say that *temazcal* even purifies and invigorates **the air, which represents the fragile human soul. The fire-water connection** creates a purifying steam. And it also represents **the world and the Earth. Upon entering a steam bath, you actually enter the breast, or the womb, of Mother Earth.** This is what they still believe today. **Mother Earth will purify and heal you with fire and water, it will bring your rebirth and you will become a new-born being.** It will bring you back to primordial perfection.

....
292 Read more about steam baths in the first book in the *Cosmic Telepathy* series.

Picturesque leaflets about Mayan medicine and the warrior-healer

In the medicine museum in **San Cristobal de las Casas**, I found a **leaflet**[293] containing simple drawings portraying the healing process of the Mayans in Chiapas and **the path of a healer-warrior**. There are explanations in Spanish and *tzotzil* and *tzeltal* languages at the back of this informative leaflet, presenting some of the methods and concepts related to healing. These simple leaflets, published by **the organisation of healers from Chiapas** and the organisation of indigenous tzeltal therapists (**OMIECH**), speak of **a wisdom which the local healers, living high up in the mountains, received from their ancestors. They still use and teach this inherited knowledge.** And their system of healing has somehow been **included in contemporary healing methods. In a similar way, the millenia old indigenous wisdom of physical and energy medicine is also used alongside classical medicine in Australia, Indonesia, China, and India.**

The offering of fish; the sacred serpent *ahau-can* sits on the top of the donor's head.

The first page of the leaflet portrays **the Goddess Ixchel,** who is the central character of Mayan medicine and **the protector of births and birthing mothers.** The Goddess appears in different forms and Native Americans believe that she can even shape-**shift into an animal** – like, for example, the ancient Slovene shaman *kresnik*. The Goddess Ixchel **connects the elements of nature and different animals and plants with diseases.** She is an ancient **water Deity** and is therefore linked to **the Moon, fertility and abundance.** Ixchel is also the protector of **weavers and healers.** Her symbols are the **rainbow, deer and monkey.**[294] In a state of trance, you enter a connection with the Gods, with cosmic and supernatural forces, **by means of sound, song, magical words, and sound formulae.**[295] These tools are also used for **oracles** – for establishing clair-knowing **telepathic abilities and divination.**

The **number nine** is written on the page. Nine represents **the nine Mayan deities – the nine fundamental levels of consciousness and reality,** which humans

....
293 *La medicina Maya pasado y presente*, Omiech, Unach, year of publishing unknown.
294 *The Mayan Gods*, no authors mentioned, Merida, 2004.
295 Ibid.

reach. On the upper part, there is a symbol of the Earth, the Earth Deity, because **the Goddess Ixchel is also the Earth Goddess.** On that drawing, she is directing the birth of a child with her hand. Healers use their hands to direct channelled life energy into those who need it. Ixchel is also **the Deity of medicinal herbs. Being the Goddess of water and life, she wears a spiral serpent-like headdress.** Her hair has the appearance of a serpent's nest.

Air diseases are shown on the second page. The element of air is marked by **the deer. In Mayan medicine, every disease is represented by an animal.** This animal can (symbolically) cause a disease, but it can also heal it. **Guacamaya, the red macaw,** which personifies air diseases, is responsible for the diseases of air.

The third page shows **fire diseases,** related to **digestive problems and diarrhoea.** The portrayed **healer wears a stick or a bone in his nostrils,** just like Australian Aborigines. This page also portrays **an ancient healer and once again the water Goddess Ixchel** with her serpent-like headdress. **The symbols of twenty days** are depicted around her. **The number twenty indicates one cycle of healing.** In the centre, there is a male-female (**androgynous and therefore the most powerful and effective!**) **Mayan healer** – a person who has managed to **unify his polarities, or dualities,** his male-female essences, **into one.** A balanced duality is also the symbol of **the dual aspect in all things, including living beings, as well as the duality of the world: hot-cold, night-day, wet-dry, etc. The healer's androgynous aspects, attained by enlightened ones,** are obviosuly exalted here. Androgyny is **an exceptional, earned gift. With it, spiritual and energy powers greatly increase,** as does **effectivness.**

Next to this holy androgynous person stands **a sacred tree, the symbol of the expanses of consciousness, which gives the healer the energy, power and wisdom to heal. Enlightened and excellent healers have to live permanently within all levels of the sacred tree.** These levels are represented by **the branches of the sacred tree.** Such healers operate out of wholistic consciousness, or the soul, which is why they are extremely effective and successful.

Besides the healer, **the incense in jars in the form of a jaguar and puma** are the central element of **Mayan medicine and their spiritual and energy power.** The puma and jaguar should be addressed with respect, offerings to them have to be made with respect. The healer's **hands reach out to sick people,** healing them with energy. Their hands also denote remote healing sessions, which, if necessary, the healer conducts for those who are absent. **Touch is not crucial.** A truly good healer can **make a diagnosis at a distance – without physical presence. Energies can be directed from wherever to wherever, which means it is possible to heal anyone from anywhere.**

The fourth page points to **the new ways of accepting old Mayan Deities.** Here, the Deity **Ixchel** is portrayed once again – **with the *guacamaya* macaw,** the symbol of air diseases or spirit, which is simultaneously also the water deity. In Catholicism, the Goddess Ixchel was **replaced by the Virgin of Guadalupe.** Offerings are placed next to her: **a cross, candles,** bottles, chickens, various **trees,** shrubs and their twigs – they are all placed on the altar together with the incense.

Today, the ancient Gods are mixed with saints and Christian Gods, with the image of Jesus Christ and the Holy Spirit, to which Native Americans bring offerings, just like they did to their ancient Gods in the past. Like **Pancho** did **when summoning rain.**

The fifth page includes a drawing, which portrays **(shamanic?) initiation and dreams of an** *ilol*. In his dreams, the future healer *ilol* is **receiving teachings and knowledge, divine wisdom on Earth.** In those dreams, **he is given wisdom and healing power. Reading the pulsing of the blood in the veins (pulse diagnosis)** is one of these skills and abilities. A telepath, or a medium, also receives messages concerning **what needs to be done and how.** In the drawing, there is also **a mountain healer** at prayer, protected by the Archangel Michael. The healer is praying for protection against the disease of his entire community.

The sixth page shows **how an androgynous healer *ilol* reveals himself to the community (when the time has come!).** Having a harmonised essence, healer **cures himself first,** during which he experiences and tests his **first knowledge. Next, the female part of his personality heals the children** – this is the first **test of his female essence.** This is how he is recognised and accepted by the community. God protects and trains him. That is why he **accepts offerings** from the patients. The Holy Trinity, the power of balance, is shown here. And the healer *ilol* is shrouded with the mantle of Jesus Christ.

On the seventh page, the **female essence of the healer shows her face. It shows the light of the day** – her daytime healing activities. **The visage in his male form is depicted as night, as teaching and healing while sleeping. The man sleeps with the wakeful presence of his spirit, soul, and heart. In dreams, his** *nagual* **guide tells the medium about the diseases of patients** who will come to him the next day, advising him what to do to cure them. The *naguals* of healers are most often jaguars**, pumas, even rats, twinkling and comets,** as well as cosmic forces, such as **lightning and thunder.**

The eighth page depicts how, since the 1950s, **drugs have destroyed traditional communities and medicine** has been pushed aside by the **pharmaceutical industry.** The page shows how **indigenous language, traditional attires, and Native American culture are being driven out of schools.** A drawing shows how **the police detained two healers, dragging them to jail.** They were accused of the possession of *peyote*[296] and other drugs, or halucinogenic mushrooms. For

---
296   Read about the Native American peyote ceremonies in the first book in the *Cosmic Telepathy* series.

centuries, *peyote* has been **a sacred plant** for numerous Mayan generations. Some *nagual* groups use halucinogenic substances **in their ceremonies to open up the awareness of higher worlds to ceremony participants.** They usually use it consciously and prudently – primarily regarding **when, where, who and how, if at all, to consume it.**

The authorities still accuse (under the influence of Christian dogmas) traditional medicine of being the **devil's work.** It is not much different in Europe. There is news on the radio **that those who perform indigenous medicine are not good.** They promote only the use of modern medicine, which does not deal in any way with people's energy. **But this is precisely the reason why modern medical treatment is only partially successful,** or even completely unsuccessful, if diseases are rooted in the energy imbalances of the spirit – of thoughts and emotions. Well, medical and pharmaceutical monopolies have a finger in the pie here. This medicine does not deal with **the causes of diseases** either.

The ninth page says: **indigenous medicine has no longer been persecuted since the 1980s. It has been increasingly recognised as effective and beneficial.** It has become a part of Mexican contemporary medical science. **Medical doctors and indigenous healers can** now **heal together.** This is especially emphasised in **San Cristobal de las Casas in Chiapas,** where the museum and the centre of Mayan medicine is located. Mayan medicine now works under the protection of Mexican government.

Contemporary Native American healers **still show great sensitivity in their perception of the energy flow of life, of the power of thought and mind.** This makes their healing **penetrating, wholistic and above all, fully conscious.** This is why they can operate successfully and above all **lovingly towards the world around them, towards people, plants, animals, and the Earth. They will miss not a single level of consciousness, not a single branch of the holy medicine tree. At least the best healers will not!** This kind of work leads both the healer and the patient to **peace, health, and to the silence of the soul.** Their work is perhaps **an echo of the old medicine of the ancient Mayans,** who, judging by their other achievements, **were able to accomplish far, far more** than we are able to even imagine today. Both, however, **knew how to heal the physical, emotional, mental, and spiritual bodies, or soul.** They knew how to travel **across the worlds of reality** on the wings of their consciousness.

While I was looking for the shaman Pancho, I met several interesting people in a little village near the **Ek Balam – Black Jaguar** temple site. The **healer** and masseur **Marcellino** was one of them. I experienced in practice their **folk medicine combined with massage, given by this local village master. He received his knowledge telepathically.** Using his **intuition and telepathy,** he received the necessary messages and guidelines about people's health conditions, as well as about **how and where to massage, how to heal, where something was wrong and why.** He attained his knowledge like all natural peoples of unspoiled consciousness usually do – **telepathically, without learning.** It is interesting to note that locals call the massage *hunku*. The name seems to derive from the word **Hunahpu,** meaning Universal life energy. **The *kurandero* (healer) Marcellino uses massage to treat all diseases, he even sets bones with it.** His touch harmonises, heals and alleviates pain. Female massage therapists are called **epiphanias.**

Healers who have acquired different healing methods through learning are usually not deemed to be good and effective healers. Enlightened shamans from different traditions claim that **information attained with the mind and memorisation is, to a great extent, unreliable and inaccurate.** Information they need in order to understand a disease and **to successfully eliminate it should be received spontaneously – in the silence of the mind.** The information which the 'learned' healers seek and choose from their memory is always **'coloured' by their personal insights, mental patterns and experiences, by their current inclinations and mere memory data impulses,** which are either only partly or not at all in tune with the problems and needs of the patient seeking help. Only **information coming from the open and silenced mind of a multi-levelled consciousness and received from the Universal Field, from the 'bank of imprints,'** can be **completely accurate and suitable.** Provided the healer, shaman, or priest is **able to attain them. Guessing and browsing through an arsenal of acquired data,** which is always limited and linked to the knowledge of the individual, **is only approximate and unreliable. True cosmic telepaths are able to draw into their minds any piece of news they need – for whosoever from wherever and whenever.** It is of no importance **if, while looking for appropriate messages, they live in the same village or on another continent, or even on another planet! Ha!** Such healing is **very rapid and effective.** I know that all of this is possible from my own healing practice.

Today, white intellectuals think in a completely different way. Having a quite narrow consciousness, they are brimming with endless information, like encyclopaedias. This is hardly surprising, as they have almost no experience of a boundless multidimensional consciousness. Only a few have it. Contemporary people are not even able to understand the difference between the two methods of acquiring information. They are satisfied with an average inaccuracy of their findings, with groping in the darkness and with their more or less (un)successful deeds (statistics says that only 30% of medical diagnoses are correct). **But our ancestors were not satisfied with imperfection, fragments, and distortion.** Wise people, **shamans, healers, and priests from the times of the great civilisations** of exceptional knowledge were people of **boundless consciousness, satisfied only with totally accurate** findings. And on top of that, these could even be proved! But in a different way. They knew how to attain them!

Not everyone is able to attain these abilities, for they **mirror the expanses of (nine-)dimensional consciousness and of a devoted connection to the cosmic Source, to the Universal Intelligence of life. The most courageous, persistent, wholehearted, and devoted discovered them.** The sages of past millennia worked, predicted, healed, and passed on their knowledge telepathically. But there is a real **danger** when someone is firmly convinced that **he is able to do all of that, but in reality, he is merely blindly following the whisperings of his own ego and mind,** which tell him that he is capable of such enviable grandeur, even though he is in fact not. And he passes to people false information about their health.

So, the village master Marcellino from a village near Ek Balam switched on his intuition and cosmic-telepathic antenna and gave a massage to my friend who had picked up a bad cold during our journey. The heat was searing and aggressive air conditioning units were humming in all vehicles, causing problems to our heated bodies. Marcellino spread a large piece of cardboard on the floor of his modest home and the therapy table was ready. An hour of his massage **cured my friend's cold** for that day and Marcellino took a childlike delight in the unexpected visit of foreigners from a faraway country. I observed his healing process. It looked like a massage, but the core of this process actually lay in balancing the energy of the disharmonious. I delighted in the heartfulness and effective therapy of this humble man.

The more contemporary Mayan methods of healing and reaching into the Primordial Field are, the more they are contaminated with foreign cultural influences and views, and the further they are from the grandeur of the ancient wisdom of antiquity. Contemporary therapists need numerous aids to be able to see, recognise, and understand better. The mind has been losing its previous depths and consciousness has been losing its grandeur. Boundlessness is being bounded, eternity is ever more estranged. The illusiveness of life is growing ever stronger, the reality of a multidimensional consciousness is ever more clouded. We are left with less and less, with so little! And what is left is greatly impoverished, uncertain, and empty.

We are left with mere empty reasoning, which does not understand the whole, which cannot make a decision, which is divided, confused and unhappy. Where and how we live within this broad array and journey along the long path stretching between ignorance and full awareness, which we call life, depends on our horizon over the expanses of consciousness, on the levels or dimensions of consciousness we are able to reach. What we know, what we experience, and how we see events in the world, what will be revealed to us and what will remain hidden from us for ever, depends on our own harmony or disharmony. If we (still) fail to see and understand, and if we (still) do not hear, it does not mean that this does not exist. Blindness and deafness are merely ours and have nothing in common with the Truth.

'**The art of a warrior** is to balance the **terror** of being a man **with the wonder of being a man.**'[297]

---

[297] Carlos Castaneda, *The Wheel of Time*, London, Allen Lane, The Penguin Press (1998), p. 100.

The life and rituals of the Aztecs and Incas

The stratification of society, the astronomical and priests' school for girls and boys

Let's take a look at how the Aztecs lived and how they nourished their shamanic abilities and knowledge. **Manuel Lucena** wrote a book titled *Así vivían los Aztecas (That's how the Aztecs Lived)*,[298] from which I drew some of the most vital information about the life of the Aztecs – the Native Americans of the modern era.

The Aztecs were a very **warlike nation; some even call them barbarian Indians.** It is said that they **sacrificed** thousands of people to their deities. Spanish conquistadors were of course quite brutal, and the Mayan and Aztec bloody sacrifices offered them an excuse to subdue them with a similar violence. They were appalled by Native American practices, claiming at the same time that, with their own cruelties, they are merely preventing and forbidding the merciless Aztec customs,[299] even though they themselves were no better.

The Aztecs were **masters of architecture and brilliant farmers.** They used irrigation systems and fertilisers to increase their yields. They were also great **builders and engineers.**[300]

Aztec society was stratified. They lived **in clans** and moving up from one social class to another was not easy. One could move up to the nobility **only by special merits,** bravery and wisdom. Aztec society was governed by a **ruler** called *tlatoani*, which means **speaker.** He had to be a good speaker and **he was the only one permitted to wear green.**[301] It is interesting to note that Egyptian priests also wore green attire (**green is the colour of the heart chakra**). The ruler's garb was adorned with **turquoise** and green precious stones. He also had **a sceptre in the form of a serpent. *Tlalocan* was a place where people spoke.**[302] Worshipping the ruler's power fostered customs, the like of which the Hawaiians had until the second half of the 20th century: **no one was allowed to look the ruler in the face, everyone** had to be **barefoot** in his presence, **no one was ever allowed to turn**

----
298 Manuel Lucena, *Kako so živeli Azteki*, Ljubljana, EWO (1994). The quotations are taken from the Slovene translation of the book.
299 Ibid.p. 82, 83.
300 Ibid, p. 76.
301 Ibid., pp. 26-28.
302 Ibid.

their back on him (this is very symbolical!), which is why his subjects always **retired backwards.**

The Aztec society meted out the worst treatment to **enslaved captives (foreigners),** as well as to Aztecs enslaved as a form of punishment, who had to wear a stick fastened behind their neck. Commoners had to serve and farm the land **until the age of 52** (until this significant and symbolic number of years).

Lucena says that **the Aztecs were not as excellent mathematicians as for example the Mayans.** However, neither the Mayans nor the Aztecs were **able to count great quantities.** It is said that all numbers greater than 400 were considered uncountable. The basis of Mayan and Aztec mathematics was the **vigesimal numeral system**, based on the number 20.[303]

The Aztecs inherited their **writing system** from their predecessors, adapting it to their *nahuátl* **language,** which had **a rich vocabulary and a simple (and melodious?) pronunciation.** Their writing system was both **ideographic and phonetic,** just like that of the Mayans. A sign and a symbol could represent a word or just an individual sound. For example, the word *atl*, which means **water,** could also be read as the letter **A.**[304]

Before the arrival of the Spanish, Aztec **pictographic** writing already showed signs of a phonetic system of recording, but its development stopped for a while after the conquest. **Scribes were highly esteemed in the Aztec society.** This is of no surprise, for they used **a magical writing of red and black colour** to draw their sacred **pictograms.** They learned this art in **temple schools.** Aztec **priests and nobility could read, but only a few could write,** whereas commoners were completely **illiterate.** They wrote on **paper made of tree bark.**[305]

The Aztecs were enthusiastic about **poetry.** Spanish conquistadors **unfortunately destroyed the numerous Aztec works of architecture and art, as well as written works.** They burnt them at the stake, for they believed that the Aztec philosophy of life was demonic, related to devil.[306]

But their writing system nevertheless produced the rich **Aztec literature**, as well as **prophetic books, calendar interpretations and historical chronicles, like** for example *Tira de la Peregrinación*, or *The Pilgrimage Strip*, which deals with the migrations of the Aztec people.[307]

The Aztecs, especially nobility, loved to play different games, and they also enjoyed **gardening,** bird **hunting** with blowguns, hunting, **writing poems, and playing music.** Aztec noble families appreciated **singing schools. Music was**

....
303 Ibid., p. 75, 76.
304 Ibid., p. 77.
305 Ibid., p. 78, 79.
306 Ibid., p. 79.
307 Ibid., p. 79, 80.

obviously a prestigious art and they had a great number of singing schools. Dance and theatre play were also taught.

It is said that the inhabitants of Aztec communities loved **gardens, flowers and herbs.** These were especially well tended in palaces and gardens.[308]

Aztec astrological knowledge was based on astronomy, which developed over millennia. Lucena claims that **the Mayan solar calendar was more accurate than Aztec and European calendars.** However, the Aztecs were familiar with main constellations, comets, and other celestial bodies. Astrology was **mainly the domain of priests,** who were convinced that the order of the Universe, the cosmic and earthly **Order according to the Gods' will, was closely linked to peoples' destinies.**[309] That is why the North American Indians, the Mayans, and Aztecs built numerous **observatories** and **recorded** their teachings and observations **in sacred scripts.**

At its core, Aztec cosmogony resembles the Mayan one; it is based on the **legends of the four Suns.** It is said that the Aztecs actually **took the Mayan myth,** which says that the Gods **created and destroyed the world four times.**[310] This myth is also known by the North American Indians.

The life of the Aztecs was directed by **an intricate calendar and a cosmogonic view** of the world and events in it. They worshipped numerous deities, many of which had multiple names. The most important was the God **Tláloc – the rain God,** as well as **Huitzilopochtli**[311] **– the war God,** which, according to a legend, came from **a mythical land of abundance (Tulan** in the Mayan tradition), from where Aztec **souls had come.** This is why I believe that bloody fights and sacrifices were added to Aztec and Mayan **ceremonies** only later. **Earlier ceremonies** must have been totally **different.** In the city of **Tenochtitlan,** priests performed various rituals, they carried out astronomic calculations and **divined the future.**

As did the Mayans, the Aztecs had **two calendars, one for religious and one for practical purposes. The two calendars coincided every 52 solar years.**[312] The **Venus** cycle was obviously reflected in their calendar. The Mayans also celebrated a **52 year 'century.'**

The author says that the renowned **Aztec Sun Stone, or the Aztec Calendar,** was discovered by accident at the end of the 18th century inside a temple in **Tenochtitlan.** The Stone measures **4 metres** in diameter and **weighs 24 tons.** At the centre of the calendar is **the Sun with the symbols of the fifth Earth's period,**

....
308 Ibid., p. 24.
309 Ibid., p. 74.
310 More about this can be found in the first book in the *Cosmic Telepathy* series, which deals with the North American Indians.
311 Manuel Lucena, *Kako so živeli Azteki*, Ljubljana, EWO (1994), p. 89, 90.
312 Ibid., p. 73, 74.

or the fifth Sun (fifth Earth).[313] The outer rings depict the symbols of previous periods.[314] It seems that **the Aztec way of thinking was not much different than that of other Native American tribes, including the Mayans.**

Among the most significant festivals were those held **every eight years**[315] (according to the cycle of the invisible Venus?).

A day in their capital Tenochtitlan was marked by the rhythms of drums and trumpets, coming from the main temple, signalling **the most important times of the day.** The first drumming could be heard **at dawn.** This was when housewives started to grind maize for the first meal. Lucena wrote that their grinding made the floor shake, which would wake up the others.[316]

It is said that the Aztecs **worked without stopping** until mid-morning, when **the sounds of drums announced breakfast time.** Then they continued to work until noon, **when there was drumming again.** This is when they headed home to eat with their families, after which they returned and resumed their work. They worked **until sunset, when the temple's drums, or gongs, announced the end of the day.** There was also evening drumming, signalling the time to rest. **Midnight drumming woke up the priests,** who went to pray and perform rites of penance with agave spines. **Then there was again drumming at three o'clock in the morning and teachers would wake up their pupils,** who had to wash themselves in the nearby canals, while the girls swept the courts and made sacrifices to the Gods. When the night was over, **the sound of trumpets and drums could again be heard at six o'clock in the morning.** A new day began and people went to work. But night work was over for priests, for the people who carried out the tasks of the soul.[317]

Maize was **the staple food of the Aztecs.** In Mexico, maize had been grown at least **7000 B.C.E.** Maize and **beans** were on table almost **every day.** Lucena says that all parts of maize were used for cooking, including stems and worms inside them. Besides maize and beans, people used **amaranth, snakes, turtles, ants, snails, worms, frogs, and supposedly even dogs, and of course squashes, potatoes and chocolate.**[318]

Cacao trees are indigenous to the tropical areas of South and Central America. The word cacao is of Mayan origin **(kakaw).** We do not know for sure who was the first to grow cacao and produce chocolate. But we do know that **the Mayans had been brewing a cacao drink at least 1100 B.C.E. and that later they invented the first hot chocolate, which was bitter.** It was consumed mostly

....
313   More about this can be read in the first book in the *Cosmic Telepathy* series.
314   Read Manuel Lucena, *Kako so živeli Azteki*, Ljubljana, EWO (1994), p. 19.
315   Ibid., pp. 62-65.
316   Ibid., p. 60.
317   Ibid., pp. 62-65.
318   Ibid., pp. 52-57.

during **rites of passage: births, marriages, as well as during funerary rites and initiations into priesthood.**[319]

The Mayans dried and roasted fermented cacao beans, after which **the powder was mixed with water. They also added spices, such as cinnamon, chilli and vanilla, to the drink.** Can you imagine the spicy chocolate flavour of this revered **ceremonial drink?** They poured the drink back and forth from one vessel to another, producing **froth,** which was especially esteemed. Archaeologists have excavated **wonderful vessels** used for storing spiced chocolate. These vessels portray kings, nobles and Gods drinking chocolate. **Commoners reportedly drank it only during feast days. At the end of the 16th century,** Spanish invader the drink balche s shipped chocolate **to Europe. In the 19th century, the English invented solid and sweet chocolate, the likes of which we know today.**[320]

The Aztecs too enjoyed **chocolate. Both the Mayans and Aztecs used cacao beans as a form of currency.** The Aztecs called chocolate **xococatl,** but their chocolate was not sweet, it was **bitter, for they did not know sugar cane at that time.** Liquid chocolate was **a ceremonial, prestigious beverage.** It is even said that the poor ate only once a day, while rich people ate three times a day.[321]

Native Americans loved to **drink** and they were supposedly very rough when intoxicated. At times they even beat each other to death when drunk or they molested their close ones. Friar Diego de Landa reported on the famous **honey wine,** which contemporary Mayan priests still bring to the altars **as offerings to the Gods and ancestors.** The friar said that the drink was strong and smelled foul.[322] Pancho too, offered to the ancient Gods and ancestors small bowls filled with mead. The bowls were placed on the ancestral altar, which he used in the abundance ceremony he led in the middle of the jungle. He called the drink *balche*.

The Mayans and Aztecs brewed **alcoholic drinks,** but they had strict rules regarding drinking. **Adults were allowed** to get drunk occasionally, whereas **young drunkards were punished by stoning.**[323] The privilege of consuming alcoholic beverages came with age.

At the age ten, children got to know their **animal – their guide *nagual*.**[324] It was believed that this animal indicated the child's life; it **guided their destiny** and determined their **dispositions.**

Aztec children were **raised strictly, even through punishment,** which was not usual among other Native American tribes. There was a commandment that

---
319 *Mysteries of the Maya, National Geographic Collector's Edition* (2008), p. 94.
320 Ibid., from p. 94 on.
321 Manule Lucena, *Kako so živeli Azteki*, Ljubljana, EWO (1994), pp. 52-57.
322 Diego de Landa, *The Account of the Things of Yucatán*, Mexico, Monclem Ediciones (2000), p. 67. The original was written between 1563 and 1572.
323 Manuel Lucena, *Kako so živeli Azteki*, Ljubljana, EWO (1994), pp. 52-57.
324 Ibid., p. 39.

children **must not mock the old, sick and lame persons, and that they must not speak too much or interrupt a person speaking.** Children were taught to be **loving and merciful, to avoid arrogance,** and **not to inflict suffering** or any other unjust deeds onto one another, and not to offend one another either. **Haughtiness was considered a sin** against the Gods. What is more, teachers warned the children that **it was not good to eat too much or too quickly.**[325]

When Aztec children were **twelve years old,** they reached the status of youths and were sent **to school. Boys married at the age of twenty, girls at sixteen.** Sons did not choose their wives, this was **the right of their fathers.** There was a commandment that they could **enter sex lives only when they were mentally and physically mature enough.** They married only with **the approval of the priest.**[326] He of course first did **astrological calculations** to establish whether the relationship really had the possibility for harmonious co-living. The priests also established **the most auspicious day for the wedding.**

Every Aztec school day ended with a big dance. The children of nobility received a different education. Temple schools were called *calmecac*. There, children were taught **astrology, calendar interpretation, divination, reading and writing, good behaviour, and discipline.** They were required **to abstain from sexual relations, to fast and to perform frequent penances.** They had to **get up four times** every night **in order to burn incense** to honour the Gods. **The warriors' self-sacrifice** included **piercing their ears and thighs with agave spines.**

The children of nobility were sent to **temple schools, where they learned reading, writing, the art of divination and astrology.** This was the very base of **elementary education. Public speaking and correct etiquette were essential.** Aztec young boys were sent to school **at the age of fifteen.** Schools for boys taught **correct speech, good behaviour, singing, dancing and military training.** This is how they trained the spirit and body. They also did ordinary chores, such as **cleaning** the school, cutting wood, maintaining canals, farming, etc. When boys were mature enough to be married, they were allowed to leave the school.[327]

The girls of nobility were educated in priest schools, but at different locations and in a way that was different from boys. But they received a similar basic education. Their **teachers were priestesses** and **most important subjects were music, dance, and the art of weaving.** They were educated in a strict manner and, just like the boys, **they had to get up at least twice a night** to sweep the temple's courts and pray. They attended school until they got married.[328]

....
325 Ibid., p. 39, 40.
326 Ibid., p. 34, 35.
327 Ibid., p. 40, 41.
328 Ibid., p. 43.

Penance without washing, musical instruments, the house of song, theatrical plays, ritual and symbolic games

The Aztecs had **steam baths,** which they used for personal hygiene, **healing** purposes and **ritual cleansing.** There were numerous public baths **in Tenochtitlan.** It is said that the Aztecs **paid careful attention to their clothing and ornaments, and they especially took great care of their bodies.**

The Aztecs loved to **adorn themselves with bracelets, necklaces, and ankle bracelets.** They liked to **pierce their noses and even their chins** so that they could wear rings made of crystal, turquoise, shells, amber, silver, and gold. These rings were called *bezotes* and they even attached them to **their foreheads**[329] (**to the third-eye area,** responsible for clairvoyant abilities). A similar ornament can be seen on Pacal's funerary mask – a flower inserted between the eyebrows, on the chakra responsible for intuitive-telepathic abilities.

The Aztecs also wore beautiful **headdresses featuring the feathers of the sacred bird, the macaw *quetzal.* But this adorning followed strict rules. Warriors** too wore splendid ornaments. Native Americans were **masters of tatooing.** Their tatooing was very painful and even dangerous. The part to be tatooed was **first coloured with a mixture of pigment and blood.** They believed that, **in this way, they would acquire divine abilities.** However, many people got infected and died.[330]

It is said that they bathed very frequently; high officials even **many times a day. Bathing was a veritable ritual,** which was encouraged since school. We can imagine how grave was the penance, limited exclusively to the priesthood class, according to which they did not bathe their bodies, not even their hair for a certain period of time. Perhaps these customs explain why **Native American warriors cleansed themselves so eagerly in steam baths before the ritual ballgame and why captives were carefully cleansed before being sacrificed.**[331] The **purity** of the body (and thoughts) was therefore **a special priviledge.**

For **priests,** a heavy **penance** was to **shave their heads at the front and sides, leaving a tuft of hair at the back of their heads;** they wore black clothes and ocassionally **did not bathe.**[332] For them, this was **a form of self-sacrifice,** as they normally paid great **attention to their external and internal cleanliness.** Young warriors also wore a tuft of hair at the back of their heads, while Aztec women

....
329 Ibid., p. 48, 49.
330 Diego de Landa, *An Account of the Things of Yucatán*, Mexico, Monclem Ediciones (2000), p. 66, 67.
331 Manuel Lucena, *Kako so živeli Azteki*, Ljubljana, EWO (1994), p. 50, 51.
332 Ibid., pp. 42-45.

sported a hairstyle similar to the Hopi women (in the form of hanging butterflies). They twisted their hair into whorls above their ears.

Manuel Lucena says that all bigger cities had **houses of song called *cuicacalli*,** where children from twelve up were taught **singing skills and dance.**[333] It seems that the houses of song were a type of a music school. **With their ingenious mouthpieces and ornaments,** Aztec (and Mayan) **clay flutes are veritable works of art.** The Aztecs too had **flutes with multiple tubes, as well as reedpipes.**

Aztec music reportedly had a double **meaning, both religious and mundane.** The Aztecs had various musical instruments. They were said to play **snail horns, clay ocarinas, flutes, reedpipes, trumpets, drums, bells and small jingle bells. The sound of conches announced the times of day and the beginnings of celebrations** (similar to India and the Pacific islands). Trumpets were traditional instruments (the Mayans had certainly used them in the classical period, probably even earlier). Towards the end of the post-classical period they were made from metals.[334]

In theatre shows, actors liked to **dress as animals,** especially **snakes, frogs, and beetles.** In a show, these animals would tell each other their adventures (in the human language, of course). Aztecs already had **professional theatre actors,** who entertained mostly noble families.[335]

Both the Aztecs and the Mayans appreciated **theatre. Of course musicians also appeared in theatre shows, using their *huehuetl* drums,** which had **membranes made of deer skin.** Spanish reporters stated that the sounds of drums in a temple in Tenochtitlan were mournful. Besides deer skin drums, the Aztecs also used *teponaztli*[336] **drums, made of hollow logs,** which were actually more like **xylophones.**

Also, they loved to play the **ballgame,** as well as games called *tlachtli* and *patolli*, the latter being a gambling dice game. The first one stemmed from a millennia old **ritual tradition,** to which the Aztecs added new elements. **The ritual ballgame turned into a competitive sports game** and even betting was introduced. Ballcourts, both public and private, were everywhere.[337]

The Aztecs played **the *patolli* gambling game** on **a cross-shaped board.** The goal of the game was to occupy, as soon as possible, the squares on the board by using **twelve pebbles – six pebbles were red and six were blue.** The board had **twelve squares,** twelve parts of the whole, which indicates **the wholeness of perfection.** Players **moved pebbles around the squares until they attained the centre of the cross.** They also used black beans, on which the number of points

....
333   Ibid., p. 81.
334   Ibid., p. 66, 67.
335   Ibid., p. 80, 81.
336   Ibid., p. 79, 80.
337   Ibid., p. 66, 67.

were marked. **The winner was the one who was the first to arrive at the central square**[338] (in the past, the central square was obviously the symbol of centredness, or enlightenment). It is said that the Aztecs were addicted to those games, some even losing all their possessions at them. The way the game was played and its symbolism speak of **its primordial ceremonial, spiritual role.** Via this game, players obviously confirmed their **desire to attain the final centre, centredness, the much sought after enlightenment.** Well, haven't enlightened **sages** always **enjoyed a special status in society?** Who wouldn't want that. Until we become enlightened, **we are unaware of the heavy burden of our ignorance.** But the ballgame and **other games** gradually **lost their original spiritual and ceremonial meaning.**

The Aztec ballcourt was I-shaped. There were stairs on its side walls, where spectators were seated. The ballcourt was **divided in two fields by a net.** The Aztecs played the game **similarly to the Mayans**. The rubber ball, called *olli*, was never allowed to fall on the ground during the game. Lucena says that the ball could be **struck with any part of the body** except for the feet and palms. **Only initial hits could be done with hands and legs.** This is why Aztec players wore **protective gear** made from deerskin: paddings for the knees, thighs and head. And the winner was of course the one who managed to get the ball through the stone ring. Aztec codices (**Codex Barbonicos,** for example) describe **competitions which became famous** and legendary. **They say that conflicts between tribes were occasionally resolved** by means of the ballgame. But even after the game became competition, it nevertheless retained **a connection to the four Deities, the protectors of the four cardinal points in the Sky.**[339] But over time, it gradually lost its original ritual meaning.

At this point, we should mention the renowned Native American **games of courage,** called *valadores*. Men, roped with lianas or ropes, launch themselves from a high pole. The rope, which is fastened to their ankles, stops them only just before they reach the ground.[340] This sport is also known by peoples on other continents. The game is a distinct risk **game for overcoming fear, a game of courage and surrender.** I watched it near Tulum. Four men in red-white festive attire **descended in spirals** from the high pole, thus indicating the four cardinal **directions in the Sky and life.**

Unfortunately, **the Aztecs believed they lived in a hostile world and that the world's existence and its balance depended on the discipline of each individual** (they were at least partially right).[341] This is why they forced their pupils to **inflict pain upon themselves.** This would strenghthen thier stoic attitude during

---
338 Ibid., p. 70, 71.
339 Ibid., pp. 68-70.
340 Ibid., p. 70, 71.
341 Ibid., pp. 42-45.

potential misfortunes. Pupils had to get up **at night and perform ceremonial cleansing.**

Manuel Lucena says that **the Aztecs set themselves the task to ensure the safety of humanity.** For this reason, they **conscientiously made offerings to the Gods,** because they were convinced that human **blood is the only food that can satisfy the Gods and reawaken the life energy of the Sun.** The more that problems in life increased, the larger was the number of victims they wanted to collect in order to sacrifice them to the raging Gods. All of this was done in order to renew **the power of the Sun.** They supposedly lived in a state of worry about tomorrow, constantly trying to keep the world in balance.[342] Their exaggerated worry demonstrates **the distortion of the ancient cosmic-earthly wisdom and teachings.**

The purpose of **intertribal warfare** was to **maintain balance in the Universe and on Earth alike.** Lucena says that **the elite order of 'the shaved ones'** was especially dedicated to this task.[343]

Just before they were **sacrificed** by the Aztecs, **captives** climbed **to the top of the Pyramid of the Sun,** to the ceremonial site located at the pyramid's top.[344]

Sacrifical rituals usually took place at the Main Temple in **Tenochtitlan** and on **the Pyramid of the Sun in Teotihuacan. Sacrifices were made mostly to the Rain God Tláloc,** who was said to live in **a paradise,** where streams flow and fruit trees grow.[345]

When the Mayan and Toltec civilisations started to mix, new monuments of time and **new accomplishments** of the two intertwined cultures came into being. But thereafter **the ancient wisdom,** which had already more or less deteriorated by then, began to be lost ever more rapidly. It sank into oblivion. Only few contemporary sages still preserve the ancient wisdom and ways of connecting to the Sky, the Earth, and the stars. **Attuning to planetary sounds dissipated.** You can read more about these sound techniques in my book about Egyptian culture.[346]

In modern era, the Aztecs and Mayans fought mainly in order **to capture enough prisoners** for their sacrifices to the Gods. Only living people had any value for them. This is why both engaged in **flower wars** in which they would take captives, 'needed' for the sacrifice.[347] Dates of the battles were preset (astrologically most auspicious dates). **As the wisdom of their distant ancestors,** who

---
342 Ibid., p. 83.
343 Ibid., p. 87, 88.
344 Ibid., p. 85.
345 Ibid., pp. 82-84.
346 The seventh book in the *Cosmic Telepathy* series, titled *The Magic of the Stars and the Keys to Life of the Ancient Egyptians and Ancient Greeks*.
347 Manuel Lucena, *Kako so živeli Azteki*, Ljubljana, EWO (1994), pp. 90-91.

had nurtured and lived a unified cosmic consciousness, **had been lost, fear grew stronger and stronger.** Not only in the Aztec society, but also among other peoples and nations on all continents. **The fear of loss, fear of darkness, fear of annihilation and death have started to paralyse the world.**

At the end of a 52-year period, when the religious and solar calendar coincided, the Aztecs went on **a pilgrimage to the mountains in order to light sacred fires.** During that time, priests closely **observed the stars** in the Sky, waiting for **the Pleiades (Siete Cabrillas) to appear on the horizon** in this terrible night, when **people** were to **repent** of their immaturities; they trembled with fear that the world might end. And when the Pleiades finally appeared in the night Sky, they were relieved, for they believed that **the Sun would now rise again** and continue its daily journey, and **the world would not end.**[348] **Then the priest gave life to the first flame of the new century.** With this flame, people **kindled the fire in their cold domestic hearths,** to ensure that life would continue without disturbances. **The Sun rose,** announcing that the Deities had accepted their sacrificial gifts.[349] **The ancient wisdom mixed with the superstition of the modern era.**

Did the Aztecs know the price of spiritual rebirth, of a new birth? In a remote past, before those ghastly physical sacrifices, had they originally endeavoured to **kindle the sacred fire of transformation** in the chest of the sacrificed person or **in their own heart,** but later forgot the original **meaning of offering the spiritual heart** and building enlightened love? Did they become so very materialistic that they literally **tore someone's heart out?** It is highly possible that the process of such nonsensical bloody sacrifices was **rooted in far more majestic ideas and visions dating back to distant eras.**

Lucena says that frequent **sacrifices** nevertheless did contribute to something good – to **an excellent knowledge of anatomy,** which fostered **the development of medical knowledge.** Priests were supposedly able to cut the heart out from a person's chest **with an extremely precise cut** in just a few seconds. The victim's pain was alleviated with **narcotics, sleeping aids, and anaesthetics.** For this, they used various **plants, hallucinogenic mushrooms, and the *peyote* cactus.** Due to frequent battles and injuries, they were **very good at setting and healing bones, as well as at treating wounds** with substances that stopped bleeding and made injuries heal quickly. Over the last centuries, Aztec healers have been called *curanderos*[350] (in Spanish). Similar to the Mayans, they too were excellent herbalists.

....
348 In a ritual sacrifice which followed, they opened the chest of the sacrificed person and took his heart out. Tinder was put in the place where the heart had been and fire was kindled. It was so after the ritual of the spiritual heart had been lost.
349 Ibid., p. 90, 91.
350 Ibid., p. 75.

Musician-priests in the ceremonies of sound and dance

The Ancient Ones claim that **life is sacred.** It is a gift from God, a lively dance and a sacred task. All forms of life and everything in life are **imbued with sacredness (of sound). Singing, performing music, and dancing** are methods and expressions of people's prayers and supplications, they are ways of attuning. **Thought is sound too,** it comes from the boundless, meta-sensory worlds of consciousness.[351]

The authors of the National Geographic special edition[352] suggest that **Mayan paintings** often portray **battles, which look like fights between supernatural forces. Warriors** were usually painted in **red or black.** Besides bows and arrows, they also used **slings, dart throwers, blowguns, axes and clubs;** for protection, they used **shields made from cotton and palm.** They also wore **cotton jackets, packed with rock salt** and had **leather or cotton bindings** on their arms. **Fights** usually commenced with fearsome **shouts** accompanied by **drums, conch-shell trumpets, and whistles.**[353]

Mayan society too was addicted to music. Music was **of extreme importance** to the Mayans. Murals **in Bonampak** are wonderful, depicting **musicians with horns, celebrating victory** after a battle (this is at least how contemporary archaeologists interpret these murals). Musicians were highly **respected** in Mayan society, which proves the claims that musicians were also great **sages – priests, or shamans.** Throughout history, Mayans were said to be **great masters and worshippers of sound tools.** Even commoners enjoyed **the sounds of drums and flutes** on a daily basis. The Aztecs, Incas and their descendants were great master musicians **and heirs to the ancient Mayan spiritual heritage.**

In their ceremonies, dances, and celebrations, the Mayans and Incas used **small drums, which they usually played by hand;** and they also used **larger drums, made of hollowed wood, which produced a profound, mournful sound; they strike them with long sticks,** which had small **rubber bulbs fastened to their tips. Striking with these sticks** produced a powerful and penetrating sound.

Aztecs also had **long, slim trumpets** of hollowed wood, with a twisted **gourd (bell)** at the end. They fashioned brilliant **musical instruments from tortoise shells,** which they struck with their palms. They even crafted **whistles from deer bones**[354] (very similar to the ones which were known in prehistoric Europe and which are, in some places, still used in folk music), **reed flutes** and **large conches.**

....
351 This edited paragraph is taken from the first book in the *Cosmic Telepathy* series, p. 317.
352 *Mysteries of the Maya, National Geographic Collector's Edition* (2008), p. 73, 74.
353 Ibid.
354 See the third book in the *Cosmic Telepathy* series.

Friar de Landa wrote that with **these instruments they played in honour of brave men.**[355]

There were always food and drinks at their festivals and dances. Feasts and drinking could last **for several days. Families** had rotas of **family banquets with food and music.** People went from one festivity to another. This was still so in the time of De Landa. **Weddings and funerary rituals** were also important celebrations.[356]

The Mayans knew two kinds of **dances.** The first one was a type of **a game with reeds,** called *colomché*. **Dancers formed a large circle and musicians accompanied them with music.** Two dancers then came into the circle, one held a bundle of reeds and **danced upright,** while the other one danced **in a squatting position.** The one holding reeds then **threw them at the other dancer,** who tried to snatch them with a small rod.

There was also **a group dance,** in which up to **800 Native Americans** took part, said the friar. They danced to the music **in long steps, holding small flags in their hands.** This was how the Mayan **war dance** looked like. **They danced all day, slowly.** Food and drink was brought to them to prevent them from falling down. But **they did not know couple dances,** in which men and women would dance together.[357]

Sacrificing to the God of fire and time

Lucena writes that, given the fact that the Aztecs worked from morning to evening, **festive holidays, work-free days** were greatly welcomed. Each month, there had to be at least one festivity, which could last several days. **Corn harvest feasts could last for ten days. Fires were lit, there was singing and dancing** (at the end of the celebration, the Aztecs **sacrificed** to their Deities **a girl, adorned with corn ears – symbols of abundance). Warriors and priests** often **performed battles** during the corn harvest celebrations. Lucena says that the **winners would then take the losers' drums, matting and cloaks.**[358]

The Incas were the successors of the great Mayan and Aztec civilisations. They built a large temple site and one of the world's miracles – the breathtaking **lost city of Machu Picchu** high up in **the Andes,** which stirs the spirit of visitors. Up to 2,000 people visit it each day. Because it is worth it. Human souls know this.

....
355 Diego de Landa, *An Account of the Things of Yucatán*, Mexico, Monclem Ediciones (2000), p. 69.
356 Ibid., p. 68.
357 Ibid., p. 69. De Landa reported about the two dances.
358 Manuel Lucena, *Kako so živeli Azteki*, Ljubljana, EWO (1994), pp. 62-65.

The booklet of a CD featuring traditional Inca music of the Andes[359] says that contemporary **Incas in Ecuador** still use the *quena* flute and reed pipes **with seven finger holes.** *Quena* is one of the oldest Andean music instruments. At present, it is most often made **from bamboo wood,** while in the past, it was made from **stone, terra cotta and bones, especially wing bones (ulnas) of Andean condors,** sacred birds of the South American Indians. *Rondador* is an Ecuadorian flute using **a pentatonic scale.** With it, musicians still today play **melodies and a harmonic accompaniment simultaneously.** If we blow the two sets of pipes, they produce **two-part** music, the sounds intertwining and merging.

Today, the Incas still play **panpipes** called *siku*, which use a **diatonic scale.** They consist of **bamboo tubes** of different lengths tied together into two rows. *Siku* usually comes **in different sizes and tunings,** producing different tone heights. Mayans and Aztecs played similar flutes.

The following fact is very interesting and revealing: the Incas supposedly **considered the best musicians** to be veritable **heroes** (still today!). Well – isn't this how it still is **today?** Young people especially see **musicians as idols.** But it is a pity that **contemporary popular musicians** and singers are light years **away from the essence and mission of the art of music; they shatter balance,** instead of restoring it. A pity and unfortunate. The revered heroism in Native American societies can also be **a trace of the untouchable respect for the enlightened wise priest-musicians.**

Drums and rattles of different sizes are very popular in the contemporary Andean music. Some date **back thousands of years.** The *bombo* drum, made from hollowed logs, covered with animal skin, comes in different sizes. *Chajchas* is a popular rattle made from goat hooves. When shaken, **this rattle-percussion** produces a sound **similar to the sound of the wind or rain,** which makes it perfect for **calling rain** during abundance ceremonies.

Under the influence of music brought by the Europeans, the Incas began to craft stringed instruments, resembling guitars, violins, and harps. The **charango,** which looks like **a small version of a Spanish guitar** or Hawaiian **ukulele,** is the only **indigenous stringed instrument** of South America. **Its ten strings** are stretched over the shell of an armadillo or over a wooden sound box. Being small, the instrument is suitable for carrying around, which is handy for **nomadic** Native Americans. The charango was mostly played by **shepherds,** who herded lamas and constantly moved from place to place.

Today, the Incas still have **different rhythms,** which differ depending on **when and why they are being used.** The most frequent Incan **dance** rhythms are *san juan, taquirari,* and *wayno,* whereas *bombo* drums usually accompany musical

....
[359] *Andes Traditional: Journey of the Incas.*

57. Stepped pyramid (called church) with a stone stela in the front.

58. A stone stela or a stone book about the temple site.

59. A stone ring – the symbolic goal of life and enlightenment.

60. The wall of the ancestors with skulls – a reminder and a warning of the power of death.

61. Resonating stone columns from Coba or the as yet unrestored Mayan lithophone?

62. Tulum on the Yucatan Peninsula (Mexico) – the northernmost temple site on a cliff overlooking the Caribbean.

63. A stone double-headed jaguar (Uxmal), the ***balam*** – a symbol of wisdom, hidden knowledge, and powers.

64. A carved feathered serpent, which also represents sound (sinusoidal) waves.

65. This dog found the best energy spot for rest, at a carved spiral on the ceremonial platform at the summit of the Pyramid of Kukulkan (Chichén Itzá).

66. The astronomical observatory (**Caracol**) in Chichén Itzá, for watching the movements of stars and planets.

67. A stone image of **Chaak Mul** waiting for offerings. Chaak Mul is the symbol of the Sun's power and initiation, the symbol of the cosmic feathered serpent, which offers the teaching and wisdom of wholistic knowledge.

68. A Mayan settlement. Hurricane winds do not destroy the straw-roofed houses, they simply blow through them.

69. The interior of a home with a fireplace and the obligatory three sacred stones – symbols of the triunity of the cosmic, spiritual, and material.

70. In Palenque, the Temple of the Cross with nine terraces clings to the dense jungle.

71. A Mayan face with flat forehead and broad 'Mayan' nose (the Palace, Palenque).

72. A carved image in a yoga posture in Palenque.

73. The Temple of the Sun in Palenque with the image of the Sun jaguar, the lord of the underworld.

74. Water magic in the river **Otolum** (Palenque); underground aqueducts were built at the Palace to prevent the little river from flooding during heavy rain.

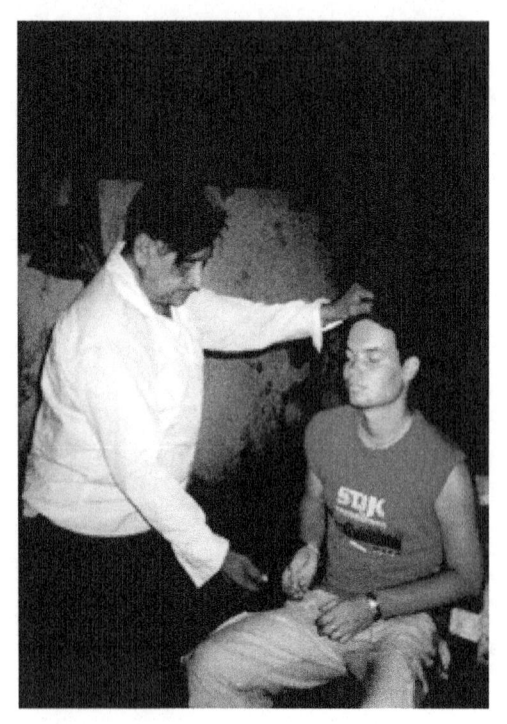

75. The shaman Candido (Mexico) performing energy **balancing; the author's son Tine is surrendering to his hands.**

76. The shaman Pancho (Mexico) blessing the author and thus supporting her research path and mission.

77. At an enchanted lake (**Laguna Encantada, Chiapas**).

78. and 79. Sailing on the enchanted lake and simple Native American rafts.

80. A meeting of the old and new worlds (Chiapas). Is harmony at all possible?

81. Dolls in the Mayan Medicine Museum, **San Cristobal de las Casas.**

82. Visiting a Mayan family near Ek Balam; the author, standing far right, in Mayan national clothes, which are still worn by the girls and women of the Yucatán Peninsula.

83. Contemporary Mayan architecture in the old Mayan style.

84. The famous church in **Chamula (Chiapas)**, where local Native Americans still perform their ceremonies.

85. Mayan cemetery (Chamula).

86. A botanical garden with a Native American sweat lodge, or sauna, located near the Medicine Museum.

87. A Native American man (**Zinacatan**) with the typical headdress with coloured ribbons prepares medicine powder (a doll in the museum).

88. An evening out (Chiapas).

89. A Mayan sweat lodge (San Cristobal de las Casas, Chiapas).

90. Drying herbs and preparing tea bags for sale.

91. The author and her travelling companion in Native American wedding costumes (the mountains of Chiapas).

92. Contemporary musicians on a decorated cart playing modern instruments – accordion, violin, trumpet (San Cristobal de las Casas).

93. A traditional Native American kitchen (Zinacatan, the mountains above Chamula, Chiapas).

94. A potter making clay bowls in the form of a sacred bird (near San Cristobal de las Casas).

95. Her wonderful pottery products.

96. A Brazilian Native American girl (**Goias**, 2012).

97. The symbol of the spiral movement and life within multidimensional consciousness and boundlessness (circled dot) – **Hunahpu.**

98. Women in festive dresses (the mountains above Chamula, Chiapas).

99. The dreamy face of a young Native American girl (the mountains above Chamula, Chiapas).

100. A sister's love (Ek Balam).

101. Native American women wrapped in shawls (Chamula).

102. A young Mayan girl (Mexico).

103. Will the world soon be better and life more beautiful?

104. The Valadores: brave men, tied to their feet, descend from the top of the pole back to the Earth (Tulum).

105. Musical instruments of South American Indians (Peru) – ocarina, reed flutes, a scraper, and a rattle made from the claws of a llama (from the author's collection).

106. A scraper–drum with a sacred bird and a scraper decorated with the sacred image of a llama and a Native American man with a horn (Peru); the scrapers are made from dried gourds (from the author's collection).

107. South American Indian reed flutes (from the author's collection).

108. Reading energy imprints among the ruins is a distinct stock-take and adventure.

109. Tine attuning to the sound of the Native American drum.

110. Clay images of animal guides – *naguals* from Chamula (from the author's collection).

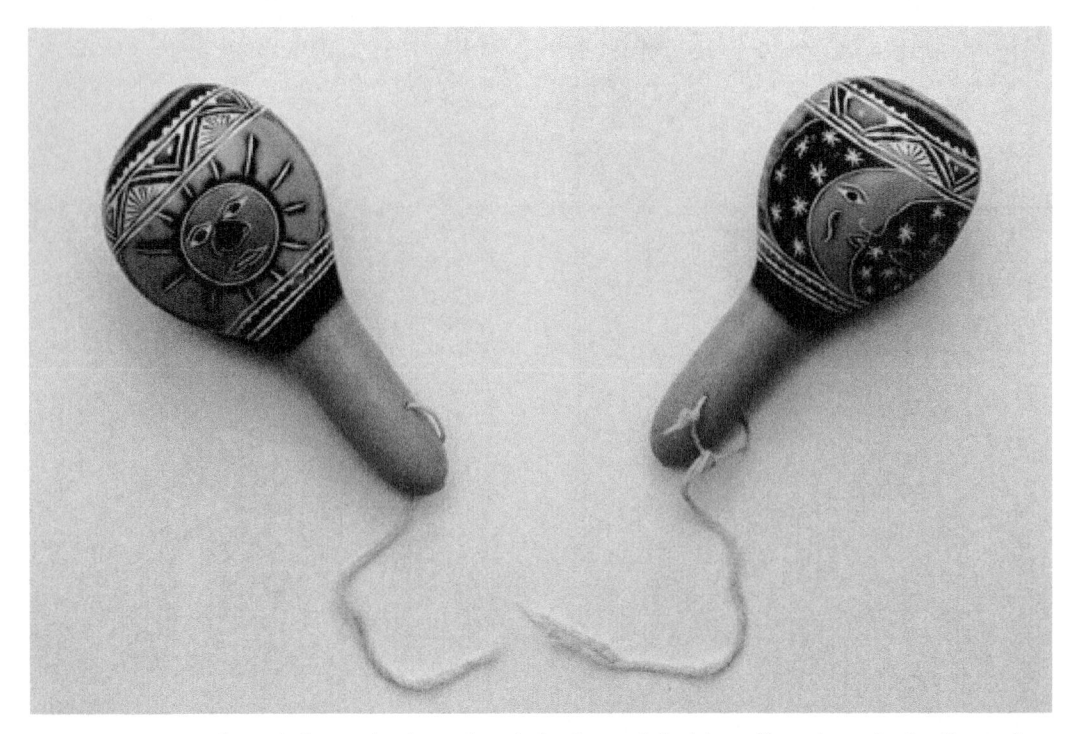

111. A Peruvian rattle made from a dried gourd, with the Sun and the Moon (from the author's collection).

112. Native American rattles with symbols, reed flutes and clay 'man and wife' flutes from Brazil.

flows in the rhythm of *sicureado*. The *aymara* rhythm is used to accompany songs. Most **rituals and religious festivals in Bolivia** take place in the *carnavalito* rhythm. *Tonada* **is a dancing and magical rhythm, a rhythm of ritual magic.**

I recently watched a TV travel programme in which a Native American **elder from Peru** was saying that **the one who is struck by lightning will become a musician-shaman.** Interesting. So, the benefits of lightning can be miraculous. Remember the introductory story about a man who became a musician after being struck by lightning.

The Aztec fire ceremony and dance on the sacred tree

Adrian Gilbert[360] described a ritual of the Aztec **Tonatac** tribe, called *danza de los voladores*. He watched this ritual, in which a group of **five young men, dressed in bright colours, climbed a 80 ft pole.** There was a narrow **platform** on its top, only **8 in. square** (this was their final destination). Attached to this platform was **a square frame, which moved about freely in the air (like the awakened ones do). The first person to reach the top stepped onto the platform and started to dance and play a bamboo flute** and a drum. Rhythm and music are the essences of life. He was joined by the others who climbed to the top and took positions around him (**enlightenment is a great gift**). They sat on the moveable frame, to which they were attached with ropes. Then, in unison, **they fell backwards from the moving frame and floated in the air. They resembled birds** (or spirits) flying around a sacred trunk (**moving along the axis of consciousness**, which is of course easier and faster if an enlightened person accompanies you). With ropes, **they made thirteen circulations around the pole** (they symbolically made a journey of one cycle, they **completed the journey**) and skillfully jumped **down to the earth (back to the physical world). The musician** was the last one to **come down to the ground. With all the dignity** of an accomplished accrobat, he joined his friends and received a well-deserved **applause.**

This ritual obviously **resembled the Aztec *xocotlvetzi* ritual,** which was described by the Franciscan friar Sahagun. **The four flying men probably indicated the four cardinal directions, or paths, four seasons and winds, four fundamental elements of the material world.** Time and time again, South-American Indians still today perform **New Fire ceremonies** at the end of each 52-year period, which indicates the movement of the planet **Venus.**

In **2005,** Adrian Gilbert together with a group of scientists cruised around the seas that surround the Mayan countries. In his book *The End of Time*, he

---
360 Adrian Gilbert, *The End of Time*, Edinburgh, Mainstream Publishing (2007), p. 75.

described **a fire ceremony,** led by the **Mayan elder Carlos Barrios.**[361] Carlos was born in the highlands of **Guatemala,** in the town of **Huehuetenango, in the land of the miraculous Mam tribe** – in a land which has perhaps **most authentically preserved the spiritual heritage, customs, and ways of living of the ancient Mayans.** Carlos closely studied his cultural heritage and became **a Mayan ceremonial priest, called** *ajq'il,* **and the leader of the Eagle clan.**

During this journey, he held the fire ceremony in a more or less abandoned town of **Cahal Pech.** He was dressed in his **white ceremonial garb:** an open-necked shirt, **a highly coloured shawl** around his shoulders and **a red cummerbund-like belt,** wrapped around his shirt. He wore his head scarf like **a turban.**

Using maize powder, Carlos first drew **a sand diagram (a** *mandala***)** on the ground in the middle of the square temple: **a circle,** which he divided, **in the form of a cross, into four parts** with lines perpendicular to each other. The two lines terminated in arrows. Using maize powder (pollen?), he then drew **a smaller circle within each field, four of them in total. And he also drew a fifth one into the centre of the diagram.** The fifth circle marked the intersection between the vertical and horizontal lines. On the east side, he drew a special **hieroglyph,** which looked like the profile of **a pyramid.** He added two dots next to it. Then he took copal **incense** out of his bag and placed a small ball of incense on each of the circles.

This was followed by **a solemn speech,** in which he said that **the glyph** he had drawn had been **used for millennia. When humanity survived the destruction of the world, four jaguars came from the Pleiades (incarnated Pleiadean souls). The Pleiadeans were in charge of teaching people.** He said that this was the period of last glaciation, during which people withdrew to caves. **They asked the jaguars, who were demigods, to clean the cosmic expanse so that sunlight could reach the Earth again** (we can also understand this in a symbolic way).

Seven altars were made on mountains. Then one of the most important healers, called **Akabal,** meaning **Venus, or the new light,** came to the country. **People started calling the Sun.** Each of the jaguars brought incense and **each took one of the corners.** The drawing represented the Creation story: **the circle is the Mother Earth, arrows denote the four directions and the central circle is the sacred place,** where the ritual was performed.

Wise members of other cultures say that every sacred place, every ritual site becomes **the centre of the Universe** during a ritual. **The four circles** represent four corners, the **four elements** – the earth, the water, the fire, and the air (**the central circle represents the ether and life energy).** The four circles inside the large circle represent **the eyes of the Great Spirit,** because **the ritual connects people with the Great Spirit, with the Intelligence of the Universe.**

....
361 Ibid., from p. 289 on.

Then the Mayan elder Carlos Barrios said: '**We don't need an intermediary. We have our own connection with the Great Spirit.**' These words say more than enough, they confirm **the conscious use of telepathic connection with the divine Source of life.**

Carlos narrated: 'And the Father **Sun arrived here on the Earth and talked to the jaguars.** He said: 'It is OK that you are creating life and we **have the responsibility for this new humanity.**' After which he added: '**Any time that you need something, you can call on me.**'

The jaguars are obviously symbolic representatives of cosmic forces, life forces, and the energies of the stars, which all nourish life on Earth. We can always connect to these forces. **Connection brings help and power.**

'But don't only call me when you have problems. Remember me also when you are happy and you have everything: when you have health, when you are prosperous and happy. Because that is the purpose of life: to be happy.' These were the words of the creative forces of the Sun. And this is also what the sacred book *Popol Vuh* says.[362] True, people usually ask cosmic, divine forces for help only when there is a misfortune or suffering. Otherwise, we tend to forget them and we also **forget to give thanks to the Great Spirit,** the God, the Intelligence of the Universe. This is what Native Americans are warning us about.

The shaman Carlos then said that **everyone wanted to attain their own goal,** but **we were destroying Mother Earth. The purpose of this ceremony was to ask for happiness, health and abundance, as well as to ask Mother Earth for forgiveness and help to find balance between the energies.**

'This is our purpose,' explained the Mayan elder and shaman. Then he explained the date (*quel sikim*) on which the ceremony was held. It was supposedly **the day of fortune, the intermediary** between people and the Great Spirit – a day on which people can ask for well-being.

'**The Great Spirit is the eagle, the condor, the *quetzal*, the bird of power,**' Carlos added.

Then he laid out more **copal** balls, **placing them around the circle** at the middle of the symbol. Then he opened a packet of candles and placed them **in groups of three** around the cardinal directions and around the great circle. He placed bigger and thicker red candles on all the arrows, **paying attention to the symmetry of the figure.** At that time **the noise of cicadas increased.** This is how, **through sound, nature supports** human endeavours, when people are in tune with the Creation and with everything that is. With the students of my school, I have experienced this support of nature countless times during ceremonies. It was always different.

362 Read the story and the interpretation of the sacred book *Popol Vuh* in this book.

Carlos lit several candles which he held in his hands and **started a ceremony in the East,** just like North American Indians start their Sun Dance. He recited **prayers,** calling upon the first jaguar, named Bolon Quitzé.

'We call on you, **Bolon Quitzé. You are the guardian of the fire of the red race. You are the guardian of the light. You are the energy of the spirit.** We are calling you because my brothers come here to sacrifice. Please **see our purpose and forgive us. We are asking that the light be spread around the Earth.** I call you, Bolon Quitzé, because you are **the energy of the light. You are the energy of the Creator. You are the beginning** and we are calling on you to **give us the power that we are your warriors.** On this date of *quel sikim*, we call the energy of the spirit of *Sikim* to help us with all our prayers, personal and communitary, **prayers for Mother Earth.** You can make possible **the Great Spirit to turn his eyes and pay attention to the small ceremony. But you don't see the quantity, you see the force, the energy and the belt of power inside of the spirit of the heart** of all my brothers and sisters. I hope you receive this energy. In essence, Bolon Quitzé, **we ask for the light to guide humanity so that we can help Mother Earth to make the transition to the five suns and five elements.** Bolon Quitzé, **thank you.**'[363]

Then the Mayan elder went on and **addressed, in a similar way, the other cosmic forces, the jaguar Gods,** who are also mentioned in the sacred book *Popol Vuh*. He invoked **Bolon Acal, who is the guardian of the black race.** The guide and guardian of **the white race** is called **Mahucutah Bolon** (in his opinion). **Iquibalam** is said to be the guardian of **the yellow race.** He addressed his prayers to each of them. The ceremony of this Mayan elder was still quite **similar to the ceremonies of his distant ancestors,** who had created the sacred book *Popol Vuh*.

Then Carlos **distributed candles and cigars** to every participant. They received cigars, just **like the mythical twins** did in the above-mentioned sacred book of Creation. Participants broke up the cigars, placing them on the pile which became **a new fire place,** marked by candles. Each participant then **spat** what seemed to be neat whisky **onto the pile.** In the sacred book, spittle is the symbol of **a new life, which has grown out of the old.** This custom reflects the mythological Creation story, in which **One Hunahpú's head,** placed in the midst of a tree, spits and impregnates a girl – who then continues the human race. Gilbert wrote that the fire burned strongly, despite the rain.

A healing ceremony followed. The Mayan priest went around the circular *mandala*. He looked each participant into their face and carried out a healing ceremony, **placing his red bag (the colour of blood and life) on their head** (where the

---
363 Adrian Gilbert, *The End of Time*, Edinburgh, Mainstream Publishing (2007), pp. 293-294.

mind resides) **and their right hand** (on the main physical assistant). He recited prayers for each participant separately, **brushing his hands down from their heads to their shoulders (cleansing their auric field and etheric bodies).** He did a different ceremony for those who seemed unwell to him.[364]

After this, he started **a general healing ceremony for the Earth,** in which he again invoked **the four jaguars and special days.** But the Mayan priest was unfortunately unable to bring the ceremony to an end, for the participants had to leave in time to catch the boat (this is how it is in a world in which there are more important things than spirit and the ceremonies of the spirit). A pity. But the described ceremony brilliantly depicts **the spiritual path *sacbé* and the role of sound in the ceremonies of life and death.**

Diego de Landa described a similar ceremony. He mentioned a similar symbol – a circle divided by a vertical and horizontal line, with five small circles in the middle. **According to de Landa, the central circle was called 'the fifth point,' or *quincunx*.** This symbolic division of the circle is the same **in rain calling ceremonies,** in ceremonies, related to the **Bacab Gods, the Gods of four directions.**[365] The names of the jaguars invoked by the Mayan elder Carlos Barrios resembled those mentioned in the sacred book *Popol Vuh*, denoting **the Fathers of the human race.**

----

364 Unfortunately, the author did not describe the way in which those ceremonies differed.
365 Adrian Gilbert, *The End of Time*, Edinburgh, Mainstream Publishing (2007), p. 295.

Magical crystal skulls

> I believe that a tree does not grow green simply because
> we think or want it so.
> But because there is an **invisible**
> and intangible **Intelligence** in it.
> **Get to know it!**[366]

At a concert a crystal bowl opens my way into the research of the crystal skulls

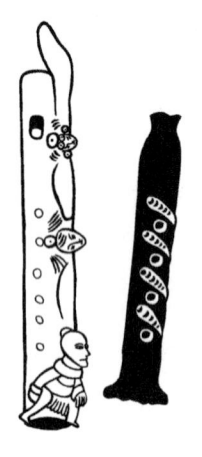

Cross flutes; the flute to the left, with a little man at its foot, is a triple drone flute.

"No, I am not going to deal with crystal skulls," I thought while preparing this book. But to what avail when **we are not actually the ones who choose** our life's tasks and events. It is our life path, or destiny as we call it, that chooses us by its own logic, a logic which is sometimes difficult to grasp. Even crystal skulls possess this power to centre and focus, which is why things turned out differently! I was simply put on a research track, regardless of whether I wanted it or not.

The Mayan oral tradition says that now – during this period of transition to the new evolutionary era of the new 'fifth Earth' and to a different consciousness – is **the time to complete our spiritual transformation as far as possible. It is time for humankind to expand its awareness and stop creating pain and suffering.** Will it manage? We have the tools: **the heart, the mind, and a boundless consciousness.** And crystal skulls are said to contribute to this process of transformation, in their own way of course. At first I wanted to avoid them while writing this book. I thought they were too contentious and mystified, because for centuries, **a net of something inexplicable, mysterious, miraculous, and incomprehensible** had been woven around them. True, I have always been drawn to researching such fields of life, but this time I had decided that there was **no need for me to go into** the field of magical crystal skulls. **But life had a different plan.** Unexpectedly, a time came for me to immerse myself in this topic. Totally,

366 Mirit, 2011.

unburdened, with all my being. **And this immersion brought me an abundance of good things.**

In the middle of September 2011, my **Vedun** Ensemble, a trio for old and meditative music and channelled healing sound with instruments and songs of the peoples of the world, staged a concert in **Zagreb,** as a part of a fair for alternative, healthy living, and fringe science. The concert room was not ready for us by the time we arrived in the Croatian capital as the previous event at the venue had overrun. That evening the **Vedun** Ensemble **was to present the spiritual wisdom and heritage of sound from various cultures of our planet to the fair's visitors.** So by chance there was enough time – which is very rare – for me to quickly check the area where numerous new-age books and other aids for self-healing and spiritual growth were on offer. I was interested to see if there was anything new in this field. Today I am only rarely drawn to books, I rely more on my telepathic abilities and inner visions, but in the past I could easily buy ten or more books in one go.

My attention was suddenly drawn to metal **Himalayan bowls.** Among them, there were **two crystal bowls,** their whiteness shining: one small and one extremely large. Himalayan bowls regularly assist at my healings and lectures, as they **quickly pull** the audience **into a more expanded attention and transcendental state of consciousness.** But at that time I had never owned a crystal bowl. I stopped in front of them and picked up a wooden mallet padded with felt, which you rub along the edge of the bowl to encourage it to start sounding. The sales person immediately jumped up: "Oh, my crystal bowls can explode! Please, don't strike them!"

I had been using such aids for many years and naturally had quite a sharp sense of how strongly I should strike or rub a bowl to induce its sound. And I was taking into account the fragility of the crystal. Every tone that came out of the displayed bowls as a result of my gentle strikes told me what kind of tool I had in my hands. They told me **about the quality of their sound** and how effective the bowls were. **The purer their tone is – the more penetrating and effective they are.** None of the sounds that were floating out into the room were **clear, rich, and pure** enough for me. But when I gently stroked the large crystal bowl, its sound utterly **rocked me into the expanses of the essence. It instantly connected all levels of consciousness into one.** There was no other option for me than to treat myself to it. I asked the price, but was told the bowl was not for sale. Oh, no! What a shame. But I kept standing there at the table, gazing at the bowl's translucency.

Meanwhile my Croatian students who had come to the concert gathered around me and explained to the sales person who I was and what I did. I was not unknown to the Croatian public. And then in a flash the lady changed her mind and was prepared to sell her personal crystal bowl, because she believed the bowl would fulfil its mission better. What a stroke of luck! Together, my Slovene and Croatian students and I came up with the money for the bowl and then it was mine – it was ours. It was there for me and for all those eager to discover their abilities and who were devoted to spiritual development. This is how **my new crystal acquisition took me into new experiences and opened up new opportunities and capabilities.**

The bowl was brought onto the stage ahead of the concert, which was due to start less than an hour later. It glistened in its crystal whiteness among the other wooden and metal musical instruments. I actually didn't have time to test its abilities before the concert. One tone sufficed. It was enough to convince me of the bowl's quality. **For years, I have been performing music in a transcendental state of consciousness, in a trance,** together with my fellow musicians – Mojka and my son Tine. **We intuitively always pick and play** instruments which suit the current moment; **ancient, forgotten and timeless shamanic instruments from different cultures** simply lie there, on display, on the carpet in front of us, **waiting to be selected when our meta-conscious channelling and telepathic thought touches them.** Then our consciousness begins to resonate in harmony with the sound images and unique tunings of those instruments from all continents. When **the guided channelled sound starts flowing through us** we turn into **medium-therapists.** The choice of a distinct colourfulness of the sound-makers and instruments which are exhibited before us is spontaneous. Every few minutes, we pick up one of them and the playing begins. The sound image changes by the minute and will **never be repeated again.** When we finish, we cannot even recall **how and what the divine Intelligence had been creating, or singing through us.** I believe that **the shaman-priest-healers and mediums of past eras**[367] shaped their healing sound in a similar manner. In this way, **they strengthened the all-connectedness between the material and non-material, the audible and inaudible – between the Sky and the Earth, Divine, and human.** Those extraordinary sound effects are enabled by our multidimensional consciousness, holographic physical senses, and meta-sensory telepathic abilities of our kind.

Somewhere in the middle of our Zagreb concert the **new crystal bowl's turn arose** spontaneously. It is quite bulky and heavy. Slowly and with great respect, I placed it on my lap and began to glide along its edge with the mallet. What happened next surprised me a great deal. The audience in the hall had been in a pretty deep trance since the opening minutes of our performance. Their eyes were closed, as they surrendered to the changing sound images and sacred songs of the different cultures which were woven into them. **A space for consciousness and**

....
367 More about guided channelled sound can be found in the first book in the *Cosmic Telepathy* series.

multidimensional awareness was open, it was open for the current moment. The bowl began to resonate **powerfully** after a few rubbings along its edge with the mallet. Its sound was **so rich and pure that I thought I was going to explode.** The sound with its crystal profundity permeated my body, as if it had **illuminated, brightened, enlightened me...** It seemed to me that **I was able to feel with still undiscovered levels of my being** and could even see sound waves **permeating me and the audience.**

I was overwhelmed by a strong energy-sound flow which intensified as we played on. I am not exaggerating when I write that this flow **connected all of us into one unified living pillar: we breathed together and felt the same way – we felt the fullness of sound and a consciousness which expanded into the unknown. Our perception of this symphony of sounds eliminated the boundaries between here and now, between eternity and the current moment. Only the fully resounding essence of life remained.** After the concert, numerous listeners shared their experience with us musicians, telling me that they had felt something similar.

I was more than satisfied that night. I knew that this was how it had to be, that **the crystal bowl had to come into my hands and that I had to go through this 'priestly' experience** in the presence of a selected audience. Around 150 listeners had together with us created **a sacred ceremonial space. They were attentive ceremony participants.**

During the following days, I often enjoyed the harmonious sound of the crystal bowl and it became ever clearer to me that **I had to go through this** singing crystal **experience at precisely that time,** at the time of carving out this book about the Mayan spiritual heritage. It was thanks to this experience that **I finally began exploring those somewhat notorious crystal skulls.** The experience **opened up for me a new path into a new awareness** and confirmed numerous hypotheses which mainstream science (still) refuses to accept. A Slovene saying says that **'thinking means not knowing.' But to experience means to penetrate into places where the mind cannot go, where thought cannot go.** Only consciousness, or the soul as folk tradition calls it, can reveal **the Mysteries of audible and inaudible sound, of life, and death.**

I first **connected telepathically** with the Mayan crystal skulls by accident, while I was reading a book titled *The Crystal Skull*[368] by **Richard M. Garvin.** It was **mid September 2011** and I was editing this book about the sound and wisdom of the ancient Mayans. **I was led gradually into** their **magic. First, I had to familiarise myself with the properties and powers of the crystals.**

....
368 Richard Garvin, *The Crystal Skull*, New York, Doubleday & Company (1973).

My crystal pendulum vanishes and prevents me from healing a horse

The death of my beloved horse Pepini (in 1993) was a very painful experience for me. It was also a very special lesson. One spring Sunday I had gone riding with friends. We raced across meadows, along streams, their banks, and pathways. Who would have thought that this would be my last ride with him. On Sunday we were riding and on Wednesday my dear horse was **dead. He had contracted a tetanus infection.** As if on purpose, the very day when the horse was dying, I had been extremely busy carrying out work for the Slovene Ethnological Society. As president of the society, I had to lead a gathering of Slovene ethnologists and was unable to delegate this task to anyone else. When my friends, who were taking care of the horse in a village in the Gorenjsko Region, told me that **something was seriously wrong, I was unable to immediately visit him. There was nothing I could do.** This gnawed at me greatly and I was desperate.

That is why early the next morning I sat on my bed and **took a quartz crystal orgone pendulum out of its pouch.** By using a bio-energetic method I wanted to release the horse from all the negative energies which had accumulated during the rapid onset of the tetanus infection. The infection had spread fast and his muscles were afflicted. So I took the pouch in which the pendulum was kept, took the pendulum out, and placed it on my lap. Even today, I can recall **a clear image of the crystal sitting on my lap. But, look, the crystal pendulum disappeared! I hadn't forgotten where I had put it!** The pouch in which the pendulum had been safely stored was still there on my lap, but the pendulum had disappeared. I searched my bed, underneath it, I spread out the duvets and pillows, but the pendulum was nowhere to be found. With my beginner's ordinary human energy, **I wouldn't have been able to cleanse the so-called bad and diseased energies from the horse in any case. Luckily for me – but bad luck for my horse. The horse died – I survived.** If, out of love for Pepini, I had done what I had intended to do, with my limited knowledge (ignorance), the **things that I would have pulled out from him would have probably killed me. The horse's harmful energy would have had to pass through me. And that would have been way too much for me at that time!**

Where did the pendulum disappear to and how? But when my friends **informed me that the horse had died, there was the pendulum right there on my bed again. How on earth was that possible?** I had been sitting on my bed, early in the morning, for two hours, meditating and sending healing energy vibrations to my horse, but unfortunately they could not prevent his death. The tetanus infection had already spread too far in his body. I needed at least another decade to understand what had happened. **I only knew that a force unknown to me had prevented an accident.** I was obviously still not allowed to leave this world. I kept saying to myself that I still hadn't done everything, neither that which had been promised to me nor that which I had promised to do at the level of my soul before this current incarnation. Later, I found out that **crystals have their own distinct and miraculous power.**

A crystal can even **dematerialise itself, which means that it changes its wave frequency and with it, it changes its dimensionality,** as we say, **its solidity. It can 'withdraw' itself onto parallel non-material high-dimensional worlds, or waves. Crystals have the power to do this,** claim sages from different cultures, who also explain that even **non-material 'energy beings,'** as we call cosmic frequency waves and frequency gifts, **can intervene.** This was without doubt an experience that **shook me as profoundly as the death of my horse.** And it also gave me new trust and awareness to **accept events which perhaps (still) cannot be totally explained** today **by the logic of the physical world** and the laws of Newton's physics. **But they are nevertheless possible!** It doesn't matter what names we give them – beings, Gods, crystal balls, the centre of the Universe, etc. The quality and powers of the **crystal balls, skulls and wands** existed at all times and in all cultures. **What was their purpose – this is what we have to rediscover.**

Pure quartz crystal is an extremely powerful energy tool, which cleanses imbalanced body energies very effectively and quickly. **It also expands our awareness** and by doing so, **it reveals a clearer perception of our physical senses, it triggers meta-sensory sensations** and also affects the restoration of **telepathic abilities.** Of course, the skulls, which **change colour and can even create sound effects and transmit heat and cold (i.e. different frequency or energy waves),** also influence the physical body, consciousness, mind, and thinking. Crystals constantly pulsate in the frequency waves of the Earth and the Universe. We say that every crystal constantly **vibrates, or 'resounds' in numerous electromagnetic waves** which are in resonance **with our brainwaves (EEG). They can impose their own rhythm, frequency, or their own sound** on our brain (or consciousness) **with the forced resonance** of the current frequency. For more than three decades, I have been researching the way crystals work, and I am still **amazed**, time and time again, **by what we are able to do with their help.** Working with them has expanded my consciousness immensely. Crystals were actually the first to **enable my life without food.**[369] And **modern computer technology** is very much based on their use.

Quartz crystals are the most sensitive solid matter on Earth. They can carry frequency waves into the human field and **transmit, to our meta-senses, imperceptible waves from the Cosmos,** the Sun, the planets and stars, which ceaselessly undulate across the cosmic expanses and nourish life on Earth. This

---
369 Check the first book in the *Cosmic Telepathy* series.

is how **a crystal can change and expand human abilities, both physical, and psychic.** Not only are crystals accumulators of earthly magnetic waves, but also of cosmic waves. **With them, humans** both **expand into the Cosmos** and **ground themselves** in the physical world. **That is why a crystal can become such an extremely powerful tool in the hands of an experienced healer, priest, music therapist or sage who is able to manage both the visible and invisible worlds. It can become a precious aid in transcending earthly limitations, especially when travelling to other (higher) dimensions of consciousness and reality.** But there are, however, **few people** on Earth **who are still able to use** these sensitive quartz crystal skulls **in their entirety, both** in their work and wholistic healing. Without personal experience, we can **scarcely guess their powers and capabilities.**

A National Geographic special issue featured a photograph of a Mayan **ceramic sculpture – an aged God** seated on a stool of bones, holding **a censer in the form of a human head.**[370] It was probably used for burning copal. When the incense was burning, **smoke poured from the God's mouth and enveloped the head. The human energy field, or auric field, and the snake-like (divine) energy which pervades the world of the living** look similar.

A translucent quartz crystal transmits **frequencies: inaudible (yet perceptible) tones across all the octaves in the Universe, both material and non-material, audible and inaudible. It expands along the path of natural aliquot tones – harmonics – which are like the invisible vibrational staircase of an infinite pyramid.**

The symbolism of the flower and the mysticism of my first connection with the crystal skull

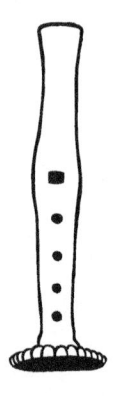

Aztec flute with a flower shaped bell symbolising the divinity of love and music.

While reading the above-mentioned book by R. M. Garvin, I was drawn to the crystal skull which was the first to have been discovered and which is reportedly the most perfect and pure. It was found by the researcher and amateur archaeologist **F. A. Mitchell-Hedges.** The skull was named after him. Immediately after a telepathic link had been created between me and the skull described in his book, I felt my **heart chakra expanding immensely.** I read on. I was pulled into **a dizziness** which we normally **feel when connecting to the Universal Logos, the Divine Being, and when we heal** with Universal life energy. I was tremendously attracted to reading Garvin's book. In my consciousness, I

....
370 *Mysteries of the Maya, National Geographic Collector's Edition* (2008), p.69.

wanted to piece together a picture of these miraculous skulls which have caused such a stir among both the lay and scientific public. Orthodox scientists of course still firmly **deny** that the skull could have any unusual abilities, especially energy abilities. But this **does not mean that they are right. I think we should believe the knowledge passed down through millennia, and the oral tradition handed down through generations,** rather than contemporary measuring devices with limited capabilities.

While reading, I soon felt – without any expectations – **a strong life energy flow running through my body** at its maximum possibility. **It wanted to immediately expand my current energy capabilities.** Well, I thought, this is something that could **open me even more to the Intelligence of the Universe** which resonates in the orchestra of everything that is. This sacred item has the power to do this. But how and why? So, I convinced myself – take up this challenge and start exploring.

To my surprise, I noticed the next morning that **my shoulders, as well as the muscles beneath my right knee were aching slightly.** No wonder, I thought. We (the Vedun Ensemble) had come back in the middle of the night from our concert the previous day. Staying out late is not good for my body and it destroys the balance I need for living without solid food. I know this very well and I feel every change quickly and very strongly. But the concert in Zagreb had finished very late. Then we had to pack up a myriad of instruments, take them to the car, then out from the car and back into the house. I sometimes feel fatigue and disharmony for a couple of days after a concert, which is why **I first attributed this slight pain in my muscles to tiredness.**

First thing in the morning, I tried out my new instrument – **the crystal singing bowl.** For the following week I didn't sleep a wink at night. I was **wide awake**, like when I work with energies for long periods of time or write deep into the night. Tired, I finally fell asleep for an hour or two at the break of day. But I nevertheless began to work early in the morning, finishing the texts about sound for this book. As I was diving into thoughts, words and sentences, which my colleague Mojka was typing on the computer, she suddenly asked me: **"What's that on your forehead?"**

I looked in the mirror, and lo and behold – there was **a red circular spot** on my forehead, two centimetres wide. It resembled **a multi-petal flower,** or the symbols which some peoples draw on foreheads when they want to **mark the area of the third-eye, the sixth chakra, which is responsible for clairvoyance, for telepathic perception.** Well, how about that, I thought, this is something! Wasn't there **a flower set on the forehead, in the area of the third eye,** on the death mask **of the king Pacal in Palenque?** What was this spot trying to tell me? First and foremost that **I should take crystal skulls very seriously**!

The next day, I read in Garvin's book that the Mitchell-Hedges skull had had a similar impact on some of the people who had got in contact with it – with this extraordinary crystal **work of art**, which is a very **accurate anatomic representation of the human skull** and an invaluable **archaeological artefact**. According to some researchers of the spiritual spheres, it is also **a remarkable tool for the expansion of consciousness and self-healing.** As for **the symbolism of the flower**, the Mayans believed that the flower indicated **the presence of the soul.**

So, my first contact with crystal skulls was **a remote, telepathic connection with the Mitchell-Hedges crystal skull.** Notwithstanding the controversy and tales surrounding this and other skulls, which continue to stir up fierce polemics, these translucent skulls are still the subject of research and testings. At the same time, they are **exceptional archaeological and cultural artefacts which cannot be denied or overlooked. They simply are, regardless of whether we understand them or not,** whether we had the possibility to experience their power or not. **The results of some of the research were allegedly never disclosed to the public.**[371] Is there **something very invaluable, something which is difficult to reach, extremely effective, and even frightening,** hidden in the skulls? I hope that we will soon uncover their powers and mysteries.

More subtle people and people of a broader consciousness are of course able to see more widely and they can feel even that which others normally cannot. But **how can science claim that something does not exist simply because it lacks the experience of all dimensions, or is still unable to penetrate – with or without instruments – into the very core, into the very essence of occurrences and items?** Futile self-oriented deliberation, denial and derision should stop at this point.

Although at first I hadn't wanted to deal with them at all, I was simply pulled into researching crystal skulls and their magical energy, whether I wanted to or not. **The path itself led me into exactly what I hadn't wanted,** what I had resisted and kept putting off until some vague future time. And this is how it should be. For such an involuntary spontaneous journey **has its own purpose and meaning. It spontaneously follows the game of life and, above all, happens when its time is ripe.** So, when I finally undertook the study of crystal skulls, I was amazed beyond belief and I would like to share my discoveries with you, the reader.

The Mitchell-Hedges skull, one of the first to be discovered

One of the first crystal skulls to be discovered was found in **1924** by an amateur archaeologist **F. A. Mitchell-Hedges** at the **Lubaantún** archaeological site, a site which had been completely overgrown with tropical vegetation. The skull is an

....
371 The British Museum seemingly never published the findings of their tests on the crystal skulls.

exquisite work of art of high technical perfection, which contemporary science is still unable to match, even though numerous imitations have started to appear. Some skulls were bought directly from **Native American priests,** while others, bought from the dealers, were only reported to have had a **previous priestly use.** It has even been claimed that the Mitchell-Hedges skull is **the most wonderful item ever to have been found on our planet. It is made from a single piece of solid quartz crystal and its detachable** lower jaw, found a few months later, **is carved from the same huge piece**, the likes of which are rarely found in nature.

At the age of 37, **Mitchell-Hedges** set out for Mexico on an adventurous research expedition. He adopted a ten-year old orphan **Anna** and enthusiastically embarked on a research journey across the Central and South American jungles, where he encountered great poverty among the Native American people, who were struggling with numerous **deadly diseases, as well as with rather non-sensical, distorted ancient ceremonies and customs.**

Anna found the skull in an abandoned and overgrown **ancient religious centre, Lubaantún,** where the ruins of a huge **amphitheatre,** which had been able to seat **thousands of people,** have been preserved until today. Now, this area belongs to **the Kekchi Maya tribes. Who knows what kind of ceremonies and customs took place there in the past?** Of course Mitchell-Hedges' passionate desire and belief that he had found the remains of the long-lost Atlantis were immediately discredited and he was accused of fraud. This battle for proof is still on-going today, due to the powerlessness and narrowness of scientific research methods. Nevertheless, Mitchell-Hedges **excavated remarkable archaeological artefacts,** carved stones, stone monoliths, figurines and beautiful **clay ocarinas.** It is still unclear today how the Native Americans, who had neither domesticated animals, nor wheels, were able to bring those huge stones to the mountain tops of the discovered city. With the bygone **science of energy and sound? That might have been the case. Lubaantún was reportedly once a large religious centre, which flourished between the 6th and the 8th centuries.** Then, the site was suddenly **abandoned,** who knows why.

Skulls have a special symbolic role in Mayan culture. They can be found virtually **everywhere:** they are carved into sacred ancestors' walls, stones and temples, while today they even come in the form of **desserts. They are symbols of life, of the circular cycles of both life and death. Not just of death,** as has been imposed by Christianity on people over the last 1,500 years, causing **abhorrence and disgust in relation to death and realms beyond death in people.** Great damage was done through this to our feeling for the natural. Whereas for the Mayans, **the skulls have a different content.** They have nothing to do with macabre death, or only insofar as death is a part of life and of the cyclic rebirth from death into a new birth. The Aztec and Mixtec **God Xolotl – Quetzalcoatl's twin** – is also depicted with a skull.

Garvin says that the Mayans **discovered the mathematical concept of zero around the year 200 B.C.E., that is 1000 years before the Hindus and other civilisations.** It was reportedly not introduced to Europe until the Middle Ages. The Mayan mathematical system is based on **the number twenty. The glyph for zero is a shell.** Obviously, the shell had a similar meaning among the ancient Mayans as it had in the Indian ancient Vedic tradition. And a **human head,** actually its detached skeletal jaw, represents **the number ten** in Mayan culture, in its language of symbols and glyphs. Of course Garvin had to ask the question of why is this so. There are no coincidences. Perhaps the crystal skull, or its importance, **brought about the emergence of the symbol for zero, for ten?** In the Mayan mathematical numerical system, the numbers **from 0 to 13** depict the heads of the most important Deities.

In the first half of the 20th century, the skull was researched by numerous archaeologists, conservators, anthropologists and museums, as well as by the media. One of them was art conservator **Frank Dorland from San Francisco.** He examined the skull for six years and was the first to **speak about the unusual sensations he experienced in its vicinity.** Those who hadn't had similar experiences of course labelled him as **a forger** and liar, and the skull was labelled a remarkable **fake.** But many were drawn to the mysterious and **inexplicable activity of that first to be discovered crystal skull** – and then by other skulls – for it had captivated them with its **magical power, being something odd, exceptional, inexplicable, and mysterious.** They were unable to simply deny its extraordinary nature due to the sensations which they themselves had experienced. And it has been the same with me. But the mystery of deliberating and guessing continues.

Its first finder Mitchell-Hedges wanted to connect the skull with the culture of the bygone **civilisation** of sunken **Atlantis.** He was naturally never able to prove this and he was **derided** by the general public. Later, scientists even accused him of having brought the skull to the site for his adopted daughter **Anna** to find it. But **none of this is** actually **important** at all! **The skull speaks for itself. It is here with all its miraculousness.** As Richard M. Garvin put it, **history** is a conglomerate of ill-timed judgements and **pitifully sad mistakes,** which, in my opinion, hinder development all too often, hinder the use of courageous discoveries to accelerate civilisational progress.

The Mitchell-Hedges skull is perhaps technically the most precisely crafted and is of extreme **perfection.** Some believe that it is called Mayan only because it was found in Mayan territory, even though it may had belonged to some other (much earlier?) civilisation. **Unfortunately, the date of the skull's creation, or** the age of the quartz crystal cannot be determined through carbon-14 dating test,[372] the test which is today used to determine the age of archaeological findings and earthly layers. That is why it is not possible to confirm to which time period the skulls really belong. Archaeologists solved this puzzle by simply classifying its origin as **pre-Columbian.**

In his book, Garvin describes **the testimonies of the art conservator F. Dorland.** He was the first to hold, examine and keep this exquisite object – the Mitchell-Hedges skull. This is how he described his experiences: "How should I describe my reaction? It was like **a cold** visceral **shock** – a minute glimpse **into the farthest reaches of elsewhere.** I felt an ancient contact – a subliminal **awareness of something which harked back to the primeval darknesses created by a Poe,** a Bierce, or a Lovecraft. The crystal skull exuded **mystery and excitement.** There was no doubt as to its **beauty** and spectacular **craftsmanship.** It glistened like an enormous sculptured diamond. And I stood transfixed as **the flame of a candle danced a fantastic orange ballet in the sockets of the hollow eyes.**"

Dorland undertook an intensive study of the skull. He totally devoted his time to it, and he was months behind in his restoration work for several years. He explained to Garvin that it was not unusual for **the skull to produce inexplicable phenomena.**[373] Of course Dorland faced great resistance from scientific circles, for his findings **shook the firm scientific dogmas and concepts,** which even today fail to reach beyond the Newtonian physical paradigm of solid matter. The laws of spirit remain overlooked. The Mitchell-Hedges skull simply **stuck out too much from everything that was known,** which is why scientific circles chose to ignore it, even accusing the finder of having manufactured or forged the skull himself. Later, **Anna Le Guillon Mitchell-Hedges,** the adopted daughter of Mitchell-Hedges, wrote a letter attesting that she had truly unearthed it among the ruins of the long forgotten city of Lubaantún – in at that time British **Honduras (now Belize).** Perhaps scientific circles have truly too much to lose if they wouldn't be able to confirm or reject the logical evidences of the skull's existence. Yet, over the last years, more and more crystal skulls and 'illogical' findings are being discovered.

Garvin also writes in his book that ancient man believed that rock **crystal of this sort was something like frozen holy water from heaven;** I would say that it symbolised **the boundless ocean waters of the Source, the Cosmic Consciousness.** "Diamonds, rock salt, crystal, and glass all went into the same bin," he wrote. And water too, of course.

It is true that today the young science of **crystalotherapy** is very well aware of the fact that a crystal is able to generate truly **magical powers of great dimensions.**

....
372 Richard Garvin, *The Crystal Skull*, New York, Doubleday & Company (1973), p. 29.
373 Ibid., p. 4.

Garvin also reminds us that, as early as **4000 B.C.E.,** the Egyptians **placed a circular piece of crystal in the centre of the forehead of the deceased prior to mummification.**[374] He claims that with this artificial and **symbolic (visible) third eye,** the newly departed could walk into the realms **beyond, into dimensions beyond death,** to the endless levels of consciousness and **eternity.**

Dorland estimated that it would have taken **four or five generations, or at least three hundred years of constant carving** to manufacture such a perfected work. Well, we won't go into such deliberations, but we will instead touch at least a little bit upon the effects the skull has. It is especially interesting to note that **the skull reacts differently** (this is what every crystalotherapist knows!) **to different people (of different levels of consciousness). It is constantly changing and producing various sensations and experiences in the people in its vicinity.** It has an especially powerful effect on those who are capable of **expanding their awareness to the realms beyond the physical world, on those who are capable of extra-sensory perception, of the expanses of cosmic consciousness.**

Even Dorland, the skull's first researcher, postulated that there certainly was **a reason** for its existence, **which everybody hesitated to acknowledge:** perhaps the skull is **an object and symbol of the wisdom in the Universe,** he thought. Why not? It could be **the data bank of time and space.** Yet these words sound alien and utterly fantastic to contemporary science, which acknowledges only the tangible material world and three-dimensional space. Even the world seen through a microscope is a certain taboo. And everything that is outside, or beyond, seems merely an empty fantasy. Garvin says that Dorland didn't want to consider any parapsychological or spiritualist phenomena, but he nevertheless believed that this was truly **a strange and miraculous object,** which fascinated people with its **hypnotic effect.** He labelled it as **a special magnet which drew to it people of all sorts.** In my opinion, it draws people who can be **in resonance and harmony with it.** Some specimens of the skulls allegedly even resided in the treasuries of the Knights Templar.

People who observed the skull for some time, like Dorland, showed a tendency to go sound asleep or to experience a certain **dizziness.**[375] In my opinion, it is precisely this dizziness which attests to **the state of an expanded consciousness and to the flow of the omnipresent life energy.** The skull caused **the pulse to quicken** in some people (their heart chakra was expanding due to an increased energy flow), some even **saw images in it** (images of an expanded consciousness). **Cold, or cold vibrations,** are the frequency-vibrational waves **beyond the material**

....
374 Ibid., p. 7.
375 Check Garvin's book.

world, which pertain to the levels of spirit and high dimensional worlds of consciousness. In them we can, if we attain them, connect to any information or event (to **energy imprints in the Field**) **in the past, present** and even in the **future** that has not yet been fully shaped. Because everything is **wholistic and permanently all-connected. Limits reside only in our three-dimensional mind, experience and body. Beyond, there are no limits.**

Some researchers and media believe that in the distant past, the skull was used by **high priests during their occult work and healing. The frequent use of clear crystal** indeed attests to this possibility, for throughout human history (and also today), it was of immense help **in healing, as well as in restoring clairvoyant and telepathic abilities.** This knowledge has somehow managed to come through to our era, which is why **crystal balls can still be found in today's tales about 'sorcerers.'** Brass mirrors for example have this role among Siberian shamans, for with them it is possible to look into the present, past, and future. But contemporary sorcerers are nothing other than **sages of exceptional abilities and a broad consciousness, sages who are able to step into timeless worlds beyond the material.** Christianity has branded them as nuisances, as heretic pagans who must be banished or eradicated as soon as possible.

The Mayans, similar to the ancient Egyptians, allegedly **placed quartz crystals at the summits of pyramids, in order to strengthen the life energy field** and to accelerate the **healing** process. Crystals can certainly also be used for **the expansion of consciousness and for travels to non-material dimensions of reality and spirit.** All of this is of course possible, although contemporary science is not yet able to research, let alone confirm it, for it still doesn't have sensitive enough measuring instruments with which to perceive all **the invisible and inaudible high-frequency waves – 'the music' from the Sky, from the stars, on Earth.** But our body and meta-senses are precisely that. This is why both **Brazilian and Filipino cosmic surgeons usually call upon the support of powerful crystals during their psychic operations, in which they channel the gifts from the Universe and even the essences of immortal souls** (in the past, such support could have been attained also by means of crystal skulls). Both believe that they are the heirs of the Atlantean heritage, of **perfect knowledge.** Millennia ago, some ancient shamans (including the Mayan ones) were able to perform utterly **miraculous sound-surgical procedures on the human body and psyche,** and if needed, **they were even able to operate on themselves visibly or physically in this way.** But I will write more about this in the sixth book in the *Cosmic Telepathy* series, under the topic of cosmic surgery. These remarkable gifts of **boundless consciousness and crystal tools are a magnificent proof of human spiritual powers and the mortal and immortal soul.**

The miraculous glow and sounds, the programming of crystal skulls

Once, at a meeting, Dorland described to Garvin what had happened to him in the presence of the Mitchell-Hedges skull. **Strange and inexplicable things occurred** near it. He hadn't understood why and even less had he understand – how. One day he suddenly saw **a glow, around 40 centimetres wide,** surrounding the skull. It was there for about six minutes. The skull simply began to **glow** more and more **in its auric field; who knows why and why precisely then?** Why did its **glow, which also attests to the flow of life energy through the skull,** grow stronger?

The researchers of the skull had been supposedly very disciplined during their year-long tests. **They did not use any stimulants** or drugs, they didn't drink alcohol or smoked, and their coffee was decaffeinated, which is why Dorland was pretty certain that those effects, those **visions could not have been produced by narcotics or sedatives.** The skull was illuminated by ordinary light, but **one day its auric glow grew stronger.** Although at the time Dorland **did not believe** the skull had any spiritualist or mystic powers, he nevertheless began to think that this might have been that kind of phenomenon. He thought at first that perhaps the crystal reacted in a similar way **to radar**[376] and that some sort of radar activity at a nearby air-defence installation might have activated the quartz. However, this could not have been possible since the radar had been working constantly, throughout the period that the skull had been there, so the radar could have impacted the skull at any time. But it didn't!

Dorland described to Garvin how **the auric glow started close to the skull with no colour at all.** The auric energy field, which is invisible to the majority, simply **grew stronger and was increasingly visible, resembling a shadow, like a ring around a moon**[377] (this is how we see basic auric layers). Not believing his eyes, he picked up a newspaper to focus them on print **to be certain he was not hallucinating.** He moved around the room, but **the aura continued to grow (spontaneously!).**

However, the following testimonies in his reports are the most important for my deliberations. Dorland explained: "There have been times, **when the skull was out of the vault, that sounds occurred around the house. Much like an** a cappella **choir.** No instrumental music, but **human voices** singing some **strange chants in a very soft manner."**

....
376 All of this, as well as the experiences of the first researchers, are described in the above-mentioned book by Richard Garvin.
377 Yes, this is how we see the auric field surrounding living beings and even objects.

At this point I would like to remind readers of **my experience in the Tolmin Church**, when I suddenly (telepathically) heard a mellifluous 'church' choir singing, which had not existed in the real three-dimensional world. **It resonated at high-dimensional levels of consciousness.** It was actually not a resonance, it was **the sound of consciousness.** Whereas my colleague who was there with me didn't hear a thing! I was astonished: if I can hear them so very well, why can't you. Perhaps they are practicing, I thought. But my colleague didn't hear anything. **She was not able to hear them.**

According to Vedic wisdom, these kinds of sound occur in an expanded state of consciousness. You are totally present here – in the earthly world, yet you are also beyond at the same time, in the non-material world of spirit, above the third dimension of the physical: and in that state, you can perceive the variety of differences of all the dimensions of existence. You are everything and everything is in you. You hear what your physical body and physical senses cannot hear, but your multidimensional consciousness can.

Dorland explained that there were **the bells** after the euphonious choir voices: **the sounds of bells,** sharp and metallic, and **quite high** (these sounds belong to shabd sounds, which can be heard in a state of expanded consciousness). They were not deep gongs or church bells, these were faint, **high-pitched silver bells (the frequencies of higher or broader levels of consciousness), very quiet but very noticeable. The broader (or the higher on the axis of consciousness) we are able to reach, the clearer the visible picture is and the clearer the sound picture is,** and we come to understand events within us and around us more clearly. In Vedic wisdom, such sound images of consciousness are called **shabd**, or **kalma** in the Arabic tradition.

"I had simply no explanation for these things," said Dorland.[378]

Yet, the ancient, but forgotten wisdom of age-old cultures which knew how to reach that place, had the explanation. Those travels were most often depicted by human figures or the images of Gods sitting in **a boat.**

Other times, when the skull was kept at Dorland's home **overnight, mysterious sounds occurred, and various items were found strewn about** even though the doors and windows were locked and nobody could have entered the house. Dorland kept the objects he was restoring exceptionally secure. He also witnessed other inexplicable phenomena. Occasionally, **images could be seen in the skull – other skulls, high mountains, even the fingers, hands, and faces of healers.** Such images or sounds can arise on **the projection screen of consciousness, but also in physical matter itself, when 'memories' awaken in it, or when it reflects the imprints of the mental-energy work and encoded messages and orders of its owners (priests?) or users (ceremony participants).**

....
378 Richard Garvin, *The Crystal Skull*, New York, Doubleday & Company (1973), p. 10.

One day Dorland saw **a dark spot which suddenly started to grow** and eventually covered about one-half of the skull and appeared to be **a clear black void** surrounded by bands of deep purple. **Images of temples appeared and disappeared.** This means that Mayan priests **had encrypted in it the images and energies of sacred sites.** Most probably in order to transfer to those sites the highest possible frequencies and **the most powerful possible energy charge** from the higher dimensions of the invisible Field. This had helped ceremony participants and healers. With it, they had been able to overcome obstacles more easily – they were able to **dissolve energy blocks and enter the worlds beyond.** Dorland even **photographed** the images in the skull. Of course the 20th century mainstream science was even more ossified than today's, but both simply ridicule cases with which they cannot come to grips. **Yet, the subquantum physics of consciousness is drawing ever closer to an understanding of what is happening at the levels of spirit.** The time is coming when it will be possible to clearly explain seemingly miraculous occurrences, for **the science of consciousness** is increasingly improving. And everything that was refuted will **once more** have to be **put under the microscope of a more perspicacious eye and ear.**

In an extremely broad consciousness of mind and heart, it is even possible to hear voices which actually do not exist in the three-dimensional world of physical ears: but they exist on the screen of expanded consciousness. All the spiritual traditions of our planet know this. Most often people describe these voices inaudible to the physical ear, as an angelic **choir of voices. These voices, encoded in our consciousness, can be barely heard, but are very clear, crystal clear in fact, once we begin to resonate with them.** They captivate those who hear them, just like **Homer's sirens**, or they **shake** them in an (as yet) inexplicable manner, like **the connection to the soul or to higher levels of consciousness** shakes us. They touch people's hearts. People who hear them, **know that these voices exist,** even though they don't exist in the physical world. **They exist in a different state of alertness and in a different reality, equally important and as real** as the solid tangible world. **This is not a hallucination. They belong to the highest degree of the cosmic-earthly symphony of frequency undulation and have an extremely strong power of radiation and penetrating energy.** People who can hear them, or are able to invoke them into their consciousness, draw **miracles** into their lives.

The energy flow of cosmic frequency waves can be felt stronger at night, because at that time the flow is less disturbed by the usual vibrations of people's everyday activities and thoughts. Also pain is felt worse at night. **Physical activities calm down, our perception increases, especially meta-perception.** So, our expanded consciousness can hear and see that which our physical ears and eyes cannot.

If the skull was really **used by Mayan priests** in the past, this crystal tool for spiritual growth and therefore for healing too, ought to work in a similar way **to today's computers,** which are also based **on the 'memory' of installed crystals.** Like computers, crystal skulls can still today **store the information about the distant ceremonies of priests, as well as information about the thoughts and actions of ceremony participants.**

Crystals can also be programmed for an activity, for a certain vibration quality, of which thought and the healing flow of life energy are a part. A crystal skull can be a veritable **bank of information** from the past which **can be read** in the present. Yet, this is **only** possible **at an appropriate level of spiritual development, when our mind is perspicacious enough to do this.** This is what **every contemporary healer** has to know even today.

I think **the translucent black spot**, which occasionally occurs in the centre of the skull, **might well be the encrypted perception of an awakened (priest?) person, who sees and connects to the all-full emptiness of Nothing,** which we call **the Source, the Centre, the Divine Essence, the Intelligence of the Universe, etc.** Everything emerges out of it and it sustains everything that is. Those who **connect to it, become part of it,** part of the all-encompassing Field, of the energy **Ocean.** With it, people **rejuvenate** and immeasurably **strengthen their life force and healing power, their perception and in-born talents: people thus become magi, alchemists, miracle workers beyond compare.**

Crystal skulls have also been found in other cultures, or they once existed in other cultures. And all civilisations associate them **with the wisdom of Atlantis and Lemuria, or with the enlightened wisdom of ancient ancestors.** Legendary Atlantis and Lemuria may well be simply **symbols of perfection and completeness.** Tools for growth, such as crystal skulls, were said to **awaken** within people **undiscovered dormant abilities** of which they were as yet unaware. Native American shamans, the descendants of both the ancient Mayans and North American tribes, say that **people who are able to read the skulls' contents (its programmes imprinted in the crystal),** people who are able to read the data imprinted in the crystal, **the energy imprints, the sound-vibration codes or picture messages,** will extract utterly **incredible information about the past, present, and future. And this information is unimaginable to the contemporary mind.** Time limits disappear in this data bank.

Native American prophecies which have been safeguarded for millennia hold the memory of the purpose and use of crystal skulls. These prophecies say that the skulls are here on Earth to **help humanity awaken into a new era, because they expand people's ordinary awareness into the realms beyond and awaken them from sleep into enlightened consciousness.** Oral heritage says that the skulls **are an exceptional tool for awakening into the new golden age, the age of a more expanded consciousness,** which will gradually begin **after 2012. The skulls reportedly bring peace** to all living forms on Earth, to everyone who sings their inaudible and audible song of the Earth and the eternal Universe here and now.

The skulls are especially important **during the time of the completion of the 13 *ahau* and 13 *baktun*** according to the Mayan calendar, when the cycle of the fourth Earth is nearing its end and fulfilling itself in the fifth Earth, and when humanity is invited to **experience a broader multidimensional spiral consciousness.**

Crystal skulls - the computers or library of the past and tools for extra-sensory perception

Crystal skulls, as well as crystal and Himalayan metal bowls, are distinct **tools for spiritual growth and the healing of the soul and body.** They are in fact distinct **computers of the past,** which link the world into a whole. **They tell stories of the past** to those who are able to read their contents, and **they also explain the laws of life.** Especially today, when light and enlightened sound are rapidly expanding within more and more awakened beings, or souls, when **the wisdom of our ancestors is returning.** A time is gradually being created when **seemingly miraculous things** will be **ever more accessible and clear.** The descendants of the ancient Mayans say that now is **the time for the prophecies to be fulfilled.** The time is coming when **the unconditional love of the soul will once more balance the Sky and the Earth, and all living beings on Earth.** We are entering an era which will once again **sing praises to the light of sound,** to the sound waves of light, to the awakened consciousness, or the **celestial** (high-dimensional) levels of the soul. This is why we are coming to understand more and more the remarkable nature of these ancient crystal aids, these age-old computers. There's actually nothing new here – **only form and appearance are changing.** Modern computers simply no longer take the form of human skulls.

Science is highly sceptical about crystal skulls and ridicules all the findings which have been transmitted by crystal skull keepers throughout the world. Due to technically limited measuring devices, the skulls' contents and effects **still cannot be proved.** Crystal skull keepers are scattered **on all continents.** As the scientific paradigm accepts only that which is visible and tangible, and **which can only be proved if it can be repeated countless times** (even though spiritual science knows that **nothing can be repeated**), modern scientists prefer to throw such findings, deliberations and knowings into the bin of fantasy and new-age non-sense. **Nobody actually lends an ear to the legends passed down through millennia, to the chosen wisdom and skull keepers, to seers** who still live also among Native American peoples and speak of the importance of those miraculous objects which are **exceptionally valuable for humanity and evolution on Earth.** Such behaviour does not, of course, honour orthodox science. **If it is still unable to research the high-frequency levels of spirit, it does not mean that the high-frequency world of energies and life does not exist.** Science really shouldn't be mocking the invisible realms of thought, emotions, and the spiritual parameters of life. And people who perceive worlds beyond the material are unable to appreciate such narrow-sighted claims, absurdities and the 'glorified' scientific theses.

Ancient **legends** are coming to light which speak of a symbolic fulfilment regarding the formation of the skulls: **in all traditions, a circle built by the number twelve (twelve skulls) is a symbol of fulfilment, completion and perfection, it is also a symbol of the nine-dimensional consciousness which resonates with it, a symbol of awakening, or enlightenment;** while **thirteen** (according to legends, represented by a skull in the centre of the circle) is a link which connects **the beginning and the end, life and death, into one cycle. Twelve is the sacred number of the divine fulfilment into a whole, the number of the return to primordial wholeness.** If we observe how our life is unfolding, we will soon realise that we are **strongly determined by the number twelve.** Fulfilment which usually begins in the tenth part of our life's cycle, or when passing from one decade to another, **ends in the twelfth part.** Humans were designed to live for at least **120 years.** Our year comprises **twelve months,** day has **twelve hours,** night too, humans reportedly even have **twelve pairs of ribs.** And when we look up into the Sky, we see **the twelve signs of the zodiac,** the twelve different qualities for experiencing the world – i.e. the twelve signs which determine human nature. **The European tonal scale,** or the backbone of sound language, consists of **twelve semi-tones.** When we **multiply this perfection by perfection, we get the alchemistical magical number (12 × 12) – the 144 octaves of the Universe, dimensions, or fundamental frequencies of differentness.** This number reflects the number of different sound qualities, or octave qualities, in our physical world.

Mayan legends, which have been passed down orally and are still today **kept by Mayan elders, priests and healers,** say that **the number twelve achieves its fulfilment in the number thirteen – 12 + 1 = 13.** A completely new cycle reportedly began in **2013,** a new beginning, a new level of existence, a new era, **life with a new consciousness,** etc. The number 13 opens and explains **the relationship between the Earth and the Cosmos.** Some crystal skull guardians claim that there are **four sets of thirteen skulls (4 × 13 = 52,** which is itself an important

Mayan number).[379] This is also what the legends claim. And reportedly these sets will be **rediscovered** in the light of the spiritual enlightening of human evolution. Their powers are said to unite into **a powerful all-connected generator of the Earth's evolution.** Some say that there are **24,** or even **72** crystal skulls on the planet, waiting to be discovered, **to come together in an energy cycle** – in a sacred circle – and take humanity into the broader consciousness of a golden age. The skulls are actually **waiting for contemporary priests who will be able to activate them (completely!) with the expanses of their consciousness, and will be able to revive the eternal and timeless wisdom of the past for the future.** This is what the stories of the mythical crystal skulls are whispering. **Siberian shamans** are said to keep and revive the ancient wisdom in a different way: **by 'reading' the imprints, the essences of the immortal souls of the Ancient Ones, in the kurgans, or mounds. They bury themselves alive in tombs in order to safeguard the knowledge and wisdom for their descendants.**[380] The body is nullified, but consciousness remains alive and alert.

We are therefore living at a time in which it is **impossible to escape transformation.** If we want to avoid it, we will draw dissatisfaction and pain into our lives: we are living during the Earth's cycle of **the accelerated awakening of ancient wisdom, knowledge, spiritual knowings, songs and rituals of the past,** which keep **the messages from previous millennia.** And **even today** these messages can **lead** us along the path of spiritual maturing and can help us.

Crystal skulls are remarkable archaeological and art objects, as well as powerful tools for spiritual growth and healing. They are said to be a **service for the transfer of knowledge from a distant past into contemporary time.** This is also what a number of spiritual teachers, healers, and shamans claim. With the skulls' help, humans can even rise to cosmic levels and can read from **the cosmic library of sacred knowledge.** Why not? After all, **everything is possible. Even though we are still unable to understand** and explain how. Two decades ago, even I didn't think that one day I would be strolling across the cosmic expanse. So, let us allow the possibility that beyond everything we are familiar with, there is an ocean of differentness, an ocean of differences, and an infinite number of new and different possibilities.

Tools, such as crystal skulls, which are reportedly distinct **sacred objects, or power talismans,** are **priestly tools** of admirable technical perfection and artistic beauty. **Along the axis of consciousness, they open the human mind, heart and consciousness to new worlds, to other non-material dimensions – to levels**

....
379 Detailed information about crystal skulls and prophecies can be found on the numerous websites of the skulls' keepers; www.crystalskulls.com.
380 Check the third book in the *Cosmic Telepathy* series.

beyond the material world. Legends as well as the contemporary testimonies of priests, healers and skull caretakers claim that they have **an immense magical power.** The skulls also have a magnetic ability **to attract those people who are today able to work with them.**[381] **When the time is right,** of course.

Every skull has reportedly its own unique properties. Some people compare them to **books in a library,** or they suggest that every skull is a comprehensive library. In a wider context, however, every skull possesses its own vibration qualities and can be compared to **chapters in a book. All skulls are like books on the book shelves of the Universal, the Divine.** They were allegedly used primarily for **the occult work of priests, shamans, or healers** in their rituals, prayers, during healing treatments and for necessary knowings and visions, as well as **during the centering and focusing of intent and for the manifestation, or actualisation of visions and ideas.**

I think that crystal skulls – transmitters of life energy – **heal the heart, the mind, as well as the physical body. They open inner hearing, or clairaudience** and inner sight, or **clairvoyance, along with telepathic abilities or awareness.** Work with them **brings awareness, peace, and joy.** They are like an all-encompassing **matrix, or portal for the awakening of cosmic memory, or cosmic (enlightened) consciousness.** They belong to the family of powerful, if not the most powerful, **telepathic tools,** because they **strengthen physical and spiritual power, the free flow of life energy** to those who work with them, as well as to all who are present. They also **expand consciousness** to unimagined heights. They are veritable **radars for the waves of the Intelligence of the Universe, or life,** with which it is possible to **penetrate into the data bank (akasha,** or the information system about everything that exists), in the bank of energy imprints of **everything that has happened not only on Earth, but also in the Universe.** Every event leaves its imprint, its energy shadow, in the universal Field. That is why crystal skulls were indispensable for **divination.** Yet, the knowledge of **how to capture eternity, the centred sound, or the Intelligence of the Universe** which we call divine, **into a crystal,** will of course remain a puzzle which will probably not receive scientific confirmation for a long time. This sound will only be revealed by a handful of individuals. But **ancient Mayans** were undoubtedly **masters of how to hide the mysterious and how to reveal the concealed,** they were masters of how to hear the inaudible and how to recognise the **waves** of the life energy flow.

Remember **the exceptional abilities of crystals,** their **acoustoluminescence.** Crystals can **change light into sound, and sound into light.** Crystal skulls are distinct **converters of different frequency waves (cosmic, earthly, human) across the dimensional levels, or worlds of reality,** across different frequency waves,

---
381 Check the testimonies of numerous skull caretakers at the above-mentioned website.

which we call dimensions. They work like **resonators, like catalysts or oscillators** – special instruments which **resonate with cosmic and earthly waves, but also with the frequency patterns which have been programmed in a crystal. They can even impose the encoded frequency wave lengths (or patterns)** which have been placed in them by their guardians, **to other objects, beings, and the environment. In line with the resonance laws,** these patterns then begin to resound with the imposed resonance and they **attune** everything around them **to their own (new) note,** for example to the absorbed vibration, or tone of cosmic consciousness and to the memory of the priest-programmer, or healer-programmer.

Actually, it is not people resonating with crystal skulls, but primarily the skulls resonating with people! **A skull gets activated** when a person has attained a broad enough awareness in their consciousness, an awareness that is **near to the bank of Truth. It opens its treasury, its mind. Its programmed contents awaken and its activity is triggered; it starts to vibrate, or resonate and it draws into resonance all the people who resonate with it.** This is how a thought, or **the program of a vision which had been imprinted in it,** is amplified – for example an idea or a vibration (tone) of cosmic consciousness. I think that crystal skulls do not belong to people, not even to their guardians, although they are keeping them physically, but I think they **BELONG TO THE EARTH AND HUMANITY AS A WHOLE.** Everyone can resonate with them, **everyone can enter into their treasury of memory** and into the codes of the timeless wisdom about the laws of life. **There is only one condition: that a person attunes, or aligns to the skull's frequency and that they, in their mind, embrace eternity, cosmic quality, universal quality, etc.**

Crystal skulls - symbols of life and death, detectors of good and evil in life, myths and fairy tales

As we have seen, crystal skulls **answer our questions and are tools for seeking the truth of our existence and our own mission. They are a distinct transformer, intermediary and amplifier of the frequency waves of primordial life energy** without which there is no life. They transfer this energy into our physical bodies and the physical world. The skulls actually expand our consciousness and raise its vibration, which is why people see, hear, and understand more or more broadly, which is why it seems to people that the skulls are delivering messages to them.

If **a person with bad or evil intentions** comes near a skull, the skull will amplify them, so this poor person might begin to **feel nausea**, perceiving his or her unkindness even more strongly. This is the reason why, **at their first contact**

with the skull, some people **became afraid** of its accompanying effects and even associated the skull with doom and death. **The Mitchell-Hedges skull** was named **the skull of doom or the skull of death** by its former owner, whereas its present owner changed its name to just the opposite – **the skull of love.** This is in fact simply a distinct **mirror** which reflects the spiritual impulses of the observers. **Both the good and the bad will be amplified in the vicinity of this crystal resonator, or oscillator. A reflection, or an echo, having the same frequency,** will be mirrored – in line with the laws of resonance.

So crystal skulls 'behave' differently with different people. Their effects depend on **how open, or closed, the observer's consciousness is, which opens, or closes with regard to their whole-heartedness. Loving and spiritually open observers experience unusual and miraculous experiences, while closed and bitter people simply get an opportunity to see a reflection of themselves,** their lacks, and **weaknesses.** Crystal quartz pendants can **pull distorted energies from the environment, or from a diseased person. They can store them and pass them on.** For example, to the wearer of that pendulum. I made this mistake only once. I had a crystal drop on me at night. A diseased person was lying next to me. Fortunately, I sensed how his disease was being transferred from him onto the crystal and then to me, so I immediately started to cleanse. It is preferable to give up wearing crystal quartz jewellery, which we would otherwise have to clean on an hourly basis.

Skulls are symbols of mind and consciousness. In Mayan culture, they are also a symbol of life and death, of purity and translucence. Visible darkening and changes in colour can occur in some parts of the skull depending on how it resonates with the current moment or with people in its vicinity. When activated, many skulls even **change their weight; while their inaudible vibration flow, or sound, can become visible,** when higher frequencies convert to the frequency waves of the (three-dimensional) material world and physical senses. It is a two-way process.

With the frequency waves of their consciousness, observers can awaken, or amplify, the crystal vibration abilities of a skull, of its programme. As if we were standing in front of a castle with innumerable gates, waiting for one or more of the gates to open. Perhaps none of the gates will open. **We cannot foresee** which gates will open and what we will encounter, or get to know, behind the gates. We are familiar with the **technology of crystal programming,** but the technology of programming crystal skulls remains quite unknown to us, even though they resemble each other in many areas. This remarkable knowledge was certainly **employed at the very least by enlightened sages, by priest-healers whose frequency waves unenlightened people are simply (as yet) unable to**

attain. It is only through high-frequency waves that it is possible to reach into the world of lower (material) frequency vibrations. The opposite is not possible! That is why skulls impact people in their own, seemingly miraculous way, and unenlightened people cannot expect any unusual changes in the skull or around it. But the skull is of course **a brilliant assistant and guide, a tool for transformation and self-realisation,** for those who are close to a quantum leap into enlightened consciousness.

Traces of this long-lost exceptional **technology of crystal programming** have been retained in **fairy tales about sorcerers, miracle workers,** until today. **Crystal balls, which work in a similar way** and reflect human properties, often appear in them. But they are nowhere near as miraculous. However, in those fairy tales, we can nevertheless sense what that 'sorcery' is about, at least a little bit. Today, it belongs to an inexplicable magic, although it is as **natural** as for example night and day, or the seasons. But what counts here primarily is our own experience. With crystals, including crystal skulls, we can draw nearer to the tracks of that which is miraculous, but completely natural.

Crystal skulls can **impact any crystal** and, according to some guardians, **twelve skulls can** even **activate** totally new crystal skulls manufactured today, **through their ancient encoded, programmed knowledge. This transfer of content is possible.**

First a telepath gratefully asks and clearly expresses the intent – the best would be for the benefit of everyone. And he or she connects to the high-frequency sound of the crystal skull and **attunes to it, begins to resonate in the same (frequency) symphony. Every undulation is sound.** Sooner or later every telepath finds their own way of entering, their own way of healing souls and bodies with it. And the Cosmic Intelligence, or the Universal Logos of life energy, will wash over anyone, healing them in their own unique way. **Everyone will receive exactly the vibrations they need for their balance.** It is like a computer rearranging its (sound) qualities. People **in tune** with a skull always feel **an increased energy flow** through their bodies and sense **crystal clear thoughts** (the term is still alive – '**a crystal clear thought!**'), with which they can create and actualise their visions. A skull is a distinct **portal between the worlds of spirit and the material world,** a bridge to the harmony of the visible and invisible, a tool for tuning the audible and inaudible, and it is also a proof of synergy – synchronicity.

Some say that a crystal skull is **like a computer memory stick.** With it, it is possible to transfer information from one computer (from the Intelligence of the Universe) to another (to the human mind). That is why today some people **transfer the imprinted, programmed content** from the thousands of years old crystal skulls **to newly manufactured and carved crystal skulls.** This was the case with the Tibetan skull called **Amar,** which a High Lama carried across the Himalayas.[382]

Skulls' powers for the completion and fulfilment of ideas **are best activated by the energy support of the full moon. When the moon is new, programming of intentions is effective. The power of fulfilment increases as the moon waxes.** These effects of the power of the moon's waxing and waning are known in all cultures. Almost all civilisations were familiar with them, including Celtic-Illyrian and ancient Slavic peoples.

Thirteen skulls for the activation of the portal of time and sound, their use in rituals

Occurrences in crystal skulls were also documented by **Karin Tag,** who holds a PhD in holistic sciences, from Frankfurt. She founded the **Seraphim** Institute and patented **a photon camera,** which can record barely visible occurrences in crystal skulls. Karin is also a guardian of one of them, the skull called **Corazon de la Luz, the Heart of Light.**

F. N. Nocerino was the first to discover **legends concerning thirteen skulls.** The legends say that **more and more crystal skulls** will be discovered, which means that there will be more and more important **spiritual 'books' about the expanses of consciousness** which will help to form **a new consciousness, or the wisdom of the new era. Thirteen skulls were brought together** in Los Angeles **on 11th November, 2011, activating a distinct portal into the new era.** According to the Mayan calendar, that day marked **the path or the possibility for a transition into something totally new.** The event itself was said to have **awakened** within people their **cosmic memory, their cosmic consciousness.** Many skulls together naturally have a stronger impact not only on both human and earthly energy fields, but also on **the Earth's crystalline grid. The stronger the 'elfin energy-sound yarn' is, the more clearly humanity becomes aware of the high-dimensional levels of existence, of the nine-dimensional consciousness of people and reality.**

In his book, R. M. Garvin describes the story about the first skull to be discovered, found in Lubaantún by F. A. Mitchell-Hedges and his adopted daughter Anna. This first discovered skull, named after its finder, is perhaps still the most brilliant. It still shines among all the later discoveries, and it is the only skull with a detachable jaw. Mitchell-Hedges and Anna both died some time ago,[383] and the

....
382 In different languages, the word *amar* supposedly means to speak, to love, to say, as well as immortal.
383 Anna died at the age of 100.

skull's **caretaker** is now **Bill Homann,** who changed its name from the skull of the doom to **the skull of love.** Homann is convinced that the skull is **here to help humanity find its contact with the heart and consciousness of oneness more easily. The skull is still changing,** it produces or facilitates various feelings, visions and **sensations** within observers. **It has an especially strong impact on people with greater sensibility and meta-sensory abilities.** Can you imagine the shock of those who were among the first to view the skull, when **a flame was flickering in its eye sockets**, or when it **changed colour** by itself, **when it emitted noises and mellifluous sounds, when it emanated hot and cold vibrations, or when it caused a mysterious dizziness and excitement** which usually occur in expanded states of consciousness?[384] Of course a variety of strange things **inexplicable to the ordinary mind** occurred in this remarkable object, which shows no trace of mechanical grinding. That is why the mind turned these occurrences into a mystery, and it even began to fear them. Today's mind is still unable to discover how ancient masters actually manufactured these wonderful crystal skulls.

Mitchell-Hedges claims in his autobiography that the skull was used **in esoteric rites by indigenous shamans, especially in the centre of pyramids even in the millennia B.C.E. Changes in the clarity of the crystal were especially miraculous** within one of the skulls which he kept, **as it most often became clouded in the area of the third eye (the centre for inner sight), at the top of the head and near the temples, where the centre of the brain for inner, telepathic hearing and meta-sensory perception is located.** Perhaps these light effects also worked on those cranial parts, or centres, of its guardians and priests?

The skull had **a particularly special effect** on people when **its interior part somehow clarified into a void of Nothingness.** There, **images of faces, temples and events would** occasionally **appear and disappear.**[385] The void of Nothingness – the absence of everything and an all-pervading presence at the same time – is the goal and **supreme achievement of everyone. The energy flow in the skull grew particularly strong at night and the skull would then usually begin to shine in its auric glow.** The clarity of its interior, which arose out of a previous whiteness, **acted like a magnet on everyone who gazed at it. This visible void of fullness is at the same time an imprint of the wholistic perception of an awakened priest,** who has been connecting, with his multidimensional consciousness, to the Intelligence of the Universe, to the Centre of the Universe, to the void of Nothingness.

In his book, Garvin summarises Dorland's research findings[386] and includes Dorland's claims that the interior of this pure and balanced crystal skull is composed

....
384   Check Garvin's book.
385   Dorland meticulously photographed all of this.
386   Dorland began researching it in 1956.

of **arches and light pipes,** which act as **concave and convex** lenses channelling light from the base of the skull upwards, into its eye sockets. I believe that they also play **a part in creating sound effects and directing sound vibrations to the top (the seventh chakra) and into the environment.** I also think that the skull can act like a distinct **accumulator and amplifier of sound, similar to the skilfully manufactured tube of a flute.** Images appear and disappear in the light of sound, and people occasionally have the feeling that **the skull is glowing,** or **burning.** This is of course also possible. Every reiki master, every master of cosmic resonance, knows this, provided they are **connected to the all-present life energy and the Universe. All bodies begin to glow** – both mine and those of the participants – when I perform **initiations of cosmic resonance** which has developed from traditional reiki. **The cosmic fire of life energy heats and illuminates everything, while humans can direct, or re-direct, this flow.**

When looking from the skull's upper surface, **a ribbon prism in the centre of the skull and pinpoints of light at the rear of the eyes** can supposedly be seen. The Mitchell-Hedges skull has been exceptionally **perfected, its eyes flicker and glow, as if alive, and the jaw opens and closes, and even nods approval or disapproval.** It was said the priests themselves moved it with a string. Did they want to say that **death is not frightening** – it is actually ever present in life – that death is in fact **a part of life and that human consciousness continues to live and move even beyond death?**

The skull, or the head, is certainly – beside the heart – **the most important part of a human being.** Humans can live without arms or legs, but not without a head. Thoughts originate in brains, which keep them, **because brains capture and convert signals from the environment, along with difficult to perceive visions, or 'messages' from the Divine Logos.** The head is a distinct symbol of the human species, it is also a mark of the **meaning of life,** which facilitates **the expansion of consciousness** and a revelation to people on Earth of the material–non-material parameters of existence. It is through the experiences in our life that **we learn how to move beyond life and death,** and we also, especially today, learn how to **get rid of the acquired dread of death.**

Given the fact that, unfortunately, **the date of their creation cannot be determined through carbon-14 dating test,** we are unable to state in what types of rites the skulls were used. Some clairvoyants suggest that it is **impossible to enter into the time of their creation,** while others associate them with the period of the **great flood** during the time of such legendary civilisations as **Atlantis and Lemuria.** These two civilisations, with their utterly fairy-tale technological and spiritual perfection, still dwell **in humanity's ancient memory and its cell memory.** Deep in our soul, in our consciousness, their myths make us feel **a yearning for** a better, or broader awareness, for a more complete and perfect – Atlantean – way of living.

It is in fact not known for certain whether the skulls are actually Mayan. We only know that they were **found on Mayan lands.** But, of course, they may as well be much, much older, having been brought from somewhere else. Perhaps one day we will be able to find out for certain **where they came from and how they were created. The tools of our consciousness might be of immense help** in this.

Testing crystal skulls, their lightness and invisibility

Extremely hard quartz crystal **cannot be carved with knife, it is even very difficult to grind it.** Incorrect pressure can crack it. **Crystal grows in spirals,** which can be right- or left-handed, and is actually a **hexagonal** prism with special **accumulating or dispersing properties. Its spiral motion encompasses the symbolism of the Earth's evolution and life itself.**

Quartz crystal is used in **contemporary electronic devices, especially in modern computer systems, where its role is to memorise and control frequency waves, because it is a resonator which reacts to cosmic and earthly waves, as well as to the inaudible vibrations, or waves, of thoughts and emotions.**

Today's computers and I are not in tune. If I try to work with one, **my balance gets shattered** (its vibrations disturb me). If I spend time next to a computer, it ceases to work (because my energy-frequency field disturbs it). It also comes to a halt if I protect myself against its radiation, which feels to me extremely destructive, primarily in the areas of the throat and heart. That is why my writing is transferred to a computer by others. **Obviously there is no harmony between computers and me. But I don't have any problems with attuning to the Cosmic Intelligence** (even though it works at far, far higher frequencies). I **also resonate brilliantly with crystal skulls.** Clearly, there is something in computer technology which is not in tune with me (and with people) – its waves, or radiation, destroy our energy fields. That is why people are tired or have sore eyes after long hours of working on a computer. Computers impose their own frequencies which are unkind to humans.

The Mitchell-Hedges skull, as well as many other skulls, was **tested in the Hewlett-Packard laboratories,** where computers and quartz oscillators are tested daily and where their growth, or their axis, is examined. The contemporary art of crystal carving **follows the natural axis of the crystal** to avoid cracking it. Yet, scientists in the above-mentioned laboratories discovered that the Mitchell-Hedges skull had been carved **with total disregard to its natural axis,** an axis which is so important to today's manufacturers. The skull is made in its own unique way. **It** was carved with regard to the three horizontal veins in a left-handed growing crystal. When looking at it, one researcher even said that the skull simply **shouldn't have been.**[387] It flies in the face of currently available technology and accepted scientific norms and beliefs.

Garvin included another interesting piece of information. When the skull was immersed in **benzyl alcohol, it became invisible. Extraordinary!** If we could **raise the frequency spectrum** of an object, or ourselves, **into the spectrum of gamma rays for example, this item (or we) would become invisible, non-material, or in fact etheric.** So invisibility is not completely impossible. **We have to change the frequency – and then we will be in another world, in another dimension, or reality.** This is also what numerous fairy tales and stories of different cultures speak about. Similarly, it is possible to change **weight, to change solid matter into the non-material, into an etheric mist, and also to overcome gravity,** which is what I do in yogic sidhi levitation. That is how I know this is not a utopia. **A rock weighing several tons can become ridiculously light.** So there is only one puzzle left – **how to achieve this** with objects. And **with which frequency, which sound?** Did the Mayans know this, as well as for example the Tibetans and Egyptians?

Traces of this forgotten knowledge of **frequency manipulation of solid matter objects** can be found in all cultures. With it, it is possible to **decrease the density or weight** of an object.[388] **It is increasingly likely that the megalithic scientists were able to move stone blocks weighing several tons using the technique of weightlessness** and place them at their pleasure in a chosen temple form – in a circle or a pyramid. Such scholarship belongs to **the forgotten knowings about sound and sound technologies.** Today, many are trying to revive it.

When the Mitchell-Hedges skull was rotated **in alcohol** and viewed through a polarised filter, it exhibited **a brilliant rainbow of colours – especially around its eye sockets and the nasal cavity and mouth regions.** It was also discovered that the jaw was made **from the same piece of crystal** as the skull itself. When **the laser was directed at a point in the middle of the nose cavity (under the centre of telepathic perception and insight), the entire skull became fully illuminated. But unfortunately, laboratories failed to perform any acoustic tests.** These tests would perhaps be of extreme importance for revealing the skull's capabilities. It was estimated that the skull was at least **1000 or 1200 years old.**

The Mitchell-Hedges skull, as well as some others, were also **tested in the British Museum in London,** but the results of the analyses were never shown to the public. Who knows why? Being self-centred, scientists have often claimed that the

....
387 Richard Garvin, *The Crystal Skull*, New York, Doubleday & Company (1973), p. 87.
388 More about this can be found for example in the third book in the *Cosmic Telepathy* series, which deals with Siberian shamans.

Native Americans were incapable of such precise and exquisite workmanship. There were even speculations **that the skulls had perhaps been manufactured in Europe in the 14th century,** when the art of crystal carving was flourishing. Which is why they simply classified the crystal skulls as being **pre-Columbian,** claiming at the same time that **the Miztecs** for example were **excellent crystal carvers** and had a good eye for symmetry.[389]

Garvin wrote that the Mayan builders of pyramids and temples, which had in many aspects even surpassed similar ancient Egyptian works of art, **used the juice of a plant, or plant-based pastes, to soften and mould the stone.** Even today, archaeologists marvel at the **incredible precision with which stone blocks were fitted perfectly** to form the huge stone formations of a temple. They explained that certainly **no cutting tools were used in the building process.** Well, these pastes have not yet been discovered, but this doesn't mean that we won't discover them one day, or that they didn't exist in the past. Let things run their course. More about miraculous pastes can be read in the chapter about Mayan healers and healing processes.

When a newspaper cameraman, J. R., **photographed**[390] the **Mitchell-Hedges skull,** he had the **shock** of his life **when he started to take a print from the negative.** He was surprised by a sudden shattering **explosion,** the like of which he had never experienced before. Frightened, he ran out of the laboratory. What had happened? Had he perceived a **breaking out of the energies which were present, or a distinct energy-sound fusion?**

Mitchell-Hedges maintained that his skull was used by **a high priest of the Mayan civilisation prior to 1600 B.C.E.** Legend has it that he took the skull into the depths of the temple and **concentrated on it, willing death.** They say that death always comes to someone connected with it.[391] These words can of course be understood in many ways. **The realms beyond death have a much higher frequency** than the physical world. Anchoring a death vision, an awakened priest who is able to master both the material and spiritual worlds, might wish to **leave his earthly life and become enlightened. He moves to the realms beyond death, to the levels of the soul.** Or, they were thinking of **the death of the old, bad, and outlived.** But this doesn't mean that we should associate the skull with evil, or with a horrible death, as his first finder did. What is more, in the vibrations (beyond death) which are higher than our ordinary material ones, our **ego starts to fall apart and everything that is still not perfect begins to die. That is why death and near-death realms are the greatest teachers.** If we still don't understand the

....
389 Richard Garvin, *The Crystal Skull*, New York, Doubleday & Company (1973), p. 85.
390 Ibid., p. 90.
391 Ibid., p. 91.

process and refuse to accept it, we can have **strange feelings, or even nausea.** Or we can embrace the process with great **gratitude,** by which we speed up the process and can complete it. **The process of becoming aware is continuously on-going in the material cosmos. If we resist it – it hurts.** Competitive people who **mostly want praise, refuse to face their weaknesses.** Praise leads them away from their core and **if there is no praise, they are unhappy, for their ego feeds on it.** What is more, these people are ferocious and **angry,** ready to **fight** anyone who whispers to them that the truth is different. Such people **need shock, pain, or the vicinity of death, to sober them up and shift them.** To make the events in their lives clear.

New fields of study have emerged over recent decades, which touch upon spiritual teachings more closely. One example are **psychic and acoustic archaeology.** Those possessing the skill of extra-sensory perception, or intuitive-telepathic abilities, are able to locate **items being searched for.** This is how **Nick Nocerino,** a pioneer in crystal skull research, found one. He telepathically knew, or 'saw,' where to dig. This is how we can look for lost items. **Psychometry** can also be of help here – a method for knowing or **reading the information, or energy imprints (the history), in objects.** Siberian shamans called khams do this with **bones. Metaphysical ecology, a study of the relationship between humans, the environment and the energy that is present,** is also steadily gaining a reputation.

There is truth in legends. We only have to hear it. But contemporary scientists are unfortunately all too often deaf to it. The purpose of this ignorance is not clear to me, as it is precisely the stories, fairy tales, and legends that are **living witnesses, veritable libraries of the past.** They have been preserved through to today precisely due to their lyrical power and importance.

Cosmic, open consciousness chooses neither papers, degrees, nor a plethora of data. It comes to both beggar and PhD, to a king and a pauper. Certificates, or recognitions, are of no value within it. **It is validated merely by consciousness itself.** Luckily, there are more and more PhDs who are bravely turning over a new leaf, increasingly **taking into account folk testimonies and even their own mystical experiences.** Some even believe that **true scientists are those who allow themselves an insight into the mythical, mystical, even into the completely unknown.** But these people encounter great difficulties principally due to the fact that today's authority and **decision-making power** lies in the hands of **unenlightened people** whose judgements are immature and erroneous, and who, on top of that, even **legalise imperfection.** It was different among the ancient Mayans.

In his researches, the scientist Garvin discovered that **the temperature of the skulls never changes,**[392] even if placed in a refrigerator for example. **Skulls constantly change colour and transparency** and Garvin says that they even exhibit

---
392 They maintain a constant temperature of 70 °Fahrenheit.

their own unmistakeable perfume and bless us with its **odour or unusual sounds.** Sensitive people can sense their **distinct vibrations and the pulsing of both heat and cold. This is what every healer and shaman,** as well as the students of my school, **need to know.**

The Mitchell-Hedges skull changes visibly all the time. Especially **the front part of the skull which often turns cloudy.** Garvin is convinced that the skull is able to plant, or better – **to transfer – its thoughts (encoded energy imprints of a priest's thoughts?) into the human mind; it can cause tightness throughout the chest area, a tightening of muscles, an accelerated pulse and high blood pressure; it can even leave a bitter-acidic taste in the mouth.** All of this is but sensory **evidence of the skull's energy-vibration work.** Pressure or tightening in the chest area can be felt due to **an increased flow through the heart chakra.**

When this first discovered skull is observed, **not only does its auric field begin to change,** it also starts to grow (its radiation, it energy starts to grow). While **dark spots near its temples** attest to yet another occurrence in the skull. **The dark area in the centre of the skull increases and vanishes in an inner void. Isn't human life like this,** emerging into the light of day and disappearing into the darkness beyond death, in the non-material realm of the soul?

Garvin also thinks that the skulls are here to **serve spiritual growth,** the expansion of consciousness, to **lift the veils of a deeper, higher truth. With them, humans penetrate their universe.** I would say – **the centre of themselves.** Let us remember that human **senses are holographic** and constantly **connected to everything that exists.** That is why, as we say, it is possible that the flutter of a butterfly's wings causes changes on the other side of the world. The skull **connects the worlds in a holographic way. And the human crystal centre reveals the beauty of existence** and the physical world, the purpose of our life's journey, of life and death, of **being and non-being.** In Chichén Itzá, **a ball** from the late Classic period was found with **a human skull inside it.**[393] This fact is especially revealing and explains the symbolism of the ball which is associated **with the head, with the mind** which resides in it.

The skulls of course **greatly surpass our abilities and understanding. They help observers to transcend, to move beyond the boundaries of life and death, to move beyond any need for proof** which becomes completely superfluous and non-sensical in the expanses of the abstruse. Crystals carved in the form of a human skull are among **the most mysterious, beautiful, intricate and miraculous objects of our world.** Some claim they are **more than 10,000 years old.** They are a distinct tool, a computer, or **an ancient telephone for a conversation with the Universal Logos, or God. They influence us, even if we don't want that or are not aware of it.** They were so **sacred** that **only a priest was allowed to touch** them.

....
393 Semir Osmanagich, *The World of the Maya*, Sarajevo, Svjetlost (2004).

Crystal skulls as vehicles for the spirit and new-age tools

Well, **contemporary caretakers** – spiritual teachers – can perform the same role as priests in the distant past. Without priestly attire though. Having been invited by Anna,[394] the medium **Simon Alexander** reportedly triggered, or **channelled, a vision** in which he saw the skull being **used in a ceremony. Priests** in the ceremony **were constantly repeating a word. I logged into the sound weave of this vision and I heard that sound.** Such visions are of course still possible and accessible. It is most likely that the priests were repeating different sound **codes, keys for unlocking the data bank, and the energy treasury.** The pioneer of crystal skull reasearch, **F. N. Nocerino,** also believed that skulls were distinct devices which could be **activated through the use of colour and sound.**[395] **Colour, sound,** even thought and feeling, are but **inaudible (high) frequency waves (therefore, light and sound) which, through resonance, trigger co-oscillation, or action. We only need to know the right frequency key** which will open the door into subtle realms and the invisible data bank about **everything that was, is, and will be.** The sound I heard resembled the sound, or the humming of Creation, **the mantra AUM.**

Crystal skulls are also **distinct vehicles of consciousness (soul), or spirit boats,** which take their worshippers and users **across the boundless ocean and eternity into the joyful realms of deep peace.** That is why their caretakers **carefully cleanse them in water and charge them with the radiation of the full moon. By blowing on a skull,** they dissolve any impure energies in the crystal. Honouring (that is **energising**) them **with prayers and ceremonies** is desired, especially on precisely determined days in **the Mayan calendar (on the day of the *keme*,** which is intended especially for **revering skulls**). Past and present caretakers light **incense** to their skulls, and they constantly **guard them against the impure energies** of those who are not yet suffused with the pure, high enough (**high-frequency**) life energy of compassionate love and wide open consciousness.

Contemporary guardians claim that skulls are excellent **receivers and transmitters of the ancient (forgotten?) mysteries of our planetary ancestors. They are protectors and guides into the consciousenss of oneness. They build a wholistic field of collective oneness. They belong to the age-old, forgotten technology of the wisest persons of our planet. And the backbone of this technology is perhaps precisely sound,** or sound (energy) frequency waves and their **modulation.** Quartz crystal enables the establishing of a powerful field of expanded

....
394 Richard M. Garvin, *Kristalna lubanja (The Crystal Skull)*, Zagreb, MISL (1997), p. 116.
395 Nocerino died in 2004. He made the skulls popular in 1980 and was the only person to have worked with several hundred skulls. Check his websites.

consciousness. In line with the laws of acoustoluminescence, it turns **white light** into **a spectrum of rainbow colours and into audible sound.** The process can also run in reverse: a crystal **turns the rainbow diversity of sound back into the white light of high-dimensional sound, the cosmic whisper.** This is how the skulls revive clair-perception – clairvoyance, **clairaudience, and visionary abilities** – within people.

Today, lyrical and symbolic **names** have been given to **the skulls, which have different vibrational qualities, abilities,** and shapes and are made from different types of crystal. The most exquisite skulls are certainly those which were estimated to be thousands, even **10,000 years old.** These were the first to have been examined in **the British Museum** in London and in a Paris **museum** (the Musée de l'Homme). Two of the most famous and remarkable are certainly **the Tibetan skull Amar** and the skull **Max** which was used by a Mayan priest in Guatemala for healing, prayer, and rituals. Also renowned are the skull called **Sha-Na-Ra from Mexico** and **Portal de la Luz,** the Portal of Light, which is made from smoky quartz and is kept by **Joshua Shapiro.** Jaap van Etten is the caretaker of the skull named **Ti** which came from Tibet. **Corazon de la Luz,** the Heart of Light, came **from Peru** and is kept by **Karin Tag** in Frankfurt. The skull called **Sam from Brazil constantly changes weight** and a very massive skull was named **Einstein.** There are of course many more such skulls. I have listed only some of the most esteemed ones.

There are also **the twin skulls** from California: **El Aleator** and **El Za Ra** (the Daughter of Light). When they came to their present guardian **Susan Isabelle,**[396] the two skulls were full of **stains and impure** energies. Susan explains that she was given the skulls by Native Americans in Central America, who recognised her as the reincarnation of a person from Atlantis. At first she didn't know what to do with them, so she put them away. The skulls had waited for six months before she remembered them. One day, she set off to a mountain together with her spiritual aspirants and took the box containing the two skulls with her. At the top of the mountain, Susan opened the box and saw that **the skulls were absolutely clean.** She is convinced the skulls **healed each other.** Today, they shine in their crystal clarity and **change colour** all the time. **Pink and blue interchange with crystal white** in rainbow colours, and you can even see into the interior of their brains. It may as well be that they were changed and cleansed by **the energies of the site, of the mountain,** as well as by the contemporary **ceremony** performed by the people who were there.

Susan placed them **on an altar** on the mountain and **a telepathic voice** told her to put them together. At first she refused to do so, saying that they were **too**

---
396 After years of experience with crystal skulls, many guardians wrote books about their findings.

hot (which attests to the presence of a strong energy flow) and that she would get burnt if she did it. But when she heard the same order once more, she did as instructed. And the two little skulls **came together – to form the perfect shape of a human heart.** Her hands were glowing strongly (probably like when cosmic resonance is activated, or when we are in a healing connection to the Primal life energy). This is how **she became the keeper of the Mayan human heart** made from two small twin crystal skulls. Susan is convinced that, **in this time of transformation, the skulls heal humanity and open the doors into new dimensions, into a time which lies ahead, into a new consciousness of the Earth.** Cyrstal skulls are said to take us to **a new beginning,** into the era of a new Earth with a completely different consciousness.

Working with crystals and sound during the process without food and liquid

Crystals have **changed** my **life** as well. Following several months of working with them, my consciousness expanded (or my frequency increased) to such a degree that **I didn't need food any more.** This happened in December 1994.

At the end of **September 2011,** I, along with the most devoted students of my **Veduna** School, headed to the island of **Murter** in southern **Dalmatia** (Croatia). Eighteen of us stayed for a week in the wonderful apartments of one of my Croatian students. We were nourished by the beauty of the wonderful environment of the Adriatic Coast, which, in my opinion, is one of the most beautiful in the world. **The Adriatic** is certainly one of the most beautiful and clear seas, full of interesting islands, lagoons, and marvellous beaches. The landscape by the azure blue sea inspired us, giving us joy and commitment which accompanied our one-week feat – **four days without food and liquid.** Day and night, I guided the participants, who all wanted to test themselves in this not so easy **initiation-trial**, through the cleansing of despair and through **the sensuous and mental storms which were triggered in the process.**

We followed the examples of ancient civilisations and also some of today's cultures which are still in harmony with nature. We delved into this **four-day initiation ritual without food and liquid,** after an initial gradual preparation, of course. My **crystal bowl** came in very handy. Each day we met three times, with everyone talking about what was happening in them. Such rituals lead to **a powerful and rapid transformation; they build faith and strongly cleanse the emotional-mental blocks caused by stress and trauma.** Being without food is easier than being without liquid. But if we embrace, openly and without a doubt, the presence of the Intelligence of life, of **the cosmic-earthly essence and its waves, this Intelligence is capable of feeding us,**[397] nourishing and sustaining us.

In such processes without food, we don't use our life energy for digestion and metabolising, which is how **all that energy becomes available for raising awareness, for maturing spiritually and being creative.** During the process, our physical body requires less and less attention, while our spirit, our consciousness, **expands as far as it is able – along the axis, or tree, of consciousness, further into the unknown, into the realms of higher dimensions. Our awareness, mental abilities, and physical capabilities expand vastly.**

Within one week, we slowly entered this four-day process without food and liquid, and afterwards we also slowly stepped out of it. Only those who truly wanted this journey and were connected to the Earth and the Universe, those who were **ready to hear where they were stuck in the illusions** which had brought them problems and unhappiness. An extensive **stock-take of emotions, thoughts, and actions** took place, together with **accelerated energy healing.** There were floods of tears at each meeting. Suppressed pain was released first by one participant, then by another. **I played my crystal bowl** during our meetings and we sang songs from different nations, accompanied by me playing the Greek **bouzouki.** I can play melodies on the bouzouki which are otherwise played on the Balkan tambouritza, the Mediterranean mandolin, the Slavic balalaika and the Turkish-Greek dzura. **The sound** of the crystal bowl and the soft sounds of the bouzouki **opened the participants right up. They connected ever more as a loving spiritual family and with themselves – into the deepest layers (Xibalba) of themselves.**

Soon, whether it was day or night stopped mattering. The process of **becoming aware and cleansing** was happening all the time. What we received during this initiation process was of **immense value.** It is not easy to endure an abstinence from physical food and liquid, but nevertheless, everyone who trusted in the Intelligence of the Universe and in the flow of life **received precisely what he or she needed.** Four days was just right. North American Indians have a similar process – **the Sun Dance** under the scorching Sun, dancing the entire day after an evening's hot sauna.[398] Or when they set off to a remote place in nature for **an inner quest.** They do this in order to look inside themselves more easily!

When being without food, our **alertness expands strongly.** As far as it is possible. **This trial requires the trust of the initiate and a level of spiritual**

....
397 I described my more than ten years' experiences of living without food in my first book *Life without Food and the Timelessness of Spiritual Messages of the North American Indians.* A similar ceremony of the North American Indians, which is still alive today – the Sun Dance – is also described in that book.
398 More about mastery over mind and the cleansing of the emotional body can be found in the next three books in the *Cosmic Telepathy* series.

maturity. **Trust** increases by the day. I also revealed my messages or insights to the participants, so that they could **identify the reasons for their problems more easily.** And my sixteen years' experience of living without food has given me substantial knowledge about the way human beings react to such extreme conditions. Many things come to the surface. And everyone can begin to see **how they have been living, thinking, fighting, or tying themselves up in knots.** White people want to understand first in order to be able to surrender more easily, to immerse themselves in **the unknown.** Numerous natural peoples are able to do this without painful dissecting and pigeon-holing.

Faith in the Intelligence of the Universe, in the omnipresent life energy, grew among the participants. A similar effect happens on my other courses, and even during concerts and lectures, as I always work on the supporting waves of the omnipresent energy (life) flow. But when the process was over and as we consumed our first cups of kompot and soup, we were overwhelmed by **an immense delight, a joyful faith in life, in ourselves, and in our own spiritual power.**

Self-confidence grew by the day. **Nothing is impossible,** reverberated from this experience. **Everyone realised that** if we had managed to go through such an exceptional **trial, we could do anything, because something truly majestic and inexplicable is watching over us,** something which descends into the human spiritual and material world – especially during **the cosmic initiations** which the participants had received in previous years, or during courses for attuning to the Intelligence of life via **cosmic resonance,** which **makes even atheists turn into grateful worshippers of life's waves.** My painful and successful shamanic initiations after a venomous snakebite and broken ribs helped everyone **strengthen this knowing.**

People's experience without food and liquid surpassed all their previous experiences, **as it demanded a complete surrender and trust,** the same as that needed by for example initiates in sarcophagi and pyramids, in deserts and tropical rainforests. It became clear to all of us that **everything is possible with the support of the Intelligence of the Universe!** This was the most important knowing of this initiation.

With such a connection, we are able to cross boundaries, tear down those walls and limits set by our mind, by our physical body, and by commonly accepted patterns.

Spirit is always more powerful than the physical body. Thought and emotion are the directors and architects of our lives. We are what we think; we will achieve what we believe. But if we despair and think that we can't do something, we will attract into our lives precisely that – failure and disappointment. **Faith in ourselves and in the omnipresent Intelligence and life energy,** also called **the**

Divine Essence, which makes us alive, which sustains, balances, heals us and makes us aware, gives **an immense power, because our visions are no longer hampered by fear and despair. This is the very core** of those processes in which crystals and music are indispensable. When **we attain the level of total acceptance, or surrender, miracles** begin to **happen** in our lives, miracles which are usually not revealed to people who go round in despair, fear, and lack of trust. But by not admitting to themselves that they have failed, they usually criticise and condemn those who are able to attain such miraculous events and **the abundance of balance and attunement.** These deserters from the journey of life find such processes a non-sense and unnecessary clutter.

In this process without food, my participants touched both **the ultimate and the mortal, the transient and the eternal** at the same time. The proximity of the beyond is **revealing and fulfilling.**

Everyone felt it was difficult to leave after the week-long process, they felt that such **openness to the spheres of spirit, the spheres of multidimensional consciousness, is well worth living permanently.** Which is not easy in an ordinary life. Experiences of this kind reveal to us **entirely new insights, unexpected visions, even new missions, talents, and destinies.** By looking from a broader perspective or symbolically, from top-down, we naturally see much better, and above all, a true **understanding of the events in our lives is much clearer to us.** So we departed with joy in our hearts and with a promise (to ourselves) that we would **treat ourselves to more** such initiation-trials in future. And thanks was given to my crystal bowl, to my playing and singing, which had opened up all the participants. Some had cured their year-long problems and diseases, including diabetes and a chest tumour.

I am convinced that **the ancient Mayans** were **also** familiar with similar initiation rituals. **The energy flames, the flames of consciousness,** rising from the head of the captain of the (**winning!**) team in the ball game, illustratively speak precisely about such experiences.

Ways of connecting and working with crystal skulls

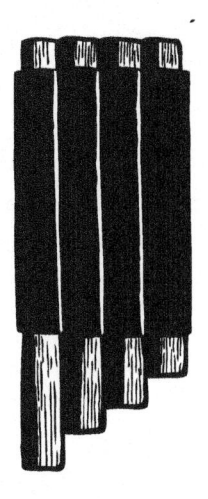

The levels of connection with crystals and crystal skulls are different. It is possible to connect with a skull via memory, telepathically. By revealing **the skull's memory, we touch its content. Through a telepathic connection,** our ability to attune to its imprints, contents, or programmes, will be determined by our depth, by our susceptibility. However, crystal skulls usually work in a different way – **they are the ones that establish the connection with us,** whether we want it or not. This **happens when the time is right,** when we are **in tune** with the skull and we are **ready for its gifts and 'messages.'** When the **Intelligence of the Universe, which reverberates in it, needs us.**

Four-chambered bone flute

However, crystal skulls are accessible to everyone. But their accessibility, or **the number of their accessible layers,** will depend on each individual person, on **the depth of the person's consciousness and whole-heartedness.** The skulls may be even totally **inaccessible.** Or they can shine in all their splendour. Most contemporary caretakers tend to only look after them physically, but a few are also able to work with the skulls' help.

Even these mysterious and magical items **travel** somehow **along the axis of consciousness** – from their physical caretakers to priest-activators. Each station which leads them to a person with a broader consciousness is a new challenge – important for both the person and for the entire energy field of the Earth. **Anyone who has a crystal skull** in their vicinity, or anyone who is able to connect with a crystal skull and perform energy work with its help, is constantly **receiving its exceptionally powerful energy support for their spiritual growth and self-healing.** Folk tales of course describe events within a skull and around it in an engaging and **symbolic way.** In order to understand what these tales are telling us, we have to read between the lines, between the metaphors and symbols. We have to read through the labyrinth of colours and sounds.

In **September 2011,** I was honoured that one of the discovered skulls **'chose' me for its mysterious work.** Then together with a group of participants, we tested its power and magic, which words cannot describe.

Many important things were revealed to me during my telepathic research of crystal skulls. For a long time for example, I dealt with the question of why the

Mayans **tied and pressed their skulls.** And here are my experiences of **connecting to four ancient crystal skulls** at the first autumn course at my Veduna School in early **October 2011**: all 50 course participants – including me – continuously felt a strong **pressing sensation around our heads. As if a tight blindfold was covering our third eye and our temples – the centres for inner sight and hearing,** which were expanded to the highest possible limits of a person's abilities and thus **opened up clair-perception.** Then it occurred to me that a blindfold over the forehead and around the head might be **indicating a readiness and desire for the expansion of one's abilities, for spiritual growth** and the opening of the third eye. Siberian shamans are familiar with something similar today; by placing a scarf over their forehead **they symbolically close (or open) their third eye,** whenever they wish to do so. When they no longer want to look at the madness of the world, they tie a scarf over their forehead. While by pressing their heads, the Mayans obviously expressed a desire to open **telepathic clair-sentient abilities.** The blindfold around their head helped them to constantly **direct their attention to the third eye – the centre of clair-perception. Attention is the energy which supports the process and accelerates it.** This is so simple, I thought. Why hadn't I realised this before?

A clear quartz skull called **Grandmother Rainbow** confirms this discovery in a picturesque way. It has a small human figure carved on its right side, **the top of whose head extends to the top of the crystal skull. Both heads merge.** It seems as if the artist wanted to say that this naked little human being **wants a permanent connection** to the magical power of the crystal skull, to the omnipresent Divine power and life energy which undulates through the skull.

As I have said, there are **different levels of connecting to the crystal skulls.** The weakest connection is visual contact, which doesn't produce any special effects on the spirit and body. Next is **memory and telepathic link,** which triggers a series of manifold effects and sensations. But when a skull (the programme imprinted in it, or **the skull's vibration waves**) connects to a human being, the unimaginable, unexpected and miraculous start to happen. This does not happen through a person's will, but through a person's consciousness. Through a higher Intent, through the incomprehensible Programme of resonance.

But a skull can of course remain a completely **inaccessible, totally numb, or seemingly dead item** – merely an interesting archaeological artefact. Nothing more. If this is a person's wish or if he or she is unable to activate it. The skull possesses an extraordinary **Intelligence – a crystal programme** which was created, or imprinted in it by **the greatest sages, the greatest minds of mankind.** The skull had been considered **an intelligent being** who merits respectful handling. Today we occasionally say something similar about contemporary computers with in-built crystals.

When a skull is **activated, its 'dormant memory,'** its hidden undulation, gets transferred into the material world and the human mind. The skull can even transmit the imprints of **cosmic waves, the sounds of the planets and planetary constellations, the Sun, the Moon, and the Earth. It is the vibration codes of our consciousness and awareness that awake the skull. If these codes or frequencies, are not correct, the skull's doors simply won't open.** But the skull will reveal the realms of **multidimensional Consciousness** to those who manage to step through its portal; **they will observe events within themselves and in the environment on the skull's crystal screen, like in a mirror. They will see images in time, space, and in timelessness beyond time. Like on a TV screen.** With the help of the skulls, **the awakened person** – a priest or a shaman-healer – can even change and **modulate the frequency-vibrational flow of life energy, of thoughts and emotions. They can correct distorted mental patterns, degenerated patterns of disease and disharmony. The modulation of frequencies,** which a crystal **will make even stronger,** enables **harmonisation – attunement and healing.**

Our planetary ancestors still possessed this knowledge, **but we have long forgotten or banished it** from our awareness. Because we are smarter and more enlightened than our ancestors. But is this really so? We have invented numerous technical devices instead of developing our sensory and body radars, our telepathic abilities and psychophysical power. **We have actually made our existence more difficult with countless machines and aids, instead of opening in ourselves a screen for looking into different dimensions of the world and for listening –** as did Mayan priests, Hindu rshis and jyotish astronomers. We are not smarter! Rather the opposite. It seems as if, throughout evolution, we have **increasingly burdened ourselves with a growing myriad of various items** and their logistics. And in doing this, we have forgotten that **the X-ray abilities are in fact within us already, along with a TV screen, radar, telephone, amplifiers, the eliminators of harmful radiation and a gramophone.** We have forgotten that we don't need apparatuses which are difficult to move and access. The ancient Mayans, although they had neither wheels nor metal tools, were able to accomplish exceptional civilisational achievements in both the material and spiritual worlds. **The axis of consciousness,** which reverberates also within crystal skulls, can be understood as **a sound-colour spectrum of the harmony of the Universe,** which we perceive with our eyes and ears.

Working with crystals resembles what **cosmic telepaths do when they make a connection to the Divine Intelligence, the Source, the Universal Mind, or the Logos of life.** The effects which caretaker-healers, or shamans, experience in their bodies and senses are: firstly **dizziness, or even being hypnotised** – as the entire being has to adapt to a different, new vibration-energy flow. They can feel **a cold shower of high-frequency vibration of the spirit or the heat of earthly physical waves, strong radiation, or pressure** (of high-dimensional wave patterns) **on the third eye** which is responsible for our intuitive telepathic awareness; a strong **expansion of the heart chakra**, which manifests as pressure on the chest; they can also feel **pressure at the top of their heads**, on **the seventh chakra**, which connects us to non-material divine dimensions. **Spontaneous insights and visions** can occur, which are important for our lives, for our healing and work; we might suddenly discover that **we know something that we have never learned or experienced before – our dormant abilities are being awakened;** we suddenly **remember our distant past,** events from our childhood become alive in our thoughts, as well as other memories from **our planetary past;** we see, feel or attract **pictures from the Earth (from the Big Bang on),** and even those from other planets and the cosmic expanse; we feel connected to **the collective consciousness of the timeless and immortal, the eternal. We understand the cycle of life and death more fully and we thereby lose the fear of death or annihilation.** Our physical senses can perceive this high-frequency flow as **smell,** or even as **taste,** but primarily as **shivers** on our sense of touch, on our skin.

We receive messages that are important for our lives **through dreams,** whereas **stress** and unhappiness are often **cleansed through nightmares;** we might experience **a faster heartbeat and higher blood pressure.** We sense **the all-connectedness of time, space, and humanity, which is why we perceive the past, the present, and the future simultaneously.** If we are tired, sick, and unhappy, and on top of that irritated, sad or desperate, we will feel **muscular pain,** which indicates that **destructive emotions are being dissolved.** The releasing of **blocks in the heart** is felt like heat and **pressure on our chest.** Our **knees** are connected to the heart and heart chakra, which is why during emotional stress we can have the feeling that, at least occasionally, **our legs cannot support us and our knees hurt. Rainbow colours** can pour across the front of our eyes and **we can hear the voice of consciousness with our telepathic inner hearing** – both the voice of our own consciousness and that of the cosmic (Divine) Essence – we can hear 'divine sounds, divine music.' During a telepathic connection to the Source, or to the crystal skull, we can perceive **a sound** which our physical ear cannot hear, but the telepathic radar of our meta-consciousness can – we hear **the primordial sound of Creation,** which was also heard by the ancient Vedic rshis, who encoded it in the sacred word **AUM,** while the Mayans captured it in the sound code *hunahpu*.

My obsession with skulls and my work with four skulls in the cosmic cross

And what is humanity actually **doing** at this very moment? **Some are discovering the new at an accelerated pace, rushing towards it, while others, being stubborn, are quarrelling and fighting,** because they are convinced of the rightness of their own opinion and **refuse to change** themselves. Yet, both groups are **seeking tools to heal the spirit and body, to find balance in their lives.** In different ways, joyful or painful. Both are becoming aware of **the laws of peace and abundance, both are seeking happiness and reviving timeless wisdom which is invariably the same for all people in all times.** They are seeking in either a good or bad way.

We are learning how to listen. A restless spirit hears little or will distort what is heard, while a frightened, angry, or jealous spirit hardly hears anything. If we harbour feelings of fear and guilt, we are simply deaf to the earthly life and especially to the higher dimensions of spiritual reality. We hear only half of any information or only its parts. The whole remains unknown to us. Perhaps we see a tree, but not the wonderful forest.

Here is an example of what listening with only half an ear looks like: Špela and Katra are going for a walk. Špela tells to Katra to take an umbrella with her, in case it rains that morning. But Katra hears only the first part of Špela's words and takes her big colourful umbrella with her on the trip, even though the Sun is shining. She had forgotten that it would have been sensible to check if it was actually raining and whether the forecast was bad. So the umbrella gets in her way all day and puts her in a bad mood. Instead of having it to protect her in case of rain, the umbrella became redundant and annoying clutter. **This is how most people live – with good reactions in the wrong place and at the wrong time. Such a life is indeed very tiring.**

Native Americans say that **we are learning how to listen carefully to the events in our lives throughout our life, even throughout all our lives. It is our life's challenge to be able to hear the current moment in its fullness.** Fear and lack of compassion, competitiveness and ambitions, envy, jealousy, and other unloving emotions **blur our sight and hearing.** That is why **life remains an unknown to us and we feel it as a heavy burden.** Along with sound, wonderful crystal skulls are tools for attentive listening and for seeing through the curtains of time. The world would be poorer without them.

I began making corrections to this book during the week after the four-day process. A slight panic suddenly came over me back home in Slovenia: how will I manage to do everything I need to do – a new academic year will be starting soon, which means that I will be busy preparing courses and doing sound surgery, and will have less time for my writing, to which I am immensely devoted. What is more, deadlines for submitting the text to the publisher were ever closer. **But crystal skulls started to obsess me** after my return from Murter, as I was finishing the book. My colleagues Mojka and Dani brought to my desk web pages containing data about thus far discovered crystal skulls. I accumulated the information about the skulls which had been found, verified and tested, or were as yet unknown. And which were fulfilling their purpose once more. Luckily enough, there is not much information on the web about people's experiences of working with the skulls. That suits me well, because I don't want any alien or unverified thoughts to be seeded in my mind, which might then unwittingly, from my memory level, colour or dictate **my experience of the crystal sound.**

A week after this process without food and liquid on the island of Murter in Southern Dalmatia (Croatia), a new intensive course, one of a cycle of nine, was scheduled to take place. For many years, I have been delivering an **intensive cycle of courses** to spiritual seekers, called *A Nine-level Initiation Journey through Nine Levels of Consciousness – 'The Great Mysteries of Sound Surgery'* or *the Shamanic Jump into the Challenges of the New Era with the Wisdom of the Peoples of the World.* During those courses, I familiarise people with **the magic of sound** and the wisdom of ancient civilisations and cultures which still hold much that is **important for contemporary people.** Many things have fortunately survived until today, even though **white people managed to successfully forget a similar knowledge long ago.**

When we together get to know the purpose, and meaning of ancient rituals and their contents, we are not only delving, or rising, into the subconscious and meta-conscious levels, **we are also discovering our mission and role here and now.** With my Vedun Ensemble, I usually play **ancient instruments** from the cultures which are being revealed that day. And we also dance in the rhythms of the forgotten **sacred ceremonial dances** of the past. The essence of these courses is primarily **to become aware,** as intensively as possible, **of the overlooked laws of life, to reveal those subconscious contents (of Xibalba) within us that destroy our peace and make us sick, or, on the other hand, make us happy and bring well-being.** We learn about the subtle **levels of our soul.** As our ancestors would put it, we constantly **stroll up the ladder, or the pyramid, of nine-dimensional consciousness.**

So, on the 8th of October, 2011 we embarked on a new cycle of nine intensive courses, which would help the participants **to get to know themselves.** I perceived telepathically that I should tell people about **the Mayan crystal skulls.** But the week before, I hadn't known exactly **how my presentation of, and healing** with them would show up. I had a meeting with the publisher on Friday morning before the course. My colleague Dani also came to the meeting and put some more web pages about as yet discovered crystal skulls on the table. I went through the pages and a clear **flash of insight** suddenly came to me – **a telepathic message which directed me to four less known skulls.** I found out later that all four had been confirmed as being **ancient.** They were probably several thousand years old or even more. This piece of information still remains a mystery, as it is not possible to determine the age of crystals. My telepathic insight connected the following skulls, which featured on three different pieces of paper: **Ami, Synergy, Mahasamatman, and Mayan Crystal Skull.** That was it! I realised that those four skulls **connected four important levels of consciousness,** which are also symbolised by the four directions and four fundamental vibrational essences of the material world. By connecting them and performing energy work with them, **a new** paradigm is created, **a new power of penetration – for the new time of a more awakened spirit.**

Ami is an unusual skull made of dark purple amethyst. Reportedly a Mayan priest had worked with it in the past and his agent brought it to the USA from **Mexico.** It had last belonged to **the Mixtec people.** At the turn of the nineteenth into the twentieth century, it was reportedly given to the Mexican dictator P. Diaz as a gift. It later changed hands. The skull was examined at the Hewlett-Packard laboratories, where they discovered that, **similar to the Mitchell-Hedges skull, it was made with disregard of the natural axis of the crystal and that it was impossible to produce the skull with any of the percussive or pressure tools known at the time.** And the Mayans didn't have wheels either. After the fall of the dictatorship, the skull was put up as collateral against a loan which was in fact never repaid.[399] It was not seen in public for decades, as it was carefully concealed. A group of businessmen in the USA had acquired it in **1985,** and it was later sold for an astronomical price[400] to an anonymous buyer.

My eyes first fell upon this skull. **It drew me in with its incredible power** despite its somewhat gloomy appearance, due to its dark purple colour. I was unable to pull away from it for some time. I soon realised why.

This dark purple amethyst has **a large circular indentation around the temples and ears.** I came to understand its purpose. **To open the inner hearing, the telepathic abilities** of both the person who works with it and people to whom the skull's power is intended. It also serves as an important **link to the Primordial life energy, to the vibrations of the Universal Logos.** The skull is purportedly still **waiting for its caretaker, for a person who knew how to activate it.** As you can imagine, I became obsessed with it. The very moment I saw it and realised its

. . . .
399 Information was taken from the web.
400 The skull was on sale for one million dollars.

value, a silent desire emerged in me to one day hold it physically in my hands and work with it. **To be able to be its caretaker.** But one million dollars – even if I sell everything I have, I could not afford its ear, let alone the skull itself. **We shall see how this story about crystal skulls in my life unfolds in the future.**

When I gazed at Ami, **my energy field began to expand** immensely, and I increasingly sensed it as being **'mine.'** I telepathically received a message that from then on the skull should hold **a place of honour** at my intensive courses, as well as during my everyday therapeutic work with crystal skulls. It needed to be placed **to the North** in the lecture room and in my meditation room. **I was greatly honoured. Since then, I have felt myself to be caretaker,** even though I do not possess it. **Or she is taking care of me, because she works through me.** I thank you thirteen times for this opportunity. Thank you for choosing me.

Then I had to place the photograph of a skull called **Synergy to the South.**[401] Its caretaker is from **Arizona. George**, its first owner, wanted to produce a copy of this skull, but he soon gave up when he discovered that this is practically impossible. A young man explained to him in Spanish that the skull had been kept by a much loved **Catholic nun in Peru** in **the early 1700s.** This was obviously as far back as the memory of the villagers reached. The nun was quite old when she died. She had given it to a boy and his father, telling them **to take great care of it, because the skull was 'an inheritance from a lost civilisation'** and was a symbol of the **transcendence (or supremacy) of the Soul over death,** just like the Christian cross. So the skull is therefore a distinct **symbol of immortality and illumination. Someone who works with the cosmic serpent of life energy is attuned and rejuvenated,** which means that they are moving away from death and disease and, **at the same time, operating without fear of death. People with a broad consciousness do not fear death.** They understand the laws of life, which is how they are able to move beyond the limitations of their fears. That is why they can lightly move through both the earthly and the beyond, the material and spiritual. So, the nun ordered the boy and his father to **safeguard the skull carefully until the person who would be able to activate its encoded content came to get it – and to then share its message with the world.**

The ancient crystal skull Synergy resounds and shines **in different shades of colour.** To our ancestors, the skull was said to be **a symbol of life, a symbol of the immortal soul who overcomes death time and again, reviving itself. Encoded memory** of the past, a memory which is as unique as humans themselves, still lives even in human **remains,** in bones and skulls. **The DNK record,** which is the **imprint** of the Intelligence of life, is still present in them. And what is more, **crystal**

....
[401] Its owner is Sherry Whitfield Merrell. She often travels with the skull throughout the United States.

skulls themselves hold the encoded memory of ancient sages. The Synergy skull lacks prominent eyes, nose, and cheeks. It is somehow expressionless and universally human at the same time. It doesn't have a precise shape, which means **it can represent anyone, or everyone.** It is somehow the **genderless** essence of a human being, bestowing **awakened androgyny** upon its caretakers and ritual participants, the balance of male-female energies within one being.

After I connected to it, I experienced that it does not only help to restore **all-connectedness, but it also opens inner sight – insight into life. It overcomes fear of life and death. Becoming aware of the all-connectedness of everything that exists** is an important moment of experience, it is **an echo of the awakened multidimensional consciousness, oneness, and wholeness.** And connectedness also enables an effective **attunement** and harmonisation.

Then my eyes stopped at the skull named **Mahasamatman**. It was obviously named in the Vedic tradition. *Maha* means great, *atma* means soul. Mahasamatman was apparently the name of an Indian prince. Its present caretaker is **a musician** and clairvoyant **telepath, Kathleen,** who is said to be a clairaudient **medium.** She could channel before she became the caretaker of this crystal skull. Kathleen nicknamed it **Sammie Girl.** She often performs meditations with it throughout Europe. According to Kathleen, the skull was **materialised from Universal Light.** This is also possible, after all. The Master and avatar **Sai Baba** convinced us of this for years. I witnessed this possibility among the balian **healers in Indonesia,** as well as among Native American **shamans in Arizona.**[402] This skull is one of the lesser known skulls; it was found **in Amazonia, in Brazil,** where the Native American **priests** of the local indigenous people were its guardians for a long time. It is reportedly one of the most activated skulls. Kathleen says that with it, her abilities expanded greatly. I was told that Mahasamatman is an especially powerful **medium for entering the meta-conscious,** the levels of expanded consciousness, the frequency levels above the physical, or three-dimensional, level of reality, for entering the field of high tones. **It is primarily priests and healers who have access to those levels. If they are enlightened, there are no limits.** The skull with the name of an Indian prince placed itself **to the East.**

A skull named **Mayan Crystal Skull** made of clear quartz was placed **to the West.** Its **whereabouts** are currently unknown. Its **origins** are also unclear. The stories say that it perhaps came from **Guatemala** or was excavated in **Honduras** around **1910.** It resembles Ami a little. And just like Ami, it ended up in a pawn shop. It is said to have originated in **Mayan culture.** According to my insights, its presence pulls people into the levels of **the subconscious, to Xibalba,** as the Mayans would say. I think it has an extremely important role **in healing and**

---

402 Check the first and fourth book in the *Cosmic Telepathy* series.

spiritual growth, as it helps people to **cleanse pain, suffering, resentment,** and other emotional-mental clutter **that has been suppressed in the subconscious.**

When we connect all the four skulls together, Ami and Synergy **open our inner awareness – inner sight and inner hearing, so that we can hear the messages of our meta-conscious, of our soul, through which the Cosmic Intelligence is whispering.** With their energy support, we can then go deep down into ourselves, **to the levels of the microcosm and the subconscious where our nightmare, blocked unhappiness and suppressed fears dwell.** This is how **our balance, wholeness, and perfection are restored** in the presence of all four skulls. What is more, together these skulls have one more ability: they can **connect a human to his or her soul family, or monad.** With the monad, we can become aware of our soul contract more easily.

So, the challenge was set and the message communicated. Our first initiative with the crystal skulls took place on a Saturday in the middle of October 2011. There, all the messages I had received became alive within each of us. **Our heart chakras were expanding, which is why we felt an exceptionally strong pressure on the chest.** There was also a very strong pressure **on the third eye** (the eye of **clairvoyance**), on our inner hearing, **the inner ear** which enables clairaudience. **The centre for the subconscious, the *medulla oblongata* at the top of the spine, yielded to the powerful Universal life flow and filtered into our memory the most painful traumatic imprints which had been locked in** long ago. **They now emerged to the surface of our consciousness and swam away, like they had never been there at all. They made room for new, more joyful feelings and more loving energies. The release of emotional clutter brings healing and a more expanded awareness.**

All the participants felt a strong pressure on their **third eye** and on the top of their head – on **the seventh chakra,** which connects us to the Primal Intelligence, to the Divine Being. We sensed an immense **joy,** which we, while dancing and through our spontaneous sound play at the end of the course, together poured into an invigorating vivaciousness.

When connecting with Ami and Synergy, **an invisible headband was pressing us on our foreheads,** in the areas of meta-sensory hearing and sight. When focusing on Mahasamatman, **we sensed hardly anything, because meta-conscious is very difficult to sense** and I also perceived that the skull was being **used elsewhere in a ceremony** with its present caretaker **at that very moment.** When we connected to the Mayan Skull, everybody felt as if they were being pulled **somewhere far away, or extremely deep down. Far away into a tranquil remoteness.** At first, only a few people unconsciously resisted this soul journey. The majority didn't, which is why they were able **to perceive,** unexpectedly, **the answers which they had been** seeking for a long time. The four skulls, **working together**, triggered in us **an elated feeling of love and grace, reflecting meta-sensory Mercy.**

After cleansing and relaxing their bodies, the thirty-three course participants and a little girl called Eli – perhaps a future healer – who was, together with her parents, always present at my courses, embarked to the level of **the first dimension – into the Earth's core crystal.** Then we tuned to the Earth's centre, made of the element **iron**, following which we aligned to the vibrational qualities of **the ancient crystal skulls. Organic iron** must have oscillated **in our blood** during this process. **Every vibration echoes in its related matter.** With ceremony and respect we entered the Earth's core crystal, **the Matrix of all life forms** in it. We set off on **a nine-level initiation journey**, the purpose of which is to find **balance, harmony, and attunement.** Stepping lightly, but with commitment, we walked up and down the vertical axis of consciousness, as if we were climbing the branches of the tree of consciousness, the tree of life. **Resonance was enhanced** in this way – a harmonious resonance with primordial perfection, with the purpose of our lives – **with the Divine Plan and our own primordial essence.**

I believe that in the distant past **spiral inter-dimensional consciousness was activated in the same way. That was how people healed themselves and others.** The skulls helped to open cosmic doors, the cosmic portal into the silence of the mind, into the (still) **unmanifested energy Field,** out of which everything emerges. This is **the Field of Truth** where we can become aware of **who we actually are and why we are.**

So, **the cross** of the four skulls had been set up, the four directions opened. The crystals, in the form of human skulls, **connected to the Earth's core crystal and its crystalline grid. They connected to our heart chakras and the Source, the Fountain of life.** And this shared grid, or network, this invisible orchestra, began to reverberate **with a harmonious resonance, nourishing and strengthening the energy flow** through all of us **to the highest possible limits.**

Repeating this journey and this centring of the Sky and the Earth along the inter-dimensional axis of consciousness is **a signpost to complete perfection, which points to directions and paths across innumerable octaves of reality.** When we manage to align ourselves, we feel **gratitude and awe; we transcend the limitations of time and space and we comprehend the planetary dreams of perfection and the contracts of the soul.**[403] And those priest-shamans, healer-musicians who are totally connected, devoted, are allowed to actually **enter the matrices, or codes of the bodies, the cell memory,** the encoded information of matter. **DNA double helixes are the codes of the Universe and the Universal triggers in them**

....
[403] More about life, death, and the contracts of the soul can be found in the fourth book in the *Cosmic Telepathy* series.

necessary changes. That is why a completely different awareness can be developed and **disease can be eliminated.** But only **when we are truly ready for this.**

During initiations and ceremonies, awakened healers and priests **practise and restore resonance, harmony and other forms of attention,** working together with people who have not yet attained this. They activate people's dormant cosmic-earthly **telepathic abilities and awaken the alertness** required for entering into the **galactic library of the eternally present wisdom of the soul.** And **the primordial sound of Creation (the tone G)** is the frequency wave which resonates with the tone of the Earth's rotation and which **renews the primordial matrix of perfection, which is itself encoded in every being and in every cell. Thus, the primordial sound of Creation balances and heals** that which is out of balance or diseased.

In this way, people can restore their **given, but still unrecognised abilities and talents. We return to the cosmic memory, to the collective mind of the whole and the all-encompassing cosmic consciousness. We discover our soul's connection with all forms of life.** At the same time, these soul contracts are **different sound qualities** which resonate in various **octaves,** or **colours.** Our holographic senses and the unveiled **meta-senses awaken the memory of soul contracts and trigger in us a yearning for spiritual growth and for a return to Primordial perfection.**

In the emptiness of Nothing, we can create at will. We can hear our soul, we can see everything as a soul – a universal code. It is in the beauty of the love of the soul that willingness happens and surrender is actualised. But when we doubt, everything remains concealed from us. To create in the silence of the mind and from within the levels of multidimensional consciousness or the soul, is **a healing and a true feast.** Everything is possible then. Even **materialisation, manifestation, and dissolving become possible and easy.**

The higher, or the broader, we go, the faster our field vibrates. We perceive this as something more subtle, less visible, less audible, etc. Though the trials in our lives, **we continuously rise** towards realms which we have not yet attained, towards the expanses of our givens; we discover our new talents and we are ever **happier and more peaceful.** Nagging and anger disappear. **Then every cell begins to resonate with those newly discovered tones.** And when we attain **a complete harmonious resonance** with the Earth, the Source (Hunahpu) and with every 'superstring' of our being, we have **completed our journey.** We have attained our own **frequency maximum and we begin to resonate with the frequencies of the Galaxy, planets, the Sun, our solar system, with the frequencies of the stars, the Earth,** spirit, and matter. **Unique sounds which we have never heard before** begin to resound in us. **We remember!** We remember our distant **past and we also get to know the matrices of a future** which is right now being shaped into a new reality. Through **the portals of spirit,** we enter beyond time and space into **the**

silence of the creative Field and we touch the songs of the stars. **Establishing a connection with the glue of love and with everything that exists becomes a joyful act. We are finally able to manage the world of bodies and matter according to our own will.** We have attained **the abilities of a shaman, priest-healer.** Of a musician, or a poet, playing on all the strings of life.

The days following the described experience were filled with **a tranquillity** beyond compare. I was especially amazed by the fact that all **worry had simply evaporated.** A serene peace came over me and everything that needed to be done **unfolded easily and by itself,** but at the same time most **effectively** and **faster** than usual. And above all, everything unfolded completely without any stressful hurry. **A feeling of solemnity interchanged with humility of the knowing: all desires had disappeared. There was no need for anything! An all-embracing peace. I simply am. We simply are.**

I hadn't believed the caretakers when they said that **the skulls bring heavenly peace to people.** Even though I experience this **grace of Mercy** during my courses, lectures, and concerts, the crystal skulls have literally projected me, together with my students, up **the 'celestial ladder' of consciousness – being an additional help, challenge, and impulse.**

The Earth is spiralling up into ever faster, or higher, frequency waves, or awareness. That is why we occasionally get the feeling that **we are always in a hurry, overtaking ourselves.** We can also sense **sudden changes in our understanding and reactions.** That is why from time to time we start moving furniture and flower pots around the house, and feverishly search out new clothes and colours. And above all, we **respond to the stressful events** in the world **in a** more loving and **less upset way.** We donate our clothes which bind us to our past to people who need them or cannot afford to buy them, because when they wear them, those clothes won't bring up the traumatic memories which are linked to our experiences.

In August 2011, I was pulled **into silence** with crystal bowls and skulls. Everything that was necessary **was ground down** and I was **drawn to my new personal quantum leap, into a totally new awareness of working with crystals and sacred crystal tools. With their scent of cedar wood,** the four guiding skulls showed me the way **beyond enlightened consciousness. Because the path of our maturing on Earth does not end with enlightenment.** Enlightenment is only the beginning if we learn how to see and listen to the invisible and inaudible, the intangible, and even to that which is seemingly unattainable and impossible.

During the following days, the crystal skull **Ami** was constantly present in my consciousness, its energy **shook, warmed, and cooled** me. I grasped that it was **not** at all **necessary to have it beside me. It was not necessary to have any of the skulls beside me. A telepathic link is enough! Spiritual guardianship** can be established at a distance. **We don't need space ships** to travel across the Universe and the dimensions of our own being, across the dimensions of reality. **We need only an open heart and a wide open consciousness.** Our 'Ancient Ones' would add that it has been so for thousands of years. **Crystals, crystal bowls, and skulls are just aids, distinct vehicles of consciousness, or soul: they are only a surgeon's tools, tunnels, and short-cuts** to infinity and eternity. **Work with them is never ending.** They can always resonate in a higher frequency, they can always reveal something new – or something old. They are infinite and **boundless** at their core, just like the human spirit.

I shall keep praying to the Cosmos until it gives the skull back to us

My connection to Ami somehow faded after the intensive course **in October 2011.** I got in touch with it again on **the 8th November, 2012.** It was two days before the intensive course *Great Mysteries of the Sound Surgery or the Shamanic Journey into the Centre of the Heart and Soul* (10th November, 2012), during which I guided the participants to sense **the first and second dimension** of our reality. The connection with the skull had in fact been established a week before, but it was at its strongest two days before the course – the second Thursday of November. The **glands in my armpits and ovaries were** extremely **painful!** As never before. I perform **sound-energy surgeries** on Thursdays. All of a sudden, Ami **began to shine in my soul, it brought about a true explosion in my energy field.** After that Thursday morning **the energy serpent** flowed ever more strongly. This invisible serpent was removing, from me and the participants, everything in our energy and physical worlds and in our souls, that stood in our path.

This time Ami – this dark purple beauty made from **amethyst quartz,** which reportedly belonged to **the Mexican Mixtec culture** and was found near Mayan ruins – showed up as a miraculous magic wand. Without any prior notice or warning. It is perhaps the only dark purple amethyst skull to have **large circular indentations on its temples near the ears** – it looks so **different** from all the other skulls – and this skull was here all of a sudden. **In the dimensions of time and space.** In Slovenia, in Ljubljana. Of course not physically, but it was nevertheless present with all its power. For years, the skull has been **waiting for a caretaker who would know how to activate it.** Who would know how to activate it!?

I just **can't believe that the skull chose me. That it chose us!** A group of people who came to my **Veduna School** to acquire tools for spiritual growth and help in (self-) healing. I gave my **first therapist course** for students of the school at the end of **July 2012.** Most of them had been expanding their awareness and consciousness in the school for several years, some even a decade or more. Almost **fifty people** took part in this course for therapists. It was time. Did Ami 'turn up' telepathically in order **to share its gifts and exceptional power with these new-age therapists of a cosmic consciousness?** Or perhaps it resonated with me, because my book about the boundless singing links of the ancient Mayans had been truly finished (only the chapter you are reading was added just before it went to print). I simply could not imagine that the skull had been confined in a vault for years and kept by nine businessmen. Well – there's that number nine again. An anonymous person finally bought it in 2009. But it is, however, obviously **still waiting to start resonating with all its registers.** It just cannot be true that **I became its caretaker! The skull** actually **became mine and ours, it opened up sight, hearing, and a portal into the silence of the mind to everyone.**

When preparing for that Saturday's intensive course, I delved deeper into its core. And the very moment **I became aware that I was now accepting the energy-telepathic guardianship of this wonderful skull, which opens inner hearing and meta-sensory telepathic abilities,** something **struck me through my ears and between the eyebrows,** like lightning, like a white-hot spike. Juices started gurgling like crazy in my stomach, as if they were trying to say that yes, yes, your perception is correct. **My voice once again changed.** It was changing by itself, especially when I was doing sound surgery. I heard **different sounds** in my head which became more and more loud: they were like a whistle, or a thought, even like **crystal clear sound and light. A crystal white light. My heart** pounded occasionally, as if it was trying to escape from my chest. Is that some special way of saying hello?

All of a sudden, I felt an immense desire to hold the skull in my hands. And that **our connection would be permanent** this time. **The flow was growing stronger and stronger. Would my body be able to endure it?** Slowly, an energy connection was being built between us. A telepathic thought, a message, illumined me on Friday evening. Hey, this **skull is actually mine!** I know it **from my memory and visions.**

"What do you think you're doing?" said my mind. "How could the skull be yours?"

"It is mine, **I know it from Palenque, where it served in the hands of local priests.**"

I heard my firmly determined voice: "**I want it back!**"

Oh, and yes, its name is not Ami. Its Mayan name is **Hanibku. So, go to your ancient memory and activate it in the old Native American way: connect it to the vibrations of the Pleiades, Orion, Galactic Centre ...** Let it be so!

At the Saturday's intensive course, after I had explained the most basic things about the as yet discovered crystal skulls, we set about connecting to Ami, now Hanibku, and activating its abilities. **We connected to the Centre, to the Source of life, with the help of the light-sound codes of cosmic resonance** and we embarked on **a multidimensional shamanic journey into the emptiness of Nothing. Into the fullness of Silence.** In the middle of the ceremony room, we placed a **clay vessel with fire in it** and put **three sacred stones** around it. Further out, we made **a circle of twelve stones and surrounded them with crystals.** We made **a crystal grid** and the largest and most powerful crystals were placed in the corners of the room, **at the four cardinal points.**

As soon I told the group that we were then connecting to it, the skull began to **work powerfully through all of us. Cries of pain, of cleansing, crying from being touched** were soon heard as if with one voice. Everything happened in an instant. The room was filled with **solemnity, honour, respect, bliss, happiness, gratitude, and a sense of belonging** to the skull and to this ceremonial spiritual family. **Tears from being touched** coursed down the cheeks and the skull **'performed' truly incomprehensible things: it healed the most deep-rooted energy blocks** suppressed deep down in the darkness of the subconscious, of Xibalba. **Physical defects, little lumps and growths** disappeared. The participants **became aware of their suppressed fears. Doubts** dispersed. We felt **stinging in the heart** (which **healed energy blocks caused by stressful experiences**) and rasping on **the solar-plexus (the chakra responsible for mental processes), the spine** was warmed and cleansed. **Hot energies** interchanged with **cold.** Even our **teeth** ached and dark stains on them disappeared (mine too). I can only say that the skull's work was **crazy powerful and completely unexpected. I had never experienced anything like this before!**

We danced around the central mandala in two large circles. We swayed while we listened to a pleasant Native American music, melting in its sweet rhythms. A growing **dizziness** led us to **a semi-trance. Grace and Mercy.** A sharp **cry of pain** was heard occasionally when a participant **suddenly experienced a cosmic surgery.** I touched everyone with my hands, like I do during surgeries and through my fingers I felt **a burning energy scalpel. My skin glowed hot** as if it had been burned. **Sweat** poured from me, even when I wasn't actually hot. The participants told me later that **my touch was as sharp as a knife.** Sharp as never before. Obviously **the power of this energy scalpel had considerably increased when aligned to the skull.**

My shamanic initiation with the snake venom some three months before (10 weeks) **had given me this extraordinary ability** and opportunity to connect to the crystal skull, **a majestic tool, a link, or telephone link to the Primordial**

Intelligence. Without the skull, there would probably have been no such wondrous connections.

When our therapeutic group became **harmoniously aligned** with the help of the crystals, sound and star essences, **we rocked into the magical** work of the dark purple skull. The skull **revealed a miraculous technology of sound and soul; it dissolved, like a laser, even those emotional and karmic traumas** which had been pushed deep down. Not only traumas from this life, but also painful memories from our experiences in a distant past. From our previous lives. But this time, **the pain** which had been encrypted for so long **was finally released,** and the participants watched it being dissolved from a safe **distance as unaffected observers.**

Time disappeared, space was of no importance, matrices of perfection, completeness, and health were anchored in everyone. **Silence and peace drove away fear and worry. Contact with eternity** was present. The silence of Emptiness worked on us like a dessert. **Spontaneous regression** switched on. **Light changed into sound and sound changed into light. Unexpected renewal and rejuvenation took place.** All of this became even more intense when I took **the crystal bowl and began singing,** and when Mojka, Tine and I played **shamanic drums** and Mayan instruments together. Then I again felt a strong **gust of energy running from one ear to another, creating an empty-full circle around my head.** One of the participants felt the same and he called this feeling a nice emptiness. I would call it **the fullness of emptiness.** Others described this expansion of the energy field and **the pressure of an invisible headband around their heads** as if **their heads were expanding** or as if they were sitting **within a great cocoon.**

After we had **activated all the portals** we had opened over the previous decade both in Slovenia and abroad, **we penetrated** even deeper **into the energy grid of the Earth and the Cosmos.** The cosmic serpent of life energy was ever more intense and **heat interchanged with showers of cold.** Everything unfolded in a **more powerful way, more quickly, and precisely.**

Those participants who had difficulties in opening up and **were therefore still unable to open themselves, experienced this sudden process of the expansion of their being initially through nausea and sweating.** Then it exploded! Bang! And the man who'd had difficulties in expressing himself, because he had been closed, was now able to **speak easily** of his pain.

Ears itched, throat chakras ached (bridges to high-frequency realms of spirit were being opened), **a cosmic infusion** of invisible vibrations flowed into emotional chakras in the area of **the coccyx. Our heart chakras expanded** to the highest possible limits, we felt a **stinging in our heart, pulses raced,** there was great **pressure** behind the eyes, **on the third eye.**

"Wow, I am going to explode!" a lady shouted.

The participants had felt all of this in a milder form **during preparations throughout the week before the course,** especially **from Thursday morning, the day of the sound surgery, when the skull had been activated.** At that time participants reported: **it was as if their heads were in a vacuum (in the emptiness of Nothing).** Preparations for this majestic connection had taken place not only days but also weeks before. **The spine and throat** (the centre for communication) were being cleansed, muscles **and bones ached, intense pins and needles** permeated the energy paths of the physical body. **Glands – the antennae** for invisible cosmic waves and the links to the Primal life energy – informed us of this invisible process. Especially **reproductive glands,** such as the ovaries, as well as **adrenal glands and those located in the armpit.**

At first I didn't feel tired at all, **my body merely radiated more and more and my eyes became bloodshot,** which always happens **when the flow is so strong** that the body is barely able to handle it. My eyes had never been so red. The shamans say that this is how they have to be, because it means that **the flow is strong enough. Red eyes are shamanic eyes.**

Some participants **relived the most painful traumas of their lives** during this Saturday **connection ceremony,** but this time, **they observed them completely without fear.** They discovered with relief that the traumas **had finally left.** And then **feelings of love, peace, joy, and connectedness** washed over them. **Everyone felt connected with everything.** Their souls whispered: everything is as it should be.

Some felt intense **Mercy and were touched** by the sight of the photograph of Ami – well, Hanibku as the Mayans would say. **Tears of happiness** came over them and **they felt the skull's (energy) presence** with all their being. From time to time, energy flows **struck like bolts of lightning** through their bodies. An increasing **heat** was warming us and we occasionally felt **shivers,** which signalled **the presence of something Higher.** Some felt that their **feet were heavy,** that their **body ached,** some felt a growing dizziness, which **pulled them into a deep trance. They simply couldn't move;** even standing was difficult. **This is how it is during invisible cosmic surgery.** The body is in a subordinate role and is therefore weak. But only for a time. After the surgery, it is strengthened.

We felt the strength and **penetrating power** of that crystal skull; **we experienced an alignment to all levels of consciousness and existence, a clairsentient path to the Silent knowledge of the Universe. Together, we awakened the dignity of all-connectedness.** However, our connection to the Source of life will be successful and **effective only when** humans sacrifice or **annihilate all their weaknesses.** Such is the human path to **happiness and abundance** – both in the past and today. **There are no short-cuts. Techniques for connecting to the Primal**

Essence are as old as the world. Contemporary people are now rediscovering their value. But **a true connection can happen only when conditions for it have been established.** Today's techniques of connecting (for example, the new-age technique of connection called The Reconnection), which promise **miraculous healings** are misleading. Miracles can **happen only when all emotional clutter has been eliminated and mental patterns and illusions dissolved. Hence the miraculous still depends on the expanse of human consciousness,** because it is **the connection along the axis of consciousness** which enables the connection to the Divine Logos, to the Universe and soul.

The skull is ours! We felt it as ours. **It doesn't matter where it actually is! It was activated for our good. It chose us.** But, before that, we had been the ones who had chosen it. **The therapeutic group had reached a level of spiritual maturity that allowed a connection to it. We solemnly promised to guard it with respect** wherever it may be, even from a distance, and **to work with its help for the benefit of humankind.** We also expressed the wish **that it would come to us.** In whatever way. Until then, we will **connect to it telepathically.** At a distance, as we say.

A long-term and devoted course participant said: "**My life got a new meaning** following the connection to Hanibku during the Saturday ceremony. I feel **solemnity and am deeply grateful** to be among its guardians, among those who have this invaluable opportunity to heal and expand with it. **I shall keep praying to Cosmos** until it has had enough of me and gives the skull back to us, until **it comes back to us.**"

Beautifully expressed, indeed, in a symbolic way. I was not the only one to perceive that I carry this skull in my heart and soul. Some said that they would give their lives for it and that they **would give their lives** in order to protect it.

The participants told me later that they **felt safe within this connection, they felt relaxed, loved,** and above all, **TRANSFORMED.** They experienced **the tremendous power of the energy waves of the Source (the Feathered Serpent – Kukulkan and Hunahpu as the Mayans would put it).** They felt the processes of **letting go, their weaknesses were being dissolved, they forgave themselves and others, and of course, they felt the vicinity of the Home of the soul,** as we call it. Some experienced **oneness** and felt **everyone** present that day **as one being of the one Great Soul. They saw everything as the essences of this Soul, of Universal Consciousness.** My soul was singing: **finally!** The spiritual seekers who had surrendered to my guidance had finally experienced by themselves what I had been speaking of and elatedly describing to them.

A synergy of events began to unfold. The understanding of life increased and **the wish and will for further transformation** emerged.

"My ego finally managed to kneel down before the skull and now **wants to be better by the day**," said a middle-aged man. Many discovered **a new responsibility** in themselves – **the responsibility for their spiritual growth and for life on Earth.**

Some **left their physical bodies** and, for the first time in their lives, experienced **the dimensions beyond, the mortal and immortal,** the higher levels of consciousness, or soul. They felt their **infinite power, the power of spirit.** Pressure and tingling **between the eyebrows**, on the third eye, were followed by **an enhanced sensitivity of the senses. Visual and aural abilities** increased. **Sound got different dimensions. Insights** into life's events followed one after another. And, just like it had happened to me at my first contact with crystal skulls, **small lumps** appeared **on the forehead**s of some of the participants – **a sign of telepathic communication and the opening of the third eye.** King Pacal from Palenque also had them.

Towards the end of our Saturday ceremony with the crystal skull, the connection with the skull Hanibku (Ami) caused me to **channel an important spiritual message in verse.** Hanibku had to come to us, to the Slavs, I thought. I also captured a new message, **an order** actually: **I need to fully realise the ancient sound technology** which will soon be **the technology of the new era,** even though it is as old as the Earth. And I need to write **a new book** about my experiences with crystal skulls. The skulls are important, because they expand people's consciousness and awareness, so that they can **perceive the Silent knowledge of the Universe, the Soul of the Universe;** so that they can hear the grass grow. **Hear the song of the Earth and of Heaven.**

I was very, very tired when everything was over. I packed away the instruments and crystals with great difficulty. I don't know how I got home and to bed. My body was 'burned out' from the immense energy flow. But I felt extremely **peaceful and happy.** Not only that evening, but also during the following days. That was it – **a quantum leap into the new!** It happened a month before the Mayan prediction of such awakened possibilities. **I was delighting immensely in the forthcoming surgery,** which would prove to be much **more effective and penetrating! And a small lump,** which had appeared on the sole of my foot after the exertions of the shamanic initiation with snake venom and broken ribs, **disappeared that night. A painful spot on my heart meridian too.** Not only the participants, but also I **changed** during this intense transformation with the crystal skull. I can scarcely sense what the connection to this wonderful crystal skull will bring me. And I had been against it so much at the beginning! Not any more. I am infinitely **grateful** to it and **I look forward to all experiences with it.**

That is how I experienced, together with 45 therapists, **the very summit of the spiritual pyramid** on the 10th of November, 2012. **The view is broader from the top, you see to all sides.** The crystal skull Hanibku revealed **a new chapter**

in my sound surgery and healing – of people, animals, and the Earth. It not only brought awe and thankfulness, but also **delight and fulfilment**; it brought **a new page in the book of life and the penetrating quality of sound, song, and movement.** A week later, **I led the group into the beneficent silence of Nothing during the initiation of the Galactic Centre.** The Hindus would say – into the group **Samadhi**. But only those who were ready were able to experience it. **The mind was finally totally silent. The harmony of soundlessness gives deep peace, health, and wholeness. And the wholeness of all-connectedness is a human's greatest well-being. A miracle without boundaries.**

At the end of my reflection on crystal skulls, I just can't but ask one more question: hadn't all that had flowed through my consciousness and mind and which had been put on paper, **already been written down somewhere – in the past or perhaps even in the future, in the cosmic library of all past events, or of all future events yet to be experienced?** Isn't that which I am discovering and writing about only **an echo of a distant wisdom which the sages of a distant past had imprinted in space and also in crystal skulls?** Why do I feel such a great urge and passion to awaken this knowledge, **to re-imprint it, to write it down once more,** and thus make it available for the initiates of my school and my readers? Why do I have to preserve this wisdom for our physical world? **Simply – because I have to.** It doesn't matter why. Perhaps I will **never find out.** Perhaps it will be completely revealed to me unexpectedly, or at levels of the soul, at levels beyond death. Our ancestors are bestowing gifts upon us, and we bestow those gifts upon our descendents. Why? Only the divine Source, the Plan of life, knows that.

Crystal skulls are intended for **connecting to the Source, to the Intelligence of life, for renewal, wholistic healing, transformation, and rebirth. They are a link to the Logoi of the stars and planets.** They heal aching souls and hearts. To the earthly world, they give the sound of **the matrix of complete cosmic memory and timeless wisdom.** They bring **the spirit of eternity** into time. They help to build **a collective consciousness** and **wholistic spiritual teaching** for all cultures and people. **They make people aware via the sound yarn of life, they teach them to carefully listen. They attune people and the world.** They are, besides sound, the most excellent tools for **the expansion of consciousness into the realms beyond, into the dimensions of life and death.** They are an incomprehensible and very **effective surgeon's tool.** In the hands of a shaman and musician, **they begin to resonate in the rainbow of the frequency waves of the Earth and the Cosmos.** Moreover, **they dissolve everyday rigidity and the pain of ignorance. They open new dimensions in the sound-energy surgery.** They even enable **materialisation and dematerialisation – the creation of material and non-material forms and the instant dissolving of distorted physical growths. They lead to a consciousness** of oneness and to the perfection of the being which we call human. They teach us **the wisdom of our ancestors.** In people, they awaken **gratitude and awe, a joyful peace, Truth,** as well as the beauty of inter-dimensional all-connectedness. **They teach the humanity how to travel across the dimensions of time.** They **awaken spiritual and energy power** in crystal skull caretakers and their ceremony participants, **they also awaken their dormant abilities, the fullness of awareness and a passion for travelling across the worlds of time and timelessness.** A **song of eternity sings in the crystal skulls,** invigorating the sacred serpent of invisible waves and rhythms, **fanning the flames of the sacred fire of transformation and devotion.** They revive the knowledge of the multidimensional technology of sound and soul. That is how the beauty and **miracle of life on Earth** is revealed. And awe turns into **thankfulness** for perhaps the **most brilliant treasure of the humankind** – crystal skulls, which **open portals into a new and better life, into the thirteenth Heaven,** as the Mayans would say. **May humans once again hear the cosmic whisper here on Earth and may they create miracles, according to the will of their awakened consciousness, in the silence of their minds.**

The ancient Mayans, people of a cosmic consciousness, experienced and lived all of that, they knew how to travel into both the Galactic Centre and their own centre.

I give thanks to the Universal Logos for singing with me the song to the Earth and the Sky!

I give thanks to my soul, my yearning assistant, who guides me to the very essence and to important discoveries!

Brilliant musical instruments, the singing crystal bowl and magical crystal skulls – thank you for finding me! Thank you for existing. For fulfilling me and inspiring me to bathe in the beauty of existence.

ETERNAL CHALLENGES BETWEEN THE WORLDS OF THE PAST AND FUTURE

The ritual initiatory path of the 'Ancient Ones' and the ancient Mayans

The cosmic university for the expulsion of fear and evil

The greatest gift of living
is **an initiation into the mysteries of life.**
**The initiation rite is an invitation
into the memory and full awareness of spirit.**
Initiation is an act of **courage** and hidden **curiosity**
to know what dwells on the other side of the body.
The initiation ritual is a penetrating act,
the whispering waves of a sound not yet embodied in the mind,
restoring bridges across dimensions of reality
with its depths.[404]

Mayan astronomer observing the symbols of the Sun and the Moon; above are the glyphs *kan* and *imix* (drawing taken from the book *The Cosmic University of the Maya* by M. A. Vergara).

Let us now **encapsulate** everything written above **into the Mayan Creation story** and delve deep into the spiritual symbolism of their initiation ceremonies and their **quests for better and more complete selves.**

The Mayan **story of Creation** and life, also revealed in the sacred book *Popol Vuh*, has kept its meaning and value until today. The Mayans still tell it to their children: **so that they will not forget, will not go astray, will remember,** etc. In the past, Native Americans did not punish their children. They rather **taught them by means of stories.**

In an interesting, symbolic, and mysterious way, the Mayan sacred book *Popol Vuh* speaks **of Creation and the human journey** through the labyrinth of life.

While the face of the Earth was only a little brightened, **before there was a Sun,** there was **one who puffed himself up** named **Seven Macaw.** /.../ ... in

---
[404] Mira Omerzel - Mirit, poem *Initiation into Mysteries*, taken from the book *Zvočne podobe prebujene ljubezni*, Vrhnika, Dar Dam (2012). The initiatory journey of the Mayans or any other spiritual seeker is described in the book **The Warrior's Path of a Black and White Jaguar** (in print), in the form of a tale.

the days and months before the faces of the Sun, Moon, and stars could truly be seen. /.../ This was in **the era when the flood was made because of the effigies of carved wood** (cold-hearted people). Now we shall tell how Seven Macaw died /.../ This is the beginning of his **defeat.** This is the shaking of the day of Seven Macaw **by the twins** (symbols of the world of duality), named **Hunahpu and Xbalanque.** They were simply gods.[405]

Hunahpu is One Blowgun Hunter (constantly moving), who is also **the God of the Dawn. Hunahpu** is the only God that is **not presented** in material form (people gave the name God to the laws of life). **Alom** is the Mother Goddess, **the Great Mother,** She Who Has Borne Children and **Quaholom** is the Father God, **the Great Father,** He Who Has Begotten Sons. This happened before the first mother and the first father of the Mayans were born. **The story of the downfall of the prideful ones has been passed down through generations.**

For a long time, **the *Quiché* people** ruled over other Native American peoples on the sacred mountain. In Guatemalan dialects, the word quiché also means 'the land of many trees' and forest. **When their time came** (when their accumulation of experiences on Earth was completed), **the four great chiefs passed sacred teachings and great wisdom to their sons. They handed them symbols – Bundled Glory, a bundle with unclear content** (eternal spiritual wisdom is invisible, intangible). The old rulers bade farewell after their task had been completed. **They sang the song named Our Burial and told their offspring to follow their path and visit the places where they had come from (to return to divine perfection, to the Home of the soul; to attain enlightenment).** This was how the chiefs said goodbye. **Thus was the disappearance and end of the first people who came from across the sea** (from the worlds beyond) **in the East**[406] (symbolically, **life begins** in the East and souls are said to come into the material world from there). This was how the first Fathers **died.**

The nations had been defeated and their glory came to an end. But they still **remembered their fathers and worshipped the Bundled Glory.** And one day, they headed to the East, where their fathers had come from. They arrived to the **wise lord of the East,** called **Nacxit,** who gave them the emblems and symbols of their lordship. These were the names of **the tokens of their glory and lordship** (tokens of the power of spirit and body): **throne** (the symbol of wisdom and spiritual power), **bone flute** (the voice of ancestors), **drum** (the instrument of all the rhythms of consciousness), **yellow stone** (the symbol

....
405 *Popol Vuh*, electronic version (2007), pp. 78-80. Notes in brackets are mine.
406 Ibid., p. 241.

of Holy Trinity, or divine perfection), **Jaguar Paws** (the symbol of watchfulness and power), **snailshell rattle** (the symbol of the spiral undulation of life energy and life itself), **Macaw Feathers** (the symbol of versatility and abundance), etc. **All these they brought when they returned and they also brought the writings of Tulan** from the other side of the sea[407] (these were symbolic images – **the visions and teachings of the multidimensional 'shamanic' consciousness, which they received through telepathy**). The Quiché Mayans used them to write down their tales in a vivid way.

The Yaqui ancestors **had nothing of their own,** but they were **enchanted people** in their essence, says the sacred book *Popol Vuh*.[408]

Hundreds, even thousands of years B.C.E., people from different Mayan countries maintained and nourished their inherited life's and spiritual **heritages, which began to be lost at an ever faster pace at the beginning of the Common Era. But they were never completely lost.** Despite an ever greater oblivion, spiritual truths continued to be kept, especially among those who understood them and passed them on. These truths were revived through ceremonies, in the **Great Mysteries**. For centuries, for millennia, **initiated spiritual seekers,** priests, healers, musicians, and spiritual teachers **helped to expand the consciousness of the chosen initiates.** They have managed, through to today, to preserve the fundamental **teachings for a harmonious life, effective healing, accelerated spiritual growth and well-being.** Yet, **that which is the most subtle** and perhaps the most precious probably **sank into oblivion** a long time ago. **It is maintained only in the bank of imprints (in the akasha) and at the high-frequency levels of a sage's consciousness.** And in the souls of rare contemporary shamans.

Hundreds, even thousands of years ago, the inherited and mystery teachings **helped people to attain the art of total awareness, a mastery of handling the mind, thoughts, emotions and body; a mastery** which had fostered their **return to a unified galactic consciousness, to the Centre of the Universe and their own soul.** And **the properties of sound,** both **audible** (songs or creative sound plays) and **inaudible** (energy-vibration flow) sound, effectively **centred people along the axis of consciousness, which enabled them to attain enviable abilities and invaluable insights** into events and life on Earth.

In different historic periods, the secret spiritual knowledge of the planets, the Universe, the Earth and life on it taught people about attuning to the multidimensional Reality and the Source of their own existence. All of this was done so that people could discover a harmonious resonance with the Divine

----
407 Ibid., pp. 243-244.
408 Ibid., pp. 199-200.

Intelligence of life, with the Universal Logos of life, as well as to understand current events, to master themselves and the challenges and problems in their life, and to invoke into their lives everything they needed: perhaps just rain, which allowed **the growth of maize** and abundance, or some other kind of benefit; but primarily **wholeness, joy, and peace.**

The Great Mysteries have kept the difficult to understand Secrets. Their essence is made of a revered and carefully kept knowledge of connecting to planetary and cosmic (frequency) waves, which lead the community into a harmonious co-oscillation with the resounding Universe. This echoes in each of us, in our every cell, every thought, and makes people sensitive enough to perceive the frequency-vibration waves of **the rhythms of the Universe, the Earth, and life.** When we listen to them attentively, our **intuitive abilities** and meta-sensory perceptions of **cosmic telepathy are strengthened.** But we only receive **the gifts of clair-perception** when **the complete frequency field, the complete sonic field of all levels or dimensions of consciousness and reality, resonates and echoes** in our multidimensional consciousness. Then, **we are able to read the codes, or the laws, of life,** physical and spiritual alike, audible and inaudible.

The wise knowings of the Great Mysteries of our planetary ancestors, including the Mayans and their descendents, have been handed down **from generation to generation, from initiate to initiate.** Both within themselves and in others, the descendents of great sages are creating **a network of nine-dimensional consciousness, a holographic resonance – co-oscillation, or co-resonance** with the Earth and the entire Universe. **A harmonious attunement of the wide open fields of consciousness aligns human thought with the Universal Logos, to the Intelligence of the Universe, the cosmic Consciousness/Mind, or God,** as we say. The Great Mysteries awaken within people a sensitive channel for the above-mentioned **mediumship, which brings the spiritual** (invisible, inaudible intangible, unfathomable) **and the material** (visible, tangible) **into an indivisible whole.**

I am convinced that ancient Mayans, as well as our ancient **Slavic ancestors and other peoples and nations, were closely familiar with the wisdom and laws of a joyful existence and abundance, about which we today unfortunately know very little.** But certainly **many people performed ceremonies in the ancient sacred way** during the last centuries B.C.E. at the very least. And they devoted considerable **attention to the actualisation of the galactic human being,** whose broad abilities are unfathomable to us even today. **The exceptional Mayan achievements from a distant past, which we intuit,** rather than know, confirm **this forgotten knowledge which we are again seeking so eagerly, discovering it at least in** fragments (but which is opposite to the logic of profit). This great knowledge is also demonstrated by admirable Mayan **technology** – without wheels, metal tools or draught animal power – which current technology **still cannot match.** Their architectural skills, astronomical-mathematic teachings and especially their manufacture and use of crystal skulls[409] stand out. But unfortunately **we are no longer familiar with** ancient Mayan **sound technology**, which seems also to be **extraordinary and admirable.**

The revealing of the unusual and miraculous abilities of all levels of the human mind and consciousness is the very foundation of ancient knowledge. To permanently live all our givens and dimensions is an eternal challenge. Contemporary archaeological, ethnological, anthropological, historical, linguistic, and spiritual explanations of their art, along with the art of inscribing monuments, they all attest to such quests undertaken by our ancestors and the Mayans. **The heritage of Izapan** belongs to **the oldest Mayan cultural-historic nucleus.** According to some researchers,[410] it had **kept the spiritual wisdom of the ancient era** far into the new era. Only a few **remnants** of this ancient wisdom **continue to live today,** at least **in a fragmented form,** among contemporary Mayan descendents. I experienced some of it during my stay among them. Yet, those remnants **barely witness the very essence of the ancient ceremonies and knowledge. I would never have been able to approach their knowledge without several decades of my own personal spiritual maturing,** which I described in the first book[411] of this series.

In the past, the ancient Mayans reportedly performed numerous **initiation ceremonies which the minds of material-oriented contemporary people can hardly grasp.** Something similar is perhaps happening with the knowledge and ceremonies of **other cultures** and civilisations, in other sacred and ceremonial sites and temples on our planet. But if we delve deep down, with our **spiritual eyes,** into the preserved historic messages and the interpretation of the **symbolism** with which especially all of **art, including music,** is suffused, if we descend deep down into the very core of their (religious) representations and philosophy of life, and if we connect the above-mentioned with **the eternal laws of spiritual questing, as well as with our own experience, we will soon extract their gist, which is very, very far away from our contemporary way of life and our understanding of the meanings of life, its rhythms, goals, and purposes.**

....
409 If the skulls were Mayan at all. They might as well belong to even older civilisations. But the Mayans certainly employed them in their ceremonies, healings, and divinations.
410 More about this can be found in two brilliant works: *Maya Cosmogenesis 2012* by John Major Jenkins and *Maya Cosmos* by David Freidel, Linda Schele, and Joy Parker.
411 *Life without Food and the Timelessness of Spiritual Messages of the North American Indians.*

The initiatory path of returning to the original Source of Creation - into the essence of the Primordial wholeness

The Universe is a myriad of frequency waves, **energy vibrations**, which are but **a boundless number of sounds, of non-material life forms.** All of these vibrations have their own **spirit, their own spiritual energy.** Their own **Great Spirit**, as Native Americans would say. And this spirit has a name in contemporary Mayan culture: **Rajaw Juyub' – the spirit of things, the keeper of the Universe,** which shapes **the Heart of the Earth and the Heart of the Sky.** The Mayans can perceive him in the rustling of leaves, the murmuring of waters, in roaring winds, in hidden winds, etc. **He is everywhere, throughout nature, and he has no form. He is in a whistle, a crackle** which appears and disappears. They say **he appears when someone violates nature's laws.** Which means that he is also the fair **law of cause and consequence.** Whoever sees him, or get to know him in some other way, is enchanted; **as if sleeping with open eyes**, say contemporary Mayans.[412]

He can also come to us in dreams, he talks to people or addresses them in the form of awakened consciousness. It is believed that if people who do not respect the laws of life repent, they will live a long time. Rajaw Juyub' can even take the form of an animal, to put it symbolically. And of course, this power is also in animals, flowers and trees, etc. The primordial Intelligence Rajaw Juyub' constantly **judges people's conduct, teaching them patiently** (those who do not live in line with those unwritten laws face problems). He is the Supreme judge, **the Supreme law of existence.**

In Chichén Itzá, I found a book by M. A. V. Calleros,[413] entitled *The Cosmic University of the Mayas – The Initiatic Route of the Mayas.* I was extremely happy, as the book is a brilliant spiritual summary of this age-old cosmic vision. The work was written by the above-mentioned indigenous expert on Mayan material and spiritual culture. The author is obviously a man of broad consciousness and rich spiritual experiences. I shall never forget the mysterious smile of the old Native American man who sold this slim volume to me. His eyes, his look and words were saying: **Finally – someone who is interested in more than just mere external appearance of the local sacred sites. Thank you! Go on, research. It is worthwhile.** And my look answered: **I promise, I will do my best**, as much as I can. Thank you for this book, it is very important to me, because I wish to find out

---
[412] Check Rigoberta Menchú and Dante Liano, *Honey Jar*, Toronto, Groundwood Books (2006) pp. 25-26.
[413] **Miguel Angel Vergara Calleros**, the founder of the **Kukulkan Academy** in Merida, Yucatan, in Mexico, also founded the **Haltun-Ha** Centre for Mayan studies. He is a respected **spiritual teacher** and authority on Mayan culture, who devoted his attention mostly to the studies of the Mayan calendar and codices, Mayan astronomy, philosophy, art, ancient ceremonies, and sacred ceremonial centres – to **the cosmic vision of the Mayan Universe.**

primarily how the ancient Mayans thought, how contemporary Mayans think, and not how foreigners, who tailor the only valid science, think. I read this slim volume in one sitting in the shadow of the Great Pyramid in Chichén Itzá. Yes, **this is it**, my consciousness whispered. Miguel is right. Finally someone who does not merely describe the pyramids and temples! The book confirmed my silent awareness and spiritual knowledge about the initiatory journey of everyone of us. I thank you!

By taking into account Calleros' findings and some of the data on Mayan culture presented by J. M. Jenkins and M. Ruiz about Toltec wisdom, I will now take a short journey through the understanding and insights of **the initiatory travels of ancient Mayans in Chichén Itzá. They were probably quite similar to the spiritual heritages and initiatory ceremonies of other planetary spiritual seekers, warriors from antiquity on different continents and in different cultures.** In some places, I will also refer to the book *Maya Cosmos*,[414] a book by several authors, who attempt to explain the rich Mayan symbolism. But we must begin at the beginning.

The sacred Mayan book *Chilam Balam of Chumayel* speaks of the human spiritual journey and life's knowings in a way quite similar to other esoteric texts of this world. It says that we are **born through the word of God, through the primordial sound**, which resonated when there was no Sky and no Earth. The word *itzá* supposedly also means '**sacred man**,' and *itzaes* means 'ancestors.' So the renowned sacred site **Chichén Itzá is the temple of ancestors, the cosmic university of the Mayans.** Its pyramidal complex is actually one of the most sacred **pilgrimage destinations** of the ancient Mayans. For centuries, hordes of pilgrims swarmed to this sacred site **on the evening of the spring equinox (20th March)** to **revere spiritual rebirth, the arrival of the new, to revere a new birth on the ruins of the old, through sound, dance, prayer, and through ceremonies to bring awareness.** That is why Mayans built majestic temple structures whose purpose was to attract people from far and near to this sacred journey. So, temples and pyramids are buildings where enlightened **Masters impart life's wisdom to the yet unawakened people, where God socialises with people, and the divine socialises with the human.**

> An awakened consciousness illuminates the mind,
> expands the heart, the eye and the ear;
> it brings you the gifts of **abundance** and bestows **silence** upon you.
> **It inspires you** for the journey into the wide open and near by,
> into the unfathomable **worlds beyond the usual,**
> and into the worlds of beyond and the non-material,
> into the boundless expanses of mind, of **totally new insights and ideas;**
> it guides you into the all-full void of Nothing,

....
414 Its authors are David Freidel, Linda Schele, Joy Parker.

where silence is creating forms and desired abundance.
**Within the sonic fullness of the primordial, perfect and complete,
dances the enlightened life,** which is the only one truly worth living,
as it knows not pain and suffering,
because it simply does not allow them to enter.
With awakened consciousness, there are no tormenting quests, no questions,
Let alone demanding proofs and (self-)confirmations.
**Enlightened consciousness is harmoniously full
and completely aware of the game of life.**[415]

An initiatory ceremony is the path of the ceremonial dying of (still) unawakened seekers and warriors. **It shows them how to live perfectly and fully.** But not only in dreams and in the labyrinth of expectations. **It teaches them to surrender to the flow of life.** The initiatory journey starts by bringing to life the **primal creative force of life,** which creates, shapes, and maintains everything in the material world. Ceremony participants **revive the perfection of the Source, the matrix of everything, the primordiality without errors or distortions.**

The Cosmos is alive and intelligent, and so is life within it; equally miraculous is the memory of both our birth and the purpose of Creation. Both have to be **revived, renewed** time and time again. As in the Sky, at the very Source, so on Earth. That is why the 'map of the events in the Sky,' revealed in the Mayan calendar, also reflects the mundane on Earth.

The unveiling of the soul and ego begins in darkness

Once a young man came to me and said,

"Dear Master,
I am feeling strong and brave today,
**and I would like to know the truth
About all of my–attachments.**"

And I replied,

"Attachments?
Attachments!

---
415 Mira Omerzel - Mirit, poem *Awakened Consciousness Enlightens Your Mind and Brings You Silence*, taken from the book *Zvočne podobe prebujene ljubezni*, Vrhnika, Dar Dam (2012).

Sweet Heart,
Do you really want me to speak to you
About all your attachments,

When **I can see so clearly**
You have built, with so much care,
Such **a great brothel**
To house all of your pleasures.

You have even surrounded the whole damn place
With armed guards and vicious dogs
To protect your desires

So that you can sneak away
From time to time
And try to squeeze light
Into your parched being
From a source as fruitful
As a dried date pit
That even a bird
Is wise enough to spit out.
/.../
Hafiz knows
The torments and the agonies
That every mind on the way to Annihilation in the Sun
Must endure. /.../"[416]

    As we have seen, the revealing of the ego and the seedling of transformation begin in the dark depths of our subconscious, or unconscious, in the darkness of problems in our life, **in the darkness of our soul,** in the dark underground temple of our consciousness. **'The Lords of the Underworld,' Lords of Xibalba,** of our unconscious mind, help us reveal our **essence through the ritual ballgame,** through our playing with life's riddles, through the agony of our fears in the **fire** kingdom – in *bolon-tik.* Through the game at those levels, **we get to see for ourselves the Mysteries of life and illusion, the absurdity and fatality of fear. Fear is the absence of love, it is the gloomy illusion of our ego, which bargains with truth and runs away from facts!** It is a reflection of the worthless and **unreal game of our mind.**

．．．．．．．
416 Hafiz, poem *And Applaud*, taken from the book *I Heard God Laughing*, London, Penguin Books (2006), pp. 5-6.

Also, Mayans had the *xibalba ocot* dance, the dance of the demons. With it, they tried to get rid of **demonic torments (namely the destructive contents of the subconscious),** which arise out of the underworld (or from the subconscious): symbolic and picturesque sowers of misery, stranglers, and shedders of human blood.[417] **These torturers resurface time and time again, disturbing our emotional-mental peace.** They even renew themselves and attract similar painful experiences, according to the laws of resonance. People know **how difficult it is to get rid of an addiction and destructive bad habit** – smoking or a fiery temper, for example. Something within us attracts them and maintains them with great power. Even when we see how and where we are wrong, we are usually unable to simply **say no.** Destructive content will not disappear. Such destructive contents have first to be **revealed, we have to acknowledge them and fight them, until they disappear.** This is how the fight with the Lords of Xibalba goes.

Like in many other cultures, **the sacred initiation path *balamkanche*** often began **in a cave, in the dark underworld, which is symbolic of a penetration into our unconscious** and into those contents which are difficult to access. And it is also a symbol of penetrating **into the expanses and depths of spirit,** into the as yet undiscovered layers of our psyche. The cave and its darkness are at the same time a metaphor for **the womb** and a metaphor for **the primordial darkness in which life was conceived.** The Underworld can also be the very foundation of our spiritual growth, out of which emerges rebirth, the birth of light out of darkness. Here, humans, suffused with physical and spiritual powers, **have to first face their ego, they have to explore it, in order to get to know themselves, their mind, their thinking patterns and the reactions which derive from those patterns.** In the darkness of Xibalba, humans check **if they are (already?) loving enough** and **compassionate** enough **towards others and towards themselves. Are they able to say no,** when necessary?

In the darkness of the ceremonial cave, people have to **face their fears, which are created by suppressed painful emotions, thoughts, and ego. There in that cave, they have to take a careful look at their beliefs, their inherited and acquired patterns and egocentric impulses. If people are afraid – they don't live fully:** and certainly they **live neither peacefully nor happily.** The North American Hopi Indians still build underground temples called *kivas*, where, through ceremony, they can **return to the Source** deeply, to the primordial darkness of primal perfection. Our **prehistoric ancestors** on the territory of today's Europe also had similar underground temples.

....
417 *Popol Vuh*, electronic version (2007), p. 103. In order to understand the content, read the chapters which speak about the dissolving of our emotional-mental deposits and about the mastery of the mind in the fifth book in the *Cosmic Telepathy* series.

Step by step, initiates move along the sacred path of self-recognition and rebirth, following the guidelines and inscriptions carved onto the temple's walls. Through their mysterious language of symbols and images, these carved warnings offer explanation and make the initiates aware. Warriors of spirit are drawing ever closer to the final station of this path, to the sacred site of **the Great Mother Ceiba** (the birth-giving life force), which is also the symbol of **the Sky, the Source.** Ceiba teaches the spiritual warrior about **the Mysteries of the fire kingdom and of the 13 heavens (*ox-lahum-tiku*).** There, in the cave, in the Earth's womb, **a human's psychic balance and their connection to the Great Mother Ceiba begins to be built – their connection to the undulating life energy.** There, **a conscious connection between above and below,** between spirit and matter, begins to be built.

In order to attain enlightenment, or ascension, and to awaken all the levels of their soul and their still undiscovered dormant abilities, the initiates must first descend deep inside themselves, into all the earthly spheres of the Great Mother, into manifold life experiences, trials of darkness and horror.

The sacred *ceiba* tree also denotes this process of transforming darkness into light, despair into trust, animosity and fear into love. Ancient Mayans brought **offerings** to the *ceiba* tree – including sacred stones and clay artefacts. **A hollow clay heart** was said to represent a pure **soul, devoid of illusions of the material world and conflictive duality.** But this can be reached only if seekers manage to dissolve their **egocentric and unloving contents and the fake mask of their personality,** which is made up of a myriad of **self-loving and distorted representations,** degenerated ideas and gloomy thoughts, which are, on top of all that, **imbued with fear, emotional unrest and memories of pain and suffering.**

Ritual dying and self-sacrifice

The transformation of the incomplete
cannot be avoided,
you have to dissolve
that which does not hold truth,
and **invite into life**
that which clears your spirit.
Which is why **every evolution is revolution,**
and every revolution evolution.
Spiritual warriorhood in the field of changing –
for the better, of course –
is the eagle's gift of all-encompassing consciousness,

waking up, **wanting to guide you,**
to accompany you into the silence of wise actions
and into the grandeur of true knowledge.
And know – **if you do not yet understand** the laws of life and growth,
it means that **you still do not know how to listen well.**
Life, which is a series of moments of learning,
therefore **asks you**
to pluck up your courage
and leave the apparent safety
of your experiences,
of the known
and the well-kept;
to dive into a new adventure
of future events and **the unknown.**
The old, having long outlived its purpose, the imperfect,
things that lack awareness
and are **not loving enough**
have pushed you into the discontented greyness of your existence.
It is time to read
a new, live book of experiences.[418]

Everyone lives on a specific developmental level of consciousness. But they are constantly making their way, moving forward, sloughing like a snake and thus growing spiritually, undulating on the waves of the river of the boundless ocean of innumerable possibilities and opportunities. By delving deeper into the events in their lives, initiates **come to understand the causes of their problems and leave distortions behind;** they consciously leave behind the old, the unenlightened, the painful and sick – an entire ocean of all this! They learn to accept the death of the old, the insufficient, the death of their illusions, their hell. They accept the dying of everything that is bad and as yet incomplete, surrendering to the current moment, to a more harmonious resonance in ever higher octaves of existence.

They seek themselves, because they forgot their own essence who knows when, or they lost themselves in the labyrinth of trials. This can easily happen, if you don't have **a wise teacher** at your side (and there are only a few of them in the white man's culture), to warn you about what you are actually doing.

People move through their lives and through the resounding (frequency) Universe more or less without a real awareness. But they are constantly

. . . .
418 Mira Omerzel - Mirit, poem *Transformation Cannot be Avoided*, taken from the book *Zvočne podobe prebujene ljubezni*, Vrhnika, Dar Dam (2012).

changing their understanding and reactions to the situations in their lives; they even repair the accepted understanding, if necessary. They transform their experiences, the contents of their lives and ways of living, building a bridge of compassion, and a power of kindness. They revive the forgotten, the overlooked and the still undiscovered, dormant abilities within themselves. They come to understand how to surrender to the abundance of the Universe. That is the reason why they are sending out, into the ether, to the Sky, their requests and **prayers for help,** which are called *pom* among the Mayans. *Pom* is the most exquisite food **for the Gods.** As they say, **it opens people's hearts and expands their consciousness,** connecting them to the Highest. With it, we **activate our attentiveness and alertness, the new dimensions of our eye and ear.**

When initiates are ready, they decide **to cross the lake, river, or the sea** – the all-encompassing **Field of Consciousness, the Eagle's emanation,** according to Don Juan's teaching. **In this Field of the new, they receive a 'baptism,' an initiation with water, which is a symbolic act of purification and an act of immersion into the fullness of oneness.** They receive the priest's **teachings about the great secrets and the wisdom of the Great Mysteries** of life. After a hot steam bath and preparations for this initiatory adventure, the seeker, now physically and spiritually purified, sets off **to the sacred sites** of the nearby temple complex. In Chichén Itzá, for example, to the Temple of the **Phalli,** dedicated to worshipping **the Goddess Mother Ixchel,** who is at the same time **the Goddess of birth, rebirth, fertility, pregnant women, and healing.** She is **the benevolent Moon Goddess,** helping at **the birth of the initiates, or adepts.**

It is said that, in their prayers, the Mayans also turned to two sacred names: **Itzen Kaan,** which means 'I am the substance of the Heavens,' and **Itzen Muyal,** or 'I am the dew of the clouds' (according to M. A. V. Calleros). Poetic are these phrases, deep and heart-felt. The two names are also very powerful and piercing **sound codes.** When they resonate in your mind, **they balance the human energy field and expand** your thoughts into the boundless Field of life energy. Connecting to this Field, to this central system of life, is very important. In this way, everyone can **switch onto the inexhaustible and eternally present source of life energy and power.**

In their own unpleasant way, **the lords of Xibalba (the energies of the Underworld** and of the darkness of the unconscious) help people to consciously dissolve their emotional and mental sediments, so that, **in the process of self-sacrifice, spiritual seekers can die within themselves,** or better, that **all the negative within them can die.** While on this path, initiates pray **to Gods for help, asking them for the support of the Universe, of God.**

An **initiatory ritual is a journey across the sacredness of the serpent. It also depicts the cosmic serpent itself –** *kinich-ahau,* **who is the spiral of life.** The cosmic serpent – **the solar Logos, the Creator** – is a symbol of inaudible frequency-energy undulation across the Universe and across everything that lives. At the same time, it is the symbol of the **omnipresent spiral movement** – in humans, in every single cell of living beings, as well as in the Earth's evolution, in the rhythms of life, in the cycles of transformation, and in the pulsing of the galaxy and Cosmos, etc.

Next, initiates visit different **temples and pyramids, which are imbued with the energy imprints** of ancient ceremony participants, who had been praying there, who had been delving deep into their life, **receiving the wise teachings of those who had already walked the length of this path and were well familiar with it.** In temples and sacred sites, initiates and warriors receive the teachings which are necessary for their **resurrection from the dead, or better – from 'the deaf.'** In each temple or sacred site, they receive a certain **knowledge for the successful sloughing into an authentic human being of a wholistic knowledge (knowing), without masks, the knowledge of the jaguar.**

Enlightened human beings are called *halach-uinik* in Mayan tradition. **In their battle of ceremonial dying,** they have the support of prayers and **invocations – the invocation of different 'vibrational qualities or Gods.'** And they also have the support of rich **symbolism** in the temples, which speaks to their souls, acting like **a warning and reminder. The artistically crafted symbolic images of divine characters** are carved in stone and arranged throughout the sacred place. **Mythological tales and sacred books** (like *Popol Vuh*, for example) also speak to them – tales, which the Mayans had first listened to in their childhood and subsequently many more times.

The book of holiness is kept in the subconscious too, or better – it is kept in people's meta-consciousness. Its spiritual contents come to life when we seek answers to our questions, thus helping us to understand the current situation and events. Symbolism, carved or put into words, together with selected rhythms and ritual song contents, **created by our wise ancestors,** shape mental representations and **energies which open our consciousness and mind.** At the same time, they **revive a hidden spiritual awareness within people.** When seekers touch them, they revive within themselves the necessary **insights, they invigorate in themselves the flow of the energy of the Field of Consciousness,** which in turn supports them effectively.

The Mayans say that, **in the canoes of life and death, Gods are the 'rowers' of human lives. Deities** (read: cosmic forces or energies) **are aware of themselves and they sustain the world with their presence and attention.** Very nicely expressed! **People return this attention to the Gods through their ceremonies and prayers. They try to understand 'divine messages' – the effects of laws and barely perceptible waves, and try to place them in the visible world of forms.** In ceremonies, they feel the snake-like flow of cosmic life energy, which is why they 'colonise' the celestial expanse with images of Deities.

Tulum – a bridge for messages from the past

The final week of our stay in Mexico was spent awaiting the forecasted **hurricane Emily**. Hurricane winds often rage across the Yucatan Peninsula. All flights had been cancelled, and it was most likely that we wouldn't be able to fly home to Europe on the scheduled date. We had spent the last weeks of our stay among the Mayans of southern Yucatan and in Chiapas, but the time of our departure was approaching, so we set off to the peninsula's north. Once again we travelled in comfortable Mexican coaches towards the coastal town of **Cancun**, the location of the international airport.

The closer we came to the northern coast, to the Caribbean, the more fallen trees and open roofs we saw by the road. The hurricane, the likes of which have been occurring here for hundreds or even thousands of years, **had ravaged this area only two days before**. It had paralysed transport and cut power lines. Our plan was to return to traditional Mexican style houses in a small village near Cancun, where we had stayed before heading south. But traffic was at a standstill, settlements along the road were in darkness and without any visible signs. **Huge, centuries old trees were lying on the ground** in front of wooden houses. Tourists had already left this place and the owners of the tourist complex were pretty scared. **Using astronomical calculations and clairvoyant forecasts, ancient Mayans had been reportedly able to foresee the arrival of hurricanes in advance** and had thus been able to prepare themselves in time. The architecture of their homes had been designed to resist even raging whirlwinds.[419]

The sacred site **Tulum** is situated on the Caribbean Sea. The word tulum is said to mean **wall**, as the town is surrounded by a wall with five gateways. The largest building is called **El Castillo** (the castle). It is decorated with figurines and masks of the divinities of **Venus and the Sun**. This ancient Mayan city was occupied for a very long period of time, reportedly even after the majority of Mayan towns had been abandoned. The temple complex **Tulum was one of the last outposts of Mayan civilisation. It was reportedly established around the**

....
[419] The great storm Sandy ravaged New York in the night of 29th/30th October, 2012. In November, water storms hit Slovenia too.

year 1200 and continued to exist until the 16th century. It was once a religious and trading centre.[420]

It was strange to walk now along the lonely paths **next to the Caribbean Sea**, looking down from the temple at a sandy beach that had been eaten away by the waves. The hurricane had cleansed the surroundings quite thoroughly, **giving me an exceptional opportunity** which I could not have hoped for otherwise. The northernmost temple site Tulum was closed, and a couple of days after the ravages of the hurricane, it was still not ready for visitors. But there were no visitors anyway. In the late afternoon, my friend and I crawled under a rope, which was symbolically closing the entrance, marking the boundary between the usual paths and the archaeological complex. With great pleasure, we strolled from building to building. They were lonely now, bathed in the glow of concealed light coming from the stormy clouds. Hordes of tourists from all over the world would normally be walking around here, making the site look like a vast anthill.

Slowly and with attention, we walked through the entire temple site without being disturbed. We reached its northernmost point, where **a large temple perched atop a cliff**, which rose steeply from the sea. The rough sea hummed beneath the temple ruins, and its big waves crashed fiercely against the rocky cliffs, telling the story of the power of nature and the sea.

The wind was still roaring ominously and howling through the rocks. Yet, now in Tulum **reigned a peace, a certain natural silence and the millennia-old presence of centuries old invisible (energy) imprints or records.** After the storm, which had cleansed the Earth and the Sky, these records of ancient ceremony participants were more **clearly readable and pure, and above all – they were still there, ingrained in the memory of the timeless stone, in the rocky walls and arches.** Dark grey and blue clouds were still drifting across the evening sky, testifying to the recent storm, covering the blue celestial dome, which occasionally revealed its dark blue colour. Rare beams of light descended from above and painted the surface of the sea with an unusual, mysterious, almost blue-green colour. My amazement at nature's painting palette was boundless.

Peaceful, I sat down on the edge of a stone wall and all of a sudden, I looked up at the Sky. Totally unexpectedly, I saw a strange **light sign**. Several moon rays were travelling down from the Sky, like a beam or **a ladder of light.** They were descending towards the temple site, penetrating the dark clouds. The departure point of this beam grew broader and lighter by the minute.

All of a sudden, I sensed that I was being pulled into a transcendental state of consciousness, into **a trance**, and that I was, without intention or prior warning, **merging and melding with the inaudible vibrational imprints of the temple.** A

---

420 *Mysteries of the Maya, National Geographic Collector's Edition* (2008), p. 97.

telepathic connection was established within a few minutes, enabling me to discover these hundreds, even thousands of years old, energy imprints. My **medium channel** opened up and allowed me to sense them. My meta-sensory perception opened up. **I spontaneously started channelling the messages of 'the millennia old records of the sages,' which were anchored in this site.** My friend switched on his mobile phone's voice recorder to capture them. The light beam which had come from the Sky **brought the ancient memory of an all-connected consciousness. It encouraged my consciousness to recognise or read** the energy messages and enabled me to understand them. It was the day before the full Moon, **20th July, 2005.** It was **9:15pm.** A strong wind was still blowing, but now lacked the power to destroy.

These were my **words**, channelled **in a state of trance:** "The ancient Mayans were able to **create a light beam**, similar to what you are looking at now. On it, or with it, **they travelled with their consciousness to non-physical levels, to the vibrational worlds of other stellar and planetary constellations, to the Home of their souls and the abodes of the immortal essences of their ancestors. They travelled by means of a (frequency) ray of light, which the priestesses created in their consciousness and mind.** Sometimes all the **ceremony participants**, the entire community, took this journey, sometimes only selected **priests**. To create and maintain this light ray, **they mostly used the broadest and the most piercing cosmic consciousness of female energy,** the high frequency waves of the **priestesses**, who were at that time always ready to **establish contacts with the great Cosmic Consciousness, Intelligence, Mind, or Logos.**"

I stopped for a moment to observe again nature's artistry around me. Then my expanded transcendental consciousness, connected to the meta-time dimension, began to dictate the following words, received **in a medium's shamanic trance:** "The wall on which you are sitting was once part of a sacred site, where a special **sacred object** was kept. This object, **in the form of a trident, was used to communicate between people and the Earth and the Sky; it was also used for multidimensional journeys across time and space, for journeys across the simultaneous, parallel, and multidimensional worlds or levels of consciousness.** There were also other objects, used in ceremonies, which facilitated **astral travel**. They were kept in this small place (which was once covered), where you are sitting right now – in this narrow niche, in a stony box covered by a wooden lid (it resembled European wells). Here, they performed **ceremonies of offering and supplication.** (The edge of this rocky overhang, beneath which the sea roared and where boundless horizons opened up, reminded them of abrupt finiteness). From there, **priest, the leader** of the winning team in the ballgame, could set off on the journey back home, **to the Home of his soul, into the Galactic Centre. He was centred within himself, he found his own centre. Temples were built as multi-layered structures,** which can be most easily described as **the system of a tone scale. The foundational floor was based on the Earth's tone, on the basic tone,**[421] while everything that followed, in the material world, had **a sound which was similar to harmonic partials, to aliquot tones, which follow or resonate across the octaves of the universes** – through to the very summit, to **the Highest.**" So simple, natural and magical at the same time!

"The ritual dance, which was danced here, unfolded **in the form of a spiral. A spiral** was thus made, which **anchored the vibrations of Cosmic Consciousness to the Earth and among people.** Movement, or dance, **grounded the intention and desire for aligning to the highest frequency of consciousness, which was an always accessible gift for all initiates and ceremony participants.** Regarding the realm of sound ceremony, **voices and drums were used; large conches** were blown."

With my inner ear, I heard the piercing sound of conches and drums. It seemed to me that those sound waves would take me further and further away. The thought continued: "Mayans were **masters of connecting the Sky, or Cosmos, and the Earth.** But they made one big **mistake** in their history. Their mistake resembled the one **the Tibetans** had made. **They began to conceal the great wisdom from each other and priests hid from people, they began to hide the mighty knowledge of how to attain life harmony, joy, and abundance. And above all, they began to hide the wisdom of connecting to star frequencies** – symbolically to star beings or cosmic vibrations (also called Master Teachers of the Universe). The ancient Mayans gave them countless **names of Divinities. They should have spread this sacred knowledge among the people, so that the entire planet might wake up.** Yet, around the beginning of the Common Era, priests and rulers **started to withhold it for themselves** in order to gain enviable power. As a result, a symphony of **disharmony, duality, and despair** began to resonate instead of one of harmony." The initiated priests started losing the support of the divine Source or Logos. The supporting vibrations of spiritual well-being started to withdraw and the ancient Mayan civilisation began to lose its wisdom which had been passed down through millennia. The civilisation sank into the poverty of spirit. Decline was inevitable.

The sacred place on which you are sitting right now was once part of a big ceremonial site, part of **a portal between the Sky and the Earth. The revered bridge in the form of a trident was a sacred site for connecting to the immortal essences of the souls of the deceased and to ancestors, who bestowed spiritual power to people who consciously embarked on an inter-dimensional journey across time and space into timelessness and spacelessness – into the worlds beyond.** This bridge was, above all, intended for initiates of the carefully kept rituals

....
421 The tone G.

and for initiates who joined **the ballgame. The priest of the winning team, who was the wisest or the awakened chosen person, had the support of all the other priests from both teams.** They helped him to return to the Home of his Soul on the wings of his consciousness, to the resounding consciousness of countless dimensions. This is how the Mayans returned to the primordial Home of the Soul, as well as to the Pleiades, which expands the hearts of everyone, and to Orion, Sirius, etc."

I took a deep breath. These messages of consciousness felt so familiar and close to me! They were a very important part in my piecing together of the image of distant events. But this was not to be the end. My telepathic experience and reception continued. When there is a real, **clairaudient** reading of the **Silent knowledge of the Universe** present, you cannot switch it off at all.

"During the time of the ancient Mayan Mysteries, **a network of temple sites** was connected with specific cosmic and star vibrations," continued my inner voice. "**Palenque** was connected with **the Pleiades, Tulum with the North Star, Coba with Arcturus, Chichén Itzá with Vega, Tical with Sirius, Ek Balam with Betelgeuse (Orion) and its twin Uxmal with Rigel (also Orion).** This is what the ancient Cosmic wisdom says. The pyramids and temples of **Ek Balam** are one of the most important sacred sites **for connecting with the wisdom of the soul and the multidimensional consciousness, for channelling the soul's messages in both directions.**" I later captured yet another piece of news: **Chichén Itzá is the link to the entire galactic – star and planetary – family, Ek Balam** is the linking thread **to the Galactic Centre** or black hole, while **Tulum** is also a station on the earthly-cosmic sacred path to other galaxies (especially to **Andromeda**). **Coba** connects ceremony participants with the constellation of **Gemini and with the energies of Kryon.**[422]

"Each of the larger temple sites has its less mighty 'servants.' Smaller accompanying or supporting temple sites are everywhere. Thus was created **a network of temples and sacred places, which was connected to the energy network** of the Earth, its non-material energy coat and to the Cosmic inter-dimensional network, or **the all-present Consciousness of the Cosmic Mind.** Junctions, or sacred sites, are located on the most important intersections of earthly and cosmic radiation. **Ceremonies on those sites maintained the celestial beam – the axis of consciousness between the worlds of reality, or telepathic connections between earthly beings and planetary vibrations, or cosmic beings. This was also how the bridge for teleportation to the worlds beyond was established.** Yet, this was only possible at a certain level of consciousness, when one's heart was sufficiently wide open for this network world of frequencies or energies." So, all of this is moving **across the**

....
422 More about this can be found in the seventh book in the *Cosmic Telepathy* series.

cosmic octaves, ennobling everything on Earth, I thought. Am I dreaming the Truth or is **the Truth dreaming** through me?

And the voice went on. "**Knowledge will come back, because it has to come back**," continued my telepathic voice. "It will slowly emerge through the spiritually most developed or open people on Earth, through healers and shamans of a heightened consciousness. With their own consciousness, with their own radar, they will be **able to read information about ancient wisdom and the achievements of our ancestors' consciousness through their own consciousness. Pancho and Don Juan de la Cruz** are two such souls." A smile sneaked onto my face.

Then I came to understand the following: "**Don Juan de la Cruz is already** receiving information, but he is not yet able to link it to his new **(Christian) faith, in which there is no anchoring to the cosmic consciousness.** Which is why he understands but a small part of this returning tradition. But his consciousness will soon expand to the point that he will be able to accept things which he had not acquired through Christian teachings. **Pancho** does not have such problems, he is completely **open and broadly accepting. He never lost his connection to the cosmic.** While **Candido,** even though he was a teacher of many shamans in the Yucatan, as they say, will not receive this old-new information. The expansion of his consciousness has finished." I pondered. And the images of all three men danced before my eyes.

The silent voice of my consciousness started again: "The shamans and healers **Pancho and Don Juan de la Cruz know each other,** but not physically. **Only at the level of the soul. They occasionally cooperate at higher levels of consciousness.** They worked together in their past lives too. They have been born into the region of today's Mexico many times. And once again they have important roles here." Yes, that's totally clear and understandable, I thought.

"The ancestors of the Native American tribes who still live in the Yucatan were different people. **Their spirit had a different sound.** Information which is flowing in this moment, relates to the period **before the Common Era: between 700 and 500 BC**," explained my telepathic dictation.

"**The temple site in Tulum was a lighthouse in the ancient Mexico,** it was the northernmost temple site, a very important temple site, which was obviously connected to **the North star** (and other galaxies). **But the blessing of well-being had left, because the ancient Mayan priests did not share their knowledge with the wider community. Their requests and prayers lost the support of (energy) forces which could manifest, ground or actualise those prayers.** So, accidents, conflicts, struggles for power, tribal wars, problems with food and hunger, etc. were ever more frequent." **But those who had managed to develop a broad inter-dimensional cosmic consciousness, all the way to enlightenment, most probably** consciously departed to non-physical parallel worlds and to levels beyond death, explain the Mayan elders. They continue to be centred **in primordial perfection.**

The hurricane had cleansed, partly at least, the Tulum archaeological site of the intrusive energy imprints of numerous hordes of tourists. At least for a short while. So when I visited it at the end of my travel in Yucatan, **Tulum was a veritable living monument and a true library of the messages from the past, a firm monument to bygone connections to the cosmic Source of life.** Here, it is still possible to feel a permanent connection to the vibrations – to the Deities and powers, to put it in the old way – to the energies of the North star and intergalactic routes, which still exist here as a trace of past ceremonies. These **imprinted, carefully downloaded and powerful vibrations** of previous Native American rituals, the devout prayers of spiritual warriors, initiates, and ceremony participants are waiting. **Like the dormant Briar Rose, they are all waiting for a new opportunity for the ancient Mayan (and other planetary) sacred sites to revive their role and power.** This revival is only possible by **using the heart-full open consciousness of people who will be able to recognise this alliance and allegiance and who will know how to realign to the Cosmic Intelligence and to everything that exists, or to put it in a more picturesque way – to the Gods, the smiths, and the lords of time.**

"Another tool helping them was **the guided sound of trance-consciousness, relaxed movement or elated dance, the piercing sound of conches and horns, the rhythms of drums, the sounds of stone litophones and the enchanting sound of clay and wooden flutes. All of this stimulated dancing in spirals, in order to bring down the very essence and the life power of the Cosmos on Earth, through the spiral sound of many octaves. To ground the wisdom of the Source, the Mercy of the Universe, the divine Logos or Intention – for a happy life and the necessary awareness.**" The vision waned. It left a space for my pondering.

This channelled communication ended just as suddenly as it had began. Upon my return to a usual state of consciousness, I added: "Wow, what was that?"

Some mediums can be faintly aware of what had happened in trance, while others do not remember anything at all. I am fortunate to be in an aware state when I am receiving healing energies and meta-sensory messages. Perhaps I do not always recall every detail, but the gist is invariably revealed, my mind remembers what is necessary. Everything unfolds **as if in a dream,** which runs through my mind, leaving there **a barely perceptible memory.** After my channelling in Tulum had finished, I didn't know for some time what exactly I had been saying. There was only a slight imprint. **I had lent my consciousness and mind to the cosmic consciousness, in order to receive the messages** which had to come through me. Fortunately, everything was recorded. And so I was once again here and now, in the usual state of consciousness.

Meanwhile, the Sky grew even darker, evening had arrived. I became greatly **tired. Events in trance had touched the deepest levels of my being, they connected my conscious and unconscious levels, my mind, and soul.** But the immense energy that flows through me while channelling, usually makes my body tired. **Mere imaginative thinking would never leave such powerful imprints and an exhausted body.**

Thanks to Tulum and to the light beam for **the messages and insights about the eternal waves,** thanks **for the challenge of a cosmic-telepathic reading on the Mayan ruins.** I am grateful for all the thoughts, which I could not completely understand at first, but which I appreciate immensely today. Slowly, one after another, those thoughts were **explained in the months and years following my return home,** when I started 'digesting' intensely all my experiences in Mexico and Chiapas and when I started to study some of the books on Mayan culture which I had brought back from my journey in this magical land of the Mayans. I will attempt to explain this sensitive cosmic consciousness on Earth in the following chapters.

I am grateful for everything I experienced, for all the insights on Mayan culture which occurred before I actually wrote down the lines about the wisdom of **this exceptional galactic civilisation, which revered the mind and the heart of all-connectedness and which, millennia ago, sought the Centre of the galaxy, the very centre, the centredness of themselves.**

The gathering of the wise Masters and Gods in Tulum and in the sacred temple of seven gates in Chichén Itzá

This is what Native Americans say: "But very early in life the child began to realise that wisdom was all about and everywhere and that there were many things to know. **There was no such thing as emptiness in the world.** Even in the sky there were no vacant places. **Everywhere there was life, visible and invisible, and every object possessed something that would be good for us to have also – even to the very stones. This gave a great interest to life.** Even without human companionship **one was never alone. The world teemed with life and wisdom;** there was no complete solitude for **the Lakota.**"[423]

Let's imagine a ceremony in one of the most brilliant Mayan temple sites – in Chichén Itzá. **Chichén Itzá** was, like **Cozumel,** one of the largest Mayan **oracle sites** and had a similar role to the ancient Greek **Delphi.** The name **Chichén Itzá** denotes **ancestors and water** (claims Calleros), or **the primal fertile liquid (the**

....
423 Luther Standing Bear, *The Land of the Spotted Eagle,* University of Nebraska Press (2006), p. 14.

ocean waters of life energy), which moistens the mouth of the sacred well. This very sentence illustrates the initial meaning of this sacred site, this temple complex. Mayans say that the Deity **Chaak** resides there – **the Deity of rain and abundance,** who was said to **live in sacred springs, rivers, lakes,** enabling life with rain (water). Human life is also nourished at the spring, in the primordial **Source** of life. In addition, **Chaak is a brilliant character in the celestial or cosmic game within the flow of the Field of Consciousness.** He appears **in countless forms,** just like nature herself: in the form of **rain,** sacred rivers, and **as lightning, thunder,** etc. That is why he has to have at least **three faces,** three visages of **the Sacred Trinity – the cosmic, spiritual and earthly.** The number three also denotes a multitude and the **connectedness** of the physical and non-material worlds.

The sacred complex Chichén Itzá is shaped according to the symbolic **image of the cosmic serpent.** The cosmic serpent wears **golden feathers of the sacred bird** *quetzal,* which embodies **universal wisdom,** inspired by the divine spirit of the Universal Consciousness (gold is the symbol of **perfection and purity**). The sacred serpent **invites us into the realms of the perfect soul.** Which is why on this path, adepts **meditate** devoutly, **diving deep into the Great Spirit** of their initiatory path, **into the very purpose and meaning of their lives. They revisit their own quests, questions, wayward paths, illusions and the quality of their lives.** In order to do this, they need time, peace, and silence.

Here, the Gods (read: cosmic life energies or forces) **live in the sacred temple of the seven golden doors. These doors represent the physical world and the seven human bodies** (the physical one and the etheric bodies), as there are seven ray qualities of the material world. Deities are dressed in **the pure gold of the Holy Spirit, the essence of the Cosmic Consciousness.** So, the temple of the seven doors is the place where **the most sacred transformation** of the initiate's or adept's path **on Earth** unfolds.

As I have mentioned before, **the emotional and mental energy vibrations of ceremony participants** have been preserved in the temples and pyramids through to today. They have been **imprinted on the site and stone. The strongest are the imprints of enlightened** and wise builder-architect-priests, as well as the imprints of other exceptional visitors and, of course, of all **awakened musicians,** who blessed this sacred oracle site with their music and **healing sounds. Nothing,** especially not 'lower sound frequencies,' **can delete that which has 'the highest frequency sound.'** For millennia, stone temple structures, stelae and large stone statues have absorbed imprints of events, emotions and the thoughts of people who were there in the distant past. And for hundreds, even thousands of years, these structures have silently 'waited' for the open minds and hearts of visitors, offering the possibility of **discovering and embracing the messages which had been imprinted in them.**

People who are aware and whose consciousness is broad enough can read these distant energy messages. They can also receive the support of the supporting frequency-energy imprints of the awakened ones, the imprints which have been downloaded over the centuries. They will thus receive the inspiration for their own enlightenment process. They can even become enlightened. It is said that at sacred sites, everyone can receive a message, which is **'whispered into the stone and into the breath of eternity.'**

Initiates can at any time **absorb the frequency records of the ancient ceremony participants, as they are still preserved in the temples,** having resisted oblivion over millennia. These records are **like an invisible computer record,** which is transferring the eternally imprinted **wisdom,** the records of supplications and events, **to new generations of initiates** with open hearts and consciousness. Initiates embark on the road **Xibalba-Bih, the road of respect and of overcoming fear,** with a desire to totally banish fear and **to open up totally to the flow of unconditional love.**

With hope and faith, humans walk **the white road of spirit** – the *sacbé*, which is also a synonym for **the Milky Way.** They walk the road which leads to the Gods, **to perfected beauty, to divine levels of awareness, to all the dimensions of existence.** This road also leads **to the invisible energy flows, or 'beings'** – to the guides or **Lords of 'the Sky,'** who 'dwell' or 'resonate' in temples and at sacred sites, at least occasionally, but especially during ceremonies and cosmic events like the Equinox and Solstice. **When called and desired,** these beings **begin to resonate in the souls of those who invoked them** – in the souls of initiates and ceremony participants.

Invisible and inaudible, yet still perceptible **messages of distant spiritual seekers and their intentions** are still imprinted in stone. And their intentions were most probably quite **similar to the quests of contemporary** spiritual warriors. After all, here **on Earth, we are all on a similar life journey.**

They say that from time to time, **a new little light** is lit on our planet, as if **new lights would appear on Earth: a new awakened being starts to shine, a being who has actualised himself in the cosmic consciousness,** shining in all its mighty light. This has been so throughout different periods of the Earth's history, in various cultures and civilisations.

Love is the sound of joy,
the joy of existence and co-existence,
the joy of listening, the joy of carefully listening to the wisdom
and the whisper of eternity,
to the teachings of our predecessors,

to the heritage of our ancestors,
who walked the Earth long before us
and experienced the riddles of life in a similar way,
even though living conditions in their time were totally different,
more modest, yet at the same time richer.[424]

The Mayans say that the sacred site **Chichén Itzá** consists of **seven temples of light**, where the spirit of great people and **awakened ancestors** is still living. **The initiatory path is the path of the ancient Mayan cosmogenesis,** a path across **the cosmic, earthly, and personal Creation.** On this path, people remember **the birth of their soul within the inaudible sound of the Logoidal Consciousness or Idea.** They remember **their birth 'through word (or sound) of God.'** This journey, this **return back to the Source,** was devoutly worshipped by our distant planetary ancestors and, in some places today, it still is by contemporary people. At least by some.

The more we are aware of the benefits of this journey and transformation, **the easier, the fuller, and the more interesting our life will be. The further our (telepathic) memory (the bellows of powers) is able to reach, the more miraculous and exceptional our paths will be.** Our distant ancestors transmitted to their descendants the very memory of the Great cosmic act of **the Big Bang, when primordial sound** created and **shaped the worlds at the beginning of time,** when there was 'no Sky and no Earth.' This was when **the primordial bang and sound** created everything, including life (energy) power and everything that exists within the Universe and on Earth. And **this inaudible sound of the Universal Consciousness is still ceaselessly creating, shaping, re-shaping, sustaining, dissolving, even destroying if necessary.** Mayans say that **the Creator is crying, shaping** life with its **tears;** or that the Creator is **sprinkling its 'blood,'** its own **life essence,** thus blessing the Earth with its infinite power.

The Native Americans of North, Central and South America, including the ancient Mayans, describe **human birth** in a symbolic way. Humans are said to emerge out of **maize dough**[425] **and the blood of a rattlesnake.** Maize – a Native American staple food – nourishes the physical body, while **the cosmic serpent, the cosmic life energy** nourishes **the spiritual body and soul.** The elements of the material and spiritual essences create life. The young Deity of abundance – **the maize God Chaak** – is therefore **the God of both rain and abundance.**

The first being to be created was said to have been **androgynous,** it was both male and female. It has an important role in Mayan rituals. **Life energies and**

....
424 Mira Omerzel - Mirit, poem *Love Is to Listen to the Teachings of Our Ancestors*, taken from the book *Zvočne podobe prebujene ljubezni*, Vrhnika, Dar Dam (2012).
425 This is also described in *Popol Vuh*.

essences are **balanced** in androgynous genderless beings. And **Gods – cosmic creative forces – are also genderless or bi-gendered. Gender and sexuality is known only in the physical world of duality.** But an awakened human being lives within this precious wholeness. That is why almost all civilisations of this world describe **the first Deity as an androgynous being, as energy** which creates male and female essences and shapes the world of duality and polarity – **the world of apparent opposites, which must be unified.** When we complete the cycle of our life's journeys and we finally **return to our own primal perfection, we regain the balance of an androgynous being. Conflicting polarity finally disappears.** Only androgynous beings are allowed to climb to the top of the sacred tree in fire ceremonies, as **they have already attained the summit (of consciousness).**

Mayans teach about **the cosmic gathering of Cosmic Teachers or Masters of all races, all times and dimensions, or worlds.** They also teach **about immortal, indestructible vibrations (read: beings) of perfection.** It is said that they all gather in the sacred oracle site Chichén Itzá and in other temples. There, they reportedly **bring to life the Great Mysteries** of humanity, **in order to teach people about the wisdom of the feathered serpent, the wisdom of the cosmic Source and existence.** That is why the feathered serpent – the most brilliant and precious symbol of the ancient Mayans and other Native American tribes – is worshipped with devotion. And the images of serpents in temples and their surroundings are reminders – to ensure **we don't forget the divine spiral flow of life, not even for a moment.**

Tribute to the divine Hunahpu, Itzamna, Kukulkan, the mythical twins, monkey, the planets and stars

'Open the door, a novice has arrived!
Offer me a cup of wine and walk with me
for a while,
You don't mind long distances because
on the way **you lay your traps,**
and **plan** how to break my heart.
You fulfilled hundreds of my wishes, yet **my heart
still hungers for more.
Your kindness warms and blesses everyone**
even the Sun bows before You.
Please, let me be Your slave and **silently walk
by Your side.**

> I will find new meaning in every joy and sorrow.
> In that silence
> I will hear the voice of spirit, and freed
> from this world
> I will see **another order** where **the end is
> another beginning.**'[426]

A trumpet in the form of the jaguar, denoting a wise priest.

Hunahpu is the Shaper, the supreme Creator God and the creative force of the Universe. In the physical world, divine force, or divine power, consists of **the four cardinal points of the cosmic cross,** which are denoted by four **colours: red,** which marks **the East** and the upcoming **life; black** indicates **the West,** the underworld, underground and **the darkness of ignorance; yellow** is the colour of **the Sun** and the symbol of **a balanced perfection; white** symbolises **death, the return** to the worlds beyond and the realm of immortal souls of our **ancestors and enlightenment.** Each direction has **its own teachings for life.**[427] None should be overlooked by people. And gazing into the polar Hunahpu symbol, which is similar to the Chinese **yin-yang,** relaxes and inspires. That is why initiates **meditate with its picture in their minds.**

The God **Itzamna, 'the old God,'** the Deity with spiral pupils in his square eyes, is the **messenger and son of the Creator,** which means he is also the Creator himself, **the creator of everything** in the Universe and on Earth. The Mayans say that besides Hunahpu, **the Creator – the God Itzamna –** is the God to which our **grateful attention** should be dedicated. The two represent our earthly **ancestors** who lived in the remote past, and they also represent **the celestial dew, the**

....
426 Rumi, *Hidden Music*, London, Thorsons (2001), p. 34.
427 Read more on this topic in the first book in the *Cosmic Telepathy* series.

Heart of Sky, the Primordial Father, and eternity. And **the lizard** is Itzamna's earthly image.

God Itzamna personifies the power of the Sky; he derives his power from the Universal Cosmic Consciousness and Mind. He enables life, even though he emerges out of infinity. The lord Itzamna comes **from light, from above,** helping people to restore **enlightened consciousness.**

> 'White people think that **the Moon** is simply a Moon – we call her **our grandmother.** They believe that **thunder** is simply a thunder – we call it **our grandfather.** For them the Sun is a large fire ball – we know it is **our brother.**'[428]

The Deity of the Sky, **the Sun God,** also called **Kukulkan, or Quetzalcóatl – the star of Venus,** is unfathomable to humans. It is **the hero who 'invented the world.'** The world is constantly **fed and sustained by the Sun's light,** which enables life and the photosynthesis of plants, through which food for other beings is created. That is why **the Sun is sacred. By means of the sacred axis,** or the sacred tree, **it connectes the underworld (the subconscious), the Earth (consciousness) and the Sky (meta-consciousness, the meta-sensory realms of Consciousness and the levels of the soul).** That is why the sacred axis, which can have the form of a tree, **cross, or a pyramid, links everything into wholistic oneness.** Whereas the Sun and the above-mentioned symbolism remind humans that they are **cosmic children on Earth.** That is why a tree and a cross are obligatory elements in ceremonies. With them, human spirit **rises** and stretches out into the realms of the soul **more easily.**

On depictions, we recognise Kukulkan by his **pierced nose.** The Mayans carefully **offered to primordial divine forces their own juice of life, their blood and even parts of their bodies.** This was **a sign of devotion and selfless sacrifice** of all that is still not good or perfect; **offering was proof of an exceptional oblation, self-sacrifice, and consecration. Especially priests and rulers,** who were in the past the wisest and **enlightened,** as well as their wives, **pierced their noses, tongues, lower lips and even penises,** as a sign of respect for the cosmic creative forces. With this, they wanted to show not only **devotion,** but also their **strong will to overcome pain.** Offering blood and parts of their body, or better – themselves, was **a reflection of the philosophy of life which stresses that spiritual principles are more important and more powerful than the material world.**

....
428 Willie Tehorwirate Thompson/Bitter Branch, 12 years; taken from the book *Tudi trava ima svojo pesem*, Radovljica, Didakta (2000), p. 169.

Mayan tradition says that **the first human being** was **without knowledge. A cyclic evolution** unfolds on Earth, with its ups and downs, with its destructions. And there are many downs. **Each 'down' is a lesson, which lifts** the person, or people, who have hit rock bottom. **Incompleteness is erased,** enabling a **new** beginning and something **better.** During the first days of life on Earth, humans were said to have no real knowledge, no real awareness of why and how to live. Yet, there were extremely wise people living on Earth already thousands of years ago. The first people, **the Ancient Ones,** were entrusted with **the 'God's' name.** In all traditions, this name is **a sound code,** which **should never be pronounced in a loud voice. The code is like a mantra which speaks to our consciousness and mind, broadening it. The sound of the God's name can be extremely helpful** to people who walk the white path of awakening. By not pronouncing the Creator's name, we **preserve the grandeur of the incomprehensible,** inexpressible, and untouchable.

A legend says that **Itzamna** arrived to the holy Earth to pass down to his children the timeless cosmic wisdom and **sacred teachings of well-being and happiness.** Creation tales also explain and confirm the brilliance and eagerness of Mayans **studies of the movements of celestial bodies and of the effects of their energy-vibrational flows of inaudible sound on living beings.** The Mayans built their knowledge of stellar paths and of the harmonisation of cosmic-earthly rhythms into different systems (**calendars**), according to which people's lives, cosmic and earthly cycles, all ceremonies and everything in the Universe unfolds.

The Father, the Creator, the Lord Itzamna is said to have walked on the sacred Earth together with the beings who were first created. He taught them; he taught everyone who had remained on the sacred Earth and **had not broken divine laws,** cosmic laws, and for whom **life was sacred.** They were **the Itzaes, the distant wise planetary ancestors** of Native American peoples. This is what their spiritual heritage claims. **The Ancient Ones, who were the first to discover the mysteries of existence, taught their descendants about the fullness of life; they built temples and revealed the sacred sites of power** – locations with the supporting earthly and cosmic energy radiation. **So that people would never forget and would always remember the true values of life.** And their successors continued to visit these sacred sites to know and **better understand life** and that which was written **in sacred books and in the temples of time.** Mayan legends respect the need of those who lived in the remote past to discover and attend to **life Truths** – the only Truths which enable joyful and fruitful harmony. **Tribute to ancestors** and to the divine forces was therefore an **obligatory** part of ceremonies.

Different cosmic frequency vibrations, or energy vibrations, were said to have collaborated in the creation of life forms on Earth. These vibrations were given the names of various deities on the Native American Olympus. These names are **sound formulae** with an inconceivable and **inexpressible power.** The mighty **celestial dragon** is one of them.

The Gods created the world of duality and the legendary Hero **Twins** (the symbol of humanity), who won an important and extremely valuable earthly battle when they defeated the lords (or **the enemies of peace and happiness), their fears and their ignorance**, following which they returned to the Sky: like **the Sun – like the power of omniscience, like the light of all-seeingness, the Venus' power of kindness. Human beings,** beings of apparent opposites, beings who are learning to transcend the opposites inside them throughout their lives, were created by the divine image of these mythological twins. The twins **fought life and death** in a serious of trials. At the end, they managed to **defeat the Deities of darkness – all that was negative inside them. They managed to become enlightened, awakened within the eternal and unchangeable Truth of existence.**

Being the symbol of unhappy and **divided human beings** and of **succesful players in the cosmic-earthly ballgame,** in the game of life, death and **transformation,** which cannot be avoided, twins **encourage people for their own battle** in the game of life. When they throw the ball high up in the air, they flirt with the invisible spiritual world. When they **hit the ball through the stone ring,** they **won the battle and arrived to the goal – to awakened consciousness; they completed their schooling on Earth. They overcame envy, anger, worry, sorrow, jealousy, etc.** They have banished all of that from their lives for ever (this is what every human being needs to do). But first they have to **trick the Gods of death, their unhealthy ways of living and thinking.** Only then can they rise to **enlightened consciousness.** They attained the immortality of all-connectedness and returned to 'Heaven,' to their own perfection, to the perfection of existence.

Long ago there were four brothers: Ch'owen and Jun B'atz' were farmers, who worked hard and **Jun aj Pu and Ix B'alam Kej** were hunters, who slept till late and worked only a little. Jun aj Pu and Ix B'alam Kej hunted **in the mountains and they told stories.** That is why Ch'owen and Jun B'atz' **got angry** with them and wanted to teach their brothers a lesson: they forced them to walk across a field of thorns and they also took them to a field where ants poured from a huge anthill. But Ch'owen and Jun B'atz' were punished for treating their brothers badly – they turned into **howler monkeys, who were allowed to return to their original undistorted form only during village festivals.** And so it was that they **returned** to the village to **play** with their brothers and chat with them. Since they lived in the mountains, **they had learned the secrets of the mountains, trees, streams, and they shared their knowledge with the villagers.** The monkeys made faces and chased them with their tails, which made the villagers laugh. And that is why today, when **dancing at a village festival, a few people always dress up as monkeys**, entertaining children and villagers. This story was told by **Rigoberta Menchú** in the book *The Honey Jar*,[429] in which she in a modern way retells the ancient Creation story, which is also recorded in the ***Popol Vuh.***

Referring to **Darwin's teaching,** white people claim that we descended from monkeys, whereas Native Americans believe that **monkeys are living images of people who were drowned (in their ignorance)**, but still possess divine forces.[430] In a symbolical way.

Yet, the lively **monkey, the supporter of the Sky, the protector of the written word, computation, writers, and artistic creativity in the service of the Gods,** resides on the Mayan Olympus. It is close to my heart. Why? Perhaps it reminds me of the broadness of free artistic work or of **the liveliness of a researching mind** or the fact that I was born in year of the monkey (in Chinese astrology)? Perhaps its witty vivaciousness and friskiness remind me of the essence of life's journey? Monkeys do resemble humans a little, but they are very different at the same time: as if they would be small and slightly disfigured human beings. This is how it seems to people. **People who live with the above-mentioned distorted destructive emotions and thoughts** will sooner or later distort their lives and their primordial image which is perfect at its core. **They will get unwell. And this is when they need to renew their knowledge and find balance on the sacred mountain or a pyramid.** When they do find it, they have to share their **wisdom with all those** who are still walking, blind and deaf, around the world.

At sacred sites, participants in initiatory ceremonies **bow to different stellar and planetary beings.** Especially to **the Earth,** the Sun, the Pleiades, Orion, **Venus, and the Moon.** The latter carries female principles, female fertility and **sensousness,** which is personified by the rabbit also in the Mayan culture, because rabbits breed fast.

Venus, one the brightest stars and the harbinger of the morning twilight and **first dawn,** reminds people of **the first and much anticipated enlightened light!** How could we possibly overlook it? May **the light of consciousness and happiness** shine, like Venus, in the darkness of suffering! And, of course, we cannot overlook **the male principle of the Sun,** which enables life to all living beings on Earth. According to Native American representations, the Sun's image is woven into the God **Itzamna, Kukulkan, or Quetzalcóatl.** When it rises, time and time again,

....
429 Rigoberta Menchú and Dante Liano, *The Honey Jar*, Toronto, Groundwood Books (2006), pp. 32-37.
430 *Popol Vuh*, Slovene translation, Ljubljana, Mladinska knjiga (1994), p. 19.

it **returns to the Sky, to the light of day,** from the darkness of the underworld, or subconsciousness, **from the darkness of ignorance** and life's problems. **It thus creates the rhythm of a cyclic time. It travels along the cosmic road, which is the path of the Sun, the path of light and good. It is guided by the love of the planet Venus,** the wonderful divine solar being which is well worth worshipping. For **love is the most reliable compass. It leads people into the light of living and the light of spirit.**

The feathers of **the sacred** *quetzal* **bird and eagle** are sacred, just like the Great Spirit of life is sacred. That is why warriors **adorn themselves with their feathers.** They also decorate the images of the solar Deity with the colourful plumage of the *quetzal* bird (macaw) and with eagle's feathers during ceremonies. Birds are free spirit beings, flying between the Earth and the Sky, under the stars and the Sun. They are well worth of the power of the **jaguar,** which was, besides **eagle,** a revered divine being and a metaphor for **the freedom of enlightened consciousness.**

The pineal gland - a link with the energy of the Sun and planets

The pineal gland is the human's principal link to the cosmic, stellar, and planetary vibrations and to the light and energy of the Sun. It is stimulated during ceremonies and when we are **connecting** to cosmic waves, forces and energies. Life energy is constantly flowing through the energy vortices (chakras) along our spine, at the base of which **the cosmic fire**[431] sits dormant – the mighty life **energy of the enlightened consciousness,** waiting to be awakened **through the fiery breath** of warrior's **full awareness,** waiting to **connect the earthly and the cosmic, spiritual, and physical waves into oneness,** waiting to **awaken a person's dormant talents and all their as yet undiscovered abilities. The work of our glands, which are antennae for the reception of different cosmic and planetary frequencies or rhythms, is increased during ceremonies.** Which is why they can be slightly **painful,** especially to the touch. Aligned persons will feel **an increased energy flow through their body** – like pins and needles, a gentle electric current, warmth, **heat, or cold.** Energies which harmonise our **physical bodies** can be very **hot,** while **cold** frequencies tune our mind or **psyche.** When receiving these energies, ceremony participants can **sweat** considerably or they can feel great **heat,** but in the next moment they can shiver with a veritable **cold fever,** and nothing will warm them up. **High-frequency cosmic energies can be truly very icy.** Yet, both heat and cold perform an important **cleansing and invigorating work in the bodies of the mediums.** Warriors cannot influence them.

....
431 The enlightened consciousness *kundalini*, according to Hindu tradition.

At sacred sites and temples, warriors endeavour **to stop the restless flow of their thoughts** and attain a meditative silence. Let me mention at this point **brainwave coherence (EEG = 8-10 Hz/the tone G).** Coherence between the two hemispheres brings the desired peace and creates the possibility for **effective healing and the realisation of our ideas.** When our brainwaves are coherent or when listening to the sounds of **the tone G, we can feel the expansion of the energy flow** in our body **as pressure on our cranial bone. As if an invisible band would be squeezing our forehead or skull.** Such squeezing is often felt by my students during **meditations which include cosmic resonance, and during sound surgeries and cosmic initiations,** or when **subtle cosmic energies are being transferred into the material body.** So is there anything strange in the fact that the Mayans expressed the desire to feel this **invisible energy band on their heads** by wearing a visible band or fold? With head pressure, Mayans indicated that they were **familiar with the effects of the snake-like flow** of the all-present life energy. And perhaps they also wanted to **express their desire for the coherent (synchronous) work of their spirit,** coherence between the left and right hemispheres, which enables the mighty life energy flow to run through the body. In any case – at sacred places, initiates **surrender to this pressure, they enjoy the flow that runs through them.** But spiritual integration of the left and right hemispheres can be slightly painful.

In a state of brainwave coherence, it is possible to rapidly and **effectively heal ourselves and others.** Brainwave coherence is created also **in the enlightened consciousness of oneness, in the transcendental state, in shamanic trance.**

In January and February **2008,** I underwent an unusual process. It happened a few days after I had begun to consciously **channel the sound surgery of all bodies,** which helps to heal other people. When the surgery descended from the highest levels of consciousness into the physical world, unusual things began to happen inside my cranial bones. This grew ever more evident and stronger by the day. I had a strange feeling of **squeezing and broadening at the same time.** I knew such processes from before. They were clearly evident and equally very intense during **yogic levitation,** which I had practiced on a regular basis until the first years of the new millennium. Yet, the processes were even clearer and stronger this time. It was not until some days later that I telepathically perceived that **an accelerated harmonisation of the frequency waves of the hemispheres** was happening as the result of the cosmic surgery, which had come into my life as a harmonising healing technique. It was obviously the right time for such a process, or there was a need for it. Perhaps this was happening, because I had **'earned'** it with the development of my consciousness? Perhaps the process began by itself due to the work of universal forces, which were preparing me for the above-mentioned cosmic-telepathic work of cosmic surgery and were expanding my energy-physical abilities? Well, such processes and feelings did not stop in the years that followed, they only **grew stronger. The power of my energy flow increased immensely in the following months, as did the effectiveness of my (energy) work, my new cosmic-sound resonance.** Even **my teeth changed** overnight. I had the feeling that my teeth were actually **moving in my jaw.**

Soon after, I was guided to carry out **the first cosmic initiation – connecting the Earth and our galaxy, the Milky Way.** The destination point of this connecting was **the Galactic Centre.** Together with course participants, I experienced great **peace** and the feeling of a joyful **wholeness and connectedness.** I had occasionally experienced both before, but this experience was now much stronger and more comprehensive. Together with my course participants, I experienced a veritable **nirvana of existence and of my own essence, a bridge to the centre of myself.** During initiations and courses, we were centred in both the Galactic centre and in the Centre of ourselves. These Mayans were clever, I thought. It is a pity that their exceptional **technologies for operating on spirit and body are lost.** But perhaps not forever, perhaps they will be revived. I am convinced that **many things are** already **coming back.** I perceive this also in my consciousness, in my spiritual research and work. **It comes by itself,** when it can come or when it has to come. And **when conditions for it are created.**

Perhaps the enlightened Mayan **priests and rulers** demonstrate and display **their status and attained (supreme) levels of consciousness** with their multi-coloured body decorations and **cranial deformations which shaped the serpent head (*polcan*)?** While connecting the two hemispheres and all levels of consciousness, we can feel vibrational waves of cosmic and earthly energy and the waves of the Cosmic Mind, which we call **Gods,** as well as cosmic telepathic processes, insights and the messages of the Primordial Intelligence, like a pressure on our head, third chakra and third eye. That is why we first have the feeling that we are about to explode. Our body feels our 'dialogue' with the Intelligence of the Universe, the Logos or God, between the eyebrows. How much we will receive depends on the degree of our openness or surrender, but the flow invariably flows **to the maximum possible extent.** As far as it goes and as far as it is possible. We are like a tube or a pipe. The flow will run through as much as the tube allows. Well, eager warriors will **delight in this pressure and will surrender to the flow as much as they can.**

The Mayans believed that **cross-eyed people had received the divine initiation of the Sun – the star which illuminates and enlightens.** Let me say that **the technique of conscious squinting (cross-eyeing) can quickly move us into a transcendental state of consciousness, into the consciousness beyond, into trance.** This is how I experienced it. When I was learning to drive a car, I had to

drive reverse for a long time one day. And **my look crossed** somehow. After a few seconds, I felt that I was being **pulled into a trance.** Well, I thought, this is something. And I continued with this experience. Trance was not unknown to me at that time, but such a rapid entry into one was. This event warned me about the experiences and myths of the ancient Mayans. The initial meaning and purpose of squinting are probably lost today. Yet, it is maybe still possible to discern the **ancient foundations** of this long-lost philosophy, which **once had a totally different purpose and meaning.**

The magic of love and death and cosmic feathered serpents in the ballgame

> "**I am love's musician** playing for joy
> I comb **the beard of happiness**
> and pull **the moustache of sorrow.**
> **When my core is touched by music**
> **love's wine begins to flow.**
> In this temple of fire my **blood**
> **is melting the snow** from my body.
> It is spring, it is time for action,
> **It is time to throw away all false pretences!**"[432]

In Mayan mythology, the jaguar, or *balam*, symbolises the power of boundless wisdom. It represents **night in the cosmic space,** in the Universe. It also denotes planetary movement and the cosmic aspect of the Universe – **night in the cosmic day.** What is more, *balam* is **a priest, who is able to flawlessly interpret cosmic laws, the will of the Gods and the laws of the four directions in the world of duality.** Priests had to be **able to connect people to the magical powers of the above-mentioned dimensions of consciousness and reality.** That is why *naguals*, the guides, **direct ceremony participants and perform initiations** – they **let the initiation flows of cosmic and earthly energy run** through them. Nobody can perform priestly tasks if they are unable to do this. Even though they are the only ones who know what they are doing and what is happening on Earth, in people and in the Universe, **they will never abuse their abilities and powers. Priests (who are also musicians at the same time) are always available to people.** And it is impossible to **contradict** their visions. They also lead the ballgame.

---
[432] Rumi, *Hidden Music*, London, Thorsons (2001), page 58.

The Cosmic spirit, the Intelligence of life, or the serpent, is a metaphor for **cosmic life energy and spiral movement** throughout the entire evolution of the Universe, the Earth and in the evolution of every person. This Cosmic spirit can be seen in stone sculptures on the sides of the **ballcourt,** called *Pucbal-chah* (according to Calleros). The four serpents on the sides of the ballcourt symbolise **the four cardinal directions and the totality of differentness. They also symbolise the seemingly opposite parts of the whole.** Serpents and **colourful sacred birds** *quetzal* move in spirals across the Earth and air, reminding people of the invisible and inaudible **spiral codes of life, which permeate our cells.** Serpents on the sides of the ballcourt **inspire** participants **about the cosmic-earthly game of life and to surrender to the divine power of nature's frequency waves.**

The word *kaan,* which in the Mayan language denotes the number **four** and **the serpent,** is anchored in the God of abundance – in **the young maize God Wahan-chan-Ahaw.** Ceremony participants ask him for the necessary well-being – both spiritual and material. And **in temples, the cosmic serpent of primal life energy visibly descends from the Sky into our divided world of painful opposites, reviving and invigorating it, ennobling it with its galactic wisdom. It whispers of the magic of a galactic human being,** of initiates and priests. The **sacred rattlesnake's scales, in the form of heart,** talk to our **soul, which dwells in our heart,** telling us to open up and **lay bare the pain and the most luminous content alike.**

Our galaxy – **the Milky Way,** is like a windmill; it is the Source of birth and **the place of rebirth.** In it sits the heart of the great cosmic being, the heart of everything that exists, **the Heart of Sky – Huracan,** as the Mayans say. The snake's **mouth** looks like dark fractures, like **a black hole** in the centre of our galaxy, the Milky Way, which **devours the unhappy contents** of beings who return there **after death,** thus enabling their **rebirth and a new (broader) consciousness** and awareness.

A meditative connection to the snake-like cosmic life energy, which I call **cosmic resonance** and the Buddhists call *rei-ki,* **is very beneficent, purifying, and healing; it makes us aware.** In my Veduna School, the students of cosmic resonance experience both **rapid healings of even the most difficult diseases and veritable cathartic changes.** So long as they surrender to this flow. But people who still have a closed heart and mind and **do not allow changes in their life,** usually soon **run away** from the life game arena. **Courage is needed to look into ourselves** and for transformation. Becoming aware of our mistakes is **not pleasant.** It can be truly **annoying** and very **tiring.** But it cannot be avoided in the sacred ceremonies of **becoming aware. In this way, wise knowledge** comes back to human consciousness **from the Consciousness of the galactic Great Mother,** from the stomach of creation, **from the Galactic Centre,** the cosmic junction or node centre. **Centred consciousness is a magnet and the very goal, in which everything is (still) harmonious and complete.**[433]

The feathered serpent is also a symbol of a connection to ancestors and Gods, to creative forces, to the principles of life. Which is why **different peoples of the world place the serpent into the symbolic centre of their ceremonies.** The cosmic serpent often has **two heads. Each head in a world.** The world of duality has two heads, **two faces** – spiritual and physical. Heads are usually turned in opposite directions. **One dwells in the material world, the other in the world of spirit.** The serpent's physical body **slithers on solid soil,** but the feathers (of its spiritual body) allow it **to rise to the non-material levels of spirit and the Source.** To the Great Spirit, as Native Americans would say.

This is exactly why the feathered serpent is the symbol of our conscious work on ourselves. The spiritual world (our thoughts, visions, emotions, and even dreams) **shapes and transforms the material world.** There lies the source of everything. **The energy serpent is infinite, boundless,** its power and vastness are inconceivable. **The double serpent, or entwined serpents, denotes the connectedness of the worlds, as well as creative oneness, love and swimming with the spiral flow** – not moving against it, which is always painful and full of obstacles. Intertwined flow is **miraculous and healing.** The ancient **medical symbol** – two serpents entwined on a pole – indicates that **always both worlds have to be healed,** the physical body and spirit alike. Through the two sacred serpents, ceremony participants absorb into themselves the essences of duality and the weave of the earthly and the cosmic (soul).

The cosmic arena, the sacred serpents' **game court,** is like a splendid manor, pyramid, and **Sun temple.** The Sun emperor is worshipped with **dance and music:** with wooden and clay **flutes, rattles and drums, conches and gongs, with stone xylophones, etc. With conches, priest-musicians mark the end and the beginning of a ceremony, and they even 'bring the dead to life'.**[434] Including those who are asleep.

In the earthly game, **Mother Earth, Father Sky, and Grandfather Sun** take part in the form of **fire. The Universe communicates through light and sound,** transmitting to the Earth the energies of the frequency waves from the Source, the Galactic Centre. According to contemporary claims, this Centre is somewhere in the area of **the black hole.** What is more, the Centre, the Source of life, has **its own sound,** which priests captured in their sound codes and mantras. Native

....
433 More about the mastery of mind and the cleansing of emotions can be found in subsequent books.
434 Ancient Hindus and Indo-European peoples shared the same belief.

Americans say that the invisible **sound of the planets' movement** is a brilliant imaginary **'game of the Gods,'** a miraculous and magical game.

During initiation ceremonies, **rulers, shamans, and priests sprinkled their blood** onto the ground. By doing so, they enabled the continuation of life, expressed their gratitude for life and awakened the creative forces of the Universe. **Blood, a symbol of life, fertility and creativity** in the physical world, is also the very essence of every incarnated soul. **In initiations and ceremonies, a symbolic offering of the heart and blood sacrifice, which later degenerated into senseless and mere physical sacrificing, was a distinct act of devotion and proof of being ready for spiritual transformation, or dying. This builds an increasing harmony in human beings and in the entire cosmic expanse.**

The consciousness of humanity is expanding. The Universe too. With drops of their blood, warriors **pledge to offer their heart, their compassionate love to the world and to themselves.** But first they have to **develop this unconditional love within themselves.**[435] True love is far from what we today call love, because we merely think of **sensuous love, which is most often restless and chaotic. True unconditional love is stable, fully aware,** eternally compassionate, and generous to everyone. **The love of the soul** is **grace and mercy,** which never loses touch with all levels of the earthly and the cosmic (spiritual).

In the ballgame, players run towards the goal

The above-mentioned sacred **game, or the ball ceremony,** was an especially important part of Mayan rituals at the ceremonial temple sites, like for example **Uxmal, Coba, Tical, Chichén Itzá, Izapan, Tulum, Palenque, Ek Balam. In it, players (priests) 'run towards the goal'** in a ritual way. In this game, using a caoutchouc ball, priests demonstrate and perceive **the reflection, or the echo, of the cosmic-earthly drama,** and they delve into it. All of this in order **to focus on their intentions and wishes and to direct the energy of attention, which is creative power, into them.** They strive to pass the ball through a ring on the pyramid's wall and so to arrive first symbolically at **the goal.** Before the game, players purify themselves in a ritual hot **steam bath** (sauna).[436] **Dressed in their finest vestments,** the players **symbolically embark on a ritual journey,** which has a purpose and goal – **to attain perfection and enlightened oneness. Their wish is thus expressed clearly, its fulfilment follows.** The one who manages to

---
435 More about unconditional love can be found in the following books in the *Cosmic Telepathy* series.
436 Read more about Native American sweatlodge and its purpose in the first book in the *Cosmic Telepathy* series.

throw the heavy rubber ball through the ring first, returns as the winner – first in a symbolic way, then in reality – **to the Galactic Centre, to the Home of the soul, to complete awareness. Life is completed, pain overcome, conflictedness banished.**

The stone **ring** is a picturesque symbol and metaphor for the human life journey along the cyclic flow of life and death, across untold trials, initiatory passages, or bridges, which are chiselled through our compassionate behaviour and kindness. **The ball is a symbol of life and of the human endeavours to attain this awakened goal and total surrender, a symbol of a wide open cosmic consciousness and the divine within ourselves. It is a sign of our attunement to the universal creative principles and laws.**

Priests – players in this ritual ball game, in which the ball can be heart-shaped – ardently play in the middle of the temple. They wear **the game's gear:** leather **padding** to cover their legs, **yokes, rings, arm protectors, distinct crowns and headdresses** as well as **protection for their faces.**[437] **During the game, players constantly touch the ground with their knees,** as this is how incarnated **souls are constantly touching the planet Earth,** for they live in the material world. Players endeavour to throw the ball through the ring. If the ball **falls on the ground, everything starts anew** (just like in life itself) and again, players have to be purified in the hot sauna, in which they stream with sweat. The winner is the team which is the first to throw the heavy rubber ball through the stone ring attached to the pyramid's wall. They have attained their goal. **Following which the captain of the team was supposedly sacrificed.**

Seven serpents, resembling flames or tongues of light, rise from the throats of (sacrificed?) headless bodies, the like of which are depicted, or carved, into the temple's walls. Modern researchers, who are far away from the primordial initiatory wisdom, are perhaps wrong in their interpretation that these serpents represent **gushes of blood from the decapitated.** A more subtle spiritual interpretation would instead present them as **auric symbols of light, the aura of the light beams of the seven etheric bodies** which surround the physical body, or rise from it. **The higher the flames go, the greater spiritual power a player has.** A broad aureole confirms **the enlightened state of consciousness of the player, or the priest 'winner,'** and also that of an individual who, through the ballgame, becomes a priest, having **attained the final goal of his life path – self-realisation.** It is more probable that these people were not sacrificed or beheaded, but instead they had earned **the expansion of their consciousness and with it, a broader auric field.**

On some archaeological monuments male players are depicted **with erections, in a fertile form.** They wear **royal symbols of the Loving Magic**[438] on their shoul-

....
437 The gear is described also in the sacred book *Popol Vuh*, electronic version (2007), p. 106.
438 According to Calleros – Miguel Angel Vergara Calleros, *Chichén Itzá: The Cosmic University of the Mayas*, Merida (1998).

ders, which lead the players to the seven beams of light, to the seven serpents of light – the symbols of their mastery over and connection to all the bodies and energy centres, or chakras, a connection between the seven earthly levels and the seven fundamental cosmic rays of Creation.

A male-female androgynous, complete being celebrates their attunement to the cosmic-earthly laws of life, the main principle of which is compassionate love. The awakened ones have managed to bring together the world's oppositions and differences to make an undivided and complete image. **Life is no longer tormenting them, for they now understand, know, hear, and see** sufficiently clearly not to be affected any more by the mind of ignorance. And within the embrace of the material and non-material, within their love act, **there is nothing more majestic than love!**

The perfection and beauty of human completeness is reflected in the winner's feeling of harmony, imbued with love. Unconditional love does not make demands, it is watchful and sacred, but above all, it is attentive to everyone and everything. The Divine Source illuminates the love couple (similar to Hindu tantra yoga) – the world of humans and God – with love, which is the link to the Intelligence of life.

Fiery flames rise in the middle, **above the vertex of the seventh light beam, or the energy serpent of the auric body of the headless human**. Players receive these flames upon entering the worlds beyond the physical, when they start living permanently within the abilities of their expanded consciousness and unconditional love, when they become one with all the levels of the soul and reality. When they are awakened, as ancient wisdom puts it, **they transform their mind and their perception of the world and they come to see the true meaning of life and events. Their mind becomes one with the Cosmic Mind. Reality is revealed to them in its totality.** They start thinking with all the registers of the soul and with a liberated – not stuck in patterns and representations – spirit, **with a mind,** which is not bound by the illusions acquired through their upbringing and education.

In their divine **marriage with the Creator**, spiritual seekers and **warriors become aware of their numerous still undiscovered abilities and possibilities**, of the unknown levels of existence and their own divine essence. Their consciousness and awareness expand immensely, they vastly **enhance their spiritual and energy power, which is the best protection against the deaf and violent world**, and especially against the intrusion of various lies and distortions into their mind. It is a connectedness without attachment to anything that creates harmony and happiness. The power of our open flow, the power of our spiritual power, increases in proportion to our unveiling of higher levels

of consciousness.[439] Yet, the perfect, the unified is neither higher nor lower, it is **simultaneous.**

The number of players is symbolic too: seven on the left side and seven on the right side; 7 × 7 means **49 levels or nuances of consciousness, perception, and understanding. Human egocentric behaviour and mind need to finnally die, so that something new, something better can be born through this connection to the highest consciousness, which is love.** Our soul is our guide through these necessary changes, but **our intellect opposes the changes, for it wants to hold on to old rigidities** and behaviour patterns. Thus begins **the battle between the ego and the soul,** a battle for and against change.

> **The wall is an invisible field of delusions,**
> **false imprints and unhappiness,**
> which get in your way, **not allowing you to breathe.**
> The strength of this wall is fortified by
> **sorrow and worry,**
> **by lack of power and fears.**
> With time, the wall becomes so strong,
> that you start **believing**
> it simply has to be there,
> that it cannot be removed.
> **The wall of destructive emotions and thoughts**
> **undermines your everyday happiness,**
> **it veils your view**
> **and leads you into unhappiness.**
> This is how it goes until you **come to see** the wall
> until you **admit** to yourself its existence,
> until it becomes truly disturbing and redundant.
> Its existence is **revealed through illness,**
> **numbness,**
> **through vanity too.**
> **When you finally recognise the wall,**
> **only then does the real battle for its destruction start,**
> bringing you back to a distant unpleasant memory,
> which is robbing you of many benefits.

---
439 We simply name them higher and lower, but they are only different, having a different frequency vibration. Higher – lower, lower – upper are just expressions, which we use to define and describe the three-dimensional physical world, in order to communicate more easily.

Fortunately, the imprints of the wall now resemble **only a pale shadow of the
pain suppressed long ago,
which follows you silently,**
which pities you
and does not want to surrender that easily.
So, be more persistent than your past
and **build a new, lighter and better life,** without walls,
**in the future.
Pain can be overcome by fate in life and in the divine Plan,
by fate in your destiny**
and – despite everything – **in goodness.**[440]

This is one of the poems which utterly poured through me one October night in **2011.** The poems were titled *Zvočne podobe prebujene ljubezni (The Sound Images of Awakened Love).* Similar to priestly music and prayer, their purpose is **to open the mind and the heart, to guide through the processes of transformation straight-forwardly.** I wove some of the poems into this book, for they perform **their priestly role** in the form of verses. In their rituals and transformational processes, the ancient Mayans probably also **used the help of poems and spontaneous guided sound, and listened to the sound of the verses of their priests,** who led the rituals and oversaw the process of becoming aware and changing.

The wall of skulls, a warning from predecessors, or ancestors, stands in the middle of the ballcourt. **The death of the team's captain is only symbolic; it is the mystical death of human distortions and masks. Death is not actual, it is spiritual. Only old perceptions of the world die, perceptions which the player has finally managed to grow out of.** Everything **that makes us unhappy,** everything that causes illness and problems has to die sooner or later. Day and night, we are fighting with the Deities of annihilation, or death. Agonising spiritual content needs to die, such as **wrath, recklessness, greed, lust, gluttony, envy, jealousy, pride, arrogance.** This is also what Native Americans teach.

The wall of skulls, the wall of the dead, near the ballcourt suggests the eternally present spirit of enlightened ancestors, who speak to living people, encouraging, and awakening them. Flowers in the skulls indicate **the beauties and gifts of life, an element of which is also the realm beyond death. Death is the fountain of life, which liberates the spirit and fosters the fullness of awareness.** Every flower is a perfect form, **a mandala of the cosmic idea, and therefore a symbol of perfection and completeness.** The head or the soul of the awakened

....
440 Mira Omerzel - Mirit, poem *In Front of the Wall*, taken from the book *Zvočne podobe prebujene ljubezni*, Vrhnika, Dar Dam (2012).

one, decorated with flowers, **celebrates the person who is finally able to entirely understand the Mystery of life and to interpret eternal truths.**

The heads of the seemingly decapitated players, crowned with the flames and flowers of light, of energy, are **surrounded with majestic aureoles, with the energy glow of perfect beings.** They say that **it is from there that the rays of cosmic consciousness of the enlightened ones return to the Sky, together with the beams of energy, which feed** human beings, the environment and the Universe. They rise into the Sky and radiate from human physical bodies, indicating that this being has just **experienced the death of the old,** the death of that which was insufficiently loving and conscious. **Annihilation is only symbolic, it is spiritual. The soul is immortal and eternal,** even though the body dies.[441]

The skulls in the centre of the ballcourt correspond with the rings and arches in the higher parts of the temple. There, **during the equinoxes** (according to Calleros) **the Sun creates a game of light and shadow, the game of life and death.** At the same time, the arch is the point in the ballcourt where **sound waves are transformed and poured into a new sound image.** Ceremony participants thus listen to the distinct **resonance phenomenon of the changing sound. The sound is also transformed – just like human life –** if someone **claps or shouts** under the temple's arch or in front of the Great Pyramid. The clapping and shouting **turn into the sound of the sacred bird** *quetzal*, which reminds participants **to remember their connection to the world of the spirit and Gods.** And that difficulties in life can turn into a euphonious song in a conscious person. This travelling and changing sound resembles the human journey **up and down on the ladder of consciousness.** Instead of earthly clapping, they can listen to the sublime **voice of the sacred bird,** which is a divine messenger and a distinct **reminder that everything in life is constantly changing and must change until we attain painless perfection.**

Mayans say that the brilliant acoustics of this miraculous temple architecture turns **sound into music (*pax*)** and enables **singing (*kayab*).** Even death, or **the dead,** are said to **encourage living people with inaudible sound,** which becomes **audible** through song and through the playing of instruments. **They sing a song of human spiritual victory, of the supremacy of light over darkness, of awakening and the attunement of the Earth to the Universe.** The sacred bird sings a song about co-existence with the Galactic Consciousness, with cosmic consciousness, which is well worth living.

Seven players play on the left side of the ballcourt and seven on the right side. A human being also consists of **seven subtle energy bodies,** which are intertwined, spanning from the material to the most subtle levels of the being of consciousness, or

....
441 More about life, death and soul can be read in the chapters of the fourth book in the *Cosmic Telepathy* series.

soul. Priests from the distant past (at least B.C.E.) were most probably **not beheaded** in the ballgame, as contemporary scientific simplifications of Mayan spiritual wisdom interpret. True, **the team's captain** is depicted or carved into the stelae and walls as **headless. Beams, or gushes, rise from his throat, symbolising the seven streaming auric rays of light,** the seven fundamental shape giving (energy-frequency) **rays of Creation,** the likes of which are also known in other spiritual teachings of the world. The physical eye can recognise them in **the colours of the rainbow.**

Everyone has to pass through numerous deaths in their lives. Life is (ceremonial) dying. That is why the players in the ballgame symbolically die and are then reborn. This happens when they manage to totally leave behind, or overcome, the old, the negative and the insufficient. The seven cosmic rays of creation, the seven rainbow or auric vibrational qualities, or inaudible sounds, are also **seven different fundamental frequency (shape-giving) waves which build the physical world.** Each vibration has its own colour, sound, density, and translucence. They are depicted by the beams which stream out of the priests' throats, and at the same time, they are depictions of **the creative forces of the Universe** and of the seven most important energy waves, which we also recognise **in the seven basic colours and in the seven tones of the European scales.**

Radiation from the winner's throat looks like **the aureole of an enlightened one.** The seemingly **beheaded captain could be the (leading, most important, spiritually the broadest) person, who has managed to stop the ceaseless babbling of mind and the eternal parasitical thinking** that arises from countless inherited patterns and expectations, all of which kill human happiness. The depictions therefore illustrate **initiation, spiritual transformation, rebirth into a new life: life with a new consciousness – without the disturbances of usual thinking.**

In the heart, in the soul of the winner, the internalised **awareness of all the dimensional realities** merges with the Source. **The warrior is now able to 'read' data from the bank of energy records** with his high-dimensional, high-frequency **etheric bodies. With them, the phenomenon of cosmic telepathy became possible, even the surgery,** in which the surgeon's work is performed by the primal life energy itself.

Every auric, or etheric, body ends and begins in **spinal marrow, which is the pillar, the path** and protection or sheath of subtle energy undulation through beings. **And every pillar of light is symbolised by the serpent.** Every energy pillar (or etheric body) vibrates, **resounds in its distinct frequency,** in its sound, or note: these pillars resonate **as the seven colours of the rainbow or as the seven basic notes in a tone scale. Each frequency brings its own gift: it has its own special, unique effect.** And these vibrational qualities of the seven basic levels of the physical world also resonate **in the notes and music** which accompanies the rituals.

Initiation, or the shamanic jump to the Sun, means total surrender to the game of life (destiny) and to the eternal existential Truths, or God. The conscious merging of human consciousness with the divine Consciousness of the Cosmic Mind is called **'marriage with God.'** It is the surrender of everything – including ourselves – to the Mysteries of life. **When we accept life as it is, transformation can begin** and we can repair that which is not good. **The gifts of the cosmic energy serpent,** the gifts of the waves of the inaudible cosmic sound start flowing through our mind and body, opening the cosmic-earthly portal, the time-space doors, into the fairytale (high-dimensional) worlds of spirit.

Snake descendants in the play of light, darkness, fire, and water

The sound of love is a messenger between the Sky and the Earth,
between the spirit and mind,
between all forms of life,
visible and invisible pictures;
it is the messenger, which **ceaselessly whispers eternal wisdom,**
encouraging you
to let go of ruinous follies.[442]

Two entwined spiral serpents are often depicted at numerous **sacred sites** of different peoples of the world, including those of the Mayans. **With their entwining, these serpents illustrate the sacredness of oneness, which wants to be anchored, or grounded, into the world of duality and to become one in the material world.** The two serpents denote the mysterious, magical, and mystical. **A serpent-like entwined cosmic monster haunts** the world of the living and causes people to be unhappy only until the two poles – the material and the spiritual – **consciously merge into one, into one being.** This braid of two serpents illustrates not only **the polarity of the forces of the Universe and nature,** but also the duality of the male and female natures, which can merge into single 'being' and into twins too.

Mayans have a simple, yet powerful **symbol of Creation: the zero or the circle,** which illustrates a connected macrocosm and microcosm. **The macrocosm,** or Cosmos, consists of the Sun and the planets, while **the microcosm** is represented by the Earth and humans. That is why **an egg is often the material and visible symbol of Creation.** It has its **sound image** too: the syllables or sounds HE and

....
442 Mira Omerzel - Mirit, poem *The Sound of Love Is the Messenger between the Sky and the Earth* taken from the book *Zvočne podobe prebujene ljubezni*, Vrhnika, Dar Dam (2012).

HU in the Mayan world. **The circle means eternally renewing life, the cycle and the medicine circle of life; the cyclic emergence and disintegration,** and also the structural form of atoms and elements (water, fire, air, earth and ether, or cosmic essence).

Dancing in a circle therefore has a symbolic weight and a spiritual meaning too, just like **the round ball,** round play, the coiled serpent and **the eternal return to the beginning, to the original base note** in music. If this is **the note G, sound will have an increased intensity and power.** The circle and circular form are **the very foundation of cosmogenesis among the Mayans** and many other cultures. A circled dot (similar to the Egyptian sacred **Eye of Horus**) also denotes the **Primordial Principle, the essence of life and the light of the primal sound, Cosmic Consciousness itself,** which is simultaneously also **the sexual symbol of emergence and birth on Earth.** A circled dot is **the divine eye,** which indicates the following thought: **I in the Cosmos, the Cosmos in me.**

Mayans say: if a plant does not die and does not shed its seeds, which would have fallen to the ground, that plant will no longer be able to grow again (according to Calleros). **Something needs to die, so something new can emerge.** Near the ballcourt stands a T-shaped **wall of skulls,** called *tzompantli.* It denotes the God Teotl and represents **the great breath of life and the sexual energy of new life. Death does not haunt life. The serpent** – the symbol of ancestors and life – therefore represents **the sexual fire and the cosmic fire of spiritual transformation.** On Earth, both are indispensable. Fire – tantric or spiritual – also denotes **the wish to eliminate ignorance** and spiritual immaturities. **By showing love** towards others and towards everything that exists (including the extra-terrestrial dimension), people **grow to be more mature and wise beings,** beings with a new psychological content and way of thinking, with **a more complete understanding of life. Love changes people,** both inwardly and outwardly.

Cosmic serpents, or the serpent-like flows of energy, come from everywhere, out of everything that lives, including the inside of bodies and spirit. **The fire of sexual alchemy,** which was also practised by the ancient Mayans, **bestows the missing and invigorating energy upon the body** in a special and supplemental way, **and it also provides the essence of the opposite sex. It thus expands the mind and consciousness of both lovers.** All of this is also fostered by **the sacred fire of a conscious transformation, which burns both within us and around us.** The sexual fiery energy of love can turn **into enormous spiritual and physical power,** which complements and joins the energies of both sexes **into a whole.** It brings the lovers together and **lifts them onto the highest levels of consciousness.** At least for a moment – **in the orgasmic merging and unification,** in which beings **touch the Absolute, or God, Silence, and Emptiness.**

At the temple's ballcourt in Chichén Itzá, ceremony participants can admire **six great stone arches.** These arches represent **the rotation of the Earth in relation to the Sun's movement.** Corners in the south of the ballcourt are important recognisable points of the setting Sun, especially at **the Summer and Winter Solstices** (according to Calleros). The ballcourt itself and its centre are **symbols of the Earth's cyclic movement at the equinoxes, captured in a material form.** At the equinoxes, rays of light from the setting Sun always shine upon the same areas of the eastern or western arch. **The precession of the equinox encompasses the 33 sacred days of Equinoctial light and darkness.** These days are well worth making use of, for they are a time to delve into our lives and **a time for the great changes** which a warrior needs to carry out. **The number 33 is the sacred number of the Triune, of the three-fold Triunity.**

During that time, participants can watch the light effects of **the light-and-shadow play** at **the Great Pyramid of Kukulkan,** when rays of light slither straight down from the Sky (the Source) to the Earth along the large **stone serpents on the stairway.** These 33 significant days begin on **the 5th of March** and last **until 6th of April,** claims Calleros. **A new earthly and life cycle** begins. Nature starts to wake up and similarly, **humans** are said to **wake up too. And snakes,** the earthly representatives of invisible worlds, come out during spring days.

The rubber ball used in the priestly ritual game is said to represent **the moving Sun.** Archaeologists claim that the ball, which flies in arches above the ballcourt evokes **the annual movement of the Earth** in relation to the movement of the Sun. The Sun is dying as it passes from the East to the West, and **it stands at its centre point during the precession of the equinox. The ball, just like the Sun, constantly travels from one side of the celestial, or life, ballcourt to the other.** All year round. Brave spiritual warriors in initiatory rituals pass the ball, **dressed in exquisite ceremonial clothes, to mark their worthiness for this cosmic and earthly game,** a game which offers them the opportunity and possibility for transformation and a deep understanding of events on Earth and in the Sky.

But the ball might also denote a conscious **seeker of Truth, who wants to discover the meaning of life, attain his enlightened goal and fulfil the contract of his soul. The heart-shaped rubber ball is burned** at the end of the ceremony. Doesn't this act of burning, **which marks the end of the game, signify the ultimate elimination of the imperfect?** There is nothing left to be burned, nothing more to dissolve! **The self-sacrifice of the player-priest** is over. The player then shares this attained knowledge with everyone who wants to listen, and he also shares with them his **new powers,** which he received in this game and with which he can brilliantly **heal** people and **see clearly** their past and future.

The feathered serpent, which represents **the invisible divine power and the dormant serpent-like life energy *kundalini*,** which, like the *shakti* (female) life energy, waits in the coccyx, is therefore an image of the exceptional **power of enlightenment and light of devotion, which shines in the emptiness of darkness.** During the transformation processes, the feathered serpent descends to the Earth and rises to the Sky. The Sky was named **Kaan** – the serpent, and the ancient Mayans called even themselves *kaan*, or **the serpent people.** With their brilliant name, they tried to preserve the ancient philosophy of life and the purpose of existence. By using this name, they constantly reminded themselves that they were **cosmic children, the children of the cosmic serpent on Earth. And that they should never overlook their origins and their invisible cosmic-spiritual substance.**

The darkness of the underworld and the wall of skulls or **the wall of the dead,** is a silent reminder of **the darkness of the ego and of the unconscious shadow self,** which needs to be transformed within people of the past and future alike. **We can free ourselves from the bad and the insufficient using the mysterious power of the cosmic energy serpent and its fire of life.** In a hidden and symbolic way, **symbols and sacred sites** portray everyone's mysterious journey **into the centre of their own core.** With their grandeur and **the rich language of forms of various artistic reminders and signposts,** they invite people to the earthly school of experiences and trials. **They are an invaluable tool for the liberation from the chains of the physical world, the chains of a destructive attachment, and from everything which does not testify to the unconditional love of the cosmic-earthly consciousness and game.**

In the ancient philosophy of life, the limited and the stuck are depicted by the image of a horrible **'cosmic monster:' a serpent or dragon, which devours that which is (still) not good,** which is still not illuminated, or enlightened. Our distant planetary ancestors from different traditions of the world tried to **kill this dragon, the monstrous evil within themselves.** They tried to eliminate their limitations, reveal life's mysteries and revive within themselves the wonderful abilities of multidimensional consciousness, the joy of freedom. They tried to earn well-being and transform themselves into wise beings, capable of the multidimensional journey of the soul. They wanted to open the portals of time and space which lead into different dimensions of reality and timelessness, where the wise ones can even meet the essences of the souls of ancestors and wise teachers of all times and dimensions. Entering the world of spirit and miraculous consciousness **during our life time** is **a challenge** worth taking. **Living the fullness of spirit on Earth** is an immense wealth and opportunity.

In the Temple of the Eagles and the Jaguars spiritual seekers can experience a cathartic purification, which is an exceptional gift. The eagle (consciousness) and the jaguar (the power of attention) symbolically hold the initiate's **heart in their**

claws, clutching it (according to Calleros). The heart in a jaguar's paws signifies the **death** of the ceremony participant and player in the ballgame (of life). It means **the death of immaturities,** which need to be transformed into the divine (awakened) qualities of **Quetzalcóatl, or Kukulkan,** as soon as possible. **The jaguar tears out the heart of the person being awakened, just as the suffering and heartache of the trials in our life teach us about the good and the bad. Trials are especially difficult immediately before enlightenment. The jaguar tears out and destroys the illusions and delusions of our earthly attachments and our lack of awareness. This is how the jaguar saves people from their rigidity and despair, showing them the path towards the renewal of the lost oneness. The jaguar and the eagle** are wonderful images of the divine spirit residing in Native American hearts.

When humans are going through **the agony of suffering,** the jaguar, eagle, and serpent inspire them to **open their hearts and embrace the visions** which follow after they have let go of earthly illusions and lies. People lie all the time, even if they are just small white lies, but they are **not at all aware** of this. They think that this is how they can avoid unhappiness and gain the affection of other people, but they could not be more wrong. **Even the mask of kindness can unfortunately be a lie.**

The Deity **Kukulkan,** which is said to also represent **the elementary beings of nature,** is the central character of numerous tales and legends, which Mayan grandmothers narrated to their grandchildren. These are tales of cosmic wisdom, or of **the serpent which comes back to people, teaching them and bringing peace.** This brings back to me what my grandfather used to ask me before putting me to sleep: **'Do you want to hear the tale about the never-ending snake or the one about the (spiral) glass snail?'**

Both tales carry the symbolism of a spiral, they have a similar content. But to no avail: if I chose the tale about the never-ending snake, my grandfather wanted to tell me about the snail; if I chose the story about the glass (invisible!) snail, he said he would rather tell me the story about the snake. Only now have I come to understand that with this **word game,** he wanted to tell me that **both symbolically speak of similar things (about the spiral energy of life)** and that whatever I choose, **this spiral will always be here. It will perhaps be different each time – yet it will always exist.** For this type of game, Native Americans have chosen the snake or the sacred bird *quetzal*, which spirals through the air. How could the warriors of light but remember **the stories, songs, and fairy tales of the sacred snake,** which their parents and grandparents used to tell them, or which they whispered to each other somewhere in the jungle or by a river?

The tales and myths of Creation and resurrection pass wise guidelines for spiritual transformation and for the renewal of complete awareness in the soul. Warriors, who become the centre of the Universe during the ceremony, become the sacred axis, the link between the worlds. This is why **the altar** in the centre of the sacred site is tied with **four** crossed ropes, which denote **the world of duality (2 × 2) and its polarity;** and they also denote **the sacred tree of wisdom,** its top reaching into the clouds, to the heights of the unknown, invisible and unfathomable, into the difficult to reach, etc. **The tree attached to the Sky awakens the yearning of the soul.** This was also how the healer and shaman **Pancho** prepared his altar which served to invoke the rain God Chaak. The past is obviously still alive in contemporary rituals.

In the temple complex of Chichén Itzá, there is an **observatory** for watching the paths of the celestial bodies and for listening to cosmic and earthly rhythms and waves. By taking into account the precise and comprehensive Mayan calendar, it was **easier to recognise on which station of consciousness, or destiny, a person lived.** Moreover, the astronomical calculations of the priests determined **the best time for ceremonies,** for marriages, for sowing and harvesting, for the birth of the new, etc.

The sacredness of water springs and the Venus temple, the temple of the warrior's courage

When **the living water**
nourishes the earth,
when spring comes,
we plant corn seeds
of all kinds,
corn, **which gives us life.**
The living water of mother Earth
wakes the seeds into new life.
They will sprout and grow
in the clear light of the Sun,
praying for rain,
stretching their hands to the four directions.

That is when
rain makers
will send forth their sultry **breath,**
masses of **clouds** will come to us from afar,
with their stretched rainy hands
they will caress the corn
they will reach down to it,
embrace it with refreshing water,
with living rain.

> **Where the paths of rain makers come together,**
> **like a waterfall, rain**
> will take sand and silt with it,
> and will wash out ravines in the hills,
> bringing tree trunks to the valleys.
> Water will rush down from all the hills,
> **flooding the planting holes**
> **of mother Earth.**
>
> **May my prayer be fulfilled.**[443]

With these words, the **Zuni** Native Americans not only called, but also created the abundance of rain – food for the corn.

In their lives and during ceremonies, humans have to **connect to all the elements of the material world.** This is why **the earth, sacred fire, sacred water, sacred springs, and the winds of the four directions** are of special importance in ceremonies and cleansing rituals. At temples and **sacred sinkholes (*cenotes*)** ripples the sacred water, which is also the symbol of life, **body fluids** and of the boundless ocean of life energy. Water represents **the flow of life and the free flow of life energy in the body. If the flow is blocked, people get unwell.** In sacred waters resides **Yumil-Chaak – God the father and the rain God. Rivers and wells are valuable for ritual purifications and (self-)sacrifices.**

The well itself is the very **heart of ritual worship** and of the spiritual journey **along the white path.** It is the place to which Mayans respectfully brought their offerings and where they offered their **fears and wishes** to the water, as they did to fire. This is why the Mayans usually symbolically offered something from their own abundance: **food, precious stones, gold, wooden items and works of art, weavings, clothing, dishes, fruits, flowers, etc.** Even animal and human bones and skulls were found at the bottom of these sinkholes.

But the most important sacrifice and self-sacrifice primarily take place in our minds and at different levels of our consciousness and conscience, where seekers consciously release their negative sides. They want to live a divine life without imperfections and poverty. But they attain this only **after they have fully understood the laws of devotion and unconditional love.** Then, their **self-sacrifice is a true deed of respect and a conscious offering of gratitude. And the 'Divine Order' rewards them with abundance!**

....
443 A Zuni prayer for rain, taken from the book *Tudi trava ima svojo pesem*, Radovljica, Didakta (2000)

Giving requires receiving. In order to be able to receive without problems, we first have to learn to give and respect others as we respect ourselves. What is more, we must allow ourselves to live as we feel is right and not as others tell us or as is expected of us. Realignment with cosmic laws will always support the seekers and will bring them **peace, harmony, happiness, abundance, etc.**

In their ceremonies, Mayans bow to **the Sun, the Earth, Venus, the Pleiades, Orion,** etc., and they connect to their **language of sound. Venus – Nahek** is certainly one of the most significant Mayan Deities. Venus is the great rising and setting star, which is seen as the bright **Morning star and Evening star.** In the sacred book *Popol Vuh* they look forward to it like **dawn, the much anticipated dawn of awakened life.** The appearances and disappearances of the Sun and Venus in the Sky encourage humans **to become aware of not only the repeating cycles of life, eternal births and deaths, but also of the creative ideas of the Universe and always new opportunities for growth, for dawning. The two stellar images raise hope and eliminate despair** which destroys the will for life. **Humans look the Creator in the eye.** At the crack of dawn, warriors feel the especially **pure and powerful cosmic energies** of the new day; they sense **the power of renewal, the great Creator's – Kukulkan's – work,** its ideas, which are realised and built on Earth by the four elementary forces of life and by the invisible fifth force – the ether. When they merge with them, warriors feel **the very essence of the material world, their own essence.**

Time and time again, wise humans are said to **return – symbolically and in their thoughts – to the rising Morning Star.** They are **re-born** through its rising light and beauty and they are **enchanted by the ever more miraculous abilities of the jaguar – balam, or 'sphinx'** (according to Calleros) **– the being of the four basic buildings blocks of the material world.** The sphinx's face, or head, is said to be the material proof of the **water** element; **the heart** is the jaguar, which is the reflection of **the fire; the feathers** of the sacred bird *quetzal* are the symbols of **air (and spirit),** the claws of the jaguar's, or eagle's, paws are the Earth. When, in their spirit, warriors **bring together the apparent opposites of differentness, they themselves become the Creator, they become boundless creators, who master the magic of life** and start to live the eternal **law of Creation and incarnation.**

> **"We are healers, wise men from the East!**
> **We have cured many from sorrow and blindness,**
> we uproot the cause of all pain.
> **We bring the dead to life** because
> we have learned our skills from Christ,
> ask those who have witnessed our signs.

> We mix our medicine from plants of paradise
> and need no instruments
> for we run through the body like thought.
> **We are the healers of spirit** and
> do not look for reward.
>
> But before we leave,
> remember not to speak of us, **guard your words**
> for this world is full of unfriendly ears."[444]

The awakened healers *ilols* and *chilams* (prophets and clairvoyants) can **see and know what others (still) do not see**, they perceive the current **states of the spirit and body, health and illness; they perceive what people think and feel, and even the events in the world, on Earth and inside it, the events on the stars and in the Universe.** They use the texts of **sacred books** to nourish and maintain these abilities, and they also use **transcendental states of consciousness, channelled and carefully selected sound, sacred songs, revered rituals and initiations, ritual dance, magical (sound) formulae and words, the colourful sounds of musical instruments, even whistling, shouting and conscious breathing.**

Large **stone cylinders** were found **in Coba;** they are actually stone columns, which were most likely parts of a large **lithophone.** This is what some people claim. Who knows what effect playing on it had on people? And they also used **different drumbeats, shaking, clapping, blowing, focused prayers, symbolic offerings, aromatic essences, herbs, living fire, smoke, and rich symbolic depictions** which spoke to the unconscious etc. These are all **helpful tools along the initiatory path** of transformation and awakening, for they open the spirit and move the outcrops of our thoughts and feelings.

Beside those in Chichén Itzá, temples in **Tical, Izapan, Cozumel,** etc. are also popular ancient Mayan temple and oracle sites. All of these temple complexes feature exceptional architecture and have **a similar purpose** as they did in the past. Numerous Mayans and their descendents (especially those with a more open spirit) still visit them on a regular basis. There, they **delve into themselves, they worship eternal wisdom and seek answers** to their questions.

Today, Mayan priests still connect participants in ceremonies and sacred initiatory paths with the barely perceptible sound vibrations of the Earth, Cosmos and the Source, and they also explain the riddles of life to people. Answers can even be signalled by **sacred animals, by animal *naguals*.** In them, or through them, people recognise hidden **talents – their talents and those of**

---

[444] Rumi, *Hidden Music*, London, Thorsons (2001), p. 127.

other people, they recognise **the abilities of which they are still unaware and their unconscious drives.**

The Temple of warriors and courage is the most important **temple of wisdom.** Every pillar, with its symbolic depictions of serpents, hearts, claws and feathers, represents one of the above-mentioned **spiritual skills of full awareness and knowledge of life's lessons.** The temple of warriors **celebrates will, courage and the victory of awakened self-awareness (self-realisation).** There, the journey of life **reveals** to initiates **the meaning of everything they had experienced, including pain and suffering; and it rewards them for their courageous introspection with insights.** There, warriors reach a point in which they **can fully comprehend and live the existential laws** and teachings of **the Great Mysteries** – the laws of **the serpent and the spiral.**

When warriors have fully mastered their emotions, thoughts and mind, they stand in front of the doors into the new, on the threshold of boundless opportunities for silent happiness and infinite creativity. They have attained the state in which they can create great and exceptional works with unconditional love and without limits, in accord with their wishes, which are now in fact totally in tune with the divine Idea, with the Universal Plan of life. The calculating ego is finally overcome. The enlightened ones begin to serve humanity and the Earth, for they themselves have now become ingenious and effective Creators.

Initiates who receive **the multi-levelled initiations of the adepts of light** need to be **totally devoted to the Cosmic will, the Divine will, to the creative vision, to the spiral of the Universe – to the serpent, to put it symbolically,** which personifies the Cosmic Intelligence, the invisible Blueprint of the Higher Will, or destiny. Through countless battles and lives, warriors of light and spiritual seekers are carved into **perfect adepts of light. The character of Chaak-Mul** indicates initiatory transformation – spiritual, cosmic, solar, and earthly transformation, which offers to humans **the revelation of life's mysteries. The Great Mysteries are thus complemented and fulfilled.**

The carved **Chaak-Mul** (in **Coba,** for example) sits in a distinct posture which resembles a coiling serpent. Eager spiritual warriors are also **often depicted as if they would be emerging from a feathered serpent, from the undulation of primal life energy. This denotes the birth of a metagalactic human being – *halah uinik*, the genius of boundless opportunities and all-encompassing consciousness, the master of all his givens, talents, and powers, which all reflect the divine. The etheric bodies and the seven energy centres (chakras) of such a person are totally open, they are glowing and are permanently connected to the Cosmic Source of life, to the Cosmic Mind. With enlightenment, warriors have completely fulfilled the task of their lives** and have connected all **the nine** levels of consciousness which humans are able to attain. They have attained the broadest possible cosmic, or galactic, consciousness.

The spiral feathered serpent – **Kukulkan** or Quetzalcóatl, and also **the Morning Star (Venus), are the bringers of dawn, the bringers of the light of enlightened consciousness, the keys and compasses to spiritual and material treasures of expanded consciousness, the signposts** to exceptional **spiritual powers and miraculous abilities** of earthly beings. Initiates **soar above their problems and chaotic life**, as the awakened ones or like the bird **phoenix**. The feathered serpent and its shape-giving power are now revealed to them as **the guides** of their life, **the *naguals* of their soul.**

Embarking on the path of a warrior requires a conscious decision, persistence, discipline, and courage for looking into your own mistakes and lacks, which is of course not easy. Everybody wants to be a kind of 'superman.' And the majority of people are actually convinced that that's what they already are and that they lack nothing. Their heads are full of information which can be found in encyclopaedias and on the internet. **The 'supermen' of the modern world are convinced that they are incredibly smart and brilliant because of their vast knowledge: because they have filled their memory to the greatest possible extent. Yet, memorisation and overflowing brains are not intelligence** – not the intelligence of the mind, neither emotional, nor social or artistic intelligence, neither meta-sensory nor enlightened intelligence, etc.

But when we think of warriors, we speak of **the meta-sensory intelligence of cosmic, galactic human beings, who are aware of both the visible and invisible, of both the audible and inaudible on Earth and in the Universe. This intelligence offers to their guardians the power of a medium, healer, musician-shaman, prophet, omniscient telepath. Without the learning** and memorisation of burdensome information. **Only attentive insights into our immaturities and a thorough and courageous battle for something better will lead us there.** This is also how the battle for the realisation of the broad **consciousness of the modern era** unfolds. But contemporary Mayans still believe that they have in fact **never lost the galactic consciousness of the whole.**

The warrior's tools for spiritual growth are above all attention, love for truth, near-death experiences, chiselling by means of relationships, painful trials in life, compassion, kindness, becoming aware and above all, persistence. All of this guides them through the labyrinth of their weaknesses. The ballgame seems like a distinct prayer, a reminder and method for anchoring a focused intent. And sacrifice is the metaphor for transformation.

The pyramid of Kukulkan in Chichén Itzá - the temple of the Divine Consciousness

> It is dawning, may the fires blaze
> and **the souls awaken!**
> May **the dawn of faith** announce
> what warriors desire so very much.[445]

The most sacred part of the warrior's path leads them to the summit of the pyramid of Truth. The initiations of supreme transformation **take place at the top of the Pyramid of Kukulkan,** which is the largest and the mightiest temple in the entire complex in Chichén Itzá. Kukulkan is **the Creator,** the mighty **Shaper, the supreme God,** the bringer and giver of awakened consciousness. **Enlightenment is like a fiery thunderbolt.** They say that Kukulkan **awards it only when he wants.** It can't be received in any other way. Bargaining with him is not possible.

Ku means **God,** *kul* is **worship** and *kaan* denotes **the infinite, celestial, serpent-like and boundless** (according to Calleros). *Ku-kul-kaan* is therefore **the Cosmic and serpent-like boundless Being, the Intelligence of life, the Divine Source.** His name is **a sound code,** a key which expands our consciousness and opens our heart and energy centres. The Pyramid of Kukulkan is the temple of the supreme, **inexpressible, and boundless Creator, who is worthy of the golden splendour of the light of the Sun and of the sacredness of the wise ones – a self-realised and enlightened human being** with a broad cosmic consciousness with exceptional abilities, **'made in the image of the Creator.'**

In the past, devoted warriors **meditated for several days and nights** in temples or pyramids, surrendering to the transformational energies of the sacred site and to the process of **becoming aware.** In silence, they telepathically received **insights and visions.** Their experiences were **beyond describable, beyond the usual human experience.** At the pyramid's top, where the final platform is, warriors could experience **a genuine contact with themselves, with their as yet undiscovered nature and the contents of their spirit and soul.** They rose to the Sun and realised their **shamanic jump to the Sun.** It was their own **breath,** unique as human beings, that took them up to the heights. They could leave their bodies for a while. **Their boundless spirit, their soul, was able to exit the physical body and chains of the material,** and rise to the high-dimensional levels of reality, to the realms of **the conscious Universe,** where we can meet wonderful **(energy) images and**

---
445 Mirit, November 2012.

characters which both human consciousness and Divine Consciousness paint on the canvas of the mind.

The Pyramid of Kukulkan is **the mirror and destination of the initiates' multi-layered path across different levels of consciousness, which direct them to the very top.** The pyramid's orientation is 17 degrees to North-East (due to the Earth's axial tilt) so it can **capture the rays** of the rising and setting Sun at summer and winter Solstices. The rays visibly indicate **the emerging dawn of a new evolutionary cycle, of a new human being and the ritual death and holiness.**

Not only is **the pyramid** (similar to Egyptian pyramids) **a large Sun calendar on Earth,** it is also **an energy collector, where the cosmic and earthly pulsation can be powerfully felt.** This pulsation is enhanced particularly inside the pyramid, under its coat. Which means we can feel it more there. Pyramidal forms **amplify and convert** cosmic frequency waves, **cosmic radiation and cosmic initiations into sound, thus bringing them into the human sensorial and material world.** This allows ceremony participants to bring together the material and non-material with the Source more easily. They offer people **an opportunity to resonate within all their registers, or givens.**

Warriors who have reached the top of the Pyramid of Kukulkan in Chichén Itzá had to climb **91 stairs,** as this is the number of steps on **each of the four sides** of the Great pyramid. The pyramid's sides, which symbolise **the four cardinal points, four seasons, four elements, the sacred cross of duality,** speak to them in their own way. There are **five** important steps beneath the top – one on each side, plus the temple platform on the top. These five steps indicate five **additional days of the Mayan calendar: the last and most important five days in the annual cycle (91 × 4 = 364; 364 + 1 = 365 days).** These days are **the most sacred in a year.** And **the very last day** is the sacred day which marks **the end of something and the beginning of something new.** During these five days, **the world is open to the new, absorbing the re-birthing powers of a new cosmic-earthly cycle, of a new year.** At that time, humans are extremely **receptive to the (new) divine impulses and rhythms.** Which is why they need to seriously think **about what they will wish for and what they will banish while on the platform.** This was also how the ancient Egyptians understood **the rhythm** of time and year. Today, this significance of the last calendar days is still respected by the Balinese people.[446]

At spring and autumn **precessions of the Equinox,** when the rays of light **illuminate large stone serpents** located at the sides of the staircase, **33 triangles of triunity** shine on their heads. The **heads** of feathered serpents also signify **the nine planets of our solar system,** which, just like the Earth, appear in the darkness of the cosmic incubator of the infinite. Every feathered serpent denotes

---
446 Read the third and seventh book in the *Cosmic Telepathy* series.

nine-dimensional consciousness, nine dimensions or levels, of reality, which humans are able to attain and which incarnated souls are able to perceive in the material world. The number nine is an important and sacred Mayan number, a symbol of hidden and mysterious spiritual (esoteric and occult) powers.[447] The levels above the ninth are difficult for human consciousness to imagine. We call them the Absolute, or the zero (primal) field.

The pyramid comprises **20 levels,** which symbolise the 20 days of the Mayan month *tzolkin,* or the 20 basic **cosmic rhythms.** Each of them has its own givens, characteristics and contents. Warriors have to pay attention to all of them. The pyramid is decorated with the images of **the Water God Father Yumilchaak with three faces (of the Holy Trinity)** on each side. They speak to spiritual warriors, telling them to delve into **the Source, into the Cosmic, spiritual, and physical alike.**

Similar to the number 9, **the number 12 ($4 \times 3 = 12$) is the number of perfection** in numerous traditions of the world. **It marks the marriage between the matter and the spirit, or God.** This number is by itself divine. We get it by 'multiplying' the symbolism of the four elements, **the four cardinal directions, by the three** – the number of **the holy trinity.** The sacredness of the number 12 can also consist of the symbolism of the sum of **9 + 3,** which indicates **the spiritual and the Divine simultaneously. Nine is the number of the highest,** broadest **level** of consciousness **which humans can attain.** If we add three levels to it, we reach the all-full **Emptiness of Nothing, the First Principle.** The sacred Mayan number **13** signifies **the return (into a new incarnation),** transition into the new, a new beginning, a passage into a new wave, **a new curve in the spiral movement,** which is always higher than the previous one. Having all of this **in mind helps the warriors to climb the steps of the spiritual pyramid more easily. By using number symbolism,** warriors and the world **open up to the new.**

The Pyramid of Kukulkan, the tallest pyramid in Chichén Itzá, is the most sacred place in the entire temple complex, it is the very heart of Chichén Itzá. It is similar in Coba, Palenque, Tical and other temples with the eponymous great pyramids. **This is the most sacred meditative and praying place, a place for ritual initiatory transformation,** where **tuning to the vibrations of the Gods and Masters of light, tuning to the Earth and the stars is most effective, because it is nourished by the majestic creative force of the Universe,** which descends into the thoughts and reverence of ceremony participants. And that which exists in our thoughts becomes **the seed of reality.** Sooner or later, thoughts get materialised in the physical world. **The sound of our thoughts becomes reality.** Which is why warriors **shape their thoughts and wishes with special care at those locations.**

....
447 *Popol Vuh.*

What is more, the pyramid's summit is an open window, **a portal into the infinite multidimensional stomach of creation, into the Primal Silence.** We travel there. We have to score the goal, whether we want it or not. Humans have to **piece together and complete all the parts of the mosaic – of their personal, planetary, and Universal mosaics alike. They have to discover all levels, all dimensions of themselves, they have to centre themselves within at-one-ment with the divine and thus fulfil their earthly mission.** They have to attain the Galactic Centre of their life.

The ancient Mayans and our distant planetary ancestors obviously lived far more **consciously.** Their lives were suffused with the wisdom of galactic consciousness. I am hereby speaking primarily of warriors **who lived before the Common Era.** Later, their great knowledge began to be lost more and more. Yet, far into the modern era, at least some **individuals have continued to attentively align and resonate with time, the Earth and the Sky, with the environment, timelessness, and eternity.** They wanted to become as excellent as possible receptors and transmitters of primal perfection. They were able to discover the Truths of existence and attain **crystal clear thinking, which is enabled by brainwave coherence (EEG 8 and 40 Hz), which is the vibration of the halo effect, the vibration of the telepathic insights of a shamanic trance. In it, they set up their clear cosmic telepathic abilities, they opened the limitations of the mind and replaced them with the galactic spirituality of all-connectedness and with resurrection qualities.**

In the past, **mediumship** was greatly **revered** and most sought after, **enlightened priests and rulers were deeply respected.** Whereas today, intellectuals, limited to the use of only one side of their brain (only the left side – the intellectual-analytical one), **scorn people who are able to activate both sides** (including the right side – the sensitive, meta-sensory and intuitive side). In the past, only those who were able to live within **the synchrodestiny of both sides decided** on the matters of life. But today, primarily those previously mentioned intellectuals are valued, and their decisions are often wrongful, based on a one-sided mind and incomplete understanding. Mayans and the sages of other cultures and times would send them to learning and transformation onto the first, beginner's pyramidal step on the initiatory path of development. **As a result of this incompleteness, the world is out of balance, full of wars and atrocities. It is time that all of this changes and that humans once more re-align with all their givens.** It is time for us to once again experience, in large numbers, the gifts of awakened consciousness and **realise the aeon-long planetary dreams of the cosmic-galactic human being with exceptional abilities.**

The Earth and the solar system are coming back to their original positions in the galaxy, they are returning to the resonance with their own source of boundless opportunities 'made in the image of the Source.' And they awaken within us the (primal) memory of the cosmic origin of the soul – symbolically, the memory of the Father Sky and of the primal state of a complete soul. Different traditions of the world claim that **high-frequency shape-giving forces, or energies, which open human consciousness and mind,** are constantly emanating from the Source, from the Centre, to the Earth. And **people's compassionate love nourishes,** or feeds, the frequency Universe, **the Universe's orchestra of (undulation) forms** and strings. True love **gives meaning to our life's journey** and to spiritual growth. It endows the awakened ones with **joy, abundance, beauty, and Truth;** it shows them the path of **how to live and why, why make the effort on Earth, where we are going and whence we came.** Sooner or later, we will all have to **return to the Cosmic Heart,** to the Source, or God, **to the Heart of Sky,** as Native Americans say.

> "I remember coming out upon the northern **Great Plains** in the late spring. There were meadows of blue and yellow wildflowers on the slopes, and I could see the **still,** sunlit **plain** below, reaching away out of sight. **At first there is no discrimination in the eye,** nothing but the land itself, whole and impenetrable. **But then smallest things begin to stand out of the depths –** herds and rivers and groves – and **each of these has perfect being in terms of distance and of silence and of age.** Yes, I thought, **now I see the Earth as it really is; never again** will I see things **as** I saw them **yesterday** or the day before."[448]

If these words make sense and are at least a little bit close to us, it means that we are already **accepting the conscious return to the Home of the soul and are discovering the shaman-healer and perhaps even the musician within ourselves.** We are soaring into the Sky, like smoke rises from the offerings. Our essences are the favourite perfume of the Gods, as the Mayans would say. Life chisels us, so that each day we are able to **resonate** ever more beautifully and piercingly **in harmony with everything that exists.** No longer do we resonate in this way only at festive rituals and meditations, but **increasingly throughout our lives.**

The Cosmic Mother and the Cosmic Father are said to merge within us, when the doors of our consciousness will be completely open, when our awareness will be completely open. Journeys through the portals of time, space and consciousness are inevitable. But when we will manage to open them, when we will come to understand the teaching of the Great Spirit, of all the laws of existence,

....
448 Scott Momaday, *The Way to the Rainy Mountain*, Albuquerque, University of Mexico Press (1969), p. 17.

this depends on us. The basic (**frequency/energy**) undulation of our solar system **is constantly changing** and the Field of consciousness, human consciousness, and awareness are changing with it. **The lost 'Silent' knowledge of the Universe is once again becoming accessible.** Like the *nik-vakinel* sages, or **those who know, we see and hear ever more clearly through the curtains of time and we are discovering the wisdom of the Real beyond illusions. It is well-worth trying to resonate and live in harmony,** in harmony with ourselves, with other living beings, the Earth, the stars, and the entire galaxy. **This is the message of the Ancient Ones.**

> They rejoiced greatly when they saw **the Morning Star.** It came forth glittering before the face of the Sun. /.../ **They wept** bitterly as they waved their censers, burning the sacred copal incense before they saw and witnessed the birth of the Sun. /.../ As one they turned their faces toward the coming forth of the Sun. The bloodletters and sacrificers were kneeling.[449] This is what the sacred book *Popol Vuh* says.

The Morning Star is a symbol of awakened consciousness, which moves us to tears.

The time in which we live requires **rapid changing. The future requires a totally new, different, much broader consciousness,** and above all, it requires **the revelation of our dormant abilities.** Yet, this **new is actually old.** As old as people and the world. **Only the names and symbols which inspire people** and help them to realise what they should do **change.** Today we will perhaps replace **the ancient symbols** of the jaguar, eagle, and serpent with something else: with the computer, aeroplane, train, mobile phone, camera, etc. Even though the language, words, concepts and **life style** change, **the content and the purpose of life's journey remain the same.** Everything **that is not compassionate kindness – needs to be dismissed.** And the new should bring us a much more **joyful and full living.**

May the ancient dreams of the Mayans and of **our planetary ancestors come true,** may they awaken those who are still sleeping in the darkness, so that they too would soon become enlightened and start resonating in harmony with the whole, with everything visible and invisible, audible, and inaudible, etc. Moaning about life does not make sense and is totally redundant. May life itself reveal to us that which is beneficent and miraculous.

> "**You see, I am alive,** I am alive!
> I stand **in good relation to the Earth**
> I stand **in good relation to the Gods**

....
449 *Popol Vuh*, electronic version (2007), p. 214.

I stand in good relation **to all that is beautiful**
I stand in good relation to the daughter of Tsen-tainte
You see, I am alive, I am alive!"[450]

Sacred is the Mayab land, says the sacred book *Popol Vuh*. **May the entire world be sacred, and truly sacred!**

....
450 N. Scott Momaday, *The Delight Song of Tsoai-talee*, taken from the book *In the Presence of the Sun: Stories and Poems*, New York, St. Martin's Press (1993).

Hunahpu – the centre of the Universe and life

The Mayan symbol Hunahpu in the rituals of centredness

The intelligent Centre of the Universe sings in the human heart,
it echoes **in our consciousness** and everyday **thoughts,**
it is reflected **in tones and sonic intervals,**
sensitively awakening you **into different worlds.**

The abstruse essence, the centre of life
speaks to you in every attentive moment –
look into yourself, into your shadows and expectations,
lay bare your tormenting **illusions** and redeeming **visions,**
start living your own compassionate centre.

When you are centred, you are fulfilled and happy,
harmonious music resonates within you;
the magnificent sound images of the Sky on Earth
are **the warp and weft of the mighty flow,**
which is always piercing and inexhaustibly mellifluous,
harmonisingly inspiring and eternal.

So, look into the ancient wisdom,
which speaks and sings of **the Centre of Harmony,**
of the harmony of life, joy and abundance,
it will show you the path of love and non-violence.[451]

....
451 Mirit, May 2012.

It is more than self-evident in the sacred book *Popol Vuh* that **Hunahpu represents the centre of the Universe, the Source, the Primal Intelligence of life.** If we read the book with the eyes of the spirit, the images of this mighty sacred character become clear to us. Hunahpu is **the code of the Universe, the key, which shapes, opens, builds, sustains, and renews** all levels of life on Earth. It is the centre and the magnet, which **attracts,** with an immense power, **the wide open consciousnesses of spiritual seekers.** Hunahpu is therefore **the very core and essence of the Universe, of all forms in it. It is the primordiality and fundamental energy,** out of which everything is built – it is **the Consciousness of the centre and the heart.**

Hunahpu – the sacred symbol of duality and polarity, a symbol of merging with unified oneness.

The sound waves of the word Hunahpu are a timeless echo **reflecting the Source, the Sky on Earth** (the Chinese call it **Tao** or **Dao**). It is the very source, the sound undulation of the fundamental **harmony, of the Universal Order.** It is **the energy vibration** and building block of every word, all speech, and all music. Hunahpu is **the Consciousness of the Universe, the Mind of the Universe.** At its core, it is **constant movement, eternal undulation** across the levels, or dimensions, of the Universe, across the material and non-material worlds. It is the abstruse **macrocosm, which is reflected in microcosm – in every body cell of living beings, in every thought, vision, even song.**

The sonic essence of the word Hunahpu **opens the doors of consciousness, building and ennobling the world, inviting humans to return to perfection.** When undulating through human bodies, it brings **the power of transformation and freedom, and it reminds people that they are cosmic beings, children of the Sky and the Earth, descendants of the indestructible spirit** in the material world. Hunahpu, also called **the cosmic butterfly, is the oneness, to which enlightened people return with their consciousness and of their own will.** It is the very principle that **inter-dimensional travellers seek and meet in higher octaves.** The soul **yearns** after its pulse, after **the rhythms of the Universe.**

Hunahpu is the zero point of Primal energy, out of which everything emerges. It is the source of miracles. This timeless source never dries up, it **undulates eternally across time and space, shaping, connecting everything with everything, making us aware, healing us.** And this distinct *perpetuum mobile*, this indestructible source of life, **is also the top of the tree of life, which symbolically wakes people up from their dreams, from lives without awareness.** Native

American tradition says it pours into our world through the energy of **the Sun and Mother Earth**. The energy of Hunahpu is also in **the human and earthly electromagnetic field**. It is said to possess not only creative power and sustenance, but above all **the ability to harmonise and strengthen life** on Earth, as well as **the power of rejuvenation**.[452] It indicates the cosmic black hole and its **strong gravitation field, where time almost stops or where there is no time, and in the vicinity of which humans keep their youthfulness.**

Hunahpu is **the very heart of the orchestral music of the Universe**, which is persistently echoing and playing within people. People and other **living beings are musicians, either more or less talented, in this great frequency orchestra. Its sound undulation** across dimensions, across time and space, constantly **creates, shapes and is eternally changing. Its waves must flow through living beings lightly and unimpeded.** If people have **blocked this flow** with their minds and emotions, **Universal life energy cannot reach all body cells and strings, which is why people are unhappy and unwell.** But we have to know that **we are the ones who set up these energy blocks** – mostly with our destructive emotions and deeds, such as **fear, worry, anger, control, accusation, doubts; by distorting the Truth, with lies,** as well as with the inappropriate treatment of our body, with straining and bad **food**. Spiritually **immature, unloving and dead relationships** also block the flow.

The Mayan symbol with its entwined black and white spirals embedded on a black-white Field (of differences), which is divided into four parts, reminds people of **the Primal Principle Hunahpu. It inspires them.** The symbol was created **so that people might not overlook or forget that we are one with the Divine Source, with the Universe and everything that exists.** In the past (and still today in some places), Mayan ceremonies helped participants **centre themselves within this Source of life, to understand and see clearly the path of their own life.** People who are consciously connected **to the energy of Creation**, to Hunahpu, and who allow its free flow, **see the Truth. They are centred in Silence, in the Field of life.** They have attained **full awareness and are therefore able to sense, always on time and attentively, what they have to do and when, what is right and what is not.** They are able to **act appropriately** at the right time. **They are not outside the flow, they are in it. They see the very core and their own shadows,** their distortions and bad sides, **they understand the messages** which relationships and situations in their lives offer them. **It is not easy to live the Truth, yet it is worth living it. Truth is the grandeur of the current moment. Do not overlook it! When we are in contact with the Truth, there are no regrets,** even when we are experiencing

....
452 More about this can be found in the chapter *The Big Bang initiates time, expanding space dimensions and enabling the journey to the black hole.*

pain, or when it seems that everything is wrong. **We know that everything is just as it should be,** that suffering is warning us of our mistakes, teaching us wisely.

When my son was in hospital, he kept repeating the following words: "Mum, everything is exactly as it should be. I see this and I feel this. **Without these problems, which I brought upon myself when I did not know how to act, I would never have been able to find the power for change in me.** Now I feel **free,** like I would again be **at a point** where I can **choose** freely again and where I can **choose something completely new.**"[453]

He was able to **solve the health and life problems he had on the verge of death quickly and very effectively** due to his very **conscious connection** to Primordial life energy. During his illness, he was persistently connecting to the Primal Intelligence of life and energy (with the help of the light-sound codes of cosmic resonance). **Even thinking about it is healing. Symbols are the high-dimensional language** of the intangible and invisible reality, they are **keys for entering the Field of all possibilities and innumerable opportunities.** They are keys for entering **the sea,** as folk tradition would put it.

By gazing at it (at Hunahpu, for example) for a longer time, or if we are **initiated into it,** the symbol **can raise, or expand, the vibrations of our consciousness.** We thus **build our own Universe,** our own **microcosmic galaxy, or orbit. We become the inexhaustible Source of harmony – the source which creates boundlessly.** A consciously established connection to the Source of life **enables us to be nourished by the energy we need. It makes us free. A permanent connection to the Source Hunahpu is called enlightenment.** This connection can be felt as a powerful **vibrational, electric flow through our body,** when we think about it. We feel an energy similar to the one we felt when we were **in love. Which is why enlightenment is a sort of permanent state of being in love.** We say that we have **butterflies** in our stomach. **The cosmic butterfly – Hunahpu!**

I guided my students to experience **the light-sound code Hunahpu** and its power in **May 2012.** A few days before the initiation, most of them had felt **a strong pressure in the third eye, an occasionally accelerated pulse, a strong expansion of the heart chakra,** and even a fluttering of the physical heart. All of these sensations grew stronger especially **during the initiation.** A few days earlier, I had felt **a strong pressure between my eyebrows,** exactly at the point of the third chakra. A pressure was there and I had the feeling that even my cranial bone was painful. During the initiation, most of the students felt **an enchanting joy and great personal power.** It was **as if they had been lifted or expanded,**

....
453 I described this story in details in the sixth book in the *Cosmic Telepathy* series (*Spiritual and Sound Surgery in the Portals of Attunement of the Aboriginal People of Australia, Brazilians, and Filipinos*).

they told me later. Well, this is what actually happened. **We rose into the sea of the Primal waves on the wings of our consciousness** and we descended back to the Earth – **transformed. Every trip there changes people.**

Our **eyes were burning** for a while during the initiation ceremony (and also before it), which is proof that an extremely **strong energy** flowed through our bodies, **the kind of energy our bodies had not been used to. The silence of emptiness flourished in our minds.** And other sensations occurred when we pulled the Primordial life energy of Hunahpu into the physical world and asked for its energy, which is ceaselessly creating and **making us** deeply **aware. Stressful thoughts began to be released from the subconscious and strong prickling occasionally occurred in ears. Nausea** occurred **in the plexus,** as the third energy centre is connected to our thoughts.

Fears and other traumatic feelings were being increasingly released from the subconscious. Distinctly physical frequencies were tearing through our legs and the strong **cold of high-frequency waves** ran through our bodies. This cold then changed, in waves, into **warmth and heat. Hunahpu revealed itself to be the Huracan, a hurricane wind of consciousness, a fire of spiritual transformation, but also pure joy, peace, silence and love.** These essences **lifted from our unconscious everything that was still not unconditional love.** They inspired us.

Hunahpu is the centre, the energy central system of universal vibrations, or various frequency patterns. It is the matrix of life, the light-sound code of consciousness and mind, which is present in time and space, and of course also **at the timeless levels of the higher dimensions of reality and consciousness.** The centre Hunahpu is **weaving the net of sound yarn,** which Native Americans in North and Central America call **cobweb or Spider Woman – a mythical being.**

I was very happy to come across a thin volume by **Ann D. Less,** titled *Mayan Map.*[454] The author made a distinct Mayan map on the basis of a knowledge of Mayan symbols and numbers and on the basis of **Hunbatz Men**'s thoughts about Mayan calendars and on the basis of the Mayan oracle *Return Path to the Stars* **written by Ariel Spilsbury and Michael Bryner.** She attempted to explain the Mayan **Cosmos based on thirteen numbers and twenty Mayan symbols (of the *tzolkin* calendar).** I simply could not believe it. It was as if I was reading my own thoughts and channelled notes! The Intelligence of the Universe was obviously whispering similar knowledge and thoughts through both of us.

In the above-mentioned book Ann D. Less also talks about **shadows, about the miracles of primordial energy and, like me, she believes that knowledge of the symbolism of numbers and symbolic images opens human minds and**

....
[454] Ann D Less, *Mayan Map*, Hoče, Skrivnost (2012). I came across the book before this book was published, in May 2012.

explains to us where we got stuck or caught, it explains where we are experiencing our **shadow,** our pain in life and **why. To live consciously is of course sensible.** According to Less, the centre of the Universe – Hunahpu, which she calls **Hunab Ku,** represents not only **the source of human energy, but also events in life.**

We should of course not go against this energy. It is sensible to **free ourselves from our chains,** from our emotional and mental riddles, which prevent life energy from running through our bodies. Mayan symbols and numbers can help in this in order that **people can fight the challenges** in their lives **more easily.** They show them **how to follow their destiny, their path.**

Ann D. Less wrote the following thought:

> "Accept yourself as you are. You are unique, different, and special.
> You are the love you are looking for in another person."

True, **life is like a mirror of unique differences,** spiritual contents, and miracles, which we create ourselves. It is our given to develop compassionate, **unconditional love** within ourselves and to share it with others.

The human being is like a galaxy, like a little Universe. The gifts of the great spiral galaxy, the gifts of the great Universe, pour through the human galaxy with the help of light-sound cosmic resonance, through co-resonance between humans and the Universe. People are able to travel with their consciousness into other dimensions of reality. But, in order to attain this, they first have to annihilate all the obstacles on their path to the Source – to Hunahpu, to the cosmic serpent. Like a seed of the Universe, humans light the flame of their transformation at Hunahpu's cosmic fireplace. It is in the darkness of their lives that they discover and create the light of the cosmic fire.

When you are aligned - you are happy and boundlessly creative

When you are connected to the Source, you feel that everything is exactly as it should be. You have **no doubt.** Because **that which is happening right now, actualises you** and is therefore the most effective tool for those transformations and changes which are needed to remove suffering. But this certain thought comes by itself, when it happens. This thought is **not created by our mind,** which usually wants only false confirmations that everything is fine, and which is trying hard to **sweep our challenges and problems under the carpet,** or into the unconscious (into Xibalba, in the Mayan tradition). **But when you know for sure** what you must do and where the path is leading you, you have a feeling of **sitting in a loop,** in a figure of eight: the refined flow **in your heart is merging** with the earthly river of life consisting of coarser vibrations. Together, they **form the material world. **The cosmic and the earthly are being braided in your heart centre. **Like a cosmic seed of the Intelligence of the Universe, you are now reflecting the eternity** of spirit on Earth. **The Earth is like an incubator** and you are a seed, which grows and develops by itself into a precious plant, a wonderful flower or a mighty tree.

Never allow your **ego and mind to manipulate you, to fake ignorance and lie to you.** Until you see their game, they will **feed on your emotions,** especially unloving emotions, on anger and worry, thus creating your **false self-image. When you are lying to yourself, you are not focused. You are outside the flow, outside the river of life, and you do not know the Truth. Which is why you see everything in a distorted or erroneous way.** Better you do not create a false image of yourself and the world, even if you take pleasure in it. **Be what you are. Do not live with a mask.** Putting on a false image, a false mask (of importance, power, of being the best) are just **excuses for your own mistakes, ways of avoiding your current trials. Listen carefully! Trust and do not doubt the school of life.** Do not run away when you should be watchful. **Be a watchful jaguar. Observe yourself.** If you are lying, you will sooner or later **turn into exactly what you have created in your lies or fears. Do not bargain with the Truth, do not distort it and do not negate it, or it will hurt** – soon. With pain, life teaches you that you are lying. But unfortunately, the majority of people **are not** at all **aware that they are constantly lying** – especially in order to be **accepted.** And then they of course complain about life.

Do not expect, do not make demands, do not control the flow of life! Do not play victim and do not create resentment, because such behaviour **is not centred in the source of the Truth.** It is outside it. And if you live **outside it, you are swimming against the flow and life is difficult. Do not compete with the flow and do not compete with others. If you do, you will be negating difference,** which is a mirror of the Intelligence of life.

A student once said to me: "Oh, **there is so much clutter in my subconscious** that I am simply unable to open the doors to it." True, this is how it is with most people.

Someone else told me this: "How can I be calm, if **I feel anger when I wake up in the morning and even go to sleep angry?"** Yes, how, indeed? Certainly not in this way.

Another student discovered this: **"If I am not afraid, I attack. But if fear comes over me, I run away."** This is how it usually **goes.** But none of this holds true. Instead, **we need to wakefully face the trials of our life. Because then, we will not fall out of balance,** we will live and **be centred,** we will live happily in the flow of life.

Do not **sulkily** walk past your partner or boss **because something had not happened as you wanted or expected. Take problems and misunderstandings as a challenge:** you can **test your tolerance and kindness** with their help and through your reactions. If you have sufficient tolerance and kindness, you will be able to converse without anger or feelings of **guilt.**

It is also well-worth thinking about in **which mental and emotional patterns you are stuck.** Perhaps an unpleasant experience is right now **calling your attention** to a painful event from your distant past. **Cleanse it. Check why you are holding on to something so stubbornly, or why are you afraid of something. Is it truly worth-while – or is it just your old habit of reacting that is leading you into conflict with yourself and with others?**

Think about **what you are losing and what you are gaining by moaning, what you are giving and receiving.** Are you even able to talk about something without stubbornly persisting in your own opinion? **Do not hold onto the old. Go into the flow,** into the river of life, into the cosmic serpent of life, the University on Earth.

Feel this undistorted flow, this undistorted sound (message) of the Universe and the current moment; feel its power and grandeur. Every challenge, even the most painful one, carries within it a secret and grandeur, it is the key to something better. As soon as you wake up, **align with the Sky and the Earth,** and perhaps even with the rising **Sun,** like a Native American. **Feel the peace and happiness of all-connectedness and centredness in your own life. You are not alone!** You are a humble part of everything that exists. **Express your gratitude. Rid yourself of your anger with the feeling of gratitude.** Perhaps you will even feel both at the same time for a short moment, but then the scales will tip to the side where happiness and well-being are. **May challenges and problems only be majestic moments. Find their hidden meaning.**

Today, we unfortunately **no longer live in a connection to the Source of life. And we no longer see, hear and feel the Primal waves (Hunahpu) in everything, we do not search for a higher meaning of events.** Who is still trying to carefully hear **common denominators, the rhythm of life, and cosmic pulsing?** Nobody has in fact taught us **how to be** – just be.

> **Be connected to the Source in every single moment,**
> **and be attentive to everything,**
> be loving towards everything
> and **act out of the centre**
> – of yourself and of the Universe.[455]

....
455 Mirit, 2012.

The harmonious ratio 20 : 13 in musical intervals and in Mayan music

The Mayans were reportedly well aware of **how important personal spiritual growth and transformation are for happiness in the lives of everyone.** They are in fact the only reliable compass throughout life, which **will surely lead us one day to clear perception and freedom,** after which we yearn. The Mayans also understood **what great power carefully chosen tones and sounds have during this transformation.**

Human consciousness is like the wind of the Universe, like a spiral movement or the inaudible sonic whirlwind. Cosmic resonance aligns us with the beneficent sounds of the heart; yet, it can only do this if we know how to listen and be compassionately watchful; if we are able to hear the rhythms of the Universe in our everyday life and live in peace, in the silence of our own self.

Human beings themselves are actually the centre of the Universe. They place themselves into the centre of the Universe, when they perform ceremonies, when they meditate, love, pray, or heal (themselves) with all-present life energy. Life turns around them. When centred, they are the utmost creative designers of their own dreams. Dreamers, who dream their dreams into life and live them. But, without a connection to the rhythms of the Universe, they are helpless and poor, unhappy and often unwell. But problems will sooner or later force them to discover a way of aligning with the energy of the Universe, to find the Truth, to discover the meaning of life and to break through the polar world of differences and separation.

Humans are creators, who experience the current moment and create the present: re-shaping the past for the benefit of the present and future. It is crucial to be in harmony with the moment, because it is in the present that we are alive the most. The ancient Mayans reportedly tried to live in the current moment as consciously as possible. But the current moment is unfortunately quite unclear and chaotic during hurry and stress. The Mayan time was once much more peaceful than today's time, while a Mayan day consisted of more than 26 hours (50 minutes each hour), which meant it was longer than today's day.[456]

So, did the Mayans **have more time or did they simply know how to use it better** than us? On the wings of our consciousness, we are luckily able to escape, at least occasionally, from the chains of time. What is more, to live in the current moment means to **dissolve our emotional troubles and weaknesses, it means to**

---

[456] Ann D. Less, *Mayan Map*, Hoče, Skrivnost (2012), p. 11.

forget the past and open up to the future. **In this very moment, we are creating everything which is yet to come.** May our life's flow and our run through life always be **gratefully open and fully conscious.**

Even **Mayan pyramids are distinct calendars,** especially those **dedicated to the Sun.** Using the play of sunlight and shadows, they accurately show time and indicate annual time periods. Time is the current moment and **the attention of the earthly moment.** For ancient Mayans, pyramids were supposedly also doors into **the worlds of other, different (non-material) dimensions.** They were the link to the Primordial life energy, to the undulation of Hunahpu. Pyramids in fact remind us that **we and our lives are like pyramids,** because we are ceaselessly moving higher and higher. **We dream and we touch the songs of the stars, we yearn for abundance and happiness until we attain them.**

Inside the pyramid of Kukulkan in Chichén Itzá there is a smaller pyramid, in which lies **a jaguar,** the green-eyed Chaak-Mul. A pyramid inside a pyramid denotes **the Mayan cosmic law,** which was also valid in other ancient cultures: **as above, so below, or the great is mirrored in the small.** This mirroring also goes in the opposite direction – **the small builds, or composes, the great.** In addition, **the jaguar in the pyramid represents balance between humans and the Earth, a balance in both their personal Universe and in the unfathomable galaxy called Hunahpu. At the same time, the jaguar addresses human alertness, wakefulness.** The pyramidal form itself is said to symbolise the balance **between human mind, soul and the Universe, the audible and inaudible Universe alike.**

Cosmic order is reflected also in the frequency ratio of the Mayan sacred number **13** and the *tzolkin* (the number 20), in **13 : 20 or 20 : 13,** which denotes **the frequencies of the flow of life and our thoughts,** and primarily **the frequency waves of the Hunahpu energy,** which we are constantly receiving on Earth.[457] The ratio of the numbers 13 and 20 builds **the frequency of the Universal order, the Universal law. We all supposedly vibrate in a frequency similar to that of the Source and the Earth, which is why we feel connected (at least occasionally!), and we often even think and perceive in a quite similar way.** Yet, this similarity occurs only when we are in total **resonance with the flow of life, with the sound of life, which is the Truth itself.** Then, we are the Truth and we are complete. But mostly we at least **try to resonate in the same tone as the totality.**

20 : 13, the basic ratio of cosmic vibration, is **the frequency matrix of life.** The ratio of the two numbers reportedly demonstrates, or echoes, **the primordial cosmic undulation in the material world.** Of course, the relationship of the two frequencies matters – as **20 : 13 or 13 : 20.** The relationship **20 : 13 (or 5**

---
457 Ibid., p. 10.

divided by 3.25) equals **1.53846153846153846153846...** The sequence **15384 is repeated into infinity and inifinity (Hunahpu) is reflected in it.**

If we **divide 13 by 20 (13 : 20), we get 0.65.** In Mayan symbolism, **13** was both the number of the beginning and end alike; **the border marker between cosmic and earthly levels, between the octaves of universes; the silence of emptiness, out of which everything emerges, which counts everything, and which does not count at all.** It is quite likely that the ratio **20 : 12 or 12 : 20** was even more important (this is *tzolkin* in relation to **complete perfection**, which is the goal of our lives). This ratio is **hidden in the ratio 13 : 20.** The ratio **20 : 12** equals **1.666666...**, where **the 6 in the decimal places repeats into infinity.** This relationship can also be expressed with the fraction **5/3 (5 : 3)**, which is **the interval of the major sixth** (the ratio between the first and sixth tone of the diatonic scale).[458]

But if we divide 12 by 20 (**12 : 20**), we get exactly **0.6,** which is expressed by the fraction **3/5 (3 : 5).** This number is not reflected in a clear interval ratio. But, according to the universal law **'as above, so below'** (and also 'as below, so above'), this relationship is **mirrored in both directions equally, thus reflecting the relationship between a human being and the Cosmos.** At its core, the ratio **3 : 5 is the same as the ratio 5 : 3. The cosmic echoes in humans and humans expand into Cosmos.**

The ratio **5 : 3 (1.6666...)** illustrates the important interval ratio of **the major sixth. When the ratios are divided or multiplied by 2, we stroll across the octaves, we stroll up and down, across the octave levels of reality, climbing the terraces of the pyramid of consciousness.** We **descend** along octave ratios, when five parts are divided by three parts, and we **rise** along the octaves, when these two numbers are multiplied.

If the number **20** (*tzolkin*) **is divided by 12 (20 : 12), we get 8 : 5, or the minor sixth,** which is exactly **1.6.** Both ratios are clearly very important. One denotes the major sixth and the other the minor sixth. The numerical and tonal ratio of **the symbolic infinity** (and also **eternity**) of **the major sixth** echoes in this interval. **The interval of minor sixth is final and bounded,** as is the physical world. The symbolism of the number **6 arises from the Source** and together with it creates the number **7, the number of physical manifestation.** The number 12 comes from the symbolism of the number 13 and represents **the Source, perfection. Within the magic of 13, the number 12 illustrates the beginning and the end, the new within the old.**

Singing and playing in parallel sixths is known in almost all cultures. It obviously **sounds mellifluous** to our ears. And probably also to our soul. This

....
458 Miroslav Adlešič, *Svet žive fizike (The World of Living Physics)* – book 2: *Svet zvoka in glasbe (The World of Sound and Music)*, Ljubljana, Mladinska knjiga, 1964.

is interesting: **wooden or clay Mayan flutes,** rescued from oblivion over the last centuries and ending up in different museums around the world, most often resonate **within the span of the sixth** or **in the intervals of a sixth or third,** with the accompaniment of a drone, provided by an additional tube.

The interval of the major or minor third is the interval which completes the sixth into an octave, into a complete set, which is also repeated into infinity. The same goes for the opposite. Another interval, which is mellifluous to our ears, is the third, which complements the sixth in the octave. This is how **the Holy Trinity (the third)** of the cosmic, spiritual and physical realm is built through sound – in both material manifestation and in the audible field (**octave**).

Singing and playing music in parallel thirds has been quite a usual musical practice in the past and the present. **Sounds in sixths and thirds obviously denote and confirm the beneficent harmony – the echo of the Universe, which caresses, calms, and heals.** People find the sonic ratios of sixth and third simply **beautiful. And beauty reflects the fundamental essence and the eternal Truth. This is how cosmic laws echo in earthly sounds and tones. Euphony received its sound persona in sixths, thirds, and octaves. Fundamental cosmic laws, valid both in the Universe and on the Earth alike, are reflected, or echoed, in sixths, thirds, and in octaves. Mayan music** testifies to this, as it is composed of the sonic ratios of thirds, sixths, and octaves, which are **the very intervals of resonance, of harmony.**

Let me repeat once again the thought of a Mexican shaman:

"I cling to nothing, so I will have nothing to defend. I have no thoughts, so I will see. I fear nothing, so I will remember myself. /.../ I will dart past the Eagle to be free."[459]

....
459 Carlos Castaneda, *The Wheel of Time*, London, Allen Lane, The Penguin Press (1998), p. 190.

A metagalactic human being and the consciousness of the Galactic Centre

The centrifuge of transformation grinds and revisiting the values

Changing is the salt of life,
Letting go is its spice;
changing validates the depths of our spirit,
and letting go confirms our penetration into the realms of the soul.[460]

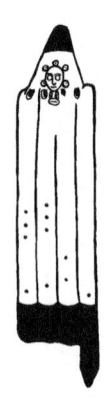

Human beings intuit their hidden abilities, but they do not dare use them. That is why warriors say that man's plight is in **the counterpoint between his stupidity and his ignorance.** Man needs now, more than ever, to be taught **new ideas** that have to do exclusively with his inner world – shamans' ideas (of ancient wisdom), not social (spiritually devalued) ideas, ideas pertaining to man **facing the unknown.**[461]

Four-chambered flute

"It can't get any worse than it is," complained the voice at the other end of the phone line.

"Why do you think so?" I wanted to know.

"Can't you see that **everything is falling apart? It's never been as bad as it is now**," my ex-husband kept trying to convince me while I was wishing him a birthday.

"No, it is not about that," I wanted to explain to him. "Everything is changing rapidly and dramatically. It's as if we are living in a centrifuge which grinds and grinds in order to grind up everything that is of no value. **Only if you cling tightly to the old and to what has long been outlived, you will feel as if you are on a rollercoaster** which is spinning and turning and which you cannot stop."

I couldn't help myself, I had to try to explain to this desperate man **what is actually happening on Earth** these years, months, days. For years, I have been closely observing and sensing events on Earth and in the Cosmos. My telepathic meta-awareness brings

....
460 Mirit, September 2012.
461 Carlos Castaneda, *The Wheel of Time*, London, Allen Lane, The Penguin Press (1998), p. 277. Notes in brackets are mine.

me the necessary explanations. **The centrifuge of transformation is indeed ever stronger and faster.** It hasn't shaken us like this for a long time. In this way, it is simply offering us **more opportunities which facilitate the collapse of things which are not valid.** Through the storms of **sudden and fierce trials, the power of transformation** which exists, which 'is in the air' as we say, **leads us to new insights,** to insights which we have perhaps been seeking or awaiting for years, or even decades. **It directs us to the decisions** which we have been **postponing** for a long time, even **far too long,** or to the right moment for which we have been waiting and yearning.

In 2012, according to the calculations of the ancient Mayans, **the Earth will return once more to its original, starting point in the galaxy,** where it had been at the very beginning of its creation. Both great rshis and Mayan astronomers claim this. The return to its starting point happens approximately **every 26,000 years.** With incredible insight, the Mayans were not only able to accurately calculate both **the evolutionary path and the level of consciousness of humanity on Earth – since the Big Bang** through today, they also worked out **the Earth's movement across our solar system and the Universe.** Not only did they foresee in details **the journeys of the planets and stars** across the cosmic expanses and paths, they also foresaw **the evolutionary levels of life on Earth.**

They even laid out, perhaps like no other earthly culture, **the cyclical journeys of human souls** in relation to the movement of celestial bodies. They did all this primarily **in order to understand at which point in this earthly evolution a human being currently lives and what additionally needs to be done** to attain the final station of awakened awareness. They wanted to know **where, when, and how the cycles and the current moment meet and mutually align or distance themselves.** They also wanted to know when 'the dark night of the soul' – a period of multiple trials – will happen, and when the vibrational (divine, symbolically) **support 'from the Sky' is auspicious for people and when not. Every frequential-vibrational (sound) pattern is unrepeatable and repeatable at the same time;** every pattern carries within itself its **unique shape-giving abilities.** Some, for example, build the physical world, while others make up the spiritual world. That is why every wave brings **unrepeatable gifts and distinct experiences.**

The discoveries of modern astronomy and the state-of-the-art telescopes, computer simulations and other devices used to observe the Universe, which is incredibly far away and invisible to the naked eye, demonstrate that Mayan astronomers, without any complex technical aids, were capable of a striking **accuracy** which shows only 'minor calculation errors' of few seconds within a hundred-year cycle![462] Truly incredible. This is indeed a great feat, but one which was obviously

....
462 According to the above-mentioned books *Maya Cosmogenesis 2012* by John Major Jenkins and *Maya Cosmos* by David Freidel, Linda Schele, and Joy Parker.

not impossible for them. At least some people **managed to develop an enlightened introspection, their inner telepathic-x-ray insight, with which they could 'capture' even information from** the high-dimensional reality **beyond time.** But there's more. **They 'grounded' the knowledge** acquired in this way **in a time-space parameter.** Similar powers were also known to Vedic rshis, to Native American Ancient Anasazi, and other sages of the world.

In the very distant past, the ancient Mayans were able to calculate that **on the Winter Solstice of 2012, the Earth would return to its departure point in the Galaxy,** from where it had started its journey. This is what J. M. Jenkins claims. Jenkins also claims that in December 2012, there will be **a conjunction of the Solstice Sun, the Earth, and the Galactic Centre** – the heart of the Galaxy. **The Solstice meridian will cross the Galactic equator in the Milky Way and separated it into two halves.** That is why the year 2012 (as well as the years before and after it) marks a special **cosmic event.** On the Winter Solstice, the Earth will **enter into resonance, or co-oscillation, with its own point of origin, with the Galactic Centre in the Milky Way.** It has been said that this shift, this new position of the Earth will **align human consciousness even more closely to the pulsing and rhythms of the Galaxy, and bring humanity back to its galactic family of all vibrational forms, of all life forms, to oneness. It will restore humanity's full awareness of the cosmic-earthly play, the ancient memory of primordial perfection,** and even the memory of the very first impulse of the Universe, **of the Source itself. Of the cosmic, or galactic, consciousness.** It has been said that **this new consciousness will completely change our views of the world and life.** That is why **consciousness** will **expand immensely** around this important year, and with it, human perception will expand too, for we are parts of the magnificent existential **Mystery of the Whole.**

So, were the ancient Mayans right when they completed **the Great Cycle in 2012, thus marking the end of an era, the end of a level of consciousness?** I think so. They were certainly right about one point: **we are now in a vortex of transformation of everything that is. We are experiencing an exceptionally rapid spiritual awakening from an unenlightened sleep** which is causing so much suffering in the world.

It has been said that especially **after the year 2000,** humans will **increasingly open up to an ever more rapid spiritual transformation, thus restoring the fullness of awareness and the memory of the entire planetary evolution. They are said to be reviving their link to Cosmic Intelligence, to God,** as we call it. The concept of God refers to the invisible **Intelligence of life and the cosmic-earthly laws** of existence. This book is yet another distinct proof of this (pre-)experience. My daily spiritual experiences, as well as those of many other seekers, attest to what I have written. Those experiences are enriched with sudden and unexpected **insights** which validate the text.

So, for example, numerous people have been experiencing in various ways that which the Mayans call **Hunahpu, the return to the Galactic Centre, to the enlightened galactic consciousness. This reaching of the Source and personal centredness is symbolised, in a picturesque way,** by a stone ring on a pyramid's wall next to the playing court of the priestly game, and also by the ceremonial ballgame itself, as well as by other games. **The ballgame** reflects human spiritual endeavours and the superior goal for which Mayan warriors strived thousands of years ago.

An increasingly mass awakening of new-old values is happening on Earth, and these values bring us ever deeper knowings of what kind of beings we are, where we are from, why we are living, and what is the purpose of life. We are obviously waking up from a long sleep. Stars are no longer merely poetic metaphors, they are a reality which is ever closer to us. Anyway – in light of everything that has been happening in the world, at the end of the century, at the end of the millennium, at the end of 'the Fourth Earth,' or 'the fourth Sun,' as Native Americans would call it – can anybody today doubt the fact that **something exceptional** is taking place?

Intolerance, profit-oriented endeavours and narrow-sightedness cause conflict. Distorted values or the countless devaluations which humanity has created particularly over the last hundreds and even thousands of years, **are falling apart turbulently. We are becoming aware of human illusions and non-sense at an accelerated pace. At least, some people are.** The illusory world is falling apart, rapidly and fiercely as never before. But **if people are of a more alert and flexible nature and are able to listen to themselves and the world around them, they won't get stuck, persistently and painfully, in their old and senseless destructive (mostly inherited family) patterns. They won't sink into the same non-sense** as those people who are utterly immersed in their old and erroneous right opinion. Today, **a much needed upheaval of humanity's ethical and moral values is happening in all cultures and societies.** Everyone is literally rushing through their **personal stock-take of the good and the bad,** through revisiting their false and valid **representations, visions, ideas, and emotions.**

We are therefore experiencing human universal and evolutionary upheaval which has probably not been matched in history. And everyone believes their own suffering is the greatest in the world. Yet similar things are happening in all countries, on all continents, in all spiritual teachings and **religions,** etc. That which has revealed itself to be **unwise and immature or not tolerant, compassionate, and loving enough – towards all forms of life,** towards all beings and even the planet

Earth itself – is being dissolved. That which is not loving enough, or that which humanity has **transcended during their continuous spiral expansion of consciousness.** In fact, this makes **the revival of the old** and the already experienced **new** at the same time. **We stand at the threshold of a new era, new consciousness and a different philosophy of life. And the carving of the new can be painful – just like every new birth!**

Well, this is where we are, you could say. Where? We are standing **at the gates which open up new realms and new dimensions of living.** We are already pressing our noses and foreheads against the doors of the unknown. **At least one part within us wants to enter.** The other part **unfortunately does not yet dare** enter. All the turbulence and pain which is currently happening on our planet is but **a battle between different proportions of good and bad, of old and new, as well as a battle in our relationships.** There is a battle going on in which everyone, whether they want it or not, has to **revisit and lay bare their philosophy of life and the way they work and live.** And in what manner this taking stock will unfold – **easily or painfully** – depends on **the rigidity or flexibility** of a person. First everyone fights primarily their own battle, **they reveal their own destiny, their mission in life, concealed talents, their hidden contents suppressed into the subconscious. Perhaps right now at this very moment, we are experiencing a collapse of the ideas which we cherished yesterday and which we nourished for years, even decades,** convinced that they were the best. For yesterday we thought them to be the only acceptable ones. But the flow of time is showing us a different face. **Mental-emotional clutter is falling apart, so that something new, better, broader, something more harmonious can come into being.**

Both the Mayans and the Aboriginal peoples of Australia claim that **humans have to reawaken the memory of the complete perfection imbued with love, which originates in and comes from the first creative sound of the Universe.** We should attune to the mighty creative forces and to our own perfection within us! In order not to forget, **people of different cultures revive this memory of the beauty of perfection in their Creation myths, ceremonies and songs: like the mythical twins** who play the ballgame and play with the Gods, losing and winning. But in the end, they manage to **overcome the evil (within themselves) and break free from division and suffering.**

We are at the threshold of a birthing of a new consciousness,[463] in a time of intense changes at all levels of life and consciousness. We are **in a centrifuge** that grinds mercilessly. The wisdom of Native American tribes is based on the spiritual heritage of the past which, hundreds, even thousands of years ago, predicted **the**

....
463 Some of the following edited paragraphs are taken from the first book in the *Cosmic Telepathy* series.

extraordinary nature of our time. It foretold **a transition to 'a new golden age,' to cosmic consciousness, a transition to a time which requires human awakening, the presence of all dormant abilities,** the revival of forgotten knowledge, and **a focus on the spiritual principle of living.**

The new is opening up: **a new, broader consciousness and a more full awareness. Right now humanity is creating a new reality. A new future.** And this process is unfolding through countless **conflicts and upheavals.** Even the Earth is shaking. There are earthquakes and floods. Natural catastrophes are changing the surface of the Earth. There is an earthly and social **revolution** going on, which is actually **an evolution of consciousness.**

Human consciousness is a creative field of Cosmic Intelligence which cannot be manipulated. The wisdom of Native American prophecies, especially the wisdom of those forecasts which are related to the renowned **Mayan calendar, is a veritable navigation across the frequency waves, the pulsing of the Universe,** across the so-called Divine, as the folk tradition would put it, or the cosmic **Plan. It is a profound philosophy of the natural rhythms of human evolution** and humanity's most important document for the study of **thousand-year cosmic-earthly periods.** This is also claimed by **Dr Carl Johan Calleman**[464] and **John Major Jenkins,**[465] both great authorities on Mayan culture. The Mayan **insight into the multidimensional reality** of the Earth's history and human evolution is piercingly accurate and exceptional, similar to the ancient Vedic wisdom. By getting to know them, we illuminate and explain events on Earth throughout the aeons.

When humans love deeply and unconditionally enough, their mind calms down at least for a moment. The feeling of love simply drowns out the mind. And within this love, they touch **the silence which is all-knowing and miraculous.** That is why we say that **love is blind. When we, through love, reach 'our galactic centre,'** we both merge with and are permeated by the primal (divine) vibrations of the Universal Intelligence; folk tradition would say with **nine, or twelve, levels, or realms (dimensions), of existence (Heavens). Within which, there is simply no room for doubting. Even wishes disappear.** They are no longer needed and are redundant. **Resistance to the unknown and to eternal changing also disappears in the silence of the mind. We have overcome our resistance** to the flow of life, a resistance which gives birth to the problems in our life, for it is based on the illusion of the seeming and on the defensive fear which refuses to see reality.

Fortunately enough, **the evolution of mankind develops in a distinct spiral, in a snake-like motion, as well as in a stepped, pyramidal way** (across different

....
464 Carl Johann Calleman, *The Mayan Calendar and the Transformation of Consciousness*, Rochester, Bear & Company (2004).
465 John Major Jenkins, *Maya Cosmogenesis 2012*, Santa Fe, Bear & Company (1998).

levels of consciousness, across the terraces of the spiritual pyramid). We are climbing **ever wider or ever higher – ever more consciously,** and especially ever more lovingly. So we ask ourselves, **why are there so many atrocities** on this planet then? **Suffering and pain,** both at a personal and planetary level, occur mostly when, or where, people are **unable to see, or refuse to see what needs to be changed. That is why they don't allow changes either to themselves or to others.** They continue to firmly hold onto their worn-out beliefs and that's why they keep quarrelling and fighting. **They are still unable to see the complete Truth or they are (still) unable to understand all the laws of existence. And they run away from a revelation of reality (at all levels!), from themselves and from new insights which are knocking on their conscience and consciousness, whispering to them what needs to be changed.** They prefer to bury themselves in the old clutter, like an ostrich buries its head in the sand. **They don't see the point! They become blind and deaf** to the events in their lives and environment. **And of course, they blame others for the unhappiness in their lives.** They do not know that it is primarily they themselves who are the **directors** and **screenwriters** of the story of their life.

"So, look, **why do you think it is necessary to continue to manage your business in the same way your father and grandfather did?**" I continued my phone conversation with my ex-husband. Together, we have been researching old and forgotten Slovene folk instruments, reviving their sound on the concert stage, for almost three decades.

"**Times are very different now.** You should look carefully at what is happening," I explained to him. "**What was true yesterday, is perhaps no longer valid today and shall be even less valid tomorrow.** Your grandfather was a blacksmith, your father had a locksmith business, you are a mechanical engineer, you passed beyond mere metal objects to more subtle levels. You can even reach up to intangible music. Aren't locksmithery and manufacture of sailing boats and aeroplanes similarly far away from each other? **But this doesn't mean that our son has to continue with all that!** It is not necessary for both of you to **drown in the greyness of the current philosophy of life and business mentality**, which is today the only one valid on Earth, mostly for the white race, who, scrambling for profit, recklessly **destroys other cultures, and especially the environment, nature, and other living beings.**

The contemporary economy is falling apart, this is more than obvious. Nobody can simply (and without consequence) take from somewhere in order to possess or earn more. **Working with compassion for the benefit of others has virtually disappeared.** This means that humanity is breaking the fundamental, universal law of existence – the law of a compassionate unconditional love, which has been valid on Earth for millennia and which dictates that humans receive and attain happiness, peace, and abundance primarily when they are able to give

to those who are without, or those who perhaps have no possibility to achieve the necessary abundance in life. **When human beings create with the thought of raising the life quality of themselves and others."**

I hear a deep sigh at the other end. I pause a little, then continue: "Everything is falling apart at an increasingly fast rate, and **it needs to fall apart. And believe me, I am sincerely happy about that. Society is based on false values,** which are even taught at university. Society is, above all, based on the most glamorised delusion which says: **take if you can and what you can,** and don't worry about the consequences this will have for the environment, for others and the Earth!? Better **stop complaining."** I comfort him. **"Sit down, calm your mind and treat yourself to some silence; meditate, listen to the silent voice of your consciousness, your soul,** and hear what it whispers. Perhaps it is telling you to **replace** steel with the harmony and euphony of voice and instruments? You are a musician, you know that **sound moves the world; it also moves all who treat themselves to a harmonious resonance. Feel what the moment wants to say to you and what it requires of you! Perhaps you need to forget the idea implanted in your mind by others,** that you should never get out of the business which your father and grandfather pursued. **Know that you should give up that which is hindering you in your spiritual growth** and which is marring the happiness in your life. **Isn't now the right time for a thorough audit, the time to embark on the next adventure in your life,** and to begin dealing with different things, or at least in a totally different way? To start doing or **creating that which makes you happy?** Only through that, will you be **successful and happy.**

When you manage to hear what is right for you, what is in harmony with you, then **a feeling of peace and great gratitude** for what life is offering you will wash over you. But first you have to ask yourself **whether you want the answer** to those questions at all, whether you want the answer **of the Intelligence of the Universe, which your soul knows. Do you dare to allow the Intelligence, the Cosmic Mind/Consciousness, to whisper the eternal Truth into your ear and mind?"**

Again, there was a silence at the other end of the line. But I thought it was worth sending those thoughts out into the space and consciousness of my interlocutor. Let them stay there at least in the form of **energy imprints,** as a hidden **memory** in the mind, **which can suddenly become alive and wash over** the person who aligns with those imprints. That is usually when the person says: "You know, **I have come to understand something** today..."

Unfortunately, however, listening (or reading) does not necessary mean **hearing. In order to actually hear, we first need to have a full awareness of the entire content of words, along with an open mind and the sensuous perception of our heart.** This holy trinity builds firm foundations and it also builds the

Wisdom which our distant ancestors, including **the ancient Mayans,** nourished for millennia and **handed down through generations to prevent their descendants from wandering in the dark. We all need this Truth,** so that we won't constantly just ask questions of why this and why that, why precisely in that way and what on Earth can we do to be more peaceful, happy, and rich in both spirit and material abundance. **The wisdom of the past echoes in the present and speaks to us so that we can hear more clearly how to live, what should best be done or abandoned,** what supports our personal spiritual growth, **the fullness of our life,** and what enables **the necessary well-being.**

The purpose of the present series of books is to lay bare this ancient wisdom, which can be of invaluable help to contemporary people in their quest for eternal truths. When we comprehend them completely and begin to live them, we will actualise and enable **a dignified life.** Not only for ourselves, but also for other people. **We mustn't think that our ancestors were ignorant! They knew far more than we do today** about the life's and cosmic-earthly laws – despite today's apparent progress, which is mostly technological. Yet, with regard to an **understanding of the subtle levels of life, we have regressed greatly over the last few thousand years. Let us not discard the ancient Knowledge for the sake of our arrogance,** or due to a belief that we have already attained the pinnacle of all opportunities, and that we are the very crown of Creation. Get real.

There was once again a deep silence on the line. It seemed to me I could hear tongues of flame rising from the brain, from the top of my interlocutor's head. Then I heard a voice of relief: "Yes, yes, **I know** ..."

But at that very moment I had the feeling that **this 'I know' perhaps wouldn't last longer than a few minutes, at the very most a couple of hours.** Then, it could once again happen that the lifeline offered to the mind would disappear, **the offered thought would sink into oblivion.** And the world would continue to turn as usual. This is how it goes with the majority of people, **until their understanding is mature enough and pops the cork out of the overfull, or jam-packed bottle, brimming with assorted clutter,** made of pain, suffering, deafness, etc.

When its content starts flowing over the rim, **a word and an attentive thought can trigger a dance of awareness, a sudden dance of thoughts and much needed change.** Then the world begins to turn in another direction, it begins to resound in a different colour (vibration). **It is well worth giving this a go** and allowing the dance and spinning. **You never know how full this bottle of your life is right now** and when its contents will spill over and so bring into your awareness the necessary **meta-sensitive messages.** This is when **the aha moment occurs – oh, I know this.**

Getting to know the cosmic-energy influences of both individual time cycles and evolutionary cycles makes us more alert, and, above all, more **centred in the**

right place at the right time. It brings us an understanding of **the transformation processes, of spiritual growth, and rapid change which leads us into the new,** into a better life, and a new era. The Mayan insights into events on the planet and in the Universe, their symbolism and ceremonies, are an accurate **'map' for the understanding of the current moment,** of the history of mankind and the evolution of spirit.

We have witnessed rapid changes in this new millennium, especially **after the year 2000.**[466] We increasingly have the feeling that **time literally flies, sweeping away everything that was bad and outlived.** A completely fresh wind had already begun to blow during the last year of the previous millennium – in **1999**, which was **a turning point**. The Mayan prophecies, their calendar, state that **humanity 'entered' the galactic underworld** in January 1999.[467] Interesting indeed: in that year, without knowing the Mayan calculations, I put in place a series of important changes in my life, including saying **no** to my spiritually immature partner. It was precisely in January 1999 that **I asked for an appropriate spiritual Teacher** who would guide me in my revealing of **the laws of life**, in my spiritual learning, and discovering ancient wisdom. And I got it. But not a physical one, a cosmic one – it was **the Consciousness of the cosmic – a telepathic link with the divine Intelligence of the Universe, with the Masters or lords of the Universe** (this is simply **what we call them symbolically**!), who whisper to everyone who is willing to listen. After that, I started **reawakening my own still dormant abilities of spirit** in a rapid and accelerated way. And **an avalanche of interesting and very precious experiences and insights** poured over me. That is how I know, out of my own experience, that **the levels of transformation foreseen by the Mayans (in their calendar) are completely correct.** They have their weight and worth and their timing is pretty accurate.

Humanity reportedly entered into the era of **a more intense alignment with the cosmic, or galactic, consciousness** as early as **1994**, which was the year of my first spontaneous experience of life without food. That was when **a holographic, or wholistic, awareness of the nine-dimensional reality, an awareness of all the levels of our consciousness,** began to be awakened within spiritually prepared people. And this awakening is still unfolding. The main purpose of my writing is to encourage it. **The spiritual dimensions of our existence are** unfortunately **completely overlooked by the science that is valid today. But we are nevertheless reawakening that which was lost long ago,** who knows when and why – **our complete nine-dimensional consciousness and awareness.**

....
466 More about Mayan and Hopi prophecies and transformations can be found in the first book in the *Cosmic Telepathy* series and in my book, still a work in progress, titled *S pozornostjo jaguarja ali sove v novi čas* **(With the Watchfulness of the Jaguar, or Owl, into the New Era)**.
467 Check the works of the above-mentioned authors.

The energy of life and life itself murmur like water – symbolically like an ocean or river. When we find ourselves **in a whirlpool of thoughts and intuitive-telepathic insights,** which is usually especially strong just before important shifts in our lives, we are like water **just below boiling point.** We should not despair, even though the most difficult part is to squeeze those very last drops into the bottle. Those drops then make the bottle's contents spill over and trigger **a shift. Don't despair, instead add the strength and fire of transformation – courage, will, a clear thought and silence, in which you can hear a clear thought, the whisper of the Spirit/Consciousness/Soul/the Universal, or divine, Intelligence. Don't abuse stimulants** (alcohol, drugs, sensual pleasure), for they will **take you even further away from the solution.** Then you shall attain the goal.

It is good to know that **just before the Centre (before enlightenment?), or below the boiling point, we reach most deeply into the denied contents of our consciousness (or subconscious), which is why the battle is fiercest at that time.** We don't want to face once again the pain that was suppressed long ago, so we keep pushing it back into our subconscious. And in the subconscious lies the most difficult and dark content, blurring our sight of reality. Yet painful thoughts **and emotions cannot last for long** when we are close to boiling point, when the bottle is almost full and **we have truly had enough.** They have to resurface and be exposed. **Don't suppress them, rather take a look at them, accept them and free yourself from them!** Unexpectedly, or **when you least expect it,** the grey fog of your sliminess will flow over the rim of the bottle and **make you lighter,** like nothing else can. **Play this game – with the ball or without it – play it in full awareness and with integrity – as a spiritually mature and brave warrior seeking freedom.**

I want to **hearten** my readers **for this battle which cannot be avoided.** Sooner or later, everyone will have to become aware of it. That is why I want to share my **stories about the releasing** of the old and outlived, my stories about **listening to the flow of life energy and to the Intent, or the Intelligence of existence,** which is eternally present and which nourishes the entire field of life.

We are usually the ones who bring **problems** upon ourselves, mostly because **we refuse to hear, or we (still) don't know how to draw from the all-pervading Field.** In a similar way, **we don't know how to ladle out** energy **food (prana) from the boundless ocean of the invisible frequency waves** of the all-pervading life energy. This energy could feed us, it could heal us, make us complete, so that we could live without the usual solid food. And **we also (still) don't know how to read** the thoughts and **messages within the information Field, within the sound yarn** which suffuses everything. All of this is not only possible, but it is going to be increasingly more understood and ever more frequent in the future. **Everything is possible in the silence of the mind.** This knowledge, however, seems **lost and** utopian to many people. **But it isn't! It has just been banished from our minds, but it is still here — as a heritage of the past and the timeless wisdom of our ancestors. It is well worth delving into it!**

The return of lost abilities

Not only have contemporary humans lost their connection to ceremonial practice, they have also lost their connection to the Universe and an awareness of the cosmic dimensions of their own essence. They may have lost **the memory of cosmic consciousness of oneness,** but fortunately they still carry it within 'the archives' of their soul. **They lost the sensitivity needed to perceive the frequency Universe of the cosmic orchestra,** of which they themselves are a part. They lost the sensitivity of the body and senses to perceive inaudible cosmic frequencies and sounds. But today humans **wish to restore these overlooked and long lost abilities of the meta-sensory.**

Ancestors living millennia ago were physically and spiritually far more sensitive than we are today. They possessed abilities, awareness, and **knowledge which we today are unable to even fathom.** Not only that: our belief that, in the past, people lived in ignorance is erroneous. We are wrong because our opinion primarily relies on ever greater technological progress, which of course is not spiritual progress. **True, we have advanced technologically, but spiritually we have considerably regressed.** However, in this exceptional time of extremely rapid changes, we are again **reviving our dormant abilities and the forgotten spiritual values of our ancestors,** which have been pushed deeply into our subconscious – into our meta-conscious – and are waiting to be revealed.

It is time to regain wholeness; it is time for us to regain those lost abilities of which numerous age-old sacred texts speak. In fragments at least, these texts **keep the memory of the human's past spiritual grandeur and of important knowledge** which has in some places managed to somehow survive in a fragmented form until today. Yet, **unfortunately, no religion, no spiritual teaching on this planet has managed to preserve and bring into our time the complete Truth of this ancient wisdom. Fundamental Truths have been simplified and increasingly forgotten** throughout time and over the history of the last few thousand years. They were simplified by priests, so that the masses could understand them more easily. But as a result, they lost the primordial essence of a wholistic awareness. And in some places, those simplified and distorted Truths even turned into **illogical dogmas, into mundane and religious commandments and non-sensical claims.** This is why numerous spiritual creeds and testimonies of the world's **religions** can unfortunately **lead us away from the wholistic perception** of Truth, away from the goals of spiritual seekers and warriors, away from an understanding of the very essence of life. **But luckily, we carry the undistorted Truth within our soul's ancient memory, and we are gradually revealing it through spiritual transformation and our life experiences.**

Today, everything is changing at a rapid pace: people, the Earth, animals, plants, nature itself, even planets and their movements, the Sun, and even the location of the entire solar system. Yet, **the Cosmic, or Galactic, Consciousness of the Source, the Universal Intelligence of life – Hunahpu as the Mayans would call it – pervades everything that exists on the Earth and in the Universe alike.** It guides us towards the as yet unrevealed and unknown. It often happens that we are **frightened by this unknown,** for our usual mind relies mostly on the solid visible world and our past experiences. **That is why humans of a more narrow consciousness feel safe principally within the framework of the known, understood, usual.**

Everyone is an important piece of the immense dimensions of the Universe. Our usual linear **mind is unable to grasp** its expanses. **But the clarity of our mind and thoughts is improving and expanding by the day.** Our life's journey is **slowing down and accelerating** at the same time. **We are spinning in the spiral vortex of our galaxy,** where we dwell both on the physical planes of our planet and at spiritual levels, in the Home of our soul. **Conflict is increasing and is being eliminated at the same time.** It is ever stronger, so that its **torments** might grind us to such a degree that we **could finally dare to step out** of that which is tormenting and hindering us.

Today humans are consciously returning to the expanses of cosmic consciousness, the seed of which **develops into the beauty of a being.** The primordial seed is waiting to blossom once more. **'Created according to the divine image,'** as we say, we are opening our petals – our countless and exceptional abilities sleeping within us. People are **expanding their consciousness and are developing alongside the expansion of the Universe,** alongside the Intelligence that pervades it. **We expand, we observe, we react and act, we laugh, we cry and sometimes we even get angry if we don't understand, if we are not patient enough.**

Galactic consciousness is a wide open consciousness of the restored memory of the Cosmic Principle and of all our earthly and personal pasts, of all our incarnations, our experiences, all our distant and close life experiences, of all our givens and abilities. Millennia ago, our distant **ancestors,** or those souls on Earth who had restored the awareness of the cosmic, or galactic, consciousness, knew **the foundations of the awakened, enlightened (cosmic) consciousness;** they lived with the described wisdom and shaped **the codex of its laws. Their wisdom was far broader and deeper than today's scholarship.**

We are waking up from a gloomy sleep like Briar Rose. We are reliving the deep sleep of the unaware mind, the lack of awareness within the darkness of modern life, which is far away from the wisdom which we call awakened cosmic awareness. This is even more relevant for us, **white Westerners who have spent the last two thousand years in the agony of bloody fights for power, authority and principally material goods,** and also in the darkness of Christian doctrine which, throughout history, has been unable to communicate the clear thoughts, messages and teachings of the great adepts and teachers. **We lost the dignity of a compassionate co-existence with other** people and ethnic groups, with different spiritual teachings and other life forms.

Being increasingly cut off from respect for diversity, we have ultimately lost even self-respect, a feeling for ourselves, for other people, and especially for animals, plants, and the Earth. This is why our planet cannot live fully, and it cannot survive either. The last traces of the great spiritual wisdom of our ancestors are being lost in egocentric strivings, and we can only intuit, rather than understand, this wisdom located in those **heritages** which have been preserved until today. Yet, it is **still here,** within the higher levels of our awareness, of our soul: a silent witness and a warning which says that **it is possible to live in a different way,** and to perceive the world in a completely unpredictable and above all, **a more loving way.** We are even able to sense the subtle vibrations of the Earth and the cosmic expanse, we can perceive the refined transcendental sound of thoughts, of consciousness, emotions, and soul. And when our minds turn again to the barely perceptible (divine) Source of life, the disturbing babbling of our mind stops. We begin to feel the fullness of life and joy, the silence of resonance.

But people who, willingly or not, are constantly mired in the disease of thinking, are deprived of those refined sensations which are like the enchanting music of the Cosmic Intelligence, the Divine Essence. The entire Universe, as well as **life in it, is connected with invisible (energy) threads – the threads of a cobweb,** as the Native Americans would say. We feel **separation** only in our physical bodies, **while our spirit, our soul, are like radar and compass for the boundless expanses of the unfathomable. They are veritable connectors between the worlds, the dimensions of reality.** When we touch the abstruse realms of higher levels of consciousness, **our soul begins to resound more fully.** Within the inner **peace of self-recognition** and with an awareness of the meaning of life, we begin to **experience our soul, our awareness, as an indispensable guide.**

Our galaxy – this wonderful **spiral formation** of so many stars, which sky watchers count in billions and trillions – has enabled the existence of the world we live in. **We belong to a small, difficult to describe, part of Galactic Consciousness in the physical world, which during our life time, lives, inspires, and creates** in linear time and three-dimensional material space. **Cosmic, or Galactic, Consciousness is encoded in our very core. It is like the chromosome of our soul's essence in the material world, it is the stimulator** which leads us unerringly in the direction of spiritual growth – **until our mind awakens within all of its grandeur in a human consciousness.**

Listening to the messages of the Universe

In order to awaken the galactic consciousness (which is a part of the Great Galactic Consciousness, or Mind) within ourselves, we encounter and fight with numerous states and levels of our own awareness and actions, as well as with our subconscious. **We gradually travel across the bridges and portals (dimensions) of spirit into ever more interesting spiritual worlds of reality. During this, our personal experiences and knowings bring us insights into the purpose and meaning of the spiritual heritages of different natural peoples of the world and the sacred texts written by those who had walked the path of human transformation before us. We are getting to know the fundamental Truth of the Universe, of our existence and life;** we are increasingly discovering the new and **dormant possibilities of the spirit and the abilities** of our own boundless essence. **Our consciousness is interlaced, or suffused, with an awareness of the meaningfulness of everything that is. But the loss of memory of both our own and the Earth's evolution,** which unfolded over aeons, created a firmly **anchored fear and worry** for our lives and survival. **We cannot orientate ourselves,** for today's teachings teach us solely about the laws of Newtonian physics in the material world. **Who knows when we lost almost everything we need to know about life, Creation, and the world.** This loss of memory probably started **at least during the last two thousand years; one day this knowledge, handed down through millennia, simply disappeared, just like the Mayans** and their exceptional culture.

But fortunately, by expanding our consciousness, by cleansing ourselves of fear and emotional problems, we become increasingly capable of hearing the messages of the Universe, of hearing the frequency waves and energy vibrations from the multidimensional universal expanses **which we reach, or better – which reach us. The care of our body and spirit serves the awakening,** which will one day finally bring us **a complete and undistorted understanding of life and its events,** along with an understanding of everything that exists in the Universe and on Earth.

Unconditional love of the soul is the driving force of the Universe, it is its **glue and the dowry** which was bequeathed to us at the time of our birth, when we were born into the physical world as a little part of the universal, cosmic and galactic spirit. **The conditions for hearing the subtle sound and messages of the Cosmic Mind, of the omnipresent Consciousness, are an open mind and heart, along with flexibility in our thinking, acceptance of the current moment and of everything that is, especially that which is different,** as well as a feeling of **connectedness to the Earth and the Cosmos. It is not easy to hear (with attention).** Humans have to thoroughly **re-examine all their thoughts, emotions, and patterns, even their unconscious impulses, and embrace their givens,** which were bestowed upon them **so that they would truly hear.** The cosmic essence of life is the driving force.

Those who do manage to surrender to the pulsing flow of the cosmic energy of life will be able to hear **the earthly rhythms and their own rhythms** alike, and will be able to surrender to them. **When we work in harmony with the entirety of Existence, everything resonates and echoes in line with the laws of resonance, or co-oscillation, in a mutually supporting connectedness. But it cuts and aches when we are in dissonance, in disharmony with the current moment and the pulsing of the Universe.** This is still known today by Aboriginal people, the descendants of the ancient Mayans, the noble souls of North American Indians, high priests of Indonesia, by Asian and Pacific cultures, African tribes, Slavic shamans, and healers etc. It was mainly us, 'the white Westerners,' who forgot this great knowledge; **we are almost the only ones destroying this world.** Our planet, our Mother. Peoples in harmony with nature are simply unable to do this.

But the wheel of evolution is turning in the opposite direction. **We are once more yearning for an awareness of all levels of reality, for the perfect Truth and a renewing co-oscillation with the Source of the Universe, the Earth and ourselves.** Our ancient memory is awakened through this yearning; **a memory which was not born from the mind, or intellect, but in the transcendental consciousness of our soul, in the first principle of a telepathic resonance with the Source, with the Cosmic Intelligence – with Hunahpu. We are returning to the fullness of awareness, to the expanse of oneness** which will reconnect us to all the parameters and meanings of life, to a life we deeply want: **a life imbued with joy, harmony, health, peace, etc.**

An indestructible **desire for a happy co-existence** has dwelt in the human soul for hundreds, even thousands of years. But it seems that **the compass** which ought to lead humans to this very happiness has **long been broken,** or at least it has failed to show us the right direction. **The great majority of humankind is unfortunately racing precisely towards a goal where there is no happiness: towards a desperate scramble for material goods,** at all costs. But I hope that the other, **more enlightened, half** of humankind, still **intuits another, different,**

path. By walking this path we will one day satisfy the hidden desires of our soul. At an accelerated pace, these intuitions of something better and more majestic lead us into a research of spiritual truths and the teachings of past civilisations.

When we listen to the Truths of the Universe, those things we yesterday perceived as **sorcery,** as meaningless **shamanic** hocus-pocus and a big hoax, will increasingly **reveal themselves as a precious jewel, a remnant of past wisdom.** But unfortunately only **distorted fragments** of a greater mosaic image have been preserved; not only are they fragments, but we no longer know where they belong to nor what they are telling us. However, **a cosmic telepath is still able to comprehend them.**

It is a fact that we are the ones who have to change, **we have to change our awareness and understanding of our philosophy of life and knowledge which is the one we believe to be the only and irrefutable truth, but which is in fact mostly delusional and is a conceited misunderstanding of an unawakened consciousness.** A great part of today's modern life doctrine, and even the only glorified scientific thought, unfortunately fall into this category.

The challenges of an attuned mind, soul and heart, and the healing powers of the connection to the Universe

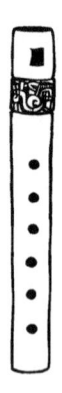

Ceremonial flute *quena* with six holes.

Prophets, spiritual teachers, healers, and shamans lived on Earth at all times; they were spiritually broadly open persons who showed people the path to eternal Truths, the path back to the Home of the soul. But those persons were **persecuted, crucified, banished, stoned** for the last two thousand years or more, as far as perhaps our historical memory reaches. It was no different during the time of the forced Christianisation of Native Americans and other peoples. **Humans are incredibly blinded by their own stupidity.** But we live in a time that enables us **to recognise, more and more easily, this dismal veiling and oppression. Every day, we can delight in something completely new.** Perhaps, an old-new awareness will arise in us, a completely **new insight** and knowing about something **that we hadn't even guessed at the day before,** let alone understood, which is why we hadn't accepted it at the time.

We are returning to the fullness of cosmic, or galactic, consciousness, and this is also what the wise men and women of different cultures claim. **We are awakening a memory which is accessible to everyone. We are embracing the**

challenge of an accelerated opening of our minds, souls and hearts. After two thousand years of **the persecution of our pagan (!?) ancestors' truths, we are finally remembering who we are, why we are, and what is the meaning of life.** With this, we are completing the 'Great Cycle,' the 'Long Count,' as the Mayans say – five thousand years of human **wandering between the light and darkness on Earth; we are completing the great cycle,** a period of spiritual development, which has a length of almost **26,000 years. We are renewing our link to the Earth, the Universe, and ourselves. Today, we are once more able to journey into the centre of the galaxy and ourselves, whenever we want to,** just like the ancient shamans did. We don't need rockets and space ships for this. **We only need to renew our weakened connection.** Not only to all beings on Earth, but also to the frequencies, **vibrations, or energies of the boundless and infinite sea, or Field,** from which everything emerges. Every culture has its own picturesque names for those frequency vibrations. They are most often called **divine beings, Masters,** or God the **Creator. And the human body is still the most sensitive instrument for their perception.**

We in fact cannot avoid perceiving the Frequency Universe. **In the inner silence of the mind, when our consciousness is expanded, awake and all-connected, we are able, just like our ancient ancestors, to feel and even hear the inaudible sound of earthly and cosmic waves, which 'resounds' outside our hearing field,** but which can nevertheless be perceived by our physical senses and especially by our **meta-sensory hearing.**

Spiritual seekers everywhere and at all times have been **connecting to the great family of cosmic-earthly vibrations – beings, or entities,** as we call them. Invisible and inaudible frequencies resonate within a majestic **choir, in the symphony orchestra of the sound weave which pervades both living and non-living nature alike.** And because we are a part of this Field, of this orchestra, everyone has to **play harmoniously, and above all, everyone has to play an equally mellifluous song,** otherwise we will find ourselves in painful disharmony and chaos. All great wisdoms actually speak about the conscious attuning or aligning of humans with the 'universal orchestra,' so that we can resonate as harmoniously as possible, and **thus avoid the suffering and pain of disharmony. Even the very thought of cosmic waves and of the sonic Source, of the symbolically divine, harmonises us. And to gaze at the symbol Hunahpu – the symbol of Silence – or to receive it through an initiation is truly beneficent and captivating.**

The symphony of the frequencies of Cosmic Consciousness must resonate within our soul, within our mind, our hearts, our feelings, and this should be embraced without any doubt, but primarily with grateful devotion. This is how we will be able to attain the mighty support of the entire orchestra, which will then play through us its harmonious, sweet melodies of existence. We call them the support of the Universe, as well as pre-destined harmony. Thought which is in harmony with, or imbued with the pulsing of the Universe, of the galaxy, our solar system, and the Earth, is always enhanced and powerful. This is how the Intelligence of the Universe and life fulfils our desires. When we, through our alignment (synergy) with the rhythms of the cosmic orchestra attain the support of the Intelligence of the Universe, which pervades and supports everything that is in resonance with it, our desires begin to be fulfilled spontaneously and in an accelerated manner; yet only if they are aligned with us, with our path, our destiny, with the totality and Divine Intent.

All material and non-material life forms, as well as numerous universes, emerge from the unmanifested Universe, the First Principle, from the Field, or the sea of all possibilities, which is symbolically like a large incubator, or hatchery. This is taught by ancient Vedic and Aboriginal wisdom, by the traditional teachings of the Pacific islands, of Native Americans, Siberian shamans, and others. Perhaps they are right. Why not listen to them? Time will tell if they got it wrong in some areas. We should accept that we (still) don't know everything! The wisdom of past civilisations was carved out by numerous generations of exceptional sage-telepaths. For thousands of years, human beings in the physical universe of the three-dimensional world have been persistently seeking a connection to this shape-giving Universe, to the cosmic soup. When we begin to resonate in complete harmony with it, new paths, new dimensions of existence open up for us. The traffic lights turn green along our path. All the while, we experience boundless enthusiasm, which is but the feeling of being aligned to the rhythms of the Universe and life, which itself pours an abundance of supporting energy over us.

Alignment can happen when we move beyond our egocentric desires and are prepared to work for higher spiritual goals and for everything that is and that lives. Then, our heart starts to beat in harmony with the cosmic Heart of unconditional love. We give without expectation and without demands. We once again begin to resonate within Galactic and Cosmic Consciousness. We have reached the goal of our earthly journey. Huracan pulls us into its vortex. And on this journey, we experience the changing of all our bodies, from the physical to emotional, mental and spiritual; and we also discover new talents within ourselves, we awaken the dormant abilities of a divine image.

According to the forecasts of natural civilisations, a golden age is ahead of us, in which people will supposedly attain the described fullness of consciousness in increasingly large numbers. At least some. Of course, we have the right not to become aware of this connection and cosmic dimension. The choice is ours. In the cosmic symphony orchestra, we can choose either a devoted co-operative play or silence. Innumerable vibrations, or symbolically 'beings,' as our ancestors named them, are reaching out to us on this exceptional journey of mass awakening. **Vibrations from the Cosmos,** which are also changing by the day, **invigorate and support us, so that we can understand, accept, allow and begin to live more joyfully the wholeness of existence.**

A conscious alignment to the above-mentioned galactic vibrations (called Hunahpu by the Mayans, and Black Sky by the Siberians), **which can even be triggered by a mere thought about our connectedness to the rhythms of the Universe, creates a healing power of balance.** A telepathic perception of **the eternally present messages about time and timelessness,** about the past, present and future, co-creates a special **medicine of spirit and body and enables a connection to the awareness of our soul. The power of healthy harmony shows us the way through changes, to multidimensional worlds, and the boundless abilities of the spirit. It also helps us eliminate our fears and emotional problems.** Within this alignment, our high-frequency etheric bodies are cleansed, which enables **the telepathic reception of information from the Field of imprints, from akasha.** With these barely perceptible sound gifts, **we are able to adapt more easily to the rapid transformation** which we are experiencing. This results in a lighter **self-renewal, (self-) healing, in the strengthening of our body and spirit and in the actualisation of harmony and our desires** – of course only those desires which are in resonance with the Plan of the Intelligence of life and our destiny.

This is how people are slowly **regaining the spiritual abilities that have been suppressed deep in their subconscious, abilities which often surprise us with utterly miraculous events** and situations which run completely **contrary to commonplace logic.** Yet, that which is unusual and seemingly miraculous is but **a reflection of an expanded (cosmic) consciousness.** Events and healings that are out of the ordinary only seem miraculous to us. Peace and wholeness come into our lives along with these miracles, and **questions like why is this so, why don't my wishes come true, disappear.** And thoughts arise like oh, yes, **I know. Finally. I came to understand events and my own actions.** I know that something truly miraculous has happened to me, something that **I have earned myself – with my attention, persistence, lovingness and compassion, and above all, with my attention to everything.**

The cosmic vibrations of galactic consciousness, or **the Galactic Centre,** are less known today, but for the Mayans they represented **the target level of the inter-dimensional journeys of their consciousness.** Humans can reach those vibrations only **when they begin to permanently live the connectedness to the galactic, or cosmic, levels of reality,** and when they begin to accept all the contents of life **unreservedly; and when even the Sky, or the cosmic, is constantly in their thoughts.**[468]

So the Universe and I are both made from the same core. This is also claimed by numerous spiritual teachings and the traditions of our planet. Every human being is in fact a spark of spirit, **'a divine spark' in time and space,** in the physical world. **A human being is a logoidal idea of the Intelligence of life, of the Absolute/Source/God which radiates and resonates within every cell, every thought and even within our memory.** People of a cosmic consciousness would say: **"Don't think only as a physical human being, think as a spirit, as a soul!"** After all, human **essence is the truth of spirit, the spirit of Truth.**

Our heart is the cosmic bridge. With our conscious spiritual growth and with **the journeys to our core, our bodily energy wave receptors, our etheric bodies which nourish the chakras,** all gain **a greater capacity** to sense and receive this high-frequency life flow on a daily basis. We say that **our soul is awakening, and our soul is actually the divine 'computer programme'** of our material body. **It is said that the Divine and the human will come together (again!) one day and play the same tune.**

The return of both cosmic memory and the cosmic initiations of perfection in the legends of Lemuria and Atlantis[469]

In the processes of the expansion of our consciousness we regain **the memory of our soul contracts, the challenges of our incarnation, tasks, and problems.** We also regain **the memory of the birth of the soul,** of the origins of our being, which when we surrender to the invisible flow, **enhance the feeling of lightness of our body.** The more we are open and receptive to the unknown, the more miraculous and beautiful things will happen in our lives, and we will discover ever more sublime things within ourselves and the world. Doubts will dissolve at an accelerated pace. A loving kindness will spread within us, along with compassion and tolerance. And life will be one great delight. It will seem to us that we are walking on air. We will want to **rise** even higher and fly to even higher dimensions, to the fairy tale realms of reality. We often dream **that we are flying.**

Cosmic, or galactic, vibrations, which also resonate in **the myths of legendary Lemuria and Atlantis,** in the myths of their perfected cultures and exceptional technology, are beneficent. These myths, known on all continents, are actually **legends**

---
468 Deepak Chopra, a physician and charismatic spiritual man, wrote a brilliant and informative book about the Hindu tradition of the need for a human connection to the Universe. The book is titled *The Book of Secrets*, London (2004).
469 More on this topic can be found in the fourth book in the *Cosmic Telepathy* series.

about human perfection. Native American and Mayan spiritual leaders claim that now is the time when **conditions for the development of human consciousness on Earth are even more auspicious than during the era of those two** highly developed civilisations of our ancestors. In the now sunken and lost Lemuria and Atlantis, in **the lost land of a wholistic consciousness,** it was **primarily priests who were said to have 'communicated'** with the vibrations of the Gods, or Masters, as well as **with** the universal **primordial frequency Field – the Centre of the galaxy (Hunahpu and Huracan),** with the Cosmos and its forces. **The heirs of their wisdom were supposedly ancient Egyptian priests and pharaohs,** as well as for example **king Solomon, Filipino surgeons, and Hawaiian** kahunas.

In both civilisations, regardless of whether they were real or not, priests were said to have surrendered to the inaudible gifts from the Cosmos **during their initiation ceremonies.** Their purpose was similar: **to accelerate the spiritual growth** of people and their own, and **to invoke the necessary healing energies.** In this way, priests, and healers, together with their followers, were said to have one day reached the enlightened goal of their journey. The mythical countries **Mu** (Lemuria) and Atlantis were some kind of promised paradise, a departure point and **a heavenly Home of the Soul, the home of perfection.** Almost all ancient cultures have resorted to the myths of those two countries, which are, today, in some places still alive in numerous stories.

The soul's yearning for perfection cannot be annihilated. Humans persistently seek perfection and they follow it, until one day they attain it – usually totally unexpectedly. We can never forget about it. That is why in the past people built **majestic temples and stepped pyramids; that is why with their myths, songs and legends, they erected magical monuments** to the immortal essences of life, **to cosmic Masters, or Gods and the masters of life, to cosmic and earthly forces – the lords of time and space, to the essences of the stars, the Moon, the Sun, the Earth, the Galactic Centre, or the Source.** All of this came out of one single desire: to be able **to align,** with their help, **more easily to the Universal Mind, the Logos,** as well as to life on Earth, to the laws of existence (the lords), or the **rhythms which pervade the Universe,** which resound in the high-frequency inner sound and **echo in life on Earth.** The ancient Mayans revered and invoked the Primal Principle **Hunahpu** and the Heart of Sky **Huracan,** as well as its representative on Earth **Kukulkan,** to help them regain **harmony and the peace of the soul** through their daily **rituals, dances, songs, myths, fairy tales, and stories,** as well as through their sacred and mysterious **initiations.** In any case – **try it out for yourself!** Perhaps connecting to the Universe, to its essences and sounds, will bring **peace and joy beyond compare to you too. It did to me.**

Cosmic initiations of a distant past, as well as those that I channel for people today, **are a permanent link to the cosmic mandala of the sounds** of the Universe and Earth. They bestow upon people **the blessings of hope and faith and help to merge the material** (physical) **and spiritual** (non-material) into a perfect and complete **wholeness, or perfection.** Perhaps right now, in an accelerated or concealed manner, everyone is consciously or unconsciously awakening within themselves **the cosmic (or female/shakti) principle suppressed for thousands of years, along with joy and delight in life.** In this way, they are, consciously or not, **preparing for the time of changes and for the new era of a consciousness far broader than what we know today.**

Everything that exists is changing rapidly. And it doesn't matter whether we give to the cosmic waves that are currently supporting us the names of different **Gods,** or **Masters, stellar or planetary Lords of the Earth, the Moon, the Sun, the Galactic Centre, of other planets and stars – the Pleiades, Sirius, Orion, the North Star, etc.** In different traditions and cultures, people have focused their sacred attention either on this or on that, but occasionally on all of them. Mostly in order **to develop their spiritual abilities and skills as far as possible** and to raise them to an enviable level, **to find permanent peace of the soul and to ensure necessary well-being.** In order to find all of this both for themselves and for others.

Cosmic initiations, which were connected to the mythology of legendary **Lemuria and Atlantis,** as well as to ancient Egypt, to the temples of Hindu rshis, to the pyramids of Mayan kingdoms and meadow temples of Native American and African tribes, European and ancient Slavic peoples, **were performed by sages of an exceptionally broad consciousness, holy persons of our planet, who helped peoples from all continents to connect to the eternal wisdom;** they helped to expand people's consciousness and awareness, so that people could understand **the multi-layeredness of truth, so that they could 'attune' to the purpose of their lives and invoke clear insights, happiness and abundance into their lives.** What we today call cultural monuments are primarily the monuments of the extraordinary and boundless abilities of our ancestors.

The question arises as to why we have forgotten this age-old wisdom of our ancestors. If it was so brilliant, **why does it no longer live in our minds?** The answer is probably the following: this majestic wisdom was **only nourished and kept by a few wise initiates. They were banished, or eradicated, by people of a more narrow consciousness and a lesser mind, as they were unable to understand and accept the sages' exceptional knowings, visions, thoughts, and planetary dreams.** The Romans for example, first killed the Celtic spiritual elite – the druids; Christians of the new era banished the ancient Slavic cosmic religion, the Chinese killed thousands of Tibetan lamas, while in Africa, Asia, on Pacific islands, and in the three Americas, white invaders and Christian missionaries first burned sacred temples, sacred books, and their worshippers. Thousands of Mongolian and Siberian savants were killed in communist Russia, the Spaniards almost completely eliminated the Mayan spiritual heritage, which thus sunk into oblivion in our era. But **fortunately, consciousness cannot be destroyed.** And everything that has happened on Earth is **still 'recorded' in energy, it is present** at spiritual levels. **Even the primordial Consciousness of the cosmic Field cannot be destroyed and deleted. That is why it is still possible to peek into this majestic millennia old knowledge and even to revive it.** By those who can manage this of course. And this is exactly what is **happening at this very moment, in numerous spiritual seekers, or warriors, too.** Once more, **the memory of people's personal, earthly, and cosmic evolution is being awakened** in them.

It is a comforting thought that **even today,** at the beginning of a new millennium, **we are able to receive** gifts that are as magnificent as those of our distant ancestors. **If only we 'remember' that, or wish to have a connection to all dimensions of reality and to the cosmic Source; if we open up to this mythical flow, cleanse our old emotional wounds, eliminate despair and fear, traumatic cell memory and painful emotions suppressed into the subconscious, if we open our heart chakra and compassionate wholeheartedness wide enough to embrace hope and faith in life and its events, to embrace the attention of the loving soul.** When we attain all of this, we will at first have the feeling that we are **illuminating our body** by the day with ever stronger light bulbs. After all, this is actually how it is and it is urgent. **The energy flow within us will increase by the day and we will be healthier and happier.**

The mysteries of the three-dimensional world are changing, yet remaining the same

In December 2012 we will supposedly be **closest to the centre of the Galaxy (the black hole),** where **gravitation** is unfathomably strong and (as contemporary scientists have discovered) **rejuvenating** at the same time. We will not be able to overlook its influence. **We will not get through** the light-sound (frequency) band we had been nearing and which some call **the multidimensional photon band without having noticed it. Nothing three-dimensional or unbalanced, can pass through without being shaken and transformed. Everything that exists is constantly changing, altering its flow, or the height (tone) of its frequency waves.** This has been so especially in the first decade of the new millennium. And all of this had already been foreseen by the ancient Mayans priests.

The climate, life forms, ocean currents, ozone layer, tectonic-seismic movements, sunspot activities, the weather, etc. are changing. **Every atom and molecular structure of life on Earth, in the solar system and the entire galaxy is changing. So the Universe is still expanding. And humans expand with it. Our solar system is shifting its position in the galaxy;** astrophysicists claim that it is returning to its **original point.** Along with it, **the qualities of the energy waves of cosmic frequency radiations** are changing, together with **the magnetic fields of the Earth, the Sun, and those of humans and their consciousness and awareness.** The more we consciously connect to the cosmic ocean of life waves or sounds, the more we welcome into our everyday life **the dimensions of spirit, the more brilliantly, faster, and lighter our personal transformation will unfold, in conjunction with planetary transformation.** Everything influences everything, everyone has an influence on the totality, and the totality is mirrored in everyone. **A new human being – metagalactic human being – is being born, who, in relation to the expanses of consciousness, will be once more closer to the exceptional spiritual dimensions of the ancient Mayans, the Aboriginal peoples** – modest inter-dimensional travellers, as well as to those of ancient Slavic and Celtic priests, Siberian shamans, past master-singers, etc. Metagalactic human beings do not resemble modern heroes or mascots – supermen, instead they are **images of satisfied, creative, and compassionate humans; images of perfection.**

The mysteries of the three-dimensional world change together with the expanses of our consciousness. **We are once more becoming more acutely sensitive, penetrating, somehow more translucent and lighter, while our consciousness is more and more illuminated and enlightened.** It leads us, in different and unique ways, to our awakened life goal, **it carries us back to the place from which we came – to the Primordial or Divine, Intelligence of the Universe and life.**

Today this journey is not much different from how it was in the past, **in the time of our distant ancestors,** who, like us, had been seeking Truth and **actualising** within themselves **the cosmic or galactic, consciousness of a meta-human being, a meta-ecologist, exceptional musician-priest-medium, and therapist. At least one part of humanity still lives this way – people who are in harmony with nature and the Universe. But the great majority of humanity is unfortunately deep asleep, criticising, bargaining, lying, stealing, and fighting. They have obviously forgotten about the age-old and eternal planetary dreams. Yet, humanity's karmic task or fate, is that everybody enlightens and awakens sooner or later.** Some at a fast, others at a slow rate. But the goal ahead of everyone is the same.

So, let us treat ourselves to a nice surprise and ride the wave of the current moment – for a better future. Dream out the best in us. The purpose of Mayan symbols, ceremonies, and invigorating sound play is to bring into life, as permanently as possible, peace, joy, attention, a healthy curiosity, and freedom. Symbols are the keys that awaken the human spirit; ceremonies are paths to the goal, selected sounds are the tool and remedy when they resonate in a loving harmony. Life is a song. And this song needs the voice of everyone, and it also needs your conscious playing.

Be the instrument and a wise musician in the majestic universal orchestra of differentness. Sing and play in harmony with it. Don't spoil the euphony by lacking compassion, that is disharmonious! But know that everyone who lives with the love of perfect wholeness, with the symphony of the Sky, humans and the Earth, will receive extremely rich gifts. May your curiosity guide you to the clarity of thought and to the devotion of the soul which opens the doors to well-being.

May the myths, legends, and stories of the past inspire your quest and dreams. To fulfil them, you have to weave into them the stars, the rhythms of the Sky and Earth, the Sun and the Moon, and the trees, plants and animals, mountains, rivers, and lakes, etc. Be connected with all of them. Everything is with you in an eternal play. May your play be light and fulfilling. If this still isn't so, allow yourself a change and invite into your life celestial characters and invisible heroes of the Earth and the Sky. Allow yourself to be conducted by the Source of life, the essence of the Universe – Hunahpu, for it knows the harmony, the way to the harmony of well-being.

And don't forget that the Universe echoes and mirrors your every single thought, returning it to you. So may the thought you send out into the world be always loving, and you shall receive lovingness yourself. Sing the world in a loving way. Always. May the sounds you create be like shining stars and like the lights of a galactic traveller on a cosmic-earthly highway, or in a canoe in the middle of the expanses of consciousness, and you shall never run out of energy, ideas, and delight. You will become the Universe, the Creator, the unique and fulfilled matrix of the Divine Source. You will become the Source – Hunahpu. You will begin to resonate with the centre of everything, with the centre of the Universe: with the energy waves of Hunahpu, which are spiralling through the Universe and through you. You are Hunahpu, the cosmic butterfly, the sound of the essence of the Universe, you are infinite at your core and above all – you are boundlessly free.

For those to whom all of this still seems alien, may this **poem of Rumi** serve as a warning and reminder:

'Those of you **who feel no love**
sleep on.
Those of you who do not feel the sorrow of love
in whose heart passion has never risen
sleep on.
Those who do not long for union
who are not constantly asking **'Where is He?'**
sleep on.
Love's path is outside of all religious sects
if **trickery and hypocrisy** is your way
sleep on.
If you don't melt like copper in your quest
for the **alchemical** gold
sleep on.
If like a drunkard you fall left and right
unaware the night has passed and it's time for prayer
sleep on.
Fate has taken my sleep but since
it has not taken yours, young man,
sleep on,
We have fallen into love's hands
since you are in your own
sleep on.
I am the one who is drunk on Love
since you are drunk on food
sleep on.
I have given up my head and have nothing more to say
but you can wrap yourself in the robe of words and
sleep on.'[470]

But we **don't have to sleep.** We can always **choose** a different way and a different journey, the exciting **path of enlightened spirit and noble love.**

....
470 Rumi, *Hidden Music*, London, Thorsons (2001), pp. 46-47.

Silence – the path and goal of spiritual warriorhood

To be able to hear yourself and the world in silence is the magic of the connection between the centre of your own being and oneness

Silence is the absence of audible sound.
It is soundlessness, harmony and euphony.
In silence, consciousness is fully awake.
We say that **in it, the soul is awake, clear, always conscious of everything.**
Yet, the silence of the mind is not only the absence of rambling thoughts,
it is **the mercy and grace of the heart.**
We say that **the compass of silence** is revealed **through love.**[471]

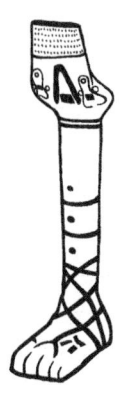

We usually think that **we know how to listen.** What nonsense! **We do not even hear those who are close to us,** we don't know what they, let alone ourselves, feel or need. We are convinced **that we know best what is right and best for others.** We are so very entangled in our own opinions, that we usually do not even ask others what they want and what they need. We simply act according to our own – usually wrong – mind, doing what seems right to us. But **is this right really right for others?** The following **yogic tale** brilliantly sheds light on this.

A ritual recorder in the form of a human foot.

A girl had been deaf since birth. One day, her parents found out that a doctor, who **could restore the girl's hearing through an operation,** was in their town. The parents took the child for a medical examination and asked the doctor for help. He said that a surgical procedure perhaps might help her, but there was no guarantee that it would be successful and not many people had their hearing restored.

But the parents nevertheless arranged a date for the operation, **without having asked the girl what she actually wanted.** After the operation, the girl **got her hearing back.** She was one of the fortunate ones – or unfortunate ones – who could hear afterwards. But the girl experienced **a tremendous shock. Before the operation,**

471 Mirit, August 2012.

she had lived in silence, which was inspiring and gentle. Now, she had to live in unbearable noise, which was everywhere. Noise was literally destroying her and she was sinking into a miserable gloominess more and more. She was even angry at her parents,[472] who, with their intrusive attention, enabled the restoration of her hearing, while at the same time, preventing her from enjoying silence, which we all need and want so much; spiritual warriors try hard to permanently attain it within themselves.

Listening to the clatter of the world is certainly not beneficial. The service, the regained gift – according to her parents – of hearing, proved to be deeply disturbing and utterly destructive. We should reflect whether what we are doing or giving to others in good faith, really is of value to them, as we may believe. Silence is a great gift too.

Sooner or later, a noisy and turbulent life will lead to silence, especially when a person has had enough of suffering, which is accompanied by the noisiness of traumatic living. Only in silence can people calm down, touch the awakened wisdom, hear all the sonic colours and shades of life and become totally aware of all its riddles. When we silence our mind, we are able to hear the subtle voice of our soul. Our thought becomes a prayer within the ocean of Silence, because silence is the fastest and the most generous link to all the levels of reality, consciousness, and soul.

Silence is not only the absence of audible sound, it is a distinct rhythm, an emptiness between sound waves, it is the alchemy of the soul. Silence is, however, also the state of a fulfilled mind, the state of a broad awareness, and inner peace. It is the link to the Intelligence of life.

Silence shapes rhythm in the flow of life, and this rhythm reveals itself when we form words and language via sound. Every language has its own rhythm and melody, which discloses the essence of those who create and speak it. Personal language is a unique melody, the rhythm of emotional and mental contents of each individual, of their consciousness, subconscious and meta-consciousness. The internalised peace of silence lays bare what we carry inside ourselves, which is why being in silence can be frightening. Silence is like a mirror, reflecting everything what we wanted to sweep under the carpet, or hide from ourselves.

Once our inner silence is attained, everything is possible. The way to stop talking to ourselves is to use exactly the same method used to teach us to talk to ourselves.[473]

I was once invited to a meeting of Slovene philosophers, where we discussed various spiritual topics, shedding light on our worldviews. The discussion started slowly and I mentioned that people can hear themselves best when in silence,

....
472 Ajahn Brahm, *Krava koja je plakala i druge budističke priče o sreći*, Zagreb, Naklada Ljevak (2010). The story includes my explanations and additions.
473 Carlos Castaneda, *The Wheel of Time*, London, Allen Lane, The Penguin Press (1998), p. 235.

which is not always pleasant, because that is when **numerous suppressed pains and spiritual immaturities emerge.** And one of the philosophers jumped up saying what rubbish I was talking. I was numb, speechless. What I said seemed very **clear and not at all controversial** to me. At that moment I knew that I had nothing to say even to philosophy professors, because their experiences and knowings were **rooted too deeply in their intellect, in the clamour of their thoughts; silence was actually unknown to them,** as were its effects. If it hadn't been so, they would have known this.

Silence is one of the parameters of sound and the final station of every sentient being. Animals want it too. I watched my little dog as she was departing from the earthly world at the age of eighteen. For months on end, I observed how she craved silence. Even animals know what silence brings.

Silence reveals the connection to our soul, to the deepest levels of ourselves. It deeply raises awareness and heals the spirit and body. That is why all past civilisations respected and **nourished** moments of silence as well as the paths leading into it. Our planetary ancestors consciously entered silence in different rituals. But **how? By means of sound, both audible and inaudible. Sound is the most brilliant tool and key, which opens doors into the field of Silence, into the all-full Emptiness.**

By using a selected sound, shaman-healers can first thoroughly **shake up auric and physical bodies,** which are then **freed from blocks, from energy blockages,** caused by the toxins of destructive thoughts and emotions. By using sound, they could **restore a free energy flow and sink into the fullness of silence.**

Every week, I see this happening during my **sound surgeries,** which I perform together with my Ensemble – with Mojka and my son Tine. I watch people who come to our therapeutic meetings tense within themselves, full of fear and pain, closed inside themselves. When **musicians** start to **guidedly create rhythms using shamanic drums,** people begin to open themselves up very cautiously. Then they **cry and shout out what had been tormenting them** and they become **ever more loud, spontaneous, and talkative.** At the end of a 90 minute surgery, during which I also help with my **therapeutic energy touch,** they simply remain lying on their mats **in a relaxed silence.**[474] **Joy** comes to their faces, their look glows and they are **grateful for the insights** they had received in silence at the end of the therapy.

Almost thirty years ago, I took up Maharishi Mahesh Yogi's Transcendental Meditation and started to experience my first deeper silence. Soon after my first meditations with **the sound code or mantra** which was given to me I began to feel **a contact with something unknown.** This unknown later became ever more known,

....
474 Read more about this in the sixth book in the *Cosmic Telepathy* series, which deals with surgeries among Australian Aborigines, Brazilians and Filipinos.

dear and inviting to me. **The sound of the mantra took me to the worlds beyond, to higher dimensions of consciousness, to the levels of the soul,** as we say. After having used the chosen mantric sounds, **a conversation in my soul, or a telepathic thought,** always started flowing rapidly **through my soul.** I always had **a notebook and a pen** beside me, in order **to immediately write down** everything I received or realised during my meditation. I received answers to questions I had been asking myself for a long time, answers were **finally made clear within the silence of my mind.** Sometimes they were brilliant **creative ideas,** sometimes simple **insights** about what I had perhaps established in a wrong way, or what I could have done better. But words of course cannot describe the silence of *Samadhi* – **the silence of Nothing** at the summit of the pyramid of consciousness.

My **gratitude** for that possibility has never left me, not even after I was able to discover the harmonising sound formulae for myself (including the Mayan ones). With them, I set off time and time again, with pleasure, on journeys **into dimensions beyond time and space, into the realms of silence and expanses of mind. Silence lays bare the waves of sound, the light of the soul; it leads, via transformation, to the holiness of freedom. That is why silence is a distinct prayer,** which reveals the path into something new and better.

When in the silence of sound, we feel love, which suffuses the Universe, the entire Creation, all living forms and beings. That is why it is to no surprise that numerous spiritual traditions on our planet – especially those from a distant past before the Common Era – **sought ways, paths, and techniques to attain centredness. Sound is this path and silence is the goal.**

To silence ourselves means to expand ourselves. It means to centre ourselves along the axis of consciousness across the dimensions of reality. On the wings of consciousness, we can climb up to the top of **the tree of life,** as our distant planetary ancestors lyrically described the expanding of consciousness. This is when **we attain the summit and we become the tree of life itself.** That is why silence is an important **window into the dimensions of the reality beyond, as well as a window into the creative world of imagination, vision and artistic freedom. Sound and silence lead us back to the Source, to the Source of life. Silence is like a time machine,** enabling to the person who has attained **the enlightened state of the silence of the mind, to travel back into the past,** into long gone past times, to **anchor themselves in the present** and telepathically hear and know **the future.**

> 'Silent knowledge **(the telepathic wisdom of channelling) is nothing but direct contact with** intent.'[475]

....
475 C. Castaneda, *The Wheel of Time*, London, Allen Lane, The Penguin Press (1998), p. 261. The note in brackets is mine.

Soundless silence is therefore nothing but the centre of every being, within whom echoes **the Galactic Centre, the Heart of the Universe, the Heart of Sky,** as the Mayans would put it. And this cosmic heart echoes also **in the heart** of every person.

A few days ago I came across a short book titled *Silence – The Mystery of Wholeness,*[476] written by the psychologist **Robert Sardello.** In it, he brilliantly describes his experiences with inner silence. He too **abandoned mainstream scientific circles and became a spiritual teacher.** He founded **a therapeutic centre,** which enables people to sense silence. I was delighted to read his book, for he came to similar findings to mine. And, of course, both of us simply renew the knowings which yogis, lamas, balians, Native American priests and others discovered long ago. What Sardello calls **silence,** I call **the Intelligence of the Universe, or the inaudible flow of life energy;** it is perceptible, even though it is inaudible. It is **the silence itself.**

The writer obviously wanted to avoid known expressions from spiritual teachings and silence was obviously the closest to him. This therapist of **depth psychology** also stresses the meaning of returning to the primordial silence, which can be **understood** primarily **through our meta-senses.** He wrote that **peace of the soul is reflected in the echo of silence,** which is the very core of the Mystery of life. He believes that **without silence, we are lost and cannot get still enough to find our way back.**[477]

Silence connects people with the centre of their own being

We can search for silence in vain or we can find it everywhere, both within and around ourselves, and of course also within the expanses of the Universe. There will always be something missing if we do not find it. That is why, even without being aware, we constantly seek what is missing – blessed **peace and the fullness of silence.** This all-full silence connects people to the centre of their own being and to the Universal Silence, which imbues people's consciousness, the Earth, and the Universe.

It is very important to attain the dimensions of silence. **If people are unable to find silence in their everyday lives, they will become impatient, unhappy, and they can get ill.** It might seem paradoxical, but nevertheless: **silence can also be created by selected sounds or sound codes (sound patterns of the magic of sound and surgery)** – by carefully chosen voices, which trigger veritable **alchemical**

....
476   Robert Sardello, *Silence – The Mystery of Wholeness,* Benson, Goldstone Press (2008).
477   Ibid., p. 8.

processes and chemical reactions in our minds, emotions and body cells. **That is why silence can also heal and deeply raise awareness.**

When in silence, we are highly creative. In silence, the world reveals itself as clear as day. When in silence, **we come to understand what our mind is unable to understand. Our mind is the headquarters of destructive noise,** which obliterates the gifts of silence, clear awareness, self-knowledge, insights, harmonising relaxation and freedom.

Noisy thinking wants to constantly prove itself. That is why noisy people are always very loud. But silence does not need this. That is why we say that **competitiveness, praise, and criticism no longer mean anything to an enlightened person, who permanently lives within the silence of the mind** (this does not mean that they do not think, but they do this in peace).

Two thousand years ago or more, **the most essential goal of life and the very core of rituals was** to attain **the level of consciousness which exists in silence. Song and sound play were indispensable tools** for the attainment of this goal. In the silence of a transcendental state of consciousness, in **a shamanic trance,** participants **experienced boundlessness and eternity, the centre of themselves, and the centre of the Universe.**

In silence, we **see the world around us more clearly. We can come to see the all-present Truth.** Silence is **experiential fullness,** offering people **an opportunity to reach their wholeness and to complete their journey.** That is why our ancestors performed rituals over and over again, **praying for the (self-) realisation within the silence of a (shamanic) trance.**

Our ancestors embarked on the journey to silence by means of song, sound, rhythms, different sound formulae, as well as by means of attentive and loving behaviour. In their initiatory rituals, when **near death, they experienced silence – their own as well as the cosmic. Near-death experiences** are an exceptional **bridge to silence. Enlightened priests and healers must be able to enter silence at any time,** they must be able to connect with its help to the source of **life energy and transfer it** into the material world, among people.

But of course restless people, or those who live **in stress, cannot experience silence and its gifts.** It simply has no value for them, just like the thought about centredness, about the axis, or dimensions, of consciousness and the world itself, does not.

Silence is the elixir of love. Silence offers **fulfilment, brought by love, which is awakened within it. Silence resonates with love and compassion.** If there is no silence and no love in people, they will pass on their **uncertainty** to others, **they will see the world in a distorted way,** in their own way. They will **blame everyone** else for their unhappiness, rather than their own bad actions.

They will mirror, or project their problems onto other people and hide behind lies.

Sardello[478] observed these processes and warned of the fact that **when we project our suppressed unconscious contents onto others, we are unaware of that.** And this is exactly how we will know that these are actually our own projections. If we are **aware of what we are doing, this means that we have touched the Truth. We should therefore recognise the differences between the imaginary and real. What we see in silence is always different from what we usually feel and think.** And this is precisely the basis for **differing viewpoints** as well as, indirectly, disputes and **disagreements** between people. **When in silence, we are on the scent of the Truth, even though it is difficult for us to accept it.** It will show itself to us **in a clear thought or in any other form. Even in the snake-like energy flow. We are able to reach it, provided we do not remain stuck in rigid thinking! We do not need to suffer in the noise of our own mind.** Beware of 'wise advisers,' who distort the knowings of great sages, cladding them with the misery of their own spiritual immaturity, or **spiritual materialism.**

When in silence, our consciousness is expanded to the greatest possible extent, our ability to feel is so powerful that it can thoroughly shake us. But not in a pejorative way. Artists, healers, and priests know **the harmonising power of silence,** its inaudible undulation, its solemn **song** at the summit of the pyramid of life. The **insights** of silence touch us so profoundly that we get the feeling that they **have literally been impressed into our body and energy field. Such an experience cannot be forgotten.** It is indelible. With it, we know that we have **touched something grand.** This is the experience a Native American has during his **inner quest in silence at the top of the sacred mountain or at the top of the sacred pyramid;** an Arab experiences it in the stillness of the desert, a Tibetan in a rocky cave, a Maya in the vastness of the rainforest, etc. And this experience **harmonises, attunes what was out of tune, it deeply raises awareness and, indirectly, heals.**

The silence of the human mind, consciousness, or soul, **pours into the ocean of cosmic Silence, into the silence of the Source.** This is when people come to feel boundless power within and around themselves. They become galactic human beings, from whom nothing can remain hidden, concealed. Their senses sharpen. A path to meta-sensory perceptions opens up. They become mediums **and telepaths** with a wide array of perceptions, they feel invisible and inaudible worlds. These expanses of silence were the aim of ancient **ceremonies** and of many spiritual techniques of ancient civilisations and cultures.

When the path of spirit opens up within silence, the flow of life energy through the body increases powerfully, complementing and fulfilling its harmonising task. A

478 Ibid., p. 14.

dance begins. **The dance of life and creative joy,** which **artists, healers and spiritual teachers** so profoundly feel and try to **pass it on to those who want and need it,** but still do not know how to reach it. This flow simply is and it **increases more and more as we grow spiritually.** But when it fills and fulfils a person, **the battle begins.** The voice of silence, which is attractive and inviting, dies down. The body feels **fatigue and deeply suppressed pain wants to liberate itself.** It simply surges up! At that time, some people **manage to release** this pain from their field, whereas others ardently **push it down,** with all their might. **A battle begins, a battle which depends on the will of each individual and above all on the depths of their consciousness.** If people understand that it would be best for them to dissolve and throw out, as quickly as possible, what they had suppressed, to allow themselves **to become aware of this suppressed content and to release it,** they will enter the heart and move one step higher on the pyramid of life. I say that they have climbed to **a higher dimension of reality. They will feel relief and they will see, hear and understand the world differently at each step, or level, of consciousness.** Such processes take place all the time, they are the very core of life, the salt and pepper of life.

When we refuse to face pain, we try to push it back, which causes tension, restlessness, and irritation. But when we have finally **dissolved all the junk** we loaded on ourselves, **we will see the world as it is,** and not as we want it to be, or as we paint it in our illusions and escapes before the Truth.

A priest-shaman and warrior must know how to consciously step out of the world of duality into the dimensions of silence and heart

The Mayan glyph *lamat* – the God of the Sky and the planet Venus.

If they want to be effective, healers, priests, and shamans must first complete the cleansing journey of their mind and emotions[479] and comprehend all the levels of inner silence. Once they have finally **merged with the sea of the universal life energy,** which is unfathomable power, **they will feel the presence of an inexplicable grandeur.** But prior to that, they need to **recognise all their projections and reflections on other people.** The problem is that it usually seems to people that **what they think and the way they see something is not related to or connected with them.** That the world simply is as they see it. They are not aware that **they are the ones who depict the world.**

---
479 More about this can be found in the sixth book in the *Cosmic Telepathy* series.

Oh, how wrong they are! And this is exactly the greatest **trap which hinders the spiritual transformation of warriors,** preventing them from becoming better and broader.[480] **The more we expand our spirit, consciousness and soul, the closer we are to the Field of Silence, the stronger and faster is the release of our fears, distorted imprints and memory,** which all reside in our subconscious and unconscious – **in Xibalba,** as Mayans would put it.

True priest-healers constantly live within the ocean of silence, which is why they always see what they need to see. They sing the song of Truth. They dissolve Untruth, which is the very core of disease, by using audible and inaudible sound, the primordial sound of the Source and cosmic life energy. They lay bare what wants to be revealed. This is what every participant in rituals attempts to do, regardless of their status or which community they belong to. This is also what people in numerous cultures are still trying to do today.

Without a connection to the Source and its silence, there is no happiness, health, and abundance. Everything is illusory and false, distorted and incomplete. But wholeness, the spiritual dimensions of oneness and all-connectedness can nevertheless flare up in the fire of transformation, in the hearts of brave and truth-loving spiritual warriors touching the Truth.

In the silence of the mind, we see more clearly, we perceive more accurately and we feel ourselves and the world in a more rich way. With it, we heal separation and painful division. But there are no shortcuts. **Only spiritual transformation enables** us to enter silence. Everything that is not the fullness of silence is less effective and less complete, and we are more dissatisfied.

Telepathic connection to the flow of life and to its silence, which is calming, nourishes the mind, increases intelligence, reveals dormant abilities, ennobles our experiences and makes us happy. Intuitive perception offers us evidence that we are not merely physical beings; **we are cosmic children, beings of spirit living in time and space and within a physical casing.** In our minds, we even carry the memory of those dimensions of existence which are difficult to reach and comprehend.

When we once again find our own centre, Native Americans would say our assemblage point, we come to feel the centre of the Universe, all its parts and the whole simultaneously. This is when silence enchants us and gives birth to **thoughts** and ideas which are in tune with the present moment. We become so very **creative** that **even we ourselves admire** that which has poured through us. I am writing these lines in this very Silence. And I am amazed. Did I write that? No, I did not. I am **only capturing these thoughts.**

....
480 Numerous spiritual teachers and psychologists write about this, as well as the author of the above-mentioned book on silence.

Gratitude and admiration are the qualities of awakened silence, the echo of the all-full Emptiness of Nothing, which is everything that has ever been, is, and will be. That is why every participant in rituals, every spiritual warrior, trains this connection, because everyone wants to discover the Truth of existence as soon as possible, everyone wants to know all the levels of their being and reality.

Only an awakened spiritual teacher, who is simultaneously a healer and priest, is capable of leading people into the world of silence and into the veiled content of the soul. Only an enlightened one can help people to find the path, which unfolds in the battle between holding on to the old and allowing the new, the better. This quest and battle is the right and duty of everyone. When people come to see all their multi-layeredness, all their levels, or dimensions, of the soul, when they experience them and start living within them, they have managed to heal (make whole) themselves and fulfil the contract of the soul, which yearns after perfection. Ancient traditions would say that they have connected themselves along the axis of the nine-dimensional consciousness. They have climbed to the top of the sacred tree. They have arrived to the top, to the final platform of the sacred pyramid, where they can delight in the majestic and enthralling energy flow of inaudible sound, which nourishes and liberates.[481]

Sardello wrote that the flow of silence (the energy flow of life energy) can be felt most powerfully in the heart. This flow, which is always present and which, over time, becomes ever more perceptible, reveals to spiritual seekers that they are also time beings – not beings in time – but beings who experience time. The heart is the best guide through the life's labyrinth of perceptions and feelings, which is why it is also the most important symbol of living in the material world – for the Mayans too. Therapists know that the qualities of living (which are also the qualities of silence and resonance with people, the world, and with the purpose of life), are most clearly revealed precisely in the silence of the mind, which is also chiselled through relationships.

The quality of life energies and rhythms is evident from speech and the flow of words. If a person is able to speak out of the silence of his mind (telepathically, as a channel), his words will flow differently from when he speaks out of his mind and usual thinking, acquired through learning. The flow, sound, and words emerging from within the centre of this person, from within the silence of his soul, are all sacred; they are the codes of Truth, the keys of life, which require from that person first to conscientiously and courageously

....
481 It is a pity that Sardello speaks only about the currents of silence, about motion, whirling, acceleration and sensing, but chooses not to speak about this current as energy, as frequency flow. He merely says that it is the flow of rhythms.

listen to the invisible and inaudible, but nevertheless perceptible, and then to devotedly pass on what he has received to others. And these worlds will be **imbued with power.**

By singing, playing, and creating sound images and formulae **in a sacred way,** a way which has nothing in common with contemporary music, **we celebrate and heal ourselves and everything that is. We express ourselves through the cosmic-earthly rhythms of words, sounds and silence; and, via the language of sound, we touch the Universal love,** which anchors us in the dream of reality. We touch the stars. Without any effort, **we start living joyously. We receive an extraordinary personal (shamanic) power and we effectively create according to our own visions and desires. What is more, we hear others well, we become clairvoyant telepaths, omniscients who able to hear the subtle waves of the Cosmos, the Earth, and of humans.** We hear the answers to our questions. **We see all living beings as souls, as beings of the same Intelligence of life, of the same holiness.**

Our distant planetary **ancestors saw and sang the world** in a similar way. They saw **the Great Spirit everywhere, including in other beings and people,** even in animals and plants. The sacred book *Popol Vuh* says that they saw what was invisible to the eye and they rejoiced in life, they surrendered to it joyously and allowed themselves to be **led by divine forces.**

To see and live the world with love means to create harmony and beauty, which does not know division, fear, suffering, and pain. It means to live within silence and peace. **The sound of the soul thus becomes permanent silence and pure happiness, while silence and sound become both highly effective tools for spiritual growth and remedies.** Those who are able to hear and feel the inaudible sound waves of primordial life energy **can direct and redirect its flow to wherever they want,** to wherever it is needed. Healers can, for example, **send it to the empty and diseased (distorted) fields of diseased people.**

This is how participants in rituals and the worshippers of life **consciously travel from audible sound to the holy silence.** On its wings, alert, watchful people can be **everywhere at the same time: in time and timelessness,** here and now, in the past and the future. **They see through the curtains of time,** say the Mayan priests. That is why they are **no longer in a hurry, they avoid clamour, mere possession no longer holds any value for them.**

The sonic flow of silence constantly nourishes and attunes the spirit and body. And attunement is the very source of happiness and well-being. Silence is the fulness of consciousness; wholistic consciousness is harmony and silence. Silence magically touches both the non-material and visible worlds. Silence can even become **a surgeon's knife and scalpel.** The inaudible

sound-energy flow is a teacher, doctor, and guide along our journey of life, revealing **miraculous, as yet undiscovered worlds and the eternally present wisdom, the Silent knowledge of the Universe, the silence of the heart, the heartfulness of silence. In silence, the heart awakens. Within the silence of our consciousness,** we can **access information about everything, from whatever time** and from everywhere.

The sound of silence, which is the peace of love, can be felt by **anyone who permanently lives within the consciousness of the heart; and those who have it in their hearts** can perceive it too. **Silence is the magic of heartfulness, the Great Mystery of life, which changes the world, the way of thinking, our views** on life and death, even our views on **pain and suffering,** and of course also on **sound and music. Silence is the magic of sound, the immortal elixir. It is well worth discovering it within ourselves.** Silence is also **the guideline and message of past civilisations** and their wise ones – shamas, priest-musicians, and healers.

> **Out of sound waves, the human quest leads to silence,**
> which discloses life and its mysteries.
> **The fullness of sound is silence,**
> it is love
> and Truth,
> the immortal essence,
> **the Field of Cosmic Consciousness,**
> boundlessness and infinity;
> it is the elixir of life,
> **the substance of the realms beyond death...**

> Sound and silence are a family,
> **the father and mother of the First Principle,**
> **the kindness of the divine Source,**
> **the language** of thoughts, songs and words,
> **the Universal Field, a telephone connection.**

> **Out of the primordial Silence, sound is born,**
> the **inaudible flow** of waves, voice and words.
> **The sound of rituals creates** silence in the body and mind.
> **The silence of the mind is a link to the Source and to the wisdom of the soul.**
> Silence is the absence of audible sound,
> but also **the majestic presence of God, which gives sound to consciousness.**

Silence is nourished by inaudible **sound flows,**
which ennoble everything,
and which reveal themselves in beauty, joy and euphony,
in fullness and heart-full consciousness of everything.
Silence is the birth-giving Consciousness,
a river of the invisible flow of life.
It is not emptiness, but **fullness,**
eternally present and healing.

Silence is a thought which does not think,
it is conscisousness, which does not ponder,
it simply is and it exists,
explains, harmonises and illuminates.

Silence is **the sea of consciousness,** its infinite Field,
all-present and all-encompassing.
Within the Field of Silence, we see others
as the light of the soul
and we hear them
as splendid **song**
with the love of the soul.

Silence is the Source and the Fountain of joy and peace.
It is a runner connecting the worlds,
the levels of reality.
Silence is the grandmother of loving relationships.

It is everything and nothing at the same time,
the mirror of existence,
the echo of reality,
the source of vision,
the fountain of destiny and purpose.

Silence is extremely **creative**
and active all the time,
deeply relaxing, bringing an awareness of the concealed content of a being.

It is therefore the very core and source of everything;
the essence, which gives meaning to and **awakens**
thoughts, emotions, body and spirit.

Silence resides in the heart,
or better – in its **centre.**
It is the all-present **consciousness of the Intelligence of the Universe,**
eliminating boundaries set in our mind,
building bridges spanning from telepathy and vision
to the earthly Truth.

It is here and beyond,
inside and outside,
above and below,
in both the audible and inaudible.
It connects our mind to our own soul,
to other souls, to the souls of the deceased.

Silence is also a rest between thoughts;
during it, **love takes over the entire stage of events.**
It seems like an ocean of wisdom, echoing in the chaos of
noise and suffering.

Silence is a bandage for the ears
for the aching soul,
offering us **the power**
to hear.

It whispers what we need to know
and answers the questions we have set.
But it can also provoke a **fierce reaction**
of the mind, body and the exposed ego.

In silence, you are **never lonely,**
even though you are alone,
for sound is **the fullness of Truth,**
which is the balm for the soul /.../[482]

....
482 An excerpt of the poem *Silence – The Fullness of Sound*, which I wrote in December 2011 for a course on silence in Slovenia.

So, let us learn once more to **live within the heartful silence of the mind, which is the pearly pure fullness of sound.**

The book was completed on the 18th day of the 11th month of 2012 – in the symbolism of the numbers for telepathic abilities, for the broadest consciousness and healing.

The promotion of this two part book took place on the 12th day of the 12th month of 2012 in Ljubljana – the number of the Holy Trinity and perfection.

Bibliography

Carlos Castaneda, *The Wheel of Time*, London, Allen Lane, The Penguin Press (1998).

Mira Omerzel - Mirit, *Življenje brez hrane in večnost duhovnih sporočil severnoameriških Indijancev*, Brežice, Primus (2011).

Mira Omerzel - Mirit, *Life without Food and the Timelessness of Spiritual Messages of the North American Indians*, Ig, Sventovid (2019).

Popol Vuh: Sacred Book of the Quiché Maya People (2007). Electronic version of original 2003 publication: www.mesoweb.com/publications/Christenson/PopolVuh.pdf.

Popol Vuh, Slovene translation by Nina Kovič, Ljubljana, Mladinska knjiga (1994).

Sam Osmanagich, *The World of the Maya*, Sarajevo, Svjetlost (2004).

Mysteries of the Maya, National Geographic Collector's Edition (2008).

Adrian Gilbert and Maurice Cotterell, *The Mayan Prophecies*, Shaftesbury, Element Books (1995).

Adrian Gilbert, *The End of Time*, Edinburgh, Mainstream Publishing (2007).

Fray Diego de Landa, *An Account of the Things of Yucatán*, translated into English by David Castledine, Mexico, Monclem Ediciones (2000).

N. Scott Momaday, *The Way to Rainy Mountain*, Albuquerque, University of New Mexico Press (2003).

Dr. Ivan Šprajc, *Quetzalcóatlova zvezda (Quetzalcóatl's Star)*, Ljubljana, Založba ZRC (2006). Spanish version of the book: Dr Ivan Šprajc, *La estrella de Quetzalcóatl: el planeta Venus en Mesoamérica*, Mexico, Diana (1996).

John Major Jenkins, *Maya Cosmogenesis 2012*, Santa Fe, Bear & Company (1998).

Miguel Vergara Calleros, *Chichén Itzá: The Cosmic University of the Mayas*, Merida (1998).

Rigoberta Menchú with Dante Liano: *The Honey Jar*, Toronto, Groundwood Books (2006).

Tudi trava ima svojo pesem: besede Indijancev in naš čas. Prijateljstvo z Zemljo: pot Indijancev, Radovljica, Didakta (2000).

Sacred Symbols: The Maya, London, Thames and Hudson (1996).

Davide Freidel, Linda Schele and Joy Parker, *Maya Cosmos: Three Thousand Years on the Shaman's Path*, New York, Perennial (2001).

The Mayan Gods, author and publication date unknown.

Monika Kropej, *Supernatural Beings from Slovenian Myth and Folktales*, Ljubljana, Založba ZRC (2012).

Jamie Sams, *Sacred Path Cards*, New York, HarperCollins (1990).
José Diaz Bolio, *The Geometry of the Maya*, Merida (1987).
José Diaz Bolio, *The Mayan Natural Pattern of Culture*, Merida (1992).
José Diaz Bolio, *Why the Rattlesnake in Mayan Civilisation*, Merida (1988).
José Diaz Bolio, *The Rattlesnake School for Geometry, Architecture, Chronology, Religion and Arts*, self-published, the year of publishing unknown.
Jeremy Narby, *The Cosmic Serpent*, New York, Jeremy P. Tarcher/Putnam (1998).
Manuel Lucena, *Kako so živeli Azteki (That's How the Aztecs Lived)*, Ljubljana, EWO (1994).
Hafiz, *The Subject Tonight is Love*, New York, Penguin Compass (2003).
Ann D. Less, *Mayan Map*, Hoče, Skrivnost (2012).
Vučedolski Orion i najstariji europski kalendar/The Vučedol Orion and the Oldest European Calendar, Zagreb, Arheološki muzej (2000).
Robert Bauval and Adrian Gilbert, *The Orion Mystery*, London, BCA (1994).
Deepak Chopra, *Quantum Healing*, New York, Bantam Books (1990).
Deepak Chopra, *The Book of Secrets*, London (2004).
Deepak Chopra, *Life After Death: The Burden of Proof*, New York, Harmony Books (2006).
Marijan Cilar, *Temelji življenja (The Foundations of Life)*, Idrija, Bogataj (2006).
Hans Cousto, *Die Oktave*, Berlin, (1987).
Dion Fortune, *Kozmička doktrina (The Cosmic Doctrine)*, Skopje, the year of publishing unknown.
Richard Garvin, *The Crystal Skull*, New York, Doubleday & Company (1973).
Richard M. Garvin, *Kristalna lubanja (The Crystal Skull)*, translated by Dragutin Hlad, Zagreb, MISL (1997).
Michel Gauquelin, *Cosmic Clocks: From Astrology to a Modern Science*, Chicago, H. Regnery Co. (1967).
Adrian Gilbert and Robert Bauval, *The Orion Mystery*, London (1994).
Hafiz, *The Gift*, New York, Penguin Compass (1991).
Hafiz, *I Heard God Laughing*, London, Penguin Books (2006).
Barbara Hand Clow, *Alchemy of Nine Dimensions*, Charlottesville, Hampton Roads Pub. (2004).
Jasmuheen, *In Resonance*, Burgrain, Koha Verlag (1999).
John Major Jenkins, *Galactic Alignment*, Rochester, Bear & Company (2002).
Pavel Kunaver, *Pravljica in resnica o zvezdah (Fairy Tale and Truth about the Stars)*, Ljubljana, Mladinska knjiga (1981).
Bruce Lipton, *The Biology of Belief*, Carlsbad, Hay House (2008).
Samuel Martí, *Music before Columbus/Música precolumbina*, Mexico City, Ediciones Euroamericanas (1978).

Rumi, *Hidden Music*, London, Thorsons (2001).

Peter Russel, *Tehnika transcendentalne meditacije* (The TM Technique), Ljubljana (1988).

Robert Sardello, *Silence – The Mystery of Wholeness*, Benson, Goldstone Press (2008).

Linda Schele and Peter Matthews, *The Code of Kings*, New York (1989).

Linda Schele and David Freidel, *A Forest of Kings*, New York (1990).

Linda Schele and Mary Ellen Müller, *The Blood of Kings*, Fort Worth (1986).

The Garland Encyclopaedia of World Music, Volume 2, New York, Garland Pub. (1998).

Iščezle civilizacije (*Vanished Civilisations*), authors unknown, Ljubljana (2002).

La medicina Maya pasado y presente, Omiech, Unach, the year of publishing unknown.

Miroslav Adlešič, *Svet žive fizike* (*The World of Living Physics*) / *Akustika* (*Acoustics*), Ljubljana, Mladinska knjiga (1964).

Miroslav Adlešič, *Svet žive fizike* (*The World of Living Physics*) - book 2: *Svet zvoka in glasbe* (*The World of Sound and Music*), Ljubljana, Mladinska knjiga (1964).

Jim Al-Khalili, *Quantum*, London, Weidenfeld & Nicolson (2003).

Ajahn Brahm, *Krava koja je plakala i druge budističke priče o sreći* (*The Cow that Cried and Other Buddhist Tales of Happiness*), translated by Zvonko Radiković, Zagreb, Naklada Ljevak (2010).

Carl Johann Calleman, *The Mayan Calendar and the Transformation of Consciousness*, Rochester, Bear & Company (2004).

Mira Omerzel - Mirit, *Zvočne podobe prebujene ljubezni* (*The Sound Images of Awakened Love*), Vrhnika, Dar Dam (2012).

The Remembered Earth, edited by Geary Hobson, Albuquerque, University of New Mexico Press (1979).

I have spoken: American History Through the Voices of the Indians, compiled by Virginia Irving Armstrong, Chicago, Sage Books (1971).

Luther Standing Bear, *The Land of the Spotted Eagle*, University of Nebraska Press (2006).

N. Scott Momaday, *In the Presence of the Sun: Stories and Poems*, New York, St. Martin's Press (1993).

ADDENDUM

About the series

In her series of nine books, which concern different cultures, Mira Omerzel - Mirit – an independent researcher and spiritual seeker with a PhD in musicology and a bachelor's degree in ethnology – describes her life experiences attained while unveiling the mysteries of life, of **audible and inaudible sound** and of the invisible energy which gives birth to and harmonises everything that is. She touches on **the wisdom of different civilisations** and **writes about her encounters with sages, healers, shamans, priest-musicians, spiritual teachers and leaders** of various peoples and ethnic groups. She visited them **particularly between the years 2000 and 2010.** She visited: **Hopi, Navajo and Apache Indians, Indonesian balians, Mayan and Siberian shamans, Hawaiian ka-hunas, Tibetan lamas and Indian jyotish rshis, Brazilian and Filipino psychic, cosmic surgeons, etc.** They identified her texts as sacred books of the future. **Mirit links the spiritual knowings of various peoples and civilisations into a unified whole, into a unique wholistic planetary wisdom.** In this series of nine books (which reflect the symbolism of the nine levels of consciousness), the reader travels into the age-old **wisdom of our ancient ancestors, who lived at a time before we began to record time.** The ancient knowledge was wrongfully identified as 'heretic' and untrue. The truth is just the opposite. **In each book** Mirit seeks to penetrate **one fundamental layer** of the past multi-layered spiritual knowledge of our ancestors. When we have grasped and accepted one **topic** (one book), we can continue our journey to the next. It is like ascending the nine steps of a Mayan pyramid. Yet, only **the totality together can illuminate the key life questions and knowings.** It can lead us to an understanding of our own (Slavic and Slovene) essence and culture, which in turn sets us free from the chaotic search for our own identity, for our planetary identity. It unveils the path to a fulfilled well-being. The time has come for us to revive it.

Summaries of the books from the series

❖❖❖❖❖❖❖❖❖❖❖❖❖

Book 1
Life without Food and the Timelessness of Spiritual Messages
of the North American Indians

In book one, Mirit describes her **journey from scientist to mystic**. The book is an account of **her experience of living without food for ten years**, which has connected her permanently with the Source and with different dimensions of our being and existence. She also touches on **ancient initiation rituals without food and liquid of different peoples**. Both in the past and today, every kind of abstinence from food has one single purpose – **the body cleansed** in that way, and devotion to the cosmic primordial force of life offer **an opportunity to connect to the Source, to our soul. This refines all of our senses (both physical and telepathic)** so that we can perceive the subtle levels of consciousness, the realms which make up our reality.
Sound, which is in fact everything, both visible and invisible, tangible and intangible, is **identified by** the Ancient Ones as **the axis of consciousness. Sound is considered a majestic tool and the technology of a distant past which brings messages and encouragements for the future.** Through the wise thoughts of **North American Indians, Mirit travels the blue road of spirit, rhythm and sound. Being frequency-energy undulation, sound is the communication system of the Universe.** It is time for us to restore and revive the forgotten **ecology of sound and the ecology of the inaudible resonance of our mind and thoughts.** In book one, the author goes into the wisdom of the **Navajo, Hopi, Apache, Cherokee and Mayan tribes**. Mirit, a researcher, artist, spiritual teacher and medium for the inaudible life energy, describes her **life journey from the bottom up, from despair**

and illness to the miraculous abilities of a human being – a cosmic telepath, medium, healer and spiritual teacher. The entire series speaks about **the quest for the lost key to happiness, abundance and health.**

The author, who is also a researcher and keeper of her own Slovene and Slavic spiritual tradition, reveals **the forgotten sparks of wisdom of various cultures; so that the knowledge of the past might help us in the future once again to attain the enlightened goal, the multidimensional awakened awareness** within the Great Mysteries of life. So that we might once again live an alignment with the cosmic, to live the Sky on Earth. **The Native American Sun Dance** connects us to the earthly and cosmic dimensions; it reveals how to attain **the watchfulness of an eagle, jaguar and snake,** how to restore **the medicine wheel and the wholistic consciousness of all-connectedness.** It shows us how to uncover our visions and the effective sound beyond the material world – the rhythm of resonance. **How to awaken our own dormant (telepathic) abilities.** The initiatory teachings of the Ancient Ones offer the possibility of **out-of-body travels** across dimensions, across the worlds of reality, whereas **Hopi and Mayan prophecies** show us the gates leading to the cosmic-earthly **evolution of consciousness and the current moment.** According to Native American prophecies, we live in exceptional times, **when human consciousness is able to reawaken within itself a knowledge dating back thousands of years. To revive it for the benefit of all** beings on Earth. **Consciousness is boundless.** We are rediscovering its keys. **And the ability to live without food** might be useful in the future.

Book 2
The Boundless Singing Links of Body and Spirit
of the Mexican Mayans

Part I
The Dimensions of Timelessness and Eternity in Mayan Culture

The Mayan culture is perhaps one of the most interesting and mysterious civilisations to have existed on Earth, but one which has sunk into the darkness of oblivion. That is why the ancient Mayans continue to intrigue us today. Their ancient wisdom, shrouded in **a mysterious symbolism,** reveals an extraordinary **grandeur of spirit.** It still inspires us today, **showing us the way into the broader consciousness of the new millennium.** As a musician, scientist and sound therapist – a medium for the transfer of cosmic life energy, as well as a guide across different levels of consciousness, Mirit **tries to open the curtains of the Mayan stage of life, primarily through the lens of sound and boundless consciousness.** The ancient **consciousness of the Mayans is increasingly becoming not only the consciousness of the new times, the new Earth,** but also **the consciousness of a better and more conscious life.** Our values, which are constantly changing, are once again turning to the wisdom of the ancient times. **The past gives meaning to and reinvigorates the future. A new human being is now being born – more joyful and spiritually less impoverished.** Out of his conscious spirit and thought **arises the current moment, gifted with peace and well-being.** With the boundless vastness of their consciousness, Mayan teachings put **sound and music** into a different perspective – **to the altar of consecration and sacredness. By grasping the past, we open the portal into understanding the present** and head towards the new possibilities that await us. Along the path, **we reveal a myriad of wonderful abilities, denied or hidden, that dwell within us.** To reveal them is our life's purpose and our **innate right. It is the purpose of our existence.** Mayan initiates had a good understanding of **the history of the Earth's evolution** and of the evolution of human spiritual development. **Mayans, who were smiths of time and timelessness, were certainly great authorities on the invisible and inaudible cosmic forces (frequency-sound waves), which are constantly creating in the Universe. Those forces are form-giving.**

Due to its comprehensiveness, the book about Mayan material and spiritual culture is published **in two parts,** although **its content represents one indivisible whole** and its chapters complement each other. In the first part, the author explains **the genesis** and the sacred book *Popol Vuh* from a spiritual perspective. She reveals **the way of ascending the nine dimensions of the axis of consciousness** (as the folk tradition would put it) – ascending through the material and non-material world and nine levels of wholeness and perfection. Mirit describes: ancient Mayan **rituals, such as rain calling ceremony, the blessing on the top of the sacred tree during fire ceremonies, the symbolism of the sacred snake and the sacred tree, which is the axis of consciousness.** She goes on to explore: **the meaning of sacred places and temples and the magic of the Sun, the Earth, the planets and stars, the priestly ball game, the power of mental-energy imprints** in the etheric body and body **cells, the symbolism of blood,** and, principally, **the revolution of a centred consciousness, of wholeness, as well as the road to the Silent knowledge of the Universe.** Climbing the pyramid is a symbol of ascending through spiritual levels, through **the axis of consciousness.** Such a journey to the top – **to the Silence – is the goal of the ancient spiritual warriors** and the purpose of their life's quest. **The old rigid mindset must give way to the dignity of oneness** with all levels of reality and with **all existing forms,** or beings. **Thousands of years ago**, the ancient Mayans consciously lived this philosophy of **aligning the mind, soul and heart.** The sacredness and forms of ancient **ceremonial sites** (including Mayan temples and pyramids) testify to the eternal Logos and **the immortality of spiritual messages. They enable an alignment with the sacred snake of the inaudible waves of energy and sound.** Ancient Mayans, as well as the sages of other cultures and civilisations, persistently sought to **rise above the limitations of time and space and attain the extraordinary abilities of galactic meta-human beings,** of complete and awakened beings who have returned to their origin and to **the Centre.**

Part II
The Sound Alchemy, Spirit, Soul, and Consciousness of the Ancient Mayans

This is a book about the long forgotten **wisdom of the ancient Mayans and our planetary ancestors.** Their extraordinary knowledge remains a great mystery for people today and their abilities and powers are still **an enigma.** This is why the book attempts to reveal **different perspectives on the Mayan spiritual heritage and on the use of sound.** As a musician, spiritual teacher, scientist and medium for inaudible cosmic (sound) waves, Mirit seeks **to remove the veil** from the Mayan life philosophy and the seemingly incomprehensible principles of their culture, **through the frame of sound, timeless spiritual laws and boundless consciousness.**

By looking at it from higher levels of consciousness, the author puts Mayan culture onto entirely **different foundations.** In her own way, **she draws nearer to the essence and principle of Mayan sound and priestly practice, with which, thousands of years ago, the wise Mayans had been creating their reality, harmonising life on Earth, healing and performing music.** The essence of ancient Mayan wisdom is also a valuable **signpost for humanity as a whole. Their cosmic or galactic consciousness** has become once again interesting and attractive in the spiritual emptiness of the modern world and its commoditisation of the truth. **Fortunately, spiritual truths are universal.** The teachings of all traditions, which are imbued with the eternal Truth, **are timeless. They are a reflection and echo of the profound life experience of countless generations,** who have been building a carefully kept and respected sacred knowledge. **Since time immemorial, wisdom keepers have been individuals of heightened** consciousness – priests, healers, spiritual teachers, artists and musicians. Musicians, who were at the same time priests, therapists, spiritual teachers and prophets, knew how to use the powers of cosmic rhythms and the breathing of the Universe within the rhythms of life for their own benefit and for the benefit of others. For them, sound was essential. It was regarded as the most important surgical tool, the most excellent tool of ancient **priest-artists and travellers across the dimensions of time, space, timelessness and eternity.** In this part, the author describes **the ritual initiatory journey of the Ancient Ones into the multidimensional (or nine-dimensional, as the folk tradition would put it) cosmic consciousness – to the Source of Creation**, to the cosmic-spiritual-physical **Triunity**. Understanding the cyclic flow of life and death is crucial to an understanding of ancient cultures.

Given its comprehensiveness, this book about the material and spiritual culture of the Mayans is published in **two parts**, although **its content represents one indivisible whole** and the chapters complement each other. The second part explains: **priests' and astronomical music schools, the role of sound and silence, the power of crystal skulls, the methods of aligning ourselves with all levels of our being and existence, transformation methods for entering into the new.** But primarily, the book addresses **the revolution of a centred consciousness, of oneness, as well as the path to the Silent knowledge of the Universe.** The writer and spiritual warrior additionally reveals all of this through **sound octaves or singing links, which, being the codes of immortality**, begin to resonate when the mind goes silent. The goal of ancient spiritual warriors and the purpose of our life's quest is **an accomplished journey across the dimensions of consciousness. Rigid old mindsets must give way to the dignity of all-connectedness between all levels of reality, between all forms, or beings.** And this philosophy of **attuning the mind, soul and heart** was attentively lived by the ancient Mayans. The author also seeks to **reveal the ancient Mysteries of the Mayans and other planetary ancestors** through the symbolism of life and death, and **the magic of love**, which is in fact the glue that binds the universal to the earthly. Like the sages of other cultures and civilisations, ancient Mayans persistently endeavoured **to transcend the limitations of time and space and attain the exceptional abilities of galactic meta-human beings – awakened beings,** who have returned to their origin and to **the Centre**. Centred human beings are able to restore their lost or as yet undiscovered powers and abilities, and so to fulfil their personal and planetary dreams.

Book 3
The Alchemy of Harmony between the Earth and the Sky
of Prehistoric Wisdom and Siberian Shamans

Prehistory is spiritually far more interesting and variegated than we dare admit. **The millennia before the Common Era were culturally and spiritually extremely rich** and **their insights** into the multidimensionality of our existence **were more complete.** The archaeological evidence – particularly **bone musical instruments** – testifies to an exceptional philosophy of primordial sound; it confirms the mythological content of life, such as the ancient bear cult. Not only in Europe, on other continents too. Siberian shamans, known as kams, even today live and safeguard this **prehistoric spirituality**. For thousands of years they have managed to maintain their **ancient customs and rituals, ways of connecting spirit and matter, and healing.** Despite various violent religious pressures and a bloody repression over the last two thousand years, Siberian shamans continue to manifest and keep, in an exceptional way, the prehistoric, **ancient mindset**, which, in its own symbolic manner, **knew how to connect human awareness, mind and ear – the cosmic and the earthly.**

The author – an artist scientist, an eager researcher of different cultures and historic periods, and an energy-sound therapist – has for many years explored the history of the oldest (bone) musical instruments to be found on Earth. In 2008, she set off to visit **Khakassian and Tuvan sages, healers and shamans.** She discovered to her amazement and joy that during her experiences among the Siberian kams she actually touched on the inherited age-old teaching. **As if she had returned to prehistoric times!** Siberian present **has never lost its heritage, the magic of multidimensional sound and consciousness, and its connection to the Intelligence of the Source, which they call Black Sky.** The modern Siberian life rhythm gives meaning to the past and leads to the future. This is also what Siberians themselves claim.

The book begins with **a stock-take of the Slavic soul.** After the initial experience of the 'singing train,' it takes us among the **kurgans in the Valley of Tsars.** Next, the book touches on **the sound laser, the vedun magi, the power of Siberian words and sound, the secret knowledge, or wisdom of the 'upper people'** and the local truth seekers. It speaks of **the sacredness of horses,** animals which are particularly close to the author's heart; it deals with **the symbolism of the nine levels of shamanic drums and prehistoric medicine stones megaliths,** which are still functioning and in use. In addition, Mirit describes a shared **shamanic ceremony** in the sacred **Kazanovka** Valley. She also describes her experience of **kamlaniye – a healing energy ceremony** with Khakassian and Tuvan shamans featuring ceremonial drums. **She performed a ceremony together with them in 'the centre of Asia,'** to ensure that the ancient **wisdom would never be forgotten.** To be revived.

The author then presents **the power of a dead shaman in a birch stump,** as well as **the yurt** – a wooden dwelling which is **a model of the Cosmos on Earth.** She explains the grace of the **cosmic vibrations of Ursa Major, the mythical drum, the blessing and ensouling of drums, as well as ceremonies at the sacred spring at the heart of a rock.** Special attention is given to **the celestial shamans' algyshes,** which are **cosmic-telepathic poems,** an inspiration of the moment, created by the shamans during kamlaniye. Among Siberian shamans, **sound is** clearly **the most important tool for connecting** to the Earth and the Source, while **the exceptional aliquot throat singing technique is a reflection of nature and a (ritual) tool** for strengthening our body and spirit. Carried on the wings of Siberian shamans' wisdom, we return to the timelessness of the mind and heart, reflecting upon and **testing** once more **our relationship with the ancient past and its knowings,** which still have the power to **bring us awareness and to teach us.**

Book 4
The Mysteries of Life, Death, and Soul
in the Ancient Vedic Lore of the Balinese in Indonesia

The book talks about the out-of-body **multidimensional journey of the wise ones in Indonesia, on Bali,** where people still live a relatively undistorted ancient Vedic wisdom. Bali is a Mecca for spiritual seekers of ancient wisdom. Among sages and healers of different levels of consciousness and teachings, among clairvoyants, seers and cosmic telepaths or **tapankan balians and taksu balians,** the author (a spiritual teacher and healer) experienced the wisdom of those who know how to cross the threshold of the physical world. In the book, the main yarn of the inaudible sound weave focuses on unveiling **the laws of life and death, as well as on uncovering the communication between the Indonesian sages and the dead. Ancient knowings about life and death are vital.** Without them, we are unable to understand the life rhythm of ancient cultures. Also, it seems that these knowings are considerably **broader and more subtle.** Who says that our insights are correct? They are far too narrow. And our experiences are a proof of that. The author relates her **near-death experiences and seeks to explain them** through the frame of an ancient perspective. She unveils the age-old way which balians use to connect to the eternal essences of dead souls and **methods for returning to our primordial Home, the Source of the soul. She explains how to attain the power of ancestors,** and how to be successful in **fighting against the destructive practice of black magic. The spiritual battles** of Indonesian priests, **materialisation and levitation (flying or overcoming the Earth's gravitation)**, which had been practiced by the author, are also described. The reader is introduced to the quest for the balance of life and body, as well as to the laws of **maintaining cosmic order on Earth.** Mirit describes the cosmic axis and the Triunity of material, non-material and cosmic, in the Balinese way. She speaks about the restoration of planetary and cosmic **powers (sidhis), about Creation and seven ray (frequency) qualities of Creation** (in the folk tradition). And of course the book primarily deals with **realms beyond death and after death, with the guiding of dead souls** to the soul planes beyond, with destiny, **soul agreements and the characteristics of a boundless and attuned consciousness, with the soul's yearning and immortality.** The text is ennobled by the author's adventures among Balinese sages. It seems that time stopped thousands of years ago on Bali. That is why newcomers have the feeling of **entering a fairy tale**, where a kind heart and an open spirit and mind reflect the ancient language and **sound-dance ceremonies of life. The people of Bali are willing to become aware of the lessons of pain and suffering. And that makes them rich and happy despite their material poverty.**

Book 5
The Timeless Weave of Mind and Abundance
of the Hawaiian Ka-huna Tradition

On one of her last travels, the author – a musician scientist, spiritual warrior and awakener, who loves dancing – visited **the Eden of sound and movement** on the Hawaiian Islands in the middle of the Pacific Ocean. Their **myths, legends, the closely kept secrets** of a wisdom handed down through thousands of years, their music, songs, tales and Mirit's encounters with exceptional sages and **keepers of ancient knowledge**, take us across a teaching which lies within all of us. Unfortunately, **buried deep in our subconscious** and at different levels of consciousness. The etheric body of sound of the Hawaiian Islands speaks of **the frequency rainbow of the majestic ka-huna tradition** and its secret teachings: **about the breath and different energy-frequency levels called aka, about Lon, the goddess Pele, the pahu drum, as well as about dimensions of sound and the powers of the Hawaiian language, its words and movement**. The author dwells particularly on the invocation and powers of **the essences of the Ancient Ones**. The most important things happen when **we connect the past with the present and direct it towards the future. Hawaiian skilful mastery over mind and multidimensional consciousness, together with an attentive use of sound,** are the most important tools of **the ka-huna navigators** across material and spiritual ocean. And of seafarers too. Mirit writes about her experiences, about the magic of the Hawaiian indigenous people and their struggle to revive the forgotten knowledge and life's wisdom. The tale of the reconstruction, voyage and success of **the legendary sailing boat Hokulea** is also described, along with 'warriorhood teaching' and the grace and skill of hula – the melding of movement (dance), music and ancestral essences into one.

The importance of **transforming emotional-mental legacy and acquired destructive family patterns** show us, in the Hawaiian way, the path to the power of **manifestation and realisation of our own wishes. It harmonises relations between female and male logos.** Additionally, Mirit describes her contact with **the eternally present essences of the enlightened ka-hunas** and relates a story **about beauty in chaos.** As in other ancient traditions, Hawaiian **initiates developed their** wisdom (huna) and mysterious, spiritual abilities for at least twenty years, in order to understand **the aloha essence of kindness and the laws of harmony** and balance. Hawaii is also home to **the magic of inaudible sound**, which is present in the huna alchemy of frequencies and in **the hula dance expression**, which is part of the ka-huna spiritual heritage and the Mysteries of life. Worthy of mention are also spiritual guides, called **amakua**, who are heirs to the exceptional abilities of legendary Lemuria (Mu). One such ability is **interdimensional journeying across the levels of consciousness.** The author-researcher also warns of the bad habits of **rigid, inflexible thinking, which can be a very serious disease.** Furthermore, there is the ka-huna **wisdom of wholistic healing and conscious transformation of reality using the power of words, thoughts, prayers and through the reciting of sacred names.** Despite Christian violence and prohibitions, **kahuna masters and menehune cosmic telepaths** survived until the Atomic era. Their knowledge can still help humans today and successfully **connect us to the essences of the stars.** Nowadays, Hawaiians increasingly **seek forms of self-sufficient and self-contained lives,** which leads them to the restoration of their age-old wisdom.

Book 6
Spiritual and Sound Surgery in the Portals of Attunement
of the Aboriginal People of Australia, Brazilians, and Filipinos

In this book, the author – a researcher, spiritual traveller and a sound-energy surgeon – takes us through the dreamtime of **out-of-body travellers, across the dimensions of Creation, reality and existence:** among Aboriginal people of Australia, who, like Siberian kams, have managed to preserve the ancient **wisdom of an attuned life** until today. Even today, Aboriginal people **go to the Sky to receive knowledge and visions,** as they say: also with the help of **mapampa,** a secret magical tool. **Initiation rites in isolation without food and water** and incredible procedures in their bodies, **enable them to connect, near death, with the highest frequency waves of their own consciousness.** This is how they touch the great auditory **Logos of the Universe,** which keeps the seeds of all forms and events on Earth as well as the imprints or information about all past events. The shamanic journey of the Aborginal **ngangkaris** across different realms reaches **beyond time** and space, to the timelessness of sound, which is why their **art is a priestly tool and a reminder,** connecting spiritual seekers with **Lalai, with the Source of life and existence,** which cannot be grasped with the mind. The story of **a sick girl** who wished to become a shaman takes us to **the medicine of spirit and the medicine of body,** and through the **seven fundamental levels of consciousness when healing the body and soul.** There, **child healers** are veritable masters.

Another miracle of the past and the present is **psychic or cosmic surgery,** which was once probably the most important **form of self-harmonisation.** It has been preserved until today particularly in Brazil and in the Philippines. It has a secret power to heal spirit and body and to **attune all the levels of our consciousness to the Primordial perfection.** Such surgery, being incomprehensible, **miraculous, but nevertheless possible,** affirms **the ancient wisdom of connecting the Sky and the Earth, the material and the non-material.** This unique **surgery** is actually a **connection between the human spirit and the Source, which resides in every cell in our body. It is a veritable surgical blade of the Logoidal Idea of wholeness.** Cosmic surgery, using no aids, is a unique demonstration and proof of **an open cosmic portal in the human heart and mind, an echo of an all-connected consciousness.** The author, initiated into the secrets of cosmic surgery, has performed it for many years. Mirit also describes her experiences in the **opening of cosmic portals within herself and the activation of cosmic-earthly portals in Slovenia, Croatia, Bosnia, the Philippines, Hawaii, etc.**

Even today, Filipino cosmic surgeons nurture their connection with the legendary heritage of Lemuria and Atlantis. They take us across **the fountain of Truth.** Furthermore, Mirit describes her first experiences of this amazing surgery among **Brazilian surgeons,** a night on the Philippine's sacred mountain **in a mythical town, divination using tree leaves,** adventures **at an enchanted lake and the sound-energy therapy of a young local medium.** She talks about the Phillipine's wholistic healing of the most renowned surgeons, about the elimination of karmic obstacles and **the mythological and legendary heritage of the exceptional abilities of the Lemurians,** who continue to inspire and awaken the consciousness of spiritual seekers.

Book 7
The Magic of the Stars and the Keys to Life
of the Ancient Egyptians and Ancient Greeks

The ancient Egyptian life philosophy is **the basis of the European Mysteries of existence, including myths, legends, customs and rituals.** The age-old concept of **Triunity** is the most important symbol of the philosophy of antiquity, including that of the Egyptians. In previous books, we travelled through notable distant spiritual monuments, **in order to understand more easily our own European – Slavic and Slovene culture,** which is anchored into time and space by Egyptian and Greek life philosophies. The Egyptian mindset was embedded in the **living Cosmos,** which is splendidly reflected in **the thoughts and wisdom of Hermes Trismegistus,** as well as in tales about **Toth, Amun-Ra, Isis, Osiris, and Horus** – the symbol of an awakened human being. Egyptian wisdom could not avoid discovering **multidimensional consciousness and the richness of the tools of sound. Atum the Creator** is the incomprehensible essence, or the intelligence of life, which is eternally creating and changing the world. **The Mysteries of Isis and Osiris are blessed with the magic of pyramids, temples, Gods and with the magic of the stars.** The magic words of power, **the sounds of sounds,** are woven into them. **The Egyptian Book of the Dead raises the awareness of the living,** preparing them for **the ritual death of all that is distorted,** of all that is not true compassion and unconditional love. The prominent **Emerald Tablets** and the teachings of Egyptian ancestors take us through **Hermes' initiations of the sacred snake,** through the rituals of the initiates. Mirit reveals her own experience in Egypt, primarily the essence of the **star spells, cosmic and star initiations,** which, concealed, continue to dwell within Egyptian artistic creations (in museums), attesting to **a great knowledge of connecting the cosmic and the earthly.** Contemporary people are simply not able to match it. **Words, or sound formulae, are the keys to life, which, through the songs and prayers of priests and priestesses of music, create the beauty of completeness and perfection, harmony, health and the sacredness of life.** In addition, the mysteries of Egyptian wisdom unveil **ways of attuning to the wholeness** and open up a path to our dormant, as yet **undiscovered abilities.** The echoes of this ancient Egyptian wisdom can still be seen **in folk customs and rituals across Europe.**

Numerous **ancient Greek sages studied in ancient Egypt**, which was a centre for teachings from all quarters of the world. Among them were **Orpheus and Pythagoras**. The ancient Greek wisdom of sacred geometry or the sacredness of proportion is imbued with the teachings of the Egyptian priests. **In a secret symbolic language**, which the author attempts to unveil to the readers, **Greek myths and legends speak of how to attain the goal of life – awakening, peace, joy and well-being.** That is why the book also touches on the myths of **Orpheus – a singer and lyre player**, who sought his beloved Euridice (a symbol of unconditional love) and divine perfection. Mirit describes **Pythagoras' quest and his priestly order, the search for 'the harmony of the spheres' – the inaudible frequency waves of the cosmic, which is embodied in the physical world.** The sacred geometry of Pythagoras leads us to the symbolism of **a multidimensional reality** and across the insights into balanced harmony, revealing the secret symbolism of sound and thought forms. **The Eleusinian and other Mysteries** only help us to unveil the eternal wisdom.

Book 8
The Sound Yarn of Love in the Fabric of Relationships
in Indo-European, Slavic, Celtic-Illyrian, and Ancient Slovene Heritages

Slavic and ancient Slovene wisdom have their roots in the indigenous Indo-European mindset, as well as in the Celtic-Illyrian and Venetian philosophy of life. **Everything is interlaced in folk spiritual culture** – thousands of years of the Earth's evolution, traces of various peoples and **the echoes of the revolution of consciousness.** This merging through time and space points to the cross-pollination of various ethnic groups and cultures and to various signposts. It is reflected also in **the Celtic-Illyrian blessings of love and spirit, in the ancient Vedic thought forms and in the penetrating ayurvedic insights into existence and ways of healing both spirit and body.** Indo-European, Celtic-Illyrian and Venetian **druidic teachings** are a reflection and echo of the **shared guidelines of the ancient philosophy of life.** They are an echo of a time before the Common Era, which, through the symbolism of **the sacred tree and sacred stones, through the first symbolic and sonic script – runes,** through the symbolism of **the circle** and through the multi-layeredness of consciousness and the boundless abilities of the mind, **indicates the past ways of travelling into the awakened cosmic consciousness of peace and happiness.** Mira Omerzel - Mirit – **a runner** connecting the wisdom of different cultures and a **wisdom keeper** of ancient Slovene spiritual knowledge – writes about her own experience of **ancient Vedic transcendental meditation** and **yogic levitation**. She talks about the essence of **cosmic-telepathic abilities**, known as **ahankara,** which descend through **our silent mind**, revealing primordial **wisdom without learning, the Absolute,** the divine silence of **the all-connected 'pure' multidimensional consciousness purusha – the light of sound.** The author takes us to the silence of the inaudible sound, to concealed thoughts and **names of Truth.** Having practiced the ancient Vedic techniques for self-harmonisation and attuning, she reveals **the power of sound and the light-sound codes of cosmic resonance.** In her search for harmony and health, life trials initially took the author to yogic techniques, to the **ayurvedic and jyotish (astrological) knowledge and understanding of cosmic rhythms on Earth, in every being, in the pulsing and cycles of life.** Jyotish – the invisible yarn of the cosmic inaudible threads of sound, **whisper yoga and the chanting of inaudible life flow,** is an extremely refined scientific procedure, uncovering the laws of existence.

In its Buddhist variation, **Vedic wisdom** has been preserved **among the Tibetan masters of sound,** who have linked this ancient teaching with **Himalayan singing bowls,** thus putting it into practice. These magnificent living beings of sound **harmonise disharmonies** and bring necessary **messages about the current moment.** Sparkling water droplets which rise from the bowls allow us to divine and read a distinct **calendar of sound.** Tibetans created musical instruments, with which they were able to enhance and orchestrate the inaudible sounds of the physical body. They ennobled them with **priestly aliquot throat singing.** The Slovene word *duša* (**soul**) derives from the Vedic word **dosha.** Our soul is our guide that helps us to recognise 'the agreements and missions of souls,' cosmic rhythms in life, spirit and body. It also makes **an embryo breathe in the ocean of the perfection of countless sonic octaves.** Indo-European lore about **agni, the fire of transformation, and about the five elements of Creation** reminds us of the cosmic essence in our bodies and cells, revealing **the techniques of cell surgery.**

Vedic wisdom is today perhaps one of the most esteemed teachings. It successfully **reveals the ancient Slovene folk culture and our existence here and now**, especially when linked with the Celtic-Illyrian spiritual heritage. The author – a keeper of the Slovene and Slavic spiritual heritage and a runner connecting dimensions – lays bare **eternal spiritual truths** through the history of Celtic-Illyrian priestly practice, which, before the Common Era, used **the power of sound,** just like many other traditions living in harmony with nature. Mirit also explains the purpose of **reed** pan pipes. **Pan pipes** – a musical instrument of the thriving Iron Age – were preserved in Slovenia as shepherds' musical instruments for several decades after the Second World War. Pan pipes **relate to a many thousands of years old story about the use of sound by our ancestors.** The author touches on the **priestly design of sacred places, temples and ceremonies,** which, in the past, helped people in their **quest for balance.** She penetrates the secrets of the Celtic and Venetian **language of sound (called ogham),** as well as the understanding of life and death, the symbolism of Gods and Goddesses and the spirits of nature, along with the symbolism of totemic animals – guides into the mysterious world of spirit and secret powers. Slovene folk culture displays **Venetian roots** and philosophy of life, which derives from the same mindset roots as the spiritual traditions of other great cultures (Vedic, Buddhist, Taoist, Egyptian, Mayan etc.). It **shows** contemporary people **the way to attunement and balance,** just like it did to our ancestors.

Book 9
The Light-Sound Threads of Songs, Myths, and Fairy Tales
of the Ancient Slovenes

The Slavic and ancient Slovene cultural and spiritual heritage is rooted in the Indo-European and ancient Vedic spiritual heritages, in Egyptian and Greek cultures. We can trace **similar quests and techniques for the restoration of harmony and health** across the centuries and ages. Mirit – today a singing academic with a doctorate in ethnomusicology – began exploring the Slovene musical heritage at the age of fifteen. In her previous books in this series she took us through the wise teachings of different spiritual traditions and **sought to lay bare the most important discoveries about life made by our distant planetary ancestors. Their knowings still hold extraordinary power and messages for the modern world.** Contemporary people are actually returning to the grandeur of the forgotten past wisdom, regarding which today we hardly scratch the surface! And all the previous books in this series about the spiritual teachings of different cultures indirectly **help to reveal the very core of our own ancient Slovene spiritual lore. For a better and a more loving tomorrow.**

The essence of ancient spiritual messages is both concealed and revealed **in** fairy tales, stories, ancient songs, in the variety of symbols, in the images of Deities and in rituals. It speaks to our soul, to our consciousness, so that the soul can remember that which it has actually known since time immemorial (also without learning)! That is why the language of the audible and inaudible sound of songs, tales, sayings and customs is sacred – **it is a sacred reminder and an indispensable guide through the labyrinth of life, which opens up the doors to happiness and abundance.** We only need to learn how to listen. In the book, the author describes her **experiences of opening 'cosmic portals or gates' leading to higher levels of consciousness, which lay bare time and space and allow us to transcend them.** Mirit also talks about her therapeutic trials and the experiences of students in her Veduna School for the development of consciousness. She describes the **miracles on the sacred mountain Krn** and the collaborative repair of (energy) damage to the archaeologically important **Vučedol site,** where not long ago war raged between the Serbs and Croats. Moreover, she describes the **ascent to the sacred tree, the celestial ladder,** or the axis of multidimensional consciousness and the eternally present urge to climb to its summit.

Magic formulae, *bajila* (magical prayers and pleas), incantations, superstitions and legends about the creation of the world, about a golden age of an all-connected consciousness, long since passed, but now returning, remnants of ancient Slovene shamans (*kresniki* and *vedomci*) – all of this has been preserved in the folk culture. They testify to an age-old wisdom of **awakening and attuning to the joyful peace of abundance**, despite the fact that, over the last two thousand years, these **testaments** of Slovene culture have seen **a great distortion of our ancestors' lore** and have **lost some of their essential elements** along the way. **Folk medicine** from the recent past is therefore still an important source for revealing the past grandeur of forgotten knowledge. Slovene folk culture has **preserved fragments about cosmic consciousness, about the exceptional and almost incredible abilities of ancient Slovene healers, touching at the same time on the struggle for the old religion.** The Slavs and ancient Slovenes eagerly protected their old faith, which required a connection between the Earth and the Cosmos, which is why it has **never been totally forgotten. Today it is possible to reconstruct it – within the silence of the mind of the silent knowledge of all-connectedness and devotion.** In the process, we are aided by **the myths of sacred stones and the gifts from the stars (cosmic initiations), by folk prayers and songs about the sun and the moon, songs about sonic masters of rhythms, about the Earth and the underworld,** the conscious and unconscious, the Creation, etc. We also have the help of **the symbolism of sacred numbers – 3, 7, 9, 12 –** which all indicate not only the multi-layeredness of beings, but also **the initiatory journey of our ancestors through the Mysteries of existence and through the powers of transformation.**

Particularly telling are December rituals of our ancestors, the messages of **Slovene, Croatian, Serbian and other European songs and fairy tales,** and of course the fragments of Slovene **customs and habits,** which all attest to a story of **a much more harmonious life philosophy** on the Slovene and Slavic territory in the past. **All traditions have identical or, at the very least, similar keys, similar ethics and symbolism,** which all speak to the human spirit and function as **a reminder and help in the processes of our awakening into enlightened cosmic consciousness. They also bring a memory from the unconscious into our conscious, and awaken dormant awareness and as yet undiscovered abilities** that dwell within each of us. Like Briar Rose, they are waiting **to be awakened.**

In Slovenia and abroad, Mirit has helped many spiritual teachers, scientists and academics to expand their consciousness and to develop spiritually. In this book she explores **the beauty and pitfalls of working with people and of teaching spirituality,** which every spiritual teacher, healer and shaman needs to know.

The triunity of the fundamental wisdom – of the **cosmic, the spiritual and the earthly** – is expressed in the Slovene tradition too: through **the 7, 9, even 12 levels, realms or dimensions of consciousness.** This tradition also attests to a similar **initiatory death of distortions** as well as to a similar symbolism of energy-frequency-sound reality and **the soul's yearning for perfection and all-connectedness.** Common denominators can also be found in its rich reminders and **techniques for awakening and wholistic healing, for the expansion of consciousness, etc.** In all cultures, or traditions, **sound is the most important tool for transformation, it is the yarn of life and the weave of our consciousness, mind and emotions, or heart. Only when in balance, these three have the power to fulfil** our visions and wishes. The ancient wisdom again offers assistance in the actualisation of human mission on Earth.

www.veduna.com
www.cosmic-telepathy.com
www.vedun.si   www.trutamora-slovenica.si   www.truta.si
www.youtube.com/user/ansambelVedun   www.youtube.com/user/katedraVeduna
www.facebook.com/VedunEnsemble/   www.facebook.com/VedunaSchool/

info@veduna.com

Other English Language Books and CDs by Mira Omerzel - Mirit, Ph.D.

Potovanje na vrh Svete gore
Pravljica o življenjskem iskanju in prebujanju iz knjižne serije »Preja večnosti duhovnih zgodb in pravljic«

Journey to the Summit of the Sacred Mountain
A Fairy Tale about Life's Quest and Awakening from the series of books 'The Yarn of Eternity of Spiritual Stories and Fairy Tales'

We are unveiling countless levels or **dimensions of soul, life and reality. The mysterious is being revealed.** The hidden inspires us. **When we move beyond our stuckness in the material world, we unveil a miraculous realm, incomprehensible to the mind.**
Mirit's **YARN OF ETERNITY** is a series of spiritual stories and fairy tales, which are all based on timeless spiritual truths and the traditions of different cultures. **The series reveals** to readers **the treasures of the soul and all-connected consciousness, the paths of spiritual transformation. It offers answers to time-**

less questions, which life presents to spiritual seekers. The book series speaks to **young children and older children alike,** or to put it another way – to all those who still feel a child's curiosity within themselves. **The age of the reader is not important.** These stories will appeal to those who haven't yet killed their inner **child's playfulness.**

The first fairy tale, *JOURNEY TO THE SUMMIT OF THE SACRED MOUNTAIN,* draws **on the Slovene cultural heritage and on the timeless warp and weft of the Slavic soul. The journey to the summit of the sacred mountain, the glass mountain,** where an apple tree grows, laden with **miraculous golden apples – symbols of the highest and perfect – is one of the most important myths and symbols of the human quest, purpose and goals of life.** Using the language of symbols, it tells of **enlightenment, of an awakening into all the dimensions of spirit and existence.** That is why the ancient Slovene spiritual journey to the summit of the mythical mountain forms the framework for Mirit's fairy tale. In it, the author flirts with the ancient **Slovene and Slavic philosophy of life,** a philosophy which, in various forms, is also known to **other cultures and teachings. Its truths are universal and timeless.**

Slavic lore has provided the backbone of the story – its poetic and symbolic idea of the journey **to the summit, to the destination, where a person, after countless trials and lengthy endeavours, finally attains the fruits of happiness and abundance.** Woven into the story are **ancient Slovene folk songs** and this yarn of spiritual messages restores the songs' original purpose – **their original sacred and ritual role.** In return, **the aural yarn of songs** gives the story its **poetic melody.** These forgotten Slovene folk songs remind eternal seekers (for this is what we all are) about the **eternal Life Plan, about destiny, at the same time warning about its inescapable laws.**

Most of the Slovene folk songs featured in the story Journey to the Summit of the Sacred Mountain **have been brought to life, in their complete sound image and without any trendy additions** or distortions, by the musicians of the **Trutamora Slovenica and Vedun Ensembles for the project** *Elfin Thread of the Sound Yarn* – a Slovene / English booklet with a double CD. In this booklet, Mirit **explains the purpose and meaning of those songs and their associated ancient rituals.**

Vilinska nit zvočne preje
Šamansko obredje naših (staroslovenskih) prednikov

Elfin Thread of the Sound Yarn
Shamanic Rites of Our (Ancient Slovene) Ancestors

A Slovene / English booklet with the explanations of the hidden spiritual content of Slovene folk songs featuring two gold CDs
Trutamora Slovenica and Vedun Ensembles
(Mira Omerzel - Mirit, Mojka Žagar, Tine Omerzel Terlep)

Two CDs and a booklet, titled *Elfin Thread of the Sound Yarn* preserve the ancient or shamanic Slovene musical heritage. The musician-therapist-mediums restore to their native culture **the previously revered, meaningful and sacred qualities.** The sounds, harmonies, rhythms and melodies of folk songs unveil the world of ancient Slovene and Slavic ancestors. Using the channelled, spontaneous sound, they **harmonise** and give sound to **Mirit's spiritual explanations of forgotten songs and rituals. That is why the booklet (68 pages) in Slovene and English, featuring two CDs, is a unique monument and reminder,** which awakens a long-concealed **memory,** while **healing our thought and spirit** at the same time. This work takes us from the wider, global context back to local **Slovene and European soil, and places the Slovene identity within the wider planetary story,** which, hundreds, even thousands of years ago, was lived by our **ancestors of a broad cosmic consciousness** and which we again seek so zealously.

After 33 years of the Trutamora Slovenica Ensemble (in 2011) and after almost **40 years** of research by Mira Omerzel - Mirit, **the musician-therapists have**

revived forgotten Slovene folk songs and rare, forgotten ancient instruments on two gold discs in an outstanding performance. They were the first in Slovenia to perform musical heritage in a forgotten, overlooked priestly or shamanic manner. Sha means wisdom and man means person: a shaman is therefore a person who knows the wisdom of life. The musicians restored the original ceremonial and sacred purpose of ancient Slovene folk songs, adding a harmonising sound, all of which was captured using a specialist recording technology in a chapel with exceptional acoustics and spatial energy. The chapel is located in the village of Tunjice near Kamnik. They imprinted all of that on gold discs, which is why when you play the CDs, it is still possible to feel the calming and harmonising sound vibrations, and sense the power of ancient sound rituals.

In her comprehensive booklet, Mirit explains the hidden spiritual and sometimes obscure content of the songs. Her shrewd comments offer a starting point from which to ponder and become aware of the timeless and eternal spiritual content of existence.

It is time for us to remember ancient Slovene musical and spiritual traditions and not to look solely for foreign knowledge. The booklet featuring two CDs seeks to preserve the spiritual and sonic wisdom of our ancestors in a form as undistorted as possible; which is why it serves as a distinct warning to the empty entertainment of popular ethno music and as an encouragement for a clearer and more truth-loving future.

WARNING: If you want to experience the unspoiled energies of the channelled harmonising (healing, guided) sound, we recommend that you purchase our CDs. The energies present within the CDs are lost to a significant extent during the process of making digital copies.

Musicians and sound therapists weave eternal wisdom into these new times, with the help of a majestic ancient shamanic musical practice – by performing music in a shamanic trance. To some of the songs, they add unrepeatable guided, channelled sound of a medium, which 'descends' through the expanded consciousness of the singer-instrumentalists, being a powerful sound tool for the harmonising primordial life energy. These pearls among folk songs and performing practices have been respectfully handed down by our ancestors through generations and through the curtains of time. In their distinct sound rituals, they used symbols and myths to awaken the laws of happiness and abundance, and to communicate important messages from the past for the future.

CD 1 comprises 4 sets: I. SHAMANIC SOUND RITES; II. THROUGH THE CURTAINS OF TIME; III. RESPECT FOR OUR ANCESTORS' TRADITION; IV. COSMIC CONSCIOUSNESS OF OUR ANCESTORS.

CD 2 has 5 sets: V. THE ELFIN THREAD OF LIFE AND DEATH; VI. MYTH AND SYMBOLISM OF SPIRIT; VII. THE AWAKENING OF HAPPINESS AND ABUNDANCE; VIII. THE UNIVERSAL LOVE OF COMPASSION; IX. THE TRADITION OF THE PAST FOR THE FUTURE.

The work of TRUTAMORA SLOVENICA, an ensemble for the revival of the Slovene folk musical heritage, has been complemented with sonic creations of the VEDUN Ensemble, an ensemble for ancient meditative music and the revival of spiritual healing sounds of the cultures of the world. To the jewels of **the sonic traditions of different peoples of the world, the Vedun Ensemble adds the subtle channelled (healing) sound of a medium,** performed in a transcendental state of consciousness.

Slovansko in staroslovensko zvočno predivo / Pojoče in duhovne vezi Slovanov in Slovencev s svetom – 1

Slavic and Ancient Slovene Sound Yarn / The Singing and Spiritual Ties between the Slavs, Slovenes and the World – 1

This CD by the Vedun Ensemble *(Mira Omerzel - Mirit, Ph.D., Tine Omerzel*

Terlep, Mojka Žagar, Polona Kuret, Igor Meglič) brings out **the ancient Slovene melos within the rich sound heritage of the Slavs.** Besides various ancient vocal and instrumental performance practices, we hear interesting, yet mostly **forgotten instruments from the Slavic world.** Jewels from the Slovene musical heritage and the exceptional aliquot throat singing (Siberian khoomei, the Balkan ojkanje singing etc.) are woven into the spontaneous (channelled) harmonising and healing sounds, perceived in **a trance play.**

The sound images of the Slavic and ancient Slovene soul are **an echo of both sensuality and meta-sensuality. A mirror of the connection between terrestrial and celestial, cosmic and inexpressible. The connection with the Source of life.** Spiritual all-connectedness requires a rich and peaceful philosophy of life, a softness of sound and tenderness. A euphony and grandeur of **tranquil simplicity. The Slavic waves of rhythms and harmonies reflect the wisdom and dignity of musician-priests – the magi of life,** and they also reflect **sound therapies** and the shaping of music. The age-old mindset of the Slavic and ancient Slovene feeling of sound is clear: we can perceive it as the piercing eye of the Sun, as the shining of the stars, or as the magical sacred crystal mountain. This **Slavic sound weave was present** in the cultures of Slavic nations, including the Slovene folk musical mindset, **until the Atomic Era.** It holds a special place within the mosaic of the musical languages and cultures of the world. A place of wise and ingenious creators, who use **the musical scene as an opportunity for spiritual immersion, cleansing and an ecstatic joy; for penetrating the mysteries of life,** sound surgery and the power of the soul. Penetrating the memory of our ancestors and the sacred. The eternal.

Slovanski melos v zvočnih podobah sveta / Pojoče in duhovne vezi Slovanov in Slovencev s svetom – 2

Slavic Melos in the Sound Images of the World / The Singing and Spiritual Ties between the Slavs, Slovenes and the World – 2

A CD by the Vedun Ensemble (*Mira Omerzel - Mirit, Ph.D., Tine Omerzel Terlep, Mojka Žagar, Polona Kuret, Igor Meglič*). **Slavic and ancient Slovene melodies and instruments are placed in the musical heritage of different cultures of the world.** Through singing and instrumental play, the CD brings in less known, yet interesting and sonically rich instruments of the past from all continents. **In a transcendental state of consciousness,** the performers elicit unrepeatable **harmonising and healing sounds** from their throats and from beneath their fingers in the instrumental play.

The ancient musical languages and cultures of the peoples and nations of the world are like a song of **the rainbow of differentness.** They are **similar** and yet so **different** at the same time. They reflect **the mindset of the ancient and mythical philosophy of life,** a philosophy in which a **tolerant listening to forms of life and sound waves** is crucial, as well as a compassionate **all-connectedness with natural cycles and rhythms,** with the dimensions of spirit, **the Universe, the Earth, the stars** and with everything that is, which in turn opens the fullness of awareness. **The link to your own soul.** Among the sonic building blocks of the musical languages of different cultures, **the Slavic expression** is recognised as **the softness of a melancholic soul,** but also as **an elated joy,** which invites you to **an ecstatic dance, elevating your spirit, expanding your consciousness, fulfilling**

your desires. In its essence, everything is sound waves. And ingeniously crafted **musical instruments** are the supporting vehicles of these waves. They support the spontaneous birth of **sound forms and codes – keys to the mysteries,** rhythms and melodic threads of the existential realms of our reality. **The family of harmonising and healing planetary sounds is an enchanting and refined alchemy,** so inspiring and calming. It is **the mosaic of historical memory** and inspiration. **Timeless in time.** A flash of the current moment.

Blagozvočje grškega buzukija v melodijah sveta – 1 in 2 /
Buzuki tudi kot beneška mandolina, ruska balalajka, turška in balkanska tambura ...

Euphony of Greek Bouzouki in the Melodies of the World - 1 and 2
Including Greek bouzouki in the styles of the Venetian mandolin, Russian balalaika, Turkish and Balkan tambouras etc.

(CD 2 is available only in MP3 format)

A CD by the Vedun Ensemble *(Mira Omerzel - Mirit, Ph.D., Tine Omerzel Terlep, Mojka Žagar, Polona Kuret, Igor Meglič)* with the melos of different cultures of the world. **Bouzouki** – this highly versatile Greek tamboura – also serves as **a Mediterranean mandolin, Russian balalaika, Balkan tamboura etc.** Besides the bouzouki, also making appearances are **Arabic gimbri, Siberian igil, Hawaiian ukulele etc.**

Vedun's themed concert, titled The Euphony of the Greek Bouzouki **in the Melodies of the World** or **Forgotten Euphony of Strings in the Melodies of the World,** emanates a very special resonance. On this occasion, the lead instrument is the bouzouki which resonates in many **different ways.** Mirit was enchanted by the bouzouki during her stay in Cyprus in 2011. Thus a new chapter began for the Ensemble's concerts. **The Greek bouzouki** is an interesting instrument, **a variation of the Arabic setar, the Turkish tamboura, the Russian balalaika, the Venetian mandolin, and the modern guitar.** It can be played similarly to all those historical forefathers. In Greece, the bouzouki is **played solely by men.** Their performance is very vigorous and often rough. However, **Mirit's fingers elicit a soft and meditative sound** that is also firm and elated – **in a woman's style.** The Greeks say Mirit is one of the few women who play it. They are amazed. **At concerts, Mirit and Igor perform melodies from different cultures, popular melodies of past times, especially old folk tunes.** The musicians improvise and channel the **harmonising sound** for the audience. Their great pleasure is to evoke what the soul and the moment seek. **They play differently from Greek musicians.** A concert, with Greek bouzouki as the central instrument, is therefore something special and unique. **A new chapter in bouzouki playing** – at home and abroad. **Tine and Mojka rhythmically accompany** the bouzouki **with the Arabic-Balkan dafs.** They also sing together with Mirit. Tine performs **Siberian-Mongolian (aliquot) throat singing**, accompanied by Igor playing **Moroccan gimbri,** the ancestor of the Greek bouzouki. Mojka showcases **many thousand year old Chinese clay ocarina xun replica,** while Mirit presents a small bouzouki-related **Hawaiian ukulele.** They perform both **throat singing in the ancient Slavic** style and free, improvised singing in the Roma style. From the classical Vedun repertoire and the multitude of instruments that the musicians normally use at their concerts, **other less known instruments** are featured at a Vedun bouzouki concert – at a concert of the forgotten euphony of strings: such as African and Siberian shaman drums, Arabic dafs, the Siberian microtonal chartan, Slavic cimbalom, various zithers, mouth and nose flutes from different cultures etc. The concert embraces several **sets** from various musical traditions: Slovene, Byzantine, Arab, Dalmatian, Greek, Siberian-Tuvan, Slavic-Russian, ancient Greek, Chinese, Balkan, Gypsy etc.

The mellifluous sounds of the vibrating strings of the bouzuki and tambouras penetrate the depths of heart and soul. They are close to the emotions of Slavic souls. When the mind goes silent, **the river of sound flows spontaneously. In the silence of trance consciousness,** we hear the refined sounds of spirit and heart, the sounds of the life field and the rhythms of the Earth, the stars and the Universe. **Meta-sensory links** become possible between musicians and their instruments, between musicians and the audience.

DVD – Zvočne podobe sveta in slovenske duše s pozabljenimi pesmimi in glasbili preteklosti / Ob 35-letnici ansambelskega delovanja in 44 letih Mirinih etnomuzikoloških raziskovanj

Sound Images of the World and of the Slovene Soul with Forgotten Songs and Instruments of the Past / Marking the Ensemble's 35th Anniversary and 44 Years of Mira's Ethnomusicological Research

The **DVD** by the trio Vedun *(Mira Omerzel - Mirit, Ph.D., Mojka Žagar, Tine Omerzel Terlep)* **with forgotten songs and instruments of the past** features **a booklet with an introductory word** in both Slovene and English by Mira Omerzel - Mirit, Ph.D., as well as **photos from the archives.** This audio-visual work was released **to mark the 35th anniversary** of the trio Vedun, an ensemble for meditative trance play and harmonising sound images of the world's cultures.

  Concerts by the Vedun Ensemble are an extraordinary experience. They are a dance of unusual ancient sounds and rhythms, harmonies, energies, feelings and colours. A mirror of the moment. Alone or with the Ensemble, **Mirit** has (during the last forty years) carried out **over 30 creative revolutions** not only in the fields of art (music), science, education, but also in the fields of seeking and teaching life and spiritual wisdom. These revolutions are evolutions in their essence, because they **contribute** significantly **to raising people's awareness and to developing the above-mentioned disciplines. All of that is reflected in the Vedun Ensemble's music, which is a powerful sound-energy therapy, following the model of ancient wisdom.** Some of the most important r-evolutions are definitely: **the unveiling, reviving, reconstruction and preservation of the Slovene roots of sound and spirit.** 'Pre-classical' music instruments and songs of the world, **ancient musical techniques and practices** buried in oblivion are also revived by the Ensemble. The Vedun Ensemble (previously Trutamora Slovenica and Truta) is the **first of its kind in Slovenia and is unique in the world.**

Their music performance is **a quest for oneness, completeness, harmony, euphony and deep internalization; a feast of diversity and similarity in the historical memory of the cultures** and musical practices of the past. The fullness of the meta-sensory dimension in their sound expression elevates the performers as well as the audience and deeply surpasses ordinary musical attempts.

An ordinary concert (as well as audio-visual creations) thus becomes much more. At their concerts and workshops, the musicians of the Vedun Ensemble weave **a sound yarn of the unrepeatable spontaneous (channelled) sound** using numerous ancient, **sacred, forgotten and rare instruments (usually as many as 100),** as well as sacred and secular **songs** from different historical periods, social strata, cultures and peoples of the world. They bring to life songs with legendary, magical, mythological, ceremonial and love themes, as well as ballads and dances. **The sound weave of the melodies of the world** is always enriched with **pearls from the Slovene musical heritage,** helping the audience become aware of **who they are, where they come from, and where they are** in the colourful mosaic of wholeness. **In the sound images of the world.** In the voices of the Earth.

As sound therapists and mediums for audible and even inaudible (but discernible with meta-senses) frequency sound waves, the musicians create music in a semi-transcendental state of consciousness, which was, especially **centuries ago, an appreciated skill of priests, healers,** travelling musicians and court musicians, who were mostly **healers of human souls and bodies. Vedun musicians bring back to the concert stage a forgotten sound-energy performance that disperses disharmonies in the room and in people.** At the same time, they restore to the music its former priestly and shamanic expanses, an **ancient quality, its harmonising power of sound,** its effectiveness and penetrating quality. Years of **Mirit's ethnomusicological field work, researches in archives and numerous journeys to different peoples of the world** were needed for every minute of their stage performance. Not to mention countless hours of the musicians' shared sonic quests and years, even decades, of their own **personal spiritual immersion.** Vedun Ensemble concerts are **an extraordinary experience. They are**

a dance of unusual sounds, rhythms, energies, feelings and colours. A mirror of the moment. Today, the **Vedun** Ensemble is also **a counterbalance to the increasingly trendy distortion of folk music heritage that was handed down through centuries** and to an empty and ever more merely technical performance of music.

Štirje letni časi - 2, Jesenski ekvinokcij / Zvočna preja s svetimi pesmimi in glasbili ljudstev sveta

The Four Seasons - 2, Autumn Equinox / Sound Yarn with Holy Songs and Instruments of the Peoples of the World

Meditative healing sounds featuring instruments of the peoples of the world; a CD with a foreword in Slovene and English by Mira Omerzel - Mirit, Ph.D., about the healing sound of musical heritage and old instruments. Vedun Ensemble – *Mira Omerzel - Mirit, Ph.D. , Mojka Žagar, Tine Omerzel Terlep* (self-published by Sventovid).

The new CD by the Vedun Ensemble – the second in the Four Seasons cycle – brings a recording of a concert, which the Ensemble bequeathed at the Autumn Equinox 2009 in the Equrna Gallery in Ljubljana. **Meditatively and in a transcendental state of consciousness, the artists and sound therapists performed folk songs and tunes of ancient sacred rituals** – notably **sacred songs** from different spiritual traditions. They enriched them with **the unrepeatable channelled healing sound of a medium**, which **spontaneously** 'flowed' through them upon this occasion. They interlaced sound, spiritual heritage and the wisdom of our ancestors in a unified sound weave.

Here is the unusual sound of the new Vedun Ensemble CD, recorded in the Equrna Gallery at the Autumn Equinox, on the 22nd September 2009. At a time when our planet was receiving exceptional cosmic frequency-vibrational support, which opens up **the cosmic bridge or portal into a spiral expansion of human consciousness, into boundless possibilities and unlimited dormant abilities of the spirit.** Into the Universal Field. We bathe in the sound which brings **gifts for self-healing,** for the expansion of consciousness and for alignment with majestic **Cosmic Consciousness,** for which **every soul is yearning** and towards which all our life's endeavours and actions move. **For thousands of years, during equinoxes and solstices, humans have opened up to and connected with the gifts of Primordial Logos,** discovering time and time again **new abilities of the spirit** or soul and drawing from the field of primordial life essences and powers.

At the Autumn Equinox, meditatively and **in a transcendental state of consciousness,** the Vedun Ensemble musicians have sung **songs with sacred themes from different spiritual traditions and cultures from all continents.** They enriched them by playing **shamanic instruments of the peoples of the world and ennobled them with the unrepeatable channelled healing sound of the medium,** which spontaneously flowed through their cosmic telepathic abilities – without the interference of the mind: **for the current moment and for everyone present.** In this way, the essence of the Source and the Intelligence of life is at its most penetrating and powerful in the music. It nourishes, balances and **attunes all bodies, as well as the spirit,** with the universal flow of life, with inaudible sound which is then grounded into **the physical audible sound.** In this way, in their distinct manner, both the performers and audience pay tribute to the wisdom of our planetary ancestors.

Using a specialist recording technology, we have preserved the presence, efficiency and healing effect of these channelled cosmic-earthly sounds, in order to share them with you when you play this CD. Just like all the CDs of the Four Seasons cycle and our other CDs, the sound you listen to **changes, calms, harmonises and heals** you – your awareness, thoughts, emotions and your physical body etc.

OTHER ENGLISH LANGUAGE BOOKS AND CDs BY MIRA OMERZEL - MIRIT, PH.D.

Štirje letni časi - 1, Letni solsticij / Veliki slušni logos Univerzuma

The Four Seasons - 1, Summer Solstice / The Great Auditory Logos of the Universe

Meditative healing sounds featuring instruments of the peoples of the world; a CD with a foreword in Slovene and English by Mira Omerzel - Mirit, Ph.D., about the healing sound of musical heritage and old instruments. Vedun Ensemble – *Mira Omerzel - Mirit, Ph.D., Mojka Žagar, Tine Omerzel Terlep* (self-published by Sventovid).

This is an exceptional CD featuring a transmission of **channelled** sound imprinted on a gold-coated CD, which alters your consciousness and fills all your bodies with energy, which in turn triggers **self-healing processes**. The CD includes an informative booklet in Slovene and English. The concert was bequeathed and recorded (live) during the Summer Solstice, on the 21st of June 2007 in the St. Ana Church in Tunjice near Kamnik. This **sound-initiatory ceremony with the instruments of the peoples of the world** serves as **self-healing and attunement with Cosmic Consciousness.**

WARNING: The CD has retained the original energies of the sound transmission. Making a copy of the CD will lose them!

Detailed information:

Here is the sound of an unusual CD, created by the Vedun Ensemble during the Summer Solstice – 21st of June 2007. The purpose of the channelled sound is to foster self-harmonisation, self-healing, the development of consciousness and an attunement with Cosmic Consciousness, for which every soul is yearning and towards which all our life's endeavours move. In all spiritual traditions, the Spring and Autumn Equinoxes (21st March and 23rd September) and the Summer and Winter Solstices (21st June and 22nd December) mark the most important moments of the year. At these times, cosmic bridges, or portals into human spiral consciousness and the boundless possibilities and abilities of spirit open up. Portals into the wholistic Universal Field. These times are suffused with the energies of the exceptional vibrations of the all-present Cosmic Consciousness on Earth. Using a specialist recording technology, we have managed to preserve the presence, efficiency and healing effect of those channelled sounds, so that you can experience them when you play this CD. Just like all the CDs of the Four Seasons cycle and our other CDs, the sound you listen to **changes, calms, harmonises and heals** – your awareness, thoughts, emotions and your physical body etc.

About the author

Mira Omerzel - Mirit, who has a PhD in musicology and a bachelor's degree in ethnology, is an independent researcher, **spiritual teacher**, musician and a clairsentient cosmic telepath - **a medium** for the transmission of Universal Life Energy - for the transmission of audible and inaudible Universal frequency waves. She is the founder of both the **Trutamora Slovenica** and **Vedun Ensembles**, as well as of **the Veduna School** – the Slavic-Pythagorean School for the Development of Consciousness and Harmonisation through Sound. She began to pursue her mission at the age of 15. She has been active in the field of **ethnomusicological** research for more than 40 years. Mirit has not only carried out ethnomusicological research into Slovene, European and the world's musical instruments and sound makers, but she also began exploring the deepest essence of sound. She is the author of numerous ethnological, ethnomusicological, ethno-archaeo musicological papers, articles, books and lectures, TV and radio programmes and series, LPs and CDs (together with the Trutamora Slovenica and Vedun Ensembles), which all foster spiritual awareness and self-healing with sound. She is also a pioneer in researching and teaching the wisdom of sound in Slovenia and Croatia. She has been a teacher to many Slovene and foreign spiritual teachers. Mirit explores and **revives ancient Slovene and ancient Slavic spiritual and sound traditions** (she is a keeper of their wisdom). She also revives the knowledge of sound and spirit of various civilisations, **linking them into a unique wholistic planetary teaching**. **Sages from other cultures have recognised Mirit as a healer-shaman, spiritual teacher, a wisdom keeper of ancient Slovene and ancient Slavic wisdom, and a runner between cultures.** Mirit is a cosmic telepath, who has **lived without food since 2000.** She is nourished by the universal cosmic life energy and can transfer it to all those who need it for their balance, health and spiritual growth.

VEDUNA
SLAVIC-PYTHAGOREAN SCHOOL
FOR THE DEVELOPMENT
OF CONSCIOUSNESS AND
HARMONISATION WITH SOUND

Great mysteries of life, the magic of sound, cosmic consciousness and the wisdom of the past

Courses and workshops, cosmic resonance and initiations, sound-energy surgeries and pranic - breatharian processes

Meditations and (self-)harmonisation using cosmic energies, Master Teachers of the Universe, with mediums Mirit and Tine and the VEDUN Ensemble

Dr Mira Omerzel - Mirit, scientist, artist, healer, spiritual teacher and writer, is the founder of both the **Veduna** School, the Slavic-Pythagorean School for the Development of Consciousness and Harmonisation through Sound, and the globally unique and exceptional **Vedun** Ensemble, an ensemble for ancient meditative music and the revival of spiritual healing sounds of the cultures of the world. She is **a pioneer in the exploration and therapeutic use of sound and music.** Mirit connects **science and art, spirituality, heritage and the past wisdom of different cultures,** theory and practice. In her spiritual school, together with her colleagues, she offers exceptional gatherings and **events** for the times we live in, during which we receive countless changes and truly miraculous gifts. Her son **Tine Omerzel Terlep** is also a **medium for the transmission of Universal life energy into the material world.** The exceptional cosmic (pranic) **surgery,** which is very rare in the world, unfolds in their presence. Mira Omerzel - Mirit is a **medium,** who has been **nourished by cosmic energy, or prana, since 2000.** Her first such experiences and gifts date back to **1994.** This special state of consciousness and of the body enables her to **perceive and channel extremely high and penetrating frequencies, which**

can dissolve even the very obstinate psycho-physical blocks and open cosmic-earthly portals. Doors into the Source of Life, into the Field of all possibilities...

Cosmic, galactic and planetary initiations also start to take place in Mirit's and Tine's presence. Through them, people receive exceptional gifts of inaudible cosmic waves, which help them to restore balance and health, the expansion of consciousness, spiritual growth and necessary insights. Selected sound is the key, the sound code leading to SILENCE – with the added support of the channelled sound of the Vedun Ensemble (the Ensemble is led by Mirit and features her musical colleagues, notably Tine Omerzel Terlep and Igor Meglič, both of whom are sound-energy therapists at Mirit's Veduna School). The musicians perform music in a shamanic trance, the sounds of which are highly effective when harmonising. With them, they restore to music its lost power and ancient sacred magic.

The material and non-material worlds are both composed of frequencies. But the quality of sound is far, far more. Sound is an alchemy of frequencies and their energy waves, a tool for the harmonisation and healing of the subtle levels of the spirit and physical body, help for the expansion of consciousness and for the activation of our meta-senses. This distinct magic of sound influences us, whether we are aware of it or not.

Using sound, or resonance, we can piece us together into a harmonious whole and attune to natural rhythms. But disharmony or our personal dissonance can make us ill. The wisdom of the world's musical traditions connects human consciousness with the archetypal unconscious realm and with the sonic patterns of meta-time. And sound connects us also to the Great Auditory Logos of the Universe and to Cosmic Intelligence, to the Consciousness of Nature. Subatomic (subquantum) physics and indeed medicine are discovering this more and more.

Sound is the key to those gateways of the 'soul and heart', which open the subtle realms 'beyond' ordinary consciousness (the transcendental levels of living) as well as the accelerated paths of self-development.

The workshops and courses of the Veduna School help to identify and solve the causes of our problems and difficulties, the consequences of destructive thoughts and emotions. They offer tools for the elimination of imbalance and pain in our lives. Through initiations, intensive courses, the exceptional (cosmic) light-sound surgery and the light-sound codes of cosmic resonance, participants activate (self-)harmonisation and (self-)healing, and awaken their talents and dormant abilities. They restore their awakened wholeness. This is in fact the very essence of our life's seeking. Mira Omerzel - Mirit, whose PhD is in ethnomusicological sciences, is a musician, energy-sound therapist, spiritual teacher, medium, writer and keeper of the ancient wisdom and knowledge. She has been researching these topics for more than 50 years. Mirit is a pioneer in the exploration of the dimensions and power of sound, and is the founder of a new scientific discipline – ethno-archaeo-medical musicology, which is unique in Slovenia and internationally. She researches the forgotten spiritual **wisdom of different civilisations,** especially the **Slavic musical and spiritual heritages.** She is the founder of the **Veduna** School and the **Vedun** Ensemble (previously **Trutamora Slovenica**). Her son, **Tine Omerzel Terlep,** an engineering graduate and **sound therapist-medium,** continues her work. Other (academic) musicians of the **Vedun** Ensemble are also **sound-energy therapists of Mirit's school.** They all work with their voices and with numerous (approximately 100) unusual, mostly **forgotten instruments** of various spiritual traditions of the world. At their courses and concerts, as well as through their CD albums, they all **harmonise the world** by channelling life **energy** and sound.

Cosmic sound-energy surgery

The exceptional, globally rare cosmic sound-energy surgery is performed by the **mediums Mira Omerzel - Mirit, Ph.D. and Tine Omerzel Terlep, MEng** (with the support of the **Vedun** Ensemble). Mirit and Tine are **mediums for the transmission of Universal life energy into the material world.** They channel **gifts** of frequency-sound **vibrations** which people need for their balance. They draw them from **the Source of Life, from the Universal Intelligence,** or the so-called "cosmic soup" – the symphony of frequencies. Or with the help of **the ancient Slavic *trojak*, which serves as a transformer of energy. Surgery is carried out at all levels of body and spirit. It dissolves emotional-mental and energy blocks** and, as a consequence, harmonises the physical body. It eliminates the destructive **effects of stress** and restlessness and **accelerates our spiritual growth.** All of that enables us to receive **clear thoughts, insights** and **visions** that are necessary for our daily life and creativity. It is recommended that you take part in **at least four consecutive surgeries.**

Courses / intensivos

This cycle of courses is an initiation journey **across the 9 levels of consciousness, of reality and of the power of transformation. The knowledge** and practice of the ancient wisdom (of Native Americans, Siberians, Hawaiians, Tibetans, Australian Aborigines, Egyptians, Greeks, Celts, Slavs, Indians, Brazilians, Filipinos, Balinese people etc.) unveils an awareness of **the laws of life and existence, offering** effective ways of restoring balance, peace and abundance. A special emphasis is placed on the **Slovene and Slavic spiritual heritages,** on the forgotten, overlooked and **miraculous Life Mysteries** of the past – for the future.

Veduna cosmic resonance

This is a multi-year and multi-level cycle (**4** basic and **12** advanced levels, or initiations). It is a cycle for **attuning** our physical and etheric bodies as well as our consciousness, or soul, **to the Source of life** (by means of **light-sound keys, or codes**). Resonance enables us to become aware of **our problems** and to **solve them** quickly. It brings beneficial **all-connectedness** and **the transmission of harmonising (healing) life energy, which is needed to restore our own harmony.** Participants receive **'tools' with which to work on themselves** and **help others.**

Veduna cosmic, galactic and planetary initiations

Initiations bring into people's lives beneficial frequencies – **energies and vibrations, which humanity needs for balance, self-awareness and joy.** We are barely able to attain these vibrational qualities by ourselves. **Mirit and Tine channel the planetary and stellar frequency-sound waves of the Pleiades, Orion, Galactic Centre, Sirius, Kryon, Gemini, Draco, Ophiuchus, Cygnus, Vega, Arcturus, Ursa Major, the Sun, the Moon and the planets of our solar system etc.** Cosmic, galactic and planetary initiations are **rare in the world**, as is **the cosmic sound-energy surgery.** They form a part of our spiritual anatomy and complement the cosmic-earthly surgery.

Concerts and CDs of the Vedun Ensemble

They are **artistic-therapeutic creations and distinct rituals.** Their **sound-energy yarn** (channelled in a **shamanic semi-trance**) creates a special experience. The Ensemble's **pioneer work**, which is **rare in the world, restores to music its sacredness.** The musician-therapists bestow upon the audience **harmonising sound images and keys, calming harmonies and rhythms, which relax deeply and expand our consciousness.** Their concerts and audio-visual creations usually feature rich explanations and interpretations of the sound images written by Mira Omerzel - Mirit, Ph.D. (booklets in Slovene and English).

Books by Mira Omerzel - Mirit, Ph.D. (Cosmic Telepathy series, Sound Images of the Awakened Love, Journey to the Summit of the Sacred Mountain, Elfin Thread of the Sound Yarn etc.)

In her books, Mirit reveals **wisdom beyond thought and audible sound, the knowledge of the past for the future.** She uses the written word to explain the long **forgotten knowledge of different cultures;** she speaks of the laws of life and survival and of the essence of sound. She also describes the experiences and trials of her spiritual journey, as well as her important and valuable experiences **among wise healers, priests and shamans of different peoples. In her stories, fairy tales and spiritual messages put into poems** (including oracle poems), **the reader is guided through the Great Mysteries of Life** in an artistic and symbolic manner. In all her books, mostly **channelled** according to a cosmic dictation, the author provides food for thought concerning **the past wisdom** of our planetary ancestors and **the knowledge of the laws of fulfilled and joyful living,** which shows a path to peace and manifold abundance.

Retreats

The purpose of **retreats** (at **Rogla**/Slovenia and at **Murter**/Croatia) is **profound relaxation, pranic-breatharian processes, spiritual growth** and re-harmonisation. Days **without usual food** and occasionally **without liquid, in silence and darkness,** as well as with sound and dance to round up the exceptional spiritual feats – these days are **magical** and extremely **beneficial** for our bodies, souls and lives. The **channelled sounds** of the current moment lead us into **the peace of the soul. Into the silence** within us. **Into harmony** with everything. Into spiritual **well-being.** All Veduna activities are **connected with sound and cosmic surgery.**

VEDUN

ENSEMBLE FOR ANCIENT MEDITATIVE
MUSIC AND FOR THE REVIVAL OF
SPIRITUAL HEALING ETHNO
SOUNDS OF THE WORLD

Therapeutic sounds of the Slavic, ancient Slovene and Balkan soul in the sonic yarn of harmonising sounds of the cultures of the world

Mira Omerzel - Mirit, Ph.D., Tine Omerzel Terlep, Igor Meglič, Matjaž Doljak
– Vedun Ensemble

You are invited to **a special celebration,** to a distinct **concert event, to a sonic feast of Slovene and Slavic roots,** which the musicians braid into **a sound-energy and therapeutic yarn of different musical languages of the world's cultures.** One of the distinct concerts of the **Vedun** Ensemble, **accompanied by the sounds of the revived and reconstructed musical languages of the past,** being **extraordinary sound therapies at the same time. Nearly five decades of Mirit's ethno-musicological researches** and cultural endeavours have now passed. The year **2018** marked **four decades of the Vedun Ensemble's work and its revival of both the ancient mysteries of sound and spirit, and the musical heritage of past eras.**

Together with her musical colleagues, **Mira Omerzel - Mirit, Ph.D., scientist, artist, healer, spiritual teacher and a medium for the transmission of Universal life energy into the material world, has broken new ground** in this field. The **Vedun** Ensemble (previously **Trutamora Slovenica** and **Truta**) was **the first of this kind in Slovenia and it is unique at a European and global level.**

Throughout history, ancient sounds, harmonies and rhythms had **an extremely significant mission:** to bestow the exceptional **power of harmonisation and (self-)healing** upon musicians and audiences alike. The Ensemble's leader Mirit is **a pioneer of the research into the power of sound and an instigator of ethno-archaeo-medical musicology** at home and abroad. Using **spontaneous, channelled sounds and the sonic logoi of the past** (for the future!), Mirit, together with her son **Tine Omerzel Terlep, who is her successor,** and other musical colleagues, **wants to return to music its former, lost dimensions and qualities.** With the variegated sounds of the Vedun Ensemble, **a lost world of once extremely respected musician-healer-priests is unveiled:** the world of Slavic **veduns,** European Celtic **oghmis and druids,** Illyrian, Balkan **lyeros** etc. They had very **important roles** in every community – **the roles of awakeners, harmonisers, healers, teachers, arbitrators etc.**

Vedun is an ensemble for the ancient and **overlooked musical heritage of the world,** bringing a **unique** dimension to the musical stage. **Mirit and musician-therapists, mostly academic musicians, who are students of the therapeutic group within Mirit's spiritual school Veduna, are like distinct contemporary bards, keepers of the world's musical and spiritual heritage.** They revive, as far as possible in their original form, sound practices that have been passed down through the centuries: from ancient **Slavic and Mongolian aliquot throat singing,** unusual sounds and **playing** techniques on **forgotten instruments of the past,** to **shamanic trance-performance,** which gives birth to **the unrepeatable spontaneous sounds of the moment,** to a sonic play of exceptional **percipience** and effectiveness.

Their musical performance is a distinct **quest for oneness, completeness, harmony, euphony and deep internalization,** a celebration of diversity and similarity in the historical memory of the cultures and musical practices of the past. The fullness of the meta-sensory dimension within their sound expression **ennobles** the performers as well as the audience and deeply **surpasses ordinary** musical attempts.

After **40 years** of work at home and abroad, the **Vedun** Ensemble (previously **Trutamora Slovenica/Truta**) continues its mission: **researching and reviving both the Slovene musical and spiritual heritage and the world's heritage of sound.** Throughout this extremely long creative period, the Ensemble constantly revealed and **unveiled new dimensions of sound and heritage, deepening their performance practice.** Their presentations include **numerous reconstructions of ancient songs, a versatile array of forgotten instruments and overlooked musical practices,** of which the especially interesting **ancient Slavic throat singing** is part. Vedun's concerts are enriched with **the forgotten melos of the Slavic and ancient Slovene ancestors and of other cultures.** Over time, their revival of the **Slovene, European and foreign ancient and folk music, combined with their wisdom,** has grown into **demanding sound-therapeutic work.** Into a distinct (self-)deepening and an experience of the parameters of sound. **Into a veritable sound-energy ceremony.** For this reason, the Ensemble is the most important tool of Mirit's spiritual school **Veduna, a Slavic-Pythagorean School for the Development of Consciousness and Harmonisation through Sound.** Together with the musicians

– Veduns, **Mira Omerzel - Mirit,** who founded the Ensemble as a teenager, bestows upon people a distinct **magic of sound. Using sonic alchemy,** the performers, just like their **ancient ancestors, help people to find a way** through the labyrinth of life. A way to their own **soul.** The musician-therapists try to restore the ancient harmonising role to musical performance. Its sonic essence and sacredness.

Concerts, sound therapies and CDs by the Trutamora Slovenica/Vedun Ensembles are artistic-therapeutic creations with a harmonising meditative sound, which musician-therapists **channel** among the audience **in transcendental state of consciousness, in a semi-trance,** in a special state of consciousness, when their **minds are silent. Trance-sounds attune the spiritual and material levels of our body and existence.** Such a musical practice was once highly **esteemed,** and in some places still is. However, it was unfortunately expelled from the world of white people a long time ago. Such **a precious sound yarn disperses and composes, relaxes** deeply and so, indirectly, **heals.** Using **instruments of different cultures of the world,** mostly from **Mirit's and Tine's collection of over 350 instruments,** the musicians **channel into the physical world the all-present Universal life energy and the harmonising sound of the current moment,** which is best described as **a spontaneous musical performance with an intense energy charge.** Interesting **ancient songs of different cultures and spiritual traditions are woven** into this sound yarn, especially pearls from **the Slavic and ancient Slovene musical heritage. Songs that have been handed down through centuries, the unrepeatable sounds of the moment's inspiration, and the colourful voices of unusual instruments, they all awaken people and expand the consciousness of the contemporary audience.** They fill people's **souls with the grace of eternity and timelessness.**

The richness of **forgotten ancient practices, singing techniques, interesting ancient instruments, as well as a diversity of musical forms, rhythms, harmonies and sound formulae of the old world,** originating mostly from the ancient times before the Common Era, are connected into **a distinct, unique concert ceremony of sound and a timeless musical yarn. As the ambassador of the Slovene musical heritage,** the Trutamora Slovenica/Vedun Ensemble have toured **every continent.** They have played **for children and young adults, as well as for demanding audiences from musical and scientific circles alike.** Weekly, Mirit, Tine and the musicians of the Vedun Ensemble perform exceptional and globally rare **cosmic sound-energy 'surgery'** at the courses of the **Veduna** School in Ljubljana (Slovenia) and elsewhere. They perform **therapeutic music in a semi-trance** and play **old instruments,** which are in fact distinct and very skilful **tools for attunement.**

At concerts, the Vedun Ensemble musicians present primarily **Slavic roots and the foundations of our history** – from the most remote **pre-history (Palaeolithic** bone flutes) to the last music to have a harmonising effect, which was preserved until the 20th century, only to then disappear from our everyday lives. More than **120 forgotten types of instruments and sound makers (over 150 in total), connected to ancient sound practices,** can be voiced on the stage. The Ensemble's work is based on **Mirit's field, archival and personal researches** and also on the ceaseless **spiritual awakening of their spiritual and musical faculties; on the sonic quests of all colleagues,** who are mostly **educators.** In addition, **Mirit and her son Tine are mediums and 'cosmic sound-energy surgeons'.** The **Vedun** Ensemble is **a rarity** within a broad creative range.

Concerts by the Vedun Ensemble are **an extraordinary experience. They are a dance of unusual sounds, rhythms, harmonies, energies, sensations and colours. A mirror of the moment.** Alone or with the Ensemble, Mirit has completed **over 33 creative revolutions** in over four decades in the fields of **art (music), science, education, as well as in the area of different searches and the teaching of life and spiritual wisdom. She has been a breatharian since the year 2000.** She lives without usual food, nourished solely by cosmic energy, by cosmic vibrations, which are sound at their core. These revolutions are in their essence **evolutions.** They contribute significantly to **raising people's awareness** and to the development of the above-mentioned disciplines. They are all **reflected in the Vedun Ensemble's music** which, following the model of ancient wisdom, is **at the same time a powerful sound-energy therapy.** Some of the most important (r-)evolutions are definitely: **unveiling, reviving and the archival reconstruction and preservation of both the roots of sound and spirit of the Slovenes** from past eras, and of "pre-classical" instruments and ancient songs of the world, early musical techniques and practices that were buried in oblivion.

Their first **imitators,** who appeared in Slovenia **within ten years of the birth of the Vedun Ensemble** (previously **Trutamora Slovenica**), unfortunately began to distort our heritage with a cloak of entertainment. The sonic and spiritual **heritage** of countless **generations of sages** from ancient times, which survived for several thousands of years, **began to be rapidly devalued during the last decades of the 20th century.** Consequently, the **historical memory** of the Slovenes and their neighbours began to be ever more lost. However, **if the remnants of the Slovene heritage managed to survive hundreds, even thousands of years, then they certainly brought important life messages and deserve to be preserved into the future: both in the museum and in the historical memory of our consciousness.**

Mirit and the Vedun/Trutamora Slovenica Ensemble have received **numerous artistic, pedagogical and scholarly awards** for their work. Like curators in the **museum of sound and life,** the Ensemble **bequeaths numerous records and audiovisual recordings featuring sound reconstructions of the Slovene and**

world's musical heritages. Bequeathed to the Slovenes and other Slavic and Balkan nations, to our inquisitive descendants and younger generation. So that we do not forget **who we are, our roots, the meaning of life, and the power that sound and music possess. What is their role? Everything is sound.** The ancient Greek priest, mathematician and healer **Pythagoras, ancient Slavic sages** and contemporary **quantum physicists claim that both our world and the Universe are composed of a symphony of frequencies.** It is worthwhile to perceive them **sensitively,** feel them with our **meta-senses,** understand them **wholistically** and **use them correctly** – for the good of all and everything.

Musical instruments

The musicians play **rare original instruments** (from Mira's extensive collection of **more than 350** instruments) as well as **replicas of historic** and pre-historic **instruments**. To perform **harmonising sound** they use **instruments from past periods** that were preserved as **folk instruments (untempered attunement)** until the Atomic Era. In addition, they use **shamanic instruments of different cultures**, which **generate a relaxing and harmonising effect** with their **tone heights and attunements**: Siberian (Khakassian) microtonal **chartan**, medieval, Baroque and folk **cimbaloms**, various European **zithers**, Byzantine and Oriental **tambouras and sazes**, Turkish **dzura** and Greek **bouzouki** (also the bouzouki in the style of a Mediterranean **mandolin, balalaika, tamboura** and other instruments), Arabic **lute**, Balkan **tambouras**, Arabic **gimbri**, Tuvan **igil**, Mongolian-Siberian **morin khuur**, Arabic **rubab**, Dubrovnik **lijerica**, Balkan **gusle**, Hawaiian **ukulele**, South American **charango**, Chinese fiddle **erhu**, Slovene **drone and violin zithers, prehistoric bone flutes** and flutes from different cultures – North American Indian and Mayan single and double flute *quena,* Native American **reed pipes**, Slavic and Slovene wooden **flutes and reed pipes**, Slavic and ancient **sopela, šurla and double flutes, duduk,** Hawaiian **nose flutes**, Slovak **fujaras**, Balkan **frula**, bullroarers and **jaw harps**, European clay **ocarinas**, Chinese prehistoric ocarina **xun**, the Vietnamese flute, Aboriginal **singing tubes, reed pan pipes** from different continents, **Persian-Indian instruments (santur** dulcimer, **sarangi** fiddle, the string instruments **esraj** and **taus, tablas** (drums), drone **tanpura/tambura, bansuri** flute, the string instrument **sarod);** the instruments from the Balinese **gamelan** orchestra (**rindik** bamboo xylophones, **suling** flutes, a **metallophone** with two bars, cradled gongs **kompler** and **komplək, kendhang** double-sided drum), Himalayan **singing and crystal bowls**, Indian **harmonium,** folk **string drum,** Hawaiian **ipu gourd drum, drums** from various traditions: Siberian **shamanic dungur drums,** Native American drums, Egyptian and Balkan **darbukas, dafs and tambourines,** African **djembes,** Macedonian **large and small tapan**; Renaissance, folk and Tibetan **horns**, ancient Slavic **urns**, Oceanian **conches**, folk **bullroarers and scrapers**, European **jaw harps, percussion implements and rattles** from various cultures, **cymbals, bells**, African **sansas, aliquot drum udu,** etc.

To perform the Slovene musical heritage they use rare original folk instruments and reconstructions of instruments, which have been forgotten on the Slovene territory: **oprekelj** (small cimbalom) and big **cimbalom,** wooden cross flutes **žvegle,** pan pipes **trstenke, zithers** (chord, drone, violin, harp and guitar zithers), **jaw harps, thick reed flutes,** clay **ocarinas,** double flutes **dvojnice, bagpipes dude** and

diple with a windbag, **tamburitzas, sopelas and šurlas** (Istrian untempered instruments), **horns** (from both animals and bark), **earthenware pot basses (gudala), little bass** (violoncello), **tambourines, drums** and a number of simple improvised sound-makers.

Besides the above-mentioned instruments, the members of the Vedun Ensemble use **medieval-Renaissance reconstructions and instruments from European musical heritage**: reconstructions of the **medieval cimbalom (oprekelj) and psaltery,** medieval **string drum,** Slovene and Hungarian **drone zithers drsovce, marine trumpet Trumscheit, the bowed psaltery Streichpsalterij** or the European medieval **bowed psaltery,** Slavic **cimbaloms,** numerous predecessors of wooden **flutes and sopelas,** various **percussion instruments and scrapers, jaw harps, earthenware bass,** wooden and animal **horns, tambourines and drums,** etc.